The Character of Credit
Personal Debt in English Culture, 1740–1914

Personal credit relations were ubiquitous in English consumer markets, binding family members, friends, neighbours, customers and tradesmen in tangled liens of mutual obligation. In this study of the social history of personal debt and credit, Margot Finn reveals the pre-eminence of social individuals – men, women and children whose ability to engage in credit contracts was contingent upon their dependent social status. Using a wide range of printed and manuscript sources, and paying particular attention to distinctions of gender and of class, Finn examines English consumer culture from three interlocking perspectives: representations of debt in novels, diaries and autobiographical memoirs; the transformation of imprisonment for debt; and the use of small-claims courts to mediate disputes between debtors and creditors. This major new study of personal debt from 1740 to 1914 will appeal to social, legal and cultural historians, literary scholars and those interested in the history of consumer culture.

MARGOT C. FINN is Warwick Research Fellow and Reader in History at the University of Warwick. She is the author of *After Chartism: Class and Nation in English Radical Politics, 1848–1874* (Cambridge University Press, 1993).

Cambridge Social and Cultural Histories

Series editors:

MARGOT C. FINN, *University of Warwick*
COLIN JONES, *University of Warwick*
KEITH WRIGHTSON, *Yale University*

New cultural histories have recently expanded the parameters (and enriched the methodologies) of social history. Cambridge Social and Cultural Histories recognises the plurality of current approaches to social and cultural history as distinctive points of entry into a common explanatory project. Open to innovative and interdisciplinary work, regardless of its chronological or geographical location, the series encompasses a broad range of histories of social relationships and of the cultures that inform them and lend them meaning. Historical anthropology, historical sociology, comparative history, gender history and historicist literary studies – among other subjects – all fall within the remit of Cambridge Social and Cultural Histories.

Titles in the series include:

1   MARGOT C. FINN *The Character of Credit: Personal Debt in English Culture, 1740–1914*
    ISBN 0 521 82342 0

The Character of Credit

Personal Debt in English Culture, 1740–1914

Margot C. Finn
University of Warwick

PUBLISHED BY THE PRESS SYNDICATE OF THE UNIVERSITY OF CAMBRIDGE
The Pitt Building, Trumpington Street, Cambridge CB2 1RP, United Kingdom

CAMBRIDGE UNIVERSITY PRESS
The Edinburgh Building, Cambridge, CB2 2RU, UK
40 West 20th Street, New York, NY 10011–4211, USA
477 Williamstown Road, Port Melbourne, VIC 3207, Australia
Ruiz de Alarcón 13, 28014 Madrid, Spain
Dock House, The Waterfront, Cape Town 8001, South Africa

http://www.cambridge.org

© Margot C. Finn 2003

This book is in copyright. Subject to statutory exception
and to the provisions of relevant collective licensing agreements,
no reproduction of any part may take place without
the written permission of Cambridge University Press.

First published 2003

Typeface Times 10/12 pt.   *System* LaTeX 2$_\varepsilon$ [TB]

A catalogue record for this book is available from the British Library

Library of Congress Cataloguing in Publication data
Finn, Margot C.
The character of credit: personal debt in English culture, 1740–1914 / Margot C. Finn.
        p.   cm. – (Cambridge social and cultural histories; 1)
Includes bibliographical references and index.
ISBN 0 521 82342 0 (hb)
1. English prose literature – History and criticism.   2. Economics and literature –
Great Britain – History.   3. Consumption (Economics) – Great Britain – History.
4. Finance, Personal – Great Britain – History.   5. Consumption (Economics) in
literature.   6. Great Britain – Economic conditions.   7. Credit – Great Britain –
History.   8. Debt – Great Britain – History.   9. Economics in literature.
10. Debt in literature.   I. Title.   II. Series.
PR830.E37.F66   2003
306.3′0942′09033 – dc21   2002041697

ISBN 0 521 82342 0 hardback

Transferred to digital printing 2004

Contents

List of illustrations	*page* viii
List of tables	ix
Acknowledgments	x
List of abbreviations	xii
Introduction	1

Part I Debt and credit in English memory and imagination

1	Fictions of debt and credit, 1740–1914	25
2	Debt and credit in diaries and autobiographies	64

Part II Imprisonment for debt and the economic individual

3	'Mansions of misery': the unreformed debtors' prison	109
4	Discipline or abolish? Reforming imprisonment for debt	152

Part III Petty debts and the modernisation of English law

5	'A kind of parliamentary magic': eighteenth-century courts of conscience	197
6	From courts of conscience to county courts: small-claims litigation in the nineteenth century	236
7	Market moralities: tradesmen, credit and the courts in Victorian and Edwardian England	278
	Conclusion	317
	Bibliography	328
	Index	356

Illustrations

1 Interior view of the Marshalsea Prison, Borough High Street, *c.* 1830. Reproduced by permission of the Guildhall Library, London. *page* 59

2 Benjamin Robert Haydon (1786–1846), *Chairing the Member* (1829). Reproduced by permission of the Tate Gallery. 71

3 Newgate Prison, *c.* 1750. Reproduced by permission of the Guildhall Library, London. 119

4 Exterior view of the begging grate at the Fleet Prison, *c.* 1800. Reproduced by permission of the Guildhall Library, London. 123

5 Thomas Shepherd (1793–1864), interior view of the Fleet Prison, *c.* 1840. Reproduced by permission of the Guildhall Library, London. 130

6 Theodore Lane (1800–28), interior view of the King's Bench Prison yard and racket-ground, *c.* 1825. Reproduced by permission of the Guildhall Library, London. 133

7 Robert Cruikshank (1795–1856), the evening after a mock election at the Fleet Prison, 1835. Reproduced by permission of the Guildhall Library, London. 136

8 Anonymous engraving of the Anti-Papal crowd destroying the King's Bench Prison during the Gordon Riots of 1780. Reproduced by permission of the Guildhall Library, London. 146

9 Notice and correspondence from the Legal & Mercantile Creditors' Association of London, 1882. Reproduced by permission of the Bodleian Library. 298

10 Advertisement for a Mortlake tea dealer and cheesemonger, depicting Samuel Johnson paying Oliver Goldsmith's debts to his landlady, to preserve the novelist from the debtors' prison. Reproduced by permission of the Bodleian Library. 319

Tables

6.1 Courts of requests judgments, 12 February 1830–12 February
1831.   *page* 244
6.2 Litigants' representatives, Boston County Court, January–
June 1848.   256
7.1 Debts reduced, Shoreditch & Bow County Court, April 1892.   313

Acknowledgments

The research and writing of this book were made possible, in the first instance, by generous financial support from a succession of institutions. Awards from the Huntington Library, San Marino (W.M. Keck Foundation), the Emory University Research Council, the Shelby Cullom Davis Center for Historical Studies at Princeton University, the British Academy–Huntington Library Exchange Scholar scheme and a year-long residential fellowship at the Newberry Library, Chicago, funded by the United States National Endowment for the Humanities, all contributed vitally to the development of this project. A Warwick Research Fellowship has now given me the time, inspiration and intellectual space to bring the book, at last, to completion.

Librarians, archivists and staff members of the Bodleian, the British Library and countless local record offices and libraries have responded to my queries, helped me to locate documents and lugged a seemingly endless succession of volumes to my desk over the years, for which I remain deeply in their debt. Julie Anne Lambert of the Bodleian Library provided much expert assistance in navigating the rich holdings of the John Johnson Collection and in obtaining photographs for the illustrations. I am grateful to acknowledge permission to use the manuscript materials listed in the bibliography.

A decade in the making, this project has benefited from critical responses by members of seminars and participants at conferences on both sides of the Atlantic too numerous to note individually. My fellow fellows at the Newberry Library during 1998–99 do, however, deserve particular mention for offering enthusiastic readings and reactions to the project and for providing a constant stream of helpful references: with their encouragement, my year at the Newberry transformed this book from an institutional into a social and cultural history. Many thanks too are due to the Newberry's wonderful staff and to Jim Grossman for making the Library such a stimulating and congenial scholarly environment.

Two research assistants, Caitlin Murdoch and Kevin Bradley, contributed valuable time and bibliographical effort to this project. Individual chapters – often in baggy, tentative and inchoate form – have been read to my profit by Penelope Corfield, James Epstein, Thomas Green, Randall McGowen, James Oldham and Susan Whyman. As the book neared completion, Matthew Hilton,

Jo McDonagh and Carolyn Steedman read the text as a whole (or very nearly that) with perseverance, acuity and wit. The book is very much the better for their efforts and encouragement. I remain fully liable for any errors of fact or judgment.

The research and writing of this book have been a peripatetic exercise, much assisted by friendships and collegiality on both sides of the Atlantic. Over the years, Sheila Biddle, David Cannadine, Carole Hahn, Leslie Harris, Ivan Karp, Corie Kratz, Henrietta Leyser, Peter Mandler, Mary Odem, Randall Packard, Cindy and Richard Patterson, Roy Ritchie, Bill and Silvia Rodgers and Pat Thane have variously and kindly provided references, counsel, cheer, food, drink and accommodation. I remain fondly in their debt. At Warwick, my colleagues in the History Department have been most welcoming, demonstrating that the brain drain from the UK to the US is not the only possible (or necessarily the best) flight pattern for a British historian. I owe special thanks to the Warwick–Oxford Commuting Group – Maxine Berg, Colin Jones and Matthew Thomson – for their advice, conversation, collegiality and sociability over the course of the past two years.

At Cambridge, Elizabeth Howard and Helen Barton ably and cheerfully steered this project into and through production. Two anonymous readers for the Press offered incisive suggestions for improvement of the text. Keith Wrightson has given enthusiastic support for the project since it (and I) joined Cambridge Social and Cultural Histories.

Warm and generous family support has sustained *The Character of Credit* (and its author) for ages. Cherie, Cody, Emily and Miles have valuably distracted me from an obsession with the past during summer holidays. My parents, always the very kindest of creditors, have also always been much more than that. This book is for them both, with my love.

Abbreviations

BLPES	British Library of Political and Economic Science, LSE
CCC	*County Courts Chronicle*
CDG	*Credit Drapers' Gazette and Trade Informant*
CLRO	Corporation of London Record Office
Commons Journals	*Journals of the House of Commons*
EcoHR	*Economic History Review*
ELH	*English Literary History*
Guildhall	Guildhall Library, London
HJ	*Historical Journal*
JBS	*Journal of British Studies*
JMH	*Journal of Modern History*
LMA	London Metropolitan Archives
P&P	*Past & Present*
PMLA	*Publications of the Modern Language Association of America*
PRO	Public Record Office, Kew
RO	Record Office
UCL	University College London Archives
VS	*Victorian Studies*

Introduction

The diarist Sylas Neville (1741–1840) was an impecunious bachelor of genteel pretensions who had dissipated his fortune in youth at the gaming table. 'Short of money & in great distress, obliged to pawn my gold stock-buckle, to carry me to town', Neville wrote morosely in his journal while travelling near Tunbridge Wells in 1768. 'Hope I shall never again be reduced to the same necessity.' Safely returned to London, Neville remained ensnared in a web of personal debt relations – his own, and those of his family, friends and connections. March 1769 saw Neville's Bloomsbury landlord, Willoughby, arrested for debt and imprisoned in a so-called spunging house in Gray's Inn Lane. 'Drank tea there', Neville recorded on the day following Willoughby's arrest. 'A spunging house, the insolence and brutality of a bailiff and his myrmidons are equal to any description I have read of them.' Forced to find new lodgings when his landlord's household goods were sold to pay his debts, Neville leased a house in Norfolk, where he established himself as a minor squire, with his former servant (now his mistress) Sally Bradford ensconced conveniently nearby. Money-troubles continued to punctuate Neville's diary entries during his Norfolk retreat. 'May God grant that I may never be more embarrassed than I have lately been!', he prayed in December 1770, reduced to two shillings of ready money. Settling his annual bills for domestic and personal consumption in January further exacerbated Neville's credit woes, revealing that his expenditure had outpaced his income by a factor of nearly four. 'God have mercy upon me!', he lamented. 'I know not what I shall do.' Successive loans from a Yarmouth bill-discounter kept him temporarily solvent, but the death of a debtor for whom Neville had stood surety again reduced his finances to disarray in August. Determined to restore his fortune by adopting a profession, Neville departed Norwich for Edinburgh to study medicine. 'Leaving so many debts unpaid hurts me not a little', he reflected anxiously in October 1771. 'It will too probably create confusion.'[1]

---

[1] Basil Cozens-Hardy, ed., *The Diary of Sylas Neville 1767–1788* (London, 1950), 45 (28 September 1768); 65 (18 and 19 March 1769); 66 (22 March 1769); 86 (3 December 1770); 89 (3 January 1771); 129 (24 October 1771). 'I find that most of my companions are in debt as well as myself',

2   The Character of Credit

The 'confusion' that surrounded Sylas Neville's domestic finances was endemic to daily economic life in eighteenth-century England. Formal and informal loans, gifts of money and of goods, begging, borrowing, cadging and ultimately flight were essential economic strategies deployed by English men and women at all levels of society during the Georgian consumer revolution, and remained integral to consumer culture in the Victorian and Edwardian years. Extended credit relations fundamentally shaped social and cultural life, and were in turn animated by social and cultural norms throughout this period. The failure of these vital liens of personal credit, as Neville's landlord Willoughby had found to his distress, was a matter of much consequence. Writs, bailiffs, pettifogging lawyers and ultimately the prison awaited debtors unable (or unwilling) to meet their credit obligations.

This book explores the character of personal debt and credit relations in modern England. By probing the depiction of debt obligations in literary sources, by tracing the evolving history of the debtors' prison and by examining debt litigation in the small claims courts that proliferated in England from the 1740s, I hope to enrich our understanding of the experience of contractual relations from the onset of the industrial and consumer revolutions to the outbreak of the First World War. Throughout this period, the function of legal institutions in regulating transactions between English retailers and their customers was both vital and highly fraught. For while liberal theorists celebrated the economic agency of autonomous individuals in the market, day-to-day experiences of commerce and the law repeatedly drew attention instead to the embedded nature of the individual's economic activities. The history of personal debt and credit relations thus underscores the inability (or refusal) of consumers, creditors, lawyers and judges to endorse the 'modern' commercial concepts of economic individualism and freedom of contract. In this context, *The Character of Credit* attempts at once to understand the constraints imposed upon and the opportunities created for consumer activity by the conflicting legal structures, commercial customs, cultural beliefs and systems of representation that shaped economic obligations in modern England.

Three broad perspectives on the history of personal debts, credits and contracts structure this study. Part I surveys the depiction of debt and credit in three related literary genres. In these chapters, evidence drawn from novels, diaries and autobiographical memoirs highlights an array of exchange activities – including instrumental gift-giving, customary retail sociability, reliance on unwritten credit contracts and purchasing by persons who lacked legal agency – that decisively shaped the character, experience and understanding of personal debts in England. In keeping with recent trends in textual analysis, literary

he noted once in Edinburgh. 'Would to God a man could live without money', 144 (21 December 1771); 148 (12 January 1772).

works feature in these chapters as dynamic, constitutive components (rather than mere reflections) of historical experience. Revealing the extent to which not only quotidian purchasing but also broader social and economic processes were sustained by overlapping networks of indebtedness, these chapters build upon the work of anthropologists, early modern historians and literary scholars who have emphasised the intensely personal (and often highly sexualised) character of credit relations in systems of economic exchange. As literary sources repeatedly attest, the cultural calculus that governed personal credit relations in England complicated – indeed, it often thwarted – the enforcement of consumer contracts, and worked to blur distinctions between persons and possessions in representations of market activity. By attending to depictions of both gift and commodity exchange in fiction, diaries and memoirs, these chapters seek to illuminate the commercial and the imaginative contexts within which the legal institutions that regulated consumer debt and credit evolved and operated.

Part II draws upon an array of institutional and governmental records to examine the changing history of imprisonment for debt, a practice that figures prominently in the literary accounts of credit relations discussed in Part I. As an instrument for enforcing civil contracts, the debtors' prison operated at the extreme end of the spectrum of legal control, functioning as a device of last resort for creditors unable to wrest payments from their customers by mutual agreement, persuasion or the intervention of friends, neighbours and family. Although hardly typical of daily credit relations, the practice of imprisonment for debt provides a particularly revealing optic for viewing changes in contractual obligations. By casting into sharp relief the contradictions that shot through contemporary understandings of the relations between economic agents and legal persons, human bodies and consumer goods, the evolving history of imprisonment for debt exposes to view key political and institutional obstacles to contractual individualism in modern England.

Part III shifts attention from the beginning and end points of consumer activity (detailed in Parts I and II), exploring instead the middle ground of retail negotiation revealed by the litigation of domestic credit contracts in summary small claims courts. Using legal materials and records derived from tradesmen's protection associations, these chapters juxtapose the pragmatic strategies used by consumers to obtain goods on credit with the counter-stratagems adopted by retailers to extract payment from recalcitrant debtors. Tensions between equity and common law and conflicts created by differences of class and gender probed in this section of the book illustrate the malleability of legal systems, the extent to which institutions designed to enforce 'free' contracts were complicit in the persistent moralisation and regulation of the retail market. Explicitly designed to modernise legal processes of debt reclamation by liberating them from customary constraints, the small claims courts established throughout England from the 1740s instead repeatedly registered and affirmed entrenched social

4   The Character of Credit

beliefs, identities and practices that constrained fully contractual consumer behaviour.

Credit and consumer culture

My focus on the period from 1740 to 1914 reflects a confluence of economic and legal developments that rendered English debt and credit obligations especially problematic in these years.[2] The mid-eighteenth century saw a significant expansion of commercial culture, as new developments in the production, exchange and consumption of goods enlarged both the extent of economic activity and the scope of economic discourse. Like the industrial revolution – which it has tended to supplant in analyses of the Georgian economy – the consumer revolution initially figured in historical writing as a rapid and triumphal development of the later eighteenth century.[3] But scholars now assign consumer activity a more extended genealogy, delineating a protracted evolution of commercial culture evident in England from at least the seventeenth century. In this revised interpretation of economic growth, while factory industry gained only a gradual and partial ascendancy over more traditional modes of production in the modern period, market-orientated consumption activities had begun to assume a central place in the lives of English men and women already in the medieval and early modern eras.[4]

The shift from supply-side to demand-side analysis in historical writing and the prominent place enjoyed by English developments in the resulting secondary literature, Craig Clunas observes, have rendered consumption 'if not

---

[2] This study focuses on England (with some attention to Wales) rather than on Britain as a whole. The significant differences between English and Scots law preclude a fully British approach to personal debt and credit at this juncture. Sustained comparative analysis will moreover be premature until historians establish a more accurate understanding of the nature of legal culture and practice in England itself.

[3] See especially Neil McKendrick, John Brewer and J.H. Plumb, *The Birth of a Consumer Society: The Commercialization of Eighteenth-Century England* (London, 1982) and Colin Campbell, *The Romantic Ethic and the Spirit of Modern Consumerism* (Oxford, 1987). For intelligent commentary on the problematic concept of the 'consumer revolution', see Jan de Vries, 'Between purchasing power and the world of goods: understanding the household economy in early modern Europe', in John Brewer and Roy Porter, eds., *Consumption and the World of Goods* (London, 1993), 85–132, esp. 89.

[4] See Peter N. Stearns, 'Stages of consumerism: recent work on the issues of periodization', *JMH*, 69, 1 (March 1997), 102–17. Authors who emphasise the significance of medieval developments in consumer and commercial society in England include R.H. Britnell, *The Commercialisation of English Society, 1000–1500* (Cambridge, 1993). For early modern developments, see Joan Thirsk, *Economic Policy and Projects: The Development of Consumer Society in Early Modern England* (Oxford, 1978); Margaret Spufford, *The Great Reclothing of Rural England: Petty Chapmen and Their Wares in the Seventeenth Century* (London, 1984); Carole Shammas, *The Pre-Industrial Consumer in England and America* (Oxford, 1990); and Lorna Weatherill, *Consumer Behaviour and Material Culture in Britain, 1660–1760*, 2nd edn (London, 1996).

Introduction 5

the linchpin then a major prop of the argument, spoken or unspoken, for an exclusively "Western" (actually, Anglo-American) modernity'.[5] In this paradigm of modernisation, the foundations of England's rise to economic eminence lie in the financial revolution that unfolded in the aftermath of the political struggles of 1688, a development that transformed English government funding by erecting a sophisticated edifice of public debt and credit. The financial instruments and institutions that emerged in these years proved capable of sustaining a dramatically enlarged fiscal and military state without detracting from the economic vitality of the broader English nation.[6] Expansion of this economic base beyond the British Isles through the processes of imperialism added materially to the fortunes of England's emerging financial elite, while fostering the wider growth of an increasingly affluent (and self-conscious) 'middling sort' of persons, deriving economic sustenance primarily from trade and manufacture.[7] Modes of thinking about economic activity changed significantly in this new commercial context, a development clearly evident in Britain's disproportionate contribution to the emergence of a science of economics. From ancient times, philosophers had wrestled with the tendency of trade to corrupt public morals, but the eighteenth century saw the development in Britain of a school of political economy – centred on but not confined to the works of Adam Smith – distinguished by its moralistic affirmation of the simultaneous pursuit of wealth and virtue.[8]

Smith's magisterial *Wealth of Nations* (1776) offered contemporaries a bold reformulation of the individual's role in fostering commercial growth, but it also laid the groundwork for economic theory's enduring misapprehension of personal credit and consumer relations by positing the cash nexus as an axiomatic

---

[5] Craig Clunas, 'Modernity global and local: consumption and the rise of the West', *American Historical Review*, 104, 5 (December 1999), 1510.

[6] P.G.M. Dickson, *The Financial Revolution in England: A Study in the Development of Public Credit 1688–1756* (London, 1967); John Brewer, *The Sinews of Power: War, Money and the English State, 1688–1785* (New York, 1989); Bruce Carruthers, *City of Capital: Politics and Markets in the English Financial Revolution* (Princeton, 1996).

[7] For the imperial dimensions of these developments, see David Hancock, *Citizens of the World: London Merchants and the Integration of the British Atlantic Community, 1735–1785* (Cambridge, 1995). For the domestic impact of commercial development, see Leonore Davidoff and Catherine Hall, *Family Fortunes: Men and Women of the English Middle Class, 1780–1850* (Chicago, 1987), and Margaret Hunt, *The Middling Sort: Commerce, Gender, and the Family in England, 1680–1780* (Berkeley, 1996).

[8] The extended purchase of luxury in debates about economic growth is detailed by John Sekora, *Luxury: The Concept in Western Thought, Eden to Smollett* (Baltimore, 1977), and Christopher Berry, *The Idea of Luxury: A Conceptual and Historical Investigation* (Cambridge, 1994). For the political economists' resolution of commerce and morality, see Istvan Hont and Michael Ignatieff, eds., *Wealth and Virtue: The Shaping of Political Economy in the Scottish Enlightenment* (Cambridge, 1983), and J.G.A. Pocock, *Virtue, Commerce, and History: Essays on Political Thought and History, Chiefly in the Eighteenth Century* (Cambridge, 1985).

6 The Character of Credit

feature of eighteenth-century English retail activity.[9] In his schematic recapitulation of the evolution of money, Smith executed a rapid, unexamined leap from primordial economic transactions predicated on barter to modern market activity based on the immediate exchange of cash. '[W]hen barter ceases, and money has become the common instrument of commerce, every particular commodity is more frequently exchanged for money than for any other commodity', he asserted, implicitly foreclosing attention to the mediation of cash sales by credit contracts in consumer markets. Although Smith recognised the development of business credit as a vital component of manufacture and international trade, staple practices of eighteenth-century consumer retailing such as extended billing cycles and credit purchasing on account find no place in his simplistic anatomy of exchange. Rather, Smith depicts modern consumer marketing activity as an anonymous, autonomous form of transaction antithetical to the protracted, personal negotiations that had occurred in pre-modern systems of barter. In his idealised consumer market cash dealings reign supreme: 'The butcher seldom carries his beef or his mutton to the baker, or the brewer, in order to exchange them for bread or for beer; but he carries them to the market, where he exchanges them for money, and afterwards exchanges that money for bread and for beer.'[10]

Despite their avowed hostility to the tenets of liberal individualism, nineteenth-century critics of classical political economy typically accepted Smith's formulation of the cash nexus as the characteristic mode of modern market exchange. As Peter Stallybrass argues in a brilliant exposition of Karl Marx's day-to-day household expedients, the theorist's refusal to distinguish systematically between cash and credit in his analysis of economic individualism and exchange relations flew in the face of his personal understanding of the material operation of consumer credit in the Victorian market. Convinced that labour was the source of all value, Marx (like Smith before him) privileged

---

[9] For the limitations of Smith's theorisation of the consumer market, see esp. Joyce Appleby, 'Consumption in early modern economic thought', in Brewer and Porter, eds., *Consumption and the World of Goods*, 162–73, and Neil De Marchi, 'Adam Smith's accommodation of "altogether endless" desires', in Maxine Berg and Helen Clifford, eds., *Consumers and Luxury: Consumer Culture in Europe 1650–1850* (Manchester, 1999), 18–36.

[10] Adam Smith, *An Inquiry into the Nature and Causes of the Wealth of Nations*, ed. Edwin Cannon (1776; Chicago, 1976), 36. As Avner Offer suggests, where Smith's *Theory of Moral Sentiments* recognised sympathy as a powerful engine of reciprocal exchange, an innate tendency to 'truck, barter, and exchange' served instead to motivate transactions in the *Wealth of Nations*. See Avner Offer, 'Between the gift and the market: the economy of regard', *EcoHR*, 50, 3 (1997), 452. The limitations of the liberal conceptualisation of the market are detailed by Craig Muldrew, 'Interpreting the market: the ethics of credit and community relations in early modern England', *Social History*, 18, 2 (May 1993); Mary Douglas and Baron Isherwood, eds., *The World of Goods: Towards an Anthropology of Consumption*, 2nd edn (New York, 1996); and Margaret Jane Radkin, *Contested Commodities* (Cambridge, MA., 1996), esp. chap. 3.

Introduction 7

production over consumption in his writings, devoting scant attention in his treatises to the petty credit transactions through which the worker's household was provisioned. But as a head of household and consumer himself, Marx was palpably alive to the significance of personal credit markets. Constantly reduced to pawning his own possessions to subsidise his research, writing and domestic expenditure, Marx quite literally wrote his critique of capitalism on the credit of his own overcoat. It was only by pawning his clothes, furniture and silver that he could pay cash to settle his extended credit accounts with the butcher, baker and stationer; only by then redeeming his overcoat from the pawnbroker could Marx gain admission to the British Museum Reading Room, and thereby complete the labour which was to produce his *Capital*.[11]

If the classical and Marxist economic traditions provide only an impoverished theoretical framework for understanding consumer credit, continental social theorists have, in contrast, emphasised the pivotal role of personal debts in economic exchange, social relations and the symbolic order.[12] Since the publication of Marcel Mauss's 'Essai sur le don' in 1925, anthropologists have generated a comprehensive series of reflections on the social and symbolic function of credit obligations. In Mauss's *Gift*, credit constitutes the lifeblood of human relations, helping both to forge viable social groups and to distribute power within them. Ethnographic descriptions of exchange in Melanesian, Polynesian and Native American societies prompted Mauss to argue that the direction of economic evolution over time 'has not been from barter to sale, and from cash sale to credit sale.' In thus emphatically rejecting Smith's model of the market, Mauss drew attention to the economic significance of routine, enforced gift-giving in traditional societies. Exchanging gifts not only of goods but also of 'banquets, rituals, military services, women, children', pre-modern peoples created extended debt obligations which, Mauss proposed, emerged before and decisively shaped both barter and market transactions. These gift exchanges were rendered obligatory by notions of honour, generosity and distinction, as well as by physical reprisals for failure to reciprocate; the obligatory nature of

---

[11] Peter Stallybrass, 'Marx's coat', in Patricia Speyer, ed., *Border Fetishisms: Material Objects in Unstable Spaces* (New York, 1998), 183–207. As Marx noted in the third volume of *Capital*, 'It lies outside the scope of our plan to give a detailed analysis of the credit system and the instruments this creates (credit, money, etc.).' Karl Marx, *Capital: A Critique of Political Economy*, intro. Ernest Mandel, 3 vols. (Harmondsworth, 1981), III: 525. Craig Muldrew offers a particularly perceptive critique of Marx's failure to appreciate the theoretical significance of credit in his ' "Hard food for Midas": cash and its social value in early modern England', *P&P*, 170 (February 2001), esp. 79, 120.

[12] In addition to the anthropological tradition, discussed below, see esp. Georg Simmel, *The Philosophy of Money*, second, enlarged edition, ed. David Frisby, trans. Tom Bottomore and David Frisby (London, 1990), 479, and Friedrich Nietzsche, *On the Genealogy of Morals*, trans. Walter Kaufmann (New York, 1967), 56–71.

8   The Character of Credit

the gift relation in turn laid the pragmatic and philosophical foundations for economic conceptualisations of debt and credit.[13]

In building upon Mauss's analysis, anthropologists have increasingly emphasised the applicability of his theories to modern and to Western cultures. C.A. Gregory, assessing the development of Western commodity exchange in Papua New Guinea, argues that modernisation typically prompts the proliferation of 'traditional' gift behaviours alongside 'modern' commodity exchanges, rather than the simple progression from gift to market exchange posited by classical and neoclassical theories of development.[14] Annette Weiner's interrogation of gifts as 'inalienable possessions' points to a second, parallel strand of argument, by highlighting the resilience and viability of gift relations in Western economies themselves. Noting that a confluence of gift- and commodity-orientated conceptions of property informs even the economic theories of thinkers such as John Locke, she underlines the need to integrate anthropological perspectives into the history of Western economic development.[15] Jonathan Parry and Maurice Bloch similarly caution against analyses of commercial development that represent pre-modern exchange in terms of personal, social negotiations and modern market exchange in terms of anonymous monetary transactions. Such approaches, they assert, construct 'a false history in which what is actually an extremely general contrast *within* cultures... becomes a contrast *between* cultures – and it is on this basis that the notion of a "great divide" between the monetary and pre-monetary worlds has rested'.[16]

Historians of medieval and early modern Europe have employed these lines of anthropological reasoning to much effect.[17] Less common are historical efforts to extend these anthropological insights to the quotidian economic transactions

---

[13] Marcel Mauss, *The Gift: The Form and Reason for Exchange in Archaic Societies*, trans. W.D. Halls, intro. Mary Douglas (New York, 1990), 36, 5. For useful appraisals of Mauss's writings, see esp. Wendy James and N.J. Allen, eds., *Marcel Mauss: A Centenary Tribute* (New York, 1998), and Maurice Godelier, *The Enigma of the Gift*, trans. Nora Scott (Chicago, 1999), 10–107.

[14] C.A. Gregory, *Gifts and Commodities* (London, 1982), 4.

[15] Annette B. Weiner, *Inalienable Possessions: The Paradox of Keeping-while-Giving* (Berkeley, 1992), 155. For her discussion of Locke, see 34–5.

[16] Jonathan Parry and Maurice Bloch, 'Introduction: money and the morality of exchange', in Jonathan Parry and Maurice Bloch, eds., *Money and the Morality of Exchange* (Cambridge, 1989), 29. See similarly Viviana Zelizer's astute sociological analysis of the social dynamics of monetary transactions in the United States from 1870 to 1930, *The Social Meaning of Money: Pin Money, Paychecks, Poor Relief, and Other Currencies* (New York, 1994).

[17] Felicity Heal, 'Reciprocity and exchange in the late medieval household', in Barbara A. Hanawalt and David Wallace, eds., *Bodies and Disciplines: Intersections of Literature and History in Fifteenth-Century England* (Minneapolis, 1996), 179–98; Natalie Zemon Davis, *The Gift in Sixteenth-Century France* (Oxford, 2000); Jane Fair Bestor, 'Marriage transactions in Renaissance Italy and Mauss's *Essay on the Gift*', *P&P*, 164 (August 1999), 6–46; Ilana Krausman Ben-Amos, 'Gifts and favors: informal support in early modern England', *JMH*, 72, 2 (June 2000), 295–338; Christian Windler, 'Tributes and presents in Franco-Tunisian diplomacy', *Journal of Early Modern History*, 4, 2 (May 2000), 168–99.

Introduction 9

of modern cultures. Historians of ante-bellum America have demonstrated both the persistence of customary gift relations alongside newer market mentalities and the successful amalgamation of gifting and contractual behaviours by slave owners in the Old South.[18] But analyses of instrumental gift relations in industrial societies such as England have focused on charitable donations rather than on economic and social exchange more broadly, suggesting that gift-related behaviours were rendered marginal to the modern market by the growth of contractual individualism.[19] James Carrier offers a partial exception to this general rule of neglect, suggesting that key aspects of eighteenth- and early nineteenth-century consumer credit relations were shaped by the reformulation of earlier gifting behaviours. As Carrier observes, in the absence of formal mechanisms for evaluating financial risk, later eighteenth- and early nineteenth-century English shopkeepers' customary extension of credit to their customers was a 'decision to enter into a personal relationship of trust', and retail purchasing thus 'carried an air of gift, rather than just commodity, transaction'. Whereas Carrier posits a sharp decline in such credit relations in the course of the nineteenth century,[20] I suggest below that informal retail credit flourished in and worked to sustain later nineteenth-century consumer markets. Mauss's interpretation of the gift can in this context help to illuminate three aspects of modern English culture that are obscured by both liberal and Marxist paradigms of economic behaviour: the configuration of social power outside relations of production, the shifting conceptualisation of the individual's personhood in the consumer revolution and the central role of gender identities in systems of contractual exchange.

First and perhaps most obvious is the key part played by credit dealings – rather than property ownership or class status alone – in the creation and maintenance of social distinctions and economic disparities. Described by Pierre Bourdieu as the 'exercise of gentle violence', credit is, like obligatory gift exchange, 'an attack on the freedom of one who receives it . . . it creates obligations,

---

[18] Bertram Wyatt-Brown, *Southern Honor: Ethics and Behavior in the Old South* (Oxford, 1982), 331–9; Kenneth S. Greenberg, *Honor and Slavery: Lies, Duels, Noses, Masks, Dressing as a Woman, Gifts, Strangers, Humanitarianism, Death, Slave Rebellions, the Proslavery Argument, Baseball, Hunting, and Gambling in the Old South* (Princeton, 1996).

[19] Gareth Stedman Jones, *Outcast London: A Study in the Relationship between Classes in Victorian Society* (Oxford, 1971), esp. 251–61; Roy Porter, 'The gift relation: philanthropy and provincial hospitals in eighteenth-century England', in Lindsay Granshaw and Roy Porter, eds., *The Hospital in History* (London, 1989), 149–78. Peter Shapley, 'Urban charity, class relations and social cohesion: charitable responses to the Cotton Famine', *Urban History*, 28, 1 (May 2001), 46–64; and Richard Titmuss, *The Gift Relationship: From Human Blood to Social Policy* (London, 1970). For efforts to extend analysis of gifting other than through charitable exchange into the nineteenth and twentieth centuries, see my 'Men's things: masculine possession in the consumer revolution', *Social History*, 25, 2 (May 2000), 133–55, and Offer, 'Between the gift and the market'.

[20] Carrier, *Gifts and Commodities*, 92, 93.

10　　The Character of Credit

it is a way to possess, by creating people obliged to reciprocate'.[21] English debt obligations forcefully illustrate this point. Novels, diaries and memoirs, which offer especially rich evidence of the prevalence of gift and credit relations in eighteenth- and nineteenth-century England, repeatedly demonstrate their implication with wider disparities of power in English society. By awarding differential credit terms according to perceived differences of personal character and social standing, tradesmen not only responded to consumers' efforts at self-fashioning but also helped to position these individuals within hierarchical social relations. As the consumption of luxury and semi-luxury goods increased apace, debt courts and debtors' prisons emerged as particularly contentious sites of interpersonal dispute. Empowering creditors such as tradesmen to seize and imprison the bodies of their debtors without benefit of jury trials, the debt law was a byword of arbitrary authority, figuring in English culture as a synecdoche for the violation of personal liberties. As conceptions of personal autonomy gained primacy in economic, political and legal thought, the function of gifts and debts in sustaining unequal power relations became increasingly problematic, spurring intense debates over the court system's role in adjudicating consumer contracts.

A second set of insights suggested by Mauss's approach to debt and credit concerns the persistently social character of modern economic relations. In *The Gift*, Mauss draws attention to the constant slippage between the category of the person and the category of the thing in pre-modern systems of exchange. Gift and credit relations in these cultures share a tendency to animate objects and to objectify persons, endowing goods with human characteristics and incorporating human bodies alongside material possessions in networks of circulation. Blurring distinctions between individuals and their possessions, exchanges based on gift and credit effectively construct webs of obligation in which economic values are embedded within social systems and shaped by cultural beliefs, rather than circulating freely through goods in purely economic markets.[22] Slavery now offers perhaps the most familiar illustration of this phenomenon, but personal debt relations arguably made the modern market's confusion of things and persons more obviously manifest on a daily basis to English men and women. By seizing men's bodies for their debts, the civil law substituted persons for things in market exchange, allowing the human body to serve as collateral for goods obtained not through productive labour and the cash nexus but rather through the operation of consumer credit. Distinctions of

---

[21] Pierre Bourdieu, *Outline of a Theory of Practice*, trans. Richard Nice (Cambridge, 1977), 193; idem, 'The economy of symbolic goods', in his *Practical Reason: On the Theory of Action* (Stanford, 1998), 94.

[22] See for example Mauss, *The Gift*, pp. 46–7, 65; and idem, 'A category of the human mind: the notion of person; the notion of self', in Michael Carrithers, Steven Collins and Steven Lukes, eds., *The Category of the Person: Anthropology, Philosophy, History* (Cambridge, 1985), 1–45.

Introduction 11

age, class and (most crucially) gender further complicated the troubled relation between things and persons in English markets, for the bodies of the children, servants and wives who routinely purchased goods on credit for the male heads of their households were exempt by law from imprisonment for these debts.

Gender constitutes the third aspect of debt relations illuminated by a shift in emphasis from neoclassical to anthropological concerns. Liberal economic treatises depict the market as a public arena for economic man: in Adam Smith's description, the butcher carries 'his' meat to market to obtain bread and beer, through the exchange of money, from (implicitly male) bakers and brewers.[23] Excluding both the butcher's wife and consumer credit from consideration, this model of the market fits well with later eighteenth- and nineteenth-century formulations of domestic ideology, in which married women occupied a private sphere (centred in the home) separate from the public world of trade and politics.[24] But this idealised vision of the market accords ill with English economic practice as chronicled in primary sources that range from account books, diaries, memoirs and novels to commercial correspondence, press reports and court records. In these documents, women assume a twofold economic role familiar from cultural anthropology, serving both as objects and as agents of exchange.[25] In a host of contemporary texts, representations of sexual relations and the marriage market draw attention to the descriptive limitations of separate-spheres ideology and demonstrate the enduring interpenetration of gift and commodity exchange in modern English society. The prominent role in these sources of women as agents in the circulation of goods through gift-giving and credit networks likewise illustrates the crucial location of the consumer market at the fluid interface of the public and private spheres.

Law and literature

By emphasising the qualitative difference between cash and credit transactions and by attending to the social and symbolic significance of economic exchange, the anthropological perspectives on debt discussed above complement recent trends in literary analysis that inform the interpretation of consumer activity offered in this book. Where historians have been slow to investigate the material function of credit in modern consumer markets, literary scholars

---

[23] The broader implications of economists' abstraction of gender identities in models of the market are anatomised by Julie A. Nelson, 'Abstraction, reality and the gender of "economic man"', in James G. Carrier and Daniel Miller, eds., *Virtualism: A New Political Economy* (Oxford, 1998), 75–94.

[24] Davidoff and Hall, *Family Fortunes*, offers the classic interpretation of domestic ideology in England.

[25] See Bordieu, *Outline of a Theory of Practice*, esp. 58–71; Marilyn Strathern, *The Gender of the Gift: Problems with Women and Problems with Society in Melanesia* (Berkeley, 1988); and Weiner, *Inalienable Possessions*.

12   The Character of Credit

have repeatedly underlined the cultural significance of representations of gifts and credit in eighteenth- and nineteenth-century texts. In their writings (as in the anthropological literature), gender, power and a persistent confusion between things and persons figure centrally in English economic exchange. From the later seventeenth century, notions of femininity were essential to the literary representation of public credit institutions in the financial revolution.[26] As private credit came to loom ever larger in the public mind, male and female literary commentators played relentlessly on the perceived nexus between sexual restraint and economic probity, conflating feminine chastity with virtuous credit dealings and equating lapses in female propriety with financial insolvency.[27] Gift relations surfaced persistently in these literary engagements with the market, lending a broad spectrum of credit dealings a distinctly erotic charge.[28]

Above and beyond the analytical insights offered by new historicist considerations of debt and credit in fictional writing, attention to literary texts as primary sources offers a crucial corrective to histories of exchange modelled on the classic treatises of economic theory. To study the history of eighteenth- and nineteenth-century consumption through the autonomous labourers, tradesmen, merchants and industrialists featured in *Capital* or *The Wealth of Nations* is to encounter a fictional market predicated on economic individualism and the anonymous cash nexus. To read Richardson's *Pamela* (1740), Elizabeth Gaskell's *Ruth* (1853) or Anthony Trollope's *The Way We Live Now* (1872) is instead to witness the workings of a credit economy – familiar from the daily lives of novelists and countless other English men and women – in which exchanges effected through borrowing and lending, gifting and purchasing on account, were shaped by both dense networks of social relations and intrinsically unstable conceptualisations of the individual self.

If the density and the character of references to gifts and credit in literary records particularly recommend these texts as sources for the history of personal debt relations, their utility is further augmented by a cluster of integral links between imaginative literature and the law in eighteenth- and nineteenth-century England. Lawyers and failed lawyers were among the most prolific writers of

---

[26] Sandra Sherman, *Finance and Fictionality in the Early Eighteenth Century: Accounting for Defoe* (Cambridge, 1996), 40. See also J.G.A. Pocock, *The Machiavellian Moment: Florentine Political Thought and the Atlantic Republican Tradition* (Princeton, 1975), 452–7, and Paula R. Backscheider, 'Defoe's Lady Credit', *Huntington Library Quarterly*, 44, 2 (Spring 1981), 89–100.

[27] See, for example, Daniel Defoe, *The Complete English Tradesman* (1726) (reprinted Gloucester, 1987), esp. 133. The impact of the financial and consumer revolutions on literature is detailed by Liz Bellamy, *Commerce, Morality and the Eighteenth-Century Novel* (Cambridge, 1998), and Catherine Ingrassia, *Authorship, Commerce, and Gender in Early Eighteenth-Century England: A Culture of Paper Credit* (Cambridge, 1998).

[28] For the eroticisation of exchange in literature, see Lewis Hyde, *The Gift: Imagination and the Erotic Life of Property* (New York, 1979).

Introduction 13

fiction in these centuries, a circumstance that worked to introduce and highlight legal themes in the novel for generations.[29] The material conditions of literary life – the sheer poverty and reduced circumstances experienced by all but the most successful authors – further reinforced English writers' association with the law, and ensured that personal experience with the legal institutions that regulated credit relations extended as well to women. Pawning, money-lending, small claims litigation and imprisonment for debt are not only potent metaphors for unequal power relations in novels and memoirs, they are also the pragmatic means by which writers negotiated their lives as consumers and producers in English markets.[30]

More broadly, law and literature are linked discursively, for law is constructed 'not only as rules and policies but as stories, explanations, performances, linguistic exchanges – as narratives and rhetoric'.[31] The narrativity of legal argument inherently lends the law literary form, character and content: as texts, law's stories share essential structural and functional attributes with imaginative writing.[32] In deploying legal lines of argument, English novelists (and English litigants) had at their disposal not only knowledge garnered from their personal encounters with the law in social and economic life but also the rich narrative potential of legal discourse itself. Just as novelists such as Henry Fielding and Charles Dickens used legal settings and circumstances as mechanisms for propelling their narratives forward, so too legal writers such as Sir Henry Maine attributed the evolution of English law over time to the emergence of so-called legal fictions – the rhetorical devices deployed by lawyers in the courtroom to conceal disparities between the letter and the operation of the rule of law.[33] Recognition of the strategic uses to which legal fictions could be put extended easily from the novel to the courts. In the myriad small claims tribunals in which

---

[29] Valentine Cunningham, 'Unto him (or her) that hath: how Victorian writers made ends meet', *Times Literary Supplement*, 11 September 1998, 13; John Sutherland, *Victorian Fiction: Writers, Publishers, Readers* (Basingstoke, 1995), chap. 8.

[30] Edward Copeland, *Women Writing about Money: Women's Fiction in England, 1790–1820* (Cambridge, 1995), and Nigel Cross, *The Common Writer: Life in Nineteenth-Century Grub Street* (Cambridge, 1985) offer excellent analyses of the impact of personal debts on literary life and literature itself.

[31] Paul Gewirtz, 'Narrative and rhetoric in the law', in Peter Brooks and Paul Gewirtz, eds., *Law's Stories: Narrative and Rhetoric in the Law* (New Haven, 1996), 2.

[32] James Boyd White, *Heracles' Bow: Essays on the Rhetoric and Politics of the Law* (Madison, 1985), 95.

[33] For Fielding and Dickens and the law, see esp. Jan-Melissa Schramm, *Testimony and Advocacy in Victorian Law, Literature and Theology* (Cambridge, 2000), 72–82, and Randall Craig, *Promising Language: Betrothal in Victorian Law and Fiction* (Albany, NY, 2000), 77–119. Maine's understanding of legal fictions is detailed by Alan Diamond, 'Fictions, equity and legislation: Maine's three agencies of legal change', in Alan Diamond, ed., *The Victorian Achievement of Sir Henry Maine: A Centennial Reappraisal* (Cambridge, 1991), 242–55. For a broader assessment of the significance of the 'law and literature' movement for historians, see my 'Victorian law, literature and history: three ships passing in the night', *Journal of Victorian Culture*, 7, 1 (Spring 2002), 134–46.

14   The Character of Credit

shopkeepers and their customers disputed consumer debts, litigants sought to advance their respective claims precisely by turning the internal inconsistencies of the law to their advantage. Together the common-law principle of coverture and the customary extension of prolonged retail credit by English tradesmen invited plaintiffs and defendants to exploit the conspicuous contradictions of the law of contract. By coverture, a married women's legal and economic identity was subsumed under her husband's legal agency, and wives in consequence lacked the ability to enter into credit contracts on their own behalf. But under the 'law of necessaries', a proviso contained within the law of coverture itself, wives enjoyed the right to pledge their husband's credit for 'necessary' (but not 'luxury') goods.[34] At once legal nonentities and legally acknowledged agents for their husbands, married women – like servants and children – were living illustrations of the common law's incoherence, of the inability of textual definitions of the legal person adequately to describe and contain the daily activities of men and women in the consumer market.

Conflict between common-law and equitable conceptions of justice was of pivotal importance in English small claims litigation, both conceptually and at an institutional level. As a legal doctrine, equity is the meliorist principle by which legal rules may be mitigated to ensure the realisation of the spirit or intention of the law. Privileging judicial discretion over precedent, equity looks not only to the legal cause but also to the human person, tempering the strict enforcement of contractual obligations by taking particular cognisance of the defendant's character and circumstances. The institutionalisation of equity in medieval and early modern courts such as Chancery and Requests saw the creation of jurisdictions in which judges repeatedly declined in their rulings to adhere to the letter of the common law. Here married women, while not recognised as full legal persons, were accorded a degree of legal and economic agency which was to be adopted by the common-law courts only in the later Victorian years. Conceptualised as courts that exercised the sovereign's 'conscience' as opposed to the strict letter of the common law, equitable jurisdictions 'formed a hinterland between what contemporaries considered to be the private and public spheres of life'.[35]

The abolition of Requests in the 1640s, the increasing calcification of legal procedure in Chancery and the unification of common-law and equitable jurisdictions in the High Court with the passage of the Judicature Acts of 1873–75 have encouraged legal and literary scholars to write the history of English equity in the modern period as a narrative of decline and fall. With the Judicature Acts, Dieter Polloczek for example argues, the anachronistic instruments of 'Equity

[34] For the law of necessaries, see my 'Women, consumption and coverture in England, c. 1760–1860', *HJ*, 39, 3 (September 1996), esp. 708–10.

[35] See Tim Stretton, *Women Waging Law in Elizabethan England* (Cambridge, 1998), esp. 25–9, citation from 11.

Introduction 15

became absorbed into law . . . essentially for purposes of egalitarian reform'.[36] Attention to the history of local small claims litigation – as opposed to a restricted focus on equity in the central courts of Westminster – suggests instead a pattern of legal evolution in which the equitable considerations that informed petty debt litigation gradually transformed legal practice in the superior courts of common law. The local small claims courts – dubbed courts of requests or courts of conscience to reflect their equitable character – that proliferated throughout England from the 1740s adhered from the outset to discretionary principles of justice, giving equity a new lease of institutional life that was preserved and expanded with the establishment of the national county-court system in 1847. Allowing married women to appear in court on behalf of their husbands in small debt cases and permitting interested parties to serve as witnesses in disputes over petty credit contracts, these inferior equitable courts were at the very forefront of legal innovation. Their history diverges from the narrative line of received accounts of legal reform in which parliamentary politicians at Westminster and legal theorists at Oxbridge and the Inns of Court serve as the chief agents of modernisation, suggesting instead that legal reform was often pioneered and powered from below and in the localities.[37] Where Sir William Blackstone, Lord Brougham and Sir Henry Maine now occupy pride of place in the pantheon of modern English legal reform, *The Character of Credit* emphasises the decisive part played by an ill-assorted array of legal characters – canny married-women shoppers and their indebted husbands, irate tradesmen determined to collect their unpaid credit accounts and small claims court judges (themselves husbands and consumers, debtors and creditors) who enjoyed unusually wide discretionary powers in determining the outcome of petty consumer disputes.

Whereas changes in the operation and perception of public debt and credit had earlier underpinned the financial revolution, changes in the status and experience of personal debt and credit were central to the transformation of law and economy that marked the producer and consumer revolutions.[38] In his *Ancient Law* (1861), Sir Henry Maine famously identified the transition 'from *Status to Contract*' as the distinguishing feature of 'progressive societies', and boasted

[36] Dieter Polloczek, *Literature and Legal Discourse: Equity and Ethics from Sterne to Conrad* (Cambridge, 1999), 8.

[37] For the significance of politicians and theorists to legal reform, see esp. Michael Lobban, 'Henry Brougham and law reform', *English Historical Review*, 105, 464 (November 2000), 1184–215, and idem, *The Common Law and English Jurisprudence* (Oxford, 1991). A. James Hammerton offers an especially perceptive analysis of the ways in which legal reform was shaped by social and cultural forces outside the realms of high politics and legal theory in *Cruelty and Companionship: Conflict in Nineteenth-Century Married Life* (London, 1992), esp. chap. 4.

[38] For the shift from a public preoccupation with public credit to concerns about private credit at mid-century, see Julian Hoppit, 'Attitudes to credit in Britain, 1680–1790', *HJ*, 33, 2 (June 1990), esp. 312.

16   The Character of Credit

that Victorian culture was 'mainly distinguished from that of preceding generations by the largeness of the sphere which is occupied in it by Contract'.[39] Historical analysis of the modern contractual order celebrated by Maine has however lagged behind the leading frontiers of the history of criminal law.[40] For the early modern period, the pioneering work of Christopher Brooks has located disputes over debts and contracts at the very heart of English litigation, suggesting 'that the civil law is even more important than the criminal law in maintaining the social and economic relationships in any society'.[41] But a dearth of comparable work on civil (in the sense of non-criminal) law in the modern period has impeded the emergence of a dynamic social and economic history of personal contracts in the era of the consumer and industrial revolutions. P.S. Atiyah's influential assessment of the century from 1770 to 1870 as a period marked by 'the rise and fall of freedom of contract' illuminates key intellectual and political currents that shaped the modern evolution of civil law, and new studies of the parliamentary reform of commercial law now provide solid foundations upon which a broader history of nineteenth-century contract may be constructed.[42] But historians have been slow to extend the source base of this new history of law beyond the pages of the Parliamentary Papers, *Hansard's Parliamentary Debates* and the legal periodical press. In consequence, with the important exception of recent work on marriage and divorce law,[43] our understanding of personal contracts in nineteenth-century England has been governed overwhelmingly by a top-down perspective. In sharp contrast to the criminal law, the history of modern civil contracts has privileged lawyers and politicians over litigants, producers and substantial merchants over consumers, men over women, and the propertied over the poor.

[39] Henry Sumner Maine, *Ancient Law: Its Connection with the Early History of Society, and Its Relation to Modern Ideas* (London, 1861), 170, 304.

[40] Stretton, *Women Waging Law*, 4. See also David Lieberman's astute analysis of the limitations of current legal interpretations of the history of contract, 'Contract before "freedom of contract" ', in Harry S. Scheiber, ed., *The State and Freedom of Contract* (Stanford, 1998), 89–121, 322–9.

[41] C.W. Brooks, *Lawyers, Litigation and English Society since 1450* (London, 1998), 27–62, citation from 28.

[42] P.S. Atiyah, *The Rise and Fall of Freedom of Contract* (Oxford, 1979). Essential recent works that explore the political and legislative background of commercial law reform in the long nineteenth century include Timothy Alborn, *Conceiving Companies: Joint-Stock Politics in Victorian England* (London, 1998); V. Markham Lester, *Victorian Insolvency: Bankruptcy, Imprisonment for Debt and Company Winding-Up in Nineteenth-Century England* (Oxford, 1995); Lobban, *The Common Law and English Jurisprudence*; and Patrick Polden, *A History of the County Court, 1846–1971* (Cambridge, 1999).

[43] See esp. Ginger Frost, *Promises Broken: Courtship, Class and Gender in Victorian England* (Charlottesville, 1995); Hammerton, *Cruelty and Companionship*; Gail Savage, ' "Intended only for the husband": gender, class, and the provision of divorce in England, 1858–1868', in Kristine Garrigan, ed., *Victorian Scandals: Representations of Class and Gender* (Athens, OH, 1992), 11–42; and Erika Rappaport, ' "A husband and his wife's dresses": consumer credit and the debtor family in England, 1864–1914', in Victoria de Grazia and Ellen Furlough, eds., *The Sex of Things: Gender and Consumption in Historical Perspective* (Berkeley, 1996), 163–87.

Introduction 17

A central claim of this study is that the expansion of consumption in modern England was powered in significant part by personal credit relations which, as they proliferated, subjected the received rules, practices and institutions of the civil law to increasing strain. The key role of credit in industrial growth and large-scale trade is a commonplace of economic history,[44] but we know relatively little about the dimensions of routine retail credit, informal borrowing and money-lending in the broader population. Craig Muldrew's detailed exposition of early modern retail practice has decisively demonstrated the ubiquity and instrumentality of sales credit prior to the eighteenth century, and suggests a variety of ways in which the culture of credit in Tudor and Stuart England militated against the strict enforcement of contracts.[45] In contrast, historians of the eighteenth- and nineteenth-century consumer revolutions have largely discounted the role of credit in shaping the purchasing process.[46] Cultural historians and exponents of cultural studies in particular have paid scant heed to consumer debt, tending to assume either that cash payments were typical in the retail market or that credit, where prevalent, was incidental to the structure and meaning of commodity exchange.[47]

---

[44] See esp. Martin J. Daunton, *Progress and Poverty: An Economic and Social History of Britain, 1700–1850* (Oxford, 1995), 247–52; Julian Hoppit, 'The use and abuse of credit in eighteenth-century England', in Neil McKendrick and R.B. Outhwaite, eds., *Business Life and Public Policy: Essays in Honour of D.C. Coleman* (Cambridge, 1986), 64–78; Pat Hudson, 'Financing firms, 1700–1850', in Maurice W. Kirby and Mary B. Rose, eds., *Business Enterprise in Modern Britain: From the Eighteenth to the Twentieth Century* (London, 1994), 92, 107–8; and Peter Mathias, *The Transformation of England: Essays in the Economic and Social History of England in the Eighteenth Century* (London, 1979), 88–115.

[45] Craig Muldrew, *The Economy of Obligation: The Culture of Credit and Social Relations in Early Modern England* (Basingstoke, 1998), esp. 174.

[46] Pawning represents a significant exception to this general rule of neglect. See esp. Beverly Lemire, *Dress, Culture and Commerce: The English Clothing Trade before the Factory, 1660–1800* (Basingstoke, 1997), 104–12; Paul Johnson, *Saving and Spending: The Working-Class Economy in Britain 1870–1959* (Oxford, 1985), 165–88; and Melanie Tebbutt, *Making Ends Meet: Pawnbroking and Working-Class Credit* (Leicester, 1983).

[47] Thus, for example, Thomas Richards devotes attention to the relation between consumer goods and 'spectacle', 'charisma' and 'kitsch', but declines to address the credit mechanisms by which goods were obtained. Thomas Richards, *The Commodity Culture of Victorian England: Advertising and Spectacle, 1851–1914* (Stanford, 1990). See similarly Rachel Bowlby, *Carried Away: The Invention of Modern Shopping* (London, 2000). Social historians have similarly obscured the significance of consumer credit, alternately arguing that it collapsed in the later nineteenth century or that its rise dated from this period. For the former argument, see for example Bill Lancaster, *The Department Store: A Social History* (London, 1995), 9. For the latter argument, see Judith Walkowitz, *City of Dreadful Delight: Narratives of Sexual Danger in Late-Victorian London* (Chicago, 1992), 47, and John Benson, *The Rise of Consumer Society in Britain, 1880–1980* (London, 1994), esp. 4. For a broader discussion of the problematic historiographical association between credit markets and modernity, see Philip Hoffman, Gilles Postel-Vinay and Jean-Laurent Rosenthal, 'Information and economic history: how the credit market in old regime Paris forces us to rethink the transition to capitalism', *American Historical Review*, 104, 1 (February 1999), 69–94, and their *Priceless Markets: The Political Economy of Credit in Paris, 1660–1870* (Chicago, 2000).

18   The Character of Credit

The history of small debt litigation offers a particularly useful corrective to these viewpoints, for the rapid proliferation of petty debt courts in England from the 1740s to the 1840s (and beyond) is a salutary reminder of the vital and continuous role played by trade credit throughout the successive phases of England's protracted consumer revolution. Important parallels link these developments in the civil law to the transformation of criminal process. In criminal law, summary courts – tribunals that dispatched justice without recourse to the much-vaunted common-law institution of trial by jury – bore an increasing burden of litigation from the eighteenth century onwards, playing an essential part in the legal regulation of property relations.[48] The parallel development of hundreds of summary small debt courts reinforced this line of evolution away from jury trials in English property law, while helping to rescue much civil litigation from the labyrinthine complexities and extortionate costs of the established courts of common law and equity. Instituted throughout England and Wales by a succession of parliamentary statutes, the local courts of requests (also known as courts of conscience) that mediated increasing numbers of small-scale contractual disputes from the 1740s, and the national county-court system that supplanted them in 1846, testify to the central importance of credit transactions for working- and middle-class producers and consumers in this period.[49] It was, significantly, these summary small claims jurisdictions (whose defendants derived overwhelmingly from the lower and working classes) which continued to commit consumer debtors to English gaols until the later twentieth century, despite the formal abolition of imprisonment for debt at common law in 1869.

Character and credit

'Character' serves in the title of this book as a metonym for the fluid constellation of attributes recognised as signifiers of personal credit in the eighteenth and nineteenth centuries. At one level, my choice of this term simply reflects eighteenth- and nineteenth-century usage. Where early modern debt relations

---

[48] See esp. Norma Landau, *The Justices of the Peace, 1689–1760* (Berkeley, 1984); Robert B. Shoemaker, *Prosecution and Punishment: Petty Crimes and the Law in London and Rural Middlesex, c. 1660–1725* (Cambridge, 1991); and George Behlmer, 'Summary justice and working-class marriage in England, 1870–1940', *Law and History Review*, 12, 2 (Fall 1994), 229–75.

[49] For the courts of conscience, see W.H.D. Winder, 'The courts of requests', *Law Quarterly Review*, 207 (1936), 369–94; H.W. Arthurs, *'Without the Law': Administrative Justice and Legal Pluralism in Nineteenth-Century England* (Toronto, 1985); Brooks, *Lawyers, Litigation and English Society*, esp. 59–62, 68; and Paul Langford, *Public Life and the Propertied Englishman 1689–1798* (Oxford, 1991), 158–60. For the county courts, see esp. Paul Johnson, 'Class law in Victorian England', *P&P*, 141 (November 1993),147–69; Polden, *History of the County Court*; and G.R. Rubin, 'Law, poverty and imprisonment for debt, 1869–1914', in G.R. Rubin and David Sugarman, eds., *Law, Economy and Society: Essays in the History of English Law* (Abingdon, 1984), 241–99.

Introduction 19

had been predicated on conceptions of mutual trust,[50] modern consumer credit was shaped most decisively by notions of personal character. The diary of the historical painter Benjamin Haydon illustrates contemporary understandings of the significance of character for credit. Notoriously insolvent and repeatedly imprisoned for debt, Haydon returned again and again in his journal to the problematic character of personal credit. Upon his release from the King's Bench prison in 1830, he pointedly recorded the adjudicating judge's remark in court that nothing had 'passed this day which can reflect the slightest on your character'. Again 'Harassed to death' by his debts in 1834, Haydon – 'for the sake of my character with the nobility' – desperately begged credit from his landlord to prevent bailiffs from seizing his goods.[51] Character functioned in Haydon's legal and domestic dealings, as it did in English culture more broadly, at once as the basis upon which lenders extended credit to borrowers and consumers and as a broader social and cultural measure of personal worth. Perceptions of personal worth, in turn, registered the successful use of goods and services obtained on credit to construct creditworthy characters. Credit thus reflected character, but also constituted it.

Haydon's diary suggests a second connotation of character significant for this study. Immured in the King's Bench in 1830 and urged by his friends to exchange his lodgings inside the prison walls for the liberty of 'the Rules' – a precinct outside the prison structure itself to which creditworthy debtors could be bailed – Haydon demurred. 'My Friends wish me to go into the Rules', he reflected, 'but here is a perpetual fund of Character! that will break into my mind at after periods of life.'[52] For Haydon, the characters of the debtors' prison were to inspire a series of marketable sketches and paintings of the King's Bench, just as personal encounters with the prison spurred the creation of fictional debtor characters in the successful novels of Fielding, Smollett and Dickens. Deidre Lynch's analysis of *The Economy of Character* helps to unpack the significance of this second set of connotations by situating the evolution of character in imaginative literature alongside the linked histories of the consumer revolution and the rise of the novel in the literary marketplace. Character was a well-established concept in eighteenth-century labour markets: the character (or reference) provided by a servant's former master or mistress

---

[50] See esp. Muldrew, *Economy of Obligation*, 125–6, and idem, ' "Hard food for Midas" ', 85.

[51] Willard Bissell Pope, ed., *The Diary of Benjamin Robert Haydon*, 5 vols. (Cambridge, MA., 1960–63), III: 473 (19 June 1830); IV: 219 (27–30 August 1834). As Jan-Melissa Schramm notes of English legal practice, 'Evidence of character and reputation were also of probative evidentiary significance in eighteenth-century trial proceedings. "Credit" resonates with a variety of meanings, tying that which is worthy of belief or assent to characteristics of social respectability and economic solidity.' (*Testimony and Advocacy*, 70).

[52] Pope, ed., *Haydon Diary*, III: 449 (3 June 1830).

20   The Character of Credit

was a vital passport to gainful employment.[53] But character, Lynch suggests, acquired new meanings, forms and values in the later eighteenth century. 'New commodities, available in new kinds of spaces, put pressure on the norms and the categories that people had formerly invoked to explain the material world and to make its artifacts meaningful', Lynch observes. 'In this context, people used characters . . . to renegotiate social relations in their changed, commercialized world, to derive new kinds of pleasure from the changes, to render their property truly private, to cope with the embarrassment of riches.' Novel-writing was a key component of this development. By the early nineteenth century, fictional characters had become 'the imaginative resources on which readers drew to make themselves into individuals, to expand their own interior resources of sensibility'.[54] Benjamin Haydon's professed willingness to remain within the walls of the King's Bench for the sake of its 'perpetual fund of Character' thus reflects a wider cultural awareness of the uses to which representations of the self could be put in the market for imaginative goods, as in markets for items of consumption.

By the Victorian period, the idea of character pervaded English society and culture. Constantly invoked by economists and politicians, character 'was, notoriously, the favoured explanatory element in the analysis of different human fates'.[55] Contemporaries clearly understood character to constitute an essential form of social capital. 'Character is property', Samuel Smiles proclaimed in 1871. 'It is the noblest of possessions.' For Smiles, character formation was integral to the making of individual identities, and credit relations provided an essential test of individual characters. Emphasising that character development was 'under the regulation and control of the individual', Smiles cited 'the exercise of constant self-watchfulness, self-discipline, and self-control' as crucial mechanisms for maintaining both personal character and personal credit. In Smiles's pantheon of historical characters, moral and manly individuals stood opposed to the temptations of consumer credit, which were predicated on hierarchical social connections and outdated customs rather than the modern verities of possessive individualism. For Smiles, personal debt was ultimately a form of theft.[56]

Prescriptive analyses of debt and credit relations, such as those advanced by Smiles, successfully capture liberal ideals that animated debates on personal

---

[53] Tim Meldrum, *Domestic Service and Gender 1660–1750: Life and Work in the London Household* (Harlow, 2000), 51–65.

[54] Deidre Lynch, *The Economy of Character: Novels, Market Culture, and the Business of Inner Meaning* (Chicago, 1998), 4–5, 126.

[55] Stefan Collini, *Public Moralists: Political Thought and Intellectual Life in Britain 1850–1930* (Oxford, 1991), 90–118, citation from 96.

[56] Samuel Smiles, *Character* (1871; London, 1997), 6, 9, 11, 180–7.

Introduction

character in modern England, but they fail to convey the tenor of exchange relations in either domestic settings or the market. Determinations of individual creditworthiness in England only rarely reflected precise knowledge of individual wealth: personal credit was a fluctuating identity concocted by a shifting range of interested parties from a fluid series of representations of the self. Creditors sought constantly and unsuccessfully to read debtors' personal worth and character from their clothing, their marital relations, their spending patterns and their perceived social status, attempting to assign stable cash values to consumers in markets continuously buffeted by the vagaries of credit. Legal definitions of personhood, agency and contract, far from serving to fix these individual economic identities, worked actively to subvert and multiply them. By subsuming a varied assortment of family members under the legal identity of the male householder, the law of contract liberated much credit purchasing from the immediate oversight of legally responsible individuals. Creating (in a quintessentially postmodern manner) artificial legal persons liable for economic acts of which they often had no direct knowledge, coverture and credit generated a welter of conflicted narrative opportunities in the courtroom, where plaintiffs, defendants and judges competed vociferously to construct credible representations and interpretations of market activity.

The historical parameters that impeded economic characters' ability to enter into free contracts as autonomous individuals provide a leitmotif of each of the three parts of this book. By situating the interpretation of novels, diaries and memoirs alongside the institutional history of contractual disputes, I hope to extend the insights of literary scholarship to the legal and economic history of consumption – without, however, allowing analysis of texts, narratives and symbolic representations to obscure the more material workings of market exchange. Within social and cultural history, as attention to production and supply has been displaced by a preoccupation with consumer demand, scholars have tended, in the words of Jan de Vries, to treat the world of goods as a realm in which 'the triumph of the will of the consumer can overcome any scarcity, where budget constraints don't exist (and where love never dies)'.[57] More broadly, recent years have seen an increasing dichotomy between studies of consumption as 'business' and studies of consumption as 'culture', a trend that Roy Church has argued creates 'a hinterland between these two sets of concerns and approaches which, while not entirely overlooked, has attracted much less interest'.[58] *The Character of Credit* attempts to bridge this widening

---

[57] Jan de Vries, 'The industrial revolution and the industrious revolution', *Journal of Economic History*, 54, 2 (June 1994), 255.

[58] Roy Church, 'New perspectives on the history of products, firms, marketing, and consumers in Britain and the United States since the mid-nineteenth century', *EcoHR*, 52, 3 (August 1999), 405.

historiographical divide by integrating analysis of the business and the culture of consumption. For only by combining culture and economics, law and society can we understand the full repertoire of consumer activities that powered the English economy in the very long nineteenth century, and comprehend the full spectrum of economic agents who participated in the construction of consumer modernity in these years.

Part I

Debt and credit in English memory
and imagination

1   Fictions of debt and credit, 1740–1914

Eighteenth- and nineteenth-century English novelists were obsessed with debt and credit. Grounded in writers' daily experience of literary and consumer dealings, this fiscal fascination was also sustained by an enduring network of symbolic linkages between fictional narratives and credit markets. As Catherine Ingrassia has argued, early eighteenth-century novels circulated as commodities in 'a marketplace influenced by fancy, desire, and the brief attention span of consumers'. Based on narratives which readers knew to be 'unreal', the emergent genre of the novel was associated by contemporaries with the new financial instruments of public debt and credit, devices that 'existed discursively, to be accessed on the page and recreated imaginatively in the mind of the investor'.[1] The increasing ascendancy of realism over sentimental, gothic and romantic lines of narrative in nineteenth-century novels only reinforced this early association between fiction and the instruments of public credit. 'Money and fiction, both representational systems relying on credit, are also often interchangeable: money as the fiction of gold or of absolute value; fiction as a commodity, exchangeable for money', Patrick Brantlinger has observed. 'In behaving like money, the realistic novel is a perfect simulacrum of a social order based on nothing more substantial than public credit and "speculative commerce".'[2]

Like public credit instruments, private credit relations animated modern literature, becoming increasingly central to imaginative writing with the rise from the 1740s of the sentimental novel. In feeding the growing market for literary products, novelists played an instrumental role in the evolution of market culture: the history of the novel in this period is in many ways a history of the

---

[1] Catherine Ingrassia, *Authorship, Commerce, and Gender in Early Eighteenth-Century England: A Culture of Paper Credit* (Cambridge, 1998), 6. See also Colin Nicholson, *Writing and the Rise of Finance: Capital Satires of the Early Eighteenth Century* (Cambridge, 1994). Later eighteenth-century conceptualisations of public credit and the private individual are explored by Peter de Bolla, *The Discourse of the Sublime: Readings in History, Aesthetics and the Subject* (Oxford, 1989), chap. 4.

[2] Patrick Brantlinger, *Fictions of State: Culture and Credit in Britain, 1694–1994* (Ithaca, NY, 1996), 144, 168. John Galsworthy's conceit of the Forsyte family as a stock exchange that traded in 'a sense of family credit' illustrates the persistence of this trope. See John Galsworthy, *In Chancery* (1920; Ware, Hertfordshire, 1994), 135.

26 Debt and credit in English memory and imagination

commodity told through commodified fictions. But in helping to create market culture novelists also continually explored market values, and repeatedly found them wanting. In fiction, disputed personal contracts and debt obligations function to move plot lines forward with drama and rapidity, literary representations of gift and consumer activity raise essential questions about the moral valence of economic obligations and legal institutions provide strategic settings for analysis of the individual's conduct, sensibilities and social standing. Economic only in their initial formulation, personal debt and credit relations in the novel constantly expose the social and cultural forces that constrained contractual individualism in English market culture.

This chapter offers a selective survey of the representation of personal debt and credit in modern English fiction. Although focused on novels that encapsulate the 'bourgeois' sensibilities that came to dominate English realist fiction, this vantage point comprises literary works that exerted a significant impact upon plebeian and propertied audiences alike.[3] Fiction provides a vital perspective on personal debt and credit relations, for novels were essential imaginative tools with which English consumers probed the lineaments of individual character and the moral limits of market exchange. Circulating alongside liberal treatises on law and economy, novels illuminated models of economic behaviour that cast the verities of contractual liberalism into doubt. Where legal theorists and political economists modelled their economic systems upon cash transactions, strict contracts, autonomous individuals and market mechanisms, novelists elaborated a more capacious view of economic behaviour derived from the practices of daily life. Gifts and commodities, equity and common law, credit and cash, animated things and objectified persons both vied and coalesced in fictional writings, generating a vision of exchange that refused to be contained within the narrow conceptual confines of the liberal market. In this manner, the fictional record helped to create a sustained discourse on consumer society that repeatedly challenged the tenets of possessive individualism.

From custom to contract? Rereading *Pamela*

Samuel Richardson's *Pamela; or, Virtue Rewarded* offers an appropriate starting point for analysis of economic discourse in the modern novel. Issued in five successive editions between 1740 and 1741, *Pamela* enjoyed immense success both as a commodity in the literary marketplace and as an extended commentary on commercial relations in England. Rapidly inspiring a 'Pamela rage'

---

[3] For the 'bourgeois' character of fictional realism, see esp. P.J. Keating, *The Working Classes in Victorian Fiction* (London, 1971), and Franco Moretti, *The Way of the World: The* Bildungsroman *in European Culture*, trans. Albert Sbragia, new edn (London, 2000). The substantial and sustained engagement of plebeian writers with canonical literary works is detailed by Jonathan Rose, *The Intellectual Life of the British Working Classes* (New Haven, 2001).

Fictions of debt and credit, 1740–1914

that saw images of its eponymous heroine used to market consumer goods such as fans and teacups, the novel affords a prime example of the thematic and material engagement with market culture that shaped English fiction from its origins. In Nancy Armstrong's influential analysis of gender relations and the development of possessive individualism, indeed, Richardson's novel features as a key literary vehicle of truly modern economic sensibilities, 'a form of writing that helped to create this concept of the individual'. By constructing a narrative in which the legitimacy of contractual relations – including marriage itself – rested on notions of individual agency, Armstrong argues, Richardson sought to supplant the traditional corporate values of the gentry and aristocracy with the market-orientated mentalities which (she believes) reigned within the middle class. 'Caught up and redefined within the figure of the contract, the whole idea of will becomes individual, sexual, and internalized; it becomes, in other words, the volition required before any consensual contract can take place', Armstrong asserts. By validating private domesticity, *Pamela* 'held forth the promise that individuals could realize a new and more fundamental identity and thus free themselves of the status distinctions organizing the old society'.[4]

Employed as a domestic servant by a gentry family in rural Bedfordshire until she is sequestered on a landed estate in Lincolnshire, Pamela Andrews is however an inherently unlikely icon of modern market culture. To be sure, Richardson's novel is relentlessly concerned at an imaginative level with paper credit and financial speculation.[5] But the attention lavished by Richardson on descriptions of elaborate gift exchanges significantly complicates Pamela's relation to modern market mentalities: Richardson's affirmation of the new instruments of public credit is matched in the novel by his endorsement of highly traditional personal credit relations centred on gifting activities. As in the Westernising cultures analysed by anthropologists, individualist and contractual lines of reasoning operate in this novel only alongside the persistence – and affirmation – of time-honoured systems of moral accounting antipathetic to purely profit-orientated economic exchange. For although Pamela readily adopts modern vocabularies of commercial calculation, she is exceptionally loath to endorse sexual activities predicated on capitalist reasoning. Only by

---

[4] Nancy Fix Armstrong, *Desire and Domestic Fiction: A Political History of the Novel* (Oxford, 1987), 30, 114, 98. Richardson's resistance to bourgeois modernity is emphasised by both Christopher Flint in *Family Fictions: Narrative and Domestic Relations in Britain, 1688–1798* (Stanford, 1998), chap. 4, and John Zomchick, in *Family and the Law in Eighteenth-Century Fiction* (Cambridge, 1993), chaps. 3–4. For the ways in which gender complicates representations of the individualist self in *Pamela*, see Carolyn Steedman, *Past Tenses: Essays on Writing, Autobiography and History* (London, 1992), esp. 2–3.

[5] Ingrassia, *Authorship, Commerce, and Gender*, 138. Her chapter on *Pamela* offers an excellent anatomy of the novel's engagement with the world of public, as opposed to private, credit (138–65).

28 Debt and credit in English memory and imagination

setting a higher value on her virtue than on economic assets such as employment, savings and possessions does Pamela succeed in resisting Mr B's illicit sexual advances and in becoming his lawful wife. Three interrelated themes shape this confluence of old and new value systems in the novel. *Pamela* is an object lesson first in the moral and political force of debt obligations, second in the social function and symbolic significance of gift and commodity exchange, and third in the limited capacity of common-law notions of contract to order and contain social and sexual relations.

Debt obligations not only pervade the text of *Pamela*, they provide the basic channels along which Richardson's plot lines develop. His heroine's sexual vulnerability, the fulcrum around which all action in the novel hinges, flows directly from her family's failed finances. By standing surety for two of her brothers, Pamela's parents incur legal liability for debts 'not of their own contracting', lose possession of their small country school, are 'forced to take to hard labour' themselves and compelled to send their daughter into domestic service. The claims of mutual obligation and liability frame the novel's development: familial values, not the tenets of possessive individualism, propel Pamela into the market, and repeatedly trump individual acquisition in Pamela's accounts. Dispatching four guineas as a gift to her parents, she earnestly desires them to pay 'some old debts with part'; justifying her own refusal to accept a gift of two guineas proffered by Mrs Jervis, Pamela piously observes that the housekeeper 'pays old debts for her children that were extravagant, and wants them herself'.[6] Efforts to avoid and liquidate personal debts preoccupy Pamela throughout the novel, but they serve to register her allegiance to a moral economy in which abstract legal doctrines of contractual liability are often less compelling than the claims of reciprocal social relations. Links to family and friends, as Naomi Tadmor has argued, were essential for – not hostile to – conceptions of virtuous individuality and 'character' in eighteenth-century novels (as in English society and culture more broadly).[7]

Although his heroine is scrupulous in fulfilling her own economic obligations, Richardson resists representing personal debts as emblems of personal failure. Rather, in keeping with centuries of Christian doctrine, literary and historical texts of this period typically denote debts as 'misfortunes' and describe debtors as 'unfortunate'. By underlining the inevitable vicissitudes of the human condition, representations of personal debt as a species of misfortune emphasised the power of charity and divine providence – not the force of

---

[6] Samuel Richardson, *Pamela; or, Virtue Rewarded*, ed. Peter Sabor (1740, 1801 edition; London, 1980), 475, 44, 108. Subsequent citations are referenced parenthetically in the text. I focus here on Part I of the novel, in which personal debt and credit obligations are more central than in Part II.

[7] Naomi Tadmor, *Friends and Family in Eighteenth-Century England: Household, Kinship and Patronage* (Cambridge, 2001), esp. 94–7, 255–6.

individual economic volition – to release debtors from their obligations. From Wycliffe's bible in 1390 to the Geneva bible of 1557, the interpretation of debt as an unavoidable misfortune of fallen man was rehearsed in the English version of the Lord's Prayer, which urged the Deity not to forgive sinners' trespasses, but rather to 'forgive us our debts even as we forgive our debtors'.[8] Pamela's repeated references to her parents' economic liabilities as 'misfortunes' partake of this conventional wisdom. Celebrating their 'resignation to the Divine Will amidst the extreme degree of disappointment, poverty, and distress, and the persecutions of merciless creditors', she declines to subscribe to a belief system in which individual agency and contractual rights are paramount (213). 'They are honest: they are good: it is no crime to be poor. They were once in a very creditable way: they were never beggars', she proclaims tellingly. 'Misfortunes may attend the highest' (419). Pamela's world view specifically distinguishes between insolvency and crime, refuses to dichotomise between the moral virtue of the debtor and the creditor, and underlines the liability of all mortals – regardless of social status – to financial failure.

Richardson's strategic use of imprisonment for debt works to buttress Pamela's recognition that the rigid enforcement of legal contracts, unless tempered by equitable Christian forgiveness, tends to advance immoral purposes rather than to promote economic justice. Depicting the debtors' prison as a site of arbitrary power and illicit sexuality, *Pamela* participates in a tradition of fictional representation that was to endure until the 1860s. When the local cleric, Mr Williams, is discovered conspiring with Pamela to effect her escape from captivity, Mr B swiftly invokes the arbitrary debt law to secure his own control over Pamela's person. By arresting Williams for a money debt which he 'had intended never to carry to account against him', Mr B at once isolates Pamela from her protector, endorses strict contracts over moral obligations and exposes the law as a means to nefarious sexual ends (201, 292). The negative moral valence Richardson assigns to this abuse of contractual authority is signalled by Mr B's compensatory largess when he capitulates to Pamela's refusal to become his mistress and seeks instead to make her his wife. Accepting Williams's bond in lieu of his person for the unpaid debt, Mr B first liberates the parson from his 'misfortunes' by freeing him from prison and then returns the cancelled bond to Williams as a token of contrition for his 'vindictive conduct' and 'cruelty' in resorting to the law (344).

The gift of this cancelled bond is only one instance among many exchanges in which Richardson juxtaposes traditional and more modern systems of circulation. Held captive within the walls of Mr B's secluded estate, Pamela has few opportunities to purchase new commodities, but enjoys access to a seemingly

---

[8] Delloyd J. Guth, 'The age of debt, the Reformation and English law', in Delloyd J. Guth and John McKenna, eds., *Tudor Rule and Revolution: Essays for G.R. Elton from His American Friends* (Cambridge, 1982), 70.

30   Debt and credit in English memory and imagination

endless succession of secondhand gifts. From the first pages of the novel to the
happy resolution of her plight, she obsessively details the receipt of presents
that register the moral character of her social relations and serve to distinguish
this traditional, personal means of credit accumulation from the anonymous
mechanisms of the modern market. In *Pamela*, moral valuations and social distinctions, rather than purely arithmetic calculations of profit, are the subtext of
economic activity, and the gift is in consequence the natural form of exchange.[9]
At the outset of the novel, the gifts Pamela receives upon the death of her mistress – Mr B's virtuous mother – offer material evidence both of the affection
she has earned and of her high status (or credit) within the household. Already
accustomed to receiving presents from her mistress of 'clothes and linen, and
everything that a gentlewoman need not be ashamed to appear in', she is now
inundated by a cascade of presents from Mr B himself (45). Within two days,
Pamela possesses a veritable armoury of gifted clothing. A 'suit of my late
lady's clothes, and half a dozen of her shifts, and six fine handkerchiefs, and
three of her cambric aprons, and four Holland ones' are presented to her on one
day; on the next, her gifts include 'two suits of fine Flanders laced head-clothes,
three pairs of fine silk shoes . . . with wrought silver buckles in them; and several
ribands and top-knots of all colours; four pair of fine white cotton stockings,
and three pair of fine silk ones; and two pair of rich stays' (49–51).

Customary presents such as these were standard perquisites of domestic
service in eighteenth-century England, and propertied men and women alike
routinely gifted and bequeathed items of clothing to servants of both sexes.[10]
By transferring clothing from mistresses to maidservants, such gifts of textiles
helped single women to accumulate trousseaus and to attract suitors. But gifted
goods were also essential components of the exchange systems that worked,
outside the formal market, to sustain unequal power relations in English society. In gift exchanges, as Pierre Bourdieu asserts, 'Wastage of money, energy,
time, and ingenuity is the very essence of the social alchemy through which
an interested relationship is transmuted into a disinterested, gratuitous relationship, overt domination into . . . *legitimate authority*.' By fostering notions
of personal indebtedness, gift exchanges serve to inculcate deferential patterns
of behaviour: 'Until he has given in return, the receiver is "*obliged*", expected
to show his gratitude towards his benefactor.'[11] Richardson's heroine is fully

---

[9] As Mary Douglas and Baron Isherwood argue, it is within the realm of gifting (as opposed to
commodity exchange) that 'moral judgment of the worth of people and things is exercised'. Mary
Douglas and Baron Isherwood, *The World of Goods: Towards an Anthropology of Consumption*,
2nd edn (London, 1996), 38.

[10] Anne Buck, 'Buying clothes in Bedfordshire: customers and tradesmen, 1700–1800', *Textile
History*, 22, 2 (Autumn 1991), 228. See also below, 82–4. Contrast Flint, *Family Fictions*, 183–4,
337–8.

[11] Pierre Bourdieu, *Outline of a Theory of Practice*, trans. Richard Wise (Cambridge, 1977), 192,
6–7.

alive to these dynamics of power and repeatedly evinces a precise understanding of the behavioural boundaries which, by demarcating proper and improper gift exchanges, distinguish moral from immoral personal relations. A gift of his mother's stockings from Mr B thus elicits Pamela's maidenly consternation not because the gift itself – a legitimate legacy from her former mistress – potentially bears sexual connotations, but rather because the male giver chooses to adopt a suggestively clandestine mode of presentation by refusing to use a senior female servant as an intermediary. As Pamela reports to her parents, 'I was inwardly ashamed to take the stockings; for Mrs Jervis was not there: if she had [been there], it would have been nothing.'[12]

Pamela's adherence to a proper moral economy of exchange is further evidenced by her recognition of the potentially liberating value of the commodity form, in contradistinction to the onerous debt obligations born of coercive gifting behaviours. When Mr B's relentless pursuit marks his presents indelibly with immoral sexual obligations, Pamela replaces this gifted finery with goods purchased with her own reserves of accumulated cash. By acquiring Scots cloth, stuff, calico, flannel, two round-eared caps, a straw hat and knitted mittens from a pedlar and a neighbouring farmer's wife, Pamela emphatically declares her determination to reject a life of luxurious depravity for the humble honesty of labour within her parental home. 'I believed myself to be more obliged to do this', she earnestly explains, 'as he expected *other* returns for his presents, than I intended to make him, so I thought it was but just to leave his presents behind me, when I went away' (76–7).

Expanding this simple moral accounting into a more complex ethical calculus, Pamela divides her possessions into three discrete parcels, each animated with distinctive symbolic associations. The first parcel, composed of gifts received from Mr B's mother, is itemised together with 'blessings . . . on my lady's memory for her goodness to me', but is nonetheless rejected, for 'Those things there of my lady's I can have no claim to, so as to take them away; for she gave them me, supposing I was to wear them in her service, and to do credit to her bountiful heart.' The second parcel, composed of presents offered by Mr B himself, is likewise unacceptable, its moral villainy so conspicuous to Pamela that the clothes assume the character of a sentient being in her analysis. 'So they were to be the price of my shame, and if I *could* make use of them, I should think I should never prosper with them', Pamela proclaims sternly. 'So in conscience, in honour, in everything, I have nothing to say to thee, thou *second, wicked* bundle!' The third parcel is also personified in her extended disquisition on economic probity, but offers a striking contrast to the moral valence borne

---

[12] Richardson, *Pamela*, 51. Later in the novel, she justifies acceptance of a gift from Mr B by the role played by Mrs Jervis, whose motives she believes to be honourable, in mediating the exchange (121).

by the second bundle. Composed of Pamela's righteously purchased goods, it figures as 'my dear *third* parcel, the companion of my poverty, and the witness of my honesty' (110–11). In all this, Richardson's novel offers not a narrative of the triumph of possessive individualism, but rather a case study in the partial transition from gift to commodity, from status to contract, in modern England. In *Pamela*, the tension and the interplay between gift and commodity exchange are key moral markers of relations between characters, providing a symbolic shorthand by which Richardson signals the value he ascribes to the choices made by individual agents in the economic and social sphere.

Significantly, in distinguishing among her possessions along these moral lines, Pamela describes her judgment as being based on 'a point of equity and conscience' (111). Rejecting common-law conceptions of contract, she invokes instead the legal principles that animated the informal small claims courts – appropriately denominated courts of conscience – that operated in a handful of seventeenth-century jurisdictions and were to proliferate throughout England from the later 1740s. In its appeal to equitable principles, Pamela's adjudication among the competing claims of debt and credit attached to her personal possessions speaks to strands of legal reasoning that were disproportionately associated with women in literature, as in the English courts. Like Portia in *The Merchant of Venice*, Richardson's Pamela personifies what Richard Posner describes as 'the spirit of equity – the prudent recognition that strict rules of law, however necessary to a well-ordered society, must be applied with sensitivity and tact so that the spirit of the law is not sacrificed unnecessarily to the letter'.[13]

If Pamela's resort to equitable reasoning suggests her determination to preserve moral systems of accounting within English market culture, the ultimate resolution of her contest with Mr B emphatically affirms the legitimacy of this received economic reasoning. To her frustrated master, Pamela's subservient position in his household marks her sexual availability precisely because domestic service conventionally entailed an extended series of unpaid obligations, including advances on wages and the receipt of gifts: in asserting Pamela's supposed debt to him, he revealingly describes their relation as 'a long reckoning to make up' (225). Having repeatedly failed to effect her seduction by exploiting the disparity of power inherent in customary gift-giving, he seeks to gain her compliance by resorting instead to the logic of commodity relations. In a series of contractual clauses larded with the language of possessive individualism, Mr B offers Pamela (in return for her virginity) 'irrevocable possession' of

---

[13] Richard Posner, *Law and Literature*, revised edn (Cambridge, MA, 1998), 109. Posner is generally sceptical of feminist claims that equitable law tends to be more beneficial for women than common law, but substantial historical evidence confirms this association in England. See esp. Amy Erickson, *Women and Property in Early Modern England* (London, 1993); Tim Stretton, *Women Waging Law in Elizabethan England* (Cambridge, 1998); and below, chaps. 5–6.

Fictions of debt and credit, 1740–1914   33

'a present of five hundred guineas, which you may dispose of as you please' and an estate in Kent 'clear of all deductions ... in full property to you and your descendants for ever', an exchange that he insists signifies the 'value I set upon the free-will of a person *already* in my power.' Pamela's rejection of this thinly concealed, contractual reconfiguration of the gift relation predictably reiterates her broader rejection of fully monetarised systems of value. 'Money, sir, is not my chief good: may God Almighty desert me, whenever I make it so', she asserts. 'To lose the best jewel, my virtue, would be poorly recompensed by the jewels you propose to give me' (228–9).

Pamela's persistent ambivalence toward both money as a marker of value and the contract as an instrument for enforcing social and economic obligations ensures that the restoration of moral order in the novel can be effected only by an appropriate marriage between conventional gifting and emergent commodity relations. Armstrong has interpreted Pamela's alliance with Mr B as evidence of 'the birth of a new ideology whereby power arises from within the individual', an ideology which triumphs in this novel over more corporate, aristocratic systems of patronage.[14] But the patterns of exchange associated with Pamela's marriage to Mr B are constructed instead from a bricolage of old and new economic practices. Precise notions of individual property rights untrammelled by moral obligations are evident – but not ascendant – in the later portions of the novel. Mr B thus employs the language of contract when he scrupulously insists that the annual sum of two hundred guineas for charity, which he intends to give his wife for her 'own use, and of which I expect no account', will be disbursed to her quarterly by his steward. 'I myself would make you the quarterly payment with my own hands', he explains, 'but ... if I did, it would rather have the look of a *present* than a *due*: and no pecuniary matters shall be permitted to abase my love to my wife, or to be supposed to engage that affection, which I hope to be sure of from higher merits and motives' (391). In marrying Pamela, moreover, Mr B undertakes to discharge her parents' debts, and thereby brings the cycle of financial obligation that had initially propelled her into his household full circle. Designed to ensure that his wife's family maintains 'a creditable appearance', this generosity is justified by Pamela in language that recognises the legitimacy of contractual obligations. Noting that each creditor will 'be paid to the utmost farthing, and interest besides; though some of them have been very cruel and unrelenting', Pamela acknowledges that 'they are all entitled to justice' (381, 489).

This concession to the justice of strict contracts is however situated within a wider network of exchange activities in which social and moral calculations continuously undercut purely legalistic thinking. Far more conspicuous than his commitment to contractual nicety is the seemingly endless stream of

---

[14] Armstrong, *Desire and Domestic Fiction*, 133. See also 127–8.

34   Debt and credit in English memory and imagination

conventional gifts that flow from Mr B to Pamela and her family upon their engagement and marriage. First to be accepted (and lovingly detailed) by Pamela are the two parcels of gifted goods which she had earlier rejected as tokens of Mr B's illicit campaign against her virtue; silks ordered from a mercer in London and the jewels previously worn by Mr B's mother complement these gifted items of female property (336–7, 382, 488). Ensuring that Pamela obtains the standard possessions that brides in fashionable circles acquired from friends and family, these exchanges also deploy objects strategically to incorporate her person into her husband's family line.[15] Now inducted into the gentry herself, Pamela promptly signals her acceptance of its characteristic exchange mechanisms by conferring a succession of wedding gifts, nicely graded to reflect distinctions of status, upon each of the servants in Mr B's household (381, 476, 484–8). Rather than rejecting the economic values of a passing aristocratic social order, *Pamela* integrates gifting and commodity practices in an effort to preserve aspects of the traditional moral economy within England's burgeoning market culture. By attributing human characteristics to material objects, underscoring the distinctive moral implications of old and new exchange regimes, questioning the concept of individual liability and the role of strict contracts, and contesting the legitimacy of creditors' sweeping legal powers over personal debtors, Richardson's novel reveals with exceptional clarity moral reservations about modern market culture that were to exercise English novelists and to shape English law into the twentieth century.

Gifts and commodities; persons and things

The slippage between gifts and commodities, and between persons and things that informed economic thinking in Richardson's *Pamela* remained a persistent feature of English fiction into the Edwardian era. Literary historians have drawn attention to the popularity, from the second half of the eighteenth century, of novels in which animated objects – sofas, watches, pins and hackney coaches – feature as protagonists, allowing authors to explore the circulation of commodities through characters figured as things.[16] Although these novels helped to integrate new market processes into imaginative literature, gift relations

---

[15] Richardson, *Pamela*, 336–7, 382, 488. For the gift of clothing and jewellery to elite brides, see Marcia Pointon, *Strategies for Showing: Women, Possession, and Representation in English Visual Culture 1665–1800* (Oxford, 1997), esp. 15–58.

[16] See esp. Liz Bellamy, *Commerce, Morality and the Eighteenth-Century Novel* (Cambridge, 1998), chap. 5; Christopher Flint, 'Speaking objects: the circulation of stories in eighteenth-century prose fiction', *PMLA*, 113, 2 (March 1998), 212–26; and Deidre Lynch, 'Personal effects and sentimental fictions', *Eighteenth-Century Fiction*, 12, 2–3 (January–April 2000), 345–68. These novels often displayed the same preoccupation with personal debt and credit as those with human characters. See for example Anon., *The Adventures of a Watch* (London, 1788), esp. 16, 31, 139–41, 156–7, 158–60.

continued to exert a powerful moral purchase over economic reasoning in the novel. Gifts afforded authors opportunities to explore exchange relations outside the cash nexus and within the domestic sphere, proving an especially useful mechanism for the fictional representation of women's debt obligations. But gifting was also an essential device for depicting market activity in the novel. Both the marriage market and retail credit transactions shared essential features with traditional gift exchange whilst also participating in processes of commodification. By including gifting activities within their models of the market, rather than building their fictions upon the polar oppositions between barter and the cash nexus favoured by economic theorists, English novelists underlined the social meanings and significance of contemporary exchange relations. As in the gift behaviours traced by cultural anthropologists, the personification of things and the objectification of persons featured centrally in their explorations of these themes, which saw gift exchange expand beyond the traditional horizons of *Pamela* to encompass new dilemmas of personal debt and credit generated by modern conceptualisations of class, sexuality and individualism.

Fanny Burney's *The Wanderer: Or, Female Difficulties* (1814) illustrates the multiple utilities of gift exchange as a tool for exploring personal debt and credit relations in early nineteenth-century fiction. Placing in the foreground the gift's role in the marriage market, this novel draws particular attention to the means by which gifts create liens of debt and credit in the economy of sexual exchange. Like Pamela, the impoverished refugee heroine of *The Wanderer* – first known as Ellis but later revealed to be the genteel Juliet Granville – lives in a constant state of moral and economic debt until her fortunes and rightful place in society are restored through marriage to the romantic hero Harleigh.[17] Like Pamela too, Ellis is propelled into the labour market by debt obligations that subject her to sexual attacks from elite men. Reduced to accepting charity from a succession of strangers, she espouses a version of the labour theory of value, resolving to 'have recourse to the most labourious personal exertions, rather than spread any further the list of my pecuniary creditors'.[18] Here as in Richardson's novel, however, purely contractual relations fail to preserve the Wanderer's character: paid employment neither liberates Ellis from the economy of sexual exchange nor locates her unambiguously in the impersonal world of the market. Rather, as imagined in Burney's novel, modern labour and commerce constantly intercalate gifting behaviours into contractual exchange.

---

[17] As Catherine Gallagher has argued of Burney's *Cecilia*, 'That single women, like readers, are just naturally in debt is one of the novel's most fundamental assumptions.' Catherine Gallagher, *Nobody's Story: The Vanishing Acts of Women Writers in the Marketplace, 1670–1820* (Oxford, 1994), 244. See also Miranda Burgess, 'Courting ruin: the economic romances of Fanny Burney', *Novel*, 28, 2 (Winter 1995), 131–53.

[18] Fanny Burney, *The Wanderer: Or, Female Difficulties*, ed. Margaret Anne Doody, Robert L. Mack and Peter Sabor (1814; Oxford, 1991), 108.

In *The Wanderer*, the language of debt and credit allows Burney to capture this transactional hybridity: obligations flow in her narrative from monetary debts with precise values and costs, from gifts in which differences of status and sexual power are more significant than precise calculations of profit or loss, and from retail transactions in which gifting and market mentalities are densely interwoven.

Ellis's economic vulnerability initially compels her to accept gifts of hospitality, assistance and money from a succession of persons to whom she is linked by neither family bonds nor ties of mutual acquaintance, and which thus violate her cardinal rule 'to avoid all obligations with strangers' (281). She attempts to bypass the dangers of the economy of sexual obligation by eschewing credit offered by a succession of unmarried men, appealing instead for assistance to Lady Aurora Granville. But this appeal itself subjects Ellis to unwanted amorous advances from Lady Aurora's brother, who attempts to press his attentions on her by initiating a series of gift and counter-gift exchanges. ' "Won't you wear such a bauble for my sake" ', Lord Melbury urges Ellis when she rejects his initial gift of a diamond ring. ' "Give me but a lock of your lovely hair, and I will make myself one to replace it" ' (139). Thwarted by Ellis's refusal to accept his presents and his person, Melbury (like Mr B before him in *Pamela*) attempts to trap her within his home.

Now fully alive to the potential dangers of charitable gifts, Ellis seeks to remove herself from these interested claims by entering the cash economy as a music teacher, an attempt to pay her debts with money earned by her own labour that is thwarted by the conventional expectations of the consumer credit market. Lacking capital and credit of her own, Ellis relies upon female patrons to supply her with both social credit (to cultivate a clientele of wealthy students) and trade credit (to obtain a musical instrument, food, lodging and clothing). Economic debts insistently elide with social obligations in Burney's novel. Miss Arbe's introductions to the Sussex social elite create 'essential obligations' that require Ellis to suffer the 'continual intrusion and fatigue' of her endless visits 'without a murmur'; Miss Bydel, 'in return for paying the month's hire of the harp', exacts from Ellis 'the private history of the way of life, expenses, domestics, and apparent income, of every family to which that instrument was the means of introduction' (240). Burney's representation of her protagonist's relations with her tradesmen reveals the extent to which Ellis's financial independence rests upon reticulated ties of debt and credit. When Ellis loses favour with her elite patrons, her landlady promptly asks her to settle her unpaid account for lodgings, a request that precipitates a cascade of 'little bills' from other local tradesmen now chary of her credit. Suffering 'the most sensible mortification, from her inability to discharge, without delay, a debt contracted with a stranger, upon whose generosity she had no claim; upon whose forbearance she had no tie', Ellis in turn attempts to collect the debts owed to her by her former music students, only to find that this vulgar request violates the norms of the elite credit economy. Lady Arramede indignantly refuses to pay her debt before the annual credit cycle enjoyed by upper-class consumers has been completed. ' "She...said that you might apply to her steward at Christmas, which was the time, she believed, when he settled her affairs; but as to herself, she never meddled with such insignificant matters" ', Ellis is informed by an intermediary (276, 298).

The moral dissonance between Ellis's professed determination to act as an autonomous economic individual and her unthinking acceptance of trade credit is exposed by Mr Giles Arbe, an elderly bachelor who persists in urging Ellis to accept his own offer of financial assistance. Ellis harbours the illusion that her market exchanges with tradesmen are liberated from onerous personal obligations by their contractual form, but Arbe emphasises instead the ways in which the consumer credit system distorts the conventions of gift exchange rather than supplanting them entirely. By creating a chain of unpaid debts that place the onus of obligation upon precisely those creditors least able to sustain their debtors' refusal to make repayment, retail credit relations subvert the hierarchies of power and obligation properly preserved by traditional gift exchanges between the lesser and the great. When Ellis cites her policy of avoiding gifts offered by strangers in declining his loan, Arbe is quick to identify the flaws in her moral reasoning. ' "Have you not an obligation to that linen draper, and hosier, and I don't know who... if you take their things, and don't pay for them?" ', he retorts. ' "Well, then... won't it be more honest to run into debt with an old bachelor, who has nobody but himself to take care of... ?" ' (281–2). Here, as in *Pamela*, equitable reasoning serves to distinguish proper from improper credit contracts. Ellis, 'struck with the sense of unbiased equity' of Arbe's comments, is caught between the competing claims of gender and class transgression as he relentlessly exposes the exploitative character of the credit obligations that sustain her fictive personal autonomy. ' "Well then, which is most equitable, to take openly from a rich friend, and say 'I thank you;' or to take, under-hand, from a hard-working stranger, whom you scorn to own yourself obliged to, though you don't scruple to harass and plunder? Which, I say, is more equitable?" ', Arbe insistently demands (331).

When the revelation of Ellis's true identity enables her at last to marry Harleigh, their union is marked by gift exchanges and debt repayments which, by interweaving gifts with acts of calculative accounting, attend to the needs of a social economy that is simultaneously customary and modern. 'Even Mr Tedman, when Harleigh paid him, with high interest, his three half-guineas, was invited to Harleigh Hall', Burney observes of one tradesman creditor. 'No one to whom Juliet had ever owed any good office, was by her forgotten, or by Harleigh neglected. They visited, with gifts and praise, every cottage in which the Wanderer had been harboured' (871–2). James Thompson, emphasising the market-orientated aspects of Burney's fiction, reads these credit relations as evidence that economic obligations function in *The Wanderer* to urge the necessity of separate male and female, public and private spheres of activity.[19] But attention to debt obligations as aspects of a social system of economics rooted at once in market and gift relations complicates this easy interpretation. For although Ellis suffers unwanted advances from moneyed men when her debts force her to seek employment in the market, her sexual vulnerability in this public setting is no more striking than the harassment she endures within the seclusion of her patrons' stately homes. Rather than securing Ellis's chastity, the domestic hearth constantly provides Burney with an appropriate context for the location of seduction narratives: the disparities of power inherent in gift relations centred in the household ensure that sexual danger lurks as alarmingly in the private home as in the public sphere.

Far from illustrating the benefits of securing women in a private sphere insulated from debt obligations, Burney's novel emphasises the instrumental, public ways in which virtuous women such as Juliet and Lady Aurora deploy gifts, credit and sociability. Based on the home but radiating throughout the locality in wider circuits of family, friendship and obligation, the credit activities of Burney's female characters depart significantly from the narrow domestic intimacy prescribed by separate-spheres ideology. In this, Burney's fictional economy attempts to theorise a gendered model of exchange that moves beyond abstract models of the market to take cognisance of the practices of daily life. 'Through the exchange of compliments, gifts, dinners and teas with other elite families, the genteel reaffirmed their gentility and maintained a wide public acquaintance', Amanda Vickery has noted of Georgian exchange relations. 'Sociability was one of the means by which the public was regulated in the home.'[20] Harriet Guest has recently suggested that literary scholars' disproportionate focus on the novel has unduly popularised 'the thesis that middle-class women were in the second half of the eighteenth century increasingly confined to domesticity by the demands of propriety', and argues that attention to other literary genres will instead reveal contexts in which 'domesticity gains in value as a result of its continuity with the social or the public, and not only as a result of its asocial exclusion'.[21] As Burney's *Wanderer* however attests, this enriched representation of the complexities of domesticity can readily be found in the Georgian novel itself. Here – if we discount political economists' simplistic models of the cash nexus and recognise the salience of debt and credit obligations – we see the inherent instability of boundaries between public and

---

[19] James Thompson, *Models of Value: Eighteenth-Century Political Economy and the Novel* (Durham, NC, 1996), 159, 167–74, citation from 159.
[20] Amanda Vickery, *The Gentleman's Daughter: Women's Lives in Georgian England* (New Haven, 1998), 222–3.
[21] Harriet Guest, *Small Change: Women, Learning, Patriotism, 1750–1810* (Chicago, 2000), 15.

private, market and home, inscribed in the competing, overlapping claims of gifts and contracts, persons and things.

As representations of gift relations in Victorian novels demonstrate, moreover, neither the increasing ascendancy of separate-spheres ideology in domestic relations nor the increasing purchase of economic liberalism in the market succeeded in displacing the gift from its pivotal place in fictional representations of exchange in the later nineteenth century. Elizabeth Gaskell's *Ruth* (1853) is typical of Victorian novels in reviving but also reconfiguring the arguments of Richardson's *Pamela* and Burney's *Wanderer* for an audience more fully attuned to the demands of modern markets and the tensions of class relations. Like Pamela, Ruth Hilton is the child of insolvent parents: 'a series of misfortunes' bankrupts her father and drives Ruth from the security of her rural home into employment in an urban dressmaker's shop.[22] Rendered sexually vulnerable by her father's debts, Ruth is chronically incapable of distinguishing among the different moral meanings of her gift and credit relations. The scene of her seduction establishes the central tensions between economic and social obligation that structure the novel as a whole. When Bellingham, her would-be seducer, orders her a pot of tea at an inn, Ruth's unwillingness to flee the scene without discharging her debt for this mere commodity outweighs her dawning recognition that her virtue is at risk. 'She thought that she would leave a note for Mr Bellingham, saying where she had gone, and how she had left the house in debt, for (like a child) all dilemmas appeared of equal magnitude to her; and the difficulty of passing the landlord while he stood there . . . appeared insuperable, and as awkward and fraught with inconvenience, as far more serious situations.'[23] Failing to distinguish between law and equity, Ruth confuses strict contracts with moral probity, thereby sacrificing her sexual purity.

Led to her ruin by a false understanding of personal debt and credit relations, Ruth is redeemed in the course of the novel only by learning to negotiate the competing claims of moral and immoral obligations. Although her novel is set within the Nonconformist commercial community rather than among the Anglican landed elite favoured by Georgian novelists, Gaskell relies upon gifts rather than commodities to precipitate her character's moral awakening. Throughout her pregnancy, Ruth's inability to accept presents that register her dependent status within society at once indicates her inadequate moral comprehension and, more broadly, allows Gaskell to question the virtues of market-orientated values of independent agency. Mr Bradshaw, the wealthy local

---

[22] Elizabeth Gaskell, *Ruth*, ed. Angus Easson (1853; London, 1997), 33.

[23] Ibid., 53. Gaskell's use of tea to signal the perils of Ruth's situation is especially apt. As Elizabeth Kowaleski-Wallace has argued, the eighteenth century saw the tea table develop 'as a gendered site' where 'the "fluid" female body in question was thought to "leak," or overflow boundaries'. *Consuming Subjects: Women, Shopping, and Business in the Eighteenth Century* (New York, 1997), 21–2.

40 Debt and credit in English memory and imagination

Nonconformist patron of Ruth's pious guardians, offers Ruth gifts of textile goods that include delicate cambric for her unborn baby and a handsome silk gown for herself: if she 'had chosen, she might have gone dressed from head to foot in the presents which he wished to make her, but she refused them constantly' (130–1, 156). In keeping with Bradshaw's strict moral character, these gifts are offered not as inducements to sexual transgression but rather as symbols of proper class relations. Bradshaw is 'possessed with the idea of patronising Ruth', 'his favourite recreation was patronising' (156, 174). Railing against these unwanted offerings because they signify her subservience, Ruth echoes Burney's Wanderer in insisting that she 'cannot see why a person whom I do not know should lay me under an obligation'. Her guardian, the Christ-like preacher Benson, promptly corrects her misapprehension that she can live in society without accepting the restraints imposed by gifts, credit and mutual obligation. ' "It is a delight to have gifts made to you by those whom you esteem and love, because then such gifts are merely to be considered as fringes to the garment... adding a grace, but no additional value, to what before was precious... but you feel it to be different when there is no regard for the giver to idealise the gift – when it simply takes its stand among your property as so much money's value" ', he reasons, only to urge Ruth to follow his own example by accepting Bradshaw's gifts and patronage (131–2). As Ruth's own moral reasoning matures, she attempts to accept her Christian obligation to receive gifts and credit, rejecting the Smithian paradigm in which virtuous exchange occurs when independent agents meet as equals to obtain commodities in cash markets. Thus, 'when Ruth saw how quietly and meekly Mr Benson submitted to gifts and praise, when an honest word of affection, or a tacit, implied acknowledgment of equality, would have been worth everything said and done, she tried to be more meek in spirit' (174). Gaskell, predictably, represents Ruth's successful redemption at the end of the novel by marriage to a man whose affection for her has been marked by presents to her illegitimate son, gifts which – together with their attendant social obligations – Ruth now appropriately accepts with willingness and gratitude (257).[24]

In *Bleak House*, also published in 1853, Dickens rehearses themes explored by Gaskell, but attends in particular to the ways in which male characters' moral failings are illuminated and expressed by their relations to gifts, debts and personal credit. Harold Skimpole's inability to recognise the mutual obligations that inhere in gift exchange – and his corresponding inability to negotiate the consumer credit system – stand at one extreme on the spectrum of debt relations depicted through gifting in *Bleak House*. Described by his patron John

---

[24] George Eliot's novels further elaborate the problematic relations among gifts, gender and sexuality. See Steven Dillon, 'George Eliot and the feminine gift', *Studies in English Literature* 32 (1992), 707–21, and Jeff Nunokawa, 'The miser's two bodies: *Silas Marner* and the sexual possibilities of the commodity', *VS*, 36, 3 (Spring 1993), 273–92, esp. 285–90.

Jarndyce as 'a child', 'unfortunate in his affairs, unfortunate in his pursuits, and unfortunate in his family',[25] Skimpole accepts endless gifts but repudiates all sense of personal obligation. Refusing to acknowledge his identity as a debtor, he perversely plays upon the mutual ties that bind parties in the gift relation by assuming the character of a creditor in his dealings with Jarndyce and his circle. ' "I don't feel any vulgar gratitude to you. I almost feel as if *you* ought to be grateful to *me*, for giving you the opportunity of enjoying the luxury of generosity" ', he asserts. ' "For anything I can tell . . . I may have been born to be a benefactor to you, by sometimes giving you an opportunity of assisting me in my little perplexities" ' (91–2). Skimpole, masquerading as an autonomous individual, offers a parodic endorsement of economic liberty when Esther and Richard prevent his imprisonment by paying his debts. ' "I ask only to be free" ', he proclaims, rejecting his obligations to friends and family even as he relies upon these social relations to obtain credit in the consumer market (97).

John Jarndyce serves as Skimpole's economic foil in the novel, but for all his generosity he too displays a problematic engagement with the economy of gifts and credit. Where Skimpole perennially resists his character as a debtor, Jarndyce indulges in constant subterfuge to deny his identity as a giver of gifts and hence as a creditor. Before meeting his wards Esther and Ada for the first time, Jarndyce pre-empts any expression of thanks for his charity and hospitality, insisting that they 'take the past for granted' and meet 'without constraints on either side' (80). Like Skimpole, Jarndyce mistakes the obligatory character of gift exchange: acknowledgments of gratitude and dependence, as Gaskell was at pains to argue in *Ruth*, are essential to credit relations for they ensure that gifts register social obligations that will endure beyond transient acts of mere economic exchange. Jarndyce's misunderstanding of his role as a benefactor is manifest most clearly in his troubling tendency to treat persons as if they were things. When Jarndyce 'gives' the orphan Charley to Esther as a maidservant, Dickens reiterates the character of the exchange as a gift transaction. ' "I am a little present to you, with Mr Jarndyce's love" ', Charley insists. ' "If you please, miss, I am a little present with his love, and it was all done for the love of you" ' (385–6). The perils of objectifying persons – as opposed to the pleasures of personifying things – in gift exchange become fully evident when Jarndyce mistakenly asks Esther – in love with a younger man – to give herself to him in marriage. Seeming to abdicate yet again his obvious role as Esther's creditor, Jarndyce insidiously draws attention to her obligation to him by couching his proposal in the language of profit and loss. 'I was the last to know what happiness I could bestow upon him, but of that he said no more; for I was always to remember that I owed him nothing, and that

---

[25] Charles Dickens, *Bleak House*, ed. Nicola Bradbury (1853; London, 1996), 88.

42   Debt and credit in English memory and imagination

he was my debtor, and for very much', Esther records uneasily of his proposal (691). Loath to accept his proper place in the distribution of charity and credit, and prone to confuse persons with material objects of exchange, Jarndyce is an inappropriate partner for Esther, who breaks her engagement to him and enjoys a happy marriage with her original suitor.

Like Dickens before him, Anthony Trollope created a mixed economy of gifts and commodities in his novels, according moral value to his male protagonists not by their identities as either debtors or creditors but rather by the tenor of their conduct within either of these symbiotic roles. In *Framley Parsonage* (1861), Trollope distinguishes among his characters by contrasting their strategies for negotiating unpaid bills. Willingness to receive appropriate gifts is central to Trollope's moral calculus of character and credit. His hero, Mark Robarts, occupies the middle ground of Trollope's spectrum of insolvency. Led into debt by the devious politician Sowerby, he is redeemed by the love of his wife and his acceptance of money given freely – despite Lady Lufton's reservations that his 'character as a clergyman should have kept him from such troubles' – by his aristocratic patrons.[26] Sowerby, preserved from the debtors' prison only by the privilege of his parliamentary seat,[27] exemplifies the stereotypical evils of the modern credit system: he is 'one of those men who are known to be very poor – as poor as debt can make a man – but who, nevertheless, enjoy all the luxuries which money can give' (68). Attempting unsuccessfully to recruit his fortunes by marrying money, Sowerby is rescued from debt only by purely contractual expedients: the heiress Miss Dunstable, declining to become his wife, agrees instead to become his creditor, by lending him money at interest (288, 325–6). The impoverished Reverend Crawley, 'a strict, stern, unpleasant man, and one who feared God and his own conscience', represents an opposite extreme on the credit spectrum. Reduced by 'undeserved misfortune' to 'a weary life...of increasing cares, of sickness, debt, and death', he fails to manifest proper moral calculation not by falling into debt, but rather by refusing to avail himself of traditional gift relations once he has done so. Unwilling to accept charitable presents for his impoverished wife and children, Crawley is wedded to autonomous individualism and distanced from the teachings of his church: he 'felt a savage satisfaction in being left to himself...and...had certainly never as yet forgiven the Dean of Barchester for paying his debts'. By refusing to acknowledge the established analogy between debtors and creditors, on the one hand, and errant sinners and the compassionate Deity, on the other, Crawley subverts the very cosmology that his religious vocation is intended to uphold. 'It is very sweet to give; I do not doubt that', he churlishly insists. 'But the

---

[26] Anthony Trollope, *Framley Parsonage*, ed. David Skilton and Peter Miles (1861; London, 1984), 521.

[27] By 12 & 13 Will. III c. 3, MPs were immune from imprisonment for debt during parliamentary sessions.

taking of what is given is very bitter. Gift bread chokes in a man's throat and poisons his blood, and sits like lead upon the heart' (190, 188, 266, 431).

In the later Victorian and Edwardian years, as economic theorists increasingly questioned the tenets of classical liberalism, sexologists challenged received understandings of individual desire and feminists launched strident public campaigns against the objectification of women, fictional depictions of gift relations expanded further to accommodate new understandings of exchange and economic personality. Oscar Wilde, flirting with utopian socialist critiques of alienated labour and commodity exchange, elaborated a 'new Individualism' in this context, rejecting 'prevailing Victorian valorizations of use and utility' and expounding an 'erotics of consumption fully premised on a relationship among producers liberated from the mediating moment of exchange value'.[28] Radical in its departure from received representations of utilitarian exchange, Wilde's *Picture of Dorian Gray* (1891) is also innovative in rewriting the conventional narrative of heterosexual gifting to examine processes of objectification generated by same-sex relations between men. The portrait, a gift from Basil Hallward to Dorian Gray, feeds off and destroys its subject, recuperating for homosexual desire the narratives of female objectification told by previous generations of novelists through the immoral gifting behaviours of fictional male seducers. As Dorian becomes enamoured with his own picture, his portrait begins its monstrous transformation from thing to person. Now enjoying 'a life of its own', Dorian's portrait both assumes his physical attributes and bears the marks of the moral decay of his character.[29] Confusion between things and persons multiplies apace until the novel reaches its dramatic conclusion. Having killed Basil Hallward to protect the secret of his newly assumed, objectified identity, Dorian repeatedly refers to his former friend as a 'thing' (180–1). His own demise, appropriately, is effected when Dorian (in destroying the portrait) is killed and exchanges identities again with the picture. Restored to represent Dorian 'in all the wonder of his exquisite youth and beauty', the portrait reduces its subject to an object. Only the material possessions found on his person allow Dorian's servants to identify him. Whereas the alchemy of virtuous gift exchange animates objects with the spirit of their donors, immoral gift and credit relations reduce persons to inanimate things.

John Galsworthy's *In Chancery* (1920), set at the turn of the century, resituates the gift relation in its prevailing heterosexual context, but reworks romantic and realist critiques of female objectification to incorporate later Victorian and

[28] Carolyn Lesjak, 'Utopia, use, and the everyday: Oscar Wilde and the new economy of pleasure', *English Literary History*, 67, 1 (Spring 2000), 201. For the broader context of these shifts in turn-of-the-century representations of consumption, see Regenia Gagnier, *The Insatiability of Human Wants: Economics and Aesthetics in Market Society* (Chicago, 2000).

[29] Oscar Wilde, *The Picture of Dorian Gray* (1891; New York, 1998), 132. Wilde specifically identifies the portrait as a gift rather than a commodity: ' "You know the picture is yours, Dorian. I gave it to you before it existed" ', Hallward remarks (32).

44   Debt and credit in English memory and imagination

Edwardian feminist developments. Soames Forsyte's efforts to rehabilitate his failed marriage to Irene are based on his fixation with property and commodities, but they assume the form of inappropriate gift exchanges. The diamond brooch he purchases as a birthday present for Irene is represented as the means of obtaining one 'thing' only, a son; Irene's rejection of this instrumental, dehumanising gift relation sends Soames in despair to his office in the City, where he mourns 'his domestic bankruptcy' (102). His later loveless marriage to Annette takes the form of a commodity purchase transacted in a calculative market free of affective ties. 'Her beauty in the best Parisian frocks was giving him more satisfaction than if he had collected a perfect bit of china, or a jewel of a picture; he looked forward to the moment when he would exhibit her in Park Lane', Galsworthy writes of Soames's second marriage (188).[30] Alert to the dangerous obligations that attached to debt relations in sexual markets, Georgian and Victorian novelists had none the less sought to reconcile market and gift exchange. Galsworthy's feminist critique of patriarchal subordination, in contrast, suggests the fundamental incompatibility of either system of exchange with egalitarian marital relations.

Equity and the dissolution of marriage feature centrally in the novel, as Galsworthy's reiterated references to Irene's liminal suspension 'In chancery' during her marriage to Soames suggest (50, 177). Jolyon Forsyte's rejection of property in women is framed both by his repugnance for contemporary marriage law and by Galsworthy's broader critique of the disjunction between contractual and equitable principles of legal reasoning. Overhearing Soames speak of his estranged wife, Jolyon reflects with distaste, ' "Well, we all own things. But – human beings! Pah!" ' (50). Equitable antagonism to contractual thinking serves as the overarching theme of political commentary in the novel, whether directed at public events or the intimate power struggles of the domestic economy. When Soames argues with his niece over the rejection of British suzerainty that precipitates the Boer War, he insists that ' "a contract is a contract" ', but June, like Pamela before her, counters this claim with the language of legal equity. ' "Contracts are not always just . . . and when they're not, they ought to be broken" ' (71). Describing the Victorian era as 'An epoch which had gilded individual liberty so that if a man had money, he was free in law and fact, and if he had not money he was free in law and not in fact', Galsworthy integrates this critique of the marriage market with a wider attack on the ascendancy of freedom of contract (190).

As figured by successive novelists from Richardson to Galsworthy, gift relations provided a conspicuous counter-narrative to both liberal and socialist

---

[30] Soames's description of Annette as a piece of china plays upon an association, evident in English culture from at least the early eighteenth century, between women as desiring consumers of chinaware on the one hand and as desired sexual objects on the other. See Kowaleski-Wallace, *Consuming Subjects*, esp. 53–68.

theories of exchange. Where classical political economy privileged autonomous individuals, freedom, cash and contract, fictional descriptions of gifting instead prized social groups, cultural constraints, credit and moral obligations. Like the first volume of *Capital*, in which Marx expounded the theory of commodity fetishism, English novels represented the economic system of their times as capable of transmogrifying things into persons. But where Marx, fixated on the evils of the market's cash nexus, saw the animation of objects by the processes of commodification as a dangerous development which necessarily entailed the objectification of persons,[31] contemporary novelists – by turning to the gift – often found cause to celebrate the personification of things as a symbol of a form of social exchange that resisted control by the market. As in Mauss's 'archaic' societies, successful gifts animate objects with the spirit of the persons who offer them and play a central role in the reproduction of society through marriage. These fictional representations of social credit were neither uniformly positive nor unchanging over time. Troubled by the instrumental use of gifts by men to objectify women, novelists were also increasingly sensitive to the gift's implication in hierarchical, aristocratic structures of power with which male democratic culture was ever more frequently at odds. Wilde's horrific portrait of Dorian Gray's depraved existence among a coterie of aristocratic bachelors and the soulless inadequacy of Soames Forsyte's attempt to purchase the affections of his own wife are emblematic in the contrast they provide to the happy gifting occasions that had earlier marked the successful marriages of sentimental and romantic heroines in Georgian fiction. This increasing unease with gifts in a market culture developed in parallel with a gradual contraction of sociable gifting behaviours in the course of the nineteenth century.[32] The central significance of fictional gift exchange however lies not in its utility as an index of historical change but rather in the novel's historical role in enriching discursive constructions of economic identity.[33] For gifts worked in English novels not by accurately reflecting economic practice as a whole but by selectively capturing and reconfiguring aspects of exchange – seduction, betrothal and marriage, debt, credit and obligation – which were vital to social relations and consumer culture but only inadequately accounted for by the economic theories that circulated, alongside the novel, in academic treatises, parliamentary debates and the newspaper and periodical press.

---

[31] Karl Marx, *Capital: A Critique of Political Economy* (1867), trans. Ben Fowkes, vol. I (New York, 1976), 163–77.

[32] See below, chap. 2.

[33] For an analogous line of argument about the creative dissonance between fictional representations and historical experiences of Victorian exchange relations, see Kathy Alexis Psomiades, 'Heterosexual exchange and other Victorian fictions: *The Eustace Diamonds* and Victorian anthropology', *Novel*, 33, 1 (Fall 1999), 93–118. More broadly, the historical work performed by the novel in this period is explored by Franco Moretti, *Signs Taken for Wonders: Essays in the Sociology of Literary Form* (London, 1983), esp. 9–21.

Commodities and credit; wives and debt

Although later eighteenth- and nineteenth-century novelists continued to use gift transactions to revisit themes of social obligation and sexual objectification, they also moved beyond this persistent trope by exploring exchange in new retail settings and by assessing the credit dealings of wives as well as unmarried women. Supplied with abundant goods through a constant traffic of interested gifts, Pamela had enjoyed easy access to the world of things while evincing only a limited acquaintance with the modern consumer market. Richardson's reluctance to frame his narrative with mundane accounts of retail activity reflects a broader unease with market culture characteristic of English novels in this period.[34] But as retail institutions and commodity transactions multiplied in the later decades of the eighteenth century, shops and shopping came to feature with new prominence in English novels. Ironically, this development of new sites for the analysis of debt and credit relations worked to entrench established lines of argument about the proper limits of economic individualism more consistently than it advanced new interpretations of consumer culture and personal autonomy. In the novel, as in wider historical markets in which works of fiction were produced and circulated, the social character of retail credit helped to ensure that economic transactions continued to be shaped by the moral economies of gift exchange. Trade credit reformulated gift obligations, even as it promoted the proliferation of consumer purchasing.

Two early fictional explorations of retail settings and trade credit established essential thematic frameworks upon which novelists – among a host of other social commentators – would continue to elaborate for decades. In *Joseph Andrews* (1742), Henry Fielding's retelling of Pamela's plight from the perspective of a virtuous male servant, the gentlemanly Mr Wilson recalls his misspent youth by chronicling his credit relations with his tailor. ' "The character I was ambitious of attaining, was that of a fine gentleman; the first requisites to which, I apprehended, were to be supplied by a taylor, a perriwig-maker, and some few more tradesmen, who deal in furnishing out the human body" ', Wilson explains to Joseph Andrews and Parson Adams. ' "Notwithstanding the lowness of my purse, I found credit with them more easily than I expected ... but I have since learn'd, that it is a maxim among many tradesmen at the polite end of the town to deal as largely as they can, reckon as high as they can, and arrest as soon as they can." '[35] Here Fielding invokes not only the characteristic trade practices of elite shopkeepers – extended credit and inflated prices to

---

[34] Bellamy, *Commerce, Morality and the Eighteenth-Century Novel*, 130. See also John McVeagh, *Tradeful Merchants: The Portrayal of the Capitalist in Literature* (London, 1981), 83–100, and James Raven, *Judging New Wealth: Popular Publishing and Responses to Commerce in England 1750–1800* (Oxford, 1992), esp. chaps. 5–6.

[35] Henry Fielding, *Joseph Andrews*, ed. R.F. Brissenden (1742; London, 1977), 196–7.

compensate for the unpaid accounts that resulted from this facility – but also the parasitic relationship between character and credit in retail settings. Trade credit was determined not by known quantities of capital but by perceived qualities of character. An assumed identity sustained by the very commodities which it allowed consumers to purchase on credit, character was constituted in significant part by tradesmen's continuous valuation and revaluation of their customers' status and social connections. Retail credit was consequently prone to suffer from tradesmen's loss of confidence in character, as Fielding's Wilson discovered when his diminished resources – 'My clothes grew shabby, my credit bad' – induced his tailor to arrest and imprison him for debt. Fielding's moralistic commentary on this legal enforcement of retail contracts is expressed through the pious Parson Adams. ' "How can such a wretch repeat the Lord's Prayer where the word which is translated, I know not for what reason, *trespasses*, is in the original debts?" ', Adams expostulates. ' "And as surely as we do not forgive others their debts when they are unable to pay them; so surely shall we ourselves be unforgiven, when we are in no condition of paying" ' (211). Christian pieties, not market mentalities, inform Fielding's assessment of retail credit and underline his resistance to the dictates of possessive individualism.

In *The History of Miss Betsy Thoughtless* (1751), Eliza Haywood's representation of her female characters' relations with the mercers, drapers, mantua-makers and milliners who supplied elite women with textiles offers a pendant to Fielding's depiction of the snares of indebtedness set by gentlemen's tailors. As an adolescent, Betsy Thoughtless is introduced to credit relations by Mrs Mellasin, a habitué of the pawnshop whose immoderate credit purchases and adulterous sexual liaisons ensure that her husband – Betsy's guardian, Mr Goodman – is arrested for his wife's unpaid debts. Now deprived of her guardian's protection, Betsy makes a miserable marriage, and as a married woman occupies herself with shopping. Glimpsing a variety of silks through the window of a shop and 'tempted to step in', she is invited into the mercer's private parlour.[36] Beguiled by his merchandise, she purchases silk for a nightgown and is introduced to the mysterious Mademoiselle de Roquelair, who proves to have been seduced both by the mercer's goods and by his person. In a scene that prefigures the dominant seduction narrative that was to emerge in plebeian small claims court litigation in the nineteenth century, Haywood neatly anatomises the problematic relations entailed by women's conflicting identities and obligations as consumers in both sexual and retail markets. De Roquelair's voracious sexual appetites are stoked and satisfied by the daily practices of consumer purchasing. The mercer, a stock character of the textile trade in his

---

[36] Eliza Haywood, *The History of Miss Betsy Thoughtless*, ed. Christine Blouch (1751; Peterborough, Ontario, 1998), 572.

48 Debt and credit in English memory and imagination

'amorous complexion', acts to type by improving upon 'the advances she made him; he frequently came to her under the pretence of bringing patterns of silks, or other things in his way of trade ... without raising any suspicion in the family' (578). Travelling continually between their shops and their clients' homes to exhibit the latest merchandise, take measurements and deliver their finished wares, artisans and shopkeepers defied the supposed boundary between private and public realms to subject women to a barrage of illicit consumer temptations.

As later eighteenth-century novelists increasingly exploited the fictional potential of retail settings in their writings, shopping provided a convenient metaphor for women's simultaneous participation in retail credit transactions and the marriage market. Lexicographers trace the first appearance of 'shopping' as a gerund to the early diaries of Fanny Burney, whose fictional protagonists experience credit purchasing at once as an essential form of sociability and as a dangerous threat to their personal characters.[37] Financial and sexual disasters join seamlessly in this context, as fictional protagonists' immersion in a range of social, sexual and economic markets multiplies their opportunities to assume the characters and credit of their family, friends and patrons. In *Belinda* (1801), Maria Edgeworth signals her heroine's perilous position in the marriage market by contrasting the moral credit she loses through her sexual objectification and the consumer credit she gains through association with the very women who compromise her character. Under the tutelage of her scheming aunt, Belinda is ' "hawked about everywhere ... and her accomplishments ... as well advertised as Packwood's razor strops." '[38] Her ability to obtain goods without consumer credit of her own reflects and instantiates her false position on the marriage market. By living in the elite household of Lady Delacour – herself hopelessly in debt – Belinda obtains easy credit with her patron's tradesmen and is carefully schooled to reject 'the vulgar idea of *ready money*' (35).

For women characters, the moral repercussions of the credit market are further complicated by the close articulation among men's debt obligations, marriage and female sexuality. Women's wealth and women's bodies function as the common coin of debt repayment in the English novel, as prudent mothers, sisters, lovers and wives repeatedly rush to rescue their feckless menfolk from ill-considered obligations. In *Amelia* (1751), Fielding's heroine pawns her clothes and jewels to compensate for her husband's losses at the gaming table; first Lady Elliot and then Lady Russell exercise the financial foresight that maintains Sir Walter Elliot's solvency in Jane Austen's *Persuasion* (1818); the orphan Laura pays the protagonist's college debts in Thackeray's *Pendennis* (1850), and is

---

[37] Kowaleski-Wallace, *Consuming Subjects*, 91.
[38] Maria Edgeworth, *Belinda*, ed. Kathryn J. Kirkpatrick (1801; Oxford, 1994), 25. For Packwood's razor strops, a byword of the eighteenth-century advertising craze, see Neil McKendrick, John Brewer and J.H. Plumb, *The Birth of a Consumer Society: The Commercialization of Eighteenth-Century England* (London, 1982), 145–94.

Fictions of debt and credit, 1740–1914   49

later rewarded by marriage to him.[39] In this over-determined system of credit relations, marriage often features in fiction – as indeed it functioned in aristocratic
finance – as a means of paying men's debts with women's money.[40] In *Amelia*,
the nefarious Captain Trent supports his extravagant household by pimping for
an aristocratic rake, a livelihood that originates in his willingness to prostitute
his own wife. When Trent encourages Fielding's protagonist, Captain Booth,
to carry 'his goods to market' in a similar fashion, Booth recoils in horror.
Entrapped however by loans from the very men determined to supplant him in
his wife Amelia's bed, he is easily removed from her side by the machinations
of his antagonists, who employ the corrupt instruments of the legal system to
secure Booth's imprisonment for debt.[41]

In fiction as in social life more broadly, wives' position in the symbolic
economy of personal debt transactions was always Janus-faced. Highlighting
women's economic agency in the domestic economic sphere by creating virtuous wives who rescue men from unwise credit transactions, English novelists
also drew repeated attention to married women's legal capacity to saddle their
husbands with onerous debt obligations. Thackeray's *Vanity Fair* (1848) explores the tendency of retail credit to compromise marital fidelity with a degree
of frankness that resonates with the increasingly worried tone of consumer commentary that emerged in the press from the later 1840s in the context of wives'
new public visibility as agents for their husbands in the county courts. Creating
a series of linkages between women's adulterous sexuality and their extravagant
economic expenditure, Thackeray depicts Becky Sharpe's sexual misconduct at
once as a pragmatic strategy in her repertoire of household provisioning skills
and as a fundamental threat to domestic life. Unable to command sufficient retail
credit on her husband's income alone, Becky willingly prostitutes her body to
an aristocratic patron to obtain luxurious goods for her home. Local tradesmen
are fully complicit in the open secret of her deception, offering her consumer
credit precisely because they observe 'the Marquis of Steyne's carriage-lamps
at her door ... in the blackness of midnight'. When the illicit lovers conspire to
remove Colonel Rawdon from his wife's side by imprisoning him for debt in
a spunging-house, the subversive consequences of the circulation of women's
bodies in the credit market become fully apparent.[42]

---

[39] Henry Fielding, *Amelia*, ed. David Blewett (1751; London, 1987), 441, 481; Jane Austen,
Persuasion (1818; London, 1965), 40–5; William Thackeray, *The History of Pendennis* (1850;
London 1972), 231.

[40] The social and economic practices that laid the groundwork for literary representations of elite
women as bearers of credit are detailed by H.J. Habakkuk, *Marriage, Debt, and the Estates
System: English Landowning 1650–1950* (Oxford, 1994).

[41] Fielding, *Amelia*, 456, 475–6, 226, 344, 374–5, 478–9 (citation from 226).

[42] William Thackeray, *Vanity Fair: A Novel without a Hero*, ed. Geoffrey and Kathlen Tillotson
(1848; London, 1963), 432. As Andrew Miller comments, 'Thackeray's term for the practice of
manipulating people and social procedures to get something for nothing is, or course, "credit":

50 Debt and credit in English memory and imagination

If wives' credit dealings served as a focal point for the analysis of gender relations and domestic sexual transgression, masculine credit relations in the novel typically functioned instead to interrogate the changes in class and status wrought by economic modernisation. Just as novelists used gifting behaviours to illustrate the ways in which exchange could maintain vertical ties of status within society, so too representations of masculine retail credit worked to suggest that market-based consumer activity would obliterate the necessary distinctions that preserved social order. Ignoring the pervasive evidence – not least the evidence of novels – that extended credit relations had shaped the consumer markets of the Georgian period, Victorian and Edwardian male novelists insisted that their own era had witnessed the birth of credit and the death of cash. In *The Struggles of Brown, Jones and Robinson* (1862), Trollope anachronistically claims that 'the ready money principle' of earlier decades has given way to a new and subversive retail system in which 'Credit and credit only was required.'[43] In *The Way We Live Now* (1872) Trollope again depicts shopkeepers' willingness to accept false tokens of consumer worth as a violation of established customs and usages that had earlier secured Engand's national prosperity. The insolvent patriarch of the Longstaffe estate is much beloved of local tradesmen, who base their evaluation of his credit on his high level of conspicuous consumption and a canny calculation that 'the owner of a property so managed cannot scrutinize his bills very closely'. In contrast, Trollope's hero, Roger Carbury, who 'had never owed a shilling that he could not pay', is solvency personified, and suffers by comparison in their esteem.[44]

To later Victorian and Edwardian novelists, this perversion of commercial credit posed a particularly alarming threat, for by jeopardising tradesmen's ability to distinguish between solvent and insolvent customers, modern credit practices appeared to imperil not only determinations of the individual's moral character but also the broader workings of the global exchange that rested upon the sum of these individual credit profiles. In *The Way We Live Now*, the suicide of Augustus Melmotte suggests that shopkeepers' increasing tendency to mistake the semblance of wealth for its substance threatens the stability of wider capital markets. The unstable edifice on which Melmotte builds his reputation as a man of global wealth rests upon an unwise extension of credit

---

Becky lives her life – social and erotic as well as economic – on "nothing a year".' Andrew H. Miller, *Novels behind Glass: Commodity Culture and Victorian Narrative* (Cambridge, 1995), 40.

[43] Anthony Trollope, *The Struggles of Brown, Jones and Robinson: By One of the Firm* (1862; Oxford, 1992), 36.

[44] Anthony Trollope, *The Way We Live Now* (1872; Oxford, 1982), 50. As Elaine Freedgood argues, the later nineteenth century saw not a new acceptance of the permanence of financial risk (posited by theorists of modernisation), but rather the evolution of new textual strategies for containing financial risks. See her *Victorian Writing about Risk: Imaging a Safe England in a Dangerous World* (Cambridge, 2000).

Fictions of debt and credit, 1740–1914   51

by local tradesmen, a circumstance that nicely illustrates the concatenation of individual credit transactions that underpinned the market in the novel. By providing him with lavish furnishings, gems, horses and carriages, tradesmen ensure that 'in the City Mr Melmotte's name was worth any money – though his character was perhaps worth but little' (33–4). H.G. Wells brought these fears to their logical conclusion in *Tono Bungay* (1909), in which fictional credit loses all relation to capital and character. 'The old merchant used to tote about commodities; the new one creates values', Edward Ponderevo comments of the increasing distance that divides objects and their signifiers in modern credit culture. 'He takes something that isn't worth anything – or something that isn't particularly worth anything, and he makes it worth something.'[45] Where credit born of gift relations had worked to fix individuals in stable social matrices arrayed in orderly hierarchical ranks, the retail credit that catalysed commodity exchange in consumer markets promised to free fictional characters from their mutual obligations, subverting sexual propriety, destabilising social order and fomenting economic ruin.

Bodies and contracts; novels and prisons

If retail settings afforded novelists an effective vantage point for examining the social repercussions of market activity, prisons arguably constituted the premier site for fictional explorations of the relations of class and power entailed by personal credit. As coercive institutions of confinement, prisons have long offered effective settings for fictional revelations of character,[46] but the persistent salience of the debtors' prison in English novels is none the less surprising. In a century that saw significant changes in literary form and focus – most notably, the shift from sentimental fiction to first romantic and then realist modes of writing – the longevity of this trope is noteworthy. Male and female, reputable and dissolute, propertied and penniless – a host of fictional characters suffer arrest or imprisonment for debt in a tradition that begins with Defoe's *Moll Flanders* (1722) and stretches from Richardson and Fielding to Dickens and Trollope in the 1860s. Dissimilar in their tastes, beliefs and behaviours, the courtesan Miss Forward in Haywood's *Betsy Thoughtless*, the charlatan hero of Tobias Smollett's *Ferdinand Count Fathom* (1753) and Oliver Goldsmith's virtuous Dr Primrose in *The Vicar of Wakefield* (1766) all share this fate. Resort to imprisonment for debt as a plot device in Ann Radcliffe's *Romance of*

[45] H.G. Wells, *Tono Bungay*, ed. John Hammond, (1909; London, 1994), 140, 118. William Kupinse elaborates these themes in 'Wasted value: the serial logic of H.G. Wells's *Tono Bungay*', *Novel*, 33, 1 (Fall 1999), 51–72.

[46] For the broad history of authors' fascination with the prison, see Martha Grace Duncan, *Romantic Outlaws, Beloved Prisons: The Unconscious Meanings of Crime and Punishment* (New York, 1996). Duncan's analysis, however, ignores essential historical distinctions between criminal and debtors' prisons.

52   Debt and credit in English memory and imagination

the Forest (1791), Charlotte Smith's *Letters of a Solitary Wanderer* (1801) and Jane Austen's *Sense and Sensibility* (1811) testifies to the persistent purchase of this usage in gothic and romantic fiction.[47] In early Victorian novels, imprisoned debtors continue to haunt the literary canon: Charles Dickens's *Pickwick Papers* (1837), *David Copperfield* (1850) and *Little Dorrit* (1857) all draw heavily upon the fictional and institutional traditions of imprisonment for debt. Insolvents who suffer (or seek to evade) imprisonment for their unpaid debts are likewise prominent among the characters in Thackeray's *Vanity Fair* (1848) and *History of Pendennis* (1850), just as they occupy centre stage in Trollope's *Three Clerks* (1858) and *Framley Parsonage* (1861).

Not least among the factors that contributed to the currency of the debtors' prison in English fiction was the enduring relevance of this institution to the lives of English novelists. English contract law allowed creditors who were owed sums of more than forty shillings to arrest and imprison their debtors' bodies for safe custody. Although the law sharply restricted creditors' access to debtors' estates and incomes, it gave them exceptional powers over debtors' persons: creditors willing to pay the considerable costs of the common-law courts were empowered to imprison their debtors without trial for extended periods as a coercive inducement to payment.[48] A site to which men of property convicted of no crime had been committed for centuries – but from which more plebeian debtors were largely excluded by the disproportionate legal costs of their incarceration – the debtors' prison offered novelists a socially acceptable institution of confinement, a gaol to which a gentleman might be consigned without irreparable prejudice to his character.

From the middle decades of the eighteenth century, the commercialisation of literary production rendered writers themselves increasingly conspicuous within the walls of the debtors' prison. For although changes in copyright conventions had begun to secure authors' property in their writings, and thus fostered novelists' ability to sell their manuscripts as commodities in the literary market,[49] the vagaries of literary fashion ensured that novel-writing failed to provide a sufficient livelihood for the bulk of its practitioners. Henry Fielding received £183 for *Joseph Andrews* (1742), £700 for *Tom Jones* (1749) and

---

[47] 'The Romantic imagination is in large part an imagination of confinement', Nina Auerbach observes. *Romantic Imprisonment: Women and Other Glorified Outcasts* (New York, 1985), 7.

[48] See esp. Paul H. Haagen, 'Eighteenth-century English society and the debt law', in Stanley Cohen and Andrew Scull, eds., *Social Control and the State* (New York, 1983), 222–47, and Joanna Innes, 'The King's Bench prison in the later eighteenth century: law, authority and order in a London debtors' prison', in John Brewer and John Styles, eds., *An Ungovernable People: The English and Their Law in the Seventeenth and Eighteenth Centuries* (New Brunswick, 1980), 250–98, 371–87.

[49] John Feather, 'From rights in copies to copyright: the recognition of authors' rights in English law and practice in the sixteenth and seventeenth centuries', in Martha Woodmansee and Peter Jaszi, eds., *The Construction of Authorship: Textual Appropriation in Law and Literature* (Durham, NC, 1994), 191–209.

Fictions of debt and credit, 1740–1914

£1,000 for *Amelia* (1751). But for most Georgian writers, payments for fictional works ranged from two to ten guineas per novel.[50] The value of Victorian authors' property in their fiction, similarly, varied dramatically between high and low extremes. Trollope earned over £68,000 in his career as a novelist and Thackeray's publisher offered him an advance of £1,000 after the success of *Pendennis*, but George Gissing, who estimated his modest living expenses at £120 per annum, was paid only £2 for *Workers in the Dawn* (1880), £30 for *The Unclassed* (1884) and £15 for *Isabel Clarendon* (1886).[51] Nigel Cross has neatly captured the essence of the paradoxical relationship that obtained between novelists and their fictional property in this context, noting that 'as authorship began to establish itself as a paid activity so imprisonment for debt became an occupational hazard'.[52]

The 1740s, indeed, saw the emergence of an increasingly symbiotic relationship between the novel and the debtors' prison. As the commercialisation of novel-writing lent authors income and credit that brought them within the grasp of the debt law, they sought to turn these experiences to financial and fictional account in their writings. The constant interplay between Henry Fielding's personal debts and his fictional strategies illustrates this nexus. As both the scion of a landed family and a successful purveyor of commercial fiction, Fielding stood at the intersection of old and new conventions and experiences of imprisonment for debt. His father died a debtor within the precincts of the Fleet prison, and Fielding himself – hounded by creditors throughout his life despite the commercial success of his novels – died insolvent in 1754. Imprisoned for debt for a fortnight in 1741, Fielding was entangled in debt litigation yet again in 1742 and 1743.[53] His novels repeatedly capitalise on these incidents, crossing and recrossing the broken line between biographical fact and imaginative fiction as Fielding's characters tread terrain that he had traversed before them as a debtor. In *Joseph Andrews*, written as Fielding hid from his creditors in Charing Cross, the protagonist's journey from London to his parental village is slowed by a succession of debts which he is unable to pay without charitable assistance, while the tale-within-a-tale told by Mr Wilson recapitulates the credit woes of Fielding's own life in the metropolis. In the autobiographical *Amelia*, Captain Booth's unpaid debts propel the novel's action from the provinces to

---

[50] Cheryl Turner, *Living by the Pen: Women Writers in the Eighteenth Century* (London, 1992), 113–14.

[51] Valentine Cunningham, 'Unto him (or her) that hath: how Victorian writers made ends meet', *Times Literary Supplement*, 11 September 1998, 12–13.

[52] Nigel Cross, *The Common Writer: Life in Nineteenth-Century Grub Street* (Cambridge, 1985), 39.

[53] Donald Thomas, *Henry Fielding* (London, 1990), 140, 160, 111–12, 151, 159–61; Martin C. Battestin with Ruthe R. Battestin, *Henry Fielding: A Life* (London, 1989), 72–3, 251–3, 288–9, 295–6, 352, 369, 609; Hugh Barty-King, *The Worst Poverty: A History of Debt and Debtors* (Stroud, 1991), 81.

54   Debt and credit in English memory and imagination

London, where Booth (like Fielding before him) seeks haven from bailiffs in the privileged regions of the Verge of the Court, but fails to elude arrest.

Fielding's intimate familiarity with imprisonment for debt was rehearsed again and again in the life stories (and the novels) of his contemporaries. John Cleland was committed for debt to London's Fleet prison in 1748, and used this enforced leisure to write his scandalous *Memoirs of a Woman of Pleasure* (1748–49);[54] Tobias Smollett – like his fictional Count Fathom – suffered imprisonment in the King's Bench, London's largest and most exclusive debtors' prison.[55] In the 1760s, Oliver Goldsmith, deeply in debt to his landlady, was spared a personal encounter with the debtors' prison only when Samuel Johnson intervened in his affairs, discharging the novelist's rent by peddling the manuscript of *The Vicar of Wakefield* – replete with its scenes depicting Dr Primrose's imprisonment for debt – to a London bookseller.[56] Johnson himself, twice imprisoned for debt, played an instrumental role in exposing the injustice of this practice to public view in his writings, excoriating the broad iniquities of creditors' arbitrary powers, and decrying writers' disproportionate vulnerability to them.[57]

Although the common-law conventions of coverture rendered wives immune from personal liability for their debts, women novelists were active alongside men in promoting the literary currency of the debtors' prison. For single women, widows and wives who sought to maintain their families by publication, imprisonment for debt was a lived experience rather than merely an appealing imaginative setting for fictional narratives: when the novelist Eliza Parsons petitioned the Royal Literary Fund for assistance in 1799, she had already been confined in a debtors' prison for two years.[58] The popular and immensely prolific writer Charlotte Smith first encountered the debtors' prison as a young married woman in 1783, when her husband – incapable of living within a generous parental allowance of 2,000 pounds a year – was committed to the King's Bench. Initially sharing her husband's confinement in prison and later joining him in Normandy when he fled to evade his creditors, Smith adopted poetry and novel-writing as means to restore the family's finances. Dunned by creditors and harassed by bailiffs to the last, she returned repeatedly to the dilemmas of debt and credit in her novels, subjecting her characters to legal processes

---

[54] William H. Epstein, *John Cleland: Images of a Life* (New York, 1974), 61–7. In his later *Woman of Honor* [*sic*] (1768), he was at pains to denounce the practice of imprisonment for debt. See Epstein, *John Cleland*, 63.

[55] David Hannay, *Life of Tobias George Smollett* (London, 1887), 122–3.

[56] For Goldsmith's rescue by Johnson, see E.H. Mikhail, ed., *Goldsmith: Interviews and Recollections* (London, 1993), 32–4, 53–5.

[57] Robert DeMaria, Jr, *The Life of Samuel Johnson: A Critical Biography* (Oxford, 1993), 194; Nicholas Hudson, *Samuel Johnson and Eighteenth-Century Thought* (Oxford, 1988), 181–4.

[58] Edward Copeland, *Women Writing about Money: Women's Fiction in England, 1790–1820* (Cambridge, 1995), 198, 204.

and institutions of confinement of which she boasted considerable personal knowledge.[59]

Trends in fictional form worked alongside these biographical incidents to insert the debtors' prison in later Georgian novels. From the later eighteenth century, the rising influence of humanitarian and gothic themes created a literary context in which economic vulnerability acquired an easy and emotive resonance.[60] Women writers' troubled negotiations between their authorial and familial obligations lent financial dealings a particular edge in their fictions. Caught in networks of debt that were at once emotionally charged and materially based, Catherine Gallagher argues, Fanny Burney and Maria Edgeworth 'stressed the superfluity of their fictional representations and indicated that the more credit they gained by writing them, the more they owed the public', perceptions of their literary and economic worth that these authors linked 'to the pressure of a seemingly unpayable daughterly obligation to their fathers'.[61] Gothic sensibilities provided especially fertile ground for the development of themes of personal debt and credit in women's fictions. 'Certainly the gothic literature of the 1790s, both in novels and short magazine fiction, concerns itself with the pressing dangers to women from debt: harassment, humiliation, confinement', Edward Copeland has observed.[62]

Like their Georgian predecessors, Victorian novelists drew upon a rich store of personal experience when they resorted to the debtors' prison in their fiction. Charles Dickens's father John, an improvident clerk, was confined for debt in London's Marshalsea prison in 1824, declared insolvent again in 1831 and rescued by the intervention of his son from a third period of incarceration three years later. Tales recounted by Dickens's mother, who resided with her husband in the Marshalsea, provided the young novelist with a fund of information on debtors and their plight which he continued to exploit from *Pickwick Papers* in 1837 to *Little Dorrit* in 1858.[63] Contemporary novelists who enjoyed more exalted social origins than Dickens none the less shared his close familiarity with the debt law. Thackeray, like the hero of his *Pendennis*, was heir to a considerable fortune, but amassed gambling debts in excess of £1,500

---

[59] See Judith Phillips Stanton, 'Charlotte Smith's "literary business": income, patronage, and indigence', in Paul J. Korshin, ed., *The Age of Johnson: A Scholarly Annual*, 1 (1987), 375–401, and Lorraine Fletcher, *Charlotte Smith: A Critical Biography* (London, 1998), 30, 62–4, 105, 153, 202, 211, 294, 311.

[60] For these developments, see Markham Ellis, *The Politics of Sensibility: Race, Gender and Commerce in the Sentimental Novel* (Cambridge, 1996), esp. 87–8, 108, 115, 119, 130–1, 135, 182, 184–5.

[61] Gallagher, *Nobody's Story*, xxii.   [62] Copeland, *Women Writing about Money*, 7.

[63] C.R.B. Dunlop, 'Debtors and creditors in Dickens' fiction', *Dickens Studies Annual*, 19 (1990), 34; Angus Easson, 'Imprisonment for debt in *Pickwick Papers*', *The Dickensian*, 64, no. 355 (May 1968), 111–12; Diane Elam, ' "Another day and I'm deeper in debt": *Little Dorrit* and the debt of the everyday', in John Schad, ed., *Dickens Refigured: Bodies, Desires and Other Histories* (Manchester, 1996), 157–77.

56 Debt and credit in English memory and imagination

at Cambridge, and was removed in disgrace by his guardians to retrench his expenditure on the Continent.[64] Trollope, the son of an unsuccessful barrister, was rendered miserable in childhood by his father's inability to pay his school fees and his mother's peripatetic efforts to earn an income through literature. Their household goods seized by bailiffs, the family fled to Belgium to escape its creditors. Upon his return to England in early manhood, Trollope as an impecunious civil servant continued to be hounded by moneylenders and duns, a fate shared in his novels by protagonists such as Charley Tudor in *The Three Clerks*, Mark Robarts in *Framley Parsonage* and the eponymous hero of *Phineas Finn*.

No less significant than the persistence of imprisoned debtors as characters in English novels is the substantive continuity that marked fictional portrayals of debtors' prisons as institutions. The decades spanned by these novels saw a fundamental transformation of the literary representation of criminal prisons. As new models of penitential confinement were sketched by architects, elaborated by politicians and endorsed by philanthropists, idealised visions of the model reformatory challenged and undermined established literary images of the criminal gaol as a ramshackle, disease-infested seat of oppression, dissipation and vice.[65] In contrast, the conventions that governed fictional representation of imprisonment for debt evolved little in this period. Despite the clarion call to reform articulated in 1766 by Goldsmith's Dr Primrose in *The Vicar of Wakefield*, debtors' prisons – as depicted in English novels – remained largely insulated from the rising tide of penal reform.[66] Viewed as administrative units, the gaols created by Fielding and Smollett are of a piece with the institutions that were to be inhabited by the fictional debtors of the Victorian era. Far from developing (with the criminal prison) from disorderly and archaic institutions of mere confinement into active, modern instruments of discipline and reform, fictional debtors' prisons continuously fluctuated between two extremes of representation, alternately figuring as venal sites of exploitation in which contractual oppression ran riot and as economic backwaters that served, worryingly, to protect their inmates from the demands of the modern market.

[64] J.Y.T. Grieg, *Thackeray: A Reconsideration* (Oxford, 1950), 48–50.

[65] See esp. John Bender, *Imagining the Penitentiary: Fiction and the Architecture of Mind in Eighteenth-Century England* (Chicago, 1987), and Keith Hollingsworth, *The Newgate Novel 1830–1847: Bulwer, Ainsworth, Dickens, and Thackeray* (Detroit, 1963).

[66] In his 'Prison reform and the sentence of narration in *The Vicar of Wakefield*', in Felicity Nussbaum and Laura Brown, eds., *The New Eighteenth Century: Theory, Politics, Literature* (London, 1987), 168–88, John Bender argues, to the contrary, that Primrose's reform activities betoken a radical departure from the unreformed prison, presaging its imminent replacement by the penitentiary in fact as in fiction. But Primrose's effort to effect reform within the prison through religious devotion is unique within the debtors' novel rather than representative of an emerging trend, and debtors (unlike criminals) were not subjected to properly penal regimes until the later nineteenth century, a century after publication of Goldsmith's novel. See below, chaps. 3–4.

In the first of these two conventions of representation, unreformed and unrepentant prison officers expose the oppression and futility of English debt law to public view. Ruled by arbitrary power for personal profit, the debtors' prison emerges in this strand of writing as a world of overlapping private fiefdoms rather than a Foucauldian institution in which officials dispense an ordered justice enshrined in the statutes of the realm. Fielding's *Amelia* offers an early example of this school of representation. Confined for debt, Captain Booth suffers a series of arbitrary exactions from the bailiff, who actively connives against his prisoner's release. Coercing his captive to purchase meat and wine at exorbitant prices, the officer dispatches his minions to a succession of attorneys 'to try to load his prisoner with as many actions as possible'. The bailiff 'had no more malice against the bodies in his custody than a butcher hath to those in his', Fielding comments with caustic irony. 'As to the life of the animal, or the liberty of the man, they are thoughts which never intrude themselves on either' (317). In this interpretation, the petty oppressions of the debtors' prison were corrosive of larger liberties, for by valuing property rights over personal freedoms imprisonment for debt objectified the male prisoner and struck directly at the much-vaunted Englishman's birthright in liberty. Violating constitutional freedoms and the precepts of Christian compassion, the debt law mistook persons for things, misfortune for misbehaviour.

A second, more roseate vision of the debtors' prison however circulated in eighteenth- and nineteenth-century novels alongside this tradition of condemnation. Gentility and social status played an essential part both in establishing this strand of representation and in maintaining the traditions upon which it was based in historical debtors' prisons. Precisely because imprisonment for debt captured not only the truly indigent but also (and more typically) propertied individuals who were unwilling or temporarily unable to liquidate their capital to discharge their obligations, England's larger debtors' prisons boasted an appealing array of amenities for their more privileged inmates.[67] All of the larger gaols allowed moneyed debtors to lodge separately from lowly 'common side' debtors by paying for the privilege of private rooms on the 'master's side' of the prison. Ranging from spacious private apartments to racket courts and convivial wine clubs, the attractions of these prisons helped debtors to preserve their status within the gaol by providing an array of markers by which inmates signalled their social capital to fellow prisoners and to prison officers. Customary fees levied by 'colleges' of debtors for food, wine and personal services helped to register the debtors' prison – in sharp contrast to criminal gaols – as an appropriate site for middle- and upper-class narrative fictions.

Ardently defended by inmates themselves, these traditions helped to sustain a persistent image of the debtors' prison as a haven from economic adversity. In

[67] See below, chap. 3.

58   Debt and credit in English memory and imagination

Ferdinand Count Fathom, Smollett's description of London's debtors' prisons as 'mansions of misery' captured the essence of this image, depicting these institutions as a somewhat seedy variant of the exclusive gentleman's club. When Fathom is committed to the King's Bench, the prison's elite debtors depute Captain Minikin to familiarise him with the social landscape. ' "You must know Sir, that exclusive of the *Cannaille* ... there are several small communities in the gaol, consisting of people who are attracted by the manners and dispositions of each other: for this place, Sir, is quite a *microcosm*" ', he proclaims proudly.[68] Even Goldsmith's Dr Primrose, imprisoned for his debts in a less exalted county gaol, discovers his fellow inmates in the enjoyment of surprising freedoms. Expecting to hear 'nothing but lamentations, and various sounds of misery', Primrose instead finds 'all employed in one common design, that of forgetting thought in merriment'. Having paid a customary 'garnish' to purchase liquor for his fellow inmates, Primrose is consoled in adversity by the daily presence of his wife and children. He soon assumes a position of moral authority over his fellow prisoners fully consonant with his clerical identity and social position, recreating in the gaol a hierarchical community that reflects his proper standing in the world beyond the prison walls.[69]

In all this, Goldsmith – despite his avowed zeal for reform – draws attention to an appealing form of social life that endured in the prison novel well into the Victorian period. Thackeray invokes this tradition of confinement in *Vanity Fair* when he imprisons Colonel Rawdon in a spunging-house owned by Mr Moss of Cursitor Street. 'There were dirty trays and wine-coolers *en permanence* on the side-board, huge dirty gilt cornices, with dingy yellow satin hangings to the barred windows ... vast and dirty gilt picture-frames surrounding pieces sporting and sacred', he notes of Rawdon's accommodations (511). Dickens was obsessed with these indices of prisoners' borderline social status, drawing attention again and again to the troublingly liminal gentility of his imprisoned debtors. In *David Copperfield* (1850), Mr Micawber is imprisoned early one morning in the King's Bench, but is 'seen to play a lively game of skittles, before noon'. Sharing his confinement with family members who live 'more comfortably in the prison than they had lived for a long time out of it', this archetypal debtor is rapidly inducted into a social club, 'in which Mr Micawber, as a gentleman, was a great authority'. Goldsmith's Dr Primrose had signalled his superior status by preaching sermons to his fellow inmates on the reformation of morals; so too Micawber (like John Dickens in the Marshalsea of the 1820s) asserts his natural authority by initiating a campaign to petition Parliament for the reform of the debt laws.[70] In the absence of official oversight and discipline

[68] Tobias Smollett, *The Adventures of Ferdinand Count Fathom* (1753; London, 1990), 242.
[69] Oliver Goldsmith, *The Vicar of Wakefield*, ed. Stephen Coote (1766; London, 1982), 152–64, citation from 153.
[70] Charles Dickens, *David Copperfield* (1850; New York, 1981), 152, 154–5.

1 Interior view of the Marshalsea Prison, Borough High Street, c. 1830. John Dickens (father of the novelist Charles Dickens) was imprisoned here for debt in the 1820s. (Reproduced by permission of the Guildhall Library, London.)

from the official keepers of their prisons, these fictional characters enjoy styles of life and levels of authority that recapitulate, through a distorted optic, the dominant pastimes, pretensions and obligations of the social elite in the wider world that lies beyond the prison walls.

In *Little Dorrit*, Dickens brought this convention to its peak in his description of 'that superb establishment, the Marshalsea hotel'. (Illustration 1). Here the genteel pretensions of the 'Father of the Marshalsea' increase in inverse proportion to his financial fortunes. 'Brought up as a gentleman... if ever a man was', William Dorrit develops 'a new flower of character' in confinement by engaging in elaborate rituals to preserve 'his forlorn gentility'.[71] Dr Haggage, who delivers the infant Amy Dorrit within the prison that houses her insolvent parents, celebrates the liberties that inmates supposedly enjoy by virtue of their confinement. ' "We are quiet here, we don't get badgered here; there's no knocker here, sir, to be hammered at by creditors and bring a man's heart into his mouth" ', he exclaims. ' "Nobody writes threatening letters about money, to this place. It's freedom, sir, it's freedom!" ' (53). Far from encouraging debtors to meet their obligations, the convivial life enjoyed by the 'collegians' who rule

---

[71] Charles Dickens, *Little Dorrit* (1857; Oxford, 1982), 79, 53, 61.

60   Debt and credit in English memory and imagination

the Marshalsea and its 'Snuggery' is inimical to the recognition of contractual commitments. 'It was evident from the general tone of the whole party, that they had come to regard insolvency as the normal state of mankind, and the payment of debts as a disease that occasionally broke out', Dickens observes with some disquiet (73).

Depicted alternately as sites of archaic oppression and as havens from the modern market, debtors' prisons worked in the novel not to associate debt with crime, but rather to undercut the legitimacy of strict contractual claims enforced by legal processes. In the novel, even female debtors whose dishonoured economic contracts reflected their compromising sexual behaviours could figure as 'unfortunate' rather than malign characters. In *Betsy Thoughtless*, Haywood's Miss Forward is deserted by her paramours and propelled into the gaol by 'debts my luxury contracted' amid 'guilty pleasures'. But despite the illicit provenance of her debts, she figures as a fitting object of feminine charity and, assisted by Haywood's protagonist, obtains her liberation from prison. In novels of the romantic era, the established linkage between debt and female sexuality similarly underlines the difficulty of demarcating rigidly between moral and immoral economic obligations. Eliza Brandon in *Sense and Sensibility* is provoked to adultery by abuse, divorced by her husband, reduced to penury and imprisoned for debt. But Austen's description of Eliza as 'unfortunate' militates against any strict equation of sexual and economic virtue in the novel. ' "Regard for a former servant of my own, who had since fallen into misfortune, carried me to visit him in a spunging-house, where he was confined for debt" ', Colonel Brandon explains to Elinor in detailing his family history, ' "and there, in the same house, under a similar confinement, was my unfortunate sister." '[72]

Anthony Trollope's *Three Clerks* likewise highlights the instability of linkages among debt, credit and character, insistently emphasising the ability of even weak-willed fictional heroes to suffer imprisonment for debt without permanent damage to their social and marital prospects. In its plot, delineation of character and final resolution, Trollope's novel encapsulates the characteristic ambivalence toward credit displayed by debtors' novels from the 1740s to the 1850s, rehearsing earlier writers' persistent unwillingness to assign fixed moral valuations to personal debts and their social consequences. In his initial chapters, Trollope situates the three clerks within a matrix of debt and credit relations that continues to shape their status, behaviour and representation throughout the novel. Henry Norman is removed from his college at Oxford and put to work at the office of Weights and Measures as a clerk when his older brother's extravagance at Cambridge leaves his father without the financial means to pay for his education. The second of the three clerks at the Weights and Measures, Aleric Tudor, also suffers the consequences of unpaid family debts from an early age,

[72] Jane Austen, *Sense and Sensibility* (1811; London, 1959), 223–4.

Fictions of debt and credit, 1740–1914   61

spending his youth in Brussels, where his father – like Trollope's – flees to avoid his creditors. Charley Tudor, the third clerk, personifies the confluence of social and economic valuation in nineteenth-century English society: he is introduced by the author as a man who 'could not rid himself of his companions, nor of his debts, nor yet even of his habits'.[73]

The contrast between Aleric Tudor's fate and the fortunes of his cousin Charley is striking. Aleric borrows money from the fiscally responsible Henry Norman early in the novel, and uses these funds to engage in illegal speculation. Enriched by these profits, he enters into a succession of increasingly immoral credit transactions, abusing his power and privileged knowledge in both the public financial market and the private marriage market to sustain an increasingly extravagant lifestyle. Led by his illicit credit dealings to embezzle the fortune of an heiress for whom he is a trustee, Tudor is convicted in a criminal court and committed to Millbank penitentiary. Trollope is careful to distinguish this criminal institution from the debtors' prisons that recur in the fictional record, marking Millbank as a plebeian institution unfit for gentlemanly characters (519). Tarred by the brush of criminal confinement, Aleric Tudor is fittingly exiled to Australia, rather than returned to the genteel English social sphere upon his release.[74]

Although Charley Tudor also suffers imprisonment for his financial misdeeds, his consumer debts and credits fall within the elastic bounds of acceptable gentlemanly economic behaviour and prove compatible with idealised romantic love and marriage. Ensnared by petty debts, Charley Tudor lives in fear of arrest by his tailor and the rapacious bill-discounter, Jabesh M'Ruen. Yet Charley's debts and indiscretions clearly signal his moral superiority to Aleric Tudor, for his actions reflect the values enshrined in traditional gift obligations in their repeated refusal to objectify persons. Aleric Tudor encourages his cousin to redeem his financial position by marrying the heiress Clementina Golightly, advancing a line of argument that echoes both Burney's *Wanderer* and Thackeray's *Vanity Fair* in equating the false expectations of mercenary marriages with the normal operation of the consumer credit system. ' "Where was your honesty when you ordered the coat for which you know you cannot pay? or when you swore to the bootmaker that he should have the amount of his little bill after the next quarter-day, knowing in your heart at the time that he wouldn't get a farthing of it?" ', Aleric urges against Charley's scruples (312). Trollope's hero, however, rejects this easy conflation of human relations and commodity transactions, resolutely declining 'to look upon himself as a marketable animal, worth a certain sum of money, in consequence of such property

---

[73] Anthony Trollope, *The Three Clerks* (1858; London, 1993), 3, 8, 19.
[74] For later Victorian novelists' increasingly problematic engagement with the tradition of romantic criminal confinement, see Nicola Nixon, 'The Reading Gaol of Henry James's *In the Cage*', *ELH*, 66, 1 (Spring 1999), 179–201.

62   Debt and credit in English memory and imagination

in good appearance, address... as God had been good enough to endow him withal' (192). The immediate consequence of this refusal to marry money is Charley's imprisonment for debt, and his temporary exclusion from the home of his beloved Katie Woodward. But unlike Aleric Tudor's fraudulent financial dealings and incarceration in Millbank, Charley's liability for mere consumer purchases and his confinement in a gentlemanly gaol feature as venial economic sins. Liberated from incarceration by the long-suffering Henry Norman, he succeeds in amending his financial fortunes by writing tales for the periodical press, and happily marries his middle-class sweetheart.

Conclusion

Legal practices such as imprisonment for debt lent themselves readily to fictional scrutiny in Georgian and early Victorian England. Novelists' constant struggles to secure their own bodies from seizure by their creditors insistently highlighted the arbitrary nature of the debt law; formal legal training, moreover, as John Sutherland has observed, provided a common 'entry point into novel writing', constructing a 'wide bridge' between law and fiction.[75] Discursive engagements with contractual morality in fiction were further fuelled by the persistent slippage between legal and literary explorations of the nature and utility of fictions. Jeremy Bentham's excoriating critique of so-called legal fictions – the procedural devices which (not unlike the principles of equity) allowed litigants to enter false pleas to gain jurisdiction or redress denied by the strict letter of the law – spurred sustained debate not only in the legal profession but in the novel, ensuring that the legal fictions that underpinned practices such as speculation in financial markets, imprisonment for debt and wives' suspended legal personhood under coverture were understood to be 'preserved in every sphere of daily life: economic, political, social, and domestic'.[76]

Sensitive to the power exerted by legal fictions in day-to-day contractual relations, English readers and writers were drawn to literary fictions as narrative mechanisms for mediating and integrating their own life stories. As Franco Moretti has argued of the European *Bildungsroman* more broadly, 'the novel exists not as a critique, but as a *culture of everyday life*'. Not least among the challenges confronted by novelists in the new market cultures of the long nineteenth century was the task of crafting dynamic fictional characters – men and women linked by dense social networks, who actively embodied diverse personalities rather than merely occupying static, individuated roles. As fictions

---

[75] John Sutherland, *Victorian Fiction: Writers, Publishers, Readers* (Basingstoke, 1995), 162.

[76] Marjorie Stone, 'Dickens, Bentham, and the fictions of the law: a Victorian controversy and its consequences', *VS*, 29, 1 (Autumn 1985), 125–54, citation from 150. For the legal history of legal fictions, see J.H. Baker, *The Law's Two Bodies: Some Evidential Problems in English Legal History* (Oxford, 2001), chap. 2.

of debt and credit repeatedly demonstrate, novelists' compelling response to the autonomous individual posited by classical political economy and modern legal reasoning was the 'polyparadigmatic character', a contractual social agent defined by heterogeneity, contradiction and 'a perennial disequilibrium of... symbolic and emotive investments'.[77]

The debt and credit relations that underpinned both gift and market relations in England proved highly problematic, for these personal obligations continually exposed to view the inability of either the commodity form or the economic contract to distinguish effectively among the competing moral and legal claims of things and persons in modern exchange. For decades, the legal vagaries of imprisonment for debt provided English novelists with a convenient shorthand for describing the inadequacies of contractual obligation. As criminal penitentiaries loomed ever larger in the public imagination and as plebeian consumers displaced gentlemanly inmates in the debtors' prison, middle-class novelists were to abandon these sites of representation, but they continued to underline the multivalent meanings and character of personal debt and credit relations in their fiction. Patrick Brantlinger has emphasised 'the tendency of most Victorian writers... to treat debt as a matter mainly of personal culpability',[78] but this argument mistakes the moral dynamics that governed fictional approaches to the realm of corporate and government finance for the more tolerant consumer moralities that shaped individuals' daily credit dealings. The enduring presence of extended credit in the novel (and in the historical consumer market) provided writers with a host of narrative opportunities for reading individuals' misbehaviours as 'misfortunes'. In this, the fictional record paralleled the representation of debt and credit found in contemporary diaries and memoirs, and worked together with these documents to create a sustained literary engagement with consumer society that privileged notions of reciprocity and gift over strictly individualist conceptions of property and contract.

---

[77] Moretti, *Way of the World*, 35, 42, 39.

[78] Brantlinger, *Fictions of State*, 141. For the fictional parameters that shaped novelists' antagonism to high finance, see Norman Russell, *The Novelist and Mammon: Literary Responses to the World of Commerce in the Nineteenth Century* (Oxford, 1981), 150–5, and McVeagh, *Tradeful Merchants*, 128–9.

2 Debt and credit in diaries and autobiographies

Like novels, diaries and autobiographies trace their genealogy to the account book, and share that genre's preoccupation with calculations of the individual's fluctuating balance of personal debts and credits.[1] Records that convey – however incompletely and selectively – both the mundane practices and the affective meanings of the market, these documents resonate with (but also extend significantly beyond) the register of fiction. As in novels, the boundaries between the market and the household were repeatedly ignored in these texts, as authors whose social backgrounds ranged from the poorhouse to the peerage drew attention to the inevitable interpenetration of social relations and economic exchange. Tradesmen who travelled to the home to ply their wares, consumers who enjoyed convivial hospitality extended by shopkeepers, commodities that circulated through processes of gift exchange and credit practices that configured debt as an ongoing social relationship rather than a purely legal obligation all linked the consumer activities recorded in diaries and memoirs to the moralised interpretations of economic exchange privileged by writers of fiction. Reading and writing practices worked to reinforce these linkages. In a diary kept in the 1750s, the Sussex shopkeeper Thomas Turner recorded that his wife read Richardson's *Clarissa* aloud while he entered the day's retail transactions into his account book; a century later, the London gentlewoman Henrietta Halliwell-Phillipps noted in her diary that her daughters read *Little Dorrit* to her as she transcribed manuscripts for her husband.[2]

References to the function of writing as a means of establishing personal character further link journals, autobiographies and novels discursively, as do writers' reflections on the parallels that obtained between their own daily

---

[1] For the interlinked histories of the account book, diary, memoir and novel, see esp. J. Paul Hunter, *Before Novels: The Cultural Contexts of Eighteenth-Century English Fiction* (New York, 1990).

[2] Naomi Tadmor, ' "In the even my wife read to me": women, reading and household life in the eighteenth century', in James Raven, Helen Small and Naomi Tadmor, eds., *The Practice and Representation of Reading in England* (Cambridge, 1996), 165, 169–70; Marvin Spevack, ed., *A Victorian Chronicle: The Diary of Henrietta Halliwell-Phillipps* (Hildesheim, 1999), 334 (10 February 1871).

Debt and credit in diaries and autobiographies 65

lives and the imagined experiences of fictional protagonists.[3] When the young Rebecca Solly attempted 'as well as I shall be able to delineate my character' in 1800, she resolved to write an annual summary of her moral development in a diary and commonplace book. 'For a young person to estimate their character is perhaps no easy task but let not its difficulty discourage me', Solly recorded solemnly. Fiction provided an essential model for this exercise in identity formation: the entries that Solly titled 'Manners & Morals', 'Marriage' and 'Character' are filled with extensive quotations from Richardson's *Clarissa*.[4] Solly was not unusual in turning to fiction to frame and shape her evolving sense of self. The diary kept in 1878 by Judge H.T. Atkinson of the Leeds county court is punctuated by references to his engagement with the world of fiction. In January the judge read Trollope's *Can You Forgive Her?* (1865), which – despite its 'improbable situations, impossible characters, and very doubtful morality' – he was unable to put down; February saw Atkinson chair a lecture on Charles Dickens attended by five hundred of his fellow Leeds residents. In October, resolving to pay off an assortment of his accumulated small debts, he was struck by the personal relevance of the economic lessons taught by Goldsmith's *Vicar of Wakefield*. 'If the fathers of ruined families could be put to the question or brought to confession, ninety [per cent] at least of them would own that their primary embarrassments (like those of the Primrose family) arose from the wish to keep up appearances', he reflected sadly. 'Vanity would be found to be a more fruitful source of misery than vice.'[5]

Plebeian authors' sense of self and their understanding of the economy, as Jonathan Rose's detailed exposition of working-class memoirs clearly demonstrates, were likewise closely imbricated with their efforts to assimilate, interpret and refashion the rich intellectual heritage bestowed by the English novel. Ben Brierley's youthful employment as a piecer in a Lancashire cotton mill was enlivened by his introduction to the fiction of Charles Dickens: access to his manager's copies of the serialised *Pickwick Papers* both relieved the tedium of industrial labour and prompted him to become an author in his own right.[6] Other readers who found inspiration in Dickens's novels for their own efforts to narrate a meaningful life story through autobiography came from equally

---

[3] Lynda M. Thompson highlights 'the cross-dressing and the rivalry between the genres of the novel and the memoir' and these works' attention to definitions of 'character' in *The 'Scandalous Memoirists': Constantia Phillips, Laetitia Pilkington and the Shame of 'Public Fame'* (Manchester, 2000), 1, 81.

[4] Bodleian, MS Johnson.e.7, Commonplace Book and Journal of Rebecca Shaen, née Solly (1800–55), 69, 125–40. For the role of novel-reading in female self-fashioning in this period, see Jacqueline Pearson, *Women's Reading in Britain 1750–1835: A Dangerous Recreation* (Cambridge, 1999), esp. 19–20, 122–51.

[5] Bodleian, MS Eng.misc.e.940, Diary of H.T. Atkinson, 1878, 124 (6 January 1878); 161 (12 February 1878); 404 (11 October 1878).

[6] Ben Brierley, *Home Memories, and Recollections of a Life* (Manchester, [1887]), 21–2.

66 Debt and credit in English memory and imagination

modest backgrounds. They included a leather-bag maker, a miner, a docker's daughter and a laundress's son. 'Perhaps Dickens's most important gift to the working classes was the role he played in making them articulate', Rose concludes. 'He provided a fund of allusions, characters, tropes, and situations that could be drawn upon by people who were not trained to express themselves on paper.'[7]

Scholars once hailed autobiography as the quintessential genre of modern individualism, but recent research has revealed the limits of personal autonomy in English autobiographical texts.[8] Victorian feminists' memoirs, for example, situate identity formation within 'collective experience entrenched within a collaborative endeavour', while Victorian literary women's memoirs reflect 'the distinct historical experience of women as unequal and selfless subjects'.[9] Working-class autobiographies likewise diverge from the narrow and solitary paths of autonomous individualism. Carolyn Steedman's analysis of the life stories extracted from indigent workers by parish officials underlines 'the autobiographical injunction' that propelled these 'enforced narratives' into being and describes such plebeian memoirs as reflections of 'a history of expectations, orders and instructions rather than one of urges and desires'.[10] Regenia Gagnier concludes that the 'functional use of literacy' in working-class memoirs displays little overlap with 'the aesthetic of detached individualism' that marks the elite male autobiographical canon.[11]

The conflicted relations between autonomy and social obligation in diaries and personal memoirs afford the historian a series of essential perspectives on the problematic processes of individual self-fashioning. More prosaically but no less vitally, these sources illuminate the texture and practice of economic exchange in everyday life, helping to unpack the ensemble of procedures, tactics and transactional modalities that Michel de Certeau denominates 'the art of practice'.[12] By highlighting the great diversity of strategies used by contemporaries to obtain goods, diaries and memoirs attest to the unevenness of

---

[7] Jonathan Rose, *The Intellectual Life of the British Working Classes* (New Haven, 2001), 111–15, citation from 114.

[8] See, for example, Trev Lynn Broughton, *Men of Letters, Writing Lives: Masculinity and Literary Auto/Biography in the Late Victorian Period* (London, 1999), esp. 9, and, more broadly, Roy Porter, ed., *Rewriting the Self: Histories from the Renaissance to the Present* (London, 1997).

[9] Pauline Polkey, 'Reading history through autobiography: politically active women of late nineteenth-century Britain and their personal narratives', *Women's History Review*, 9, 3 (2000), 484; Mary Jean Corbett, *Representing Femininity: Middle-Class Subjectivity in Victorian and Edwardian Women's Autobiographies* (New York, 1992), 100.

[10] Carolyn Steedman, 'Enforced narratives: stories of another self', in Tess Cosslet, Celia Lury and Penny Summerfield, eds., *Feminism and Autobiography: Texts, Theories, Methods* (London, 2000), 28.

[11] Regenia Gagnier, *Subjectivities: A History of Self-Representation in Britain, 1832–1920* (Oxford, 1991), 42.

[12] Michel de Certeau, *The Practice of Everyday Life*, trans. Steven Rendall (Berkeley, 1984), esp. 29–76.

market-oriented commodification. For like novelists, English diarists and autobiographers proved intensely reluctant to abandon the market to the possessive individual, refusing – in the face of considerable ideological pressure to the contrary – to disengage 'the social' from 'the economic'.[13] Representations of debt, credit and exchange in these documents demonstrate the resilience of myriad moral economies – shaped and mediated by social individuals enmeshed in webs of personal debt and credit – in modern English market relations.

Benjamin Robert Haydon and the social life of credit

The voluminous diaries of the historical painter Benjamin Robert Haydon (1786–1846) offer an historical pendant to the fictional model of the social economy delineated in Samuel Richardson's *Pamela*. Written self-consciously with an eye to their conversion into a marketable memoir, Haydon's diaries are a sustained exercise in intertextual apologetic, larded with references to fictional and historical characters whose financial plight mirrored his own. In entry after entry, Haydon probed the antinomies created by the dual character of credit, which features in the Haydon diaries alternately as a dangerous, degrading source of obligation and as an inevitable component of moralised economic exchange. By detailing the pragmatic mechanisms through which he obtained work materials, household provisions and consumer goods and services alongside his reflections on the social meanings of economic activity, these texts situate Haydon's debt and credit relations at once within the imaginative realms of fiction and the mundane practices of everyday life.

The son of a provincial bookseller, Haydon was placed under the tutelage of an Exeter accountant as a youth in preparation for entering the family business. Soon disgusted by commerce, he left Exeter for London in 1804 to study at the Royal Academy, where his overweening ambition and grandiose sense of self rapidly alienated the art establishment. In London, Haydon's descent into debt was swift, profound and permanent. Contemptuous of lucrative portrait commissions and only modestly successful in executing the massive historical paintings which he held to represent the pinnacle of artistic merit, Haydon owed £600 to an assortment of creditors by 1812. In the following years, his obligations mounted precipitously, reaching several thousand pounds by the early 1820s. Seven times arrested and four times imprisoned for his unpaid

---

[13] In contrast, Mary Poovey argues that the early Victorian years saw commodification decisively demoralise the market as 'the social domain had begun to be conceptualized as a collection of responsible, disciplined individuals'. Mary Poovey, *Making a Social Body: British Cultural Formation 1830–1864* (Chicago, 1995), 3, 22. See also the critique of Poovey's approach in Lauren M.E. Goodland, ' "Making the working man like me": charity, pastorship, and middle-class identity in nineteenth-century Britain; Thomas Chalmers and Dr. James Phillips Kay', *VS*, 43, 1 (Summer 2001), esp. 599–602.

68   Debt and credit in English memory and imagination

debts, Haydon was driven to suicide in 1846 by the combined forces of financial ruin and manic depression.[14]

In his diary, personal debts provide a battlefield upon which the artist waged a self-righteous campaign on behalf of high art. On 7 January 1822, Haydon was 'Out the whole day to see & pacify discontented creditors'; three weeks later he was driven from his studio again 'to battle with creditors, & to get the next month as clear as possible in order to work'.[15] Tradesmen seeking payment invaded his hearth with distressing frequency, each distinguished by his own character as a creditor. As Haydon reflected despondently on his dearth of cash in April 1824, his baker 'called & was insolent', the landlord appeared and was 'kind & sorry', a butcher loomed 'respectful but disappointed' and Haydon's tailor – always a gentleman's last refuge in adversity – was 'good honoured & willing to wait'.[16] Patience, indeed, was characteristic of a surprising number of Haydon's lenders. For despite the notoriety of his many arrests and successive imprisonments, Haydon enjoyed considerable success in convincing creditors to defer payment or legal action. Connection, the retail convention by which tradesmen habitually extended long credit to middle- and upper-class consumers in return for loyal patronage of their shops, lay at the heart of his success, allowing Haydon to continue to extract goods and loans from creditors to whom he was already substantially in debt. Liberated from the King's Bench prison in 1836, Haydon promptly ordered a new canvas from his supplier Brown, 'a worthy fellow, who abused me for not settling . . . the last balance', but promised to deliver the ordered goods. 'Brown & I have been connected for 30 years, and have had about 40 regular quarrels', Haydon observed knowingly of this longstanding relationship.[17]

Haydon's landlord, Newton, was by far the most sympathetic of these connected creditors, caught in a perpetual debt relationship with his tenant that was at once calculating, affective and social. Repeatedly generous in deferring collection of his rent and solicitous in protecting Haydon's art supplies from seizure by the bailiffs, Newton advanced the painter countless sums of money to ward off more importunate creditors. The exchange of gifts and courtesies worked together with formal loans and cash payments to enmesh the two men in ongoing mutual obligations. When Haydon's wife Mary was delivered of a

[14] See David Blayney Brown, Robert Woof and Stephen Hebron, eds., *Benjamin Robert Haydon 1786–1846: Painter and Writer, Friend of Wordsworth and Keats* (Kendal, 1996). Haydon's suicide precluded completion of the autobiography, but a posthumous compilation of his texts appeared within a decade: Tom Taylor, ed., *Life of Benjamin Robert Haydon, Historical Painter, from His Autobiography and Journals*, 3 vols. (London, 1853). See also Benjamin Robert Haydon, *Correspondence and Table Talk: With a Memoir by His Son, Frederick Wordsworth Haydon*, 2 vols. (London, 1876).

[15] Willard Bissell Pope, ed., *The Diary of Benjamin Robert Haydon*, 5 vols. (Cambridge, MA, 1960–63), II: 354 (7 January 1822); II: 359 (30 January 1822); II: 368 (8–9 July 1822).

[16] Ibid., II: 471 (21–23 April 1824).   [17] Ibid., IV: 390 (24 November 1836).

son in 1835, he named the child Newton as a token of these ties; six years later, it was Newton who provided fifteen pounds for the children's school fees.[18] Cultivating ongoing relations such as these required Haydon to maintain a delicate balance between periodic offers of small sums 'on account' and resistance to pleas to pay the entire balance – an act that would, by discharging his contractual obligations, put a permanent end to the credit relation. Haggling with his baker over a bill for twenty-eight pounds in 1832, Haydon succeeded in negotiating payment in two instalments only to question the wisdom of agreeing to pay in full. 'He is just as likely, now he is safe, to behave ill as a stranger', he reasoned worriedly.[19] In a commercial environment in which credit functioned to inculcate loyalty and continued custom over time, liquidating debts was often a false economy that diminished consumers' ability to extract further loans.

Failure to maintain a creditworthy status with friends and tradesmen could have dire consequences, forcing Haydon to pawn personal possessions and, *in extremis*, the tools of his trade to put food on the family table. Books, pictures, plate, clothing and watches travelled in a seemingly endless circuit between the Haydon household and local pawnshops, causing the artist acute shame and considerable professional distress. As he recorded in 1834, having obtained four pounds by pawning his Italian art books, his wife's best gown and his children's clothing, 'The state of degradation, humiliation, & pain of mind in which I sat in the dingy hell of a back room is not to be described.'[20] Like Karl Marx later in the century, Haydon found his ability to pursue his high-minded calling curtailed by the more pressing demands of domestic credit finance. His anatomy prints, lay figures and spectacles all served, once pawned, to purchase household provisions, but only at the cost of impeding completion of his commissions.

When even pawning failed to stave off creditors, arrest and imprisonment brought legal processes to the forefront of credit relations. Suspended by ties of friendship, habit and custom, the contractual components of debt obligations were attenuated in day-to-day perception, but surfaced alarmingly when creditors' affection, patience or optimism snapped. For Haydon, as for so many English novelists, resort to the debt law represented the ultimate violation of the moral economy of exchange. Viewing the debtors' prison as an anachronistic relic of economic barbarism, ill-suited to regulate the consumer passions unleashed by modern commerce, Haydon reflected that 'The law of Arrest must have had its origin in savage times, when the novelty of money and the wish to gain it was of more consequence than the blood of Men.' Far from curbing extravagance and encouraging economic probity, the law lay at the root of false commercial credit. 'While a Tradesman has the power to arrest, he is careless of giving credit', Haydon reasoned, 'because possession of the person is such

---

[18] Ibid., IV: 304–5 (22 and 26 August 1835); V: 154 (17 May 1842).
[19] Ibid., III: 636–7 (23 September 1832).   [20] Ibid., IV: 199–200 (7 June 1834).

70   Debt and credit in English memory and imagination

an annoyance & disgrace that there is nothing he imagines a Gentleman or his Friends won't do to pay the debts, which the speculative rascality of his Tradesmen entrapped him to incur, rather than endure it.'[21] In keeping with this logic, legal expenses extracted by 'the Scoundrels of the Common Law' represented a perversion of trust by contractual formalism, and Haydon accordingly excluded them from his equitable conception of just debts. 'If, before I die, I can satisfy my old Creditors (those who did not put me to law costs & there is something of revenge in that, I believe & fear) I shall die <u>unloaded</u>', he insisted.[22]

Attempting to preserve his sense of self and his aspirations to gentility in the face of these incessant battles with tradesmen and the law, Haydon sought to recast his debt relations imaginatively. References to the debts of novelists and of their fictional characters recur throughout the diaries, inserting his own insolvency into the genteel tradition of representation fostered since the 1740s by the English novel. Hard at work in 1823, Haydon was 'obliged to sally forth to get money in consequence of the bullying insolence of our old, short, bawdy looking wicked eyed, wrinkled, waddling, gin drinking, dirty ruffled Landlady'. Associating this vulgar intrusion with fictional narratives of genteel indebtedness clearly helped to assuage Haydon's injured pride. 'Fielding should have seen the old devil', he reflected.[23] Imagining himself, in a rare moment of optimism in March 1840, as Dr Primrose ensconced within his warm family circle in *The Vicar of Wakefield*, Haydon by October was increasingly disconsolate, and dramatised instead the perils to which his unpaid debts had subjected his innocent wife. 'In my Imprisonments, great efforts were made, from her beauty, to seduce her from me, without the least effect, and she has been a solace, a blessing, & a salvation', he noted – recasting his debt relations as a narrative of seduction familiar since the eighteenth century from the fictions of Richardson, Fielding and Haywood.[24]

Like the novelists whose fiction helped to frame his own shifting self-representations as a debtor, Haydon was alert to the artistic potential of his financial dilemmas. A broker's agent who delivered a writ and a bailiff who took possession of his household goods were incorporated into his paintings in lieu of paid models; a pawnbroker who extended credit on the family plate and possessed 'a fine head of silvery hair' provided Haydon with a convenient subject for a life study.[25] Confinement in the King's Bench inspired two of Haydon's best-known works of art, both studies of the ritualised, parodic political culture elaborated by the prison's inmates. Freed from imprisonment in 'that Temple of Idleness & debauchery' in the summer of 1827, Haydon promptly revisited the gaol to make sketches for his painting of *The Mock Election*. The sale of

---

[21] Ibid., III: 471 (13–15 July 1830).   [22] Ibid., IV: 522 (16 September 1838).
[23] Ibid., II: 453 (14 January 1823).
[24] Ibid., IV: 613–14 (14 March 1840); V: 8–9 (10 October 1840).
[25] Ibid., IV: 225 (8 October 1834); V: 551 (16 June 1846).

2 Benjamin Robert Haydon (1786–1846), *Chairing the Member* (1829). Haydon's painting, undertaken after his own release from the King's Bench prison, depicts the riotous conviviality of the gaol, after a mock election held by the imprisoned debtors. Haydon himself looks down on the scene from an upper window. (Reproduced by permission of the Tate Gallery.)

this work for five hundred guineas to George IV – himself, as Prince of Wales, a notorious debtor – prompted Haydon to return yet again to the King's Bench to paint *Chairing the Member*, which he sold for three hundred pounds in 1830.[26] (Illustration 2). Personal debts drove Haydon pragmatically to labour, but they also fired his artistic sensibilities. With 'A bill due & no money' in 1842, he 'Painted in delicious & exquisite misery'.[27]

Haydon's recognition of his dependence upon economic adversity as a spur to artistic production was linked closely to his understanding of the ways in which financial obligation to aristocratic patrons both limited his personal autonomy and liberated his professional talent. 'I get vigour from despair, clearness of perception from confusion, & elasticity of spirit from despotic usage', he concluded

---

[26] Ibid., III: 215 (26 August 1827); III: 211 (15 August 1827); III: 271 (21 April 1828); III: 272 (28 April 1828); III: 319, fn. 8.
[27] Ibid., V: 178 (9 July 1842). 'Out of what a mess of indigestion, fog, debt, discontent, opposition, vice, temptations, & trial is every work of intellect accomplished.' Ibid., V: 511 (16 June 1846).

72   Debt and credit in English memory and imagination

in 1823. 'Perhaps independence would ruin me, & enjoyment in voluptuousness dull my vigour.'[28] References to elite debtors whom he encountered and befriended in the King's Bench also allowed Haydon to emphasise the genteel sensibilities and social connections inculcated by his art, while distancing him imaginatively from the plebeian 'swearing, fighting, cursing, drinking, gambling, & stumpeting' endemic to the gaol.[29] Confined to the King's Bench in 1830, he spent his evenings strolling on the racket grounds with Colonel La Tour and Major Bacon, 'both Waterloo Heroes and men of fortune and family' and railed indignantly against the 'rascally tradesmen' and solicitors who had conspired to imprison such honourable men.[30]

Just as Haydon sought to associate his own insolvency with aristocratic credit conventions by drawing attention to the high social status of his companions in the King's Bench, so too he attempted to associate his employment as a painter with the elite economy of honour rather than with the individualising exchange mechanisms of the market.[31] In his diaries, Haydon emphasised his location within aristocratic patronage networks in which gifts and loans tempered the sharp dealings of the cash nexus and silenced the insistent demands of legal contracts. Although extracting cash payment for commissioned work from the aristocrats who constituted his preferred clientele was a central goal of Haydon's professional activities, maintaining an ongoing relationship with his patrons beyond the delivery of any one painting was vital to his survival. A gift of fifty pounds from the Duke of Cleveland helped to liberate Haydon from a spunging-house in 1833; five pounds donated by the Duke of Bedford in 1836 allowed the artist to retrieve his dress coat from a pawnshop; funds provided by the Duke of Sutherland in 1837 enabled Haydon to pay his rates.[32] Counter-gifts helped to consolidate these liens of obligation. Lady Stafford intervened with her husband and secured Haydon a gift of fifty pounds with which he paid his stepson's college fees in October 1830, and Haydon duly reciprocated in December by giving Lord Stafford a picture he had painted.[33]

Social and economic forms of credit constantly coalesced in Haydon's strategic negotiations of his domestic and professional debts: in his diary, as in sentimental and romantic novels, status differentials rather than the unalloyed claims of contract distinguished proper from improper exchange relations. The manner and mode by which payment was rendered acquired central importance in

---

[28] Ibid., II: 397–8 (21 January 1823).   [29] Ibid., IV: 381 (24 October 1836).

[30] Ibid., III: 448–9 (3 June 1830); III: 472 (16 July 1830).

[31] For the gift economy associated with British artistic production, see Marcia Pointon, ' "Surrounded with brilliants": miniature portraits in eighteenth-century England', Art Bulletin, 83, 1 (March 2001), esp. 57–62.

[32] Pope, ed., Diary, IV: 118 (29 July 1833); IV: 332 (9 January 1836); IV: 419 (6 July 1837).

[33] Ibid., III: 490 (2 October 1830); III: 590 (31 December 1831).

Debt and credit in diaries and autobiographies 73

this context. When Haydon completed a painting of Romeo and Juliet for a Hull dealer in 1840, he was disgusted to find that the merchant would pay the balance due on the commission only upon receipt of the work. 'How unlike the Nobility', he reflected. 'Everything with... all of the [aristocratic] Class [is] honor [*sic*] & faith. All paid me long before the work was home.' Efforts to extract gifts and loans from mercantile patrons reinforced his distaste for market mentalities and the middling minds that espoused them. Having solicited funds from a Quaker, a businessman and an aristocrat in 1842, he returned home to find a gift of fifty pounds. 'I had written to a rich Banker, a Manufacturer, & a Duke! – who assisted me?', Haydon asked rhetorically. 'The Duke of course, and their three letters are specimens of each class.'[34]

Bolstered by adherence to a hierarchical model of social relations, Haydon's participation in extended networks of credit was also legitimated by references to the sacred meanings of borrowing, lending and gifting activities. From early manhood to his last weeks of suicidal despair, Haydon interpreted his economic, professional and moral status within a framework of particular providences. Contemplating a work in progress 'with a mind burthened with debt' in 1814, Haydon adduced his ability to complete his paintings as evidence of the Deity's special solicitude for his artistic genius, a sign 'that I am preserved for some great purpose, by my great & beneficent Creator'.[35] In this interpretative framework, the credit extended by elite patrons appeared as a particular manifestation of divine providence, and personal debts figured as the sacred instruments by which Haydon's moral character would be redeemed. In September 1834, he received substantial gifts of cash from a duke and an MP. Acknowledging that consistent prosperity 'would make us imprudent, voluptuous, & ungrateful', Haydon emphasised 'the value of affliction to a character like mine, if he has a soul to be saved'. Unpaid debts were the 'proper correctives' of worldly man, mechanisms of moral regeneration rather than tokens of lapsed economic virtue. 'They keep the creature dependent to his Creator, on whom in trouble he always calls', Haydon concluded.[36]

Like writers of fiction, Haydon invoked the lessons of the Lord's Prayer to sanctify his model of the moral economy, refusing to construct debtors as exceptional 'sinners' and debts as unconscionable 'trespasses'. Turning (as Henry Fielding had before him in *Joseph Andrews*) to the wording of the Greek text rather than the modern English translation, Haydon cited the injunction in Matthew 6:12 to 'forgive us our debts, as we forgive our debtors'.[37] The preoccupation with Atonement that marked both evangelical eschatology and

---

[34] Ibid., IV: 632 (26 May 1840); V: 135 (7 March 1842).
[35] Ibid., I: 341 (26 January 1814).   [36] Ibid., IV: 221 (3 September 1834).
[37] Ibid., III: 470 (10 July 1830). See also above, 29, 47.

74 Debt and credit in English memory and imagination

evangelical economics in the early nineteenth century added a further dimension to this received exegesis. Haydon tended toward an extreme, pre-millennialist understanding of the Atonement and its economic implications. 'For pre-millennialists, temporal misfortunes were always "special" or "particular" judgments...requiring miraculous suspensions of natural law', Boyd Hilton has argued. 'Providence always acted miraculously, and it was presumptuous to expect to comprehend its dispensations, or to seek, by rational and prudential calculations of one's behaviour, to avoid its blows in future.'[38] Promising spiritual justification not through works or secular symbols of economic success but rather through faith in Christ's Atonement on the Cross, this strand of evangelical soteriology afforded Haydon rare moments of solace as he struggled to accept his failure as an artist and a domestic provider. In 1843, lacking funds for the collection plate when he received the sacrament on Good Friday, Haydon recalled his repeated imprisonments and chronic inability to repay his creditors, but found consolation in the convinced Christian's inevitable character as a debtor to Christ. 'All these things came across me, & I felt as if my Soul was blackened, but a ray of brilliant hope supported me, & I went up in quiet self possession, believing if I believed, the Atonement would reconcile me to God, and I trust it may.'[39]

Freed by his faith in the Atonement from personal culpability for his economic failings, Haydon could argue – albeit with a defensiveness that signals the inherent instability of his assertions – that his character remained unsullied by his questionable credit dealings. The failure of any one of the 150 creditors at whose behest he had been imprisoned to oppose his liberation from the gaol thus vindicated his moral standing in 1823: 'I consider this an ordeal that has tried my character, and a test of my honor [sic], and I feel grateful for it', he recorded.[40] The success of Academicians who enjoyed public acclaim and professional profits was, in contrast, indicative of their subjection to 'the Vices of Fashion'. His debts notwithstanding, Haydon's 'moral character' had proved immune to the alluring blandishments of purely economic wealth. 'I never seduced the Wife of my Patron and accepted money from the Husband while I was corrupting his Wife & disgracing his family', he asserted, returning again to the association between debt and sexual transgression fostered by successive generations of English novelists.[41] Tortured by doubt, debt and depression, Haydon was a tissue of contradictions; as an economic character, his multiple debtor identities fluctuated wildly, between depths of appalling abasement and heights of grandiose delusion.

[38] Boyd Hilton, *The Age of Atonement: The Influence of Evangelicalism on Social and Economic Thought, 1795–1865* (Oxford, 1988), 14–15.

[39] Pope, ed., *Diary*, V: 262 (14 April 1843). See also V: 29 (25 January 1841).

[40] Ibid., II: 421 (26 July 1823).

[41] Ibid., III: 386 (7 August 1829); III: 404 (27 November 1829).

Debt and credit in diaries and autobiographies 75

Although Haydon's histrionic claims are extreme, the credit strategies described in his diaries are not the artifacts of fiction and aristocratic clientage alone. Gifting, cadging, borrowing, haggling, credit dealing, pawning and fear of imprisonment for debt recur as daily experiences in a broad spectrum of English diaries and autobiographies, testifying to the limits of the cash nexus as a descriptive model of economic exchange in consumer markets in this period. Haydon's elastic, equitable conception of just and unjust debts and his contempt for legal mechanisms of debt enforcement were, moreover, widely pervasive in English culture. These sentiments pervaded not only novels, journals and memoirs but philanthropic activity, prison administration and legal practice itself.[42] The sympathetic response accorded by other diarists to the extracts from his journal that circulated in the newspaper press in the wake of Haydon's suicide suggests the degree to which Haydon's financial and psychological state resonated with a broad spectrum of his contemporaries. Unsurprisingly, the bohemian journalist E.L. Blanchard, himself chronically insolvent, found the extracts 'intensely interesting' when he read them in June 1846, and commiserated with the plight of yet another artist – 'poor fellow!' – unappreciated by society.[43] But this compassion extended considerably beyond the narrow brotherhood of the impecunious metropolitan literati. William Lucas, a successful Quaker brewer – his sect's abhorrence of bankruptcy and insolvency notwithstanding – reflected that the extracts from Haydon's diary painted 'an affecting picture of his mind struggling against neglect and complicated difficulties till at last reason gave way'.[44] The thin and permeable boundary that separated the status of debtor from that of creditor ensured that these sentiments were widely shared. George Harris was later to preside as a judge over small claims courts in Bristol and Birmingham. But he too, in the 1840s, identified with Haydon's plight. Having lost substantial sums in railway speculation, Harris lived in constant fear of the bailiffs. 'His feelings, and apprehensions,

---

[42] Below, chaps. 3–7. Although political economists largely ignored the impact of such sentiments on consumer markets, Haydon's contemporary (and fellow insolvent) Thomas De Quincey sought to formulate a theory of exchange that would accord personal debts and their psychological effects a central place in economic life. See Josephine McDonagh, *De Quincey's Disciplines* (Oxford, 1994), chap. 2.

[43] Clement Scott and Cecil Howard, eds., *The Life and Reminiscences of E.L. Blanchard: With Notes from the Diary of Wm. Blanchard*, 2 vols. (London, 1891), I: 47 (24 June 1846). The artist Ford Madox Brown's later reading of the diaries was more ambivalent. Bundling up his wife's shawl, some household ornaments and several pictures to send to the pawnshop, Brown was at once attracted and repelled by the parallels between his life story and Haydon's. 'I am getting a regular Haydon at pawning – so long as I do not become one at cheating my creditors it matters little'. Virginia Surtees, ed., *The Diary of Ford Madox Brown* (New Haven, 1981), 115 (11 January 1858).

[44] G.E. Bryant and G.P. Baker, eds., *A Quaker Journal: Being the Diary and Reminiscences of William Lucas of Hitchin (1804–1861) a Member of the Society of Friends*, 2 vols. (London, 1934), II: 376 (25 June 1846).

76   Debt and credit in English memory and imagination

and sleepless nights and disquietudes, how like mine', he reflected on reading the account of Haydon's suicide.[45]

The limits of the cash nexus

Benjamin Haydon's diaries record an economy of expedient makeshifts, a ceaseless round of negotiations, deferrals, denials and substitutions by which he secured commodities and services for his family without the immediate – or even the ultimate – exchange of cash. The broader literature of diaries and autobiographies produced in the course of the long nineteenth century similarly attests to the constraints that limited the operation of the cash nexus in domestic exchange relations. For domestic provisioning throughout this period was sustained by modern economic mechanisms enfolded within – and often superseded by – more conventional social and cultural practices. Double-entry bookkeeping, mortgages, promissory notes, interest-bearing accounts and paper money could all promote precise calculations of economic gain. But the theoretical promise of these instruments was often thwarted by the pragmatic workings of the market itself.[46] Shortages of specie, aversion to paper money, delayed wage payments, pawning and gift-giving practices all fostered extended credit relations in modern England. Long credit, in turn, significantly complicated – and not infrequently compromised – individuals' perceptions of economic profit and loss in their market transactions.

In the eighteenth century, endemic shortages of specie encouraged reliance on barter, payment in kind, monthly or annual wage settlements, trade tokens and the truck system. The wage norms that evolved in this context significantly slowed the development of a fully monetised economy. Servants and other labourers who 'lived in' typically received much of their wage payment in kind – in the form of lodging, board, clothing and credit with their master's tradesmen – rather than in cash. Tim Meldrum argues that 'continuity in customary, mixed remuneration' rather than 'a commodification or monetisation of service' characterised this sector of the economy into the nineteenth century, fostering 'a moral economy of service'.[47] As Richardson's *Pamela* repeatedly registered,

---

[45] George Harris, *The Autobiography of George Harris, LL.D., F.S.A., of the Middle Temple, Barrister-at-Law* (London, 1888), 131 (6 May 1846). On railway speculation and middle- and upper-class debt, see R.W. Kostal, *Law and English Railway Capitalism 1825–1875* (Oxford, 1994), chap. 2.

[46] For the promise of double-entry bookkeeping, see esp. Mary Poovey, *A History of the Modern Fact: Problems of Knowledge in the Sciences of Wealth and Society* (Chicago, 1998), chap. 2. David A. Kent, 'Small businessmen and their credit transactions in early nineteenth-century Britain', *Business History*, 36, 2 (April 1994), esp. 60–1, notes the limited purchase of this accounting practice among retailers and artisans.

[47] Tim Meldrum, *Domestic Service and Gender 1660–1750: Life and Work in the London Household* (Harlow, Essex, 2000), 196, 186. See also Ben Fine and Ellen Leopold, 'Consumerism and the industrial revolution', *Social History*, 15, 2 (May 1990), 167–9.

Debt and credit in diaries and autobiographies 77

extensive, mutual debt relations between workers and their employers were the very stuff of service. Lucy Luck, a straw-plait worker who fashioned ladies' hats in mid-Victorian Luton, recalled that having been set unrealistic production goals by an employer with whom she lodged, 'whatever quantity I was short she reckoned I was so much money in her debt... and so my little money went, and when that was gone she had my clothes just for my living [expenses]'.[48] Serving to curtail workers' mobility, coercive liens of credit surface again and again in plebeian memoirs. Lillian Westall vividly recalled the oppressive conditions of her employment as the only servant of a Chiswick dentist in the Edwardian era. 'I gave my notice in the first week', she noted in her memoir, 'but a servant was obliged to stay at least one month in those days, and wasn't paid, of course, until the end of that time.'[49]

In manufacturing as in domestic labour, the chronic shortage of specie persistently discouraged cash payment for goods, services and labour. Because victuallers enjoyed ready access to substantial supplies of coin, 'an almost incestuous relationship between alehouse and employer' obtained in many sectors of the expanding eighteenth-century economy. As parliamentary pressure was brought to bear against the operation of this so-called 'truck' system in the later Hanoverian period, Peter Clark observes, 'Truck did not so much wither away... as change its shape.' Discouraged from issuing credit bills at local public houses, employers now established truck shops in their own manufactories instead.[50] Firmly entrenched in eighteenth-century labour markets, the imbrication of credit and payment in kind with the wage relation continued to feature prominently in nineteenth-century wage relations.[51]

Like workers' recollections of wage payments, accounts of the acquisition of goods in diaries and memoirs draw attention to the prominence of transactions conducted other than on a cash basis. Barter and a range of pawning mechanisms were important adjuncts of eighteenth-century commerce, and long endured as expedients for payment in lieu of currency. In Sussex, the shopkeeper Thomas Turner often paid his suppliers in kind: in 1755 he balanced an account of just under ten pounds owed to William Piper with 84 lbs of butter, a pair of gloves, three bottles of wine and a sum of cash.[52] Tradesmen anxious to bring consumers' extended credit accounts to a close, or desperate to stave off

[48] Memoir of Lucy Luck (1848–1922), in John Burnett, ed., *Useful Toil: Autobiographies of Working People from the 1830s to the 1920s* (London, 1994), 58.
[49] Memoir of Lillian Westall (born 1893), in Burnett, ed., *Useful Toil*, 216. Her employment dates from *c.* 1908–09.
[50] Peter Clark, *The English Alehouse: A Social History 1200–1830* (London, 1983), 229, 230, 317.
[51] See, for example, Henry Broadhurst, *Henry Broadhurst, M.P.: The Story of His Life from a Stonemason's Bench to the Treasury Bench: Told by Himself* (London, 1901), 52, and L.D. Schwarz, *London in the Age of Industrialisation: Entrepreneurs, Labour Force and Living Conditions, 1700–1850* (Cambridge, 1992), 118–20.
[52] David Vaisey, ed., *The Diary of Thomas Turner 1754–1765* (Oxford, 1989), 7 (11 March 1755).

78   Debt and credit in English memory and imagination

their own insolvency, of necessity accepted goods in lieu of cash. In 1836 the shopkeeper Robert Sharp noted with resignation that he and his wife 'had a Couple of Summer Rabbits from Weedley for an Oil Cask, which he...got more than three years since, so that we are now even; or at least we shall get no more'.[53] The labourers, brushmakers, shoemakers, butchers and grocers who purchased goods from George Stratford, a Chesham draper soon to be imprisoned for his debts, in 1841–43, rendered payment in coin, brushes, wash leathers, knives, forks, eggs, beer, meat and old clothes.[54] Payment in kind proved especially persistent in rural areas. Describing holidays taken in Wales in the 1890s, Molly Hughes noted the continued salience of barter in the local economy. '[T]here seemed to have been very little in the way of actual money transactions, especially from patient to doctor', she recalled; 'a good fat goose or a bottle of wine was a more common thank-offering'.[55]

The escalation of pawning, and the increasing formalisation of this trade as it migrated from alehouses to free-standing pawnshops in the later eighteenth century, played a significant role in displacing barter as a common means of acquiring goods. Pawnshops, which more than doubled in number in the first two decades of the nineteenth century alone, rapidly became a pillar of working-class exchange relations.[56] Beyond the labouring poor, pawning offered consumers who were perched precariously on the boundaries of middle-class respectability an essential supplement (or substitute) for savings and insurance. Samuel Bamford, who had risen from the ranks of labour to the penumbra of the lower middle class, placed funds in a Post Office saving account when circumstances allowed, but relied increasingly on the pawnshop as his own earnings and his wife's health declined with the onset of old age. Destitute of funds for household expenses, Bamford's wife Jemima pawned his best coat, and then redeemed the coat on the following day by pawning a satin dress – which she kept, unbeknownst to her husband, locked in a drawer as a final reserve of cash.[57]

Within the working classes, pawning remained largely the preserve of women (and children), but among debtors with middle-class pretensions male

---

[53] Janice E. Crowther and Peter A. Crowther, eds., *The Diary of Robert Sharp of South Cave: Life in a Yorkshire Village 1812–1837* (Oxford, 1997), 532 (10 August 1836).

[54] Centre for Buckinghamshire studies, Q/DA/95, Pocket Book of G. Stratford, esp. accounts of Mr Brown and Mr Rotfield.

[55] Molly Hughes, *A London Family: 1870–1900* (Oxford, 1991), 341.

[56] For the transition from alehouse to pawnshop, see Clark, *English Alehouse*, 318. The early history of pawning and its gender dimensions are detailed in Beverly Lemire, 'Petty pawns and informal lending: gender and the transformation of small-scale credit in England, *circa* 1600–1800', in Kristine Bruland and Patrick O'Brien, eds., *From Family Firms to Capitalism: Essays in Business and Industrial History in Honour of Peter Mathias* (Oxford, 1998), 112–38. For pawning in nineteenth-century working-class communities, see Paul Johnson, *Saving and Spending: The Working-Class Economy in Britain 1870–1939* (Oxford, 1985), and Melanie Tebbutt, *Making Ends Meet: Pawnbroking and Working-Class Credit* (Leicester, 1983).

[57] Martin Hewitt and Robert Poole, eds., *The Diaries of Samuel Bamford* (Stroud, 2000), 140–1 (28–29 July 1859). For Bamford's Post Office account, see 224 (28 March 1860).

participation was vital. Middle-class notions of masculinity rendered wives' public appearance in the pawnshop intensely humiliating for husbands. Ford Madox Brown's second wife, Emma, was, as the daughter of a bricklayer, considerably lower on the social scale than the artist himself, who had inherited a property valued at several hundred pounds. Yet it was Brown rather than his wife who, when necessity demanded, pawned jewellery, plate, opera glasses, his dress-coat trousers, waistcoat and silk cape – or commissioned a jobbing man to travel to the pawnshop on the family's behalf.[58] The sense of shame suffered by husbands of the middling classes when their wives were forced to resort to the pawnshop emerges clearly from George Gissing's diary. Like Brown, Gissing had taken a plebeian wife who displayed an undue (and uneconomic) fondness for drink. Having separated from her in 1883, Gissing was appalled to learn that she had been driven to pawn her clothing and her wedding-ring to pay her domestic debts. 'Henceforth I never cease to bear testimony against the accursed social order that brings about things of this kind', the novelist wrote in his diary upon returning home from the Lambeth lodgings in which his impoverished wife had died, a pledge fully redeemed in Gissing's works of fiction.[59]

Less well examined than the pawnshop itself are the ways in which the principle of pawning leeched over into daily shopkeeping practices, tending to reinforce contemporaries' perception that cash exchange was only one among a variety of available strategies for obtaining commodities. Working-class memoirs indicate that the line that divided barter and pawning in plebeian consumer repertoires was fluid rather than fixed. The memoirs of Mrs Layton, who began her working life as a baby-minder in Bethnal Green, suggest that informal pawning practices formed part of a wider pattern of purchasing often hidden from historical view by its clandestine nature. At the general shop kept by her employers in the 1860s:

Articles of clothing and household goods were brought and left, something like a pawnshop, only food was given instead of money to be redeemed when the poor things were able to pay ... I have seen a pair of children's boots left in pawn for a loaf of bread and a small quantity of butter. Babies' pinafores, frocks, saucepans, candlesticks and all kinds of articles have been brought in for food. The practice was illegal, so all articles had to be brought in when no one was about, and I was trained to help smuggle the things in.[60]

---

[58] Surtees, ed., *Diary of Ford Madox Brown*, 99 (6 October 1854); 113 (3 January 1854). For middle-class notions of masculinity, domesticity and the market, see John Tosh, *A Man's Place: Masculinity and the Middle-Class Home in Victorian England* (New Haven, 1999), chap. 2.

[59] Pierre Coustillas, ed., *London and the Life of Literature in Late Victorian England: The Diary of George Gissing, Novelist* (Hassocks, Sussex, 1978), 23 (1–2 March 1888). Gissing later borrowed Benjamin Haydon's autobiographical memoirs from the local free library (283: 11 August 1891).

[60] Margaret Llewelyan Davies, ed., *Life as We Have Known It: By Cooperative Working Women* (London, 1931), 21. See similarly Pat O'Mara, *The Autobiography of an Irish Slummy* (New York, 1933), 66–7.

80 Debt and credit in English memory and imagination

In Salford at the turn of the century the connection between pawnshop and grocery shop was also very close: the shop run by Robert Roberts' mother functioned as an acknowledged extension of the adjacent pawnshop on Saturday evenings, holding a consignment of clothing bundles for neighbouring families who had been unable to redeem pledged items before the broker closed his shop for the week. Her many protestations to the contrary, Roberts's mother was occasionally moved by compassion to lend her grocery customers cash, thereby reinforcing the functional overlap between her business and the pawnshop.[61]

If shortages of coin tended to discourage reliance upon cash in consumer and labour markets, the availability of paper money offered at best a panacea to this problem. Aversion to paper money – an unsurprising response to the frequent failures suffered by provincial banks – was both widespread and deeply rooted in Georgian England. William Cobbett's celebration of the early nineteenth century as a 'time when there was scarcely ever seen a bank-note among Tradesmen and Farmers' was a self-indulgent exercise in reactionary nostalgia,[62] but it tapped a common and enduring vein of sentiment none the less. In East Yorkshire in the 1820s and 1830s, Robert Sharp railed repeatedly against the invidious effects of 'Rags' or paper money, a form of currency that he held to reflect poorly on the character of those who relied upon it. 'Confusion attends this ragged system', Sharp fulminated; 'there was a gentleman told me only on Monday night that he would rather have Paper than Gold, I told him I had a very poor opinion of any person who preferred Rags to pure Gold, this Man I believe is a half pay officer, so I was not so much surprised'.[63] Paper money continued to cause consternation for decades. Despite his training in double-entry bookkeeping and his employment in a draper's shop, H.G. Wells evinced a reverential attitude toward money as a youth. 'I had never yet seen ten sovereigns together in my life, never touched any paper money except a five pound note, never encountered a cheque', he wrote of the closing decades of the century. 'Bank of England notes were dealt with very solemnly in those days; the water-mark was scrutinized carefully and the payer, after a suspicious penetrating look or so was generally asked to write his name and address on the instrument.'[64] Immersion in the world of goods clearly coexisted with limited familiarity with coinage, paper money and monetary calculation in English market culture.

---

[61] Robert Roberts, *A Ragged Schooling* (Manchester, 1976), 104, 17.

[62] William Cobbett, *The Autobiography of William Cobbett: The Progress of a Plough-Boy to a Seat in Parliament*, ed. William Reitzel (London, 1947), 127.

[63] Crowther and Crowther, eds., *Diary of Robert Sharp*, 128 (26 April 1827), 169 (31 October 1827).

[64] H.G. Wells, *Experiment in Autobiography: Discoveries and Conclusions of a Very Ordinary Brain (since 1866)* (New York, 1934), 148. For his training in bookkeeping, see ibid., 65.

Debt and credit in diaries and autobiographies 81

The regular exchange of neighbourly and familial gifts further undercut the primacy of contractual and monetary transactions, perpetuating older norms of reciprocity that generated social (as well as economic) forms of capital.[65] Gift-giving was, if not ubiquitous, widely pervasive in the eighteenth- and early nineteenth-century economy, where it worked at once to mark social distinctions and to maintain social solidarity.[66] Gifts given to the deserving poor were a staple of charitable endeavour. Thomas Wale, a wealthy merchant who had retired to an estate in Cambridgeshire, was among many propertied men who participated in this sector of the gift economy, recording in 1770 that he had made his tenant, William Claydon, 'a present of . . . [a] Coat and Britches'.[67] Clergymen's diaries in particular abound with reflections on the moral and social imperatives that prompted such gift exchanges. The Reverend James Newton of Nuneham Courtney made gifts of rabbits, plum-pudding, boar meat, sugar, tea, money and furze faggots to the poor, material gifts that worked strategically alongside his pastoral care for parishioners' souls. 'Called on Dame Lediard & gave her good Advice', Newton noted in 1761. 'Sent her some Pudding & wine by her Daughter.'[68] William Holland's diary detailed numerous gift exchanges made by members of his social circle, and carefully underlined the social meaning of these exchanges. 'The Clerk of Dodington who dined here I presented with a good old black coat of mine, of which he stood in need for he is but a miserable wight and drinks up everything and keeps himself as poor as a Church Mouse', Holland noted smugly one Christmas. 'However he was made desperate proud today', the parson observed of this gratifying instance of gifting to a dependant.[69] The role played by charitable gifts in maintaining social credit in the form of deference was palpably obvious to Holland. 'Miss Dodwell made a present t'other day to poor Betty Pierce of the Workhouse of a new stiff Petticoat and a new pair of stockings which the poor creature was very thankful for', he recorded approvingly of a visiting relative's gifting activities in 1799. 'She says she will go down on her knees to

---

[65] For the medieval and early modern precedents upon which such accumulations of social capital built, see Marjorie K. McIntosh, 'The diversity of social capital in English communities, 1300–1640 (with a glance at modern Nigeria)', in Robert I. Rotberg, ed., *Patterns of Social Capital: Stability and Change in Historical Perspective* (Cambridge, 2001), 121–52, and Craig Muldrew, *The Economy of Obligation: The Culture of Credit and Social Relations in Early Modern England* (Basingstoke, 1998), esp. chaps. 5–6.

[66] Amanda Vickery explores the operation of gifting as a means of maintaining sociability among the gentry in *The Gentleman's Daughter: Women's Lives in Georgian England* (New Haven, 1998); gifting practices lower on the social scale are detailed in my 'Men's things: masculine possession in the consumer revolution', *Social History*, 25, 2 (May 2000), 133–55.

[67] Henry John Wale, ed., *My Grandfather's Pocket-Book: From A.D. 1701 to 1796* (London, 1883), 143 (25 April 1770).

[68] Bodleian, MS Eng.misc.e.251, Diary of James Newton (1761–62), 1 (5 April 1761); 7 (11 May 1761); 19 verso (2 July 1761); 70 verso (1 January 1762); 38 (4 September 1761).

[69] Ayres, ed., *Paupers and Pig Killers*, 161–2 (25 December 1807).

82   Debt and credit in English memory and imagination

Madam to tell her that she will never wear it but on Sundays as long as a rag of it remains.'[70]

Calculated to instil a sense of social debt, charitable giving to the local poor provided opportunities for propertied men and women to exert power over their inferiors. After the death of her father, a Baptist minister, the spinster Sarah Thomas deployed strategic gifting to retain a moral purchase over the poor in her Cotswold village. In January 1861, she was afoot on 'Errands of mercy all day', as worsted stockings, a shift and a pinafore provided her entrée into the homes – if not the hearts – of the lower sort. 'Took a Dorcas shift to poor Jonathan Cowley's wife and found him alone, so took the opportunity of urging him to repent for his sins', Thomas recorded. 'All were grateful.'[71] Even when the givers of gifts displayed more tact than Thomas, recipients understood that gifts placed them in ongoing relations of obligation. As the elderly Samuel Bamford and his wife became increasingly reliant upon gifts from friends and patrons, Bamford grew ever more conscious of this aspect of social credit. In June 1861, he sought unsuccessfully to repay ten shillings he had borrowed from a patron, who 'declined taking them; saying ... he intended at the time to make a gift of them'. Bamford, despite his poverty, protested that 'his lending me the money when I wanted it, was ... quite sufficient obligation', but his creditor persisted and Bamford, now doubly in his debt, uneasily pocketed the cash.[72]

Like charitable giving to the poor, presents to servants were a commonplace means of distributing goods, patronage and power. Money gifts were not unusual, and could be considerable in amount, but clothing was the common coin of gifts made to servants. When Thomas Garett successfully completed his apprenticeship to an Essex clothmaker in 1754, his master recorded that Garett, 'being a very good servant', was given the very substantial sum of five pounds five shillings 'to buy him a [be]Coming suite of cloths'.[73] In May 1783, James Woodforde 'Gave both my Maids a Gown apiece of [cloth] ... of the Pea Green' colour; March 1785 witnessed him purchase half a yard of corded muslin 'for the Maids ... which I gave them for Caps'; in September Woodforde dispatched his servant Betty 'to Norwich to buy my two old Washer-women ... a new gown apiece which I intend giving them'; and October 1793 saw the parson give Betty herself 'a new Gown bought in London'. Not all such gifted items had entered Woodforde's possession as commodities. 'Gave my maid, Sally Gunton, for

---

[70] Ibid., 19 (19 November 1799).
[71] June Lewis, ed., *The Secret Diary of Sarah Thomas 1860–1865* (Moreton-in-Marsh, Gloucestershire, 1994), 69 (18 January 1861). For instrumental charitable giving in this period, see Gareth Stedman Jones, *Outcast London: A Study in the Relationship between Classes in Victorian Society* (Oxford, 1971), 241–61.
[72] Hewitt and Poole, eds., *Diaries of Samuel Bamford*, 325 (8 June 1861).
[73] Diary of Joseph Savill, in A.F.J. Brown, ed., *Essex People 1750–1900: From Their Diaries, Memoirs and Letters* (Chelmsford, 1972), 42 (20 May 1754).

Debt and credit in diaries and autobiographies 83

sitting up with me, when ill, 2. Yards of black Silk, being a hatband sent me by John Mann on the Death of his Mother', he recorded in 1797.[74]

Women played an essential role in this constant traffic in textiles, devoting time, care and emotional energy to the selection of gifts for their servants.[75] The gifts made to household servants by Faith Gray of York nicely illustrate the precise arithmetic of loyalty, affection and calculated reward that informed this mode of exchange in affluent Georgian households. The ploughman's annual wage of thirty-one pounds, paid by Gray in December 1813, was accompanied by the gift of a hat (which she valued at a guinea) as well as a guinea in cash; Gray supplemented payment of Anna Burnett's wage in December 1815 with the gift of a gown, also valued at a guinea. A cash gift of a guinea to Burnett in 1817 was followed by a 'Present to her 25 years in our service this day' of a pound and two shillings in April 1818. Upon this loyal servant's marriage three months later, Gray presented her with a gift of fifty pounds. Mary Cummings, also married in July, received the lesser – but still significant – sum of ten pounds ten shillings, 'She having been with us 5 years & 8 months' only.[76]

Domestic servants remained the beneficiaries of middle- and upper-class gifting behaviours throughout the nineteenth century. Gifts of clothing constituted the vital core of this system of exchange: despite the decline of home production of textiles and the growth of both itinerant peddling and fixed shops, servants continued to obtain many consumer commodities indirectly through gift exchange rather than directly through the exchange of cash in the market. Hannah Cullwick's recollections of domestic service during her Shropshire childhood convey both the utility and the emotive value of such presents. It was her first employer, Cullwick recalled fondly, who 'first got me out o' my school dress, & give me one of her old straw bonnets trim'd with a plaid ribbon & a new print lilac frock from Birmingham which I thought was the loveliest could be, & so it was, for I remember it well & have never seen a better nor a prettier one since'.[77] Gifts of clothing from the employers of servants played an essential

---

[74] John Beresford, ed., *Woodforde: Passages from the Five Volumes of the Diary of a Country Parson 1758–1802* (New York, 1935), 166 (6 May 1783); 199 (8 March 1785); 328 (17 September 1791); 362 (24 October 1793); 455 (27 March 1797).

[75] For the role of gentry and elite women in this system of circulation, see Vickery, *Gentleman's Daughter*, and Marcia Pointon, *Strategies for Showing: Women, Possession, and Representation in English Visual Culture 1665–1800* (Oxford, 1997). Maxine Berg details the care and attention lavished on bequests by middle-class women in 'Women's consumption and the industrial classes of eighteenth-century England', *Journal of Social History*, 30, 2 (1996).

[76] Mrs Edwin Gray, ed., *Papers and Diaries of a York Family 1764–1839* (London, 1927), 206 (December 1813 and 1815); 207 (1817, 3 April 1818, July 1818). The inculcation and display of mutual liens of gratitude by such gift exchanges is a recurrent theme in diaries. See, for example, Richard Morgan, ed., *The Diary of a Bedfordshire Squire: John Thomas Brooks of Flitwick 1794–1858* (Bedfordshire, 1987), 133 (12 October 1849).

[77] Liz Stanley, ed., *The Diaries of Hannah Cullwick, Victorian Maidservant* (New Brunswick, 1984), 35. Presents of clothing from the families for whom she laboured continued to augment Cullwick's wardrobe throughout her years of service. See, for example, ibid., 41, 123.

84   Debt and credit in English memory and imagination

role in the circulation of textile goods to rural communities. Flora Thompson's memoir of rural Oxfordshire in the 1880s and 1890s returns repeatedly to this point. 'For outer garments they had to depend upon daughters, sisters, and aunts away in service, who all sent parcels, not only of their own clothes, but also of those they could beg from their mistresses', Thompson recalled of local housewives' provisioning strategies.[78] Factory production succeeded in transforming the production of textiles along new, modern lines shaped by the cash nexus, but the distribution of these goods among the poor often relied upon more traditional means of exchange informed by gift relations.

The practice of distributing Christmas boxes – annual presents of coin or goods to servants, apprentices and the like – further reinforced the gift economy. In his diary for 1803, William Upcott, an apprentice bookseller in London, recorded 'the welcome present' of a Christmas box containing a pound, and paused to reflect on the gift's wider meaning. 'Such a gift as this to me, is like an important era of a mans [sic] life. Well worth recording', Upcott observed. 'It gives vigour to the mind – and a smooth face to the person. I was in a good humour the whole day.' The contrast between the notions of moral economy conveyed by such gifts and the strict contractual obligations of the market was striking, and was promptly brought home to Upcott by the claim upon this pound made by his 'Hyena' of a tailor, to whom he stood in debt.[79] In the following decades, gifts of coin continued to allow servants and labourers with otherwise limited access to cash to participate in market activity. Hannah Cullwick received nearly two pounds in cash through Christmas boxes in 1863. 'I put mine in the bank wi' my wages', she recorded piously; 'Mary says hern [sic] shall buy a new bonnet.'[80]

Servants, dependants and the poor were by no means the only beneficiaries of this pervasive system of voluntary exchange, for gifts of produce, textiles and consumer goods were essential instruments of elite and respectable sociability. Presents made to underlings were calculated to reward past service, to promote future deference and to underline the lesser status of the recipient, who was expected to reciprocate not by offering material objects as counter-gifts but by acknowledging and perpetuating the values and behaviours of a hierarchical society. Gifts between and among friends, family and neighbours incorporated essential features of this status-orientated world view. But they also elicited a cycle of counter-gifting, and thus ensured that the circulation of material goods flowed in more than a single direction over time. Marking honour, status and affection, these gifts, as Benjamin Haydon well knew, established liens of social credit that overlapped instrumentally with more nakedly economic borrowing and lending practices.

[78] Flora Thompson, *Lark Rise to Candleford* (London, 1973), 32. See also ibid., 155, 157, 165.
[79] British Library, Add. MS 32,558, Diary of William Upcott (1779–1845), 8 January 1803.
[80] Stanley, ed., *Diaries of Hannah Cullwick*, 145.

Rural living was especially conducive to the gifting of produce and food-stuffs. When Thomas Wale received 'a present of a young pigg' from Mrs Younghusband and 'a present of a quarter of lamb' from Mr Fisher in 1775, he 'Sent in return a basket of apples, and to Mrs Younghusband some forced meat balls'. Wale's wife, who received 'a pott of Sour Crout' from Mrs Atkins at this time, promptly dispatched 'a fattened hen turkey by the Cambridge coach' to the Atkins home.[81] Provisions sent as friendly gifts travelled impressive dis-tances: having returned to London from a visit to his uncle in Norfolk, Samuel Woodforde recorded that his uncle's friend 'Mrs Davie sent as a present a Nor-folk Turkey weighing 12 pounds.'[82] The diary of Nancy Woodforde, Samuel's sister and James Woodforde's niece and housekeeper, indicates the scale and social significance of these exchanges at the local level. Entries for 1792 docu-ment the receipt of three snipe, 'a nice Pot of Honey', 'a fine pike', asparagus, a melon and a seemingly endless succession of partridges. 'Mr Collins sent us two brace of Partridges which I think was very genteel of him, he never having been in company with either of us', Nancy recorded with satisfaction in September. 'Mrs Custance sent her love to me with a Present of a fine pheasant and a Bottle of Pickled Mushrooms and a Bottle of Preserved Gooseberries', she noted sadly two weeks later. 'We shall never have such good Neighbours again in Norfolk, their going away is the greatest loss I could meet with here.'[83]

The textiles, trinkets and fashionable luxury items spawned by England's burgeoning commercial economy also figured prominently in this gifting activ-ity, and provided contemporaries with abundant material for reflection on the systems of social signification that attached to material objects. Anne Lister's journal of life in later Georgian Yorkshire registers hares, partridges and a 'particularly kind and attentive' gift of mutton,[84] but dwells with especially loving attention on her purchases of elegant consumer items for her friends and paramours. December 1817 saw Lister acquire two 'mother-of-pearl knives with two blades, corkscrew &c &c at the end, a pair of small scissors contained in a silver sheath . . . [and] a silver pencil with a magnifying glass' for friends with whom she had been visiting; in September 1819 she ordered an eight-volume illustrated edition of *Lallah Rookh*, lined with green satin and bound in crimson morocco leather, for her lover Isabella.[85] Lister was acutely conscious of the

---

[81] Wale, ed., *Grandfather's Pocket-Book*, 169 (10 February 1775).
[82] Dorothy Heighes Woodforde, ed., *Woodforde Papers and Diaries* (London, 1932), 95 (15 January 1785).
[83] Ibid., 45 (23 February 1792); 51 (24 March 1792); 53 (12 April 1792); 55 (17 April 1792); 74 (24 September 1792); 74 (28 September 1792); 73 (18 September 1792); 75–6 (6 October 1792). Similar gifts of foodstuffs are recorded, for example, in the more modest Wordsworth household in the Lake District. See Pamela Woof, ed., Dorothy Wordsworth, *The Grasmere Journals* (Oxford, 1991), 7 (3 June 1800); 16 (5 August 1800); 29 (22 October 1800).
[84] Whitbread, ed., *I Know My Own Heart*, 150 (24 March 1821). See also ibid., 173 (18 December 1821).
[85] Ibid., 28 (19 December 1817); 99 (9 September 1819).

86   Debt and credit in English memory and imagination

shifting permutations of etiquette and economy that governed gift exchange. Shopping in York for a present to give to a soldier who – having risen 'from the ranks' to become the riding master of the local barracks – had undertaken the task of breaking her young horse, Lister dismissed silver tankards as 'too high in price', and fixed instead 'upon a pair of salt-cellars, gilt inside, very handsomely chased, very handsome' indeed, albeit secondhand. 'As far as he himself was concerned I might safely have given him money', Lister observed, 'but being now an officer he must be made a gentleman of, & the regiment would not let him take money.'[86]

Gifting behaviours persisted among the upper classes in the mid-Victorian period, as attested by the continued circulation of partridges, plants and other rural products among neighbouring gentry families.[87] But like the fictional archive, diaries and memoirs also suggest that the obligations entailed by such lateral gifting grew increasingly troubling to propertied men and women in the course of the nineteenth century. As liberal notions of personal autonomy became more current, gifts to individuals outside the immediate family but within one's social circle appear to have become increasingly problematic. Sarah Thomas expressed no qualms about her own coercive gifting to the poor, but – like the eponymous heroine of Elizabeth Gaskell's *Ruth* – was sensitive to the possibility that her neighbours' gifts were motivated by a desire to express their social superiority. When friends sent her invalid sister gifts of jelly, fish and rice pudding, 'Mrs Frise, always wanting to go one better, sent a Sally Lunn', Thomas recorded. 'I assume it was as much to show they had been to Bath as . . . [to] present a gift, but had to chastise my quite un-Christian thoughts of it.'[88] Leslie Stephen's late Victorian memoir, in which debt repayment figures as a prime feature of manly bourgeois character, registers considerable unease with his wife's incessant gift-giving to friends and family. 'As it seems to me, she had learnt so thoroughly in her dark days of widowhood to consider herself as set apart to relieve pain and sorrow that . . . she had a stream of overflowing goodwill which forced her to look out for some channel of discharge', Stephen ruminated worriedly. 'I confess that I grudged a little this incessant round of kindly services; they took, I thought . . . too much labour.' Disturbed that Julia's exhausting exchange activities had elevated gift-giving into 'a kind of religious practice', Stephen as a widower had no qualms about his own use of gifts to bind his daughters emotionally to him. 'I have given to Stella a chain which I gave to

---

[86] Ibid., 251–2 (12 and 13 May 1823).

[87] See, for example, Morgan, ed., *Diary of a Bedfordshire Squire*, 175 (14 September 1853). 'Capt[ai]n Reader sent this morning 3 brace and I disposed of them thus: 1 brace ourselves – dinner party, 1 brace to Wynter, and 1 brace to Sir William Hooker.'

[88] Lewis, ed., *Secret Diary*, 32 (7 June 1860). See similarly Mary Clive, ed., *Caroline Clive: From the Diary and Family Papers of Mrs Archer Clive (1801–1873)* (London, 1949), 181–3 (Spring 1844 and 28 April 1844).

Debt and credit in diaries and autobiographies

her mother upon our marriage; and to Vanessa a photograph by Mrs Cameron which...shows her mother's beauty better than any other', he recorded. 'We will cling to each other.'[89]

Diaries and memoirs suggest that the scale and scope of gifting among friends and neighbours diminished, and that gift exchange became increasingly formalised, in the course of the nineteenth century. Where neighbourly gifts of produce, cloth and trinkets constantly punctuate Georgian diaries, presents made to family members on birthdays and holidays are far more typical in Victorian and Edwardian sources. The commercialisation of Christmas, a process eagerly exploited by department stores, helped to foster this redefinition of appropriate gift behaviours by associating present-giving with advertising and the market rather than with day-to-day mutual sociability.[90] An entry in Beatrix Potter's diary for 1884, when her family travelled to Manchester to dispose of her grandmother's effects, reflects nostalgically upon the gradual erosion of customary gift-giving at the upper levels of society:

One thing was given me which I value exceedingly, an old green silk dress of my grandmother's which she wore as a girl. It was wrapped up in the same paper with her wedding dress, a white silk brocade...I thought at first they would have given it [to] me, but Aunt Harriet thought after she ought to keep it. I should not have ventured to ask for either, but that they spoke of giving it to the servants! It is extraordinary how little people value old things if they are of little intrinsic value.[91]

Once common among the respectable classes as a means of circulating both goods and the emotional obligations that attached to them, the exchange of clothing items now appeared to represent a relic of the pre-modern market, rendered increasingly anachronistic by the triumph of commodification.

Lower down on the social scale, diaries and memoirs again suggest a diminution of sociable gift behaviours outside the family circle during the nineteenth century. The growth of popular radicalism laid essential groundwork for this development, prompting antagonism to interested gift-giving by elite patrons. Robert Sharp, a keen critic of Old Corruption, was intensely hostile to neighbourly gift-giving rituals, which he understood to constitute a fundamental impediment to the development of personal autonomy. Dismissing the subservient behaviour fostered by gift-giving at funerals, Sharp underlined his

---

[89] Allen Bell, ed., *Sir Leslie Stephen's Mausoleum Book* (Oxford, 1977), 81–3, 97. Trev Broughton offers an incisive analysis of the gender dimensions of Stephen's engagement with personal debts in *Men of Letters*, 60–70, 180–1, note 11.

[90] For department stores and the commercialisation of Christmas, see Christopher P. Hosgood, '"Doing the shops" at Christmas: women, men and the department store in England, *c.* 1880–1914', in Geoffrey Crossick and Serge Jaumain, eds., *Cathedrals of Consumption: The European Department Store 1850–1939* (Aldershot, 1999), 97–115.

[91] Leslie Linder, ed., *The Journal of Beatrix Potter from 1881 to 1897* (London, 1966), 78 (2 April 1884).

88 Debt and credit in English memory and imagination

own independence when he declined to attend a local burial. 'Bearers were chosen and Gloves given them so that they were hired', he observed in 1827, 'but as I had no retaining fee I was a free agent, and was pleased not to give my attendance, but left the mourning department to those who were paid for it.'[92] The liens of sociable credit entailed by Christmas boxes likewise raised Sharp's hackles. Having successfully evaded both giving and receiving these customary gifts in 1830, he reflected that 'it is a satisfaction to know that I am not in the least obligated to any one for what I have had, and but to a few for their offers'.[93]

Sharp was unusually sensitive to the demeaning potential of traditional gifts, but disengagement from such exchange activities was, in the Victorian period, to become more common among petty producers and retailers. While serving as an apprentice wheelwright in the 1860s, George Bird recorded many gifts exchanged between his parents' rural Lincolnshire household and an uncle who lived outside of Norwich.[94] But few presents given to his family by friends and neighbours appear in the pages of his journal, and few of even these exceptional presents were given outside of holidays and ritualised contexts.[95] Later nineteenth-century urban diaries and memoirs corroborate this trend. Edward Harvey, a Hoxton letter carrier, was an avid consumer in local shops, but the only gifts recorded in his diary for 1859–60 other than Christmas boxes were birthday gifts exchanged with family members.[96] Winifred Burke's memoir of her working-class childhood in London at the turn of the century also suggests the restricted scope of gifting. Although she waxed rhapsodic over a Leghorn hat – 'a flower dropped from heaven' – spontaneously given to her by a family friend, it was the annual exchange of presents and hospitality within her family circle at Christmas that dominated her lengthy description of gift-giving.[97] Now associated primarily with servants, youths and the recipients of charity, customary gift-giving increasingly gave way – outside familial relations – to market exchange. Market exchange itself, however, was hardly ruled by commodification and the cash nexus. For while notions of social obligation gradually faded in

[92] Crowther and Crowther, eds., *Diary of Robert Sharp*, 134 (21 May 1827).

[93] Ibid., 292 (26 December 1830).

[94] John A. Liddie, ed., *The Diary of George Bird: Victorian Wheelwright* (Nottingham, [1982]), 9 (31 January 1865); 11 (27 February 1865); 12 (4 March 1865); 14 (25 March 1865); 25 (4 August 1865); 50 (26 May 1866).

[95] For Christmas boxes and funeral gifts, see ibid., 8 (26 January 1865); 41 (24 February 1866); and 9 (2 February 1865).

[96] Modern Records Centre, University of Warwick, MS 219, Diary of Edward Harvey, 27 (17 December 1859); 29–30 (18 December 1859); 35–6 (22 December 1859); 43–8 (27–30 December 1859); 73–6 (18–23 May 1860).

[97] 'The Leghorn hat – it crowned me princess ... To see it lying there in its fragile beauty gave me one of the Things I wanted but could not define. It fed my hunger.' Clare Cameron [pseud. Winifred Burke], *Rustle of Spring: Simple Annals of a London Girl* (London, 1927), 77–8. For her description of Christmas, see 50–74.

Debt and credit in diaries and autobiographies 89

gifting behaviours, the norms of retail practice ensured that social forms of debt and credit persistently shaped Victorian and Edwardian consumer relations.

Commodities, purchasing and the market

The triumph of anonymous consumer relations in the course of the nineteenth century is a commonplace of historical analysis: urbanisation, the increasing spatial separation of tradesmen's homes and shops and the development of new retail institutions such as department stores all figure in the literature as modernising impulses that inaugurated a new era in consumer relations. In this view, just as structural changes in production led to the commodification of labour, so too the evolution of new retail structures promoted a commodification of consumer relations. 'Mass (in the sense of anonymous) marketing appeared, as shopkeepers increasingly sought individual transactions with unknown buyers rather than extended patronage by established customers', James Carrier argues of the decades from 1800. 'Customers were increasingly acquiring objects in impersonal interactions in impersonal institutions.'[98] William Cobbett's choleric diatribes against later Georgian retail innovation resonate with such claims. 'Wens devoured market towns; and shops devoured markets and fairs', Cobbett lamented. 'All was looked for at the shops: all was to be had by trafficking . . . nothing was so common as to rent breasts for children to suck: a man actually advertised in the London papers, to supply childless husbands with heirs!'[99]

Nineteenth-century retailers laid important foundations for this modernisation thesis in their memoirs. The socialist pioneer Robert Owen, who served as a draper's assistant in the 1780s, self-consciously situated his own life story within a narrative of commercial modernisation. His first employer, a Lincolnshire draper, was a Scotsman who had begun business by hawking goods from a hand-basket but had surmounted these humble origins through a combination of diligence, reputation and attention to personal relations, cultivated by making 'regular rounds among customers of the first respectability'. Connection, rather than economic capital alone, ensured this draper's success, and sociability and gifting accordingly featured at the centre of his life story. His shop became 'a kind of general rendezvous [point] of the higher class nobility', and one particularly devoted aristocratic customer presented a favourite hunter to the shopkeeper upon his retirement from trade.[100] The establishment maintained

---

[98] James G. Carrier, *Gifts and Commodities: Exchange and Western Capitalism since 1700* (London, 1995), 75. The broader parameters and limitations of this interpretation are detailed below in chapter 7.

[99] Cobbett, *Autobiography*, 192.

[100] Robert Owen, *The Life of Robert Owen: Written by Himself*, intro. John Butt (London, 1857; republished London, 1971), 12–13.

90   Debt and credit in English memory and imagination

by Owen's London employer, in sharp contrast, sold commodities 'for ready money only'. Here numerical calculations of financial gain clearly outweighed older commercial conventions: the customers were 'of an inferior class' and were 'treated differently'. 'Not much time was allowed for bargaining, a price being fixed for everything, and compared with other houses, cheap', Owen recalled. 'If any demur was made, or much hesitation, the article asked for was withdrawn.'[101] Cash sales and fixed prices had, if only in Owen's imagination, sounded the death-knell of traditional, status-oriented retail practices already at the turn of the nineteenth century.

Later tradesmen helped to fill out Owen's preliminary sketch of retail modernisation: the construction of precisely this vision of modern market rationality appears to have been a key factor motivating memoir writing by successful retailers. Tradesmen who suffered the common commercial fate of bankruptcy dwelt at considerable length upon the persistence of localism, anachronism and personal relations in retail markets.[102] But the men who spearheaded the later Victorian campaign to legitimate shopkeepers' place in society were champions of the modernisation thesis. As 'An Old Draper' recalled in 1876, 'In old-fashioned times people used to chaffer and haggle about the price, when they wanted to buy any thing; and the healthy system of sticking to one price was just coming into vogue, and was the means of saving much time.' Fixed prices, anonymous contracts and commercial efficiency were of a piece in this analysis. Whereas early nineteenth-century shopkeepers 'seemed to depend more upon their connexion and usual customers than to seek for new ones', he claimed, now 'Greater judgment is used in buying, and the trade is so divided, classified, and thoroughly looked after, that . . . a lady may invariably get exactly what she wants without any trouble or annoyance.'[103]

Although forward-looking shopkeepers were loath to acknowledge continuity in retail trade relations, diaries and memoirs written by consumers are sensitive to the endurance of conventional commercial behaviours. Craig Muldrew and Claire Walsh have identified sociability as a central feature of early modern shopkeeping, underlining the importance of domestic conviviality in sustaining ongoing connections between consumers and tradesmen in this period.[104] Later eighteenth-century sources illustrate the continued role played by retail sociability in fostering commercial relations. As in gift relations, the confluence of commercial and social obligation entailed by such sociability complicated

---

[101] Ibid., 18–19.

[102] See, for example, Frank T. Bullen, *Confessions of a Tradesman* (London, 1908).

[103] Anon., *Reminiscences of an Old Draper* (London, 1876), 6, 142, 9. Along similar lines, see Throne Crick [pseud.], *Sketches from the Diary of a Commercial Traveller* (London, 1848), 111.

[104] Muldrew, *Economy of Obligation*, esp. chap. 5; Claire Walsh, 'Shopping in early modern London' (Ph.D. thesis, European University Institute, 2001), esp. chap. 1.

Debt and credit in diaries and autobiographies

determinations of payment for consumer goods and services. When Nancy Woodforde spent a few days shopping in Norwich in May 1792, she paid two shillings to have her hair dressed by Mr Noseworthy – from whom she also 'bought a few trifles' – before joining her uncle at the Noseworthy table for 'a very handsome Dinner'. Returning to Norwich in August, both she and her uncle again lodged with the Noseworthy family, 'where we were very comfortably accommodated with a nice Room and charmingly revived with a Mutton and . . . Porter and Wine'. In these circumstances, precise payment required an aptitude for social as well as economic calculation. 'Uncle paid Mr Noseworthy 7s. 6d. for our refreshment but Mr N. did not want to be paid but for the Wine, but Uncle would pay him handsomely on account of his civil behaviour', she recorded.[105]

The continued centrality of retailers' homes and shops as sites of consumption and social relations emerges clearly from later nineteenth-century sources. In 1851, middle-class householders who lived above or beside their shop or business premises still outnumbered those who had separated their home from the workplace.[106] Isabella Mayo's autobiography speaks to the persistence of sociability, custom and connection encouraged by these spatial arrangements, even in metropolitan London. Until debts crippled the business in the later 1860s, her family lived above their bakery in Bedford Street, where 'Shop and dining-room were divided by a partition of small-pained windows'. On Sunday mornings, the bakery served 'as a community bakehouse', a neighbourly practice precisely calculated 'to "keep together" the "custom" of the neighbourhood'.[107] Lower down on the social scale, where small family shops provided much of the working-class population with daily provisions, retail sociability prevailed into the Edwardian era. In the small shop kept by Robert Roberts's mother in Salford, personal relations remained at the heart of daily purchasing activities. 'People came then not only to shop but to talk, the weekly purchasing of from one to five shillings' worth of goods being a high social occasion', Roberts recalled. ' "And if there was any free milk going," my mother used to say, "the babies got it! You've taken nourishment from half the women of the neighbourhood!" '[108]

Consumers' private residences were also central sites of retail sociability, for despite the growth of fixed-shop retailing, shopkeepers, tradesmen and itinerant pedlars continued to conduct business in the homes of their customers. Parson Woodforde was hardly exceptional in inviting the itinerant draper Aldridge 'to dine with our Folks' after he purchased silk and cotton goods from the pedlar in

[105] Woodforde, ed., *Woodforde Papers*, 57 (2 May 1792); 66 (16 August 1792).
[106] Tosh, *A Man's Place*, 17.
[107] Isabella Fyvie Mayo, *Recollections of What I Saw, What I Lived Through, and What I Learned, during More than Fifty Years of Social and Literary Experience* (London, 1910), 21, 24.
[108] Roberts, *Ragged Schooling*, 8.

92   Debt and credit in English memory and imagination

1795.[109] Like sociability enjoyed within shops, such gifts of hospitality by consumers complicated economic relations. In 1819, Anne Lister was perplexed by the difficulty of determining the precise degree of sociable behaviour to display towards a seamstress who came to her home to fit a gown for her lover Isabella. Having offered the seamstress beer, Lister found that by general consensus she had badly misjudged her role as hostess to an economic transaction that was invested with social meaning and status considerations:

My aunt said wine & water. Tib [Isabella] wondered how I could ask such a nice woman to have beer – wine, certainly. Her father always asked Willoughby, the master-builder at Malton, & even Tomlinson, the master-joiner, to have wine. Much more should I have asked such a woman as Miss Kitson to have wine.[110]

Lister's predicament reflected habits of sociability that flourished in provincial and metropolitan areas alike throughout the nineteenth century. Molly Hughes's fond memory of the family tailor suggests the continued sway exerted by affective ties in the middle-class marketplace in the 1890s. 'Mr Neal paid periodical visits to his customers in London', she recounted. 'This kindly man was more of a friend than a tailor to both of us, taking genuine interest in the joys and sorrows of our life.'[111]

Swathed in the tissue of nostalgia in autobiographical memoirs, the sociable behaviours displayed by retailers and their customers were well calculated to foster loyalty (and thus profits) over time. Fierce competition encouraged tradesmen to deploy personal ties – rather than price differentials alone – to cultivate stable consumer relations. For Thomas Turner in the mid-eighteenth century, maintaining commercial relations with other local traders whose businesses he supplied with goods required occasional visits to their premises, where convivial behaviour worked alongside purchasing power to ensure continued custom at his shop.[112] The sense of obligation entailed by such social ties often hobbled consumer choice. It was affective, local and personal ties, Flora Thompson observed, that dulled the competitive advantage that co-operatives and other large retail outlets would otherwise have enjoyed in late Victorian Oxfordshire. 'At that time the more important village people, such as the doctor and clergyman, bought their provisions at the village shop as a matter of principle', she recalled. 'They would have thought it mean to go further afield for the sake of saving a few shillings, and even the rich who spent only part of the year at their country houses or their hunting boxes believed it to be their duty to give the local tradesmen a turn.'[113]

---

[109] Beresford, ed., *Woodforde*, 414 (24 November 1795).
[110] Whitbread, ed., *I Know My Own Heart*, 95 (30 July 1819).
[111] Hughes, *London Family*, 541–2.
[112] See, for example, Vaisey, ed., *Diary of Thomas Turner*, 184–5 (7 June 1759); 282 (6 December 1763).
[113] Thompson, *Lark Rise*, 462.

Debt and credit in diaries and autobiographies 93

The growth in itinerant peddling witnessed by the nineteenth century further reinforced the personal character of consumer relations in the modern period, reducing contemporaries' exposure to the anonymous cash nexus and purely contractual understandings of exchange. Pedlars and hawkers had been essential cogs in the distributive process since at least the seventeenth century, but they proliferated dramatically in response to the casual labour markets spawned by commercial and industrial growth, traversing both the unstable dividing line that distinguished traders from consumers and the artificial boundary that separated the market from the home.[114] In an economy in which business failure was endemic and employment highly labile, door-to-door peddling offered men and women burdened with unpaid debts the opportunity to support their families, recoup their fortunes and fashion an individual identity worthy of autobiographical reflection. The actress Charlotte Charke, whose memoir was first published in 1755, turned to a series of economic expedients that included a stint as an itinerant peddler of home-made sausages, pawning and then the publication of her own life story for profit.[115] Mary Saxby, the daughter of a London silk-weaver, was 'left deeply in debt, with a small family to provide for' upon her husband's death in the 1780s and became a pedlar of drapery and haberdashery items, travelling with her wares from Stony Stratford to London and ultimately carrying her goods to customers' homes from a shop in Olney.[116] Jane Jowitt of necessity trod a similar path. The daughter of an Irish barrister who had suffered imprisonment for his debts in the Marshalsea, Jowitt lost her fortune and journeyed to Liverpool, where she 'was advised to buy some light goods and travel on foot to London by easy stages'. Successful in selling these items, she purchased an additional stock of goods and established herself profitably as a pedlar in outlying villages before turning to literature as a trade.[117]

References to purchases made on the doorstep or in the home from itinerant merchants underline the personal character of such exchange relations. Tales of debt-driven itinerant trade recur in diaries that record the narrative lines

---

[114] For early modern peddling, see Margaret Spufford, *The Great Reclothing of Rural England: Petty Chapmen and Their Wares in the Seventeenth Century* (London, 1984), and Laurence Fontaine, *History of Pedlars in Europe*, trans. Vicki Whittaker (Durham, NC, 1996). The nineteenth-century efflorescence is discussed in D.R. Green, 'Street trading in London: a case study of casual labour, 1830–60', in John Benson and Gareth Shaw, eds., *The Retailing Industry*, 3 vols. (London, 1999), II: 115–31.

[115] Charlotte Charke, *A Narrative of the Life of Mrs. Charlotte Charke (Youngest Daughter of Colley Cibber, Esq.): Written by Herself*, intro. Leonard R.N. Ashley, 2nd edn (London, 1755; reprinted Gainesville, 1969), 70, 97, 132, 134, 137, 148, 223, 269.

[116] [Mary Saxby], *Memoirs of a Female Vagrant Written by Herself* (London, 1806), 6, 8–9, 14, 15, 51–2, 54, 58–9, 61, 73 (citation from 52). See similarly Ann Kussmaul, ed., *The Autobiography of Joseph Mayett of Quainton (1783–1839)* (Cambridge, 1986), 61, 66, 85.

[117] Jane Jowitt, *Memoirs of Jane Jowitt, the Poor Poetess, Aged 74 Years, Written by Herself* (Sheffield, 1844), 3, 11, 13, 15–19 (citations from 3, 18–19).

94   Debt and credit in English memory and imagination

deployed by pedlars to sell their wares in consumers' homes. In 1785 James Woodforde obtained oysters from 'a poor distressed old Man... [who] has bred up a large Family by Blacksmiths business but since the Death of his Wife and being 60 Yrs of Age and some of his Family not turning out Well, [is] obliged... to give up his business... and become very poor'.[118] The travelling salesman who sold Robert Sharp a silk handkerchief and fifty needles in 1827 retailed an analogous life story, claiming 'that he has been a merchant but the times have been so much against him, that he is obliged to do anything honestly for his support, he is rather a respectable looking man, and very clean in his appearance'.[119] When goods were presented at the doorstep in this personalised manner, consumer purchasing elided with charitable gifting behaviours and market activity was informed by an array of moral valuations in addition to utilitarian considerations of price.

Later nineteenth-century diaries and memoirs underscore consumers' willingness to purchase goods at the door from pedlars, who feature in these sources far more significantly than do the retail warehouses and department stores which have captivated historians of the period. In Lincolnshire, George Bird 'bought a beautiful Bible of the Lincolnshire Book Hawking Association man' in 1867; his father purchased two pieces of cloth, 'of a nice pattern', from a pedlar in 1871.[120] Margaret Penn's small village in Edwardian Lancashire was served by family shops, but it was the monthly visits of an itinerant credit draper rather than these local outlets or the department stores of nearby Manchester that introduced her to the seductive pleasures of the consumer market. The pedlar's visits saw her mother's 'will-power slowly drawn from her by the tallyman's dreadful charm... tempted beyond all human limits by the dazzling display' of frocks, pinafores, stays, chemises, petticoats, shirts, collars, stockings, linens and bead necklaces that flowed from his pack in the kitchen of their home.[121] Rural denizens were not, however, the only consumers to trade with pedlars: fond recollections of itinerant tradesmen are a recurrent theme in later Victorian (and Edwardian) urban autobiographies. In Frank Steel's impoverished mid-Victorian London boyhood, fire-stove ornament hawkers 'figured largely', peddling 'gorgeous wares of variegated paper and tinsel... an ecstasy to behold and an unfailing joy for the mind to dwell upon'.[122] Molly Hughes elaborated on this theme even as she rejected Steel's plebeian aesthetic sensibilities. 'Up and down there went, much oftener than to-day, the hawkers of various goods, each with an appropriate cry "Flowers all a-blowing and a-growing", "Ornaments for your

---

[118] Beresford, ed., *Woodforde*, 208 (29 September 1785); 499. The leech-gatherer who inspired Wordsworth's poem was another such pedlar, driven by the scarcity of leeches to begging and an itinerant trade in religious volumes. See Woof, ed., *Grasmere Journals*, 23–4 (3 October 1800).

[119] Crowther and Crowther, eds., *Diary of Robert Sharp*, 123 (6 April 1827).

[120] Liddie, ed., *Diary of George Bird*, 76 (13 March 1867); 187 (3 November 1871).

[121] Margaret Penn, *Manchester Fourteen Miles*, intro. John Burnett (Firle, Sussex, 1979), 173–4.

[122] Frank Steel, *Ditcher's Row: A Tale of the Older Charity* (London, 1939), 4.

Debt and credit in diaries and autobiographies 95

fire-stove" (unbelievably hideous streamers of coloured paper), "A pair of fine soles", bird-cages, iron-holders, brooms, brushes, and baskets.'[123] Together the winkle-and-shrimp man, the muffin-man, comic-book sellers, pot-plant pedlars, and itinerant dealers in caged birds, lavender, salt and hearth-stone are permanent fixtures of the remembered landscape of late Victorian and Edwardian retail culture.[124]

Retail sociability and the persistence of peddling worked to blur distinctions between home and market, consumer and retailer, economic exchange and social obligation, but it was trade credit above all other relations that limited autonomy and anonymity in the modern English consumer market. The cultivation of consumer loyalty by tradesmen through sociable behaviours was dictated by more than quaint notions of reciprocity and a desire to stabilise their consumer base, for the ubiquity of credit at all levels of retail trade made a degree of mutual trust integral to buying and selling. Where historians, in describing the transformation of England into a consumer culture, refer confidently to the triumph of the cash nexus, diaries and memoirs – like contemporary novels – speak eloquently instead to the continued dominion of personal credit. Extended in all directions, trade credit bound consumers, retailers and wholesalers together in networks of mutual lending that encouraged all parties to surround their contractual agreements with a scaffolding of extra-legal customs, obligations and expectations.

The practice of annual billing at Christmas encapsulates many of the characteristic features of consumer credit in this period. For persons of any standing in the local community, annual payment for items purchased at intervals on account was a standard practice. Friends, neighbours and kin expected tradesmen to extend credit to them on the basis of personal connection; tradesmen in turn relied upon this personal knowledge to facilitate evaluations of creditworthy behaviour and to enhance the sense of obligation that would promote the eventual payment of just debts. Widely pervasive, these normative expectations were also highly taxing for tradesmen. Thomas Turner commented despondently in 1757 on the complications created by the customary linkage that obtained, through credit, between his social and his economic transactions:

almost all the people in the parish . . . are so long [to] pay that no tradesman I am assured can bear it, for even the best will not pay above once a year. Then living so near my friends is I think a great disadvantage though I should be willing to lend them all the assistance that is in my power and help them in anything I can. But they seem to study nothing but self-interest, or if they have no design to take advantage, it turns out very much to my disadvantage.[125]

---

[123] Hughes, *London Family*, 5.

[124] See, for example, Cameron [pseud.], *Rustle of Spring*, 46–7; Allan Jobson, *The Creeping Hours of Time* (London, 1977), 27–9.

[125] Vaisey, ed., *Diary of Thomas Turner*, 111 (16 September 1757). For Turner's understanding of his obligations to friends and kin, see Tadmor, *Family and Friends*, esp. chap. 5.

96   Debt and credit in English memory and imagination

For theorists of political economy, autonomous individualism promised commercial profits, but for tradesmen active in historical markets 'self-interest' was a bugbear where credit was the norm. 'At home all day and but very little to do', Turner lamented three years later, 'and even what little I have is altogether trust, and my affairs are so connected with my friends that I know not how to extricate myself out of my trouble.'[126] Credit and connection secured Turner customers, but only at the price of unpaid debts and deferred payments.

James Woodforde's diary illustrates the perils that awaited tradesmen who departed from these customary retail norms and presumed to press their customers unduly for cash. Woodforde paid bills to a wide variety of tradesmen annually in December, and took umbrage when his tradesmen drew unwanted attention to the contractual character of their relations by sending in untimely reminders of his unpaid balances. His description of payment of his miller's bill nicely conveys the proper lines of authority that connected tradesmen and their genteel credit customers. Emphasising his own role in initiating payment, Woodforde wrote that the miller 'called on me this morning by my desire, and I paid him a 48 Stone Bill for Flour for my House for this Year'.[127] Failure on his tradesmen's part to adhere to this customary code of economic decorum was a declaration of independence that demanded rapid disciplinary reprisal. When his woollen-draper Smith and tailor Forster had the impudence to send him unsolicited bills for goods in 1799, Woodforde was outraged. Promptly dispatching his manservant to pay the bills in full, he fumed that the tradesmen's behaviour represented a fundamental breach in social values – a lapse which Woodforde specifically associated with the unacceptable, Dissenting face of the Protestant ethic:

I told Ben to take a stamp Receipt of each of them in full of all Demands having done with them ... It pleased me much on the said Bills being paid but the remembrance of their being sent me by them, will not be by me soon forgot having dealt with them for at least 23 Years. Smith the Mercer is a Presbyterian and I suppose Forster, the Taylor, is of the same Persuasion. I have now done with them for ever for their late shabby, ungentleman-like behaviour.

Woodforde soon acted upon this threat. When he was measured for a pair of black velvet breeches in March 1800, it was Robert Cary, not the tailor Forster, who attended upon him in his home.[128] Five years later, William Holland's response when a local shoemaker and his spouse 'rather ungraciously popped a Bill into my wife's hand that had not been a month's standing', was equally decided. Having paid the bill immediately, he noted that he would 'take care to have no bill with either of them in future for no two meaner and more greedy and shabby people I scarce ever met with'.[129]

[126] Vaisey, ed., *Diary of Thomas Turner*, 211 (18 September 1760).
[127] Beresford, ed., *Woodforde*, 315 (7 and 8 December 1790).
[128] Ibid., 469 (26 February 1799); 479 (11 March 1800).
[129] Ayres, ed., *Paupers and Pig Killers*, 116 (20 August 1805).

Debt and credit in diaries and autobiographies 97

Extended billing cycles were not the exclusive preserve of elite purchasers: a wide range of solvent and insolvent consumers enjoyed generous (and flexible) credit terms. E.L. Blanchard was chronically in debt and often forced to resort to the pawnshop, but many tradesmen extended him credit, and December 1853 thus saw Blanchard gloomily lament the 'Usual overwhelming cavalcade of Christmas accounts'.[130] Because the perpetuation of existing accounts loomed larger in many creditors' concerns than short-term economic profits, even impecunious debtors could gain extended credit from local tradesmen if they were willing to enter into personal negotiations to that end. His wife pregnant and his possessions pawned, Ford Madox Brown walked to the family grocer 'to arrange ... about not paying & getting credit' in December 1854, a strategy that kept his family supplied with provisions until late January, when Brown was able to pay an instalment of ten pounds on his grocery account.[131] For more solvent customers well known to their local tradesmen, cash sales and fixed prices were often so intertwined with credit relations and retail sociability as to lose any fixed meaning. Settling his debts several weeks after purchase did not prevent Henry Hill, tenant farmer of 200 acres in Derbyshire, from successfully bargaining to reduce established prices: the 'washing machine' he purchased on 5 July 1872 for three pounds fifteen shillings was settled for three pounds eleven shillings on 20 September.[132] Discounts, gifts and douceurs designed to encourage or reward payment of bills within a year were essential elements of tradesmen's strategic arsenals. When the schoolmaster W.E. Swift paid his Christmas bills in Cheltenham in 1898, his draper gave him a discount of five shillings for a suit of clothes purchased in 1897, and a shopkeeper offered him a penknife as a present for settling his account.[133]

George Bird's diary reveals the tangled skein of reciprocity that surrounded credit relations in the artisanal households that supplied consumers with an array of goods and services. December, January and February routinely saw Bird and his father prepare and collect Christmas bills for those customers who paid for work done in their wheelwright's shop on an annual billing cycle, a protracted process further complicated by the Birds' impressionistic accountkeeping practices.[134] But annual billing represented only one among many available credit arrangements for their customers. Most common was periodic payment on account. Robert Lambert's payment of '2/6 on account of his son's bill, leaving a balance yet to pay of 15/-', exemplifies the piecemeal pattern of payments, which encouraged retailers and craftsmen to buttress their commercial contracts with consumers by extending a range of complementary services

---

[130] Scott and Howard, eds., *Life and Reminiscences*, I: 115 (29 December 1853).
[131] Surtees, ed., *Diary of Ford Madox Brown*, 106 (2 December 1854); 118 (25 January 1855).
[132] John Heath, ed., *Diaries of Henry Hill of Slackfields Farm 1872–1896* (Nottingham, 1982), (not paginated).
[133] Gloucestershire RO, D 3981/24, Diary of W.E. Swift (8 January 1898).
[134] See, for example, Liddie, ed., *Diary of George Bird*, 10 (17 February 1865); 35 (18 December 1865).

98   Debt and credit in English memory and imagination

and courtesies to them. Small loans made to neighbour-customers, such as the 2/6 'borrowed by his wife' that Mr. Pindard repaid when he settled 'his little account' of 14/2, were means to this end, as was the 'bottle of wine for one of the children' that Mrs Bird gave Mrs Laxam – visiting the shop to pay two pounds ten shillings for a child's coffin – in 1871.[135]

Perennially owed money by their customers, the Birds were themselves perpetual debtors. Notations of payments on account for their own family purchases appear alongside the short-term loans and extended lines of credit that sustained their business activities. Late payments of rent and rates recur throughout the diary: George junior's relief when he was able (uncharacteristically) to pay the rent in full in 1873 – 'thank God that's over' – was palpable. The reciprocal nature of debt relations, however, reduced the imperative for prompt and full repayment substantially. Many of the Birds' creditors were also their customers, and the family's unpaid financial obligations thus constituted bonds that united debtors and creditors rather than purely contractual relations that distinguished them from each other. When George junior paid John Hannam for two years' unpaid rates, he noted that Hannam 'had a bill [owed to the Birds] against it for 2 l. 2 so it relaxed it'. This mutual indebtedness fostered credit relations that extended long beyond annual billing cycles. 'I went to Hannam's, he & I had a settling', Bird recorded in 1874. 'I had 37/11 to draw, never had one [a settling] since 1860'.[136] Rather than an expedient to which only devious bankrupts and insolvents would resort, failure to render full payment at the point of purchase or upon presentation of a bill was a commonplace of eighteenth- and nineteenth-century market practice.

Debt collection and the law

Sociability, personal negotiations and extended credit were normative in the consumer markets recalled and recounted in English diaries and autobiographies of the modern period. Consumers' resistance to anonymous cash exchange ensured that credit contracts figured in English memory and imagination (and functioned in English markets) as ongoing social relations rather than as purely contractual agreements. Processes of debt collection were in turn shaped fundamentally by the social character of credit relations. Framed by coercive legal mechanisms, the enforcement of credit contracts was repeatedly mitigated in the practice of everyday life by contemporaries' reluctance to countenance notions of strict contract and individual liability. Retail sociability did not preclude resort to the law: diarists and autobiographers who recognised that credit relations entailed social obligations number among the men and women who turned to

---

[135] Ibid., 185 (17 October 1871); 159 (23 November 1870).
[136] Ibid., 230 (7 May 1873); 227 (20 March 1873); 248 (4 March 1874).

Debt and credit in diaries and autobiographies

the courts when their debtors refused to pay their accounts. But the pervasive extent, fluid boundaries and social character of retail credit did temper the legal claims of contract. In doing so, these everyday meanings and practices worked to channel attitudes toward courts and prisons along equitable lines of moral reasoning familiar from the pages of the English novels.

Until the later nineteenth century, when retailers began to establish specialised debt-collecting associations, tradesmen's ability to extract payment from recalcitrant credit customers – already constrained by the norms of retail etiquette – was restricted further by limitations of time, transport, profit and personnel. Although chequebooks enabled elite Victorian and Edwardian consumers to pay bills by post, cash payment of credit accounts (requiring payment in person) remained standard retail practice. References to 'money hunting' expeditions undertaken by tradesmen on foot, horseback and by train pervade diaries and memoirs, as do disappointed notations that debtors had gone into hiding or removed surreptitiously to a new address.[137] In a retail environment dominated by small family businesses, debt collection placed considerable strain on labour resources within the shop. As a child, Mrs Scott of Stockport had been dispatched unhappily on Saturday afternoons to collect debts for her parents' drapery shop, developing 'a horror of debt' that underpinned her later advocacy of the co-operative movement.[138] Bill-paying trips made to shops by consumers possessed obvious advantages over infant debt collectors to tradesmen, but left them at the mercy of their customers' whims, schedules and perseverance. Heavy rain prevented Dorothy Daubney and her father from walking to town to pay one creditor in February 1907; Daubney called twice to pay her dressmaker's bill in July before she was able to find the tradeswoman at home.[139] Episodic and partial payment flourished in these conditions, which also reinforced the sociable dimensions of retail trade by inserting debt collection processes into domestic settings. In London, the footman William Tayler paid his tailor's bill in 1837 and also 'drank a few glasses of wine with him'; Hannah Cullwick's mistress gave the local fish-woman 'a bottle o' beer as well' when she paid her bill in 1872.[140]

When treating, cajoling and dunning all proved unavailing, creditors turned with reluctance to the law. Thomas Turner initiated legal action against debtor Darby in 1758 only when his mother – also a shopkeeper – warned him that

[137] See, for example, ibid., 7 (19 January 1865); Vaisey, ed., *Diary of Thomas Turner*, 171 (7 January 1759); Diary of Jonas Asplin, in Brown, ed., *Essex People*, 134 (3 January 1826).
[138] Davies, ed., *Life as We Have Known It*, 82.
[139] Gloucestershire RO, D5130/9/7, Dorothy Daubney Diary, 19 February, 13 and 16 July 1907.
[140] Dorothy Wise, ed., *Diary of William Tayler, Footman* (London, 1962), 10 (3 January 1837); Stanley, ed., *Diaries of Hannah Cullwick*, 214 (24 April 1872). A pedlar who plied his wares toward the end of the century similarly recalled that he enjoyed 'an abundance of free food' from customers. William Henry Davies, *The Autobiography of a Super-Tramp* (London, 1908), 266.

100   Debt and credit in English memory and imagination

Darby would soon be imprisoned for his debts by other creditors. 'Oh, what confusion and tumult there is in my breast about this affair!', Turner lamented. 'To think what a terrible thing it is to arrest a person, for by this means he may be entirely torn to pieces, who might otherwise recover himself and pay everyone their own.' The factors that militated against allowing Darby – whose debt had been due for over three years – further leeway reveal the significance of custom and connection in retail credit relations. Darby's family had 'quite forsaken' Turner's shop, trading instead with shopkeepers in nearby Lewes, while his wife and daughters enjoyed an extravagant lifestyle, suggesting that they, 'instead of getting out of debt, go farther in'. Despite these justifying circumstances, Turner remained 'prodigious uneasy' that by going to law he had gone beyond 'what is consistent with self-preservation and the laws of equity'.[141]

Turner was hardly exceptional in his distaste for the use of legal means to enforce contracts. 'I do not much admire the law for incarcerating Persons for debt', Robert Sharp noted acerbically in 1827.[142] In keeping with these sentiments, diarists' representations of individual liability and the sanctity of contract were more often equivocal than univalent. George Bird and his father resorted to the county court when their debtors could not be convinced to render payment by less coercive means. But Bird's diary is also punctuated with expressions of sympathy for debtors caught up in the tentacles of law. The draper Mason suffered bankruptcy and had his goods seized for auction by the bailiffs – 'very harassing for the poor fellow', as Bird commented in his diary – but Mason and his family remained securely within the embrace of neighbourly sociability. Mrs Bird attended Mrs Mason at her confinement in October; the Mason's infant son lay in Mrs Bird's arms when he died a month later.[143] And if quotidian gifting behaviours faded in later nineteenth-century plebeian culture, exceptional gifts and loans rendered to stave off the bailiff or the prison remained integral to the survival strategies of the poor. In East London in the 1890s, neighbours offered Walter Southgate's family temporary loans – including a sum raised by one friend who pawned her wedding ring – to save their furniture from the bailiffs; 'unfortunate' consumers who fell into debt in late Victorian Salford were also assisted by charitable initiatives undertaken by their neighbours.[144] Inability to pay debts was, in these circumstances, hardly an indelible blot on the debtor's character.

Hostility to the so-called 'bum-bailiffs' who executed the law upon the debtor's goods or person was widespread in English culture, both reflecting

---

[141] Vaisey, ed., *Diary of Thomas Turner*, 149 (21–22 May 1758).

[142] Crowther and Crowther, eds., *Diary of Robert Sharp*, 115 (10 March 1827).

[143] For their use of the county courts to recover debts, see, for example, Liddie, ed., *Diary of George Bird*, 10–11 (18 February 1865); 187 (6 November 1871); 249 (14 March 1874).

[144] Walter Southgate, *That's the Way It Was: A Working Class Autobiography 1890–1950* (Oxford, 1982), 23; Roberts, *Classic Slum*, 33.

Debt and credit in diaries and autobiographies

and buttressing reluctance to resort to legal instruments to recover payments. Robert Sharp recorded with barely suppressed glee that when Michael Clegg, 'Bum Bailiff to Teavil Leesom' sought to arrest Tommy Shaw, 'he was saluted by Tommy's wife with Fire poker and tongs', and had to defend himself with a chair.[145] The Cornish grocer George Trezise succeeded in outrunning the bailiffs who arrived to arrest him in May 1843; his capture at an inn six months later provoked a minor riot for which eight young men who had defended Trezise were charged with assault.[146] The barrister A.G.C. Liddell served on a government committee on county-court practice in 1899, and watched in horror as advocates of the introduction of pensions for process-servers submitted 'a collection of the weapons to which they are exposed' to support their claims. 'This was of varied character, and consisted of axes, clubs, pokers, rods, weights, and a large flat-iron, the last named having been dropped on a bailiff's head', Liddell noted in his diary.[147]

Significantly, antagonism to the debt law extended from debtors to the personnel of the courts. Diaries and memoirs reveal the extent to which judges and their family members were themselves ensnared by personal debts, a circumstance that could moderate their zeal for the letter of the law of contract. Charles Whitmore's persistent lobbying for a county-court appointment in the 1850s was driven by economic exigency. 'God be thanked for this huge good!', he exalted when the Lord Chancellor at last selected him to preside as judge at the Southwark county court. 'I am relieved from all anxiety about my finances for the future.'[148] Although legal reforms sharply diminished the likelihood that middle-class debtors would suffer imprisonment for debt after the 1860s, the high incidence of retail debt and credit ensured that county-court practice continued to be informed by personal fears and experiences of the debt law. Worried reflections on his own debts and those of his children recur in the diary of H.T. Atkinson. Active in mitigating the full force of the law to the advantage of plebeian debtors in his court at Leeds, the judge owed debts valued at over a thousand pounds, and dipped repeatedly into his pockets to pay county-court judgments rendered against his feckless son Alfred at the behest of butchers, grocers and landlords.[149]

---

[145] Crowther and Crowther, eds., *Diary of Robert Sharp*, 227 (12 October 1829).

[146] Richard G. Grylls, ed., *A Cornish Shopkeeper's Diary 1843: The Diary of Henry Grylls Thomas, Draper and Grocer of St Just-in-Penwith, Cornwall, and Thirteen Letters Written to His Wife between 1846 and 1854* (Mount Hawke, 1997), 58 (19 May 1843); 104–5 (24 October 1843); 106 (1 November 1843).

[147] A.G.C. Liddell, *Notes from the Life of an Ordinary Mortal: Being the Record of Things Done, Seen and Heard at School, College, and in the World during the Latter Half of the 19th Century* (London, 1911), 319 (8 June 1899).

[148] Gloucestershire RO, D45 F48/2, Diary of Charles Shapland Whitmore, 22 February 1857.

[149] Atkinson diary, 332 (31 July 1878); 350 (18 August 1878); 369 (6 September 1878); 404 (11 October 1878). For his mitigation of the law in his own court, see below, chap. 7.

102   Debt and credit in English memory and imagination

Publication of autobiographical memoirs written by small claims court personnel served to circulate officials' reservations about the extent of their coercive powers in the public sphere. The memoir of William Hutton, who presided over the late eighteenth-century Birmingham court of requests and championed its equitable style of justice, provided a much-read model of judicial self-fashioning along these lines. 'I considered the suitors as my children; and when any of this vast family looked up to me for peace and justice, I have distributed both with pleasure', Hutton reminisced.[150] Repeated parliamentary investigations into imprisonment for debt encouraged later Victorian and Edwardian county-court judges to incorporate such equitable reasoning into their diatribes against the imprisonment of merely 'unfortunate' debtors. Judge J.D. Crawford was careful to distinguish the debtors who appeared before him in the county courts from the defendants brought before the police courts. Whereas police-court cases were 'mainly concerned with drunken and disorderlies, and criminals of various types and degrees', he recalled, the debtor clientele of the county court was 'altogether different', comprising the 'very poor, very unfortunate, very foolish, and very stupid'.[151] Edward Abbott Parry, judge of the Manchester county court denounced the unscrupulous business practices of the money-lenders and credit drapers who brought plebeian debtors to his court, concluding that 'The law as it stands assists the knave at the expense of the fool.' Imprisonment for debt, Parry insisted in tones that recalled the diatribes against the debt law in Benjamin Haydon's diary, was a vestige of medieval life that sustained a system of false credit inimical to the debtor's character. 'The whole thing turns of course upon imprisonment for debt', he observed of county-court business. 'Without imprisonment for debt there would be little credit given, except to persons of good character, and good character would be an asset.'[152]

Conclusion

Judge Parry's invocation of character highlights a central tension within consumer credit relations, the troublingly unstable relations among debt, credit, character and connection. Contemporaries agreed that a fundamental nexus obtained between personal character and personal credit, but the inherent fluidity of these systems of identity, meaning and exchange thwarted the construction

---

[150] William Hutton, *The Life of William Hutton, Stationer, of Birmingham; and the History of His Family* (London, 1841), 45–6. The popularity and impact of Hutton's memoir are attested by, for example, C.P. Fendall and E.A. Crutchley, eds., *The Diary of Benjamin Newton: Rector of Wroth 1816–1818* (Cambridge, 1933), 131 (26 February 1818): 'Having read Hutton's life of himself which afforded me much amusement I mean to get a book and attempt something of the kind.'

[151] J.D. Crawford, *Reflections and Recollections* (London, 1936), 135–6.

[152] Edward Abbott Parry, *Judgments in Vacation* (London, 1911), 107, 56–7.

Debt and credit in diaries and autobiographies 103

of stable interpretations of consumer characters. To be sure, diarists and autobiographers at times advocated strict notions of contractual liability, casting aspersions on debtors for their lack of self-control and self respect. When James Woodforde learned that his acquaintance Walker was 'a profligate abandoned young man' whose creditors had issued writs for his arrest, he determined 'to break every Connection' with Walker and his associate, Mrs Davy. Concerned that his niece's 'Character (being too intimate with Miss Davy) is not talked of so well', Woodforde now cautioned Nancy 'to drop her Acquaintance by all means, which if she does not (after their Characters are so well known) she will disoblige me as much as she possibly can do'.[153] The Lancashire mechanic Benjamin Shaw, writing his memoir in the 1820s and 1830s, similarly underlined the necessary interrelation of character, debt and credit. Shaw's wife Betty was a poor household manager, trading on credit with drapers and shopkeepers and pawning the family's goods when she had exhausted other credit resources. Shaw blamed this flaw in her 'Characture' [sic] to an absence of natural female pride, which served in other women 'to Stirr [sic] them up to care & diligence, to get & save all that they can to appear respectable, & to be independant [sic], & free from any obligation'.[154] Like gift obligations, consumer credit was understood to entail servility and to curtail personal independence. Maintaining a sense of autonomy in the market posed a constant challenge to debtors in this context. Samuel Bamford, reduced by penury to purchasing a shoulder of lamb on credit, feared for his good character. 'This is much against my ideas of rectitude', he observed; 'it seems shabby, shifty, and I feel humiliated.'[155]

Bamford's diary itself, however, offers abundant testimony of the unstable character of personal debt and credit in English culture. Only months earlier, in debating the sanctity of debt obligations with friends, Bamford had cited 'Christ's directions for Salvation' by reading 'that portion of Christ's Sermon on the Mount. Matt. ch. 6: viz "And forgive us our debts, as we forgive our debtors"'.[156] Here Bamford invoked a line of moral reasoning that surfaced again and again in English diaries, memoirs and novels, undercutting notions of personal liability by numbering debt among the 'misfortunes' to which fallen mankind was necessarily prone. The Reverend James Newton, reflecting on 'misfortune' in 1761, observed that 'In our most prosperous State we are in danger of an adverse Fortune & therefore we should not depend too much on it, but act with Caution & Prudence in all our Affairs & leave the event of them in the hand of Providence.'[157] Newton's sentiments were widely current

[153] Beresford, ed., *Woodforde*, 300 (28 January 1790); 301 (30 January 1790); 302 (3 March 1790).
[154] Alan G. Crosby, ed., *The Family Records of Benjamin Shaw, Mechanic of Dent, Dolphinholme and Preston, 1772–1841*, Transactions of the Record Society of Lancashire and Cheshire, 130 (1991), 76.
[155] Hewitt and Poole, eds., *Diaries of Samuel Bamford*, 128 (8 July 1859).
[156] Ibid., 122 (18 June 1859). [157] Newton diary, 21 (7 July 1761).

104   Debt and credit in English memory and imagination

in Georgian culture, extending to encompass a capacious range of 'unfortunate' debtors. James Gatliff, who had indulged in gambling and duelling as a young man and accepted ordination as an Anglican priest in 1801 to secure an income, lived well beyond his means, fell badly into debt and was imprisoned in the Fleet. When Gatliff was liberated from the prison and wrote to his bishop to resume his living in Cheshire, the prelate responded that he 'did not consider the interests of religion in my parish would be promoted by my immediate return'. But Gatliff's parishioners evidently subscribed to a different understanding of the morality of personal debt and credit and petitioned the bishop for his restoration.[158]

For writers of diaries, memoirs and novels, debts provided both tests of personal character and texts upon which the individual's own identity could be inscribed. Benjamin Haydon returned constantly to these dual functions in his diary, adducing his financial plight as both the sign and the impetus of his artistic talent. In this as in his wider representations of character and credit, Haydon's experiences and sentiments, if extravagant in degree, echoed the life stories of a wide spectrum of less exceptional English men and women. Patrick Joyce, analysing the diary kept by the plebeian journalist and author Edwin Waugh, identifies sorrow – both economic and psychic – as 'the medium of his emerging selfhood', the means by which Waugh came to understand and exercise his 'character' and 'independence'.[159] Like Haydon's unpaid bills, Waugh's debts provided a material cause for his sorrow, but one which refused to remain within purely economic bounds. Stalked by 'that demon debt', Waugh celebrated the superior merits of 'the wealth of the true spirit' only to be confounded by the thraldom entailed by the sheer poverty of his day-to-day existence. 'O thou who hast an independent spirit, and wouldst hold thyself in all things in the honorable attitude of manly freedom, beware Debt', Waugh raged impotently. 'Shun Sin and Debt . . . If thou wouldst walk erect, beware of these.'[160]

Where credit relations insistently called attention to debtors' subordination to creditors and individuals' submersion in the social, cash sales promised to liberate consumer and retailer alike from the tyranny of character. The bookseller James Lackington, whom Michael Mascuch has advanced as the quintessential exemplar of English autobiographical individualism, sought to break decisively with retail convention in 1780 by refusing credit even 'to the most respectable characters'. This tactic, which proved immensely successful for Lackington himself, was greeted with ridicule by his fellow tradesmen, who 'thought that

---

[158] H.E. Gatliff, ed., *Stations, Gentlemen! Memoirs of James Gatliff* (London, 1938), 99, 153, 186, 273, 274–5, 281, 284–7, 291.

[159] Patrick Joyce, *Democratic Subjects: The Self and the Social in Nineteenth-Century England* (Cambridge, 1994), 24, 19.

[160] Manchester Central Reference Library, Diary of Edwin Waugh, 36 (14 August 1847); 33 (13 August 1847); 111–12 (9 September 1848).

I might as well rebuild the tower of Babel'.[161] The reluctance (and inability) of most tradesmen and consumers to follow Lackington's lead and substitute cash for credit payments played a decisive part in shaping attitudes to debt, understandings of character and experiences of individualism in modern England. Retail innovations such as cash sales, fixed prices, department stores and anonymous transactions all played an important role in accommodating the market to the constant influx of new goods generated by the industrial and consumer revolutions. Yet each of these strategies existed alongside more traditional modes of selling goods on credit. By emphasising the modern over the traditional features of the commercial landscape, by privileging the history of the cash nexus, scholars have overlooked the extent to which earlier norms of trade endured together with – and at times were lent new life by – the advent of more modern marketing practices. In doing so, they have obscured the myriad ways in which the practice of everyday life shaped and restricted contemporaries' constructions of meaningful self-identities (and enforceable contracts) in the course of the long nineteenth century.

[161] James Lackington, *Memoirs of the First Forty-Five Years of the Life of James Lackington*, 2nd edn (London, 1792), 335, 337, 336. See also Michael Mascuch, *Origins of the Individualist Self: Autobiography and Self-Identity in England, 1591–1791* (Stanford, 1996).

Part II

Imprisonment for debt and the
economic individual

3 'Mansions of misery': the unreformed debtors' prison

The century from 1760 to 1860 saw the birth of the penitentiary, but it also witnessed an efflorescence of the unreformed debtors' prison. In criminal law, a proliferation of penal statutes, an increasing reluctance to execute felons convicted of capital offences and the government's inability to transport convicts to the former American colonies combined to promote a dramatic growth of the English prison population. In civil law, the creation of a plethora of local small-claims jurisdictions, the impact of commercialisation and successive waves of economic crisis spurred by rapid economic growth similarly contributed to a significant increase in the number of imprisoned debtors – historically, the largest category of inmate in English gaols. By the Victorian era, the criminal component of the prison's burgeoning population had clearly gained ascendancy. Now numerically dominant among inmates, convicted prisoners monopolised penal ideology, marking prison life with an intrusive, reformatory impress largely foreign to the eighteenth-century experience of incarceration. But although disciplinary mechanisms designed for criminals ultimately prevailed in penal policy, their rise to even ideological dominance was halting, piecemeal and hotly contested. Like fictional representation of civil imprisonment, archival records of debtors' prisons suggest the limitations of change over time. Just as the expansion of consumer markets multiplied the personal credit connections between creditors and debtors, so too, for decades, did the protracted evolution of criminal incarceration allow the customary privileges and convivial conventions of the debtors' prison to persist (and even to expand) in the interstices of the emerging penal complex. Thus the institutional framework designed to discipline a growing body of convicted criminals also served to harbour an increasingly conspicuous population of unreformed, unrepentant and largely unrestrained insolvent debtors in English gaols.

Custodial confinement

Medieval and early modern practices of imprisonment contributed substantially to debtors' prolonged success in combating the criminal penitentiary's encroachment on their conventional rights. In striking contrast to their modern

110   Imprisonment for debt and the economic individual

usage, gaols were originally intended primarily to secure the safe custody of inmates' bodies, rather than to exact retribution for their past trespasses or reform their future conduct. In practice, this purely custodial principle was subject to constant violation, not least because the objectionable conditions of prison confinement often rendered even nominally custodial sentences effectively punitive. But the medieval definition of the prison as a place principally of safe custody was none the less of central importance in shaping the institutional culture of the English gaol. By constructing the prison primarily as a custodial site, successive political regimes encouraged prison-keepers to concentrate their energies on preventing escapes from penal institutions, rather than on regulating behaviour within them.[1]

Imprisonment for debt played an essential part in maintaining this custodial definition of incarceration over time. Practiced in ancient Babylonia, classical Athens and republican Rome,[2] confinement for debts owed to the Crown had entered English statute law by the reign of Henry II. But it was subsequent legislation extending this practice to private creditors that secured debtors a preponderant and enduring place in the English prison population. In 1283 the statute of Acton Burnell allowed merchant creditors to compel debtors to acknowledge their liabilities before a town mayor, and to distrain debtors' goods or imprison their bodies should they subsequently default on these obligations. Legislation of 1352 increased these powers dramatically, authorising creditors to arrest and imprison the bodies of debtors who had made no public acknowledgment of their liabilities, and to continue this custody until the captives agreed to settle their accounts. 'From this statute', Ralph Pugh observes, 'sprang all the imprisonings for debt, all the debtors' prisons or debtors' wards, and all the lamentations which they brought in their train.'[3]

Significantly, the statutes of 1283 and 1352 neither defined the debtor as a criminal nor interpreted debt itself as a crime at common law. Precluding the active punishment of debtors, this custodial interpretation of imprisonment for debt survived the complex legal reforms which, by the eighteenth century, had created a three-tiered system of bankruptcy, insolvency and small debt litigation in the English courts. Bankruptcy proceedings, restricted by law to merchants and traders who owed substantial sums, allowed substantial commercial men both to avoid imprisonment and to extinguish their debts in full by forfeiting

---

[1] Séan McConville, *A History of English Prison Administration*, vol. I: *1750–1877* (London, 1981), esp. 1–9 provides an excellent synopsis of the functions of the medieval prison. See also Ralph B. Pugh, *Imprisonment in Medieval England* (Cambridge, 1979).

[2] Edward M. Peters, 'Prison before the prison: the ancient and medieval worlds', in Norval Morris and David J. Rothman, eds., *The Oxford History of the Prison: The Practice of Punishment in Western Society* (Oxford, 1995), 10, 7–8, 14–15.

[3] Pugh, *Imprisonment in Medieval England*, 5, 45–6, citation from 46.

'Mansions of misery' 111

their goods for sale and paying a dividend to their creditors.[4] Persons who owed sums of forty shillings or more but were unable to declare bankruptcy (either because they failed to meet the definition of 'merchant or tradesman' or because their commercial debts were too small to meet the requirements of the statute) fell instead within the purview of the insolvency law. Creditors of these insolvent debtors were empowered by statute to initiate a suit in any one of the metropolitan superior civil courts or the borough courts of record, and so obtain the power to arrest the debtor's person. Debtors unable to obtain bail were committed to prison to await trial, a process known as 'imprisonment on mesne process'. Creditors who subsequently succeeded in proving their debts in court – as the vast majority succeeded in doing[5] – could choose between two legal options. They could 'execute against the goods' of the debtor, a process that entailed the seizure and sale at auction of the debtor's moveable chattels, or they could 'execute against the person' by detaining the debtor in prison until payment was effected, a procedure known as 'imprisonment on final process'.[6] Debtors owing sums of less than forty shillings were subject instead to summons by their creditors to appear in local courts of conscience (also known as courts of requests). Here, if impressed by the merits of the creditor's case, a judge or commissioners would order payment either forthwith or in a series of instalments. As in the superior debt courts, failure to meet such payments empowered inferior court officials to execute against either the debtor's chattels or body. In contrast to common-law insolvents, however, terms of imprisonment for these petty debtors were, from the 1780s, limited by the amount of the debt, and completion of a set prison term liquidated the debt in full.[7]

Prohibiting the seizure of debtors' lands and monies, the mechanisms of 'execution' created by successive insolvency and small-claims statutes endowed creditors with broad and arbitrary powers of arrest, but conferred only limited means with which to extract payment from recalcitrant debtors upon judgment. Affluent insolvents content to suffer imprisonment could – and did – subsist on rents, income and savings within the prison walls in defiance of their creditors.

---

[4] The evolution of imprisonment and bankruptcy legislation is usefully summarised by Jay Cohen, 'The history of imprisonment for debt and its relation to the discharge in bankruptcy', *Journal of Legal History*, 3, 2 (September 1982), 153–71.

[5] Between 1823 and 1827, creditors obtained favourable judgments in 97.5 per cent of cases in the King's Bench, 97.8 per cent in Common Pleas and 96.3 per cent in Exchequer. See Clinton W. Francis, 'Practice, strategy and institution: debt collection in the English common-law courts, 1740–1840', *Northwestern Law Review*, 80, 4 (Winter 1986), 824.

[6] Joanna Innes, 'The King's Bench Prison in the later eighteenth century: law, authority and order in a London debtors' prison', in John Brewer and John Styles, eds., *An Ungovernable People: The English and Their Law in the Seventeenth and Eighteenth Centuries* (New Brunswick, 1980), 252–3 provides the best succinct exposition of these labyrinthine processes.

[7] For imprisonment by courts of conscience, see W.H.D. Winder, 'The courts of requests', *Law Quarterly Review*, 207 (1936), 369–94.

112 Imprisonment for debt and the economic individual

In theory, execution against the chattels offered a viable alternative to execution against the body, but in practice a variety of factors made the prospect of compelling payment through extended (or indefinite) periods of imprisonment more appealing to many creditors than seizure of the debtor's goods. Debtors' tendency to disperse their chattels among friends and family in anticipation of the arrival of the bailiffs reduced the efficacy of execution against the goods, a process which was further complicated by the frequent presence of more than a single generation of adults within the home. When John Satchell, an officer of London's Palace Court, sought to execute against the goods of debtor Bramwell in 1844, Bramwell's son insisted that the property was his own, and summoned a policeman to eject Satchell from the house.[8]

As wealth and financial obligations multiplied in the industrial, commercial and consumer revolutions, imprisoned debtors increasingly crowded the prisons of England and its expanding empire. When John Howard conducted his investigations of English and Welsh gaols in the later eighteenth century, he found that debtors constituted roughly half – and convicted felons only a quarter – of all prison inmates.[9] Debtors likewise figured prominently in colonial prison populations stretching from the Atlantic seaboard to Bengal. The New Gaol built in New York in 1757–58 continued to serve as a debtors' prison – that 'unhappy mansion', 'that dismal cage', as contemporaries called it – for decades after the colonists had gained independence from British rule.[10] In Calcutta, 16 European and 238 'native' debtors were committed to prison in the East India Company's gaol at Fort William between 20 December 1796 and 20 December 1797. The number of criminal commitments to the prison in this interval reached only the relatively modest figure of 149.[11]

Although the prison conditions experienced by debtors were shaped by medieval norms of custodial confinement into and beyond the eighteenth century,

---

[8] PRO, PALA 9/1/27, Satchell v. Bramwell, 8 March 1844. See similarly PRO, HO 45/971, East Riding of the County of York, to wit: the several informations of George Gray of North Ferriby.

[9] John Howard, *The State of the Prisons of England and Wales, with Preliminary Observations, and an Account of Some Foreign Prisons and Hospitals*, 4th edn (London, 1792), 492. Most continental states also developed mechanisms for imprisoning the debtor's body: in sixteenth-century Italy roughly half of all prison inmates were debtors. See Nicholas Terpstra, 'Confraternal prison charity and political consolidation in sixteenth-century Bologna', *JMH*, 66, 2 (June 1994), 237.

[10] Bruce H. Mann, 'Tales from the crypt: prison, legal authority, and the debtors' constitution in the early Republic', *William and Mary Quarterly*, 3rd ser., 51, 2 (April 1994), 183–202, citations from 184.

[11] British Library, India Office, Home Misc. series, H/420, 'First Section of the Statistical Report', Fort William, Calcutta, 26 October 1798, fols. 311, 314. For the evolution of imprisonment for debt in the American colonies and the republic, see P.J. Coleman, *Debtors and Creditors in America: Insolvency, Imprisonment for Debt and Bankruptcy, 1607–1900* (Madison, 1974). The use of human bodies as security for debts in the English slave trade, an extreme variation of this instance of legal imperialism, is detailed by Paul E. Lovejoy and David Richardson, 'Trust, pawnship, and Atlantic history: the institutional foundations of the Old Calabar slave trade', *American Historical Review*, 104, 2 (April 1999), 333–55.

'Mansions of misery' 113

these established precepts did not entirely monopolise penal thinking before the rise of the penitentiary. From the later sixteenth century, a new and initially parallel series of carceral institutions, so-called bridewells or houses of correction, emerged in the commercial centres of western Europe. Designed specifically to contain and improve the lower orders, houses of correction were intended to address the problems of vagrancy, sloth and petty crime by setting the poor to work within a disciplined institutional context.[12] In its English inflection, the bridewell served to mediate the decline of personal servitude and the rise of contractual labour relations, helping to impress unwilling workers with the relative virtues of 'voluntary' participation in the labour market. By the later eighteenth century, England boasted perhaps 170 houses of correction. Here vagrants, pedlars, bawds and disturbers of the common peace were to be confined, whipped and set to work.[13] Fuelled by economic expansion, the bridewell system was framed and sustained by changes in legal practice that presaged the eighteenth- and nineteenth-century proliferation of summary small-claims litigation. From the seventeenth century, local justices' ability to convict an escalating range of petty offenders without jury trials provided houses of correction with an ever-expanding population of prisoners.[14]

Juridically distinct from the county and city gaols to which they were often linked by both architecture and administration, houses of correction existed at the periphery of the prison system and the penumbra of penal consciousness until the reformative claims of their advocates began to capture new attention in the later eighteenth century. By 1865, the corrective principles embodied in bridewells had successfully penetrated the wider prison network, encouraging the government to create a new category of 'local prisons' forged from the merging of local gaols and houses of correction.[15] But in the interim, the existence of bridewells arguably served as much to preserve as to undercut dominant contemporary understandings of the custodial function of imprisonment for debt. By segregating petty criminals in their own distinctive institutions, bridewells inadvertently bolstered superior-court debtors' immunity from coercive discipline in borough gaols and county prisons.[16]

---

[12] Pieter Spierenburg, 'The sociogenesis of confinement and its development in early modern Europe', in Pieter Spierenburg, ed., *The Emergence of Carceral Institutions: Prisons, Galleys and Lunatic Asylums 1550–1900* (Rotterdam, 1984), 9–77, esp. 16–22; idem, *The Prison Experience: Disciplinary Institutions and Their Inmates in Early Modern Europe* (New Brunswick, 1991).

[13] Joanna Innes, 'Prisons for the poor: English bridewells, 1555–1800', in Francis Snyder and Douglas Hay, eds., *Labour, Law and Crime: An Historical Perspective* (London, 1987), 46, 62, 86–7.

[14] Robert B. Shoemaker, *Prosecutions and Punishment: Petty Crime and the Law in London and Rural Middlesex, c. 1660–1725* (Cambridge, 1991), 166–97.

[15] Innes, 'Prisons for the poor', 42, 94.

[16] The commitment of some small-claims debtors to houses of correction blurred this line of demarcation, but did not (until the 1840s) erase it, most notably because this confinement was not accompanied by labour. See below, chap. 4.

114   Imprisonment for debt and the economic individual

If the impact of bridewells on the prison conditions experienced by insolvents was initially muted, the sharp increase in prison commitments that marked the later eighteenth and nineteenth centuries was, for debtors, of immediate significance. In criminal law, the century from 1660 saw the rapid growth of secondary punishments such as penitential incarceration. 'By the 1790s incarceration was the common punishment for offenses against property that did not involve some particularly heinous aggravation', John Beattie observes, 'and imprisonment under the right conditions carried the hopes of many for a punishment that would not only penalize the offender and deter him and others but also reform and rehabilitate him in such a way as to make possible his return to society and to home and employment.'[17] The sheer size of this increase in imprisoned convicts placed considerable strain on the fabric of the prison system: 4,446 criminals were committed to gaols in England and Wales in 1768, but 16,147 were imprisoned in 1787.[18]

Against this background, the timing of the later eighteenth-century rise in bankruptcy, insolvency and small-claims litigation rates was, for imprisoned debtors, less than propitious. The average number of bankrupts, which stood at only 44.9 per year in the decade from 1691 to 1700, had increased to 210.2 annually by 1751–60, and rose to 762.7 per year in 1791–1800.[19] Because bankruptcy procedures were designed to effect the equitable distribution of the bankrupt's goods rather than the seizure of his body, this increase served to heighten public alarm about the dangers of commercial debt rather than to swell the prison population. But a parallel rise in both superior-court insolvency proceedings and small-claims cases in the new courts of conscience produced sharp increases in the number of imprisoned debtors in these decades. An estimated 3,814 persons were imprisoned for debt in England and Wales in 1759, but at least 5,333 debtors suffered imprisonment in 1769 and 8,238 in 1779.[20]

Although national statistics for this period are elusive and unreliable, the later eighteenth and early nineteenth centuries clearly witnessed an increase of imprisoned debtors that outpaced even the rapid growth of the general population.[21] Commitment figures from individual gaols, which are often more accurate than available national statistics, help to convey a sense of the impact

---

[17] J.M. Beattie, *Crime and the Courts in England 1660–1800* (Princeton, 1986), 601.

[18] Ian P.H. Duffy, *Bankruptcy and Insolvency in London during the Industrial Revolution* (New York, 1985), 372.

[19] Julian Hoppit, *Risk and Failure in English Business 1700–1800* (Cambridge, 1987), 46.

[20] Duffy, *Bankruptcy and Insolvency*, 372.

[21] McConville, *History of English Prison Administration*, 223, discusses the limitations of national statistics compiled before 1840, and their tendency in particular to neglect the smaller local prisons. Peter J. Lineham, 'The campaign to abolish imprisonment for debt in England, 1750–1840' (M.A. thesis, University of Canterbury, NZ, 1974), 60, details the rise of insolvents within the general demographic expansion.

'Mansions of misery' 115

that this growth exerted on prisons at a local level. The King's Bench prison in London, which drew inmates entangled in superior-court litigation from across the nation, received 615 debtors in 1750, 1,098 in 1770 and 2,590 in 1788. At Lancaster Castle, which held inmates from Manchester and its industrialising hinterland, the number of debtor committals rose from 162 in 1798 to 319 in 1808 and 526 in 1818. The Borough Compter, in which petty debtors drawn from London's teeming labouring population were imprisoned by the Southwark court of requests, received 53 debtors in 1809, 381 in 1814 and 730 in 1818.[22] The contemporary rise of criminal commitments compounded the task confronting prison administrators who grappled with the pragmatic effects of these increases, and ensured that perceptions of the explosion of the imprisoned debtor population were coloured by fears of a rising tide of crime.

Prison structures

Unlike the Victorian penitentiary, which looms in the historical imagination as an impregnable, hulking fortress, the unreformed prisons that housed the expanding population of insolvents and petty debtors were characterised above all else by their fluid and porous boundaries.[23] Execution against the body was often a protracted process, a series of strategic moves and counter-moves that afforded insolvents a variety of opportunities for prevarication, negotiation and even outright escape. The dilemmas of George Scott, a Palace Court bailiff, testify to the ingenuity displayed by debtors intent to evade the prison. Attempting to seize William Lewis of Stamford Hill in 1826, Scott arrested a character 'who represented himself to be the said William Lewis and who when informed of the purport of the said George Scott's visit voluntarily surrendered himself as the right Defendant and came away to town with the said George Scott'. Having drawn Scott away from Stamford Hill, the prisoner, presumably a friend of the insolvent Lewis, revealed his true identity as William Clements, and succeeded in extracting five pounds from the bailiff by threatening to sue him for false imprisonment.[24] Debtors who lacked such resourceful associates typically relied upon personal mobility to evade execution against the body. The flight by the young Anthony Trollope's family to Belgium in the nineteenth century was

[22] Duffy, *Bankruptcy and Insolvency*, 372; Margaret DeLacy, *Prison Reform in Lancashire, 1700–1850: A Study in Local Administration* (Manchester, 1986), 61; CLRO, SC 2/6, Southwark Compter Register, 1809–18; CLRO, Letterbook of John Law, Keeper of Southwark Compter, 1819, fol. 27.

[23] For the character of the unreformed prison, see also John Bender, *Imagining the Penitentiary: Fiction and the Architecture of Mind in Eighteenth-Century England* (Chicago, 1987), esp. 13–16, and Robin Evans, *The Fabrication of Virtue: English Prison Architecture, 1750–1840* (Cambridge, 1982), esp. 11–40.

[24] See PRO, PALA 9/3, George Scott's letter, responding to complaints against his conduct, 16 September 1826.

116   Imprisonment for debt and the economic individual

only one instance in an extended tradition of evasion upheld by generations of English debtors, who secured their persons from arrest by removing to Ireland or the Continent.[25] In eighteenth-century London, debtors unable or unwilling to travel such distances could avail themselves of the various privileged sanctuaries within which, by statute or tradition, they were immune from arrest for their debts. Most famous was 'the Verge of the Court' surrounding Whitehall and St James, which sheltered both the novelist Henry Fielding and his fictional protagonist Captain Booth in the 1740s. Here a host of profiteering lodging-house keepers served a shifting population of beleaguered insolvents, providing a safe (if costly) haven in the very heart of the metropolis against the execution of the law.[26]

Once secured by a bailiff, the debtor entered an institutional matrix that was as various as the inmate population it served. Lock-up houses were first among the congeries of structures that confronted the metropolitan insolvent committed on mesne process. Maintained by sheriff's officers and lesser court officials, lock-up houses held recently arrested debtors while they attempted to secure bail or settle with their creditors. They were commonly referred to as 'spunging-houses', a term that reflected the excessive fees extracted by their keepers. Private residences secured by iron bars and elaborate locks, spunging-houses attracted the upper end of the debtor population. 'It was . . . seldom without an inmate or two of the most respectable or wealthier class of prisoners', Francis Place recalled of his father's lock-up house in London in the 1770s; 'they were . . . such as could best afford to pay for comfortable accommodation, and were willing to pay, in preference to being lodged in the Marshalsea Court Prison'.[27] The cost of such accommodation was substantial. A three-day visit to Sloman's spunging-house in Cursitor Street, the likely model for the lock-up house that held Becky Sharpe's hapless spouse in Thackeray's *Vanity Fair*, cost over five pounds in the early Victorian era, a sum several times greater than the weekly wage of a labouring man in full employment.[28]

Maintained purely as profit-making concerns, spunging-houses were concentrated – like the imprisoned debtor population – in the London metropolitan

---

[25] See Paul Hess Haagen, 'Imprisonment for debt in England and Wales' (Ph.D. dissertation, Princeton University, 1986), 312–52.

[26] The history of the sanctuaries is detailed in Haagen, 'Imprisonment for debt', 262–311; Hugh Barty-King, *The Worst Poverty: A History of Debt and Debtors* (Stroud, 1991), 5–7; and Nigel Stirk, 'Fugitive meanings: the literary construction of a London debtors' sanctuary in the eighteenth century', *British Journal of Eighteenth-Century Studies*, 24, 2 (Autumn 2001), 75–88. For the Verge of the Court, see esp. Rev. [John] Trusler, *The London Advisor and Guide: Containing Every Instruction and Information Useful and Necessary to Persons Living in London, and Coming to Reside There* (London, 1786), 157–8.

[27] Francis Place, *The Autobiography of Francis Place*, ed. and intro. Mary Thrale (Cambridge, 1972), 26–7.

[28] Anon., *Whitecross and the Bench: A Reminiscence of the Past: By the Author of Five Years' Penal Servitude* (London, 1879), 9, 19.

'Mansions of misery' 117

area,[29] where they proved especially attractive investments for members of the provisioning trades. The lock-up houses that surrounded the Fleet prison in the early eighteenth century were let at excessive rents to victuallers who, like Mary Whitwood, extracted extortionate charges from their captive guests to recoup their expenses.[30] In theory, government legislation limited the extent of such abuses from the mid-eighteenth century, requiring justices of the peace to regulate the fees charged by local spunging-houses. But as Sir Richard Phillips discovered in 1807, the provisions of this act *'had never, at least in the memory of men, been acted upon'*.[31] Lacking effective internal and external regulation, spunging-houses routinely delivered their debtors to the prisons they served in an impoverished, and often inebriated, state. In 1858, debtor Milligan, newly committed to London's Whitecross Street prison, suffered 'a paroxysm of Delirium caused by drinking... Brandy in large quantities' at a spunging-house, and attempted to take his life by stabbing himself in the chest with a knife.[32]

Superior-court insolvents who failed to obtain bail or to effect a settlement with their creditors in a lock-up house proceeded to the debtors' prison itself, where they joined those less affluent (or less optimistic) debtors who had entered the gaol immediately upon arrest. The basic typology of the prisons to which these debtors were committed was fourfold. County gaols, originally designed to hold criminal prisoners for trial at quarter sessions or assizes, served as the backbone of the English prison system from 1166 to 1878. Nominally under the control of sheriffs but subject to increasing regulation by justices of the peace from the seventeenth century, many were originally located in castles. Municipal prisons provided urban centres with a second series of gaols in which to incarcerate offenders brought before their local courts of record. Their administrative structures were highly diverse, with sheriffs, justices, mayors and corporations sharing or competing for power to varying extents in different municipal prisons throughout the country. Franchise and other special prisons served a third series of constituencies, offering structures for the imprisonment of individuals who came before ecclesiastical or manorial tribunals as well as the special courts that served some privileged mining and forest regions. Finally,

[29] The great distances travelled by sheriff's officers in arresting dispersed provincial debtors discouraged them from establishing spunging-houses. See James Pearce, *A Treatise on the Abuses of the Laws, Particularly in Actions of Arrest* (London, 1814), 62–9.

[30] Prisoners in the spunging-houses that served the Fleet paid from one to two shillings a night for a bed (often shared with other debtors), and one shilling a day for a fire; board was additional. *Report from the Committee Appointed to Enquire into the State of the Gaols of the Kingdom: Relating to the Fleet Prison* (London, 1729), 4, 8.

[31] The legislation regulating spunging-houses was 32 Geo. II c. 28. A table of fees for Middlesex spunging-houses established rates for rooms which ranged from one shilling to three shillings and sixpence per day. Sir Richard Phillips, *A Letter to the Livery of London, Relative to the Views of the Writer in Executing the Office of Sheriff*, 2nd edn (London, 1808), 179–90.

[32] CLRO, Gaol Committee Officers' Reports, Report of William B. Langman, surgeon, to the Gaol Committee, 24 July 1858.

118 Imprisonment for debt and the economic individual

some prisons located in London – Newgate, the King's Bench, the Fleet and the Marshalsea – housed superior-court prisoners drawn from the kingdom as a whole.[33] (Illustration 3).

John Howard's survey of later eighteenth-century confinement helps to bring the debtor's place within this complex reticulation of prisons into sharper focus. In successive visitations from 1774 to 1783, Howard identified a total of 128 institutions across England with debtor inmates. The distribution of debtors in these institutions was uneven, with the London metropolitan area accounting for 47 per cent of the imprisoned debtors in his sample. The King's Bench alone was home to just under a quarter of all imprisoned debtors in 1779; together with seven other prisons – the Fleet, the Marshalsea, Newgate, the Poultry Compter, York Castle, Lancaster Castle and the Bristol Newgate – it held just over half of all debtors imprisoned in England in that year.[34]

Vast differences obtained both within and among these institutions. Lacking a distinctive architecture of their own, the prisons of the eighteenth century ranged in style from the towering edifices of the county gaols to a ragged series of smaller (but numerically dominant) structures fully integrated with the surrounding urban landscape and often indistinguishable from – indeed, occasionally situated within – local public houses. 'Hovel, cottage, house, workshop, lodging house, terrace, alley, court and tenement, the most commonplace types of accommodation in towns and cities, were the identifiable forms in the construction and layout of eighteenth-century prisons', Robin Evans has observed of early eighteenth-century structures; 'the prison took patterns of so varied a character yet of such fundamental ordinariness that it could not be said to constitute a specific building type at all'.[35] At one end of this broad spectrum were the county gaols of Lancaster and York, each located in an ancient castle but otherwise strikingly different in appearance. Lancaster Castle, dating from the twelfth century, loomed over the town from a medieval mound which endures to the present day, while York Castle gaol, renovated extensively in the Baroque style by 1705, was adorned with enormous pilasters elevated on a rusticated platform.[36] Among the many structures at the other end of this spectrum were

---

[33] The characteristics of these four types of prisons are detailed by Pugh, *Imprisonment in Medieval England*, 57–139, and McConville, *History of English Prison Administration*, 5–8.

[34] Howard, *State of the Prisons*. Only prisons in which debtors were actually present when Howard visited are included in these calculations, which in consequence underestimate the debtor population. In 1779, Howard noted a total of 2,078 debtors in English gaols on the days of his visits. Of these 968 were located in London or Southwark gaols, 498 were in the King's Bench, 184 in the Fleet, 92 in the Marshalsea, 73 in York Castle, 72 in Lancaster Castle, 51 in London's Newgate, 47 in Bristol's Newgate and 46 in the Poultry Compter (486–92).

[35] Evans, *Fabrication of Virtue*, 16.

[36] Evans notes that the renovated York Castle was the first prison 'substantially constructed and detached from other buildings'. With 'pretensions to symmetry', it 'employed the repertory of classical elements', but remained unique in these respects among English prisons until the 1750s. Ibid., 41.

3 Newgate Prison, *c.* 1750. Now remembered as a criminal prison, London's Newgate housed thousands of metropolitan debtors before the erection of the Whitecross Street prison in 1816. (Reproduced by permission of the Guildhall Library, London.)

120   Imprisonment for debt and the economic individual

the tiny gaols of Rochester, Chesterfield and Walsall. Consisting in the 1770s of three rooms – 'all close and offensive' – located under the city's courtroom, Rochester gaol also extended into the prison-keeper's house, where debtors who could afford to do so could obtain a private bed. Chesterfield's prison, which belonged to the Duke of Portland, was let to his steward for eighteen pounds twelve shillings per annum. It consisted of 'only one room, with a cellar under it; to which the prisoners occasionally descend through a hole in the floor'. Walsall gaol, two rooms located under the town hall, was likewise rudimentary in design, distinguishing between its debtor and criminal prisoners chiefly by providing the former, as privileged persons, with a fireplace.[37]

The decades from 1775 to 1795 saw the emergence of a distinctive style of prison architecture pioneered by William Blackburn, who designed gaols either as a hub with radial wings or a hub facing a polygon of prison buildings.[38] But the fifty-odd prisons built to this new pattern existed alongside a plethora of existing structures, supplementing rather than supplanting the motley array of institutions of confinement. When James Neild surveyed the prison system early in the nineteenth century, he noted with discouragement the persistence of the older prison forms. At Abingdon, the gaol for debtors imprisoned by the borough court was located in the town's old gateway and lacked running water: 'a tub in one corner serves as a privy, and is emptied once a month, for which the Gaoler charges eighteenpence'. In Halifax, the gaol for the manor of Wakefield, owned by the Duke of Leeds, housed impecunious 'common-side' debtors in its 'Low Gaol', and more affluent 'master's-side' debtors in the keeper's adjacent public house. A small aperture in the room that held the common-side debtors allowed friends and family members to pass provisions in from the street. Master's-side debtors were apparently better supplied, occupying as they did four chambers in the tavern at 'the sign of the Leeds Arms', under which '*Neat Wines, The Jail House*' was inscribed.[39]

Spatial divisions within the gaol served to distribute inmates according to their social and legal status, but these boundaries were of necessity fluid and routinely crossed. Halifax's division between master's-side and common-side debtors was replicated in almost all gaols that could boast more than a single room. In the largest of the metropolitan prisons devoted exclusively to debtors – the King's Bench, the Fleet and the Marshalsea – this twofold division underpinned a serried array of distinctions, privileges and amenities that demarcated the inmate population according to economic wealth and social pretension. Among the 800 prisoners who inhabited the King's Bench in the 1820s, master's-side debtors occupied choice apartments in the so-called Statehouse, entertained their visitors at the fashionable Coffee House and spent their

---

[37] Howard, *State of the Prisons*, 268, 320, 353.   [38] Evans, *Fabrication of Virtue*, 94, 146.

[39] James Neild, *An Account of the Rise, Progress, and Present State of the Society for the Discharge and Relief of Persons Imprisoned for Small Debts throughout England and Wales*, 3rd edn (London, 1808), 65, 251.

'Mansions of misery'

evenings at exclusive wine clubs within the prison walls. Common-side debtors acted as servants for the master's-side elite, but otherwise frequented the back portions of the prison, where spiked walls obscured the daylight, open sewers ran from the privies and inmates deposited the prison slops. Excluded from the gaol's more exclusive convivial institutions, these lesser debtors congregated in the evening at the common tap, where many later made their beds upon the tables and benches.[40] The presence in most gaols of an assortment of debtors, criminals and even bridewell prisoners, however, created a shifting and promiscuous population inimical to the rigid maintenance of fine gradations. At London's Newgate, which contained 160 debtors and 326 criminals in April 1814, debtors who chose to live on the master's-side shared their quarters with felons – men imprisoned 'for every crime, and of every description', admitted to the civil side despite their criminal status upon the payment of an entry fee of thirteen shillings and sixpence and an additional two shillings and sixpence per week for the use of a bed. At Bristol's Newgate in 1815, classification was more rudimentary yet: the only effective division separating the members of its mixed population of debtors and criminals was the wall that segregated male from female inmates.[41]

The inherent fluidity of the unreformed gaol's internal divisions was, in a few select prisons, increased at the exterior walls by precincts known as the 'Rules'. Located physically outside and around these institutions but considered juridically integral to them, the Rules allowed debtors who could find two propertied persons to stand security for their good behaviour to pay for the privilege of residing in private accommodation outside the gaol itself. This option became especially attractive as the increasing number of commitments for debt produced severe overcrowding in the London prisons, among which both the Fleet and the King's Bench possessed extensive Rules. By 1792, prisoners who remained inside the walls of the King's Bench could expect to share a room with at least two other inmates. Not surprisingly, seventy of the 570 prisoners chose instead to live within the Rules. So-called 'day Rules' allowed other inmates to leave the prison to transact business with their creditors, provided they returned to the prison by 9.00 p.m.[42] In Newcastle, it was less affluent debtors (whose

---

[40] Anon., *A Description of the King's Bench Prison: Being a Brief Review of Its Constitution...* (London, [1827]).

[41] 'Report of the committee appointed to inquire into the state of the gaol of Newgate, and the Poultry, Giltspur Street, Ludgate, and Borough Compters', CLRO, Prisons: State of: Report of the Committee (1814); Anon., *The Gaol of the City of Bristol Compared with What a Gaol Ought to Be: Intended to Diffuse a More General Knowledge of the Requisites of a Good Prison...* (Bristol, 1815), 71.

[42] *Report from the [House of Commons] Committee Appointed to Enquire into the Practice and Effects of Imprisonment for Debt* (London, 1792), 34. At the Fleet, which suffered an even more acute shortage of rooms than the King's Bench, 80 of the 280 debtors were in the Rules. (Ibid., 35). The cost of gaining access to the Rules varied with the amount of the debt. At the King's Bench in the 1820s, the charge was eight guineas for the first hundred pounds, and four guineas for each additional hundred pounds of debt. Anon., *Description of the King's Bench*, 19–21.

122   Imprisonment for debt and the economic individual

possible escape posed the least financial risk for the keeper) who enjoyed access to the Rules. Here, 'as the keeper cannot find by what authority these Rules were granted, no debtors are indulged in the use of them, but those of good character, who are confined for small sums'.[43] In the West, where the Lostwithiel gaol for debtors was the property of the Duke of Cornwall as lord of the Stannaries, Howard found that 'the *rules* extend over the whole borough'.[44] Debtors with sufficient funds who were confined in provincial prisons lacking the amenities of the Rules could, moreover, pay to obtain a writ of habeas corpus and transfer custody of their bodies to the King's Bench or the Fleet. Of one hundred insolvent debtors imprisoned at Ilchester Gaol, Somerset between May 1808 and January 1810, four used this device to relocate to metropolitan prisons.[45]

Even debtors without access to a habeas or the Rules necessarily experienced the debtors' prison as a porous container rather than as a 'total' institution. For while the architectural structures of the medieval castle visually suggested effective isolation in some of the more remote county gaols, the limited functions performed by administrators of unreformed prisons inevitably promoted an ongoing influx of goods and persons from outside to service the debtor population. To be sure, a series of overlapping systems of charity within the gaol provided a rudimentary system for provisioning debtor inmates. By the Lords Act of 1759, debtors imprisoned on final process were eligible to sue for their 'groats', a sum of two shillings and fourpence per week paid by the detaining creditor to maintain the debtor in prison – a provision that clearly reflected debtors' conventional identity as victims of contractual rigour and economic misfortune.[46] From the mid-eighteenth century, many county and some municipal prisons also offered small allowances of cash or provisions to debtors who swore that they were unable to maintain themselves in prison. At the Marshalsea, where the sum provided was sixpence per diem, 184 debtors received a total of just over £151 through the county allowance system in the six months from midsummer to Christmas 1824.[47] Debtors residing in areas with sympathetic parish officers derived additional assistance from the Poor Laws. An eighty-year old debtor confined for nearly two decades thus eked out an existence in the Dolgelly gaol

---

[43] Neild, *Account of the Rise, Progress, and Present State*, 382–3.

[44] Howard, *State of the Prisons*, 398.

[45] Haagen, 'Imprisonment for debt', 161–3 describes the use of the habeas. For the Ilchester statistics, see Somerset RO, Q/Agi/17/2, Ilchester Gaol Debtors' Register, 1808–24, admissions from 2 May 1808 to 3 January 1810.

[46] The Lords Act of 1759 (32 Geo. II c. 28) replaced similar but less generous legislation of 1729 which had been initiated in the House of Lords. The amount of 'groats' was increased to three shillings and sixpence in 1797. Lineham, 'Campaign to abolish', 36–9 details the Act's uses and limitations.

[47] PRO, PALA 9/8, A list of the debtors who have received the county allowance, Midsummer 1824–Christmas 1824. By Thornton's Act of 1813 (53 Geo. III c. 113), counties were uniformly required to provide for the maintenance of imprisoned debtors unable to support themselves, whether imprisoned on mesne or final process.

4 Exterior view of the begging grate at the Fleet Prison, *c.* 1800. Kept in constant public view by devices such as this, debtors were fitting objects of charity in the heyday of the unreformed prison. (Reproduced by permission of the Guildhall Library, London.)

with money earned from carding and spinning, plus two shillings a week in poor relief granted by his parish.[48] Begging grates situated in the outside walls of debtors' prisons allowed inmates to solicit charitable donations on a daily basis from pedestrians in the street, and worked to keep the plight of imprisoned debtors constantly in the public eye. (Illustration 4).

[48] Neild, *Account of the Rise, Progress, and Present State*, 156.

124   Imprisonment for debt and the economic individual

These relief mechanisms, however, provided at best a partial means of maintaining debtors in the prison. Groats proved far easier to decree in parliamentary legislation than they were to extract from indignant creditors. From the 1770s, John Howard's successive investigations of the nation's prisons drew attention to this failure, which was exacerbated in over half of the county gaols by the absence of a regular allowance for debtors. Only one of the forty-nine debtors imprisoned at Carlisle in 1774, Howard reported, had succeeded in obtaining his groats, and the prison-keeper could recall only four or five debtors who had received the mandated payment in his fourteen-year tenure at the gaol.[49] Debtors committed for small sums by the summary courts of conscience were in any event ineligible to sue for groats, and the payments garnered by fortunate superior-court debtors were woefully inadequate to supply their basic needs. At Whitechapel's gaol, which confined inmates committed by the small debt court for Stepney and Hackney, the keeper estimated the minimum sum required to maintain a female debtor at five shillings a week in 1792. Even had the petty debtors in his gaol – which provided its inmates with neither an allowance nor provisions – been eligible for groats and successful in obtaining them, the monies so extracted would have represented less than half of this sum.[50]

Prison charities

Charitable activity was vital to the day-to-day maintenance of debtors in unreformed prisons and served further to underline the custodial (as opposed to punitive) character of their confinement. Widely current in diaries, memoirs and fictional writing, the depiction of fallen man's subordination to the Deity as a relationship between debtor and creditor was also axiomatic in philanthropic Anglican discourse and didactic literature. The author of *The Relative Duties of Creditors and Debtors* (1743) was emphatic in underlining the parallels between spiritual and economic accounting. 'For since our Sins render us obnoxious to the Anger and Vengeance of GOD, and we are thereby *indebted* to his Law, and owe Satisfaction to his Justice', he explained, 'they are very properly set forth, in holy Scripture, by the Metaphor of *Debts*; for which GOD Almighty, according to the *Rigour* of the *Law of Works*, may cast us into the *Prison* of Hell, 'till, as our Lord hath expressed it, *We have paid the very last Mite.*' Just as divine grace could rescue the undeserving Christian from eternal retribution for his spiritual deficiencies, the merciful worldly creditor could liberate the debtor from the secular confinement occasioned by his economic misfortunes. Noting

[49] Howard, *State of the Prisons*, 5.
[50] *Report from the [House of Commons] Committee*, 50–1. As women were conventionally expected to subsist on substantially less provision than men, the assistance provided by groats was clearly even more inadequate than this comparison suggests.

'Mansions of misery' 125

that '*insolvent* Debtors have not by contracting their Debts transgressed any *penal* Law, whereby they may justly be punished as *Highway-men*, *Pickpockets*, and other *Villains* who, it is certain, have a *Villanous Intention*', the author charged that 'when Men deal thus unmercifully with their *insolvent* Brethren; they do in effect blaspheme against, and refuse to submit to the Providence of God'.[51] In 1775, James Hallifax, rector of Cheddington and vicar of Ewell, imbued this line of analysis with an evangelical emphasis in keeping with the heightened religious sensibilities of his age. Even a lifetime, he proclaimed, 'would prove insufficient to satisfy the debt due to God, for the blessings of creation, preservation, and redemption, and above all for the means of grace, and hopes of glory; and should the uttermost farthing be demanded from the best of us, we must inevitably be cast into that prison where there is perpetual weeping and gnashing of teeth'. Salvation by grace thus prefigured and legitimated the debtor's secular liberation from the prison by charitable endeavour, for 'Christ Jesus came into the world to save sinners, and to restore those to freedom who were in captivity to the law of sin.'[52]

As the delivery of Hallifax's sermon 'For the Benefit of Unfortunate Persons Confined for Small Debts' suggests, the interpretation of personal insolvency as a species of misfortune served to distinguish even petty debtors in the philanthropic mind from the criminal population. Although contemporary commentators were fully aware that the individual's personal failings or dishonesty could lead to the debtors' prison, they more typically judged the inmate's dilemmas as a circumstance 'arisen from *imprudences* perhaps, from ignorance and unskillfullness; from a want of experience, or the common and unforeseen casualties and occurrences of Life'.[53] In a sermon delivered in 1774, Thomas Francklin observed 'that amongst all the miserable objects confined in the walls of a prison, many are indebted for their wretched situation there, to unavoidable misfortune ... many, most of them, indeed, to the cruel and unfeeling disposition of their merciless creditors; but few, very few, to what is too often ascribed as the cause of it, a total want of principle and common honesty'.[54] The trope

---

[51] Anon., *The Relative Duties of Creditors and Debtors Considered: Shewing the Indispensable Obligation Debtors Are under to Make the Utmost Restitution to Their Creditors; and Proposing Some Arguments and Reasons for the Gentleness and Compassion of Creditors towards Insolvent Debtors* (London, 1743), 5–6, 29, 35.

[52] James Hallifax, *A Sermon Preached at the Parish Church of St. Paul, Covent-Garden, on Thursday, May 18, 1775, for the Benefit of Unfortunate Persons Confined for Small Debts* (London, 1775), 11–12.

[53] Anon., *An Exhortation to the Debtor Released by the Society for the Discharge and Relief of Persons Imprisoned for Small Debts* (London, [1780]), 8.

[54] Thomas Francklin, *A Sermon Preached at the Chapel in Great Queen-Street, Lincoln's Inn Fields, on Saturday March 20, 1774, for the Benefit of Unfortunate Persons Confined for Small Debts* (London, [1774]), 8. Josiah Dornford rehearsed this theme in his *Seven Letters to the Lords and Commons of Great Britain, upon the Present Mode of Arresting and Imprisoning the Bodies of Debtors* (London, [1786]), iii–iv.

126 Imprisonment for debt and the economic individual

of the unfortunate debtor persisted into the Victorian era. William Hepworth Dixon, describing the debtors confined in London's Whitecross Street prison in 1850, declared 'many of them honest, and all unfortunate'.[55]

In this moral context, charitable gifting represented an obvious and fitting response to the practice of imprisonment for debt. Bequests specifically intended either to support unfortunate debtors in the prison or to liberate them entirely from confinement appeared in England from at least the fifteenth century.[56] Charity distributed to debtors at Whitecross Street as late as 1856 included a legacy from Sir Thomas Gresham's will of 1576, bequests from Mrs Margaret Simcott and Sir William Middleton dating from at least 1633 and monies derived from Elizabeth Misson's will of 1774.[57] The bequest of Ralph Carter, dated 1576, continued to finance annual deliveries of meat to metropolitan debtors until 1866: Christmas 1825 saw 500 lbs of beef distributed among 335 debtors at the King's Bench and Marshalsea prisons, and the Whitecross Street prison's 400 debtors received a pound of beef each from the Carter charity in May 1827.[58] Dame Mary Ramsey's will of 1601 bequeathed the very considerable sum of five hundred pounds 'towards the relief of the poor distressed and miserable estate of such prisoners as do or shall lie in execution or otherwise in the prisons in London and Southwark ... for the sum of forty shillings and under', but stipulated that the monies could be applied to a debtor imprisoned for a greater sum 'upon the extreme necessity and poor estate of some man's particular case ... towards whom the good report common reputation and honest behaviour ... shall move an extraordinary respect and compassion'. By the nineteenth century, these instructions had come to be interpreted with considerable latitude. The sums paid by the charity to release six debtors from the Whitecross Street prison in 1850 ranged from ten to thirty pounds apiece.[59]

In London, individual bequests of this sort were supplemented by a variety of legacies and donations channelled into the City's prisons by its guilds and trade corporations. Initially, these funds were intended to assist only insolvent members of the exclusive companies that controlled the City's political and economic structures. Ludgate prison, the preserve of debtors who possessed the freedom (or citizenship) of the City, benefited disproportionately from such

[55] William Hepworth Dixon, *The London Prisons: With an Account of the More Distinguished Persons Who Have Been Confined in Them* (London, 1850), 276. For the shifting relationship between Providentialist belief and political economy, see Boyd Hilton, *The Age of Atonement: The Influence of Evangelicalism on Social and Economic Thought, 1785–1865* (Oxford, 1991).

[56] Pugh, *Imprisonment in Medieval England*, 213. Terpstra, 'Confraternal prison charity', notes the emergence of similar charities in Italy from the later fourteenth century (221).

[57] CLRO, Gaol Committee Papers, Return of Debtor Charities, 15 November 1856.

[58] Guildhall Library, MS 10,781, Allhallows Lombard Street, Receipts for Prisoners' Relief, Ralph Carter's Charity, 1824–66, 24 December 1825, 31 May 1827.

[59] Guildhall Library, MS 13,668/1, Christ's Hospital: Dame Mary Ramsey's Gift: Account of Payments, 1824–41, extract from the will (not paginated), and Guildhall MS 13,668/2, 11 April–18 November 1850.

'Mansions of misery'

bequests, which acknowledged the likelihood that even the privileged men and women affiliated with the City's corporate system could suffer imprisonment for debt in the course of their careers in trade. John Luff (citizen and goldsmith), James Jewston (citizen and haberdasher), Amelia Heath (citizen and weaver) and Mary Wells (citizen and cooper) were among the sixty-four debtors freed from Ludgate by the charity of the Ironmongers' Company in the period May 1752–December 1761.[60] Like many of the bequests made by individual donors, these corporate benefactions had, by the nineteenth century, both risen substantially in value and come to serve a much wider constituency of debtors than the guilds had originally envisaged. The occupations of the 173 debtors discharged from Whitecross Street in 1855 were far removed from the concerns of the Mercers', Drapers', Clothworkers' and Grocers' companies that provided the £966 of charity that effected their liberation from the prison. Sarah Atlee was a 'Lady' in 'reduced circumstances', William Brooks was an omnibus proprietor, Arthur Blyth was a lodging-house keeper, George Chitty was an organist and William Cocken had been 'formerly on the turf'.[61]

Provincial debtors similarly benefited from a range of relatively open-ended charitable donations. Like Richardson's *Pamela*, Rebecca Hussey's will of 1713 registered a social rather than an individualist conception of debt obligations, bequeathing a thousand pounds 'for Charity to Prisoners that are confined for small Debts for themselves or have unhappily been bound for other Folks'.[62] County officials actively encouraged such philanthropic giving, which – in keeping with the presents of food and clothing made to social inferiors recorded in diaries and memoirs – allowed propertied men and women to acknowledge debtors as fit objects of charity while affirming their own superior status as monied members of the local elite. In later eighteenth-century Leicestershire, John Howard reported, the justices of the grand jury formally endorsed an annual collection of charity monies by the county's clergy, who organised the collection of funds for debtors in their individual parishes. Likewise in Derbyshire, 'a person goes round the county about Christmas to gentlemen's houses, and begs for the debtors'.[63] In Lancashire, Mrs Abigail Rigby's charity distributed forty shillings annually to 'poor Widows of the Town of Lancaster being Protestant, having no Pension or Relief out of the Town' and to 'prisoners for debt in Lancaster Castle'.[64]

---

[60] Guildhall Library, MS 17,009, Ironmongers' Company Charities: Volume of Signed Receipts for Beneficiaries Confined for Debt, 1718–70.

[61] CLRO, *Composite Printed Minutes of the Court of Aldermen, 1853–70*, January 1856, 2, 5.

[62] Lincolnshire Archives, CoC 2/1, Minutes of the Grand Jury, 1741–1891, Extract from the will of Rebecca Hussey, 83. By 1853, the charity's value had risen to £5,756. Lincolnshire Archives, CoC 2/6, Gaol Sessions, 1858–70, 29 December 1859.

[63] Howard, *State of the Prisons*, 314, 318.

[64] Lancaster Reference Library, MS 2311, Account Book of the Rigby Charity, 1783–1800. The charity continued in operation until 1867.

128   Imprisonment for debt and the economic individual

The active intervention of living benefactors further buttressed the distribution of funds from these legacies. Visits to prisons to dispense charity to debtors formed an integral part of the philanthropic pursuits of men and women of the governing classes. 'Mr Kent of the Borough in company with his Lady visited the Prison and enquired if there was any distress'd cases among the Debtors', the keeper of the Borough Compter noted in his journal in 1817; 'after Inspecting many of them he paid the Debts of two and they were Discharg'd: he took the Names and Residences of four others to enquire as to Character and if approved of to Discharge them also.' Twenty years later such charity was still in evidence. When the Earl of Elgin, Lady Mary Christopher and a party of their friends conducted an informal inspection of Lincoln Castle in 1837, Lady Mary left a sovereign to be distributed among the twenty-one debtors in custody.[65]

The operation of these multifarious systems of charitable relief demonstrates the limited purchase exerted within English culture by the strict legal distinction between the justifiable debts of merchants, on the one hand, and the supposedly reckless obligations of petty tradesmen and consumers, on the other. William Blackstone affirmed conventional legal wisdom when he justified merchants' and substantial traders' exclusive access to the procedures of bankruptcy – which freed the bankrupt both from imprisonment and from full payment of his debts – by arguing that only businessmen were 'liable to accidental loss, and to the inability of paying their debts, without any fault of their own'. In this interpretation, ordinary insolvents – gentlemen, professionals, farmers, labourers and the host of artisans and petty traders whose debts were too small to allow them to file for bankruptcy – were guilty of fraud, and justly merited their imprisonment.[66] Legal historians have seized upon this line of argument to explain the longevity of the practice of imprisonment for debt in England, suggesting that contemporaries' perception of the debtor's personal culpability undermined their willingness to extend the privileges of bankruptcy to consumer debtors until the Victorian era.[67] But the long history of debtor charities argues against this view. Far from serving to distinguish virtuous commercial bankrupts from recklessly insolvent consumers, contemporary understandings of the moral meanings of indebtedness united members of widely divergent social and economic groups under the shared rubric of misfortune and thereby distanced them from the rigid conceptions of personal agency, responsibility and culpability associated with modern economic individualism.

[65] CLRO, Borough Compter Journal, 1817–23, 23 December 1817; Lincolnshire Archives, CoC 5/1/3, Lincoln Castle Keeper's Journal, 1836–48, 25 August 1837.
[66] William Blackstone, *Commentaries on the Laws of England*, 5th edn (Oxford, 1773), 2: 473.
[67] See, for example, Cohen, 'The history of imprisonment for debt'.

The open prison

The depiction of debtors as victims of misfortune worked alongside the parsimony of local and national government to link the prison to the outside world. A dearth of official oversight necessitated constant visits from outsiders, who delivered meals, ale, clothing, bedding, letters, newspapers and often contraband goods throughout the day and into the night. At Ilchester, tradesmen from the town held a daily market in the gaol, where they could expect master's-side debtors to exhibit discriminating tastes. In June 1817, twenty-two debtors complained about the quality of the beer to the keeper, who 'advised them to send to the Town for samples & prices which was done & William Raymond was chosen to supply them at seven pence per Quart, being a penny above the Beer complained of & refused'.[68] Although most prisons provided common-side debtors with a bedstead and bedding, master's-side inmates traditionally rented furniture more suited to their superior tastes and station from the prison-keeper or local furniture dealers. George Howard of Davygate, York charged debtors in the Castle sixpence a week (payable, wisely, in advance) 'for the use of Chairs, Tables, Drawers, Looking-Glass, Fender, Fire-Irons, Frypan, and Candlestick' in the rooms they inhabited in the 1860s.[69] These commercial transactions fostered ties of sociability between debtors and their provisioners, a tendency promoted further by the presence of recreational facilities that included taverns or taps within many gaols. Among the debtors playing billiards, skittles, mississippi, fives and tennis at the Fleet prison in the 1770s, John Howard counted 'several butchers and others from the market; who are admitted here as at another public house'.[70] (Illustration 5).

The daily traffic occasioned by these necessary negotiations and the convivial cultural practices that attended them constantly undercut the isolation of the debtor population. In 1832, an estimated 1,500 persons visited the Whitecross Street prison each Sunday; an official suggested (no doubt with considerable exaggeration) that 3,000 visitors a day routinely passed into and out of the Fleet prison in 1827.[71] When the government sought to limit entry into the King's Bench prison in 1832 as a precaution against the spread of cholera, William Jones, the prison-keeper, explained the likely impact of this measure on the institution's internal economy in terms that nicely conveyed the porosity and privilege of confinement in the unreformed debtors' prison. 'I beg to say that

---

[68] Somerset RO, Q/Agi/7/1, Ilchester Gaol Occurrence Book, 1816–21, 7 June 1817. Local butchers were admitted to the gaol at 10.00 a.m., and offered their goods for sale at the market or 'shop' for an hour. (Ibid., 29 November 1817).

[69] York Castle Museum Archives, Printed notice of furniture rentals, York Castle, 1 January 1869.

[70] Howard, *State of the Prisons*, 219. 'The same may be seen at many other prisons where the gaoler keeps a tap', he concluded dourly.

[71] CLRO, Gaol Committee Minute Books, 18 February 1832; PRO, HO 20/2, George Watlington to Chief Justice Best, 10 February 1827.

5 Thomas Shepherd (1793–1864), interior view of the Fleet Prison, *c.* 1840. Amenities such as racket-grounds helped to attract the public to the precincts of 'open' debtors' prisons. (Reproduced by permission of the Guildhall Library, London.)

as this Prison is an open Prison, and conducted on quite a different plan to the County Gaols, it would not be possible for me to prevent the usual ingress and egress of persons', he warned, noting that essential provisions were supplied to debtors by local tradesmen. 'Independently of these objections, if the relations and friends of the prisoners were to be refused admittance, and their usual mode of obtaining their food &c put a stop to, I feel sure that a very serious disturbance would take place; indeed, I could not answer for the consequences.'[72]

No less significant than this open trade in necessary goods was the parallel economy of illicit items that flowed into and circulated within the debtors' prison. Although William Jones referred to the King's Bench as an 'open prison', most prison-keepers did place restrictions on the provisions delivered to debtor inmates in an effort to contain disorder within their walls. Virtually all Georgian gaols allowed debtor inmates to receive a quart of ale each day, and most allowed debtors who provided for themselves to purchase a daily pint of wine as well. But debtors maintained on the county allowance were in some prisons forbidden

[72] PRO, HO 20/2, William Jones to S.M. Phillips, 17 February 1832.

'Mansions of misery' 131

to augment their diet with provisions from outside – particularly perceived luxuries such as coffee, tea and tobacco – and national legislation of the later eighteenth century both abolished prison taps in county gaols and prohibited the sale of spirits within prisons throughout the nation.[73] These restrictions, although poorly enforced, encouraged the growth of an active smuggling trade both between the prison and the outside world and among debtor inmates. The journals of prison-keepers are replete with references to the discovery of these activities. At Lincoln Castle, debtor John Gostlelaw, in receipt of the county allowance, attempted to smuggle an amount of beef, pork and coffee into the prison in 1836 by having the goods addressed by his friends to a master's-side debtor; in 1858, master's-side debtor Pennington's friends sought to provide him with half a pound of prohibited tobacco and four pipes with which to smoke it by concealing them in a loaf of bread included in his customary hamper of goods. Alcohol was, however, the overwhelming favourite among the smuggled goods habitually concealed within more prosaic purchases. William Pashley, the York Castle gate-keeper, extracted a bladder with a quart of rum from a pie sent to a debtor on 7 April 1837, and confiscated a quart of gin concealed within a debtor's loaf of bread two days later.[74]

The entrepreneurial potential of this system of restricted supply was obvious to inmates and potential provisioners alike. At Lancaster Castle in 1845, county-allowance debtor Christopher Webster 'received his bottle of ale (costing 5d.) daily, & retailed it out at 3d. per glass' for a tidy profit. Habitual drinkers who supplemented their own rations with ale purchased from fellow debtors and with smuggled spirits could command substantial alcoholic resources. The official investigating one affray at Lancaster, in which a debtor was severely beaten by his companions, found 'the floor swimming with drink', and noted that 'although there were only 4 members belonging to the Room, there were $14\frac{1}{2}$ quarts of Ale, 5 bottles of porter, & about $1\frac{1}{2}$ pints of Rum'. Descriptions of debtors' drunken and disorderly behaviour provide a constant refrain in the keeper's journals. John Ceaseburn was 'fuddled' by eleven in the morning; Joseph Althorn was 'fuddled and stank of liquor'; Henry Porter – 'staggering drunk' at 9.00 a.m. in May 1842 – was reduced by 'habits of intemperance ... nearly to a state of idiocy' by July.[75] Although debtors themselves bore the brunt

[73] An act of 1752 (25 Geo. II c. 40) prohibited the sale of spirits, and an act of 1784 (24 Geo. III, sess. 2, c. 57) abolished prison taps in county gaols. At the specialised London debtors' prisons that continued to maintain taps into the nineteenth century, alcohol sales were substantial. The tap at the King's Bench, for example, sold 1,731 butts for a profit of £2,683 from 1812 to 1814. Guildhall Library, MS 659, King's Bench Miscellaneous Papers, vol. 2, Profits by the Tap for the last three years.

[74] Lincolnshire Archives, CoC 5/1/3, Lincoln Castle Keeper's Journal, 1836–48, 26 May 1836; Lincolnshire Archives, CoC 5/1/5, Lincoln Castle Keeper's Journal, 1856–60, 6 February 1858; York Castle Museum Archives, Diary of William Pashley, 1837–48, 7 and 9 April 1837.

[75] PRO, PCOM 2/443, Lancaster Castle Governor's Journal, 1842–45, 29 March 1845; 25 February 1844; 19 January 1842, 16 January 1844, 18 May 1842, 1 July 1842.

132   Imprisonment for debt and the economic individual

of the violence fomented by this customary alcoholic haze, prison officials were also at risk. In 1816, a Lancaster debtor, disarmed of the bottles of ale he had brandished as weapons in a minor riot, threatened the keeper by saying 'if he could ever catch me when sober he would break every bone in my skin'.[76]

Women played a central role in the provisioning networks of the debtors' prison. Single women carried messages and goods between the prison and the town, while married women fulfilled their wifely duties by providing meals and clothing for their inmate husbands. Exploiting the opportunities afforded by these conventionally female functions, women were especially active in smuggling goods into gaol. At Lincoln Castle, Mrs Bell sought to give her husband, who was restricted to the county allowance, a loaf of bread hidden in a greatcoat; at Bedford prison, Mrs Street was caught conveying two ounces of tobacco wrapped in a towel to her husband in November, and was discovered with a pound of clandestine plum pudding about her person in January.[77] A warder at Lancaster Castle recalled a wife who sought to smuggle goods to her husband by packing them in her crinoline, while other Lancaster debtors sent home for overcoats, which arrived at the prison gates newly lined with tobacco. When the prison's governor discovered alcoholic spirits in the debtors' rooms in 1848, his natural instinct was to surmise that 'females no doubt are the purveyors'. Troubled by the tensions roused during visits to debtors by wives and female friends, he lamented their inevitable presence. 'I wish the "ladies" could be altogether excluded [from] the Debtor's yard', he reported wearily after yet another disturbance. 'Ninety nine irregularities out of every hundred that take place may be traced to the "fair" visitors.'[78]

In many prisons, the problems occasioned by wives' visits were compounded by their residence. Although the common-law convention of coverture ensured that relatively few women were confined in their own right as debtors,[79] many chose or were compelled by economic necessity to join their husbands within the prison's walls. Despite repeated notices in 1813 banning 'the indecent practice of Debtors wives sleeping with their Husbands in a Room where there are frequently 8 or 10 persons', very few debtors at Lancaster Castle chose to 'exhibit any delicacy on this subject', and the practice proved difficult to

---

[76] PRO, PCOM 2/442, Lancaster Castle Governor's Journal, 1816–18, 24 August 1816.

[77] Lincolnshire Archives, CoC 5/1/3, Lincoln Castle Keeper's Journal, 1 January 1839; PRO, PCOM 2/293, Bedford Prison Governor's Journal, 1852–59, 13 November 1856 and 2 January 1857.

[78] Isaac Smith, *A Warder's Experience of Lancaster Castle* (Blackburn, n.d.), 21–2; PRO, PCOM 2/444, Lancaster Castle Governor's Journal, 1845–48, 28 March and 23 July 1848.

[79] Women constituted about 5 per cent of the imprisoned debtor population in the eighteenth century. Paul Haagen, 'Eighteenth-century English society and the debt law', in Stanley Cohen and Andrew Scull, eds., *Social Control and the State: Historical and Comparative Essays* (Oxford, 1983), 224. From 1857 to 1880, women debtors represented between 0.3 per cent and 2.4 per cent of all persons committed to local gaols on civil process. Lucia Zedner, *Women, Crime and Custody in Victorian England* (Oxford, 1991), 318–19.

'Mansions of misery'

6 Theodore Lane (1800–28), interior view of the King's Bench Prison yard and racket-ground, c. 1825. Women and children were constant visitors to (and often residents in) the prison during the confinement of their husbands and fathers. (Reproduced by permission of the Guildhall Library, London.)

eradicate.[80] The London prisons were especially noted for the residence of debtors' wives, many of whom – like Charles Dickens's mother in the Marshalsea prison – were accompanied by their children. John Howard estimated that the 395 debtors imprisoned in the King's Bench in 1776 had 279 wives and 725 children, of whom two-thirds resided inside the prison's walls. As a schoolboy, John Thomas Pocock repeatedly trudged the London streets to visit his imprisoned father in the King's Bench, where he and his mother occasionally spent the night. Disgusted by the drunken conviviality of a prison 'Free and Easy' in March 1827, the young Pocock returned more happily to see his father in June, accompanied by a friend and determined 'to have a game of rackets'.[81] (Illustration 6). At the Fleet in 1834, between a third and half of all men kept wives and families with them, swelling the gaol population at times

[80] Lancaster Reference Library, MS 133, Special Commission to Inquire into the State, Conduct and Management of Lancaster Castle, 1812–15, 1 and 30 January 1813, 8 February 1813.
[81] Marjorie Holder and Christina Gee, eds., *The Diary of a London Schoolboy 1826–1830: John Thomas Pocock* (Plymouth, 1980), 9 (2 March 1827), 13 (15 June 1827).

134   Imprisonment for debt and the economic individual

from 200 debtors to 400 persons.[82] Visits from mistresses and lovers added further to the tensions generated by overcrowding. At Surrey's Horsemonger Lane prison in 1836, 'Mrs Cooper, the wife of Frederick Fox Cooper (a master debtor) complained... that an abandoned female was in the habit of visiting her husband in the gaol', and the authorities were 'called to the room of J.W. Morris (a master debtor) to quell a disturbance between Morris and his wife' precipitated by visits by a female servant who had earlier been discharged from service by Morris's jealous wife.[83]

Presiding over and participating directly in this ceaseless commerce of goods and persons were the keepers, turnkeys, tipstaffs, watchmen, chaplains and surgeons who composed the prison's staff. Prison-keepers were an especially diverse group of officials, derived from a wide range of social backgrounds and active in a host of economic pursuits in addition to that of gaoler, an office which in Howard's day was typically remunerated solely by fees levied on debtor inmates rather than with a regular salary.[84] At the lower end of the social scale were the artisans and tradesmen who supplemented their incomes by assuming the rents and responsibilities of the smaller provincial gaols: a collar-maker kept the Buckingham town gaol (conveniently located across the street from his workshop) for an annual salary of five pounds five shillings early in the nineteenth century; a shoemaker maintained the town and county gaol at Haverford West; a tallow-chandler was keeper of the prison for Newcastle-on-Tyne; and a tobacco pipe-maker kept the Northampton town gaol.[85] In London, spunging-house keepers were drawn from much the same stratum of petty artisans and tradesmen. Francis Place's father (a master baker in Southwark), having been twice reduced to destitution by gambling, became the keeper of a spunging-house in the 1770s and 'notwithstanding he was an extravagant man accumulated money'.[86] Women constituted a significant minority of provincial gaol-keepers, an office which they both assumed in their own right and inherited as the widows of gaolers. John Howard noted women keepers at Chelmsford, Norwich, Reading and Worcester (among other gaols) in the 1770s, and despite legislation in 1782 that forbade the appointment of women gaolers, Neild found female keepers at the Scarborough and York city gaols in the early nineteenth century.[87]

---

[82] Howard, *State of the Prisons*, 244; PRO, HO 20/2, Return of Prisoners in the Fleet Prison, 14 June 1834.

[83] *Report from Commissioners: Inspectors of Prisons – Great Britain, 2nd Report*, Parliamentary Papers, XII (1837), 153.

[84] Of the 128 debtors' prisons surveyed in Howard's *State of the Prisons*, only 51 (40 per cent) boasted a salaried gaoler.

[85] Neild, *Account of the Rise, Progress, and Present State*, 112, 258, 380, 407.

[86] Place, *Autobiography*, 22–7, citation from 27.

[87] Howard, *State of the Prisons*, 259, 296, 337, 346; Neild, *Account of the Rise, Progress, and Present State*, 485, 545. The legislation barring female keepers was 22 Geo. III c. 64.

'Mansions of misery' 135

At the other end of the spectrum of prison-keepers were the men who officiated at the larger county and city gaols, where the combination of salaries and fees could generate substantial income. The keepership of the Cambridge city gaol, with a salary of £12 in 1807, was an unlikely investment for a man of means, but oversight of the county prison at Cambridge Castle, with a salary of £200 per annum, was clearly another matter. The keepers of the prisons at Chester Castle (in receipt of a salary of £400 a year plus fees), Lancaster Castle (salaried at £600) and York Castle (paid a £450 salary exclusive of fees) enjoyed considerable incomes.[88] Profits from salaries and entry or discharge fees were moreover augmented by income generated from the provision of goods suited to the tastes and requirements of a prison's more affluent inmates. At York Castle in the 1780s, the keeper provided gentlemen debtors with meals for eight shillings a week, and offered a graded series of less sumptuous menus to yeomen, tradesmen and artificers.[89] Men who succeeded in obtaining an appointment as a prison-keeper were often understandably anxious to keep the office within the family. The Higgin family, which governed the prison at Lancaster Castle from 1769 to 1833, was both tenacious and successful in this regard. John Higgin senior derived his income from a substantial landed estate, a mill for cotton carding and his salary as keeper; his son inherited both the landed estate and the prison office on the death of his father from gaol fever in 1783.[90] Such substantial county gaolers, as Margaret DeLacy has argued, 'needed to be, and usually were, well born, well connected, and reasonably well off'.[91]

London's lucrative debtors' prisons represented an even more attractive investment for individuals and family networks. Sons succeeded fathers as keepers at Newgate in 1752 and Ludgate in 1790; John Kirby, keeper of Newgate, helped to engineer his nephew's appointment as keeper of the Poultry Compter in 1804. From 1794 the City of London's Common Council banned the sale of City offices by their occupants, and the control of the keeperships of Newgate, Ludgate, Whitecross Street and the Giltspur Street, Poultry and Borough Compters passed thereafter to the City's aldermen. This was a considerable access of patronage on the City's part.[92] At Newgate, which received over a thousand debtors a year from 1810 to 1813, the keeper earned an average annual profit of £350 from entrance and discharge fees alone.[93] Returns were even

---

[88] Neild, *Account of the Rise, Progress, and Present State*, 124, 127, 137, 313, 539.
[89] Howard, *State of the Prisons*, 407.
[90] See Lancaster Reference Library, Higgin Family Biography File, and Lancaster Reference Library, MS 7321, Account of the Prison as Related by Mr. Higgin, Keeper.
[91] DeLacy, *Prison Reform in Lancashire*, 37.
[92] Wayne Joseph Sheehan, 'The London prison system, 1666–1765' (Ph.D. thesis, University of Maryland, 1975), 195, 213–14.
[93] CLRO, Gaol Committee Papers, Account of the Fees Payable to the Keeper of Newgate for three years, viz. from Michaelmas 1810 to Michaelmas 1813.

7 Robert Cruikshank (1795–1856), the evening after a mock election at the Fleet Prison, 1835. Male sociability at the prison tap was an integral part of life in unreformed debtors' prisons, and was an immense source of profit for the keepers of London's elite gaols for debtors. (Reproduced by permission of the Guildhall Library, London.)

higher at the King's Bench and the Fleet. William Jones, appointed Marshal of the King's Bench in 1791, maintained the office for over forty years to no small profit. Revenues derived from the fees paid by debtors who resided in the Rules alone averaged over £4,000 a year from 1815 to 1830, and were bolstered further by a host of additional charges and the profits of the prison tap. Jones's total income from the King's Bench from 1820 to 1830 was a stunning £62,969. W.R.H. Brown, the warden of the Fleet, earned £28,111 from debtor emoluments alone in the same period.[94] (Illustration 7).

The services provided by keepers in return for these fees were narrowly circumscribed. As in the Middle Ages, the safe custody of debtors' bodies formed the basic duty of the eighteenth- and early nineteenth-century prison-keeper, who was legally responsible for the debts of any inmate who succeeded in escaping from his prison. All keepers were in consequence required to post securities,

---

[94] PRO, T 90/66, Minutes of the Royal Commission on Courts of Justice: Returns Furnished by Officers: King's Bench and Fleet.

'Mansions of misery' 137

which were, at the larger prisons, substantial.[95] Aside from exercising these custodial functions, the keeper's interaction with his debtor inmates was typically limited. Until at least the 1840s, many were absent or non-resident for significant portions of their tenure, and were encouraged by convention to minimise their oversight even when present within the prison. As Robin Evans has argued more broadly of the officials who governed unreformed prisons, 'theirs was, more than anything else, a power extended over a prisoner's circumstances, not aimed directly at his conduct'.[96] Even those exceptional keepers who wished to regulate debtor behaviour had few instruments of discipline at their disposal other than the ability to place the most disorderly prisoners temporarily in a strong-room. When the debtors transferred from Newgate to the recently established Whitecross Street prison vented their dissatisfaction with the new gaol by breaking its windows in 1818, the keeper's only effective means of retaliation was briefly to withhold the meat allowance donated for their benefit by the City's aldermen.[97]

Like prison-keepers, chaplains and surgeons numbered among the less visible of the unreformed prison's officers. Many eighteenth-century prisons lacked such officials altogether: the gaols of Southwark, Huntingdon, Cambridge, Ely and Leicester were among the institutions visited by Howard in the 1770s that boasted neither a chaplain nor a salaried surgeon.[98] Although staffing levels had improved considerably by the time of James Neild's survey in the early nineteenth century, nearly a quarter of all debtors' prisons still lacked medical attendance and almost 40 per cent had no official chaplain.[99] Inadequate remuneration and supplies, moreover, discouraged those officials who were appointed from exerting themselves unduly in the prison. The Reverend Woolley, chaplain of the Marshalsea in the 1780s, dismissed the fee of a shilling per discharged debtor which he received in lieu of a salary as 'very trifling'; the Reverend Watford, chaplain of the King's Bench in the 1820s, complained of the 'trifling sum' of his fees, and farmed his office out to a curate.[100] Faced with such adverse conditions, many prison officers relinquished even the pretence of any interest in the bodily or spiritual health of their debtor inmates. When William Mann, the seventy-seven-year-old chaplain of Surrey's Horsemonger Lane prison, was asked by the Home Office's prison inspectors to detail his

[95] See, for example, printed letter from John Higgin concerning his salary, 31 October 1831, Lancaster Reference Library, D 6351, no. 24, Lancaster Castle Returns and Correspondence.

[96] Evans, *Fabrication of Virtue*, 23.

[97] CLRO, Gaol Committee Minutes, 28 November 1818.

[98] Howard, *State of the Prisons*, 253, 286, 288, 291, 310, 316.

[99] Of ninety-nine English gaols with inmates in 1800–02, Neild's *Account* identified twenty-three without a surgeon and thirty-nine without a chaplain.

[100] Rev. W. Woolley, *The Benefit of Starving: Or the Advantages of Hunger, Cold, and Nakedness; Intended as a Cordial for the Poor, and an Apology for the Rich* (London, 1792), 27; PRO, T 90/66, Letter from Edward Gibbs Watford, 13 September 1832.

138   Imprisonment for debt and the economic individual

official duties to debtors in 1837, he asserted that it was 'no part of my duty to visit them' and that he 'should be insulted' by any suggestion to the contrary.[101]

To the extent that oversight was assumed by prison officialdom at all, the day-to-day care of debtors thus fell largely on turnkeys, wardens and tipstaffs. Drawn from the ranks of the artisanate that supplied the lesser gaols with their keepers, these officers served as governors' servants rather than as employees of county or state government. At Lancaster in 1817, Higgin described his response to a turnkey's negligence in emotive and personal terms: he was 'shocked' and 'hurt' by the behaviour, and warned the offender 'that if he repeated such conduct, he must leave my service'.[102] William Brown, warden of the Fleet, was equally emphatic in 1832. 'The Turnkeys are my Servants and not Officers of the Court ... their Fees are my Fees, and [I] have always received them ever since I have been in Office', he explained to a royal commission. 'The Turnkeys are not appointed by any written Document – they are appointed & detained by me during pleasure & I can discharge them at any moment.'[103]

Predictably, given these terms of employment, petty prison officers were more often noted for their ability to extract fees than they were for their effective regulation of debtors' conduct. Tipstaffs expected to be rewarded with drink as well as cash for their trouble in conveying debtors to the Insolvent Court or the prison, where they offered a range of other services to inmates for additional payments.[104] Together the demands of such services and the small number of prison officers relative both to debtors and their constant stream of visitors precluded active intervention in inmates' daily lives. In the later eighteenth-century King's Bench, three or four turnkeys were responsible for several hundred debtors.[105] Although prison establishments expanded in the nineteenth century, they remained inadequate for the needs of institutions that were required both to house a shifting population of inmates for indefinite periods and to conduct them at frequent intervals to and from disparate courts of law.[106]

Unreformed debtor culture

The paucity of prison administration, the ready availability of alcohol and the porous boundaries that divided inmates from the outside world fostered an array of disorderly cultural practices within the unreformed debtors' prison.

[101] *2nd Report of the Prison Commissioners*, 162.
[102] PRO, PCOM 2/442, Lancaster Castle Keeper's Journal, 1815–18, 6 May 1817.
[103] PRO, T 90/66, Evidence of W.H.R. Brown, 18 December 1832.
[104] Anon., *Whitecross and the Bench*, 21, 111–12.
[105] Innes, 'King's Bench prison in the later eighteenth century', 267–8.
[106] See, for example, CLRO, Gaol Committee Papers, Returns of the Governor of the Debtors' Prison, 30 January and 9 February 1856.

'Mansions of misery'

Prison reformers and their followers clearly exaggerated the extent of this mis-behaviour, seeking to legitimate their attempts to transform the prison along disciplinary lines by exposing the evils of established practices in a highly par-tisan fashion.[107] But the records of individual prisons provide ample evidence of debtor disorder. Conflict between debtors and their keepers was minimised by the limited extent of their interactions but could, under provocation, easily escalate. When John Higgin announced that he would be transferring debtor Edward Hemingway from Lancaster Castle in 1816, Hemingway (having taken to his bed and refused to attend Higgin in the keeper's quarters) was carried naked from his room, upon which indignity he called to a fellow inmate 'with a view to cause a Riot in the Room'.[108] Violence against prison officers, al-though far less common than debtors' attacks on each other, was not unknown. Debtor William Newsome, a spoon-buffer confined at Sheffield for a debt of fourteen shillings, escaped from the prison in 1836. Apprehended in his cups at Mrs Smith's Punch Bowl a few hours later and returned to gaol, he struck the doorkeeper a lethal blow before the prison officers succeeded in securing him in the strong-room.[109]

Episodes of violence against fellow prisoners combined with more gener-alised manifestations of aggression to earn debtors a particular reputation for disorderly conduct. In the 1840s, the surgeon at Lancaster Castle admitted debtor Munday to the infirmary badly bruised by another inmate and set debtor Robinson's leg, broken in an affray with his fellows; the keeper at Lincoln Castle temporarily prevented his master's-side debtors from receiving visitors and ale in 1849 to punish them for 'making hideous noises and yelling and screeching and other outrageous modes of annoyance'. The Lord Chief Justice captured a dominant and enduring image of this riotous debtors' culture when he condemned the Fleet prison in 1827 as a 'seat of dissipation sensuality and vice'.[110]

Yet as scholars have long recognised, the unreformed prison was by no means bereft of regulation. In the absence of effective oversight by their official keep-ers, both criminal and debtor inmates elaborated and imposed their own codes of prison conduct.[111] In debtors' prisons, these systems of internal regulation were designed to preserve their privileged place within the gaol, and acted to

---

[107] Sheehan, 'London prison system', 297–8.
[108] PRO, PCOM 2/442, Lancaster Castle Keeper's Journal, 1816–18, 13 July 1816.
[109] *The Sheffield Iris*, 2 August 1836.
[110] [James Stockdale], 'An Old Lancaster Castle surgeon's journal', *Cross Fleury's Journal*, no. 109 (September 1905), 13 and no. 111 (November 1905), 12; Lincolnshire Archives, CoC 5/1/4, Lincoln Castle Keeper's Journal, 1848–56, 3 March 1849; PRO, HO 20/2, Report of Chief Justice Best, 2 March 1827.
[111] DeLacy, *Prison Reform in Lancashire*, 31–2; Michael Ignatieff, *A Just Measure of Pain: The Penitentiary in the Industrial Revolution* (London, 1978), 38–40; Sheehan, 'London prison system', 145–63.

140   Imprisonment for debt and the economic individual

insulate inmates from the interference of penal and government officials. As James Pearce noted of the King's Bench in the early nineteenth century, 'with respect to the inside of the prison, the plan is to keep everything quiet, so that there are no complaints to the marshal: if this can be done, all is well'.[112] This tradition of debtor self-government was of considerable antiquity. The City of London had recognised the right of freemen imprisoned in Ludgate to regulate their own conduct as early as the fifteenth century, and by the seventeenth century the existence of such liberties at Ludgate and other metropolitan gaols was widely acknowledged in literature on imprisonment for debt.[113] Debtors' privileged status at law as inmates held only for safe custody allowed their conventional institutions and practices of self-government to flourish even at the height of the movement for penal reform.

At prisons with substantial debtor populations, debtor self-government was conventional and highly formalised: modelling their structures of authority on the legal and political institutions that maintained order in the outside world, debtors worked within the gaol to recreate the hierarchies of rank, fortune and power that distinguished among solvent citizens outside the prison's walls. The structures within which these received distinctions were embedded were carefully detailed in written rules which – like the 'little code of laws' that Howard found in operation in the eighteenth-century Fleet – were typically crafted by master's-side debtors to exclude common-side inmates. At the King's Bench, where the thirty-seven rules that regulated the master's-side debtors were printed and presented to all new members of the self-styled 'College', meetings of the General Court were held at weekly intervals, and the College minute books were available for inspection by collegians at any time, upon the payment of a penny. The preservation of such books could serve essential purposes, particularly when prison officers sought to impose their own authority over debtor life. In 1818, when the City's Gaol Committee suspended its customary beef allowance to punish Whitecross Street's debtors for their misconduct, the officials of the Ludgate ward defended their '*Right by Ancient Usage*' to receive the meat by producing a book of rules that dated from 1729.[114]

Highly defensive in tone and intent, these institutions of self-government were designed to preserve existing debtor privileges more than to contest or mock established structures of power. Debtors in county gaols invested their

---

[112] Pearce, *Treatise on the Abuses*, 105–6.

[113] See, for example, Marmaduke Johnson, *Ludgate, What It Is; Not What It Was* (London, 1659), in John Stow, *A Survey of the Cities of London and Westminster and the Borough of Southwark*, 6th edn, 2 vols. (London, 1755), II: 694–702.

[114] Howard, *State of the Prisons*, 220; Guildhall Library, Pam 5339, Rules for the Court Erected by Some of the Prisoners in the King's Bench Prison (abolished 21 June 1779); CLRO, Gaol Committee Papers, Ludgate debtors to Sir James Shaw, 18 May 1818. The Whitecross Street prison opened in 1816 and held both the debtors previously housed in Newgate and those previously committed to Ludgate and the two City compters.

'Mansions of misery' 141

own forms of authority with both the nomenclature and the gravitas of county administration. At Lancaster Castle debtors promulgated sixty-four rules for their own government in 1772, and enforced them in a court governed by an elected debtor judge, constable and clerk assisted by debtor sheriffs, appointed by seniority within the prison. Women debtors who paid their dues were eligible for the monies and the services administered by debtor officers, but were 'excused attending the Court' by rule number fifty-six. At York Castle in the early Victorian years, the government of the debtors' 'Clifford Club' was composed of a magistrate, a clerk and two constables. The first of the printed rules distributed to all new members of the club decreed that 'on the Magistrate taking his seat, all Members [are] at once to uncover [their heads] and remain silent, and no member [is] to speak during the time the meeting is open for business, except by addressing the Magistrate'.[115]

At the smaller provincial gaols, where the social composition of the debtor population was typically less exalted, systems of self-government were also elaborated by the inmates, who in allocating privileges tended (of necessity) to rely more upon seniority than upon degrees of social or economic distinction. Birmingham's gaol for debtors committed by the local court of conscience was too confined to permit a rigid demarcation between common- and master's-side inmates, but significant distinctions of status none the less obtained. Debtors able to pay the keeper's fees slept in separate beds with clean bedding, while the remainder 'huddled together at night in one Room . . . provided with a little loose straw on a Guard bedstead', conditions a contemporary observer compared unfavourably to those in the local workhouse. Seniority brought some relief from the full rigours of this system. 'The Debtor who has been longest in the Prison is known as the King', an official investigating a riot reported in 1843, 'and (ludicrous as the statement may appear) among other distinctions enjoys that of not being obliged to take up with more than seven bed-fellows'. Public rites of initiation served to introduce inmates to these customary distinctions: at the induction of a new debtor, established inmates brandished swords, subjected the initiate to ritualised insults and exacted 'garnish' and 'chummage' payments for the provision of alcohol and a place to sleep.[116] At the Duke of Norfolk's gaol, a converted warehouse that served Sheffield's court of requests, senior debtors appointed by their peers oversaw the admission of new inmates, known as 'birds'. A male inmate paid two shillings and sixpence to the 'Garnish Master' or had 'his hat and coat taken for security' in 1838; female debtors, in keeping with their lesser means, paid an entrance fee of one shilling and threepence, or

---

[115] Lancaster Reference Library, MS 6615, A Book of Laws to Be Observed by the Court of Lancaster Castle, 17 June 1772; York Castle Museum Archive, 'Rules of the Clifford Club; To Be Observed in Clifford's Buildings by All Debtors', n.d.

[116] PRO, HO 45/775, Report of Mr. Weale, 10 December 1843, and M.D. Hill to Sir James Graham, 12 January and 6 April 1844.

142   Imprisonment for debt and the economic individual

rendered a bonnet and shawl as a pledge for subsequent payment. Having paid these dues, the new bird ascended to the lowest rung of the prison hierarchy and 'commenced nancy', becoming responsible for cleaning the debtors' rooms.[117]

Debtors' structures of self-government served a variety of pragmatic functions. The influx of provisions into the prison through the county allowance system, the visits of friends and family members and the operation of charity all encouraged a considerable traffic in goods, generating a lively market that was compromised by many inmates' shortage of ready cash. Money-lending was central to the working of the prison's internal economy, but could generate substantial animosity among inmates. Like professional pawnbrokers, the more cautious of the debtors secured the cash advances made to their fellows by taking goods in return. John Petty, imprisoned for ten years at York Castle and in receipt of the county allowance, was found in 1845 to have 'a good deal of money in his possession and several Watches & Cloathes &c which he is supposed to have purchased or taken in pledge' from fellow inmates. Prisoners who chose to lend cash without such security did so at considerable risk. When a debtor in the King's Bench dispatched a messenger to pawn a valuable clock in 1860, an inmate to whom the messenger was himself indebted seized the clock and refused to return it unless he received his money.[118] Arbitrating such disputes was an essential function of debtor governments. The first five rules adopted at Lancaster Castle in 1772 detailed the procedures by which the court was to govern debts between debtor inmates, while the contemporary regulations at the King's Bench decreed 'that any Rules and Orders made by the General Court for the Recovery of Debts contracted in this College between Party and Party, shall be deemed legal and binding to both'.[119]

Generated and executed by debtors themselves rather than imposed on them by external authorities, these ritualised forms of discipline were central to the elaborate debtor subculture that flourished in prisons throughout the nation. Rule number twenty-eight at Lancaster Castle was exemplary in its carefully calibrated severity, specifying that an inmate convicted by the debtor court of stealing from his fellows should either pay the victim twice the value of the stolen object or 'stand three Hours at the post called the rogues post every day, until the thing so stolen be rendered ... and shall have a paper fastened to his Head, signifying the nature of the crime, and likewise shall every day have two quarts of cold water poured down his arms and head'.[120] Conventions of

---

[117] PRO, HO 20/3, Extract from the Rules Made by the Debtors in the Court of Requests Prison at Sheffield, 1838.

[118] York Castle Museum Archive, York Castle Gaoler's Journal transcript, 1824–47, 29 November 1845; PRO, PRIS 10/114, H.G. Prince to Captain Hudson, 9 May 1860.

[119] Lancaster Reference Library, MS 6615, A Book of Laws to Be Observed; Guildhall Library, Pam 5339, Rules of the Court.

[120] Lancaster Reference Library, MS 6615, A Book of Laws to Be Observed.

'Mansions of misery'

debtor self-discipline were equally essential to the administration of nineteenth-century prisons. Articles seven and eight of the Marshalsea's constitution of 1814 decreed that the name of any debtor who resisted the committee's rulings was to be 'struck up in the Ale Room & other most conspicuous places in the College', and that 'no persons sent to Coventry be allowed to go into the Ale Room nor participate in any of the Advantages belonging thereto'.[121] Inmates enforced such prescriptions with vigour. An official investigating an attack on debtor Hemans at the Marshalsea in 1820 found the prisoner badly bruised and 'Hemans sent to Coventry' emblazoned in letters a foot high on the prison walls. Similarly debtors at the Whitecross Street prison joined forces 'to Cat' the property of inmates who refused to make customary garnish payments for maintenance of their wards. As described by one of its practitioners, this process required 'several persons, generally those of another Ward to disguise themselves with their bed rugs and their faces blacked and go in a body mewing like Cats, and to take away some part of his property, as his Hat, Coat, or otherwise'.[122]

Social distinction was a crucial element of debtors' rationale for the imposition of customary payments within the prison. As Dickens's *Little Dorrit* and Benjamin Haydon's diary alike attest, debtors were acutely conscious of disparities of status and rank, and were determined to ensure that the social life of the prison replicated the nice distinctions of gentility, fortune and class that obtained in the outside world. A petition signed by twenty Newgate debtors conveyed the strength of these sentiments to the City's aldermen in 1814. Seeking to defend the perpetuation of their system of ward dues, the debtors underlined both their own superior social status and the wider imperative to maintain social boundaries within the prison walls, arguing 'that from the Gaol of Newgate being the County Prison, Persons of the first respectability, from the sudden Return of Writs ... whose walk in life exempts them from depraved associates; and with whom such association would greatly add to the pain and punishment of confinement' were compelled to reside in the prison. In this context, the imposition by debtors on the master's side of ward dues served an essential social function: 'the exaction of these fees has proved the means of keeping this Side of the Prison select', the petitioners concluded with evident feeling.[123]

Although critics of the unreformed prison denounced garnish and the disciplinary modes that enforced it as conducive of riotous behaviour, the exaction of customary dues was rooted in and perpetuated by the more mundane needs of the debtors' prison. Offices such as secretary, steward and scavenger, subsidised

[121] PRO, PALA 9/8, Marshalsea Prison Rules, 8 August 1814.

[122] PRO, PALA 9/8, Memo from Inspector Hewitt, 13 June 1820; CLRO, Rep. 227, 22 July 1823, Deposition of John Duncan Bentham. See similarly CLRO, Misc. MSS. 342.3, Proceedings before Sir George Carroll and Alderman Cubitt, 12 May 1857.

[123] CLRO, Gaol Committee Papers, Petition of Newgate Debtors, 6 July 1814.

144 Imprisonment for debt and the economic individual

by fees exacted by debtors themselves, provided needy prisoners with a regular income in return for the provision of services disdained by their more affluent fellows. At the Marshalsea, the elected secretary received seven shillings a week for administrative duties that included oversight of the scavenger, a debtor paid five shillings a week for sweeping the College walks, cleaning the privies each morning and scouring the water butts and cistern.[124] Enforcing basic standards of cleanliness was a central concern of debtor self-government, a task rendered increasingly difficult by the overcrowding that ensued from the increasing number of debtor commitments. At the larger prisons, debtors enforced rules prescribing appropriate hygienic behaviour with detailed schedules of fines. Lancaster Castle debtors required persons who defiled 'the House of Easements ... by ordure, pissing, or any other evacuation' to pay sixpence into the court's coffers; York Castle debtors detailed the proper use of chamber pots and imposed a penny fine on debtors who left the seat up in the water closet. At less exalted institutions, the measures taken for the maintenance of hygiene were less formalised but no less exacting. When John Cole was admitted to the Borough Compter 'in the most wretched and filthy condition, in fact ... full of vermin' in 1818, 'his fellow Prisoners for their own protection prevailed upon him to strip and allow his Clothes to be burnt; in this state, wrapped only in two Rugs and a Coverlid [sic], he remained until notice was given to the Bailiff and he could be relieved'.[125]

Resistance by debtors to rule by their fellows was not unheard of, but neither was it normative. Although disaffected debtors and their relatives filed occasional complaints with prison officers and government officials, they more often took issue with the way that individual debtors executed their offices than with the system of debtor self-government itself. The four common-side debtors who petitioned the Marshalsea's officials against the peculations of their steward were typical in requesting that in future the donations 'may be justly and equally divided amongst those who declare on the Poor side' rather than challenging debtors' control of the distribution of charities *per se*.[126] Fear of reprisals no doubt reduced the occurrence of such complaints: when debtor Turbitt sought to curry favour with the keeper of Lancaster Castle by reporting debtors' illegal traffic in ale, he was seized by a large and boisterous crowd of inmates, who threatened to soak him under the pump for informing on them.[127]

The indifference, and indeed hostility, with which the prisons' official governors received complaints against debtors' administrative practices also served to contain opposition to inmates' customary governance. The experience of a

---

[124] PRO, PALA 9/8, Marshalsea Prison Rules, 8 August 1814.
[125] Lancaster Reference Library, MS 6615, A Book of Laws to Be Observed; York Castle Museum Archive, 'Rules of the Clifford Club'; CLRO, Rep. 222, 17 February 1818, fols. 175–6.
[126] PRO, PALA 9/8, Petition for Marshalsea Poor Side Prisoners, 29 January 1808.
[127] PRO, PCOM 2/442, Lancaster Castle Keeper's Journal, 1815–18, 31 May 1816.

'Mansions of misery' 145

group of debtors who railed against the 'pretended Power' of 'Persons who call themselves the Steward and Members of the Court' in the King's Bench in 1750 was instructive. When they appealed to the Marshal to exercise his authority against this competing system of government, he advised them 'to pay the said Garnish or Imposition and offered to pay for or lend each of them the said . . . money to pay the same: and instead of Checking or Discountenancing the said Practices or Mock Court endeavoured to support them and give the Colour of Law thereunto'. This response was replicated in prisons throughout the kingdom. In 1813 John Higgin chose to mediate major disputes among debtors in Lancaster Castle, but described his intervention as occurring 'with the concurrence of the members' and left lesser complaints to be decided by the debtors' elected officers. Thirty years later, Higgin's successor adopted much the same strategy, taking no action himself to remove debtor Lambert – who was persistently inebriated – from his office, but telling the members of Lambert's ward 'that their room might by a majority vote Lambert out, and that I would sanction such a vote'. The sheriffs of London merely affirmed a venerable tradition of vicarious oversight when they responded to complaints about the exaction of garnish at Whitecross Street in 1822. Acknowledging that the dues had never been submitted to the City's magistrates for approval, they none the less commended (and upheld) their imposition as 'conducive to the comfort of the individuals confined' in the prison.[128]

Steeped in the rhetoric of custom and ancient usage and predicated on the forms of authority that prevailed in the outside world, the cultural practices of the unreformed debtors' prison were more naturally suited to a defensive conservatism than they were fitted for effective opposition to the status quo. Michael Ignatieff, writing of the structures of self-government elaborated by criminals in the unreformed prison, describes their activities as 'savagely accurate burlesques of official ritual' resented by reformers because they 'mocked the solemnities of the law'.[129] But the burden of evidence suggests that debtors constructed their own systems of authority with little intent to subvert established norms of authority. Admittedly, debtors' patriotic celebration of national events had a patently instrumental purpose, enabling them both to justify and finance excessive bouts of drinking. The Marshalsea debtors who requested a subscription from their keeper 'to celebrate his most Gracious Majesty's Birth Day by publicly dining together' in 1837, the twenty-three debtors in Horsham

---

[128] Guildhall Library, MS 659, King's Bench Miscellaneous Papers, vol. 1, fols. 1–2, Original Affidavits on the Complaint of the Prisoners in the King's Bench Prison, 24 July 1750; Lancaster Reference Library, MS 133, Special Commission to Inquire into the State, Conduct and Management of Lancaster Castle, 5 February 1813; PRO, PCOM 2/443, Lancaster Castle Keeper's Journal, 1842–45, 30 May 1843; PRO, HO 20/, Letter from Francis Desanger and George Alderson [December 1822].

[129] Ignatieff, *Just Measure of Pain*, 40.

8 Anonymous engraving of the Anti-Papal crowd destroying the King's Bench Prison during the Gordon Riots of 1780. Many debtors delayed their flights from prison during the riots to preserve their personal property from damage. (Reproduced by permission of the Guildhall Library, London.)

'Mansions of misery' 147

gaol 'anxious to participate in the public rejoicings' at the coronation of Queen Victoria in 1838 and the Lancaster debtors who, when reprimanded for 'loud singing & noise' in 1847, told the keeper that 'they were merely celebrating the anniversary of Waterloo', clearly sought to capitalise in this manner on their putatively patriotic sentiments.[130] But other evidence suggests that debtors by and large preferred existing structures of power to radical innovations upon them. An observer of the annual mock election held in 1842 by debtors at Lancaster Castle 'for the representation of the ancient borough of John O'Gaunt' noted that the Conservative candidates emerged victorious, 'as is generally the case'.[131]

The low incidence of attempted escapes from debtors' prisons reported in prison-keepers' journals is symptomatic of debtors' broader adherence to the wider structures of authority that constrained them. The young John Higgin quashed a rebellion of Lancaster convicts orchestrated by a debtor in 1785, and drew his sword to prevent the escape of both debtors and criminals in 1788 when a wooden barricade at the castle collapsed in a storm.[132] But the experiences of London prisons during the anti-Catholic Gordon Riots of 1780 illustrate debtors' more habitual reluctance to force their liberation from the confines of the prison. The Gordon Riots saw a sustained campaign of looting in which prisons and spunging-houses became a particular focus of the rioters' animosity. The destruction of Newgate and the liberation of its debtor and criminal prisoners was followed by successive onslaughts on the Fleet, Ludgate and King's Bench prisons, the Borough, Poultry and Wood Street Compters and at least twenty spunging-houses, as well as an unsuccessful attack on the Marshalsea.[133] (Illustration 8). Although debtors availed themselves of the opportunity to flee their prisons in the Gordon Riots, they were hardly at the forefront of the crowd. William Vincent's contemporary narrative of events described the destruction of the prisons as a project that was 'not altogether improbable to be a favourite scheme of the lawless rabble', but noted that the debtors in the Fleet, far from decamping immediately upon the breaching of its walls, were 'employed all day in removing their goods, preparatory to its being burnt in the evening'. Even long-term debtors could, as men of property, evince more concern to protect

---

[130] PRO, PALA 9/8, Letter of P. Dixon, 23 May 1837; PRO, HO 20/7, Petition of Horsham Gaol Debtors to Lord John Russell, [June 1838]; PRO, PCOM 2/444, Lancaster Castle Governor's Journal, 1845–49, 19 June 1847.

[131] J. Hall, *Lancaster Castle: Its History and Associations* (Lancaster, 1843), 23–4.

[132] Lancaster Reference Library, MS 3218, Punishment Book, Lancaster Castle, 1785–89, 8 August 1785; Edward Higgin, 'Memoranda relating to Lancaster Castle', *Transactions of the Historic Society of Lancashire and Cheshire*, 1 (1848–49), 100.

[133] Details from the attacks on prisons and spunging-houses, and the value of liberated debtors' debts (for which prison-keepers were legally liable upon their escape) are found in Anon., *A Narrative of the Proceedings of Lord George Gordon, and the Persons Assembled under the Denomination of the Protestant Association* (London, 1780), 15, 33–8, 43–4.

148   Imprisonment for debt and the economic individual

their possessions than to effect their personal freedom. The crowd that forced
the gates of the Fleet, another contemporary account recorded, began to demol-
ish the prison, 'but the prisoners expostulating with them, and begging that they
would give them time to remove their goods, they ... gave them a day for that
purpose, in consequence of which the prisoners were removing all this day out
of the place: some of the prisoners were in for life'.[134]

Conclusion

The muted welcome accorded to the Gordon rioters in 1780 was rehearsed
by debtors' reception of the Chartist challenge in 1848. Inmates of the King's
Bench stoutly offered their services on 10 April to the keeper 'to repel any
attack upon the prison' by the crowds amassed at Kennington Common, conduct that earned them a commendation from Sir George Grey at the Home
Office.[135] These actions were fully consonant with the prison's Janus-faced
function as a site of unwilling containment and a haven from economic adversity. For friendless and impecunious debtors immured in the smaller provincial
gaols, the debtors' prison could offer an inhospitable refuge. But the constant
influx of goods and persons, the distribution of debtors by social status and
the existence of effective systems of self-government all served to insulate
more affluent inmates in the larger carceral institutions from the full rigours
of confinement. Intended to encourage debtors to settle with their creditors,
imprisonment for debt, as novels such as *Little Dorrit* suggested, often served
instead to confirm their recalcitrant opposition to discharging their contractual
obligations. A parliamentary committee noted with concern in 1790 that 'to
Debtors of the worst Description a Prison is no Punishment; but on the contrary
... such Persons find an Interest, or a Gratification in remaining in a Situation
full of Misery to the Honest'. Promotional literature designed to draw debtors
to particular prisons played upon this theme shamelessly. 'There are few men
who have for any length of time laboured under adversity and been subject
to the unnecessary persecution of relentless creditors', a pamphlet advertising
the attractions of the King's Bench urged in 1827, 'but have found the King's
Bench, and its rules, a happy and welcome asylum, where persecution ends.'[136]
Debtor John Marsh, imprisoned in the King's Bench in 1827 for his failure to

---

[134] William Vincent, *A Plain and Succinct Narrative of the Late Riots and Disturbances in the Cities of London and Westminster, and Borough of Southwark*, 2nd edn (London, 1780), 44, 57; Anon., *A Narrative of the Proceedings*, 27.

[135] PRO, PRIS 9/8, Queen's Prison Governor's Journal, 1847–49, 10 April 1848, and PRO, PRIS 10/113, Denis LeMarchant to Captain Hudson, 17 April 1848. For a more detailed analysis of the limits of imprisonment for debt as a radical cause in this period, see my 'Henry Hunt's *Peep into a Prison*: the radical discontinuities of imprisonment for debt', in Glenn Burgess and Michael Festenstein, eds., *English Radicalism, 1550–1850* (forthcoming, Cambridge, 2004).

[136] *Report from the [House of Commons] Committee*, 22–3; *Description of the King's Bench*, 3.

'Mansions of misery' 149

pay William Rawlings, Esquire damages awarded for criminal conversation – that is, adultery – with Rawlings's wife, no doubt agreed. Having successfully pleaded destitution to sue Rawlings for his groats, Marsh paid over the sum received to obtain a private apartment in the prison, where observers reported 'that he was living exceedingly well, and also that Mrs Rawlings was living with him, and maintaining him herself at her own expense'.[137]

The journals and correspondence of prison-keepers provide ample confirmation of the prison's function as a haven. In 1833, when the keeper of Lincoln Castle at length succeeded in negotiating with William Holewell's creditors to effect the debtor's discharge upon the payment of a portion of his debt, Holewell – who had been imprisoned for five years and four months – rejected the settlement out of hand, declaring that 'he will not pay a sixpence but will remain in Gaol'. The keeper of the Queen's Prison (formerly the King's Bench) met with much the same response when he urged debtor Ford, an inmate of several years' standing, that he could readily obtain his discharge and could rely upon the keeper's assistance to this end. 'He admitted all this to be the case', Hudson noted with frustration in his journal, 'but said that he had no wish to leave the Prison, as he would rather die there.'[138] The existence of charitable bequests and regular work within the prison offered a particular attraction to debtors who lacked stable employment in the outside world. In this context, expulsion from the prison could function as a punishment rather than a reward. In 1801, the officers of the Palace Court disciplined a Marshalsea debtor for 'making a Noise and disturbance in the prison' by forcibly discharging him against his consent.[139]

In sharp contrast to the keepers of criminal gaols, the officers of debtors' prisons were confronted with the dilemma of policing inmates who were intent to gain access to privileges within the institution's walls alongside those who were determined to leave its precincts behind them altogether. The arbitrary character of arrest on mesne process allowed debtors who wished to avoid their creditors to obtain a 'friendly arrest' from a business partner or family member, and thus to enter the prison on their own terms. Hugh Butcher, imprisoned at the Fleet in 1826, availed himself of this legal option, and enjoyed the receipt of the prison's charities for several years.[140] Resort to this device was common outside the metropolis as well: an array of provincial debtors evinced considerable eagerness to enter gaols in their localities. In 1861, a man applied for admission at the gates of Bedford's prison, saying 'he was insolvent & wished

---

[137] Robert Nathaniel Cresswell, *Reports of Cases Heard and Decided in the Court for Relief of Insolvent Debtors: . . .* (London, 1830), 158.

[138] Lincolnshire Archives, CoC 5/1/2, Lincoln Castle Keeper's Journal, 1831–35, 12 October 1833; PRO, PRIS 9/11, Queen's Prison Keeper's Journal, 1853–56, 14 March 1856.

[139] PRO, PALA 8/70, Palace Court Rule Book, 1801–02, 22 May 1801.

[140] PRO, HO 119/8, John H. Cancellor to Lord Chief Justice Best, 15 April 1829.

150   Imprisonment for debt and the economic individual

to come to gaol'. Informed that his imprisonment could only be effected by a sheriff's officer with a writ, he was turned away twice by the gate-keeper, but ultimately achieved his desired goal, being 'brought into the Prison by the legal authority at 8 o'clock far advanced in Liquor'. In a similar manner, George Leish, imprisoned at Lancaster Castle from the Salford court of record, 'delivered himself into custody' at the prison gates in 1848, as the officer of the court 'was otherwise engaged & therefore deputed the Debtor to convey his own body to Gaol'. Frederick Smith, a coal dealer committed to the prison in October 1842, had previously obtained permission to tour its interior, a visit the keeper surmised was intended 'for looking about the Debtors' rooms for some quarters'.[141] His visit was fully in keeping with inmates' frequent description of debtors' prisons as hotels. Victorian debtors at Lancaster referred to their residence (after its keeper) as 'Hansbrow's Castle Hotel' and, less grandiloquently, as 'Hansbrow's Stone Jug', while Whitecross Street prison was known both as 'Burdon's Hotel' and the 'Cripplegate Coffeehouse'.[142]

Archival records testify to the great longevity of unreformed debtors' culture in the English prison, confirming the image of disorderly (but not entirely chaotic) community life projected in contemporary novels, diaries and memoirs. Rooted in an accretion of customary usage, the structures and practices of the unreformed debtors' prison defied the norms of contemporary legal discourse, resisting the civil law's distinction between the limited liability of the merchant and the full personal culpability of the consumer. Contractual obligations were less salient in this context than were expectations born of precedent and religious belief, a circumstance that worked – together with considerations of cost – to secure debtors considerable autonomy and power within the walls of the prison. Arrayed in nice gradations that reflected established perceptions of (or pretensions to) rank, status, gender and fortune, these forms of authority were not equally available to all debtor inmates. Nor was their longevity fortuitous. Rather, as the following chapters argue, the conventional culture, privileges and practices of unreformed debtors' prisons were predicated on the twofold basis of the custodial tradition of confinement and the tendency of high legal costs at common law to focus debt litigation disproportionately on substantial rather than petty debtors. Depicted as innocent victims of misfortune and counting men of considerable property among their ranks, eighteenth- and early nineteenth-century imprisoned debtors were well placed to defend their traditional privileges from the early onslaught of disciplinary penal reform. As their numbers were swelled by tens of thousands of plebeian debtors imprisoned

---

[141] PRO, PCOM 2/294, Bedford Prison Governor's Journal, 1859–67, 8 April 1861; PRO, PCOM 2/444, Lancaster Castle Keeper's Journal, 1845–49, 26 February 1848; PRO, PCOM 2/443, Lancaster Castle Keeper's Journal, 1842–45, 27 August 1842.

[142] Smith, *A Warder's Experience*, 8; Anon., *Whitecross Street and the Bench*, 42.

by small-claims courts, however, these immunities were subjected first to increasing scrutiny and then to sustained attack. By the mid-Victorian years, this extended process of reform would reconfigure the institutional experience of personal debt, transforming a process geared to recover debts contracted by the more affluent members of society into a mechanism for enforcing the contractual obligations of the working-class consumer.

4 Discipline or abolish? Reforming imprisonment for debt

Like the literary record, the history of unreformed debtors' prisons emphasises continuity rather than the dramatic transformation of imprisonment for debt over time. By underlining the retention of customary institutional cultures and practices from the 1740s to the 1840s, this static, descriptive survey helps to explain the persistent tropes that informed fictional representations of imprisonment for debt from Fielding and Goldsmith to Dickens and Trollope. Yet the demise of debtors' prisons as sites of literary representation in the mid-Victorian period suggests the need to supplement this narrative with an analysis that recognises the significance of change over time. For although the legal definition of insolvents as prisoners confined only for safe custody endured into the Victorian period, the proliferation of inferior small-claims courts ultimately undermined the time-honoured English interpretation of debtors as hapless victims of misfortune. By encouraging contemporaries to re-imagine the innocent debtor as a culpable legal agent, the rise of small-claims litigation compromised a tradition of representation that stretched back to the origin of the novel itself. Removing the debtor's prison from the domain of fiction, this reconfiguration of the debtors' character also worked to legitimate the reform of the debtors' prison.

Trends in economic life, political culture and legal practice are of central importance in understanding these developments. Financial panics provoked by the expansion of credit trading, mounting antagonism to aristocratic habits of indebtedness, hostility to the National Debt and the rising cost of administering the Poor Laws all rendered Georgian men and women increasingly sensitive to issues of debt and credit. By the 1770s, fiscal crises had become a commonplace feature of the English economic landscape, occurring roughly every six years. More alarming in scope and scale than earlier financial setbacks, Julian Hoppit argues, these disruptions 'cast serious doubts on the strength of one part of the financial structure underpinning the growth process, for the later crises not only began to involve the whole business community, but also were mainly caused and structured by the very nature of private credit'.[1] By drawing attention to

---

[1] Julian Hoppit, 'Financial crises in eighteenth-century England', *EcoHR*, 2nd ser., 39, 1 (February 1986), 50–1.

Discipline or abolish? 153

the perils that personal debts posed not only to individuals but to national prosperity more broadly, these recurrent credit crises helped to lay preliminary foundations for a hardening of attitudes toward debtors and their 'misfortunes' that triumphed in the Victorian period.

The scandalous debts of the Prince and Princess of Wales contributed to this attitudinal shift by generating new antagonism to traditional aristocratic credit practices.[2] As radical political sentiments gained currency in the aftermath of the American and French revolutions, parliamentary debate on the Prince of Wales's incontinent credit purchasing made personal solvency a byword of virtuous patriotism in opposition rhetoric.[3] The National Debt, which rose from £238 million in 1793 to £902 million in 1816, further exacerbated hostility to the feckless economic behaviour of aristocratic governments.[4] If fears of foreign invasion helped to blunt active resistance to these trends in the revolutionary era, they failed to prevent the emergence of a vociferous radical critique of the state's mounting credit obligations. Strident denunciations of the baneful financial influence of a governing elite, itself notorious for its inability to pay consumer debts, served to personalise critiques of the rising public level of debt and contributed to new scepticism about the moral valence of credit relations in English culture more broadly.[5]

Dramatic increases in unemployment and in the cost of poor relief further stoked fears of financial crisis and helped to precipitate a fundamental reformulation of attitudes toward poverty. Reinforcing the lines of argument that had earlier prompted the establishment of houses of correction, the increasing cost of poor relief tended more broadly to reduce tolerance to economic failure. 'Eighteenth-century administrators and projectors had been inclined to see poverty as a kaleidoscope of individual experiences rather than as a monolithic social condition, and accordingly they attempted to maintain institutional responses to poverty which, in theory at least, treated every application for relief on its own merits', David Eastwood has argued. From the 1790s, however, the confluence of escalating poor rates, a manifest inability on the part of the better sort to control their social inferiors and new theories of political economy increasingly eroded this conventional wisdom. 'The poor ceased to be regarded

---

[2] The norms of aristocratic indebtedness are detailed by David Cannadine, *Aspects of Aristocracy: Grandeur and Decline in Modern Britain* (New Haven, 1994), chap. 2, and H.J. Habakkuk, *Marriage, Debt and the Estates System: English Landownership 1650–1950* (Oxford, 1996).

[3] See, for example, [A Hanoverian], *John Bull Starving to Pay the Debts of the Royal Prodigal: A Letter to the House of Peers* (London, [1795]). For the earlier articulation between debt and patriotism, see John Sainsbury, 'John Wilkes, debt, and patriotism', *JBS*, 32, 2 (April 1995), 165–95.

[4] Norman Gash, *Pillars of Government: And Other Essays on State and Society c. 1770–c. 1880* (London, 1986), 44.

[5] For radical critiques of public debt, see Iain McCalman, *Radical Underworld: Prophets, Revolutionaries and Pornographers in London, 1795–1840* (Cambridge, 1988), esp. 101.

154   Imprisonment for debt and the economic individual

as individuals who may or may not merit assistance, and came to be regarded instead as "a problem": poverty appeared less as a transitory condition than as a quasi-permanent fourth estate.'[6]

These disparate developments – the increasing elaboration of credit networks, rising distrust of the aristocratic state's reliance on borrowing to finance its own expansion and a growing belief in the salutary discipline of market mechanisms for the poor – drew new public attention to the social and political significance of personal debt and credit relations. The mounting number of debtors committed to English prisons (now bursting with convicted criminals) worked together with new theories of penal discipline to challenge the interpretation of debtors as victims of misfortune. Initially serving to generate new forms of charitable assistance for insolvent prisoners, these pressures ultimately promoted an uneasy incorporation of debtors into the criminal prison itself.

Three broad phases mark the protracted campaigns that transformed the debtors' prison from an asylum capable of protecting its inmates from the full wrath of their creditors into a more punitive institution intended to exact retribution for economic misbehaviour. In the first stage, extending from the 1770s to the 1820s, magistrates and local government officials dominated initiatives, which focused more intensely on improving prison conditions for debtors – or on removing them from the prison altogether – than on rendering their confinement punitive. Debtors enjoyed a significant degree of sympathy from prison reformers in these decades, but this humanitarian concern was increasingly eclipsed by attention to the reform of convicted felons. As prison reformers became preoccupied with debates over the comparative merits of the silent and separate systems of prison discipline for convicts, debtors were shifted from the centre to the margins of prison policy. The second phase, from the 1830s to the 1860s, saw a revival of attention to imprisonment for debt. Parliamentary efforts to reform and expand the small-claims courts now raised the possibility that this practice, far from fading with the modernisation of English market relations, would constitute an essential component of new market disciplines. This period was marked by considerable confusion in contemporaries' perceptions of debtor inmates, who occupied a range of subject positions – from hapless victims of misfortune to wilful obstacles to economic progress – in the reformist imagination. Resolved in the 1860s by the abolition of imprisonment for substantial debts and the perpetuation of imprisonment by the small-claims courts, this second phase gave way to a third period, which lasted into the twentieth century. Now largely confined to working-class debtors, imprisonment for debt was stripped of its customary privileges and genteel associations. No longer of literary interest to novelists, imprisoned debtors emerged instead as the objects

---

[6] David Eastwood, *Governing Rural England: Tradition and Transformation in Local Government 1780–1840* (Oxford, 1994), 121.

Discipline or abolish? 155

of judicial solicitude. As the debtors' prison faded from public view, the county court emerged as a prime institutional site in which contemporaries debated the morality of modern contractual relations.

Debtors and philanthropic reform

Historians conventionally date the onset of sustained campaigns to reform English prisons to the 1770s, when John Howard's selection as sheriff of Bedfordshire (and thus his appointment as governor of the county gaol) precipitated an extended effort by local notables to transform the treatment of prisoners.[7] Episodic efforts to address the condition of prisons and their inmates in earlier decades had however prefigured the key concerns that were to dominate Howard's zealous campaigns. Three central premises of reform had emerged already in the seventeenth century: a belief that custody of all prison inmates should be entrusted to salaried government officials rather than to private individuals motivated by personal profit; a conviction that prison regulations should be crafted to create an orderly environment – rather than to transform debtors' attitudes or behaviours; and a determination to distinguish sharply between the conditions of confinement suitable for imprisoned debtors and the penalties appropriate for convicted criminals.[8] Legislation of 1670 provided a clear statutory mandate to construct reform agendas that recognised the distinction between debtors and criminals, requiring gaolers to separate the two groups within the prison.[9] The failure of prison-keepers to adhere to these precepts was not a novel revelation of Howard's time: a parliamentary committee led by James Oglethorpe had already exposed prison officials' 'Barbarous and Cruel' treatment of debtor inmates 'in high Violation and Contempt of the Laws of this Kingdom' in 1729.[10] Howard's innovation was, rather, to attempt to systematise knowledge of the prison and to promote received reform agendas for debtors alongside new punitive regimes for convicted criminals.

Much scholarship belabours Howard's efforts to impose new disciplinary regimes upon criminal inmates. Sidney and Beatrice Webb established an enduring analytical framework in identifying 'the subjection of all prisoners to a reformatory regimen of diet, work and religious exercises' as the key to

---

[7] For the conventional interpretation, see Sidney Webb and Beatrice Webb, *English Prisons under Local Government* (London, 1929), esp. 32. Rod Morgan offers a judicious assessment of Howard's significance in 'Divine philanthropy: John Howard reconsidered', *History*, 62, 206 (October 1977), 388–410.

[8] Donald Veall, *The Popular Movement for Law Reform 1640–1660* (Oxford, 1970), esp. 142–51.

[9] 22 & 23 Chas. II c. 20 (1670).

[10] *A Report from the Committee Appointed to Enquire into the State of the Gaols of This Kingdom: Relating to the Fleet Prison* (London, 1729), 14. See also Alex Pitofsky, 'The Warden's court martial: James Oglethorpe and the politics of eighteenth-century prison reform', *Eighteenth-Century Life*, 24, 1 (2000), 88–102.

156 Imprisonment for debt and the economic individual

Howard's penal vision while dismissing civil inmates in a telling phrase as 'the perennial crowd of mere debtors'.[11] Michel Foucault, while rejecting the Webbs' claim that Howard's motivation was fundamentally humanitarian, rehearsed essential features of their model by emphasising the disciplinary character of philanthropists' reform measures and their preoccupation with crime. For Foucault, the punitive apparatus of the modern prison, with its 'subtle, calculated technology of subjection', was so inextricably linked to the demands of modern capitalism that 'the two processes – the accumulation of men and the accumulation of capital – cannot be separated'. Contemporaries' efforts to discipline credit relations through penal policy are ignored in this analysis. Like the Webbs, Foucault and his English acolytes failed to address the significance of imprisonment for debt for the emergence of modern market relations.[12]

In striking contrast to these twentieth-century interpretations, John Howard's treatise on *The State of the Prisons in England and Wales* lavished attention on the plight of imprisoned debtors. First published in 1777 and rapidly acquiring canonical status as it passed through successive editions, this text described both metropolitan and provincial debtors' prisons in dense detail. Howard repeatedly documented debtors' numerical predominance over felons within the gaol. In 1779, of the 4,379 inmates he enumerated in English and Welsh prisons, 2,078 (47.5 per cent) were debtors and only 798 (18.2 per cent) convicted criminals.[13] Howard's approach to imprisoned debtors can hardly be described as penitential, punitive or disciplinary in its primary emphasis. Neither the Webbs' 'reformatory regimen of diet, work and religious exercises' nor Foucault's 'subtle, calculated technology of subjection' is salient in his proposals. To be sure, Howard was determined to reform the diet of imprisoned debtors, and urged that those confined on the common-side of the prison should 'have from the county the same allowance of every kind as felons: food, bedding, and medicine'. But given the failure of many prisons to provide debtors with any allowance of foodstuffs whatsoever, Howard's plea for the imposition of a diet fails to signal disciplinary imperatives calculated to reduce debtors to the status of criminals. The philanthropist, indeed, both recognised that debtors enjoyed the 'right to send out of the gaol for liquor and other necessaries' and described this provision as 'very judicious'.[14]

[11] Webb and Webb, *English Prisons*, 37, 24.
[12] Michel Foucault, *Discipline and Punish: The Birth of the Prison*, trans. Alan Sheridan (New York, 1977), 221. Foucault simply ignored the presence of debtors in prisons; Michael Ignatieff, *A Just Measure of Pain: The Penitentiary in the Industrial Revolution 1750–1850* (London, 1978) and John Bender, *Imagining the Penitentiary: Fiction and the Architecture of Mind in Eighteenth-Century England* (Chicago, 1987), acknowledge the salience of debtors in eighteenth-century prisons, but exclude them from the narrative of nineteenth-century penal reform.
[13] John Howard, *The State of the Prisons of England and Wales, with Preliminary Observations, and Some Account of Some Foreign Prisons and Hospitals*, 4th edn (London, 1792), 492.
[14] Ibid., 30, 3–4, 26.

Discipline or abolish?

Howard's proposals for debtors' labour within the prison were likewise signally deficient in disciplinary intent. Although fully cognisant of debtors' dissipated behaviour in the prison, Howard traced these tendencies to the evils of their environment rather than to the parlous state of their souls or the defects of their characters. He stressed the need to maintain debtors and felons in 'totally separate' precincts within prisons precisely because 'the peace, cleanliness, and health and morals of debtors cannot be secured otherwise'. The provision of prison workshops 'for such as are willing to work' was necessary not to inculcate new patterns of self-discipline among debtors but rather 'for preserving their habits of industry'. Examples of industrious debtors who made good use of the few opportunities for labour provided in unreformed prisons punctuate Howard's descriptions of provincial gaols. Handloom weaving, he noted with evident satisfaction, was the voluntary occupation of imprisoned debtors at Chelmsford, Ipswich, Lincoln and Lancaster. 'At the window they sell nets, purses, laces &c: over it [is] inscribed on a stone tablet, "He that giveth to the poor, lendeth to the Lord" ', Howard noted approvingly of debtors in York city gaol. Where Foucault saw prison labour as a disciplinary instrument imposed upon unwilling inmates by prison officers, Howard highlighted officials' obstinate opposition to debtors' virtuous efforts to support their families and pay their debts through labour conducted within the prison walls.[15]

From the 1770s to the 1820s, both local and national leaders of prison reform shared Howard's view of debtors as a distinct and rightfully privileged constituency within the prison. William Smith was a prominent advocate of strict penal discipline for convicted criminals, urging that 'One solitary confinement with hard labour, would intimidate the abandoned more than ten executions.' But Smith was punctilious in exempting 'the honest, though unfortunate debtor' from such disciplinary mechanisms. Denouncing the 'barbarous pretence' by which debtors were 'ranked with criminals', Smith in 1778 described confinement for debt as 'an imprisonment, which no law can justify, no religion reconcile, no morality countenance, no reason approve'.[16] Sir George Onesiphorous Paul, the driving force behind Gloucestershire's ambitious programme to replace mere prisons with effective penitentiaries in the 1780s, echoed this analysis. Staunch in his belief that 'CONFINEMENT TO PUNISH should also be Confinement to reform: It should be a State of continual Labour, and of total Seclusion from Society; by the former to create a Habit of Industry – by the latter to force Reflection on the Mind', Paul was an avowed disciple of 'the incomparable Mr HOWARD, the presiding Genius of Reform of these

---

[15] Ibid., 24, 260, 301, 327, 432, 409, 405, 312.

[16] William Smith, *State of the Gaols in London, Westminster, and Borough of Southwark* (London, 1776), 76; idem, *Mild Punishments Sound Policy: Or Observations on the Laws Relative to Debtors and Felons . . .* (London, 1778), 53–4.

158   Imprisonment for debt and the economic individual

melancholy Mansions of Oppression and Distress'. Like Howard, Paul was determined to defend 'the unfortunate Debtor (the victim of mere Misfortune)'
from the fate of 'the convicted Malefactor', for 'as Debtors, they have broken
no moral law'. His defence of debtors' conventional immunity from prison discipline rested securely on the conviction that 'Under the *British* Constitution it
is indispensable to Justice, that Proof of Criminality under all Forms of Law,
should precede Punishment.'[17]

Paul was typical of his generation in reaffirming the conventional distinction
between debtor and criminal prisoners while working to translate Howard's
new philanthropic ideals into administrative practice. To Lancashire's magistrates, who consulted Howard's writings in crafting their campaign to rebuild
the county's prison structures, the need to distinguish between criminal and
civil inmates was axiomatic. Meeting in Preston in 1784 to discuss the best
mode of establishing 'a Gaol of Punishment' at Lancaster Castle, they began by resolving 'That the different objects of Confinement seem to mark a
distinction between Gaols of Custody and Gaols of Punishment and require
separate prisons and different regulations.' By 1786, the justices had imposed
an extended system of prison regulations at Lancaster Castle, requiring criminal
prisoners to wear prison uniforms, subjecting them to labour and instituting a
programme of prisoner surveillance.[18] But Lancashire's magistrates failed to
evince corresponding zeal in disciplining civil inmates. The Castle's debtors,
already subjected by their fellows to detailed schedules of self-imposed regulations when Howard visited the prison in the 1770s, remained exempt from
regulation by prison officials until 1812.[19]

Reformers' active endorsement of the fundamental distinction between
debtor and criminal inmates continued in the early nineteenth century, when
efforts to erect penitential prisons – interrupted by the French wars – resumed
throughout the nation. The philanthropists of the influential Prison Discipline
Society were drawn disproportionately from the Quaker community – which
routinely expelled members from its ranks when they suffered bankruptcy – and
thus were hardly disposed to view debtor inmates with especial favour. Yet, as
the writings of this second generation of philanthropic reformers demonstrate,
they too were determined to defend debtors from penal discipline. Thomas
Fowell Buxton was adamant that the 'judicious discipline' of labour, surveillance and regulation would effectively reclaim the criminal for society. But

---

[17] Sir George Onesiphorous Paul, *Considerations on the Defects of Prisons, and Their Present Mode of Regulation*... (London, 1778), 53–4, 10, 19. For the subsequent reform of the county's prisons, see J.R.S. Whiting, *Prison Reform in Gloucestershire 1776–1820: A Study in the Work of Sir George Onesiphorous Paul, Bart.* (London, 1975).

[18] Lancashire RO, QAL/1, Lancaster Castle Committee Proceedings, 1783–1848, 13 May 1784, 20 July 1786.

[19] Margaret DeLacy, *Prison Reform in Lancashire: A Study in Local Administration* (Manchester, 1986), 95–6.

despite his adherence to the shibboleths of disciplinary reform, Buxton continued to define debtors as victims of misfortune. 'Human foresight cannot always avert, and human industry cannot always repair the calamities to which our nature is subjected; surely these are entitled to some compassion', Buxton argued in 1818. Casting debtors in their familiar character as innocent 'unfortunates', Buxton used a providentialist line of reasoning to justify his selective rejection of penal discipline. 'Not an act in the statute book is to be found, by which any mode of construction can be distorted into a justification of any, even the slightest severity upon the debtor, beyond his imprisonment', he insisted.[20]

In embarking upon the ambitious construction programme that was to erect or substantially rebuild over fifty prisons in England and Wales between 1800 and 1832, the second generation of prison reformers elaborated upon but also reformulated the goals expounded by their predecessors. Whereas Howard and his supporters had emphasised the need to provide secure penal structures that would guard inmates from disease while exposing them to uplifting moral influences, reformed prisons were now designed to act more forcefully upon the behaviour and character of individual criminal prisoners. A new emphasis on penal compulsion, rendered more potent by the introduction of Samuel Cubitt's improved treadwheel in 1822, received official endorsement with the passage of Sir Robert Peel's Prison Act of 1823, which 'defined the essentials of prison discipline as due classification, inspection, regular labour and religious and moral instruction'.[21] In the first decades of the nineteenth century, as Robin Evans has argued, 'classification, inspection and labour had supplanted security, salubrity and reformation as the fundamentals of a good prison'.[22]

Because county debtors' prisons were typically located within larger penal complexes that also housed felons and misdemeanants, debtor inmates were caught up in these new punitive regimes. In the 1820s, local magistrates were repeatedly compelled to weigh their allegiance to debtors' customary privileges against the dictates of the new norms of criminal confinement. Although the culture of the unreformed debtors' prison suffered some depredations in this context, it retained its characteristic features throughout the 1820s, as the sympathetic attitude toward debtors evident in the writings of prison reformers was replicated in the actions of local prison officials. Magistrates in a number of localities began tentatively to explore the limits of debtors' conventional immunity from prison discipline, but custom and latitude continued to outweigh

---

[20] Thomas Fowell Buxton, *Appendix to the First Edition of an Inquiry, Whether Crime and Misery Are Produced or Prevented by Our Present System of Prison Discipline* . . . (London, 1818), 12; idem, *An Inquiry Whether Crime and Misery Are Produced or Prevented by Our Present System of Prison Discipline* . . . (London, 1818), 4, 6.

[21] U.R.Q. Henriques, 'The rise and decline of the separate system of prison discipline', *P&P*, 54 (February 1972), 66–71, citation from 71.

[22] Robin Evans, *The Fabrication of Virtue: English Prison Architecture 1750–1840* (Cambridge, 1982), 236, 256–60, citation from 260.

160 Imprisonment for debt and the economic individual

prescription and strict regulation in the quotidian life of imprisoned debtors. Even when reformers' restrictive impulses were evident in the county's administration of debtors, inmates' traditions of self-regulation tended to blur the lines of authority and control that were articulated through new punitive measures. A magistrate's order for Ilchester gaol, Somerset in 1825 which decreed that debtor Bartlett be removed 'into solitary confinement for 3 days, for profane cursing and swearing – abusing the keeper in the presence of the Debtors, and for abusive and highly improper behaviour to the whole ward' could be read as evidence of the newly authoritarian tenor of prison administration. But the Foucauldian significance of this incident, its ability to document magistrates' intention to impose an alien code of behaviours on the inmate population, is undercut by the next sentence in their journal, which notes that 'A letter was sent to us signed by 9 of the Debtors complaining of the said Bartlett & praying that he might be removed.'[23]

In tenor, tendency and operation, indeed, the new schedules of regulations imposed in the 1820s tended to consolidate received conceptions of imprisonment for debt as a form of safe custody alone. Whereas rules governing convicts' behaviour emphasised uniformity, compulsion and regulated labour, debtor regulations were couched in terms of exceptionalism and volition: variations on the phrase 'except for the debtors' punctuate the strictures imposed upon criminals in county and borough gaols. In Wiltshire, the rules instituted at Fisherton Anger gaol in 1822 mandated that the governor 'shall neither take or demand any Fee, Gratuity, or Emolument, save and except such Compensation and Allowance as the Debtor Prisoners confined on the Master's side of the Gaol . . . may choose and agree to pay', and prohibited the consumption of wine, ale, beer and spirits 'except in the case of the Debtors'.[24] At the Cambridge county gaol, rules approved in 1824 decreed 'That all the prisoners (except the debtors) be locked in their proper wards, cells, or rooms, when day-light terminates' and declared that all prisoners, 'except persons confined for debt', be dressed in the prison uniform.[25] Prison officers' recognition of the anomalous legal status of imprisonment for debt further compromised government attempts to reduce debtors' exemptions from penal discipline in the 1820s. 'Imprisonment is not considered by the Law as a punishment for Debt; but merely as a Security, by confining the person of the Debtor 'till payment is made', William Jones, marshal of the King's Bench, reminded a parliamentary committee in 1825. 'If the Marshal of the King's Bench were to adhere, without relaxation of any kind

---

[23] Somerset RO, Q/Agi/7/3, Magistrates' Book, Ilchester Gaol, 23 May 1825, 87. See similarly Lincolnshire Archives, CoC 5/1/1, County Gaol Keeper's Journal, 1824–31, 18 July 1827.

[24] PRO, HO 20/1, item 59a, *Rules, Orders, and Regulations, for the Government of the County Gaol and Bridewell, at Fisherton Anger in the County of Wilts* (Salisbury, 1822), 63–5.

[25] PRO, HO 130/3, Town of Cambridge. By order of the session of the 7th July 1824 the Rules and Regulations adopted.

Discipline or abolish? 161

whatever, to the strict letter of all the Rules, which have been issued at different and distant periods for the Government of the prison, it would be a place of punishment as well as Security.'[26]

The attitudes toward inmate labour encapsulated in new prison regulations speak eloquently to debtors' continued privileged status in the prison. As reformers' enthusiasm for regimes of compulsory labour mounted, county magistrates across the nation hastened to install treadwheels, on which petty offenders and felons were set to mill corn, pump water or 'grind the air' without productive purpose.[27] Debtors' exemption from compulsory labour and the tentative tones in which their voluntary employment within the prison was mooted are both striking and significant in this context. Here too inclination replaced compulsion and the conditional tense reigned supreme. The rules instituted at Bedford in 1824 convey the predominant tendency of these regulations, stating that 'Debtors inclined to work may employ themselves or be employed in the prison.'[28] In the 1820s, as in earlier decades, concern that debtors' chosen employments would disrupt order within the prison were more salient in regulations than fears that failure to labour would demoralise debtor inmates. The regulations for debtors confined in the borough gaol in Colchester thus declared 'That no Debtor shall be allowed to exercise his Trade or use any Employment in the Gaol to the annoyance of other Debtors or without the special order of the Mayor in writing.'[29]

New forms of charitable relief for debtors were also significant in mooting – and containing – debtors' subjection to a degree of discipline and surveillance in these years. Charitable bequests with few if any restrictions continued to provide imprisoned debtors with funds, foodstuffs and coal well into the Victorian period, but the later eighteenth century saw an increasing effort on the part of philanthropists associated with a cluster of new charitable associations to distinguish among inmates according to their character and moral merits. By far the most prominent of these organisations was the Society for the Discharge and Relief of Persons Imprisoned for Small Debts – known familiarly as the Thatched House, or the Craven Street, Society – inspired in 1772 by a sermon preached on behalf of imprisoned debtors at a fashionable chapel in Pimlico.[30]

---

[26] PRO, HO 20/2, William Jones, Observations upon the Report of the Hon. Henry Grey Bennett's Committee, 25.

[27] Ignatieff, *Just Measure of Pain*, 177. Twenty-six counties had installed treadwheels by 1826.

[28] PRO, HO 130/3, *Rules for the Government of Prisoners ... Bedford County Gaol* [1824], rule 9.

[29] PRO, HO 130/3, 'Rules and Regulations for the government of the Debtors' Gaol of the Borough of Colchester', [1824].

[30] James Neild, *An Account of the Rise, Progress, and Present State of the Society for the Discharge and Relief of Persons Imprisoned for Small Debts throughout England and Wales*, 3rd edn (London, 1808), 13–18. Peter J. Lineham, 'The campaign to abolish imprisonment for debt in England, 1750–1840' (M.A. thesis, University of Canterbury, NZ, 1974), 86–103 provides an excellent overview of the Society's early activities.

162   Imprisonment for debt and the economic individual

Over the course of several decades, the Thatched House Society enabled tens of thousands of petty debtors to obtain their discharge from prison: between 1772 and 1831 alone, it secured the discharge of 51,250 debtors at an average cost of two pounds, nineteen shillings and twopence each.[31] Available only to men and women whose debts did not exceed the sum of ten pounds, the charity's funds were allocated after a committee (composed of members who had paid an annual subscription of two guineas) had subjected the debtor's petition for assistance to close scrutiny. Character loomed large in the Society's deliberations: petition forms required all applicants to provide the names of persons who could attest to their *sobriety and integrity*' and the committee reserved the right to apply for further information to debtors' detaining creditors. Letters to these plaintiffs were specifically designed to distinguish between deserving and undeserving debtors, requesting their creditors to remark on '*the manner in which the debt was contracted: whether in the common and ordinary course of business, or upon specious pretenses; and of such other circumstances, as may enable the Society to judge of the Petitioner's true character*'. Inmates who applied to its funds again, the Society's fifth rule proclaimed, were to be relieved only when it was demonstrated 'that their second misfortune cannot be imputed to their own fault'.[32]

Although the Thatched House Society's determination to exclude persons who had fallen into debt 'by fraud, vice, or extravagance' from their charity presaged later reformers' hostility to fraudulent debtors, their philosophy was, in keeping with their times, predicated upon a fundamental belief in the innocence of debtor prisoners and the fractured nature of individual autonomy. Questioning the legitimacy of imprisonment for debt, their secretary and leading spokesman James Neild drew particular attention to the 'unavoidable misfortunes' that propelled debtors into gaol.[33] The Society's refusal to pay more than a composition (or portion) of the debt for which the inmate was imprisoned was of a piece with this interpretation of debtors as victims of misfortune. Rejecting the moral legitimacy of legal proceedings that enforced the individual's contracts to the full, payment of partial compositions was intended to convince creditors that it was in their spiritual and economic interest to treat debtors with compassion. 'Plaintiffs must always be losers by prosecution of Debts', they proclaimed. 'This the Society ever take into consideration; and it is a principal object of their Attention, to demonstrate to the lower class of People the exceeding Folly of being stimulated by their Passions to go to Law with Fellow-Creatures.'[34]

---

[31] Guildhall Library, MS 17,027, Prison Charities: Thatched House, A Summary View of the Money Annually Expended by the Society for the Discharge and Relief of Persons Imprisoned for Small Debts, [1832].

[32] Neild, *Account of the Rise, Progress, and Present State*, 49–57, citations from 55, 57, 52.

[33] Ibid., 52, 19.   [34] Ibid., 576.

Discipline or abolish? 163

Provincial philanthropists inspired by the Thatched House Society created a number of like-minded charitable associations to assist and liberate petty debtors in their localities.[35] In Gloucestershire, where draconian, disciplinary prison reform found many of its most staunch adherents, distinctions between 'deserving' and 'undeserving' debtors ostensibly became more salient from the 1790s. New rules designed to make the county's renovated prison structures function as an effective penitential system rather than merely as sites of containment focused on criminal prisoners, but exposed the need to exact 'a due submission' from debtors to promote 'that decency and good order which must be their common benefit'.[36] The twenty-eighth rule of the county's new prison regulations called for the formation of a committee with the express function of policing the distribution of charity to debtors. Dominated for over a decade by Sir G.O. Paul, the Prison Charity Committee established in 1792 sought to marry established practices of charitable Christian paternalism with emerging notions of individual responsibility.[37]

Deriving its initial funding from a donation of three hundred pounds made by the King to assist 'Prisoners confined for small Debts' in the county, the Prison Charity Committee operated according to many of the same principles that animated the activities of the Thatched House Society. Antagonism to the strict legal enforcement of contracts and concern that charity be extended only to debtors of good character were defining features of the committee. Its regulations urged that only a composition of the debt be paid to the creditor and that the petitioning debtor provide at least one reference 'relative to his general character, and in the case of [there being] more than one Petitioner, the Preference shall be given to the Person of best Character & who shall have behaved most regularly whilst in Prison'. To prevent the legal profession from benefiting from their largess, moreover, committee members refused to award funds toward legal fees that it deemed excessive, preferring to apply the charity to relieve the debtor in prison rather than to promote 'aggravated costs of Law'.[38]

The Committee's minutes provide substantial information on the traits used to distinguish deserving from undeserving debtor characters. Thomas Hatchett, a husbandsman who 'behaves well in Prison' and 'knows Mr Miles a clergyman in Cirencester' was judged worthy of assistance and discharged from gaol upon payment of a composition in December 1792; the shoemaker Jasper Evans, who bore 'a good Character in his neighbourhood' was relieved in September

---

[35] See, for example, Somerset RO, Q/Agz/18/1, Account Book of Small Debtors Fund, 1809–1832, and Somerset RO, Q/Agz/18/3, *Somersetshire Society for the Relief of Persons Imprisoned for Small Debts* (Bath, 1810).

[36] *General Regulations for Inspection and Controul of All Prisons . . . 15 July 1790*, 2nd edn (Gloucester, [1790]).

[37] For its establishment, see Gloucestershire RO, Q/Gc/18/1, Prison Charity Committee Proceedings, 1792–97, report of Shipping Sessions, 1792.

[38] Ibid., 3 February 1792.

164 Imprisonment for debt and the economic individual

1799.[39] The presence of social connections – dependents who relied upon the debtor's labour and family members, friends or local authorities willing to offer additional assistance – evidently strengthened the virtuous debtor's case further. Richard Pearce, a barber with a wife and nine children, was assisted by a subscription raised by his neighbours, to which the Committee willingly contributed two guineas in 1796; Thomas Williams, a farmer with nine children thrown on the Poor Laws by his imprisonment, was offered a composition of five shillings on the pound to discharge his debt, on the condition that his parish also contribute toward his liberation. Similarly, Richard Daniel, 'maintained in Prison by a Daughter who followed him to Glo[u]cester for that Purpose; appears to be a most deserving object'.[40] Far from emphasising the autonomous individual's full liability for his debts, Gloucestershire's charity highlighted the individual's immersion in social relations, and thus the injustice of enforcing contracts without attention to equitable mitigating circumstances.

Debtors whose petitions the Committee rejected displayed a predictable range of bad behaviours. When William Voice 'prevaricated on his Examination in Court' he was found 'no longer to merit the protection of the Committee', a fate that also befell the gardener Warren Davies, who 'does not give a fair and open account, nor appear to mean justly toward his Creditors'. Joseph Moreton was clearly unfit to receive the charity, figuring as 'one of the most unfeeling & unnatural Characters ever before the Committee. His cause of imprisonment being the arrest of his own father aged near 90 on a false Plea.'[41] In keeping with its avowed distaste for the legal profession's cultivation of plaintiffs' litigious tendencies, the Committee declined repeatedly to assist debtors who, like John Stephens, were confined for debts 'created by Law'. The failed farmer James Lifely, who appeared deserving of assistance when his imprisonment seemed 'attributable to the vile conduct of an attorney named Jessop', was judged worthy of disciplinary procedures instead when it emerged that he had made a false affidavit '& that on the whole it was a scheme between Lifely & Jessop to deceive the committee & his creditors'.[42]

If the Committee often upheld simplistic notions of virtuous character and conduct, members' extensive use of their discretionary powers none the less displayed their continued willingness to take cognisance of debtors' unavoidable misfortunes. When Benjamin Rogers failed to obtain a character reference from parish officials, the Committee ordered the prison-keeper to write instead

---

[39] Ibid., 17 December 1792; Gloucestershire RO, Q/Gc/18/2, Prison Charity Committee Proceedings, 1799–1816, 28 September 1799.

[40] Prison Charity Committee Proceedings, 1792–97, 11 January 1796; 7 April 1796; 10 February 1792.

[41] Ibid., 30 July 1793; Prison Charity Committee Proceedings, 1799–1816, 8 June 1802; 28 November 1806.

[42] Prison Charity Committee Proceedings, 1792–97, 10 February 1792; Prison Charity Committee Proceedings, 1799–1816, 18 January and 27 November 1799.

Discipline or abolish? 165

to a local magistrate, 'the Parish appearing to be prejudiced ag[ains]t him'. Nor were debtors with known histories of misconduct inevitably refused assistance. William Voice was denied money for his discharge because he had made a false statement of his finances in the Insolvent Court and been convicted of stealing from his fellow debtors in gaol, but 'on account of his very distressed situation . . . his Illness & Inability to work', he was awarded a modest prison allowance. And notwithstanding Edward Churchill's fraudulent conveyance to an attorney of property he wished to preserve from his creditors, he was relieved with eighteen shillings in 1802. Having subsequently proven 'industrious and exemplary in his conduct', he was assisted again by the Committee, which effected his discharge from prison in 1804.[43] Like novelists, diarists and autobiographers, prison philanthropists evinced a tolerant and fluid understanding of debtors' moral status. In Georgian prison administration as in imaginative literature and market dealings, the character of credit was a flexible construct rather than a rigid norm premised on strict notions of contract.

The distribution of charity to debtors in the half century from 1780 to 1830 – the period in which the highly personalised justice of the county magistracy was arguably at its zenith[44] – shared obvious similarities with a wider range of local administrative practices, most notably the operation of the Poor Law. Just as parish officials prior to 1834 could choose to confer on paupers economic benefits of a surprisingly 'generous and widely encompassing nature', so too prison philanthropists were willing to dispense their monies to meet a broad array of needs among distressed debtors.[45] This confluence of practice was not surprising, as individuals confined by the small-claims courts derived from the same social strata served by the Poor Laws, to which the families of imprisoned debtors were routinely forced to appeal for assistance when their breadwinners were cast in gaol.[46]

The limitations of these new debtor charities also mirrored the broader limitations of county government, based upon the voluntary participation of unpaid notables. James Neild, who made a habit of meeting with local magistrates

---

[43] Ibid., 15 December 1810; Prison Charity Committee Proceedings, 1792–97, 6 October 1796; 7 April 1796; Prison Charity Committee Proceedings, 1799–1816, 8 June 1802 and 20 August 1804.

[44] For the vitality of county government in this period, see Eastwood, *Governing Rural England*, esp. 75, 82.

[45] K.D.M. Snell, *Annals of the Labouring Poor: Social Change and Agrarian England, 1660–1900* (Cambridge, 1985), 104–37, citation from 105. Snell notes that Poor Law officials purchased a wide range of necessary goods for paupers, as well as providing them with money allowances. See similarly Tim Hitchcock, Peter King and Pamela Sharpe, eds., *Chronicling Poverty: The Voices and Strategies of the English Poor, 1640–1840* (Basingstoke, 1997). Likewise, the Gloucestershire committee ordered the purchase of a pair of shoes for the insolvent hatter William Jarnott. Gloucestershire RO, Q/Gc/18/1, Prison Charity Committee Proceedings, 1792–97, 1 August 1796.

[46] See below, 245–6.

166   Imprisonment for debt and the economic individual

when he visited provincial prisons, recalled that 'I was always received with cordiality and kindness, and as they were struck with compassion at the recital, reform was determined upon, and resolutions entered into; but after a lapse of eight or ten years, guess my surprise, when I found nothing done!'[47] The causes of this administrative indolence – the rapid turnover in the roll of magistrates, the pressure of justices' paid employments and their reluctance to enter gaols notorious as sources of infection – were widely pervasive in county government. Gloucestershire's prison charity flourished when it could draw upon the expertise and weekly intervention of Sir G.O. Paul, but as local enthusiasm for prison reform lagged in the 1830s, the Committee suffered a corresponding decline.[48] More broadly, as the English prison population continued to rise and the composition of the inmate population shifted increasingly toward plebeian criminal offenders, local initiatives and philanthropy were largely eclipsed by national reform agendas that emanated from the Home Office.

Imprisoned debtors and reformed prisons

The 1830s saw reformers' tentative inroads into imprisoned debtors' autonomy expand significantly as the central government assumed increasing responsibility for prison policy. Fears of social disorder spawned by the continued increase of the criminal and pauper populations had promoted public calls for a greater degree of deterrence in penal policy throughout the 1820s, and in 1830 the Whig ministry dispatched the philanthropist William Crawford to the United States to assess new American penal regimes based on the cellular model. Crawford, converted by this visit to the so-called separate system – in which criminal prisoners were locked in individual cells, exercised in separate yards, laboured on partitioned treadwheels and attended mandatory divine service in partitioned chapels – spearheaded a successful campaign to replace the second generation of reformed English prisons – built to optimise the classification and segregation of inmates into distinct groups according to their crimes – with prisons organised instead around cellular units that separated individual prisoners regardless of their designated position in the prison's classification scheme.[49]

The establishment of a national Prison Inspectorate and the appointment of five peripatetic prison inspectors – the most vocal of whom was Crawford himself – lent force to these individualising developments in penal policy. The

[47] T.J. Pettigrew, ed., 'Memoir of J. Neild, Esq. written by himself', *Gentlemen's Magazine* (April 1817), 309.

[48] By 1837, lack of interest had effectively disbanded the committee. See Gloucestershire RO, Q/Gc/18/3, Prison Charity Committee Proceedings, 1817–45.

[49] Henriques offers a succinct analysis of the history of separate confinement in 'Rise and decline', esp. 71–4. The American models and their European implications are discussed in Adam J. Hirsch, *The Rise of the Penitentiary: Prisons and Punishment in Early America* (New Haven, 1992), esp. 112–13.

Discipline or abolish? 167

balance of ideological power now increasingly shifted to central government officials, who worked sedulously to create a 'hermetic zone of expertise' intended to link prisons directly to the Home Office.[50] Launched 'by sheer force of unproven assertion', the separate system advocated by Crawford and his fellow inspector Whitworth Russell gained the official sanction of Lord John Russell – Whitworth Russell's uncle – and was explicitly prescribed for county and borough prisons by successive Gaol Acts.[51] Central government subsidies to local government now bolstered hortatory reform rhetoric, becoming 'an increasingly important means of ensuring local compliance with statutory obligations and ministerial directions'.[52] By 1850, Colonel Jebb – appointed in 1844 to the new office of Surveyor General of Prisons and empowered to approve all plans for prison rebuilding and erection in England and Wales – could report the completion of fifty-five prisons in compliance with the separate system, with an additional six cellular prisons under construction.[53]

Historians of the criminal prison have rightly drawn attention to the failures of the separate system, highlighting the disjunction between the draconian new policies it mandated and the persistence of entrenched administrative practices and disorderly inmate behaviours.[54] The projected expense of converting the nation's prisons from the classificatory to the cellular system was alone staggeringly prohibitive: a Select Committee of 1835 estimated that the proposed conversion would increase county expenditure on prisons by 59 per cent.[55] Bureaucratic obstacles and infighting further impeded implementation of the separate system, notwithstanding its official sanction by the government. Conflicts among the prison inspectors and between inspectors and the Surveyor General of Prisons were fierce and destructive. As Crawford, who had greeted the announcement of Jebb's appointment with open hostility in 1844, wrote irately of the inspectors' relations with him a year later, 'our being kept in entire ignorance – as we have been – of the Plans of new Prisons or of extensive alterations, in our District, is calculated to embarrass our Proceedings with the Magistrates in our Visits to the Prisons'.[56]

Against this backdrop, extending the cellular principle to debtors proved especially difficult. In the aftermath of the 1832 Reform Act, a growing conviction that the rising tide of Whig reform would sweep the practice of imprisonment

---

[50] Evans, *Fabrication of Virtue*, 331.
[51] Henriques, 'Rise and decline', 78. For the early history of the Prison Inspectorate, see Séan McConville, *A History of English Prison Administration*, vol. I: *1750–1877* (London, 1981), 170–5.
[52] McConville, *History of English Prison Administration*, 256.
[53] Henriques, 'Rise and decline', 78; Evans, *Fabrication of Virtue*, 367.
[54] See esp. Séan McConville, *English Local Prisons, 1860–1900: Next Only to Death* (London, 1994), and Lucia Zedner, *Women, Crime and Custody in Victorian England* (Oxford, 1991).
[55] Eastwood, *Governing Rural England*, 258.
[56] BLPES, Sir Joshua Jebb Papers, part 1, 3/3/5, William Crawford to Joshua Jebb, 26 April 1845.

168   Imprisonment for debt and the economic individual

for debt away altogether encouraged counties to resist government pressure to include debtors in plans for cellular confinement.[57] Brecon magistrates sitting at Quarter Sessions in 1837 were typical, resolving that 'as to the erection of a new Gaol it appears desirable to wait . . .'til the Legislature shall have determined the Question of continuing or abolishing Imprisonment for Debt as that Determination will materially affect the size and arrangement of the Prison'.[58] The new prison inspectors themselves, who viewed debtors as a secondary concern in their campaign to impose cellular confinement on criminals, were moved by the uncertainty of the 'present position of the Law with reference to the confinement of Debtors' to recommend to Russell in 1837 'that accommodation should be provided, on the most limited scale' for borough debtors.[59] In November, inspector Williams reported optimistically to Russell that 'the expected alteration of the Law of Debtor and Creditor, may render it unnecessary to provide a new building for this Class of Prisoners' in Liverpool, a sanguine prediction that Crawford and Russell hastened to confirm.[60] Twenty years later, uncertainty as to the perpetuation of the practice continued to plague efforts to build prison structures that would subject insolvent inmates to disciplinary regimes.[61]

Despite their preoccupation with criminal policy, the prison inspectors did play an essential part in fomenting new interest in debtor discipline from the 1830s. Their concern to impose bureaucratic uniformity upon a prison system riddled with particularistic privileges, to justify the expense of the separate system by demonstrating the conspicuous inadequacies of mere classification and to subject criminal prisoners to rigorous regimes of penal regulation all fostered this punitive trend. Inspector Williams's horrified report on the state of the Duke of Norfolk's franchise gaol in Sheffield, to which court of requests debtors were committed, gave voice to these concerns in 1836. The gaol's inadequacy as an institution was made manifest by the keeper's repeated appeals to the local police 'for the repression of disorders and riots', but even the debtors' more peaceable activities provided powerful testimony to the failure of mere classification to promote order and industry in the prison. Constituting a unified, segregated 'class' of prisoner, these petty debtors exhibited the worst

---

[57] Brougham's famous six-hour speech to the Commons in 1828 had done much to associate Whig legal reform policies with a programme of modernising initiatives that included abolition of imprisonment for debt. See Bruce Kercher, 'The transformation of imprisonment for debt in England, 1828–1838', *Australian Journal of Law and Society*, 2, 1 (1984), esp. 71–4.

[58] PRO, HO 20/5, Copy of Quarter Sessions proceedings at Brecon, 17 October 1837.

[59] PRO, HO 20/4, Crawford and Whitworth Russell to Lord John Russell, 22 September 1837. The government approved the provision of debtor accommodation 'on the most limited scale' a few days later. See PRO, HO 20/8, Maule to Crawford and Whitworth Russell, 27 September 1837.

[60] PRO, HO 20/4, Williams to Russell, 18 November 1837, and Crawford and Whitworth Russell to Russell, 1 December 1837.

[61] See, for example, CLRO, Gaol Committee Papers, 'Report upon the Present State and Condition of the Sheriffs Prison for Debtors, Whitecross Street' (1857), 56.

Discipline or abolish? 169

excesses of unreformed behaviour. 'On going through the rooms gambling with cards appeared to be the only occupation, except in one, where a lottery had just been drawn, the capital prize of which, had been a pair of razors', a scandalised Williams reported. Here the fatal consequences of localised power and privilege – as opposed to centralised state control – were conspicuously evident. 'These unfortunate people being uterly neglected, have formed rules of conduct for their society', Williams wrote of the debtors. 'The keeper has . . . frequently applied to the Steward of the Court, and the Magistrates, for directions, for the better government of the Prison, but they have considered it beyond the pale of magisterial interference, as being private property.'[62]

As the prison inspectors gained ascendancy, debtors' customary privileges emerged as significant obstacles to the achievement of the separate system's deterrent and reformatory goals. Conflicts surrounding the use of tobacco in the 1830s illustrate the dynamics of this conflict. Proscribed by the government for criminal inmates in 1835, tobacco was permitted – at the behest of no less a keen reformer than Lord John Russell himself – for debtor prisoners, in deference to the merely custodial character of their confinement. Selective prohibitions and entitlements of this sort were however exceptionally difficult to maintain, and debtors' anomalous status within the prison rendered punishment for the infractions that inevitably occurred highly fraught. When magistrates visiting Dorchester's gaol in 1835 found debtor Henry Chitty guilty of selling tobacco to the criminal inmate John Drew, they confronted a range of obstacles in seeking to discipline the offending debtor whilst acknowledging his privileged legal status. Drew, as a felon, was easily dealt with through the device of solitary confinement, but the magistrates were clearly reluctant to accord civil and criminal inmates equivalent punishments. Warning the debtors that they must consider their use of tobacco an 'indulgence', they punished Chitty with a forty shillings fine, to be deducted from his earnings as a painter within the gaol, and – in an obvious departure from the separate system's use of compulsory labour as a punitive discipline – also prohibited him from future employment in the prison.[63]

When debtor Andrew Robings was found to have supplied Dorchester felons with tobacco several months later, he too was fined and barred from prison employment, but the magistrates, evidently frustrated by the limited and contradictory mechanisms at their disposal, now additionally disciplined the debtors as a body by revoking their smoking privileges. The master's-side

---

[62] PRO, HO 20/3, Captain Williams to S.M. Phillips, 9 December 1836. The Duke's steward noted that reform of the gaol had been considered in 1827, but abandoned when Parliament began to debate the abolition of imprisonment for debt. PRO, HO 20/3, [Richard] Ellison to the Duke of Norfolk, 26 November 1836.

[63] PRO, HO 20/3, Dorchester Gaol, Extracts from the Visiting Justices' Minute Book relative to Debtors giving Tobacco to Criminal Prisoners, 21 July 1835 and 1 January 1836.

170   Imprisonment for debt and the economic individual

inmates promptly retaliated by appealing to the government to preserve their privileged status. Debtor William Godwin reminded Lord John Russell of the magistrates' failure to recognise the fundamental distinction between a gentleman's word and the duplicitous claims of a convicted felon. Whereas Robings was prepared to swear his innocence on oath, Godwin noted, his accuser was 'a Person who has since been tried, convicted and sentenced to be transported beyond the Seas'. The Dorchester magistrates, themselves clearly conflicted about their unauthorised policy, in turn wrote to Russell, intent to justify their departure from past practices by demonstrating their inability to enforce the separate system mandated for criminals unless they were empowered to impose new restrictions upon debtors. 'The utmost vigilance of the Keeper or Turnkey will not be able to prevent the clandestine conveyance of Tobacco from the Debtors to the other Prisoners', they maintained, '& therefore the prohibition can only be enforced, by [resorting] ... occasionally to such means as may appear severe'.[64]

Represented by Dorchester's magistrates as an 'occasional' disciplinary expedient, the prohibition of tobacco soon calcified into an official policy sanctioned by the Prison Inspectorate and the Home Office. The evolving line of government response to the smoking problem illustrates the broader process of attrition by which debtors' customary privileges were gradually eroded. Pressure to conform to the separate system intensified in August 1835, when Russell sent a circular to all county magistrates and borough justices specifically endorsing the inspectors' plans to confine all criminals in well-constructed separate cells, 'with moral and religious instruction, regular employment, and the daily visits of the chaplain and officers of the prison'.[65] This effort to subject convicted prisoners to individualistic disciplinary regimes placed prison officials under renewed pressure to contain debtors' habitually dissolute forms of sociability. Already in the autumn of 1836, the prohibition of tobacco had become a regular feature of the rules for debtors submitted by magistrates for Russell's approval, rather than a contingent disciplinary device invoked to punish debtors who had abused the freedoms conferred by their superior status as custodial prisoners. Responding to a query from the town clerk of Hull in November, Crawford and Whitworth Russell decreed that in the town's new prison rules 'the use of Tobacco should be prohibited in regard to Debtors as well as every other description of Prisoners and that on no account should such an Indulgence be permitted except in cases of Indisposition'.[66] By defining access to tobacco as

[64] Ibid., 1 January 1836; William Godwin to Russell, 14 January 1836; PRO, HO 20/3, Dorchester Visiting Magistrates to Russell, 24 January 1836.
[65] PRO, HO 20/5, *Circular of the Right Honourable the Secretary of State for the Home Department, to the Magistrates Assembled at Quarter Sessions of the Peace and to the Justices of Boroughs* (15 August 1835), 2.
[66] PRO, HO 20/3, Crawford and Whitworth Russell to S.M. Phillips, 23 November 1836. Tobacco was believed to have medicinal benefits, hence the inspectors' caveat.

Discipline or abolish? 171

an indulgence rather than a right, the inspectors sought to reduce the distance between debtors and criminal prisoners. But the wording employed in their memoranda also signalled their continued inability to ignore this distinction altogether. Whitworth Russell, addressing the complaint lodged by debtors at Warwick gaol against new restrictive regulations a few days later, was careful to present the new rules in terms of the maintenance of proper discipline within the institution of the prison, not the infliction of discipline upon the person of the imprisoned debtor. 'We are of opinion that the Regulations are salutary, and calculated to aid the discipline of the prison', he insisted, 'whilst they are in no respect oppressive or unnecessarily severe'.[67]

Efforts to extend new levels of separation and surveillance to debtor prisoners increased sharply in the wake of Russell's circular of 1835. Religious observance provided prison reformers with an obvious frontier along which to extend moral regulation from criminal to debtor prisoners. At York Castle, the magistrates sought to impose Sunday worship on debtors in 1837, denying those in receipt of the county allowance their allotment of bread when they neglected to conform to this new policy.[68] More draconian – and far more subversive of debtors' customary privileged status within the prison – were the rules submitted by the justices of Newcastle upon Tyne for Home Office approval in 1837. Having prohibited debtors from purchasing ale during their confinement, the rules specified that inmates committed by the small-claims courts who received the prison diet in lieu of providing for themselves 'must clean the Debtors Ward, carry in the coals of the other Debtors, and such Court of Conscience Debtors as may be Tailors and who may receive the prison Diet, must repair the clothes of the Criminal Prisoners'. Breaching imprisoned debtors' conventional immunity from labour, these regulations reflected reformers' growing commitment to prison discipline as a mechanism for policing plebeian market morality. 'I think the Debtors could be compelled to do such work', a Home Office official noted approvingly in the margin of the justices' proposals.[69]

Already complicated by parsimonious local officials' reluctance to fund extensive gaol renovations, the implementation of these new policies was further impeded by debtors' vociferous objections. Numbering articulate, educated and propertied men among their ranks, imprisoned debtors were – in sharp contrast to the criminal population – well placed to defend their immunity from punitive confinement. A flood of correspondence from entitled debtors served to remind the Home Secretary of the privileged legal status and the genteel social pretensions of those debtors confined to gaol for safe custody by the superior courts. In 1838, insolvents imprisoned in the Hertford county gaol pointedly observed that they were 'not aware of any existing Law that authorizes the

---

[67] PRO, HO 20/3, Whitworth Russell to Phillips, 28 November 1836.
[68] PRO, HO 20/4, Crawford and Whitworth Russell to Phillips, 14 December 1837.
[69] PRO, HO 20/4, William Crawford and Whitworth Russell to S.M. Phillips, 14 November 1837.

172 Imprisonment for debt and the economic individual

Governor of this Gaol to lock your Petitioners up in their separate cells at night the same as convicted Felons' and emphasised 'that as long as the Debtors of this Gaol are kept in safe custody the pecuniary responsibility of the Governor is satisfied [and] any further harsh treatment and restrictions ... cruel and illegal'.[70] Insistent reminders that personal indebtedness constituted a species of innocent misfortune rather than a criminal act regularly punctuated these outraged petitions. Debtors confined in Gloucester county gaol in 1840 thought 'it extremely hard to be so harshly treated, because they happen to be unfortunate men, and under a liberal government too' and insisted that 'the legislature never did contemplate the extending of such coercive treatment to unfortunate persons confined for debt'.[71]

Perceptions of social difference were fundamental to insolvent debtors' objections to new disciplinary regimes. A petition of grievances submitted by Bristol inmates made the partisan character of their disaffection palpably evident in 1840. Identifying an 'indiscriminate mixture of debtors' within the gaol as the root cause of their complaint, these inmates distinguished sharply between the disciplinary imperatives that should rightly govern the confinement of petty debtors committed by the inferior courts and the genteel sensibilities that must instead guide the treatment of propertied insolvents:

The Day Rooms are open to all classes of Debtors, from the Court of Conscience which takes cognizance of Debts of so small a sum as 4d. ... Can it possibly have been in the contemplation of any Legislature that Persons accustomed to the Social Intercourse of the higher and middle classes of Society, when through misfortune (to which all are liable) thus immured; are to be subjected to the obligation of mixing with the very lowest Grade of Persons; to take their meals at the same Table where Penury and Want are constant attendants; frequently accompanied by the most obscene Language, and the most disgusting and revolting Actions; dirty in the extreme; and even verminous? We can give no Credence in our Liability to such Treatment by any legal enactment, or civil authority, and protest against it either as Law, Rule, or Regulation.[72]

Dividing debtors into two antagonistic constituencies, this conflict channelled debate over imprisonment for debt along lines of status, wealth and class. Central to insolvents' interpretation of their proper place within the prison, these distinctions were to prove instrumental in shaping government attitudes and policies toward prison reform from the 1840s to the 1860s.

Reformers' frustration with the increasingly anomalous status of imprisoned debtors accelerated from the later 1830s, as parliamentary leaders debated the comparative merits of reconfiguring the debtors' prison along disciplinary lines or abolishing imprisonment for debt altogether. The years from 1838 to 1846 saw a flurry of legislative activity intended to resolve the protracted dispute

[70] PRO, HO 20/7, Petition of Hertford debtors, 10 July 1838.
[71] PRO, HO 20/11, Memorial of Gloucester debtors, 5 June 1840.
[72] PRO, HO 20/11, Petition of Bristol debtors, 9 July 1840.

Discipline or abolish? 173

over the place of imprisonment for debt in the modern economy. Five successive acts framed this phase of reform, establishing parameters that shaped imprisonment for debt for decades. By 1 & 2 Vict. c. 110 (1838), superior courts lost their authority to imprison debtors on mesne process – that is, before trial – but creditors gained new powers to oppose the discharge from prison of inmates who had acted 'fraudulently' either in entering into their contracts with creditors or in their subsequent dealings with the courts. A second act, 5 & 6 Vict. c. 116 (1842), widened the category of the 'fraudulent' debtor. Whereas earlier legislation had held fraudulent credit transactions to be those in which the debtor contracted without 'reasonable or probable *expectation*' of rendering payment, the new act defined as fraud transactions in which debtors had contracted without 'reasonable assurance' of making full payment to their creditors. The Small Debts Act of 1844, 7 & 8 Vict. c. 96, further entrenched the legislative category of the fraudulent debtor while taking a radical leap toward the wholesale abolition of imprisonment for small debts. By this act, Parliament prohibited the imprisonment of debtors who owed sums of less than twenty pounds to a single creditor but confirmed judges' authority to confine to gaol for up to six months those debtors – regardless of the amounts they owed – whose debts had been contracted by fraud or misconduct. Greeted with outrage by the trading community, this legislation was rapidly supplanted by the Small Debts Act of 1845, 8 & 9 Vict. c. 127. Empowering creditors to summons debtors who owed them sums of less than twenty pounds for examination before either a bankruptcy commissioner or a court of requests, this act allowed judges or commissioners to gaol debtors for up to forty days at a time if they failed to appear for examination or proved to have contracted their debts fraudulently. In sharp contrast to previous practice in the courts of requests, such imprisonment failed to liquidate the debtor's obligation to pay the litigated debt, and thereby rendered defendants liable to repeated imprisonments for the same unpaid sums. This principle of continued personal liability for small debts was confirmed by the Small Debts Act of 1846, 9 & 10 Vict. c. 95. By this statute, jurisdiction over debts of less than twenty pounds passed from the local courts of requests to a new, national system of county courts. Empowered to imprison defendants for up to six weeks at a time, county-court judges could commit these debtors to gaol repeatedly for contempt if they failed to pay their debts (or instalments thereof) after judgment was rendered against them.[73]

---

[73] David Deady Keane, *Courts of Requests, Their Jurisdiction and Powers, under the 'Act to Amend the Law of Insolvency, Bankruptcy and Execution' (7 & 8 Vict. c. 96), and the 'Act for the Better Securing the Payment of Small Debts' (8 & 9 Vict. c. 127)*, 3rd edn (London, 1845), details the legislation to 1845 (citation from 16). For the legislative context of these reforms and the creation of the county courts, see V. Markham Lester, *Victorian Insolvency: Bankruptcy, Imprisonment for Debt, and Company Winding-Up in Nineteenth-Century England* (Oxford, 1995), chap. 3, and Patrick Polden, *A History of the County Court, 1846–1971* (Cambridge, 1999), chap. 1.

174   Imprisonment for debt and the economic individual

The antinomies of debtor legislation in these years are striking. Abolishing imprisonment for debt with one hand only to restore and reinvigorate it with the other, reformers created a conflicting welter of new statutory imperatives. By defining contracts made without the reasonable assurance of repayment as acts of fraud, the legislation of 1842–46 significantly increased the potential for debtor prisoners – hitherto troped as victims of misfortune and confined, at law, only for safe custody – to be categorised instead as criminal malefactors who merited the salutary rigours of penal discipline. Yet, by abolishing imprisonment on mesne process and – however briefly and partially – experimenting with the abolition of imprisonment for 'unfortunate' debts of less than twenty pounds, reformers also signalled their distaste for creditors' persistent reliance on the debtors' prison as a coercive mechanism for enforcing contractual obligations. Shot through with contradictions, these statutes were to provide a highly unstable legal foundation for the reformulation of debtor gaol regimes in the following decades.

Two broad and interlocking trends in penal policy were apparent in the aftermath of the legal reforms of 1838–46: a sharp escalation of local and national government attempts to subject all debtors gaoled by small-claims courts to punitive confinement, and an increasing determination to distinguish clearly between merely unfortunate and actively culpable debtors imprisoned for more substantial sums through the mechanisms of bankruptcy and insolvency. Like superior-court insolvents themselves, reform-minded government officials evinced little sympathy for the debtors confined by small-claims tribunals, and it was these inmates who bore the brunt of disciplinary penal policy. As one Home Office official explained in 1845, petty debtors committed under the provisions of 8 & 9 Vict. c. 127 'are not imprisoned for safe custody alone, or in satisfaction of their Debts – But as a punishment either for fraudulent or dishonest conduct, or for a wilful disobedience of the orders of a Court of Law'. In these circumstances, the Home Secretary had ruled that 'Debtors of this class may properly be subjected to a different mode of treatment to that sanctioned in the case of those imprisoned for debt under ordinary process'.[74] Regulations for debtors confined for sums of less than twenty pounds under 8 & 9 Vict. c. 127 formulated by Surrey magistrates in 1846 reflect the increasingly disciplinary tone of local policy-making encouraged by these statutory changes. Although exempt from separate confinement and segregated from criminal prisoners, petty debtors in the Surrey county gaol were to be distanced decisively from the privileges enjoyed by superior-court insolvents. Prohibited from seeing their friends and family more than once a week and denied the right

---

[74] PRO, HO 86/1, fols. 83–4, H. Manners Sutton to I. Grace Smith, 14 November 1845. See similarly CLRO, Rep. 250, 2 December 1845, fols. 9–10, Sir James Graham's instructions to City of London officials.

Discipline or abolish? 175

to consume tobacco, wine, beer and fermented liquor, these nominally fraudulent debtors were restricted to a prison diet of oatmeal gruel, bread, soup and potatoes, supplemented with a daily ration of three ounces of cooked meat.[75]

Perceived class differences played a central part in justifying both the continued imprisonment and the penal classification of small-claims debtors in these years. J.H. Elliott, a merchant who spearheaded attacks in the press against the abolition of imprisonment for small debts in the wake of the enactment of the Small Debts Act of 1844, was explicit in his judgment. Convinced that preserving the imprisonment of petty debtors was essential for protecting the property of 'the middle class', Elliott underlined 'the feeble controlling power over the appetites, which the numerous untrained mass are incapable of exerting'. For Elliott, petty debtors and their creditors invariably represented different social classes and displayed distinctive market moralities. 'If we place creditors in one lot, and debtors in another, justice and mercy will characterise the former, as often as fraud and improvidence will characterise the latter', he insisted in anatomising the incorrigible market activities of the poor. 'Creditors, as a body, are a superior order of men... [and] the presumption of the law should be in favour of the creditor', Elliott concluded self-righteously.[76] The creation of the county-court system in 1846 provided further substantiation for this interpretation of the flawed moral character of working-class debtors. T.B. Addison, chairman of the Preston quarter sessions, expatiated upon the significant legal changes wrought by the Small Debts Act of 1846. 'No longer treating imprisonment as a necessary legal result of indebtedness, to be inflicted without regard to its moral or social consequences, the law proposes to apply it with a view to enforce payment, and in the manner most likely to effect that object', he observed. Arguing that confinement in the separate cells located in reformed houses of correction offered an appropriate punishment for county-court debtors, Addison suggested that the 'pauper population' and the class 'just above it' would provide the bulk of debtors prosecuted and imprisoned by the new tribunals. 'The treatment and accommodation due to such Persons should bear a proportion to that of the Workhouse, in which many of them must leave their wives and families; and if the discipline be more lax and the fare better than in a well regulated workhouse, imprisonment will be little feared', he reasoned.[77] Leading figures of the central government repeatedly echoed this analysis. As a Home Office official explained to inmates who petitioned against the restrictions to which they were subjected in the Whitecross Street prison in 1856, inclusion in the 'penal classes' was mandatory for all county-court debtors because 'the

[75] PRO, HO 45/1373, Rules for approval from county of Surrey, 6 January 1846.
[76] J.H. Elliott, *Credit the Life of Commerce: Being a Defence of the British Merchant against the Unjust and Demoralizing Tendency of the Recent Alterations in the Laws of Debtor and Creditor* (London, 1845), 1, 100, 187.
[77] PRO, HO 45/1810, T.B. Addison to S.M. Phillips, 1 September 1847.

176   Imprisonment for debt and the economic individual

Imprisonments referred to are not for Satisfaction of the debt, but a punishment for not paying it'.[78]

Developing in parallel with these new strictures upon small-claims debtors were the government's efforts to dismantle the legal and customary privileges enjoyed (and abused) by debtors tried for more substantial sums by the insolvency courts. Determined to use the provisions of the revised debtor statutes to cleanse the Augean stables of the debtors' prison, reform-minded government officials seized upon the culpability of the fraudulent debtor as a prime justification for remodelling the traditional institutions of civil confinement. In 1842, Parliament enacted legislation to consolidate the Fleet, Marshalsea and Queen's Bench prisons into a single institution, occupying the site of the former Queen's Bench but governed by new regulations and systems of classification mandated by the Home Office. Now denied the liberty of confinement in the 'Rules' outside the prison, the Queen's Prison debtors were to be segregated by sex and divided into separate classes that distinguished sharply between fraudulent and non-fraudulent debtors. The enabling legislation authorised the Home Secretary 'to make separate Rules for each class of Prisoners', and empowered prison authorities to prohibit inmates from sending outside the prison walls for food, drink and bedding, 'to prevent Extravagance and Luxury, and for enforcing due Order and Discipline within the Prison'.[79]

Directives to local magistrates extended the erosion of propertied insolvents' privileges from metropolitan to provincial gaols. Insolvent debtors remanded for fraud, a Home Office circular instructed chairmen of Quarter Sessions in April 1846, should be subjected to the same punitive restrictions as petty debtors committed to gaol by the inferior small-claims courts.[80] Emboldened by legislative reform, prison inspectors eagerly joined the fray. 'We are not aware of any Act which constitutes the class of Debtors called "Master Debtors," which confers peculiar privileges upon Prisoners... designated by that term', William Crawford and Whitworth Russell sternly informed Durham magistrates when inmates resisted the introduction of reformed rules mandated by the Home Office. 'Under these circumstances we are of opinion that the Governor may punish any Debtor committed under the 8th & 9th Vict. c. 127, or by Commissioners of Bankrupts for Frauds... and Debtors remanded for Frauds by Insolvent Debtors Courts, for non-compliance with the rules.'[81] Designed to dismantle the structures and practices that had allowed debtors' prisons to function as havens from market discipline, this

---

[78] PRO, HO 86/3, fols. 3–4, H. Waddington to John Shaw, 18 June 1856.

[79] *An Act for Consolidating the Queen's Bench, Fleet, and Marshalsea Prison* (31 May 1842). For debtors' petitions against these restrictions, see *Commons Journals*, 97 (1842): 287, 451.

[80] Bedfordshire RO, QGR/1/15, Circular from H. Manners Sutton, 23 April 1846.

[81] PRO, HO 45/1373, Crawford and Russell to Sir William Somerville, 21 August 1846.

legislation sought to supplant the disorderly and sociable images of debtor confinement fostered by fiction with a uniform vision of incarceration attuned to the new demands of penal discipline.

By conflating two broad categories of inmate – on the one hand, all small-claims defendants and, on the other, fraudulent bankrupts and insolvents – the Home Office worked assiduously to create a new class of inmate, the 'penal debtor'. Resting uneasily on the shifting statutory ground established by the legislation of 1838–46, the category of the penal debtor proved inherently unstable. Although plebeian protests against the infliction of discipline upon small-claims debtors were relatively rare, 'penal debtors' who boasted education, property or connection were vociferous in denouncing the new punitive regimes imposed on county-court and fraudulent debtors, unleashing a barrage of petitions to the House of Commons and the courts of law and sending a stream of letters to metropolitan newspapers. The railway clerk Charles Pollett, committed to the house of correction at Coldbath Fields by the Whitechapel county court in 1848 for his failure to pay a debt of two pounds, returned to the court upon his release to lodge an indignant complaint against the prison's governor, George Laval Chesterton. A zealous proponent of prison reform who claimed in his autobiography to have transformed Coldbath Fields 'from one of the worst specimens of corruption and misrule into an establishment distinguished for industry, order, and impressive discipline',[82] Chesterton had, Pollett claimed, greeted him with the words ' "You are sent here for correction, and correction you shall have." ' Compelled to wear the prison uniform, restricted to the prison diet and required to labour by picking oakum, Pollett suffered all the indignities of penal discipline. 'Mr Pollett said he had been degraded, and was a most injured man', the *County Courts Chronicle* reported. 'He was most reputably connected and . . . had lost his character, and should have some difficulty to obtain another situation.' Reported indignantly in the London press, Pollett's treatment was denounced in the House of Commons by Baillie Cochrane, who referred to the incident as 'a case of great oppression'. Emphasising that Pollett was 'respectably connected' Cochrane insisted that penal confinement had inflicted an unjustified 'stigma upon his character' and called for legal reforms to prevent 'unfortunate' men such as Pollett from suffering 'such gross cruelty' in prison.[83] Not content to let the matter rest with Parliament, Pollett later took Chesterton to court for having ordered his officers to cut off his hair – a routine measure of disciplinary hygiene inflicted on criminal

---

[82] George Laval Chesterton, *Revelations of Prison Life; With an Enquiry into Prison Discipline and Secondary Punishments*, 2 vols., 2nd edn (London, 1856), I: 3–4.

[83] *County Courts Chronicle*, 1 April 1848, 228; *Daily News*, 17 March 1848; *Hansard's Parliamentary Debates*, 3rd ser., xcvii, 27 March 1848, cols. 1019–20, 31 March 1848, cols. 1142–3.

178   Imprisonment for debt and the economic individual

prisoners – during his confinement. A sympathetic jury awarded Pollett twenty-five pounds in damages for his degrading treatment.[84]

Pollett was hardly alone among middling debtors in challenging his treatment as a 'penal' inmate. At the Queen's Prison, the appointment of Captain Hudson of the Royal Navy as governor was intended to secure the gaol's orderly administration, but Hudson's journals and correspondence testify to privileged inmates' tenacity in guarding their historic privileges. Constantly required to police inmates' drunken sociability and to remove illicit womenfolk from the male sections of the gaol – in September 1847 he was horrified to find 'Mr Skipp a prisoner in Bed with a female & three men in the Room with them'[85] – Hudson attempted in vain to impose the government's mandated scheme of classification upon his unruly charges. Fraudulent debtors who preferred the familiar comforts of the goal to the hostile environs of the outside world and were well practised in the art of manipulating legal processes responded to these efforts by inditing appeals to the press, petitioning Parliament for redress and lodging costly legal suits against Hudson and his officers. The clergyman Philip Herring, having cohabited in the gaol for months with one Miss Mitchell, appealed both to his MP and to the House of Lords when Hudson denied him access to his paramour in 1846, entangling the governor in prolonged and frustrating correspondence with the Lord Chancellor, the Home Secretary and the prison inspectors.[86] Chancery debtor William Cobbett was yet more incorrigible. Refusing his plaintiff's repeated offers to release him from confinement, Cobbett launched a seemingly endless succession of vexatious suits against Hudson and his officers for removing him from the insolvent to the penal class of debtors. Appearing before judges on twenty occasions between June 1845 and October 1847 to lodge his complaints, Cobbett won forty shillings in damages against Hudson from the Court of Exchequer in 1847 and gained a decision from the law officers of the Crown in 1848 that his classification as a penal debtor was indeed unjust, forcing the government to obtain yet another revision of the debt law to expand the definition of fraudulent debt transactions.[87]

Challenges such as these exposed the confusion that continued to surround the legal status of imprisoned debtors despite successive statutory reforms. In theory, the creation of the county-court system in 1846 laid secure foundations for the penal classification of petty debtors by defining their offence as contempt

---

[84] *County Courts Chronicle*, January 1850, 5–6. See similarly the letter of complaint lodged against Chesterton by the comedian Henry Gaskell Denvil: PRO, HO 45/1810, Denvil to Sir George Grey, 7 December 1848.

[85] PRO, PRIS 9/8, Queen's Prison Governor's Journal, 17 September 1847.

[86] See, for example, PRO, PRIS 9/17, Hudson to Sir William Somerville, MP, 22 August 1846; Hudson to the Lord Chancellor, 29 August 1846; Hudson to Sir George Grey, 7 September 1846; and Hudson to C.E. Trevelyan, 21 July 1847.

[87] PRO, PRIS 9/17, Hudson to Sir George Grey, 16 October and 29 December 1847; Hudson to Grey 3 January, 4 February and 15 April 1848.

Discipline or abolish? 179

of court, rather than as failure to pay the debt itself. But in practice, the public's persistent conceptualisation of county-court imprisonment as imprisonment for debt, the incarceration by the new small-claims tribunals of a small but highly vocal cohort of middling defendants alongside the mass of working-class debtors and the perpetuation of imprisonment for substantial debts by the superior courts all worked to undercut support for the increasingly disciplinary regimes favoured by the Home Office. Government officials and legal authorities themselves, moreover, continued to dispute the status of imprisoned debtors, a division of opinion that was thrown into sharp relief whenever local officials or debtor inmates challenged Home Office policy. For if Sir James Graham and Sir George Grey were secure in the belief that county-court inmates could, as penal debtors, be classed as misdemeanants, their legal advisors were not. 'I entertain great doubt as to how Prisoners committed under the 9th and 10th Vict: cap 95 section 99 are to be classed', H.H. Dodgson of the Temple informed the Home Office in 1848. Uncertain as to whether these inmates should be classified as either debtors or misdemeanants, Dodgson declined to endorse reformers' draconian classification schemes. 'Possibly he may be of a class for which no rules have been made', his review of the penal debtor's legal status concluded unhelpfully. 'If there be no rules applicable to him he must be treated as at Common Law.'[88]

Already weakened by legal challenges, the Home Office's penal policies were further compromised by pervasive sympathy for insolvent debtors among the respectable classes. Justified by Christian apologetic and nurtured by genera-tions of novelists, this sentiment was further bolstered by many prison officials' reluctance to inflict punitive discipline upon men whose social backgrounds and aspirations were similar to their own. When Parliament considered the provisions of the Small Debts Bill of 1845, Thomas Burdon, governor of the Whitecross Street prison, wrote worriedly to the Mayor of London to express his reservations. Disciplinary classification, he argued, posed two problems to prison officials, 'first the legality of classifying Debtors and secondly the amount of good to be gained, much sympathy Public and private is lavished on Debtors (in many instances deservedly so) and any change which presses on them would call forth public comment'.[89] At Lancaster Castle, the governor was likewise sensitive to the wrongs suffered by otherwise respectable inmates confined as penal debtors. An entry in his journal for 1845 noted that when

---

[88] PRO, HO 45/1810, Legal opinion of H.H. Dodgson, 27 April 1848. See similarly PRO, HO 49/9, Waddington to Maule, 30 June 1849.

[89] CLRO, Gaol Committee: Officers' Reports, Burdon to the Mayor and Gaol Committee, 7 June 1845. Even George Hicks, brought in to establish order at Whitecross Street after Burdon was relieved of his duties in the 1850s, expressed substantial sympathy for the gentlemanly debtors in his charge. See [Captain George Montagu Hicks], *The Double Doom of the Poor Debtor: To Those Who Owe Money, and to Those to Whom It Is Due* (London, 1858).

180   Imprisonment for debt and the economic individual

debtor Watkins was discharged 'he inveighed bitterly against the classification plan, which was the means he stated of compelling him to associate with characters, whose manners & language he described to have been most repulsive & disgusting'. Compassion for this debtor's plight emerges clearly from the journal. 'Mr Watkins was a man of gentlemanly manners & a regular attendant at divine service', the governor observed unhappily.[90] For some prison governors – as for many novelists – little imagination was required to identify with the outraged sensibilities of propertied penal debtors. In 1853, the governor of Bedford Gaol was forced to flee to London and to resign his post when his creditors initiated actions to imprison him for debt; James William Newham, who was later to become governor of Canterbury Prison, entered prison service as a clerk at Maidstone gaol in 1851 through the patronage of his stepfather – a wine merchant who had lived as an insolvent for months with his wife in the Queen's Prison, before being liberated by the courts as a bankrupt.[91]

Comprehensive statistics on the social composition of the imprisoned debtor population are lacking, but the available data go far to explain why sympathy for penal debtors in the 1840s and 1850s focused disproportionately on 'fraudulent' debtors committed by superior courts rather than on inmates imprisoned by small-claims tribunals. The high costs of litigation in superior courts ensured that labouring men remained a small minority of all debtors confined under the insolvency statutes in the nineteenth century, as had been the case in the preceding century.[92] Statistics compiled by the government on debtors who petitioned for release by the Insolvent Debtors Court from September 1820 to December 1821 confirm David Kent's assertion, based on a broad sample of petitions scattered in local record offices, that retailers and artisans 'always formed the majority of insolvent debtors'.[93] In the statistics from the Insolvent Debtors Court, men overwhelmingly outnumbered women among petitioners, representing 96.1 per cent of the total sample. Among the thousand debtors for whom an occupation was given, tradesmen, merchants, artisans and shopkeepers predominated: together victuallers, bakers, butchers, grocers, cheesemongers, general shopkeepers, carpenters, tailors, cabinetmakers and shoemakers provided over a quarter of all insolvents petitioning for release from prison. But

[90] PRO, PCOM 2/443, Lancaster Castle Governor's Journal, 11 February 1845.
[91] Bedfordshire RO, QGR/1/33, Report of the Governor of the Gaol, 5 April 1853; Paul Coltman, ed., *The Diary of a Prison Governor: James William Newham 1825–1890* (Gloucester, 1989), ix, 5–7, 10–12.
[92] In Paul Haagen's sample of eighteenth-century insolvents, 68% were tradesmen or shopkeepers, 7% 'gentlemen' and only 2.3% 'labourers'. Paul Haagen, 'Eighteenth-century English society and the debt law', in Stanley Cohen and Andrew Scull, eds., *Social Control and the State* (New York, 1983), 224, 240; idem, 'Imprisonment for debt in England and Wales' (Ph.D. dissertation, Princeton University, 1986), 69–72.
[93] David A. Kent, 'Small businessmen and their credit transactions in early nineteenth-century Britain', *Business History*, 36, 2 (April 1994), 50.

Discipline or abolish? 181

the great diversity of these inmates' backgrounds is none the less striking. In all, debtors derived from over 260 occupational groups, counting servants, seamen and ship-owners, comedians, coachmen and clothiers, a Dissenting minister, a gem collector, a ginger-beer manufacturer, a teacher of chess, an officer of the Palace Court and an assistant to the tipstaffs of the King's Bench prison among their numbers. Embracing a wide spectrum of the English population, insolvency emerges from these petitions as a legal experience that connected the lesser – but not the very least – members of society to the propertied great. The thirteen labourers in the sample were swamped by the thirty-nine insolvent 'gentlemen' and 'gentlewomen' who constituted the second largest single occupational group of petitioners, followed closely by thirty-four farmers or yeomen and thirty-two clerks.[94]

Supplementing these national statistics with records of actual imprisonment – as opposed to petitions for release – derived from individual gaols confirms these general outlines. Famous for its amenities, the King's Bench attracted genteel debtors from both London and the provinces, many of whom, having removed from a local gaol by the legal device of a habeas, chose to live outside the prison's walls in the Rules. Among ninety-two sampled insolvents in the Rules of the King's Bench in 1830, fully a third were 'gentlemen' and nearly a tenth were attorneys.[95] In the later 1840s, the reformed Queen's Prison continued to boast a genteel inmate population, as it had in Benjamin Haydon's day: when Captain Hudson prepared to defend the gaol against the Chartist crowds on 10 April 1848, the 'gentlemen' prisoners who 'offered their Services to assist in any way that might be required to repel any attack upon the prison' included Major General Latour, Rear Admiral Bouchin, Colonel Warner and Major Tolson.[96] Soon thereafter, Lord Harley was discharged from confinement in the prison, having gained immunity from further imprisonment for his debts by succeeding his father as the Earl of Oxford.[97] The status of superior-court insolvents as persons of property was clearly a matter of public knowledge. In 1856, Hudson reported, two burglars were apprehended in the Queen's Prison 'with housebreaking Tools and Skeleton keys in their possession and their object

---

[94] The sample was derived from the first 1,007 petitions listed in the *Returns of the Names of the Commissioners and Officers Employed in the Court for the Relief of Insolvent Debtors in England, Rules and Orders, and Other Matters Relating to the Said Court*, Parliamentary Papers, 1822 (276). The sample includes all debtors from John Archer to Henry Frieake (pages 16–45). Thirty-nine debtors were female and seven listed no occupation, yielding an occupational sample of 1,000 debtors. Where more than one occupation is listed, only the first has been counted. Labourers were the eighteenth most common group of petitioners.

[95] PRO, PRIS 10/135, Rules book, King's Bench Prison: Prisoners and Securities, 1828–30. The sample consists of all debtors with surnames beginning with A, B, C or D, excluding debtors for whom no occupation was listed. A total of thirty-one debtors were 'gentlemen' (34%); the eight attorneys (9%) were the next largest single grouping.

[96] PRO, PRIS 9/8, Queen's Prison Governor's Journal, 10 April 1848.

[97] *City of London Trade Protection Circular*, 13 January 1849, 19.

182   Imprisonment for debt and the economic individual

was to rob some of the Prisoners'.[98] Although contemporaries constantly derided the Whitecross Street prison, which provided its inmates with accommodation in common dormitory wards, for failure to offer amenities suited to men who had 'the habits of gentlemen',[99] it too housed debtors who claimed genteel backgrounds. The 173 insolvents liberated from the prison through its charities in 1855 included four attorneys, three ladies in 'reduced circumstances', two barristers, a gentleman, a gentlewoman and a 'tutor and fellow' of a college.[100]

Ascriptions of gentility are, notoriously, unreliable indices of social status and economic worth. But the records of individual gaols none the less suggest that debtors in general and insolvents in particular constituted a distinctive inmate population. At Lancaster Castle on census day in 1851, the 106 male debtors represented a total of 64 occupations, of which the five most common were gentlemen (8 debtors), grocers (6 inmates), silk manufacturers and joiners (5 inmates each) and labourers (4 debtors). In social background, these civil prisoners differed sharply from the criminal inmates with whom they shared the Castle, two-thirds of whom were either servants or weavers. On average, the Castle's debtors were also five years older than criminal prisoners and were far more likely to be married men than were convicted inmates: 84% of debtors but only 36% of criminals were married.[101] These differences were not unique to Lancaster. At Lincoln Castle in 1851, the average age of felons was twenty-five, while that of debtors was fifty-two. Here 86% of criminal prisoners were agricultural labourers, only 48% of criminals had been born in Lincolnshire and only 25% were married. In contrast, 80% of imprisoned debtors were tradesmen, and 92% had been born in Lincolnshire and were married. 'Thus the typical debtor was a local middle aged tradesman', Michael Hardy concludes. 'The typical felon was a young, unmarried and rootless labourer.'[102]

Statistics such as these reveal significant differences between debtor and criminal inmates, but they also distort the national profile of imprisonment for debt by under-representing petty debtors committed to local gaols and houses of correction by small-claims courts. By 1843, debtors imprisoned for petty sums by courts of requests had begun to outnumber insolvents committed by superior courts: there were 6,911 small-claims debtors (or 50.9% of all debtor

---

[98] PRIS 9/18, Queen's Prison Governor's Letter Book, 1852–60, Hudson to Waddington, 4 January 1856.

[99] William Hepworth Dixon, *The London Prisons: With an Account of the More Distinguished Persons Who Have Been Confined in Them* (London, 1850), 280.

[100] CLRO, *Composite Printed Minutes of the Court of Aldermen*, 15 January 1856.

[101] Lancaster Reference Library, Lancaster Castle census, 1851, microfilm. Occupations were listed for only forty-one of the ninety felons; of these, eleven were servants, eleven steam-loom weavers and five hand-loom weavers. The average age of debtors was thirty-nine years and that of criminals thirty-four years.

[102] Michael Hardy, 'Lincoln County Gaol in 1851', Lincolnshire Archives, R Box L.365.9 HAR, 93/26 (typescript), 12. There were twenty-two felons and twelve debtors in the gaol on census day.

Discipline or abolish? 183

inmates) among the 13,586 debtors imprisoned in England and Wales in that year. Both metropolitan debtors' prisons and provincial county gaols admitted disproportionately few inmates drawn from this proliferating class of debtor, a circumstance that worked to elevate the social status of their inmate populations. Among the 588 debtors confined in the Queen's Prison in 1843, only one had been committed by a court of requests. Lincoln Castle was less socially exclusive, but it too accommodated relatively few inmates confined by small-claims courts. Prisoners committed by courts of requests accounted for 64% of all debtors confined in Lincolnshire in 1843, but only sixteen small-claims debtors (22% of the debtor population) numbered among the seventy-two debtors confined at Lincoln Castle in that year.[103]

The available data consistently suggest that small-claims court inmates were drawn from lower social strata than were the insolvents who petitioned Parliament for their release from gaol. The quantifying impulse of nineteenth-century reformers spawned efforts to categorise the small-claims court debtor more precisely than 'the humblest Rank of Society', 'working people with large families' and 'Persons of the lowest Description' named in eighteenth-century accounts.[104] At the Spilsby house of correction, where debtors imprisoned by a range of Lincolnshire courts of requests were accommodated, the petty debtors committed from 1827 to 1844 represented a total of fifty-four trades, but were drawn overwhelmingly from the labouring classes. Of 451 debtors identified by occupation, 278 (or 61.6%) were labourers; together with the 27 shoemakers who represented the second most common occupation, these workers accounted for over two-thirds of Spilsby's small-claims prisoners.[105] Of 246 court of requests debtors confined at Shepton Mallet house of correction in 1843 for whom a trade was recorded, 76 were labourers (31%), 21 masons and 21 shoemakers.[106]

Statistical information on county-court imprisonment similarly attests to the predominantly plebeian status of debtors imprisoned by these new tribunals. At Wakefield house of correction, workers from the metal trades – followed by labourers and miners – dominated the debtor population.[107] The inmates committed by Shropshire county courts a decade later, although drawn from a total of eighty trades, likewise derived from predominantly plebeian occupations.

---

[103] *Ninth Report of the Inspectors Appointed under the Provisions of 5 & 6 Will. 4 c. 88, to Visit the Different Prisons of Great Britain*, Parliamentary Papers, XXXIV (1844), 216–17, 52–3, 46–7.

[104] Neild, *Account of the Rise, Progress and Present State*, 597; Howard, *State of the Prisons*, 229; *Report from the Committee Appointed*, 50.

[105] PRO, PCOM 2/400, Spilsby Gaol Discharge Register, 1826–48.

[106] Somerset RO, Q/Ags/17/1, Shepton Mallet Gaol, Register of Debtors, 1842–78.

[107] Of 363 debtors for whom an occupation was recorded from 1847 to 1849, 127 (35%) were from the metal trades, 41 (11%) were labourers and 19 (5.2%) were miners. West Yorkshire Archive Service, C118/101, Wakefield House of Correction Debtors' Receiving Book, 1847–49.

184   Imprisonment for debt and the economic individual

Of 717 county-court debtors imprisoned in Shrewsbury between 1855 and 1861, 233 (or 32.5%) were labourers and 123 (17.2%) were miners. Together with 36 shoemakers (5.0%) and 32 bricklayers (4.5%), these four occupations accounted for 59.2% of small-claims court debtors confined at Shrewsbury.[108]

Viewed from this perspective, the practice of imprisonment for debt assumes a considerably more demotic aspect than when examined from the perspective of insolvency alone. Yet these data also suggest that debtors committed by small-claims courts represented a significantly different sector of the plebeian population than did petty criminal inmates committed by summary criminal process to local gaols and houses of correction. Men convicted of petty crimes were a preponderantly youthful sector of the adult population: of 47,149 adult men summarily convicted of crimes in 1843, 25,392 (or 53.8%) were aged 21–29, and only 21,757 (46.1%) were aged 30 years or older.[109] In sharp contrast, of the 222 Spilsby debtors for whom an age was recorded between 1827 and 1844, only 23% were in the 21–29 age group and 77% were aged 30 or more.[110] The age structure of small-claims debtors suggests that these men were – like superior-court insolvents – most likely to be imprisoned for small debts when they were burdened by a family of small children. Data from Somerset, where prison officials recorded the marital and family status of small-claims debtors in 1843, confirm that petty debtors – like superior-court insolvents – were more likely to be married parents than to be rootless youths. Here three-quarters of the 252 court of requests debtors were married, and an additional 13 per cent were widowed. Only a quarter of the Shepton Mallet debtors had no children; the 189 debtor parents in the gaol claimed a total of 745 children at the time of their imprisonment.[111]

Taken together, the available information indicates that debtors imprisoned by the summary small-claims courts differed in significant ways both from the population of convicted criminals and from insolvent debtors committed to gaol through the insolvency statutes. To be sure, these populations overlapped: labourers figured prominently both among criminal and small-claims court inmates, and mature married men predominated over single youths among both petty and insolvent debtors. Petty debtors from the courts of requests, indeed, may be seen to have occupied a liminal position in the inmate population, just as they inhabited a troublingly marginal status in the institutions of the prison system itself. Neither fully culpable nor merely unfortunate, drawn neither from the criminal nor from the reputable classes, they were ill-suited to occupy either

---

[108] PRO, PCOM 2/396, Shrewsbury Debtors' Register, 1855–61.

[109] *Ninth Report of the Inspectors*, 90–1.

[110] PRO, PCOM 2/400, Spilsby Gaol Discharge Register, 1826–48. Fifty-one Spilsby debtors were aged 21–29 and 171 were 30 or older.

[111] Somerset RO, Q/Ags/17/1, Shepton Mallet Gaol, Register of Debtors. Of 252 debtors, 188 (75%) were married, 33 (13%) were widowed and 31 (12.3%) were single. Only 63 debtors (25.0%) had no children.

Discipline or abolish? 185

the old customary groupings or the new punitive classification schemes of the prison.

From mid-century, the increasing number of debtors imprisoned by the county courts combined with the debt law's new insistence that fraudulent superior-court inmates were proper objects of punitive confinement to provoke disquiet and open antagonism among debtor inmates, prison-keepers and government officials. At the Whitecross Street prison, where county-court debtors were acutely aware of the privileges enjoyed by the gaol's insolvents, efforts to enforce the Home Office's classification scheme precipitated outraged resistance throughout the 1850s. When the governor sought 'To reduce the Prison to better order' by selectively denying county-court debtors the right of purchasing a daily quota of beer, enraged prisoners rioted, breaking forty windows and hurling their chamberpots from the upper-level windows onto the courtyard below. The Lord Mayor, called in to quell the disturbance, found the prison 'in a state of siege with fragments of pottery brick bats broken window frames and glass strewed over the yards & Prisoners in a high state of excitement'.[112] Public sympathy for the Whitecross Street debtors drew unwanted attention to the reprisals exacted by City officials in the wake of such protests. In a tract dedicated (with permission) to Charles Dickens, H.W. Weston condemned 'the penal tyranny' of reform at the gaol. 'How can such a system be in accordance with His whose whole teaching was of brotherly love, brotherly kindness, the forgiving your debtors not once, not seven times, but even seven times seven', Weston raged; 'who taught us our daily prayer, to forgive our trespasses as we forgive them that trespass against us?'[113]

Efforts to eradicate these disparities of treatment by deploying charitable funds to liberate propertied insolvents from the prison escalated in this context, but often proved ineffective. At the Queen's Prison, the 1850s saw systematic efforts on Captain Hudson's part to secure the release of his inmates by offering detaining creditors a composition on their debt in lieu of full payment. At best episodically successful, these efforts foundered not only on angry creditors' refusal to discharge their captives but upon debtors' obdurate resistance to ejection from the gaol. The Warwickshire creditors of debtor Cornell had declined to accept a composition of ten pounds from the prison charities in 1848, hoping by this means to compel the debtor to transfer a small cottage to them in lieu of his debt. In 1851, Hudson's secretary wrote to offer an increased composition of fourteen pounds, commenting acerbically of Cornell's confinement that 'He seems rather to enjoy it than otherwise and I have no doubt he would consider it a punishment to be turned out of the prison where he is earning a liberal means of subsistence.' Five years later, as Cornell completed his fourteenth

[112] CLRO, Gaol Committee Papers, Report of the City Solicitor, 28 May 1859.
[113] H.W. Weston, *Protection without Imprisonment for All Embarrassed Debtors. Why Not?* (London, 1858), 12.

186   Imprisonment for debt and the economic individual

year of imprisonment, he continued to be 'industrious' despite failing health, but resolutely opposed Hudson's efforts to secure his release, evidently preferring to make 'an asylum of this place rather than have his liberty'.[114] Although Hudson's frustration with this impasse was palpable, his repeated willingness to expend time, effort and charitable funds to secure the release of recalcitrant debtors who declined to comply with court orders indicates the substantial sympathy that continued to mark attitudes toward superior-court debtors. Mary Pryce consistently refused to avail herself of legal means to obtain her liberation, but Hudson, 'Prompted by humanity alone', drew her creditors' attention to Pryce's pitiable state and attempted to negotiate a compromise 'as it would be very desirable ... to enable her to pass her few remaining days in the enjoyment of her liberty'.[115]

Confronted by the obvious failure of its policies to rid the prison of propertied inmates who declined to pay their debts, the government turned again to legislative action, decisively transforming the debt law in acts of 1861 and 1869. Both acts conceded the inability of imprisonment to police the market activities of middle- and upper-class debtors, but both also confirmed the utility of retaining county-court imprisonment to enforce plebeian contracts. By 24 & 25 Vict. c. 134 (1861), non-traders gained access to bankruptcy procedures, and the Court for the Relief of Insolvent Debtors was accordingly abolished. Upon payment of a ten-pound fee, personal debtors could now petition for bankruptcy, protecting their goods from seizure by their creditors and guarding their bodies from imprisonment while allowing the debt to be discharged for a composition of ten shillings or less on the pound. Two categories of debtor were specifically excluded from these provisions: persons sued in the superior courts for sums of less than twenty pounds and all defendants committed by the county courts remained liable to suffer confinement. By 32 & 33 Vict. c. 62 (1869), 'An Act for the Abolition of Imprisonment for Debt', superior courts lost the power to imprison defendants for debts of any sum, but county courts retained the ability to confine debtors who owed sums of less than fifty pounds for up to six weeks at a time, nominally for contempt of court. As bankruptcy petitions were, for most working-class heads of household, prohibitively expensive, the legislation of 1861 and 1869 effectively restricted imprisonment for debt to the labouring population.[116] Tradesmen, artisans, retailers, clerks, professionals and the seedier members of the gentry had formed the key constituency

[114] PRO, PRIS 9/20, Charles Colwell to Messrs Gibbs and Henley, 23 April 1851, 27 February and 11 March 1856.
[115] PRO, PRIS 9/20, Charles Colwell to Messrs Woostman and Lloyd, 16 May and 2 July 1851.
[116] For forceful analyses of the revised debt laws and their class character, see Paul Johnson, 'Class law in Victorian England', *P&P*, 141 (November 1993), esp. 158–63, and G.R. Rubin, 'Law, poverty and imprisonment for debt, 1869–1914', in G.R. Rubin and David Sugarman, eds., *Law, Economy and Society: Essays in the History of English Law 1750–1914* (Abingdon, 1984), 241–99.

Discipline or abolish? 187

of the debtors' prison for generations. They were now to be displaced definitively from the prison by working men committed by county courts for petty sums.

Imprisonment after abolition

Final closure of the distinctive metropolitan institutions that had catered to the elevated tastes and sensibilities of both historical and fictional debtors for generations emphatically registered the demise of the unreformed debtors' prison in the wake of the legislation of 1861 and 1869. Its insolvent inmates cajoled or compelled to avail themselves of the bankruptcy statutes, the Queen's Prison closed in September 1862, when the recalcitrant remnant of its fraudulent debtor population was transferred to the less salubrious environs of the Whitecross Street prison. Itself rendered anachronistic by the 1869 act, Whitecross Street was abolished in 1870 and its remaining county-court prisoners transferred to Holloway.[117] Segregated from criminal inmates but deprived of debtors' historical privileges, immunities and charities, these prisoners remained a troubling anomaly in English gaols until the passage of the Administration of Justice Act at last abolished county-court imprisonment for debt in 1970.

Considerations of cost prohibited the confinement of county-court debtors in the isolated individual cells mandated by the separate system, and until the turn of the century most inmates spent their daylight hours in aimless association with other debtors in dismal common rooms. Daily attendance at divine service, limited access to friends and family and the prohibition of tobacco all testified to the enduring legacy of the category of the penal debtor that had been constructed by reformers in the 1840s.[118] But the government's conflicted, inconsistent attitude toward debtor labour in the decades after 1869 also demonstrates the extent to which prison reform had failed to bring debtor inmates fully within the ambit of disciplinary confinement. Until 1899, compulsory labour by imprisoned debtors was prohibited, a circumstance that underlined the persistently marginal status of debtors in reform ideology and penal practice. When the Prison Commission belatedly empowered prison governors to order county-court debtors to perform labour, its circular conceded that 'As there will not be the same means of supervision and instruction as in the case of convicted prisoners, the simpler and easier tasks can properly be selected' for their employment.[119]

---

[117] For the closure of these prisons, see my 'Being in debt in Dickens' London: fact, fictional representation and the nineteenth-century prison', *Journal of Victorian Culture*, 1, 2 (Autumn 1996), esp. 220.

[118] See, for example, the description of debtor life at the turn of the century in Birmingham Central Reference Library, Local Studies, L.43.93, Winson Green Prison Newscuttings, Inquest at Winson Green, 4 February 1899.

[119] PRO, PCOM 7/491, Circular L.P. 13/1899, 16 June 1899.

188   Imprisonment for debt and the economic individual

Ironically, in the late Victorian and Edwardian years, debtors' incongruous position in the criminal gaol insulated them from the growing trend in penal policy away from deterrent and disciplinary imprisonment and toward less punitive plans of treatment. From the 1880s, Martin Wiener has argued, new doubts about 'the positive role of adversity in character development' emerged in England as thinkers reconceptualised human nature in ways that weakened the personal autonomy and moral responsibility of the adult individual.[120] Restricted to light labour, debtors were excluded from the progressive stages system – in which inmates advanced from more to less onerous labour over time and received rewards for their progress – that now increasingly supplanted reliance upon tasks such as oakum-picking and treadwheel labour in reformers' disciplinary arsenal.[121] Developing apace with the expanding frontiers of therapeutic intervention and the welfare state, the dissonance between county-court imprisonment and twentieth-century penology remained a thorn in the side of government officials in the post-war period. 'That the present state of the law as to Imprisonment for Debt…is anomalous and unsatisfactory is a proposition which will…be generally admitted', the solicitor J.A. Parker wrote to the Prison Commissioners in 1929, urging the need to abolish this practice altogether. 'The purpose of this memorandum is therefore somewhat akin to flogging a dead horse.'[122] By 1945, imprisoned debtors' status was yet more problematic. Still excluded from progression through the stages system, they were now the only prisoners denied the privilege of smoking within the gaol. Redressing this anomaly, the chairman of the Prison Commission noted, would require time-consuming consideration of the fundamental question that continued to dog this legal practice – 'e.g. what is the intention of imprisonment for debt – punitive, deterrent, reformative, or simply a form of pressure in the interests of the creditor?'[123] The legislation of 1861 and 1869 had succeeded in establishing that debtors were no longer confined merely for safe custody, but it had clearly failed to resolve the question of what purpose was to be served instead by their incarceration.

Conclusion

The transformation of prisons from institutions of passive containment to sites of discipline and reform exerted a profound effect on imprisoned debtors,

---

[120] Martin J. Wiener, *Reconstructing the Criminal: Culture, Law, and Policy in England, 1830–1914* (Cambridge, 1990), 322.

[121] For debtors' exclusion from the stages system, see PRO, PCOM 7/491, Letter of E.G. Clayton, 5 August 1899.

[122] PRO, PCOM 9/61, Memorandum upon the law relating to civil coercion, 16 August 1929. McConville, *English Local Prisons*, 361–9 offers an excellent synopsis of the contradictions of debtors' treatment in the aftermath of the 1869 act.

[123] PRO, PCOM 9/1321, Minutes re petition of Peter Mandelson, 20/2/1945 and 21/2/1945.

altering their experience in confinement and reconfiguring their identity in the imagination of the educated classes. Drawn from all strata of society but concentrated disproportionately among those who possessed accumulations of social and economic capital, eighteenth-century debtors had constituted the largest single category of prisoner in English gaols. Provided with accommodation suited to their tastes and means, visited on a daily basis by friends and family, freed from onerous labour by the services of lesser inmates and active in institutions of self-government, the most privileged of these debtors found a happy asylum within the prison's walls. A century and a half later, these propertied insolvents had been supplanted by working-class debtors committed by the county courts. Compelled to labour, restricted to weekly visits with a family member, prohibited from smoking and reduced to subsisting on the prison diet, these penal debtors were now classified – by law as by much public opinion – as culpable agents rather than unfortunate victims of circumstance. Petty debtors were themselves acutely conscious of this violation of the traditional norms that had, for centuries, governed perceptions and experiences of imprisonment for debt. George Smith of West Kilburn, a debtor released from Holloway in 1893 following imprisonment 'for the crime of being 70 years old and not being able to pay the parish rates', was painfully alive to the new penal ideologies that had displaced the philanthropic tendencies of organisations such as the Thatched House Society. As he observed in a letter of protest to the Lord Chancellor, 'we are told that Imprisonment for small debts are [*sic*] done away with but the one portion of it I can assure your Lordship is entirely done away with ... is the money that was left for the Benefit of poor <u>debtors</u> that part is entirely gone'.[124] Debtor James Beach of Hammersmith, a seventy-four-year-old joiner rendered unfit for work by bronchitis, asthma and rheumatism, invoked the trope of 'misfortune' that had earlier dominated discourse on imprisonment for debt to describe his plight and to rail against the criminalisation of inmates' status. Casting debtors as hapless victims, he urged 'an alteration in the law and treatment of debtor prisoners in Holloway not as some are treated at the present time more like Burglars or Murderers than like debtors'.[125]

The persistent argument that debtors should be distinguished from criminal prisoners in the gaol, the continued reliance upon conceptions of misfortune to describe the debtor's dilemma and the enduring memory of charitable funds that had affirmed inmates' freedom from full moral liability for their contracts all testified to these county-court defendants' determination to link their own life stories to traditions of imprisonment for debt made familiar for decades by fictional writing and insistently remembered by propertied men and women through allusions and references to classical novels in diaries, memoirs,

---

[124] PRO, LCO 2/66, George Smith to the Lord Chancellor, 13 February 1893.
[125] PRO, LCO 2/66, James Beach to the Lord Chancellor, 15 July 1893.

190   Imprisonment for debt and the economic individual

petitions and tracts. But fiction proved a poisoned chalice for county-court debtors and their partisans in the later Victorian and Edwardian eras. In the decades from 1740 to 1860, fictional representations of debtors' prisons had offered English novelists exceptionally effective vehicles for exploring the troubling social consequences entailed by new forms of economic exchange. Yet while the dilemmas of personal debt and credit continued to exercise novelists into the twentieth century, imprisoned debtors disappeared from the cast of characters that animated imaginative literature from the 1860s. In *Framley Parsonage* (1861) Mark Robarts's debts bring bailiffs to the vicarage, and in *Phineas Finn* (1869) Trollope's hero is desperate to retain his parliamentary seat precisely because his status as a Member of Parliament prevents his creditors from seizing his body as security for his unpaid bills. But imprisonment for debt – which remains an intimated threat, rather than a realised experience, even in these two novels – faded rapidly from the literary record in this decade.[126]

Changes in the debt law fostered the demise of this literary convention, not by abolishing imprisonment for debt but rather by tearing apart the reticulation of genteel associations that had helped to sustain fictional descriptions of this practice since the 1740s. Deployed alongside representations of the unreformed debtors' prison, eighteenth- and early nineteenth-century depictions of civil courts and their personnel had helped to stoke fictional outrage against the treatment of unfortunate insolvents by highlighting the inevitable tension that obtained between the strict enforcement of contracts and the protection of moral and social obligations.[127] Small-claims courts were, however, poorly suited to perpetuate this fictional tradition. Typically bereft of legal counsel, only rarely resorting to jury trials and inevitably packed with unruly, vociferous plebeian defendants, the small-claims courts lent themselves easily to the melodramatic narrative traditions that flourished in the working-class and popular press.[128] But these inferior local courts failed to engage the sympathies of English novelists. In *Little Dorrit*, the last of his debtor novels, Dickens gestured to this unexplored avenue of narrative only to highlight the inadequacies of small-claims courts as sites for middle-class legal fiction. Arthur Clenham's attorney is careful to advise his client against allowing his imprisonment to issue from the Palace

---

[126] Bankruptcy or exile to the colonies replaced imprisonment for debt as a trope and plot device, as exemplified by novels such as George Gissing's *Eve's Ransom* (1895) and William H.G. Kingston's *Millicent Courtenay's Diary* [1873]. See also Finn, 'Being in debt in Dickens' London', 203–26, and Barbara Weiss, *The Hell of the English: Bankruptcy and the Victorian Novel* (Lewisburg, PA, 1986).

[127] Prime examples include Smollett's portrayal of the King's Bench in *Ferdinand Count Fathom* and Dickens's *Pickwick Papers*, *Little Dorrit* and *Bleak House*. See also the discussion of novelists' use of corrupt legal practices to deliberate the moral valence of contractual relations, in Randall Craig, *Promising Language: Betrothal in Victorian Law and Fiction* (Albany, NY, 2000), esp. 115.

[128] See my 'Working-class women and the contest for consumer control in Victorian county courts', *P&P*, 161 (November 1998), esp. 136–8.

Court, which served as a small-claims tribunal for the city of Westminster. ' "I should prefer your being taken on a writ from one of the Superior Courts...It looks better" ', he instructs the hapless debtor. ' "This is an extensive affair of yours; and your remaining here where a man can come for a pound or two, is remarked upon, as not being in keeping." '[129] Trollope's disparaging references in the 1860s to the low status of county-court judges were of a piece with these sentiments, which echoed the dominant sentiments of contemporaries. In *Orley Farm* (1862), Felix Graham's lack of wealth and patronage suggests to his prospective mother-in-law that he can, at best, aspire to a county-court judgeship; in *Phineas Finn* (1869), only the loss of the parliamentary office that has protected his person from arrest for debt reduces the hero to thinking 'how grand a thing it would be for him to have a County Court for himself'.[130]

The prisons associated with county-court confinement were likewise the victims of selective amnesia on the part of English novelists in the aftermath of the statutory reforms of the 1860s. No longer a form of confinement suffered by unfortunate self-described ladies and gentlemen – including a significant number of novelists – in spunging-houses and exclusive metropolitan gaols, imprisonment for debt became instead a practice endured by persons of lowly social origin in penal institutions. Dickens, schooled since childhood to navigate the precise social geography of the gaol, had recognised – and resisted – the demise of the genteel debtors' prison and the rise of the penal debtor already in 1838. In *Pickwick Papers*, Dickens declined to commit his fictional characters to the gaols frequented by small-claims debtors, in which gentlemanly amenities were at a discount. ' "You can't go to Whitecross Street, my dear Sir!...Impossible! There are sixty beds in a ward" ', Pickwick's attorney advises his client anxiously. ' "You can go to the Fleet, if you're determined to go somewhere." '[131]

Contemporary observers hostile to the new county courts recognised the vital relation that obtained between the historical perpetuation of imprisonment for debt and the parallel disappearance of the debtors' prison from the novel. Protagonists of the small-claims courts turned again and again to imaginative literature in defending the reformed practice of imprisonment, while antagonists repeatedly adduced the troubling legacy of fiction in seeking to return unfortunate debtors to the central place in reformed penology which they had enjoyed in the days of John Howard. The *Traders' Herald*, worried by proposed reforms to curb county-court imprisonment in 1880, assured its readers that 'The flagrant abuse which "Little Dorrit" was written to illustrate has been

---

[129] Charles Dickens, *Little Dorrit* (1857; Oxford, 1981), 599–600, 618.
[130] Anthony Trollope, *Orley Farm*, ed. David Skilton (Oxford, 1985), 409; idem, *Phineas Finn*, ed. John Sutherland (London, 1972), 697.
[131] Charles Dickens, *Pickwick Papers* (New York, 1964), 616. The broader dimensions of these developments are detailed in Finn, 'Being in debt in Dickens' London'.

192   Imprisonment for debt and the economic individual

entirely blotted out of the statute book.'[132] The *Credit Drapers' Gazette*, whose subscribers were notorious for their use of county-court imprisonment to enforce the payment of consumer debts by working-class men and women, was equally sanguine. 'The abuses of the debtor and creditor system that belonged to the old law... furnished some of our brilliant novelists with more than one pathetic situation, rousing public opinion so much that... these abuses [have] been swept away', the newspaper proclaimed in defending the county courts from parliamentary attack in 1882.[133]

Opponents of the courts despaired of the ways in which the fictional legacy undercut their efforts to convince Parliament to abolish imprisonment for petty debts. In their interpretation, novels had promoted a baneful association in the public mind between imprisonment for debt and the shabby gentility of the unreformed debtors' prison, perpetuating an anachronistic shared cultural memory that was instrumental both in obscuring the continued imprisonment of county-court debtors and in veiling the draconian conditions now endured in the gaol by these inmates. 'Everyone should know that the old conditions of a debtors' prison recorded in the works of some of our classical novelists have quite ceased to exist', a debtor committed to Holloway wrote in 1909, railing against the severity of her confinement.[134] 'It is generally known that imprisonment for debt still exists in England, but there is a comfortable belief that the propaganda of Dickens brought about changes which reduced to a minimum the evils described in *Little Dorrit* and made it impossible for any but fraudulent debtors to be sent to prison', the *New Statesman* noted as late as 1929. 'This belief is not entirely baseless, but those who hold it will be disquieted by the high figures given in present-day statistics of debtor-prisoner populations.'[135] Where proponents of the county courts read the history of imprisonment for debt as evidence of the novel's power to effect reform, detractors of county-court imprisonment instead underscored fiction's ability to distort the historical record of legal practice.

Together, the demise of the fictional imprisoned debtor and the failure of English novelists to exploit the narrative potential of the county courts provide a salutary reminder of the highly selective uses to which law was put in English fiction. In emphasising the inherent overlap between legal and literary genres of argumentation, scholars have identified essential underlying narratives, structures and tendencies that helped to shape the evolution of English fiction.[136] But the history of imprisonment for debt suggests that an undue emphasis on the shared discursive terrain of law and literature may obscure the

[132] *Traders' Herald*, 17 January 1880.
[133] *Credit Drapers' Gazette*, June 1882, 35. See also the memoir of J.D. Crawford, county-court judge, *Reflections and Recollections* (London, 1936), 179–80.
[134] A Female Debtor, *A Summer Holiday in Holloway Gaol* [London, 1909], 15.
[135] *New Statesman*, 2 November 1929.   [136] See above, 12–14.

Discipline or abolish? 193

historical limits of this constellation of linkages in English novels.[137] Already in 1740, Richardson's *Pamela* had suggested the narrative potential of small-claims litigation: in her precise demarcation of possessions according to 'equity and conscience',[138] Pamela spoke directly to legal principles that were to vex judges, journalists and politicians engaged with problematic petty debt claims throughout the Victorian and Edwardian eras. But this available line of legal thinking failed to take root in the English novel. Loath to interrogate the social consequences of economic credit in the plebeian precincts of the small-claims court, nineteenth-century novelists increasingly averted their gaze, shifting the locus of their fictions from civil court litigants and prison inmates to the exchange of persons and commodities in gift and consumer markets. The problem of the petty debtor was in consequence channelled into and structured by alternative discursive sites and modalities. Debated in Parliament, in the courts and in the press, the petty credit transactions of the lesser sort became staple subjects of legal and political policy-making, forcing lawyers, judges, MPs and government officials to re-imagine the contractual identities of the individual along new lines of class, gender and character difference.

[137] Contrast Randall Craig's assertion that fictional representations of legal conflict are necessarily 'both more supple and more subtle' than historical legal discourse. Craig, *Promising Language*, x, 12, 69, citation from x.

[138] Above, 32.

Part III

Petty debts and the modernisation of English law

5 'A kind of parliamentary magic': eighteenth-century courts of conscience

The rise of the penitentiary played a central role in the demise of the debtors' prison, prompting a reformulation of the instrumental relations that linked the gaol, the body and the market. But if the changing nature of the prison both promoted and came to symbolise a reconfiguration of English debt relations, analysis of penal reform alone fails to convey the extent to which the institutions that mediated personal contracts were transformed by (and acted to promote) the commercial, consumer and industrial revolutions. Gaols were only the institutional apex of economic conflict engendered by credit transactions; imprisonment marked the endpoint of an extended process of negotiation that began with the sharp bargains, unwritten obligations and extended credit of the marketplace and was formalised only when the failure of these assumed contracts brought debtors and creditors into the corridors of the law through the litigation process.

Historians of crime depict the long eighteenth century as a period of rapid legal innovation and growth: the history of criminal law in this period is chiefly told in terms of the proliferation of capital statutes that formed the 'Bloody Code', a dramatic rise in criminal prosecution rates, an access of public hanging and the erection of an expanding constellation of penal institutions for those convicts who escaped both the gallows and transportation to the Antipodes.[1] The history of civil litigation is, in striking contrast, dominated by a 'great litigation decline'. Christopher Brooks's crucial research on trends in civil litigation from 1640 to 1830 has largely set the agenda for this interpretative paradigm. 'In 1640 there was probably more litigation per head of population going through the central courts at Westminster than at any other time before or since', Brooks concludes. 'But one hundred years later, in 1750, the common law hit what appears to have been a spectacular all time low.'[2]

Parallel trends marked civil litigation in the local courts of record that had successfully adjudicated petty credit disputes in the sixteenth century. Overall

---

[1] See esp. V.A.C. Gatrell, *The Hanging Tree: Execution and the English People 1770–1868* (Oxford, 1994).

[2] Christopher Brooks, *Lawyers, Litigation and English Society since 1450* (London, 1998), 27–62, citation from 29. He notes the predominance of debt cases in these courts on page 53.

197

198   Petty debts and the modernisation of English law

levels of litigation in the borough, hundred and county courts with jurisdiction over debts valued at less than forty shillings increased dramatically in the early Elizabethan era, Craig Muldrew observes, describing borough courts as 'probably the most widely used secular institutions in towns by the end of the sixteenth century'.[3] As with the central courts, however, recourse to local courts to recover debts diminished in the later seventeenth century. In metropolitan superior courts and provincial courts of record alike, legal expenses appear to have contributed substantially to this decline. Costs rose dramatically in the superior courts from the later seventeenth century, at least doubling the cost of litigation in London's superior courts between 1680 and 1750.[4] In the provinces, the decades marked by significant increases in petty debt litigation had also seen local courts adopt the precise forms and procedures of London's superior courts of common law,[5] a trend that appears to have detracted significantly from the appeal of local courts of record by increasing the cost, duration and complexity of litigation. Between the 1590s and the 1670s, average costs in Shrewsbury's *Curia Parva* rose fourfold. Unsurprisingly, levels of litigation fell sharply, dropping from an average of 1,175 actions entered in the court annually in the decade beginning in 1600 to only 78 cases per year on average in the decade beginning in 1720.[6]

Plebeian producers, retailers and consumers appear to have been progressively excluded from the ambit of the civil law in the course of the seventeenth century, a development rendered highly problematic by their active and increasing participation in the dense networks of credit that sustained English commerce. Contemporaries' awareness of the obstacles placed in the way of petty lending and borrowing by common-law procedures was first manifest in a spate of local initiatives to bypass local courts of record. In the City of London, the mayor and aldermen had recognised this problem already in the reign of Henry VIII, when an Act of Common Council of dubious legality established a so-called Court of Conscience or Court of Requests to determine claims of 40 shillings or less owed to or by 'any citizen . . . victualler, tradesman or labouring man' within the City's walls. Confirmed by statutes of 1604 and 1606, London's court of conscience specifically eschewed common-law principles and jury trials, instructing its lay commissioners to act by summary process

---

[3] Craig Muldrew, *The Economy of Obligation: The Culture of Credit and Social Relations in Early Modern England* (Basingstoke, 1998), 221, 205. From the medieval period, the lowest sum for which a debt suit could be brought in the central courts of London was set at forty shillings.

[4] Brooks, *Lawyers, Litigation and English Society*, 45–8.

[5] Muldrew, *Economy of Obligation*, 204.

[6] W.A. Champion, 'Recourse to law and the meaning of the great litigation decline, 1650–1750: some clues from the Shrewsbury local courts', in Christopher W. Brooks and Michael Lobban, eds., *Communities and Courts in Britain 1150–1900* (London, 1997), 179–98, esp. 179, 184–7; idem, 'Litigation in the boroughs: the Shrewsbury *Curia Parva* 1480–1730', *Legal History*, 15, 3 (December 1994), 105.

'A kind of parliamentary magic' 199

'as they shall find to stand with Equity and Good Conscience'.[7] Provincial efforts to bring lesser debtors within the reach of the courts in this period similarly emphasised 'equitable' principles at the expense of common law. Petty debtors in early seventeenth-century Norwich could appeal their suits to the summary Mayor's Court of Equity, which was specifically intended to serve 'where an equitable remedy may appear but none can be obtained by Common Law'.[8]

Scattered and episodic, these early local initiatives were soon surpassed by national developments. As political consensus disintegrated in the 1640s, antagonism to law and to lawyers became a central component of wider attacks on the established state. Levellers were at the forefront of this challenge, but they were hardly exceptional in calling for a reformulation of common-law practices. The Hale Commission of 1652 recommended the creation of a national network of local small-claims courts in which lay commissioners, rather than judges or juries, would adjudicate debts valued at less than four pounds.[9] The increasingly shrill criticism directed against the use of Latin in common-law courts reflected not only this concern that the law be made accessible to the common people but also a more fundamental scepticism as to the ability of common-law procedures to deliver justice. As one critic commented pungently, 'The Latin tongue is good, so is wine good in a clean vessel, but not in a piss-pot.' In 1650 Parliament decreed that henceforth law books must be published in English and court proceedings recorded in ordinary – not court – hand.[10]

The restoration of monarchy in 1660 is conventionally taken to mark the eclipse of these ambitious reform aspirations, just as it witnessed the return of Latin to the courtroom. 'The Republic was a failure because common law survived', Alan Cromartie concludes. 'The legal history of the interregnum was the history of the common law's survival, both as a guarantee of private rights and as the natural language of English political thought.'[11] As a description of high politics, this analysis has much to recommend it, but the legislative elaboration of statutes designed to regulate petty debts departed significantly from the trajectory of legal evolution suggested by this Whiggish narrative. With the Restoration, as commerce, manufacture and consumption recovered from the economic dislocations of the revolutionary years, efforts to modify and

---

[7] For the origins of the City's court of conscience, see W.H.D. Winder, 'The courts of requests', *Law Quarterly Review*, 207 (July 1936), 370–1; Richard M. Wunderli, *London Church Courts and Society on the Eve of the Reformation* (Cambridge, MA, 1981), 105.

[8] Michele Slatter, 'The Norwich Court of Requests: a tradition continued', in Albert Kiralfy, Michele Slatter and Roger Virgoe, eds., *Custom, Courts and Counsel: Selected Papers of the 6th British Legal History Conference* (London, 1985), 98–101. For similar developments in Shrewsbury, see Champion, 'Litigation in the boroughs', 208–9, and idem, 'Recourse to law', 189–90.

[9] Alan Cromartie, *Sir Matthew Hale 1609–1675: Law, Religion and Natural Philosophy* (Cambridge, 1995), 70–2; Donald Veall, *The Popular Movement for Law Reform 1640–1660* (Oxford, 1970), 170–2.

[10] Veall, *Popular Movement*, 191–2.   [11] Cromartie, *Sir Matthew Hale*, 58, 64.

200   Petty debts and the modernisation of English law

modernise the legal regulation of small-scale contractual disputes by moderating the stringent conventions of common-law process grew apace. The system of summary justice pioneered by the City of London's court of conscience now became increasingly attractive to contemporaries. From 1662 to 1685, the denizens of Southwark and Westminster repeatedly sought to obtain courts of conscience for the adjudication of debts of less than forty shillings.[12]

Significantly, where earlier efforts to simplify debt litigation by loosening the grip of the common law had smacked of Leveller aspirations, Restoration attempts to establish summary small debt courts appear to have been tarred instead by monarchist associations. Records of parliamentary debate on these proposals are lacking, but royalist tendencies are intriguingly salient among the men who sponsored small-claims court bills from 1662 to 1702. Sir Philip Warwick, Sir Thomas Clarges, Thomas Christie, Colonel John Perry, Viscount Cornbury and Sir John Kaye were all monarchists in the civil wars or associated with the Tory interest in the Restoration and its aftermath.[13] The text of Warwick's *Memoires of the Reigne of King Charles I* and the arguments of his *Discourse of Government, as Examined by Reason, Scripture and Law* – both written in the 1670s, when Warwick introduced an unsuccessful bill for a court of conscience for Westminster – suggest the lines of legal thinking that may have made equitable courts attractive to monarchist MPs. In his *Memoires*, Warwick interpreted the royal exercise of arbitrary political power as an essential equitable prerogative of government.[14] His *Discourse of Government* expatiated further upon the essential relation between royal authority and legal equity, insisting that 'A power of equity was necessarily entrusted with Soveraigns, because there would be often occasion to abate the severity of the laws; for if the extremities of contracts and penalties in laws should be always taken, laws would often be snares, and too often burthensome to be borne.'[15]

Unsurprisingly, parliamentary efforts to create petty equitable debt courts were highly contentious. Between 1662 and 1702, forty unsuccessful attempts

---

[12] The Southwark bills were attempted in 1662, 1675, 1677, 1679 and 1685; the Westminster bills in 1673, 1674, 1675 and 1677. See Julian Hoppit, *Failed Legislation 1660–1800: Extracted from the Commons and Lords Journals* (London, 1997), 56, 120, 124, 126, 132, 138, 150, 158.

[13] For Warwick, see Basil Duke Henning, ed., *The History of Parliament: The House of Commons 1660–1690*, 3 vols. (London, 1983), III: 674–5, and *Dictionary of National Biography*, vol. XX, 894–6; for Clarges, Henning, ed., *History of Parliament*, II: 74–81, and *DNB*, vol. IV, 398–9; for Christie's political affiliations, see Henning, ed., *History of Parliament*, II: 66–7; for Perry, see Henry Horwitz, ed., *The Parliamentary Diary of Narcissus Luttrell 1691–1693* (Oxford, 1972), 502; for Cornbury, see Henning, ed., *History of Parliament*, II: 624–5; for Sir John Kaye, see Henning, ed., *History of Parliament*, II: 668–9.

[14] Sir Philip Warwick, *Memoires of the Reigne of King Charles I. With a Continuation to the Happy Restoration of King Charles II* (London, 1701), 1, 57.

[15] Sir Philip Warwick, *A Discourse of Government, As Examined by Reason, Scripture, and Law of the Land. Or True Weights and Measures between Sovereignty and Liberty* (London, 1694), 7–8.

'A kind of parliamentary magic' 201

were made to ease and speed the recovery of small debts by summary process.[16] Broadsheets published in response to these proposed bills suggest the extent to which debates over political liberty and authority had polarised efforts to simplify the enforcement of small-scale economic contracts since the Hale Commission of 1652. Celebrated in the Interregnum as a corrective to the rigid forms of the common law, summary small-claims courts now figured as dangerous departures from the political guarantees promised by the Restoration or secured by the Revolution settlement. In 1675, a broadsheet opposing the erection of a metropolitan court of conscience struck a characteristic chord in asserting that the proposal 'takes away... the ancient Trials by Jury, and gives an arbitrary power to the Commissioners... without any appeal from them to any Judicature whatever... and takes from every Man his Birth-right to the ancient Law of the Land'. Where 'the Common Law' vested legal authority in 'Persons of Quality, that are Lords of Mannors', the mooted court 'vests it in Shop-keepers', the author observed contemptuously.[17] Equality before the law, the Whig mantra of the Revolution settlement, underpinned this attack on summary justice. 'This Arbitrary Proceeding, contrary to the Law of Magna Charta (being the Subject's Birthright) will bar the subject of the Benefit of other Good Laws', the author of another broadsheet prophesied darkly.[18]

This critique of summary small-claims courts nested easily within Whig political doctrine, but it failed to account for contemporary economic developments. Rather than dampening enthusiasm for reforms that would temper the scrupulous niceties of the rule of common law, the achievement of a constitutional settlement in 1688 clearly raised aspirations for legal innovation compatible with economic growth. Key legal thinkers began to question the utility of jury trials for substantial commercial disputes, and in 1698 John Locke successfully drafted legislation to speed merchants' suits through summary arbitration.[19] 'By the later seventeenth century, the rigours of the common law of contract were being relaxed in favour of the generally more forgiving customs of merchants', Christopher Brooks observes. 'The common law courts followed suit. By 1750

[16] Hoppit, *Failed Legislation*, 56, 120, 124, 126, 132, 138, 150, 154, 158, 160, 162, 164, 166, 168, 170, 172, 176, 178, 180, 184, 186, 194, 196, 206, 230, 232, 236, 240, 244.
[17] Anon., *Reasons against the Bill for Erecting Courts of Conscience* [1675], British Library press mark 816.m.15 (2).
[18] Anon., *The Lady Russel's and All Lords of Mannors, Case and Reasons against the Bill for Erecting a Court of Conscience* [London, 1707], British Library press mark 1891.d.1 (39).
[19] Henry Horwitz and James Oldham, 'John Locke, Lord Mansfield, and arbitration during the eighteenth century', *HJ*, 36, 1 (1993), 137–59. For the broader contours of these legal developments, see David Lieberman, 'The legal needs of commercial society: the jurisprudence of Lord Kames', in Istvan Hont and Michael Ignatieff, eds., *Wealth and Virtue: The Shaping of Political Economy in the Scottish Enlightenment* (Cambridge, 1983), 203–34, and idem, 'Property, commerce, and the common law: attitudes to legal change in the eighteenth century', in John Brewer and Susan Staves, eds., *Early Modern Conceptions of Property* (London, 1996), 144–58, esp. 150–1.

202 Petty debts and the modernisation of English law

they were regularly using mechanisms which eased the rules that obligations had to be performed on a certain day and which forced creditors to accept partial payments of debts.'[20]

The proliferation of petty credit contracts at the lower levels of society contributed significantly to this reformulation of law and contract by commercial culture. Between 1689 and 1691, Westminster, Southwark, Holborn, the Tower Hamlets, the London out-parishes, Greenwich, Colchester, York, Exeter, Norwich, Yarmouth and Canterbury all petitioned Parliament for summary small-claims courts; between 1689 and 1701, Bristol, Gloucester, Newcastle and Norwich all succeeded in obtaining a court of conscience for debts of less than forty shillings.[21] A sustained interval of relatively high wages for workers, Christopher Brooks suggests, impeded efforts to build upon these precedents by reducing economic pressure for the creation of new courts of conscience in the early decades of the new century.[22] The return of more precarious economic conditions for wage workers and a new recognition on the part of propertied commentators of the consumer activities of the poor both, however, proved conducive to a sustained growth of courts of conscience from the later 1740s to 1789.[23] Southwark and Middlesex at last gained parliamentary approval for courts of requests in 1749, as did the City of Westminster and the Tower Hamlets in 1750. Provincial centres of commerce and industry swiftly followed suit. Lincoln acquired a court of conscience in 1750, Birmingham, St Albans, Liverpool and Canterbury in 1752, Boston in 1753, Sheffield in 1756, and Yarmouth in 1757. Continuing apace with the creation of eight new courts in the 1760s, eleven in the 1770s and ten in the 1780s, this proliferation of summary tribunals marked a new phase in the evolution of English law.[24] Serving to return labourers, artisans and petty producers to the embrace of civil process, eighteenth-century courts of conscience also distanced the small debtor emphatically from the much-vaunted protections of the rule of law.

[20] Brooks, *Lawyers, Litigation and English Society*, 52–3, citation from 53.

[21] Hoppit, *Failed Legislation*, 160, 162, 164, 166, 168, 170, 172, 178, 180, 184, 186. The legislation was 1 Will. & M. sess. 1, c. 17 (1689, Newcastle); 1 Will. & M. sess. 1, c. 18 (1689, Bristol and Gloucester); and 12 & 13 Will. III c. 7 (1701, Norwich).

[22] Brooks, *Lawyers, Litigation and English Society*, 37. See also Paul Langford, *Public Life and the Propertied Englishman 1689–1798* (Oxford, 1991), 158–9. Impassioned defences of common-law process against the courts' equitable encroachments continued to punctuate political debate over legal reform in this interval. See John Mallory, *Objections Humbly Offer'd against Passing the Bill, Intitled A Bill for the More Easy and Speedy Recovery of Small Debts in Law* (London, 1730).

[23] For the emergence of the plebeian consumer in the economic discourse of this period, see Jonathan White, 'Luxury and labour: ideas of labouring-class consumption in eighteenth-century England' (Ph.D. thesis, University of Warwick, 2001).

[24] The geographical dimensions of the courts' growth are helpfully detailed by Langford, *Public Life and the Propertied Englishman*, 160. As Langford notes, the courts' jurisdictions typically encompassed substantial hinterlands around the designated court towns, and thus included a more extensive area than is initially suggested by the wording of their enabling legislation.

Summary justice

The creation of summary small-claims courts throughout England formed an essential part of a broader expansion of summary justice in the modern period. Where social historians previously saw 'the law' as a unified and unifying body of procedures characterised above all else by its attention to punctilious legal forms,[25] analysis of legal processes in contexts other than the central courts and the Assizes has pointed instead to the wide disparities of procedure and practice fostered by the expanding legal system's reliance upon the unpaid laymen who administered summary justice in the localities. In criminal law, as historians have turned their attention from jury trials to detail the crucial roles played by magistrates, judicial discretion has become a watchword of legal practice. Peter King's study of summary criminal hearings describes the period from 1740 to 1820 as 'the golden age of discretionary justice in England'; his assessment of the 'bewildering variety of practices' elaborated by magistrates emphasises that 'legal technicalities did not take pride of place in these courts'. Parliamentary statutes and legal handbooks, even when available for consultation, often went unread: the contemporary observer Thomas Gisborne suggested that magistrates' judgments typically relied instead 'on their own unauthorized ideas of equity'.[26] Viewed from this perspective, the proliferation of petty 'equitable' debt courts in eighteenth-century England emerges as an integral component of broader legal changes that worked during the era of the consumer and industrial revolutions to reconfigure the adjudication of property relations and contractual disputes.

References to increasing levels of trade and manufacture abound in the preambles of the petitions to Parliament that precipitated the establishment of local courts of conscience. Birmingham's successful petition of 1752 boasted that the town employed 'by Computation, above Twenty thousand Hands, in useful Manufactures, that are not only greatly serviceable to the Government, but also return annually great Sums of Money to this Kingdom, from foreign Parts'.[27] The parish of Old Swinford, straddling Worcester and Stafford, similarly drew attention in 1777 to the region's 'divers Manufactories of Iron, Glass, and Cloth,

---

[25] The classic formulation of the law as a unifying (albeit terrifying) national force is Douglas Hay, 'Property, authority and the criminal law', in Douglas Hay, Peter Linebaugh, John Rule, E.P. Thompson and Cal Winslow, eds., *Albion's Fatal Tree: Crime and Society in Eighteenth-Century England* (New York, 1985).

[26] Peter King, *Crime, Justice and Discretion in England 1740–1820* (Oxford 2000), 1, 83, 85; Thomas Gisborne, *An Enquiry into the Duties of Men of the Higher and Middle Classes* (London, 1794), cited in ibid., 85. For the expansion of summary justice, see also David Eastwood, *Governing Rural England: Tradition and Transformation in Local Government 1780–1840* (Oxford, 1994); Norma Landau, *The Justices of the Peace 1679–1760* (Berkeley, 1984); and Robert Shoemaker, *Prosecution and Punishment: Petty Crime and the Law in London and Rural Middlesex, 1660–1725* (Cambridge, 1991).

[27] *Commons Journals*, 16 January 1752, 368–9.

204   Petty debts and the modernisation of English law

and other Trades, carried on in a very large and extensive Manner', noting predictably that 'many Thousands of Persons are constantly employed therein'.[28] Within this generic framework, the vital role played by 'useful credit' among the lower orders in driving local commerce, consumption and manufacture was a recurrent leitmotif of court of requests petitions and statutes. As the Liverpool petition proclaimed in 1752, 'small useful Credit is found to be absolutely necessary amongst... Traders, Artificers, Handicraftsmen and Seamen'.[29] Producers' use of credit to maintain stable work forces – a tactic well documented in plebeian memoirs – featured importantly in the petitioning literature. In 1758, when Yarmouth's application for a court of requests was examined by a Commons committee, William Martyn testified 'That when Trade is bad, Labourers would not be able to subsist, unless their Employers were to advance them small Sums; and the Recovery thereof is attended with great Expense'.[30] Petty sums advanced by labourers to their employers in the form of unpaid wages provided the other side of this plebeian credit relation. When John Gale was examined by the Commons committee considering a Wiltshire court of conscience petition in 1779, he noted that 'it is the Custom of the Country to pay the Wages of Labourers and Manufacturers but once a Month, by which means they want Credit, and are compelled to contract Debts, which they frequently refuse to pay'.[31]

Petitions characteristically paired these paeons to useful credit with attacks on the baneful economic effect exerted by common-law procedures. Just as proponents of classical political economy denounced mercantilist devices that restricted the flow of goods, so too partisans of the courts of requests decried the obstacles posed by antiquated legal systems to the flow of useful credit. Lincoln's petition of 1750 was typical, citing the 'Discouragement, from giving Credit for small Sums to the Poor' that ensued from 'the Expense and Delay which attend the Recovery thereof, being confined to the Strict Rules of the Common Law'.[32] A stream of citizens travelled to Westminster to substantiate their petitions with evidence of the existing court system's inability to enforce petty credit contracts. Joseph Rushton and James Webb of Birmingham drew attention to the extortionate costs associated with small debt litigation in the local court of record in 1752, testifying 'that they have known Four Pounds expended by a Plaintiff and Three Pounds by a Defendant, upon Account of a Debt which did not amount to Ten Shillings'.[33] Urban elites who presided over local courts of record were often at the forefront of this effort to discredit their own tribunals' procedures. In Kirby, the mayor, aldermen and capital burgesses were among the petitioners who pleaded that although a mayor's court did sit weekly to hear claims of less than forty pounds, 'the Proceedings of the

---

[28] Ibid., 10 February 1777, 149.   [29] Ibid., 16 January 1752, 369.
[30] Ibid., 6 March 1758, 118.   [31] Ibid., 22 February 1779, 155.
[32] Ibid., 27 February 1750, 66.   [33] Ibid., 3 February 1752, 415.

same ... prosecuted in the usual and legal Forms thereof, have been found to be very tedious, expensive and dilatory ... to the great Discouragement of Credit and Industry'.[34]

In the statutes that translated these aspirations into functioning legal systems, antagonism to archaic legal mechanisms was matched by hostility to the legal profession. Bath's act of 1766 specifically prohibited attorneys from acting as commissioners (that is, lay judges) in its court and imposed a swingeing fine of twenty pounds upon any attorney who sought to act as 'Advocate in Behalf of any Plaintiff or Defendant, or to be admitted to speak in any Cause or Matter before the said Court'.[35] Restrictions such as these became a commonplace of later eighteenth-century court of requests legislation. King's Lynn (1770), Beverley (1781) and Rochester (1782) were among the many courts that prohibited attorneys from appearing in their precincts either as advocates or commissioners.[36] Removing causes from the courts of conscience to courts of common law was moreover explicitly prohibited by several of the statutes: Derby's act of 1766 forbade local creditors to bring suits for debts of less than forty shillings 'in any of the King's Courts at *Westminster*, or any other Courts whatsoever' in lieu of the new court of conscience.[37]

To replace the common-law conventions employed in local courts of record, the court of conscience literature proposed that the new small-claims commissioners should avail themselves of 'equitable' reasoning. Equity in this context referred less to the formal practices of the central court of Chancery, than to tempering the strict letter of the law by taking account of particularistic, mitigating personal circumstances. As William Blackstone, citing Grotius, declared in his *Commentaries on the Laws of England* (1765–69), equity was ' "the correction of that, wherein the law (by reason of its universality) is deficient" '.[38] Derived from the circumstances of the particular case rather than from strict adherence to legal precedent, equitable reasoning was fully consonant with the petty debt courts' role in adjudicating disputes without the intervention of lawyers. In 1689, Bristol and Gloucester's act had decreed that its commissioners should render judgments 'as they shall find to stand with Equity and good Conscience in a summary Way ... not tying themselves to the exact Forms and Methods of the Common Law or other Courts of Justice'.[39] Subsequent legislation repeatedly affirmed the virtues of equity and good conscience alongside – and increasingly in place of – law. In 1750, the Tower Hamlets act specified that its

---

[34] Ibid., 16 December 1763, 707.   [35] 6 Geo. III c. 16, s. 25.

[36] 10 Geo. III c. 20, s. 31 (King's Lynn); 21 Geo. III c. 38, s. 28 (Beverley); 22 Geo. III c. 27, s. 29 (Rochester).

[37] 6 Geo. III c. 20, s. 24. Several acts, however, specifically preserved the rights of other local courts to continue to hear small debt suits.

[38] William Blackstone, *Commentaries on the Laws of England*, 4 vols. (1765–69; Chicago, 1979), I: 61–2.

[39] 1 Will. & M. sess. 1, c. 18 (1689), HLRO.

206   Petty debts and the modernisation of English law

commissioners could adjudicate small debt claims 'as to them shall seem just in law or equity', but from the 1760s, court of conscience legislation often failed to reference the common law at all. The acts for Derby in 1766 and Surfleet in 1777 simply decreed that their commissioners should act 'as to them shall seem just, and most agreeable to Equity and Conscience'.[40]

The willingness of petitioners to abandon the protections of the common law by instituting summary 'equitable' processes for petty debt claims was closely linked to the socioeconomic profile of the courts' intended defendants. Specifically barred from hearing disputes involving real property or sums over forty shillings, the courts of conscience were explicitly targeted at plebeian debtors. In justifying the courts' creation, petitioners and legislators returned again and again to the lowly status of the petty debtors who would be summoned by the commissioners. Bristol and Gloucester's act of 1689 asserted that a similar court in its locality would promote the interests of 'poor ... Labourers and others' by preventing 'the ruin of them their Wives and Children and [preventing the] filling [of] the prison with miserable Debtors and ... [causing] great charge to the severall [*sic*] parishes' of the region.[41] Drawing attention to the ubiquity of petty credit, mid eighteenth-century statutes (like Richardson's *Pamela*, Fielding's *Joseph Andrews* and so many contemporary novels) figured debt as an unavoidable 'misfortune'. Liverpool's legislation linked solicitude for the local poor with concern to protect the parish purse. Observing that 'many poor honest Persons ... from numerous Family Misfortunes in Trade Want of Employment or Times of Scarcity or Sickness or other unforeseen Misfortunes are often necessitated and obliged to contract small debts', it claimed that the court's speedy arbitration of economic disputes would prevent the poorer sort from suffering seizure of their goods or persons, 'to the utter Ruin of themselves and Families the loss of their Labour to the Publick and the great Burden or charge of the Parish'.[42]

Over time, however, the dominant language of court of conscience legislation altered. Echoing a hardening of attitudes to the labouring population that was also conspicuous in approaches to Poor Law relief from mid-century,[43] the stock phrases employed in small-claims statutes began to shift from the trope of the 'unfortunate' debtor to depict the insolvent poor as intentionally dishonest

---

[40] 23 Geo. II c. 30, s. 1 (1749, Tower Hamlets); 10 Geo. III c. 20; 6 Geo. III c. 20, s. 2 (1766, Derby); 17 Geo. III c. 62, s. 3 (1777, Surfleet).

[41] 1 Will. & M. sess. 1, c. 18 (1689). See also the Norwich act, 12 & 13 Will. III c. 7 (1701). Like the act for Bristol and Gloucester, the legislation claimed that the court would preclude the ruin of poor debtors and their families and thus reduce the strain on the local poor-rate, an argument that again attests to the lowly economic status of the court of requests' intended defendants.

[42] 25 Geo. II c. 43 (1752).

[43] For these broad changes in attitudes to the poor, see Lynn Hollen Lees, *The Solidarities of Strangers: The English Poor Laws and the People, 1700–1948* (Cambridge, 1998), chap. 3, and above, 153–4.

economic agents. In statutes, critiques of petty debtors' invidious motives often featured more prominently than defences of the legitimate borrowing needs of the poor, and creditors' rights increasingly came to be constructed in opposition to the needs of indebted workers. The preamble of Kidderminster's act of 1772 identified workers in the town's 'large and extensive Manufactury' as 'Debtors [who] are well able to pay their respective Debts, yet . . . often refuse so to do', language reiterated in the depiction of delinquent debtors (specifically identified as iron-workers, glass-workers, weavers and coal-miners) in Old Swindford's court of conscience act five years later.[44] Only adumbrated in court of conscience petitions and statutes, these critiques of eighteenth-century petty debtors were to lay essential groundwork for the emergence of the fraudulent working-class debtor in nineteenth-century county courts.

As summary tribunals that dispensed with the cumbersome forms of customary and common law, as jurisdictions called into being in the interest of trade and manufacture, and as institutions designed to police petty contracts between employers or retailers and the labouring population, courts of conscience participated in broader trends associated with the consumer and industrial revolutions. Explicitly justified as bulwarks of local commerce and industry, these summary tribunals contributed to wider debates on the role of the legislature in promoting the wealth of the nation. Where political economists highlighted the need to free production from customary restraints, the merchants and tradesmen, mayors and aldermen who petitioned Parliament for courts of conscience drew attention instead to the imperative need to liberate 'useful credit' for plebeian producers and consumers. Like the construction of 'free' labour, however, the liberation of the petty debtor proved more fraught in practice than its advocates' rhetoric had suggested. Not least among the factors that served to complicate the new small-claims courts' relation to the modern market was their problematic treatment of the plebeian debtor's body.

Imprisoning the petty debtor

In keeping with the broadly liberalising currents that informed their world view, petitioners had emphasised the summary courts' tendency to encourage timely repayment of petty debts, rather than their ability to coerce debtors to meet their obligations. The mere existence of these tribunals, they intimated, would provide adequate incentives for a plebeian population 'well able' to pay their debts with local tradesmen. The acts which resulted from these petitions were, however, evidently less sanguine of this prospect, equipping commissioners with broad powers to 'execute' or seize the debtor's goods and body when payment failed to materialise. Together poverty and intransigence ensured

[44] 12 Geo. III c. 66 (1772); 17 Geo. III, c. 19 (1777).

208   Petty debts and the modernisation of English law

that imprisonment by courts of conscience exerted a significant impact on the eighteenth-century poor. Statistics from the Tower Hamlets court – established to serve a population of 'the most mean and Indigent' description[45] – illustrate this point. In the first eighteen months of its operation, the court issued 16,918 summonses, convened 9,310 hearings at which 4,920 payments were made into court, and effected a further 2,168 full and 2,345 partial payments out of court. Yet litigation alone failed to convince hundreds of petty debtors to meet their obligations: the court's officers issued executions against 632 defendants who refused (or were unable) to respond to their orders.[46]

All courts of conscience possessed powers to seize debtors' bodies for failing to obey the commissioners' orders of repayment, but the scope of these powers varied widely from court to court. The acts for Bristol and Gloucester in 1689 and Norwich in 1701 allowed commissioners to imprison debtors who refused to comply with their orders without bail until they paid their debt, a practice copied by Southwark in 1749 and Birmingham in 1751. Southwark's act invoked a far less benign vision of summary justice than the petitions' conventional invocation of 'good concience' suggested when it endowed commissioners with 'power and authority' 'to award execution ... against the bodies, or against the goods and chattels of all and every person or persons against whom they shall give any judgment or decree, as to them shall seem just in law or equity'.[47] Most later eighteenth-century courts specified maximum sentences for petty debtors, normally in the range of one, two or three months per unpaid debt. But debtors' inability to pay their gaol fees at the expiration of their terms could render these limitations moot, for until 1785–86 prison-keepers were empowered to retain inmates indefinitely on this account.

If the arbitrary length of petty debtors' imprisonment mirrored the experience of more affluent debtors confined to the prison by courts of common law, their place of confinement marked a new departure in the long history of imprisonment for debt. Held merely for safe custody, common-law debtors were immured in prisons designed to detain but not to discipline their inmates. But court of conscience debtors, as befitted the objects of inferior, summary justice, were in many localities denied the privilege of imprisonment in the debtors' wards of borough and county gaols – much less the relative luxury of the specialised metropolitan debtors' prisons such as the King's Bench. Doncaster's statute did specify that its court was to confine petty debtors in 'the Common Gaol or Prison' of the borough; Blackheath's act, more vaguely, indicated that commissioners were to confine debtors 'in such Publick Prison or Place of Confinement' as was provided by the court's clerks.[48] Far more common was the

---

[45] *Commons Journals*, 11 February 1752, 429; 18 February 1752, 445.
[46] Ibid., 21 January 1752, 393.
[47] 1 Will. & M. sess. 1, c. 18 (1689); 12 & 13 Will. III c. 7 (1701); 22 Geo. II c. 47; 25 Geo. II c. 34 (1751).
[48] 4 Geo. III c. 40 (1763); 5 Geo. III c. 8 (1765).

'A kind of parliamentary magic'   209

direction – at Chippenham, Derby, Surfleet, Ely and Horncastle, to name only a few locations – that commissioners confine petty debtors to 'some Common Gaol or House of Correction' in their jurisdiction.[49] John Howard recorded the presence of small-claims debtors in houses of correction at Clerkenwell, Tothill Fields, Hertford, Yarmouth, Spalding, Devizes, Preston and Kingston upon Hull.[50] Although exempt from compulsory labour, court of conscience defendants confined in houses of correction were distanced both from the charitable donations and from the established conventions of representation that mitigated the severity of imprisonment for debt for insolvents. A wealth of evidence suggests that the use of houses of correction was both intended and perceived to signal a broader effort to demarcate the experience of imprisonment for debt along socioeconomic lines.

The commissioners' ability to associate petty debtors with petty criminals in houses of correction underpinned an array of efforts – undertaken not only by officials but also by more affluent debtors themselves – to distance the court of conscience defendant from the venerable traditions of the unreformed debtors' prison. At St Albans, insolvents committed by common-law courts occupied a lodging room adjacent to the town hall, to which they were given occasional access during the day, but court of conscience debtors were housed together with the borough's felons in 'two day-rooms, and two close offensive night-rooms' with 'no fire-place ... No straw, no court, no water'.[51] In Newgate, the distinction between superior-court and summary-court debtors was established and maintained by the more privileged insolvents themselves, who selectively excluded debtors committed by the courts of conscience – as they excluded felons – from receipt of the prison's many charities.[52] Observers hostile to the labouring population were vociferous in defending these lines of demarcation. As the author of a tract advocating mandatory imprisonment for petty – but not for substantial – debtors argued in 1789, this distinction was necessitated by the 'Depavity and want of Principle which prevail amongst the lower Classes of Mankind'. The lower orders 'seldom have any Property; and when they have, they generally dispose of it, in order to evade the Effects of the Law', he opined. 'It is widely different with those who move in a higher Line of Life.'[53]

---

[49] 5 Geo. III c. 9 (1765); 6 Geo. III c. 20 (1766); 17 Geo. III c. 62 (1777); 18 Geo. III c. 36 (1778); 19 Geo. III c. 43 (1779).

[50] John Howard, *The State of the Prisons of England and Wales with Preliminary Observations, and an Account of Some Foreign Prisons and Hospitals*, 4th edn. (London, 1792), 236, 241, 257, 300, 330, 377, 435, 415.

[51] Ibid., 257–8.

[52] Josiah Dornford, *Nine Letters to the Right Honourable the Lord Mayor and Aldermen of the City of London, on the State of the City Prisons ...* (London, [1786]), 25.

[53] A. Grant, *The Public Monitor; Or, a Plan for the More Speedy Recovery of Small Debts; Where the Expediency of Effecting County Courts and of Enlarging the Powers of the Courts of Requests Is Pointed Out* (London, 1789), vii. His tract, tellingly, was dedicated to that most notorious of aristocratic debtors, the Prince of Wales.

210   Petty debts and the modernisation of English law

The relationship between these developments and the arguments propounded by theorists of economic liberalism is significant. Economic thinkers such as John Locke and Adam Smith drew attention to the central role played by human labour in the generation of national wealth, and urged that the emancipation of the labour market would increase both the labourer's personal wealth and the wider wealth of the nation precisely because labour power was itself a form of private property. Productive labour figured in this literature not only as a means of generating wealth and possessions, but also as the form that possession typically assumed for the working population, whose property in its own labour was understood to be more extensive than its property in goods. Parallel arguments for the social benefit of removing artificial restraints from the retail market developed alongside this defence of free labour, contributing to a fundamental reformulation of contemporaries' understanding of the moral valence of economic transactions.[54]

With their constant references to the benefits conferred by the rise of trade and industry, petitions for courts of conscience had repeatedly affirmed the liberal social logic of economic expansion. But by underlining the vital role played by private credit in both the labour and the consumer markets – a mundane consideration for which liberal theorists evinced little concern – these documents also highlighted the failure of employment alone to guarantee even industrious labourers a bare sufficiency of goods in times of market disequilibrium. The petitioners' repeated invocation of 'useful credit' spoke to this realisation of the new economic needs generated by the market economy. By providing unemployed workers with goods, useful credit functioned to promote free labour markets, serving as an informal substitute for earlier legal entitlements guaranteed by Poor Law settlements and access to common lands.[55] But just as the construction of 'free' labour markets in the later eighteenth century promoted the enactment of coercive legislation to enforce 'free' contracts by mandating imprisonment and compusory labour in bridewells for workers who breached their employment agreements,[56] so too the creation of 'free' credit contracts in the retail market fostered the introduction of coercive prison terms for plebeian defaulters. Here, however, the logic of labour and of consumption diverged. Imprisoned for debt, the working poor were forcefully reminded of the sanctity

---

[54] E.P. Thompson, *Customs in Common: Studies in Traditional Popular Culture* (New York, 1993), 185–351. For the social imperatives of early liberal economic thought, see Istvan Hont and Michael Ignatieff, eds., *Wealth and Virtue: The Shaping of Political Economy in the Scottish Enlightenment* (Cambridge, 1983), esp. 1–44.

[55] For the transformation of these entitlements, see esp. J.M. Neeson, *Commoners: Common Right, Enclosures and Social Change in England, 1700–1820* (Cambridge, 1992), and K.D.M. Snell, *Annals of the Labouring Poor: Social Change and Agrarian England 1660–1900* (Cambridge, 1995).

[56] Robert J. Steinfeld, *Coercion, Contract, and Free Labour in the Nineteenth Century* (Cambridge, 2001), esp. 42–3.

of economic contracts. But imprisonment itself precluded petty debtors from mobilising their most valuable reserves of private property – their labour – and thus rendered them yet more unable to honour their contractual obligations in the consumer market. The statutory limitations placed on the courts' ability to imprison petty debtors indefinitely further complicated the relation between bodies and money, payment and punishment, labour markets and consumer markets in these years. By releasing debtors who had refused – or were unable – to satisfy their creditors at the end of a fixed prison term of one, two or three months, the court of conscience commissioners effectively allowed the poorer sort to bypass the first and most essential step in the acquisition of goods as depicted in classical political economy – the expenditure of labour – and thereby to substitute the detention of their persons for cash payment.

As increasing numbers of creditors resorted to courts of requests to recover their debts, these inherent contradictions became troublingly obvious to observers. John Howard's inspections of the nation's prisons served to publicise the pitiable condition of small-claims debtors, and the activities of the Thatched House Society ensured that these critiques continued to circulate widely in the public sphere after Howard's death.[57] Locally, impulses to moderate the powers of the courts' commissioners were evident from the 1760s in the increasing prominence of statutory provisions for instalment payments, which sought to reduce the likelihood of an execution against the debtor's goods or body by allowing the court to collect the debt in small weekly or monthly portions. As recognition of the courts' arbitrary powers mounted in the 1770s, supporters invoked these clauses to underline the commissioners' beneficent care of the poor. The provision in the act for Elloe's court of 1775 specifying that the commissioners could order payment in instalments 'at any Time, upon the Request, and for the Ease and Convenience of the Defendant' was reiterated in acts for Old Swinford (1777), Ely (1778) and Horncastle (1779).[58]

In 1780, local concern that the courts were arbitrary and unduly harsh in their operation crystallised in a broad-based reform effort, as Parliament – prompted by revelations of the abuses suffered by petty debtors imprisoned by the Halifax court – considered a bill to prohibit courts of conscience from executing against the bodies of their defendants altogether.[59] Cut from the same cloth as the petty debt courts that had preceded it in other hubs of trade and manufacture, Halifax's court of conscience act complemented a range of civic-minded reforms which had been promoted by the increasingly self-confident local commercial elite since the 1750s. Merchants and manufacturers whose fortunes had grown with

[57] See above, chap. 4.
[58] 15 Geo. III c. 64 (1775); 17 Geo. III c. 19 (1776); 18 Geo. III c. 36 (1778); 19 Geo. II c. 43 (1779).
[59] Langford, *Public Life and the Propertied Englishman*, 245–7 offers an excellent synopsis of this extended campaign.

212   Petty debts and the modernisation of English law

the West Riding's dramatic rise as a centre of woollen and worsted cloth production, these men had joined forces in a series of voluntary associations to reform the administration of area workhouses and poor relief, to install an organ in the loft of Halifax's parish church, to establish a local library and to build a canal.[60] Civic virtue, however, clearly provided only part of the impetus for local notables' participation in the establishment and operation of the Halifax court of requests. A region characterised by poor soils, scattered settlements and heavy reliance by the labouring poor on the use of unenclosed wastelands, Halifax and its hinterland provided an ideal context for proto-industrial development. Supplanting the woollen and worsted production of East Anglia and the West Country by the 1770s, Halifax had profited from both small-scale domestic industry and large-scale manufacture, forms of production that initially enjoyed a symbiotic relationship but were subjected to increasing strain as the century advanced. Pitted against the more highly capitalised manufacturer, the independent yeoman clothier of the eighteenth century was to become first the handloom weaver and then the factory hand of the nineteenth century.[61]

The protracted course of this struggle among producers was marked by heated resistance, and affected credit no less than labour markets. Coining and clipping, the counterfeiting and reduction of gold coin, were endemic in the Halifax region in the 1760s, spurred both by a temporary (but devastating) collapse of the worsted industry and a severe local shortage of cash. Prosecuted by magistrates with an episodic and largely ineffectual vengeance, the so-called 'yellow trade' enjoyed substantial support from a broad spectrum of local society.[62] These tensions played directly into disputes over the proper role of state intervention in consumer markets. In 1783, crowds descended upon the marketplace from the weaving villages of Halifax under the leadership of the ex-coiner Thomas Spencer and laid siege to local grain merchants, forcing them to sell wheat and oats at a just price set by consumers. Spencer was executed for his role in the riot, but was hailed as a hero by Halifax's weavers, who thronged the roadside leading to his village on the day of his burial.[63]

In this context, the establishment of a court of conscience at Halifax in 1777 afforded the commercial and manufacturing elite an essential means not

---

[60] John Smail, *The Origins of Middle-Class Culture: Halifax, Yorkshire, 1660–1789* (Ithaca, NY, 1994), 121–63.

[61] For the economic development and social consequences of textile production in the West Riding, see Pat Hudson, *The Genesis of Industrial Capital: A Study of the West Riding Wool Textile Industry, c. 1750–1850* (Cambridge, 1986); and Smail, *Origins of Middle-Class Culture*, 51–81. Significantly, the two earlier hubs of cloth production had been among the first regions to request and obtain a court of conscience: Gloucester (1689) and Norwich (1701).

[62] John Styles, ' "Our traitorous money makers": the Yorkshire coiners and the law', in John Brewer and John Styles, eds., *An Ungovernable People: The English and Their Law in the Seventeenth and Eighteenth Centuries* (London, 1980), 189–249, esp. 208.

[63] E.P. Thompson, *The Making of the English Working Class* (New York, 1963), 64–5.

merely to critique the character but also to control the behaviour of the labouring population. The charges made in the series of petitions that led Parliament to investigate the court's operation in 1780 indicate that the commissioners had been quick to act upon the court's disciplinary potential. A petition lodged by 'several Persons' in February 1780 claimed that the court's operation had been 'very injurious' to the region, and in March, 'several Gentlemen, Merchants, Manufacturers, Traders, Landowners, and Others' directed a more pointed critique at the court, claiming that the commissioners conducted their business 'in a very arbitrary, if not illegal, Manner' and subjected local debtors to 'many Acts of Severity and Oppression'.[64] Petitions for and against the Halifax court garnered several thousand signatures, as advocates and opponents of summary justice mobilised support throughout the region.[65]

The evidence that Yorkshire MP Sir George Saville presented against the Halifax court and the Bradford gaol to which it committed recalcitrant debtors was damning. William Lee, Saville testified, had been keeper of the court's prison in Bradford for eighteen months in 1777–78, during which period the commissioners had imprisoned fifty-four persons – each for the maximum term of three months – for debts as low as three shillings and eightpence. As the Bradford gaol boasted neither prison charities nor a prison allowance, the debtors were entirely dependent upon provisions supplied by their friends and families. Unsuccessful in obtaining support from the debtors' friends, their townships and a local JP to whom he had appealed, Lee was 'at length obliged to supply them with Provisions himself, otherwise they would have been starved'. In a twofold effort to draw attention to the deficiencies of the prison system and to obtain compensation for this expenditure, Lee ingeniously attempted to turn the summary law upon itself and summoned a debtor inmate before the very court by whose orders he was imprisoned. In court, Lee 'represented to the Commissioners the Circumstances of the Case, and extreme Poverty and Distress of the Man and his Family, upon which the Commissioners made an order for Payment of the Money by Instalments'.[66]

The court's draconian order that the imprisoned debtor be charged for his own maintenance in gaol, like Saville's broader report, captured the contradictions that shot through the court of conscience's approach to debt, labour, discipline and punishment. On the one hand, the commissioners operated on the premise that labourers were 'well able' to pay their debts. In his testimony, Silas Hainsforth, a clothier imprisoned for three months in 1779, informed the

---

[64] *Commons Journals*, 8 February 1780, 579; 16 March 1780, 725–6.

[65] Anon., *Observations upon the 'Short State of Facts Respecting the Court of Requests at Halifax, &c. &c. &c.'* (n.p., [1780]), 2–3. The author claimed that 'upwards of Six Thousand Persons' had signed one of the petitions.

[66] *Commons Journals*, 22 March 1780, 746.

214   Petty debts and the modernisation of English law

commissioners that upon their admission to the gaol debtors were 'put into a Room under Ground, called *The Breaking School*... a nasty stinking Hole, without Glass to the Windows'. The commissioners, he claimed, 'put all the Prisoners there at first, in order to see if they will pay their Debts'.[67] Viewed from this vantage point, the absence of basic provisions, the dank chambers and the noisome privies of Bradford's gaol for small debtors reflect the successful achievement of a built environment, rather than negligent administrative oversight on the commissioners' part.

Prohibitions against labour within the prison worked alongside the systematic use of physical space and bodily deprivation, if not to compel debtors to meet their contracts then at least to punish them for failing to do so. Six of the debtors, William Lee noted in his testimony, had been committed on warrants that specifically ordered the keeper 'not to let the Prisoners have any work in the Gaol'. A further instruction that Lee 'keep the Prisoners close locked up' also militated against their employment. When debtors rebelled against this regime, the court's officers fell back upon bodily restraint and spatial confinement, sending Lee 'a Pair of Handcuffs and the Key of the Hole'. In all this the political economy of Bradford's petty debtors' gaol offered a sharp contrast to the principles of classical economics. For here the normal ordering of liberal theory was reversed: rather than advocating free labour as a means to generate both goods and the cash by which goods could be acquired, the court's commissioners placed artificial physical restrictions on labour to compel payments for goods which had already been obtained on credit. The failure of imprisonment of this variety to inculcate economic virtues such as self-sufficiency was conspicuously obvious to the court's detractors. The clothier Hainsworth had supported his wife and five children without assistance prior to his commitment, but his imprisonment at Bradford compelled the parish to allocate his wife and children a subsistence allowance of six shillings a month.[68]

The evidence adduced by the committee, moreover, repeatedly underlined the divergence between the socioeconomic identities of persons actually imprisoned by the court and the petitioning literature's idealised, able-bodied workers, 'well able' to pay for goods through their labour. Petitions had depicted petty debtors as male heads of households, but opponents of the Halifax court emphasised its baneful impact on female workers who occupied a precarious position within the world of paid labour. Lee testified that 'a Woman upwards of 80 Years of Age' had suffered imprisonment in Bradford for three months for a debt of thirteen shillings and threepence, and that a travelling chapman had imprisoned another female debtor, 'a poor Girl of about 18 Years of Age, who had been apprenticed out of the Town to which she belonged', for a debt of seven shillings and twopence. Debtor Hainsworth too emphasised the sheer inability

[67] Ibid., 22 March 1780, 746.   [68] Ibid.

'A kind of parliamentary magic' 215

of imprisonment to extract cash payments from such dependent petty debtors. Three 'young women' suffered three months of imprisonment for a shared debt of five shillings and sixpence, he testified, 'and when they were discharged they were obliged to leave a Pair of Stays for the Gaol Fees'.[69]

Counter-petitions designed to preserve the court's powers intact operated along three socioeconomic fronts, seeking at once to associate the court with the established elites of landed society, to denigrate the characters of petty debtors caught in the court's snares, and to exalt the rise of commerce and manufacture in the locality. The petition that had brought the court into being had specified only 'Tradesmen' among the general lot of 'Inhabitants' who would benefit from its creation,[70] but the exigencies of Parliament's investigation compelled a reformulation of this social identity. A petition in support of the court presented to the House on 6 April 1780 claimed to emanate from the 'Gentlemen, Clergy, Merchants, Manufacturers, Traders and Farmers' of the region; four days later a group of 'Gentlemen, Clergy, Merchants, Manufacturers, Land Owners, Traders and Farmers' petitioned Parliament to the same end. Given the rarity of specific references to agricultural interests in court of conscience petitions, the invocation of landowners and farmers in these documents is striking. Lest the court's close articulation with traditional systems of authority be overlooked, the first petition represented the commissioners themselves as 'the Gentlemen, Clergy, and first-rate Persons within the said Parishes', effectively removing the commissioners from the narrowly partisan interests of commerce and manufacture.[71]

Resort to imprisonment, in this view, was dictated by the failings of a distinct and disorderly subset within the plebeian population itself. Claiming that the court had successfully recovered £9,000 of unpaid debts and that it had imprisoned only forty-seven debtors for the maximum term of three months, the petitions of 6 and 10 April argued that the commissioners' discipline fell only upon the portion of the industrious population that was ill-disposed to exercise its labour power. The first of the two petitions urged that debtors imprisoned for the full three months were 'either such as were able, yet obstinately refused, to pay the Debts, or such as through riotous Living rendered themselves unable to pay, and thereby became chargeable to their own Families, instead of being the Means of their Support'. Neatly reversing the critics' reasoning – in which the court's oppression had been most obviously manifest in its abuse of defenceless women and youths – the petition represented debtors as inadequate male providers whose imprisonment, like their failure to support their dependent families, attested to a wilful abdication of economic responsibility.[72] The debtors, in this description, were men:

[69] Ibid. [70] Ibid., 31 January 1777, 96.
[71] Ibid., 6 and 10 April 1780, 763, 765. [72] Ibid., 6 April 1780, 763.

216   Petty debts and the modernisation of English law

who, when employed in the Woolen Manufacture, or other Work, will not do more than is necessary for their immediate Support, spending in Idleness a great Part of their Time, rather than earn wherewith to discharge any small Debts which they have contracted when out of Employ; and that such Persons are often unmarried, and have no Effects whereon the Debts could be levied, or, if married, have Families who can better maintain themselves without than with such Masters, their Conduct tending more to their Impoverishment than Support.

Formulated in this manner, the particularistic needs of Halifax's manufacturing interest rested within a broader contemporary critique of producers whose pre-industrial attitudes toward labour-discipline were manifest in their prodigal expenditure of time and money and signalled by their adherence to anachronistic traditions such as the observance of Saint Monday.[73]

Plebeian credit thus occupied a central – but highly conflicted – position within the model of economic behaviour constructed by the petitions. Like adherents of the classical republican tradition, the petitioners associated credit with luxury, dissipation and vice. But credit, equally, functioned as the handmaid of liberal economic development, providing a means by which unemployed labourers could be sustained in an economic system that was subject to severe short-term commercial dislocations. Where the market mechanisms of Smith's invisible hand promised to deliver wealth in the long term, credit functioned to feed and clothe workers in the short term, whether in the extended intervals between customary payment periods or in times of unemployment. The nature of the wage form, the petitioners insisted, ensured that amendment of the court's powers of imprisonment would be 'very prejudicial to the manufacturing Parts of this Kingdom ... where the Woolcombers, Weavers, and other Inferiors in the Trade, frequently and very necessarily require Credit for small Sums during their Employ in particular Branches in the Manufacture, for which they receive no Wages till the Species of Goods they are manufacturing be finished'.[74]

Although Halifax's petitioners repeatedly cited their region's specific need for a summary court empowered to imprison petty debtors, their efforts formed part of a wider, national campaign to preserve imprisonment for small debts by courts of requests. Partisans of this campaign celebrated the extension of credit to petty producers and consumers, underlined the exceptional nature of imprisonment and emphasised the unerring ability of the threat of incarceration to distinguish between the industrious and the idle poor. Useful credit was of vital importance to this defence of local courts of conscience, for the petitioners represented the creation of petty credit as the courts' primary contribution to social harmony and economic growth. As the gentlemen, traders and manufacturers of Exeter urged, it was the power of imprisonment that made

---

[73] Ibid., 10 April 1780, 765. For the broader effort to refashion eighteenth-century habits of industry, see Thompson, *Customs in Common*, 352–403.

[74] *Commons Journals*, 10 April 1780, 765.

tradesmen 'less unwilling to give that Degree of Credit to the inferior Class of People, without which they would be daily reduced to the utmost Distress for the common Necessaries of Life'.[75] Parliament's proposed abolition of the courts' imprisoning powers, they claimed, would not only deprive the labouring poor of essential subsistence goods but also place unbearable demands upon the propertied classes by increasing the burdens on the poor-rate. Norwich's petition expressed this pervasive line of reasoning most forcefully, asserting that the proposed amendment would be a 'great Disadvantage to the labouring Poor ... by putting an End to the Credit usefully given to them in such Times of Sickness or Want of Employment', and would 'increase the Poor Rates of the said City (already very burthensome) to a Degree which the middling Ranks of Tradesmen will be totally unable to Support'.[76]

The courts' use of instalment payments, these petitioners insistently claimed, provided an essential mechanism by which honest and dishonest debtors could be distinguished. A petition composed by the Tower Hamlets commissioners claimed that their court preserved labourers and artificers from starvation, the Poor Laws and 'the destructive Practice of Pawning' because 'the sober industrious Poor are always able to pay their Debts under the Indulgences granted ... by Instalments'. The 'Gentlemen, Tradesmen, and Manufacturers' of the locality affirmed this assessment, noting that instalments enabled 'the sober and industrious Poor to avoid the Coercion of an Execution', which 'only affects the idle and dissolute Part of the People, and becomes a Punishment for those faults which are the sole Cause of their Neglects'.[77] The success of instalment payments, advocates argued, was evidenced by the low proportion of their defendants committed to gaol. Exeter's petitioners claimed that its court had imprisoned a mere half-dozen debtors since its creation in 1772; King's Lynn assured Parliament that its court had resolved 1,466 debt disputes since 1770, but had imprisoned only six petty debtors.[78]

Parliament's proposal to replace execution against the body with execution against petty debtors' goods was, the petitioners emphatically declared, rendered unworkable by the dual circumstances of industrious labourers' endemic poverty and of idle labourers' habitual deceit. Petitions emanating from some courts emphasised dishonest debtors' ability to frustrate the seizure of their ill-gotten goods with 'many Concoctments' and 'fraudulent Practices' such as 'Concealments' and 'pretended Sales' of their effects.[79] Execution against honest debtors' property was likewise problematic. When not precluded by the

[75] Ibid., 6 April 1780, 762.
[76] Ibid., 10 April 1780, 767. For arguments along similar lines from the City of London, Westminster and the Tower Hamlets, see ibid., 10 April 1789, 765–6.
[77] Ibid., 20 March 1780, 734; 10 April 1780, 766.
[78] Ibid., 6 April 1780, 762; 10 April 1780, 765.
[79] Ibid., 20 March and 10 April 1780, 734, 765.

218   Petty debts and the modernisation of English law

sheer absence or insignificant value of household goods, seizure and sale of the defendant's essential possessions was complicated by the idealised depiction of debtors as male heads of dependent households that the petitioners had worked so assiduously to promote. Brixton's petitioners noted that by execution against the debtor's goods his 'Family are frequently left without a Bed, whereas the Terror of a Gaol being held out to them, they most commonly submit to the direction of the Court'.[80] Terror, indeed, lay at the heart of contemporaries' understanding of the courts' power to imprison. Southwark's petitioners protested that the proposed amendment, 'by taking away the Terrors of the Gaol', would reduce their court to a cipher. The idle among its resident silk-throwers, wool-combers and handloom weavers, Derby's petition similarly concluded, could be compelled to pay their debts only 'by holding out imprisonment to them *in terrorum*'.[81]

Shrill and insistent in their tone, these pleas were also politically efficacious. To be sure, the outcry against Halifax's court succeeded in amending its statutory powers in key respects. Provisions enacted in 1780 established a property requirement for commissioners, in an effort to ensure that the law would henceforth be administered by men of some substance. The amending act also reduced the maximum term of imprisonment from three to two months, prohibited execution against debtors' bedding and tools, empowered the commissioners to provide a maintenance allowance of up to fourpence a day per debtor from the court fees and charged them to construct 'a wholesome and convenient Prison' for their debtors. Perhaps most ambitiously, the amending act decreed that the court's commissioners were to imprison only persons whose indebtedness was occasioned by 'an extravagant, dissolute, idle or negligent Course of Life'. Prohibiting execution against the bodies of persons 'unable to pay ... from some unavoidable Accident', the act however failed to specify how commissioners were to distinguish between genuine misfortune and wilful economic misbehaviour, and made no provision to ensure that they would attempt to do so.[82]

Despite these concessions, the broad tenor of legislation in these years ultimately served to affirm the small-claims courts' right to imprison petty debtors. The bill which, by proposing to abolish this power, had initiated the petitioning campaign in 1780, received a second reading in March only to vanish from the parliamentary record.[83] National reform, when it was at last achieved in 1786, sought to regulate, calibrate and standardise the courts' powers of imprisonment – not to abolish them. Requiring that all commissioners be householders possessed of real estate with an annual value of at least twenty pounds or of personal estate valued at five hundred pounds or more, the statute lent the haphazard collection of small-claims courts a rudimentary degree of uniformity.

---

[80] Ibid., 12 April 1780, 783.   [81] Ibid., 10 April 1780, 766–7.
[82] 20 Geo. III c. 65 (1780).   [83] *Commons Journals*, 21 March 1780, 743.

It upheld the continued operation of execution against the goods and execution against the body, but specified that court officials must choose between these two options for any given debtor. Persons imprisoned by courts of conscience for debts of twenty shillings or less could now be imprisoned for no more than twenty days per debt; those imprisoned for debts over twenty shillings could be confined for a maximum term of forty days per claim. Expiration of the term, moreover, was now unambiguously to liquidate the debt, and gaolers were prohibited from charging petty debtors any fees which might result in their continuance in the prison at the end of their set term.[84]

By regulating courts of conscience in this manner, Parliament ostensibly brought summary small-claims proceedings into a closer articulation with the shibboleths of the common-law tradition, which held that the world of goods was best secured by men of property who adhered to the due processes of uniformly applicable, if highly exacting, legal procedures. But by failing to provide mechanisms for the evaluation and enforcement of these regulations and by declining to integrate the courts of conscience – through the right to appeal – into the broader systems of law that linked the summary administration of petty criminal disputes to the central courts, the legislation of 1786 also ensured that the courts would continue to operate as independent islands of justice outside the archipelago of the common law. As local small-claims courts proliferated, antagonism to this extensive autonomy was increasingly salient not merely in parliamentary petitions, committees and debates but also in the wider public sphere, where courts of conscience served as the focal point for a series of interlocking debates on the place of summary justice and equitable reasoning in the regulation of the plebeian credit economy.

Enlightened equity

Foremost among the later eighteenth-century critics of the courts of conscience was William Blackstone, the legal theorist whose *Commentaries on the Laws of England* were to the evolving science of jurisprudence what Adam Smith's *Wealth of Nations* was to the emerging science of political economy. Attired, in David Lieberman's apt phrase, 'in the mantle of the Enlightenment *philosophe*', Blackstone insistently claimed that legal understanding properly constituted a 'rational science'. Like Smith's *Wealth of Nations*, the *Commentaries* were framed by the natural law doctrines of Grotius, Puffendorf and Locke, but they were also shaped by more immediate historical concerns, reflecting a broader contemporary awareness of the sweeping tide of statutory activism that

---

[84] 26 Geo. III c. 38 (1786). These restrictions had been applied to London's courts a year earlier by 25 Geo. III c. 45 (1785).

220   Petty debts and the modernisation of English law

had marked English law since 1688.[85] To Blackstone, the growth of summary jurisdictions (for both criminal and civil causes) featured conspicuously among the troubling consequences of this legislative onrush.

Distaste for summary justice established by statute formed a leitmotif of the *Commentaries*' sustained encomium to the rule of law. An innovation 'not agreeable to the genius of the common law', the growth of summary criminal proceedings had, Blackstone observed severely, 'of late been so far extended as, if a check be not timely given, to threaten the disuse of our admirable and truly English trial by jury'.[86] Describing the constitution of the City of London's court of conscience as 'illegal', Blackstone acknowledged that the proliferation of the courts was 'a great benefit to trade', but was deeply troubled by the prospect of their continued expansion, 'as the method of proceeding therein is entirely in derogation of the common law; as their large discretionary powers create a petty tyranny in a set of standing commissioners; and as the disuse of the trial by jury may tend to estrange the minds of the people from the valuable prerogative of Englishmen [the jury trial], which has already been more than sufficiently excluded in many instances'.[87]

Blackstone's analysis echoed the arguments of later seventeenth-century petitioners against the courts, but it also spoke to more recent trends in English understandings of the protections afforded by jury trials. The century's dramatic rise in capital statutes against property crimes had seen a parallel increase in the practice of jury mitigation in suits for common felonies, saving countless petty thieves from the horrors of the gallows. As political radicalism brought increasing numbers of plebeian and popular leaders before the courts, juries proved a vital protection of political liberties, further bolstered in 1792 by an expansion of the jury's powers in trials for seditious libel. Generating intense public debate, these developments served to vindicate 'the historic role of the jury as the last line of defense against executive tyranny'.[88] James Caldwell situated his critique of the courts of conscience securely within this debate in 1794, underlining the tribunals' departure from 'the ancient and valuable privilege of the trial by Jury' and declaiming against their dangerous possession of 'absolute discretionary powers over the property and personal liberty of individuals'. For Caldwell, the commissioners' lowly social standing epitomised the courts' violation of common-law protections of property and person. 'For

---

[85] David Lieberman, *The Province of Legislation Determined: Legal Theory in Eighteenth-Century Britain* (Cambridge, 1989), esp. 13–19, 32–7, citations from 32, 37.

[86] Blackstone, *Commentaries*, IV: 284, 277–8. As he noted of summary justice in an eloquently disdainful aside, the common law 'is a stranger to it' (277).

[87] Ibid., III: 81–3.

[88] For the changing role and perception of juries in both criminal and political trials, see Thomas A. Green, *Verdict According to Conscience: Perspectives on the English Criminal Trial Jury, 1200–1800* (Chicago, 1985), 267–355, citation from 349.

'A kind of parliamentary magic'

the exercise of these extensive, not to say unlimited powers, equally repugnant to the Constitution and unknown to the common Law of *England*, no other qualification whatever is required, than that of a small pecuniary fortune', Caldwell observed derisively, 'which, by a kind of parliamentary magic, is presumed to vest at once in its possessor, all the sagacity, integrity, and impartiality, requisite for the due discharge of the arduous and important office of a *Judge*; or what is still more, that of an *arbitrary distributor* of private justice.'[89]

With its concern to underline the necessary relation between liberty and property, Caldwell's tract resonated with a long and venerable republican political tradition that linked the preservation of personal freedoms to the administration of the law by men of substantial landed wealth.[90] His critique of the courts of conscience similarly drew upon received rather than emerging wisdom in its assessment of the proper role of plebeian consumption and credit in the economic and social life of the nation. Identifying the chief beneficiaries of the courts of conscience as the unproductive middlemen – the 'publicans, petty shop-keepers, and retailers of different descriptions' – against whom the sanctions of the moral economy had been directed, Caldwell rejected the conception of 'useful credit' that pervaded the court of conscience petitioning literature. 'In manufactures...one of the greatest evils is the extension of *petty credit* amongst the poor and working classes of people', he argued, 'as by this means, not only the temptations to idleness and intemperance are increased, but the means are at the same time supplied.'[91] Where the petitioners had insisted that petty credit was both a spur to plebeian industry and an essential prop to the virtuous labourer in the inevitable periods of unemployment entailed by the vicissitudes of the market, Caldwell instead celebrated the disciplinary function of the cash nexus:

When a man is obliged to pay for what he has, it may generally be said, that what he spends, he first must have earned. In order to get drunk he must first have been sober and attentive. In order to be idle, he must first have been industrious. The evil is by this means limited, and in some degree counter-balanced. But credit operates in a very different manner.[92]

---

[89] [James Caldwell], A Manufacturer, *A Letter, to the Manufacturers and Inhabitants of the Parishes of Stoke, Burslem, and Wolstanton, in the County of Stafford, on Courts of Request*... (n.p., [1794]), 4–5.

[90] Among the many analyses of this tradition, see esp. J.G.A. Pocock, *Virtue, Commerce and History: Essays on Political Thought and History, Chiefly in the Eighteenth Century* (Cambridge, 1985).

[91] [Caldwell], *A Letter to the Manufacturers*, 6. For the wider contemporary hostility to retailers and middlemen, see Thompson, *Customs in Common*, esp. 208–11, and Douglas Hay, 'The state and the market in 1800: Lord Kenyon and Mr Waddington', *P&P*, 162 (February 1999), 101–62.

[92] [Caldwell], *A Letter to the Manufacturers*, 6–7.

222   Petty debts and the modernisation of English law

The terror of the prison, Caldwell argued, was unlikely to foster industry: given the 'little prudence and foresight' that characterised labouring-class behaviour, 'little benefit is to be hoped for in this respect, even from the terrific form of oppression itself, acting in . . . a Court of Conscience'.[93]

If Caldwell's critique borrowed arguments from Blackstone's *Commentaries*, it was directed specifically against the writings of the small-claims courts' most strenuous advocate, William Hutton of Birmingham. Together Hutton's *Courts of Requests: Their Nature, Utility, and Powers* (1787) and his *Dissertation on Juries* (1789) formed an oppositional pendant to the *Commentaries*. Part rhapsody and part rationalisation, Hutton's detailed and highly partisan defence of the courts of requests in these works and in his published memoir helped to ensure that the workings of these institutions were familiar to a wide audience beyond the corridors of Parliament. Like Blackstone, Hutton cast himself as an Enlightenment theorist of law. But in identifying equitable, rather than common-law, principles as the linchpin of liberty and property for the lower classes, Hutton's writings ran directly counter to the dominant legal apologetic of his day. 'Every man is said to have his hobby-horse; and a Court of Requests seems to be that of the worthy Magistrate of *Birmingham*', Caldwell observed acidly, comparing Hutton in his excessive affection for summary justice with a man unduly influenced by 'ardours of no common passion' for his mistress.[94]

Hutton, who served as a commissioner of Birmingham's court of requests for nearly two decades, embodied the conflicting commercial impulses that had fuelled the courts' creation and development. A self-made stationer possessed of landed property and a paper mill, Hutton exhibited many of the stereotypical traits and tendencies of a middle-class Dissenting tradesman and manufacturer. But his biography is also a forceful reminder that the categories of 'gentleman', 'merchant', artificer' and 'labourer' so carefully demarcated in parliamentary petitions co-existed and overlapped in the fluid currents of historical experience. Born the son of a woolcomber in 1723, Hutton as a child worked in a silk mill at Derby, became a stocking-frame knitter at Nottingham in adolescence and adopted the bookbinding trade as an adult. From bookbinding he progressed to bookselling, from bookselling to papermaking and from papermaking to the purchase of substantial tracts of land. Now a considerable merchant-manufacturer, he became active in local administration. As he recalled of his appointment as an overseer of the poor in 1768, 'I . . . thought myself elevated beyond my ancestors . . . They had rather been *the poor* than *overseers of* the poor.' Four years later, Hutton became a commissioner in the Birmingham court of conscience, which rapidly became his 'favourite amusement'. In the course of

---

[93] Ibid., 8. Like Blackstone, whom he repeatedly echoed, Caldwell advocated a revival of the old county-court system to determine petty debt cases (page 9).
[94] Ibid., 11–12.

'A kind of parliamentary magic'

nineteen years' service to the court, Hutton estimated that he had helped to resolve over a hundred thousand petty debt claims.[95]

Credit transactions played an essential role in Hutton's ascent from textile worker to landed proprietor. 'Bage has sent word he will be here on Monday with a Load...but [I] have neither Mony [*sic*] nor Credit', Hutton wrote to his wife in 1763. 'Since you left, another Rascal...hath failed...in my Debt', he lamented in 1779, 'this is the 15th since Christmas amounting to...nearly twenty Shillings a Day upon average'.[96] Hutton's fluctuating identity as debtor and creditor functioned as an essential component of his concerted strategy to acquire property, and was self-consciously celebrated in his memoirs. 'I had once resolved not to buy land without paying for it, which would have prevented me from running into debt; but the bent of my mind was too strong for restraint', he reflected. 'I could not pass by what I thought a bargain.' Far from disqualifying him from serving as an arbiter of contracts, Hutton interpreted his credit dealings as an apt training for his role as a commissioner of petty debts. 'Thus purchase after purchase caused me to contract debts wholesale', he concluded without apparent irony. 'I was now chosen a Commissioner of the Court of Requests, and it was prophesied I should make an active one.'[97]

Published in the immediate aftermath of the legislative enactment of national guidelines for the constitution of small-claims courts prompted by the Halifax scandal, Hutton's *Courts of Requests* offered a sustained defence of summary civil justice informed by an Enlightenment reformulation of the relation between law and equity. Hutton framed his treatise with an extended exposition on the market and commercialisation. Like Mandeville's *Fable of the Bees* and Smith's *Wealth of Nations*, Hutton's treatise was animated by the beneficent force of individual self-interest. 'Public interest proceeds from private; they are both shoots from self-love', Hutton proclaimed. 'While we serve ourselves, we serve each other.' Credit figured in this analysis as an essential instrument for fostering property and wealth by limiting financial risk. 'The more people encrease their trade, the more they must venture their property', Hutton reasoned. '[H]ow necessary it is, then, to enact such laws as will best secure that property...To multiply the Courts of Requests, and enlarge their powers, is the likeliest way to attain this end.'[98]

---

[95] William Hutton, *The Life of William Hutton, Stationer, of Birmingham; and the History of His Family* (London, 1841), 1, 3–4, 8–9, 19–20, 30, 33–5, citations from 33. Hutton valued his net worth in 1768 at £2,000 (page 33).

[96] William Hutton to Sarah Hutton, 9 June 1763 and 17 July 1779, Birmingham Central Reference Library, Hutton MS, 20/10, 20/11.

[97] Hutton, *Life of William Hutton*, 34.

[98] William Hutton, *Courts of Requests: Their Nature, Utility, and Powers Described, with a Variety of Cases, Determined in That of Birmingham* (Birmingham, 1787), 2, 153, 9. 'If we see a bargain made between the two heads...we may safely conclude it originates from self-interest; this is the enlivening principle which warms into action; the hinge upon which we turn – the pole to which we point' (page 338).

224   Petty debts and the modernisation of English law

Equity animated Hutton's representation of the smooth regulation of petty commercial contracts in the modern market. Petitions for courts of conscience had repeatedly drawn attention to the cumbersome processes of debt recovery at common law, but Hutton estimated that Birmingham's summary court could dispatch with between 130 and 250 suits in each of its weekly Friday sittings. 'Law, with its rigid fetters, binds what conscience sets free', he asserted in defending the commissioners' ability to adjudicate through common sense rather than common law. Denigrating 'the chicanery of corrupt law', 'the dull steps of the law' and the 'mazy track' followed by attorneys, he proclaimed that 'Law is at best, but a crooked path, and a man of talents can easily make it more crooked, but it is the province of equity to make straight.'[99]

Hutton's narrative recollections of cases from the Birmingham court offered an opportunity to flesh out these philosophical reflections with examples of commercial culture in the court. Like the sentimental novelists of his era, Hutton emphasised the moral imperative to temper the rule of law with equity in resolving contractual disputes. 'Law knows no attribute but that of justice; equity introduces mercy', he argued. 'Law gives a man his right; equity sees cause to deprive him of it.' To illustrate the virtues of this system for plebeian contracts, Hutton detailed a case in which 'a poor old infirm man' was sued in the court for a just debt. Having determined that the debtor defendant was terminally ill and 'not master of one penny', the commisioners requested that the plaintiff withdraw his action. When he refused to comply with this request, they exercised their equitable prerogative with tactics that were to be rehearsed again and again in the Victorian and Edwardian county courts. 'As a few weeks ... will finish ... [the debtor's] wretched existence, and as common humanity forbids us to suffer him to die in prison under our warrant', they decreed, 'we shall set the payments as low as the Court can allow, and protract the first [payment] for three months, by which time he will, in all likelihood, be removed to that place, where stern justice never frowns.'[100]

Consistently depicting summary equity as a merciful boon to the plebeian defendant, Hutton also hailed the court of conscience as an especially appropriate instrument with which to grasp the nettle of married women's credit dealings. Hutton's engagement with the gender dynamics of petty credit was conspicuous both at the level of metaphor and in his descriptions of the concrete workings of material exchange. Whereas Hutton represented the common law as corrupt, crooked and male, he claimed that 'Equity may be known by the beautiful symmetry of her figure ... though she may not always appear in the same dress.'[101] Real women, as Hutton well knew, were vociferous, cacophonous litigants in the courts of requests. Although the enabling legislation for courts of conscience made no mention of a wife's ability to appear on behalf of her husband, the

---

[99] Ibid., 88, 247, 347, 193, 348.   [100] Ibid., 106–7. See similarly page 418.
[101] Ibid., 414.

'A kind of parliamentary magic' 225

commissioners evidently chose to follow the precedent set by a variety of early modern equitable and local jurisdictions in departing from the strict letter of the common-law principle of coverture and allowing married women to participate actively in their proceedings.[102] 'A particular attention is due to the fair sex', Hutton noted somewhat ruefully. 'Their connexions with this Court are very frequent, and very loud.' Unwilling to abandon the law altogether by conferring full legal agency on married women, Hutton presaged the critiques of Victorian county-court judges when he expressed his frustration with the submersion of the wife's legal identity under the husband's legal person. 'The laws of England consider the husband accountable for the debts of the wife; though she is the sole actress, they do not suppose her to act', he recorded of the commissioners' ruling in a case involving a married woman's credit dealings. 'As this court is detached from the law, we apprehend no evil could arise from a judgment against her; but as the Courts above have not given us a precedent, we shall not venture to set the example.'[103]

A suit entered against a cross-dressing female debtor allowed Hutton at the very end of his treatise to explore these themes in greater depth. Uncertain as to the gender identity of the debtor, the plaintiff had summoned '*Elizabeth, alias John Haywood*' to the Birmingham court. Hutton clearly relished describing the defendant, whose ambiguous sexual identity provided an especially appropriate context for the particularistic reasoning of equity. Debtor Haywood, dubbed Betty John by the crowd that attended the court, 'appeared . . . in a female habit, was rather elegant . . . tolerably handsome . . . had a firm countenance and manly step, no beard, eyes susceptible of love, a voice tending to the masculine . . . and was rather sensible', Hutton reported. Although she claimed in court to be a married woman and thus pleaded her coverture as a bar to the debt, Haywood had previously dressed as a man, 'courted a young woman, married her, and . . . lived together in wedlock, til the young woman died', upon which, 'like the people of higher rank, [she] kept a mistress'. The commissioners, much perplexed by this evidence, ultimately ascribed a male gender to the problematical Haywood, who (as John Haywood) was subsequently imprisoned for failing to meet their order for repayment. To Hutton's consternation, 'incontestable proof' that Haywood 'had nothing of the man about her higher than the feet' and indeed possessed a husband in Shropshire, emerged during her incarceration. In reflecting on the broader significance of this suit, Hutton reiterated his claim that the common law obscured contractual relationships which equity could reveal

---

[102] For the appearance of wives as litigants in the central London Court of Requests (a superior court not to be confused with the petty City of London court of conscience), see Tim Stretton, *Women Waging Law in Elizabethan England* (Cambridge, 1998). Alexandra Shepard details the appearance of married women in the Cambridge university courts in 'Manhood, credit and patriarchy in early modern England, *c.* 1580–1640', *P&P*, 167 (May 2000), 90–5.

[103] Hutton, *Courts of Requests*, 256, 301–2. For a broader discussion of married women and debt litigation in this period, see my 'Women, consumption and coverture in England, c. 1760–1860', *HJ*, 39, 3 (1996), 703–22.

226   Petty debts and the modernisation of English law

transparently. In this interpretation, whereas equitable logic suggested that the person who contracted the debt – wife though she was – should be liable for its payment, common law instead conferred an artificial liability on the husband, who was 'wholly innocent' of his wife's contractual activities. 'Perhaps the error committed by the Bench was an error of right', Hutton concluded; 'they punished the guilty through mistake, who was acquitted by law.'[104]

By arguing that the court of conscience was 'beneficial to commerce', utilitarian in its tendency to encourage the essential credit that would supply the poor 'purchaser with necessaries in time of want', and salutary in its promotion of 'industry, by allowing the debtor easy payment when another court would dissolve his substance',[105] Hutton recapitulated the lines of argument advanced by the courts' advocates in parliamentary petitions. In the aftermath of the Halifax debacle, however, sustaining these claims required that he qualify his interpretation with a recognition of the potential abuses to which petty debt proceedings could be put, a task that Hutton accomplished by turning attention from the court to its prison. In describing the shameful condition of Birmingham's gaol for petty debtors – two narrow rooms in the town prison, 'emphatically termed *The Dungeon*' – Hutton sought to ally himself with the reforming zeal of the philanthropist John Howard.[106] But reform of the prisoner loomed much larger in Hutton's narrative than did reform of the prison. Noting that 'the terrible ideas of a prison' were often sufficient to effect payment, he rejected Howard's representation of petty debtors as industrious victims of misfortune and decried the unreformed gaol's tendency to promote the very 'misconduct' and 'idleness' that had produced the original debt. Logically, he argued, only the systematic introduction of labour into the petty debtors' prison – like the bridewell before it – could foster useful credit and thereby promote national wealth.[107]

Hutton's treatise on the court of requests subjected him to attack from above and below. The *Monthly Review* refuted the work's guiding principles in terms that recall Blackstone's interpretation of the threat posed to English liberties by summary justice. 'It has been observed, that an arbitrary monarchy would have many advantages over a limited one, could we be assured of being always governed by wise and good kings', the *Review* commented. 'Having seen frequent instances of ignorance, folly, and partiality, in those who preside in some of these courts, we do not look upon these jurisdictions with so much complacency as our Author does.'[108] Hutton was unconvinced by these criticisms, and in 1789 published a *Dissertation on Juries* to urge the further extension of the summary courts' jurisdiction. Here he pointedly ascribed Blackstone's antagonism to the courts of conscience to his special interests as a member of the legal profession. 'Where then is the wonder if his sentiments tended to

---

[104] Hutton, *Courts of Requests*, 425–30.   [105] Ibid., 420–1.   [106] Ibid., 64, 43–4, 64.
[107] Ibid., 67–8, 70.   [108] *The Monthly Review*, 79 (December 1788), 505.

'A kind of parliamentary magic' 227

diminish the power of other Courts, when they tended to diminish his own?', Hutton asked rhetorically. 'Was a barber ever known to decry the use of wigs, or promote long beards?'[109]

Lower down on the social scale, Hutton's antagonists were also vociferous. When Birmingham's leading radical Dissenters met in 1791 to celebrate the second anniversary of the French revolution, Church and King rioters responded by attacking their homes and businesses. Although Hutton had not attended the anniversary meeting, the crowd singled him out for attention. After ransacking his townhouse in High Street and destroying his stock, they travelled three miles to his country home at Washwood Heath and burned it to the ground. Hutton, his family and other observers all attributed these attacks to his activity as a small-claims commissioner rather than to his confessional or political identity.[110] The crowd itself was careful to ensure that this interpretation of their actions prevailed, scripting their attack to parody Hutton's arbitration of small-claims suits. Rioters looting Hutton's residence mimicked Hutton's standard statement to litigants whose causes required a second hearing in the court – 'Thee pay sixpence, and come again next Friday' – as they disposed of his possessions. 'When our furniture was being thrown out of the windows', Hutton's daughter recalled, 'the mob above cried "Who bids for this?" To which the mob below answered "I'll give sixpence and come again next Friday."'[111] The crowd that surrounded Hutton's residence added insult to this injury by bearing the commissioner away to a public house, where they ran up a score for 329 gallons of ale – an unpaid debt which they recorded against his name.[112] Hutton was clearly devastated by this attack, which struck at the core of his identity as a local font of equity. 'Do not distress thyself about my resuming the direction of the Court of Conscience', he assured his daughter in October. 'I am as likely to distribute justice while sitting on a bench in the moon.'[113]

Summary justice in the court records

Antagonists' claims that the courts of conscience represented a dangerous threat to time-honoured English liberties were often as stylised as proponents'

[109] William Hutton, *A Dissertation on Juries; With a Description of the Hundred Court: As an Appendix to the Court of Requests* (Birmingham, 1789), 1–2, 4–5, 10.

[110] See, for example, unidentified newspaper cutting, 21 July 1791, PRO, HO 42/19, item 207; Hutton, *Life of William Hutton*, 46–51; Anon., *An Authentic Account of the Riots of Birmingham, on the 14th, 15th, 16th, & 17th Days of July, 1791 . . .* (London, [1791]), 8. See also Catherine Hutton, *A Narrative of the Riots in Birmingham, July 1791* (Birmingham, [1875]), 7.

[111] Catherine Hutton to Mrs André, in Catherine Hutton Belae, ed., *Reminiscences of a Gentlewoman of the Last Century: Letters of Catherine Hutton* (Birmingham, 1891), 112.

[112] Anon., *Authentic Account*, 16–18; Hutton, *Life of William Hutton*, 46.

[113] Hutton to Catherine Hutton, 30 October 1791, in Belae, ed., *Reminiscences of a Gentlewoman*, 100.

228   Petty debts and the modernisation of English law

assertions that the courts represented an enlightened form of law suited to the new demands of a commercial economy. Hutton's experiences make the contrast between these opposing interpretations especially clear, illustrating the radical dissonance that obtained both between and among popular and propertied conceptions of 'equity and good conscience'. Although the very limited survival of eighteenth-century court of conscience records prohibits sustained analysis of these institutions, the archives of a small cohort of jurisdictions do provide material for a selective discussion of their pragmatic operation. Scattered, partial and episodic, these records confirm the potential of summary justice to exert arbitrary reprisals on plebeian debtors. But they also suggest the extent to which the courts' institutional fragmentation, their reliance on unpaid lay commissioners and their employment of corrupt court officers limited this tyrannical authority, diminishing the disciplinary power that partisans of the courts of conscience had hoped they would exercise over the plebeian credit purchaser even as they exposed new segments of the labouring population to the experience of imprisonment for debt.

The diary of Matthew Flinders, a Lincolnshire surgeon who was active in petitioning for the creation of a court of conscience for Surfleet and its surrounding parishes in 1777, adds texture to Hutton's philosophical account of the commercial impetus that spurred the establishment of summary small-claims jurisdictions. Like Hutton's memoir, Flinders's journal attests both to the writer's powerful acquisitive impulses and to the centrality of credit in his domestic and professional dealings. Each New Year began with a complacent notation of his annual profits, a careful accounting that extended from Flinders's professional to his personal life. When his wife was delivered of stillborn twin daughters in June 1777, Flinders noted 'how kind is the Providence of God thus to free us from the expense and care of a numerous family for had all our young ones lived with us, we should scarce [have] known what to have done with them, the two we have living if agreeable to Divine Wisdom, I would gladly keep, but by no means wish an increase'. Lending and borrowing to family and friends formed an integral part of Flinders's broader economic strategy. In September 1775, he noted the first of many sums borrowed by his impecunious brother – twenty pounds lent at interest 'on account of his son going to school'. Neighbours were likewise wont to turn to Flinders as a source of local credit. 'J. Kendall, an honest and industrious Labouring man of this Place, having request[e]d of me Six Guineas (to purchase a Cow) for a year; I ventured to let him have it, for which he has given me a Note with Interest', Flinders recorded in 1778. 'I thought I might safely venture as both himself & wife are industrious People.' Not all credit recorded in the diary flowed from Flinders to supplicant debtors. As a man of some substance, the surgeon naturally enjoyed extended billing cycles with local tradesmen, paying Stiles Maplesoft a pound and four shillings

'A kind of parliamentary magic' 229

on 7 October 1777 to settle a bill for shaving and hairdressing that was of two years' standing.[114]

Firmly enmeshed in local credit networks, Flinders was, from the outset, active in the Kirton division of the short-lived Surfleet court of conscience as both a commissioner and a plaintiff. He recorded the initial meeting of the court on the same day that he expatiated on the economic blessings of his wife's failed pregnancy. 'I attended the first court... [as] one of the Commissioners, this is an excellent act, for our Hundred, I do not in the least regret the money I subscribed towards obtaining the act, as it will soon repay me more; we had 12 causes, which much entertained us, it will bring the never pay villains to a little sense of honesty', he observed. 'It has already brought me I believe more than one bill.' On 19 September he had three causes in 'our Court': debtor Melliday owed eleven shillings and threepence, Brewster's man eight shillings and sixpence and William Smith fifteen shillings and sixpence. The first two of these defendants remitted the sums owed without further action before the court day; Flinders paid three shillings and sixpence in costs for the hearing of William Smith's debt, 'which together with the Bill the Court ordered to be paid in 5 weeks, but at Smith's request I agreed to take at 1s per week'. Within a few months, the court had clearly attracted substantial business, meeting for a full day on 23 January 1778. By May, however, the commissioners' flourishing trade had attracted the attention (and ire) of the Earl of Exeter, lord of the local manor and its court, who successfully appealed to Parliament to quash the new summary jurisdiction. For Flinders, the timing of the court's demise was especially unfortunate. 'As I was not possessed of a single Law Book, I thought the most useful one I could purchase would be Burn's Justice, which I have just got', he recorded regretfully upon the court's abolition.[115]

The records of the Chatteris division of the Ely court of requests lack the qualitative dimensions of Flinders's diary, but offer instead suggestive data on the effectiveness of summary debt proceedings. Here too the receipt of a summons was often sufficient to settle outstanding petty debts. Of the forty-five summonses issued – for sums as low as two or three shillings – returnable on the first two court days (23 September and 25 November 1785), twenty-five (or 56 per cent) were settled before the commissioners met. Although the records do not provide systematic information on the economic status of litigants, anecdotal evidence suggests that the court's simple processes did render it accessible to plebeian creditors. When William Black recovered a debt of one pound

---

[114] Lincolnshire Archives, Flinders 1–2 (henceforth cited as Flinders diary), MS diary of Matthew Flinders, surgeon, 1775–1802, vol. 1, 2 January 1776; 27 June 1777; 9 September 1775; 4 April 1778; 7 October 1777. See also Langford, *Public Life and the Propertied Englishman*, 247–8.

[115] Flinders diary, 27 June 1777; 19 September 1777; 23 January 1778; 18 May 1778. The act repealing the court was 18 Geo. III c. 43 (1778).

230   Petty debts and the modernisation of English law

nineteen shillings in 1790, he acknowledged receipt of the payment by signing a cross in lieu of his name in the court book. Modest fees and costs were an obvious incentive to lowly plaintiffs. The court's clerks charged sixpence for entering each cause into the books, sixpence for each summons, threepence for calling litigants before the commissioners and sixpence for each trial; the sergeants received fees of sixpence for service of summonses within a mile of Ely Cathedral (or ninepence beyond that distance) and a penny for calling litigants into the court.[116]

Each suit in the Chatteris court was heard by three commissioners, who appear to have been drawn predominantly from the middling ranks of the community. The Reverend William Holden, M.A. often heard cases in the court, but among the other commissioners only Robert Grinditch was dignified with the title of 'Esquire'. Like Matthew Flinders of the Surfleet court, the Chatteris commissioners themselves could and did enter suits to recover debts. Thomas Skools, who served as a commissioner at the court's first meeting in 1785, summoned debtor James Groon for the following court day and received payment in full before the court met; when Skools sued John Hudson in January 1786, the debt was again satisfied without a court hearing. But if the Chatteris commissioners enjoyed substantial powers as creditor-judges, the records of their rulings do not suggest that they exerted this authority unreflectively. Samuel Blackley, who admitted his debt to Christopher Walker, was ordered to pay the sum and costs in whole within two months; his debt to William Solby was also proved, but the commissioners allowed Blackley five months to meet this obligation, and the associated court costs. The commissioners ordered several debts to be paid in small instalments: John Rignall was to repay a debt of seven shillings and elevenpence (and costs of three shillings and twopence) by weekly payments of a shilling; Jeremiah Brown was ordered to repay seventeen shillings and sixpence owed to George Brooks at a rate of one shilling a week for three weeks and then by weekly instalments of sixpence. Failure to honour these orders did, from the court's second meeting, result in orders of execution. Sarah Worth was awarded an execution against debtor Masters's goods when he defaulted on his payments in November 1785, and Christopher Walker successfully sued for the seizure of Samuel Blackley's body on the same date.[117]

Where the Surfleet commissioners were swiftly disabled by the intervention of the Earl of Exeter, the Chatteris court was gradually hobbled instead by the reluctance of local men of property to serve as voluntary commissioners.

---

[116] Cambridge University Library, Add. 9358/7/4 (henceforth Chatteris minute book), Court of Requests minute book for Chatteris, September 1785–January 1792, not paginated, summonses returnable on and court days of 23 September and 25 November 1785; 28 May 1790; Index: table of fees.

[117] For Skools's debts, see Chatteris minute book, summonses returnable on and court day of 25 November 1785 and summonses returnable 27 January 1786.

'A kind of parliamentary magic'   231

Within two years of the court's establishment, the absence of a quorum began to appear in the records as a frequent cause for adjournment. Courts scheduled for 28 September 1787, 26 September 1788, and both 27 March and 18 April 1789 were postponed because of a lack of commissioners, and the volume of court business appears to have declined in response. Only a handful of summonses were issued for many of the courts in 1788 and 1789, and although there was something of a revival of business in 1790, the court book – after yet another adjournment due to a deficit of commissioners in November 1791 – fails to record any suits beyond December of that year.

While rural small-claims courts in the provinces evidently faced significant obstacles, metropolitan courts – like Hutton's urban jurisdiction in Birmingham – were often highly successful in attracting petty litigants. The court officers serving parishes such as St James's, St George's, St Martin's and Covent Garden charged a mere eightpence for a summons and two shillings and sixpence for an execution.[118] Geared to reduce legal costs to a minimum, the London courts appear to have attracted a predominantly lower- and middling-rank clientele. 'The plaintiffs and defendants of these courts are in general people so very low, that a gentleman would sooner lose 40s. than attend them', the Reverend John Trusler noted loftily in a guidebook designed for recent arrivals to the metropolis.[119] A range of contemporary evidence confirms Trusler's association of the courts with persons who lacked genteel status. Plaintiffs petitioning against the corrupt practices of the City's court in 1774 included Joseph Staines, a hatter and hosier, Samuel Harper, a breeches-maker, Mrs Jane Waine, the wife of a butcher, and William Clarke, a coachman.[120] Defendants were typically drawn from a lower stratum of society: in 1792, the keeper of the Borough Compter in Southwark described the two or three hundred debtors imprisoned in his gaol each year by the court of conscience as 'in general... young hearty Men, who are of some Mechanical Trade'.[121]

Creditors enjoyed more than purely social advantages over debtors in London's petty courts, as the Reverend Trusler was careful to note. 'Of course, it is better in these Courts to be a plaintiff than defendant', he observed, 'for if the plaintiff swears to his debt, no oath of the defendant will avail him.'[122]

---

[118] Rev. [John] Trusler, *The London Advisor and Guide: Containing Every Instruction and Information Useful and Necessary to Persons Living in London, and Coming to Reside There* (London, 1786), 153–5.

[119] Ibid., 155.

[120] CLRO, Minute book of the committee to enquire into the practice & fees of the Court of Requests & the Abuses of its officers and their servants and also the inconveniencies attending the present mode of executing the business thereof (henceforth cited as Minute book), 19 January 1774–30 October 1788, entries for 21 February 1774, p. 58; 28 February 1774, p. 65; 14 March 1774, p. 79; 21 March 1774, p. 84.

[121] House of Commons, *Report from the Committee Appointed to Enquire into the Practice and Effects of Imprisonment for Debt* (London, 1792), 26.

[122] Trusler, *London Advisor*, 155–6.

232   Petty debts and the modernisation of English law

Statistics for the City's court of conscience in 1786 suggest that this assessment was overdrawn, but accurate in its broad outlines. Of 1,443 suits brought by plaintiffs from August to December 1786, the commissioners dismissed 138 (or 9.6 per cent). The frequent claim of their advocates that courts of requests typically discouraged executions by generous resort to instalment payments is only partially borne out by the City evidence. In the sample for 1786, commissioners ordered instalment payments in 774 cases (53.6 per cent), but also lodged executions against 318 (22.0 per cent) of the debtors.[123] Although many defendants no doubt chose to settle their debts upon receipt of the order for execution, many too were cast into prison. The Woodstreet Compter alone housed a hundred debtors from the City's court of conscience in the shrieval year that began in September 1780, and over a hundred in 1789.[124] As the Borough Compter's keeper reported of the hundreds of mechanics and labourers confined in his gaol, 'where One pays the Debt in Consequence of his Imprisonment, Twenty are discharged after staying out their Time'.[125]

London's courts amply demonstrate critics' allegations that the operation of summary small-claims courts was both oppressive and degrading. In 1776, at the Clerkenwell house of correction, the surgeon William Smith found debtors committed by the City and Tower Hamlets courts of requests 'mixed with the Felons and disorderly People'.[126] Similar conditions obtained a decade later at the Borough Compter. Here the reformer Josiah Dornford found 'Men and Women Felons and Debtors are mingled together, as at the Poultry and Wood-street Compters all day; and [have] but one *convenience* for them all . . . where they all go to the *same place* in the face of each other'.[127] Citing a coroner's evidence that petty debtors in London gaols 'had died for the lack of the necessities of life' and testifying that prison officers continued, illegally, to extort fees from debtors committed by courts of conscience, Dornford waged a public campaign in the *Morning Chronicle* against the administration of courts and prisons by City officials.[128]

Yet if the metropolitan experience of imprisonment for small debts attests to the courts' ability to oppress their defendants, the City's archives also demonstrate the substantial obstacles placed by the courts' officials in the way of plaintiffs who sought to coerce payments from their debtors. The City's court was held at the Guildhall, a location that one alderman in 1774 described as 'very unfit for the purposes' and subject to an 'almost total Interruption of

[123] CLRO, London Court of Requests register book (1786), 2 August–30 December 1786.
[124] CLRO, Woodstreet Compter registers, WC1/23, WC1/41, 28 September 1780–81, 1789.
[125] *Report from the Committee*, 26.
[126] William Smith, *State of the Gaols in London, Westminster, and Borough of Southwark* (London, 1776), 3–4.
[127] Dornford, *Nine Letters*, 93.
[128] Ibid., 4–5, 87, 102–3, 109–11, 122, 125, 128–9, citations from 102–3, 128–9. Dornford's *Nine Letters* reprints much of the *Morning Chronicle* controversy.

'A kind of parliamentary magic' 233

Business during the whole Time of Lotterys [*sic*] and of taking Polls'.[129] Even creditors who succeeded in capturing the commissioners' attention in the mêlée of the courtroom found that their struggle to enforce their contracts had only begun. Beadles, who purchased the right to collect debts and undertake executions from the City, typically charged their own servants with the day-to-day business of implementing the commissioners' orders, a practice which, as a committee of aldermen admonished them in 1774, was patently 'illegal'.[130] The beadles themselves, however, were hardly men whose selection was calculated to inspire confidence. Thomas Byam died insolvent in 1790 with forty pounds recovered from court of conscience debtors in his possession, only to be succeeded in office by the hapless Holloway Brecknock. 'I am a poor unfortunate Mortal, I have been so all my life', Brecknock stated in his testimony to a committee investigating his actions in 1791. 'Tho' [I] was in Trade many years in Credit & Respect, but fate so order'd it at last I was obliged to submit to Crosses & Losses.' Brecknock's submission to his 'Distress and Misfortune' had, like that of fellow beadle James Mason, taken the form of 'making use of the Suitors Money received by them as executions'. When beadle Heylin was suspended for misconduct in 1799, he was promptly imprisoned for debt in Ludgate. Reduced at the age of seventy-two to subsistence on the prison allowance, he petitioned to be restored to his former position, excusing his errors as an innocent consequence of 'the failure of memory, which together with his other Faculties are very much impaired so as to obviate any Evil which should arise therefrom'.[131]

Together, the beadles' financial exigencies and their habit of farming debt collection out to servants ensured a wide degree of latitude for negotiation between petty debtors and the court's officers. Petitions from plaintiffs seeking to enforce summonses and orders of execution are a commonplace in the City's records. Thomas Machin, who petitioned the aldermen to compel Gilbert Eames to enforce an execution order in 1757, complained that the beadle 'behaved in a very insulting Manner to him when Aplied [*sic*] to, to do his duty'. Mrs Elizabeth Browning, who sued the birdcage-maker George Acton for eight shillings and sixpence in the 1760s, testified nine years later 'that she had frequently applied to get the said Execution served, but Mr Barber the Beadle said he had lost it'.[132] Such lapses were integral to the beadles' business and profit. George Green, repeatedly suspended from – and repeatedly reinstated

---

[129] CLRO, Minute book, 21 February 1774, 57–8.
[130] Ibid., 28 March 1774, 86–91, citation from 87.
[131] CLRO, Misc. MSS. 260.1, General Purposes Committee, Miscellaneous papers & rough minutes relating to the court of requests, 1790–1832, 31 March 1790, 21 June 1791, 19 April 1792, 15 May 1800.
[132] CLRO, Rep. 162, 29 November 1757, fols. 27–8; CLRO, Minute book, 28 February 1774, 67–8.

234   Petty debts and the modernisation of English law

to – office for misconduct in the 1770s, administered the collection of debts from his public house, the Red Lyon in Moorfields, where debtors seeking his protection from the law and creditors seeking to enforce their contracts were alike compelled to purchase liquor from his tap while negotiating their claims.[133] Debts collected from officials of courts of requests had a decided tendency to accumulate in officers' pockets rather than in plaintiffs' hands. Although the City's aldermen investigated complaints against the officials at intervals, they took few effective measures to secure the creditors' interests which they had defended so vociferously in parliamentary petitions. Like previous and subsequent investigations, the report of 1774 produced an elaborate scheme of reforms which the retention of demonstrably corrupt officers rendered entirely nugatory. Josiah Dornford, complaining in 1778 to the aldermen that John Deacon 'was so frequently intoxicated as to be almost incapable of transacting his Business', noted with obvious frustration that the beadle's embezzlement of suitors' funds was in direct violation of the court's reformed regulations of 1774.[134]

Rapacious, arrogant, arbitrary and illegal, the court officers' conduct was no more fitted to advance creditors' interests than it was designed systematically to oppress petty debtors. When plaintiff Deveaux Wall threatened to take George Green to court for failing to deliver six summonses purchased at the court office, Green reportedly 'said that he might be damned and the Court too, for that he hath bought his Place'. Called before the court of aldermen to justify his behaviour, Green denied all knowledge of the parliamentary statutes that required him to serve summonses in person, and urged the committee to consider the Christian virtues of maintaining extended delays between orders for execution and their implementation. 'Surely if a Moments reflection on the Consequences . . . was taken', he exclaimed piously, 'any Reasonable Person would certainly think it cruel to run a poor Distressed Person to Gaol from a Large and Distressed Family, when by our waiting they are often able to procure some Friend to advance the Money or some Means found to settle it with the Plaintiff.'[135]

Conclusion

Beadle Green's invocation of the trope of the unfortunate debtor clearly smacked of strategic self-interest, but it also reflected a broader public recognition of the constraints that limited contractual thinking (and contractual practice) in eighteenth-century England. Notions of moral economy and conceptions of

---

[133] CLRO, Minute book, 24 February 1774, 66–7. In this Green built upon a long-established tradition of debt collection in which the public house served as the focus for both credit networks and labour markets. See above, 77.

[134] CLRO, Rep. 179, 31 January 1775, fols. 146–7; Rep. 182, 27 January 1778, fol. 114.

[135] CLRO, Minute book, 7 March 1774, 69; 28 March 1774, 95, 102.

patriarchal authority imposed ideological restrictions on the enforcement of personal debts; so too (more prosaically) did the frequent failure of civil imprisonment to extract cash from impoverished or intransigent labourers and the tendency of extended prison terms to throw debtors' families on the parish. Administered by commissioners who lacked the social stature or economic security of the landed JPs who imposed summary sanctions on petty criminal offenders,[136] the small-claims courts were prone to the arbitrary exercise of economic self-interest. In theory as in practice, they departed significantly from the interpretation of the law popularised by Blackstone's *Commentaries*, which held that 'in free states, the trouble, expense and delays of judicial proceedings are the price that every subject pays for his liberty'.[137]

Yet neither the courts' conspicuous failings nor their significant departure from dominant legal paradigms can obscure their central place in English legal culture in the era of the industrial and consumer revolutions. Established from 1749 to 1789 not only in England but also in Ireland and in the commercial hubs of the emerging Indian empire, these courts enjoyed a renewed phase of institutional and geographical expansion in the nineteenth century, with fifty-six new courts created within Britain alone between 1806 and 1842.[138] Key legal provisions forged in these courts, moreover, migrated to and flourished in the national county-court system which was to supplant the haphazard network of courts of requests in 1846. Over a century before the common-law courts allowed interested parties to testify in civil cases or permitted wives to appear and offer evidence in their husbands' suits, the courts of conscience had accepted these equitable conventions as vital to the maintenance of useful credit among the lower orders. Pioneers in conferring a degree of legal personality on married women conventionally excluded from the courtroom, these summary tribunals were also at the forefront of new conceptualisations of imprisonment for debt. By displacing petty debtors from the privileged precincts of the gaol and confining them instead in houses of correction, eighteenth-century courts of conscience laid the foundations for a Victorian reconfiguration of the unfortunate petty debtor as a wilfully irresponsible consumer, an individual economic agent rightly subject to the discipline not only of the free market but also of the reformed prison.

---

[136] An annual income from land of at least £100 was required for county JPs. For the social and economic status of JPs, see King, *Crime, Justice and Discretion*, 117–25; for small claims commissioners' more modest backgrounds, Langford, *Public Life and the Propertied Englishman*, 234–43.

[137] Blackstone, *Commentaries*, III: 423–4.

[138] For the reform of Irish small-claims litigation in the eighteenth century, see Anon., *The Junior's Precedence: Illustrated in a New Impression of Two Acts of Parliament Made in Ireland, for the Recovery of Small Debts . . .; Shewing the Necessity of Courts of Conscience . . .* (London, 1750). The establishment and troubled history of courts of conscience modelled on the City's court in Calcutta and Madras from the 1750s are detailed in my 'Law, debt, and empire in Calcutta', *Papers of the Faculty Seminar in British Studies* (Austin, 2000), 1– 25.

6 From courts of conscience to county courts: small-claims litigation in the nineteenth century

Although the proliferation of courts of requests slowed in the tempestuous decades of the French revolutionary and Napoleonic wars, business in these summary small debt tribunals mounted steadily in the early nineteenth century. In a number of localities – Bolingbroke, Bristol, Rochester, Sheffield and Kingston upon Hull among them – this increase was promoted by successful petitions to raise the jurisdiction of existing courts from forty shillings to new limits of either five, ten or fifteen pounds. Case-loads rose in many individual small-claims courts and in the nation as a whole. In Newcastle's court of conscience, creditors had entered only 378 plaints in 1804–05, but initiated 3,921 actions in 1829–30. By the 1820s, Christopher Brooks has calculated, courts of requests throughout England 'were hearing some 200,000 cases each year, or about 2.5 times the number entertained by the central courts in London'.[1] Further increases resulted from successful efforts to establish new courts in the 1830s and 1840s. Leicester, Loughborough, Barnsley, Rotherham, Rochdale, Glossop, Belper, Preston, Bury, Brighton and Totnes were among the many urban centres to which Parliament granted a court of requests in this period.

Nationally, new interest in small-claims litigation was also evidenced by successive government ministers. In 1821, Lord Althorp introduced a bill that proposed to ease and speed the recovery of debts valued at fifteen pounds or less by creating a series of local courts, presided over by judges drawn from the Bar. Rejected out of hand by the Lord Chancellor, Althorp's bill inaugurated a quarter-century of haphazard and ineffectual legislative endeavour intended to rationalise, modernise and dignify small debt recovery throughout England and Wales. As Patrick Polden has commented of the thicket of failed legislation that preceded the passage of the County Court Act in 1846, 'the story of these bills is profoundly unedifying'.[2] For some commentators – not least

---

[1] Christopher Brooks, *Lawyers, Litigation and English Society since 1450* (London, 1998), 41–2. The terms 'court of conscience' and 'court of requests' are largely interchangeable, but the former usage was more common in the eighteenth century and the latter term in the nineteenth century, terminology reflected in this and the previous chapter.

[2] Patrick Polden, *A History of the County Court, 1846–1971* (Cambridge, 1999), 36–7. See ibid., 5–37, for a detailed survey of these attempted reforms. Michael Lobban provides an astute

From courts of conscience to county courts

some small-claims court litigants themselves – the history and conduct of the national reticulation of summary courts that resulted from this protracted legal campaign was likewise unimpressive. Advanced by their proponents as icons of legal modernity, the county courts featured in their detractors' denunciations as bastions of legal despotism in which judicial discretion routinely triumphed over the letter of the law. Imprisonment for debt, distinctions of gender, age and class, divergent understandings of the relation between character and credit and discrepancies between common law and equity all served as persistent flash-points in the nineteenth-century small-claims courts as litigants, lawyers, judges and observers sought to settle personal debt disputes without resort to juries. Lying at the heart of these conflicts was the fundamental dissonance that obtained between the autonomous contractual individuals posited by economic theory and the social and cultural world of contractual relations inhabited by the men, women and children who purchased goods and services on credit in historical markets.

An understanding of the social dynamics of small-claims courts based upon surviving court records (rather than upon printed sources alone) suggests that legal historians' conventional account of the transition from the local courts of conscience to the new national system of county courts requires substantial revision. For H.W. Arthurs, the abolition of courts of requests and the establishment of the county courts provide a prime example of the victory of legal centralism over legal pluralism in nineteenth-century England. In this dominant interpretation, whereas the courts of requests 'had existed in virtual isolation from the superior courts' and enjoyed 'virtual autonomy', the new county courts were rapidly colonised by representatives of the legal profession and integrated into the common-law tradition. The new salience of lawyers in small debt disputes underpins the heart of this assessment: 'the County Courts Act of 1846 gave lawyers a monopoly of representation to the exclusion of the "low attorneys" and other unqualified individuals who often appeared in the old local courts', Arthurs thus argues.[3] In their survey of English legal culture from 1750 to 1950, Cornish and Clark, who describe the creation of the county courts in 1846 as 'a parting of the ways crucial to the Victorian reforms of judicature', reiterate Arthurs's analysis. 'They were lawyers' courts', these authors observe of the new county courts. 'The right of representation was confined to members of the bar and attorneys.'[4]

---

assessment of the problematic contribution made to these reform efforts by Lord Brougham in 'Henry Brougham and law reform', *English Historical Review*, 115, 464 (November 2000), 1184–215.

[3] H.W. Arthurs, *'Without the Law': Administrative Justice and Legal Pluralism in Nineteenth-Century England* (Toronto, 1985), 44–5. Arthurs's important account of small-claims litigation draws upon court records of court of requests disputes but not of county-court disputes.

[4] W.R. Cornish and G. de N. Clark, *Law and Society in England 1750–1950* (London, 1989), 31, 38.

238   Petty debts and the modernisation of English law

Closer scrutiny of the relevant statutes – or even a superficial glance at county-court minute books – demonstrates the shortcomings of this pervasive line of analysis. By section 91 of the County Courts Act, lawyers were indeed empowered to represent litigants by right, while paid agents who lacked formal professional status could appear to represent creditor or debtor in lieu of a solicitor only by the leave of the presiding judge.[5] Surviving court documents, however, suggest that many judges accepted paid agents as fitting representatives of the litigants who appeared before them. Children, parents and (above all) wives, moreover, routinely appeared in county courts to represent male heads of households – as they had in the courts of conscience since at least the eighteenth century. The active participation of these unpaid agents, who were uneducated in the law but well schooled in the day-to-day lessons of personal credit negotiation, provided a significant counterweight to the creeping legal formalism that supposedly stifled equitable impulses in Victorian contractual disputes.[6] Reducing the sway of lawyers and distancing the courts' proceedings from superior-court practice, these vociferous legal agents played an essential role in ensuring that law was often tempered with equity in the county courts. County-court judges themselves – their status as trained barristers notwithstanding – were complicit in this process of mitigation, interrogating and at times openly flouting their own authority to enforce the individual's full liability for consumer contracts.

Litigants and litigation in the courts of requests

When Mary Ann Ashford, the orphaned daughter of bankrupt London innkeepers, entered domestic service in a bank clerk's family as a child in 1800, she contracted for a wage of six pounds ten shillings a year. Within a few months of her employment, however, rumours of her employer's dishonest financial connections began to circulate in the neighbourhood, and a family friend and benefactor convinced Ashford to give notice and seek an engagement elsewhere. Although she returned to her former employer's home repeatedly to collect her unpaid wages – amounting to over a pound – he refused to consider Ashford's pleas for payment until her benefactor 'summoned my master to the Court of Requests, and got it'.[7] A minor who lacked both a legal guardian and full legal

---

[5] Polden, *History of the County Court*, 36, notes the ability of agents who lacked formal legal training to represent county-court litigants, but situates the courts securely within existing superior-court traditions none the less: 'The new county courts would be courts of law as lawyers understood them but stripped of most of the rococo ornament that encrusted the superior courts.'

[6] For the most influential formulation of the argument that legal formalism increasingly supplanted equitable interpretations of contract, see P.S. Atiyah, *The Rise and Fall of Freedom of Contract* (Oxford, 1979), 388–9.

[7] Mary Ann Ashford, *Life of a Licensed Victualler's Daughter: Written by Herself* (London, 1844), 22.

From courts of conscience to county courts 239

personhood... in her own right, Mary Ashford was an ideal candidate for the equitable forms of justice championed by eighteenth- and nineteenth-century advocates of the summary small-claims courts. As William Hutton's memoir of the Birmingham court of conscience had emphasised in the 1780s, commissioners' equitable interpretations of litigants' personhood and agency were intended to bring legal redress to individuals excluded by cost or convention from the ambit of the common law. In many courts, formal statutory regulation buttressed commissioners' informal practices to advance this goal: in addition to raising the court's jurisdiction from forty shillings to five pounds, the statute that revised the powers of Sheffield's court of requests in 1808 specifically empowered its commissioners to hear claims for unpaid wages brought by legal minors.[8]

Ashford's autobiography is significant in revealing the willingness of the courts' commissioners to entertain suits – and testimony – by individuals such as infants, wives and interested parties who lacked legal agency in courts of common law.[9] A newspaper account of a suit heard in Bath in 1839 suggests the extent to which this commonsense approach to contractual disputes had become standard practice in early nineteenth-century courts of requests. The plaintiff, a Bristol tailor, had sold goods on credit to an apprentice lad, whose parents resided in Bath. Under the so-called law of necessaries, fathers – or widowed mothers – were legally liable for necessary (but not luxury) goods purchased on credit by their minor children. At law, the suit in the Bath court of requests was thus lodged against the apprentice's father, who would be held liable for payment only if the commissioners judged the purchases to be 'necessary' for a child of the defendant's social position. On the court day, however, the apprentice's father was absent, and his suit was ably defended by the youth's mother – acting as her husband's agent here as no doubt she did on a routine basis in purchasing goods on his credit for consumption in the family home. Throughout its account of the case, the *Bath Guardian* referred to the wife as the defendant rather than (as was technically true in law) the defendant's agent, endowing her with an autonomous identity denied by the common-law principle of coverture. 'The defendant concluded that she was not liable, that she had supplied her son with requisite clothing as far as her condition in life would

---

[8] *An Act for Regulating the Proceedings in the Courts Baron of the Manors of Sheffield and Ecclesall...* (Sheffield, 1842), in Sheffield City Archives, Arundel Castle MSS, S 603, page 18: 'in every case, where any wages, or any other sum or sums of money whatsoever... shall be due or owing to any menial servant... or any other person whatsoever, under the age of 21 years, it shall... be lawful... [for such persons] to sue for and recover such debt in the said Courts in the same manner as if he or she were of full age...'.

[9] Not until passage of the Evidence Amendment Act of 1851 were parties who had an interest in the outcome of most civil cases competent to testify in common-law courts. See Christopher Allen, *The Law of Evidence in Victorian England* (Cambridge, 1997), esp. 95–8. Wives and infants are discussed more fully below.

240   Petty debts and the modernisation of English law

allow, and quite sufficient for his circumstances', the paper reported, accepting without comment the wife's ability to figure as if she were a legal person for the purpose of litigation. The Bath commissioners clearly shared this willingness to suspend the letter of the law by rejecting common-law rules of evidence and accepting a wife as a competent witness and agent for her indebted spouse. Upon hearing her testimony, they ruled that the tailor had failed to exercise 'due caution by giving credit' and dismissed the suit, warning 'that parents might be exposed to ruin if children were permitted and encouraged to incur debts without their sanction'.[10]

Newspaper reports and memoirs provide vital evidence of commissioners' willingness to shape legal procedures to accommodate the partial or suspended legal identities with which key economic agents – children, servants and wives – entered the market on a daily basis. Archival records of court activity further underline the significance of this procedural flexibility for debtors in particular, by demonstrating that plaintiffs as a group enjoyed substantial advantages over their defendants. Plebeian debtor-defendants sued by propertied men and women were far more numerous than working-class creditor-plaintiffs in the small-claims courts, and suits to recover payment for goods purchased by the lesser sort typically far outnumbered plaints (such as Mary Ann Ashford's) entered by labouring-class creditors against their social betters.[11] Judgments for creditor plaintiffs, while by no means automatic, were rendered in striking disproportion to judgments that favoured debtor defendants. By far the majority of plaintiffs in Bath could enter the court of requests with sanguine prospects in the 1820s and 1830s. In over five hundred plaints heard in August and September, plaintiffs failed to be awarded the full amount of their claims in less than 10 per cent of sampled suits in 1829 and 1839.[12] In Yorkshire, at the Keighley court of requests, defendants' likelihood of convincing the commissioners that creditors' claims were unjust was also slim. Only one defendant defeated his creditor in 113 plaints heard by the court in November and December 1840.[13]

Although the courts were clearly predisposed to creditors' interests, the surviving evidence suggests that at least some commissioners continued, like Hutton in the eighteenth-century Birmingham court, to weigh the evidence

---

[10] *Bath Guardian*, 22 March 1839. For the law of necessaries, see my 'Women, consumption and coverture in England, *c*. 1760–1860', *HJ*, 39, 3 (September 1996), 703–22. For the debts of infants (persons under the age of twenty-one), see Thomas Peake, *A Compendium of the Law of Evidence*, 5th edn (London, 1822), 278–9.

[11] In two samples of several hundred suits heard in the Bath court of requests in the 1820s and 1830s, for example, labourers were roughly three times more likely to appear as defendants than as plaintiffs in 1829, and nine times more likely to appear as defendants than as plaintiffs in 1839. Margot Finn, 'Debt and credit in Bath's court of requests, 1829–39', *Urban History*, 21, 2 (October 1994), 218.

[12] Ibid.

[13] West Yorkshire Archives Service, CC1/2/1, Keighley Court of Requests Judgment Book, 1840–42, suits from 5 November to 2 December 1840. Of 125 plaints, 12 were not served.

From courts of conscience to county courts 241

with some care when meting out their judgments. Socioeconomic considerations appear to have figured prominently in commissioners' efforts to adjudicate between debtors' inability to meet their obligations and creditors' insistence that they do so, for judicial outcomes repeatedly reflect defendants' status rather than testifying to the courts' uniform determination to enforce free contracts upon autonomous individuals. At the Bath court of requests, for example, instalment payments were awarded disproportionately to labourer defendants. Of 1,102 suits heard from August 1829 to January 1830, only 215 (20%) resulted in orders for instalment payments, but labourers were allowed to pay their debts by instalments in 26 of their 56 suits (46%) in this sample.[14] Instalment payments ordered by commissioners of courts of requests could make creditors wait for months for full payment of their debts. If rendered at the rate of two shillings per week mandated by the Bristol commissioners, the labourer William Taylor's debt to shopkeeper Michael Holloway would have taken over five months to collect through the court, exclusive of costs.[15]

Plaintiffs of all social levels pursued debtors of all varieties in the courts of requests. Like diaries and memoirs, the courts' records provide abundant evidence of a credit economy that linked all social groups through the credit nexus. In Bath, defendants of gentlemanly status were sued by plaintiffs representing over sixty trades or occupations: as evidenced by these sources, butchers, bakers, grocers, fishmongers, ironmongers, engravers, druggists and fencing masters all routinely traded with genteel customers on credit. Although labourers evidently enjoyed less extensive circles of credit than gentlemen, as a group they too succeeded in obtaining goods or services from a wide range of artisans and tradesmen. Drapers and shopkeepers overwhelmingly predominated among the forty-four trades that sued labourers in the Bath court of requests, followed by bakers, cordwainers and beer-sellers, but surgeons, smiths and clock-makers also numbered among the plaintiffs who had agreed to extend these workers goods or services on credit.[16]

By the early nineteenth century, significant local disparities in how plaintiffs used the petty debt courts were already evident. In some courts, large numbers of suits entered for a given court day by any one plaintiff were the exception rather than the rule: the plaints heard in both Bristol and Bath generally adhered to this diffuse pattern of litigation. In Sheffield, in contrast, many creditors had recognised the potential – later to be exploited by Victorian trade protection associations – for the court to provide a routine mechanism of debt collection rather than an occasional instrument of last resort. On 5 December 1808, plaintiffs in the Sheffield court of requests who brought multiple suits included

[14] Finn, 'Debt and credit', 219.
[15] Bristol RO, 09303/1, Bristol Court of Requests Proceedings, 1816.
[16] Finn, 'Debt and credit', 224, 232.

242   Petty debts and the modernisation of English law

Charles Hobson, who sued three labourers, two colliers and a farmer over payment for unspecified goods; Thomas Keyworth, who sought to recover debts for shoes purchased by ten labourers, colliers and metal-workers; and John Moorehouse, who sued ten defendants, seven of them cutlers, for the provision of medicines. Although credit drapers who sold cheap articles of clothing to the poor would later emerge in public discourse as the archetypal villains of the small-claims courts, it was surgeons who were especially conspicuous among plaintiffs who brought multiple suits in the Sheffield court of requests: Hall Overend sued twenty-three debtors for medical provisions on 5 December and entered another eleven suits against his patients in the court held a week later.[17]

If plaintiffs' litigation strategies differed from court to court, so too did the commissioners' use of their ultimate sanction, the issue of an execution against either the goods or the body of the recalcitrant debtor. The alacrity (or the reluctance) with which commissioners ordered executions varied substantially among jurisdictions. In some courts, a debtor's failure to appear when summoned initially provoked only a ruling to pay the creditor by a specified date, but in other jurisdictions absence from court itself constituted grounds for an immediate execution order against the debtor. At the Brigg court of requests in Lincolnshire, Josiah Trolley sued John Jenkinson on 16 March 1810 for three pounds ten shillings and a penny, and the commissioners promptly ordered an execution against Jenkinson's goods when the debtor failed to appear to answer the summons. Recalcitrant refusal in court to agree to pay a debt likewise precipitated immediate execution orders in this court. When William Walker, also sued by Josiah Trolley on 16 March, 'refused to pay' the debt proven against him, the commissioners, 'at the request of the Complainant', ordered an immediate execution against Walker's goods and chattels. Of twenty-four judgments rendered in the Brigg court from 16 March to 8 June 1810, fully a third resulted in orders for execution against debtors' goods – five for failure or refusal to pay, and three for failure to appear in court.[18] In this context, the significance of wives' ability to appear in court in lieu of their defendant husbands is obvious: merely by making an appearance on behalf of their husbands, wives could increase the likelihood that the commissioners would consider ordering instalment payments rather than issuing an immediate execution order in response to the debtor's absence from court.

Threatened executions against debtors' goods and chattels were effective means of compelling a significant minority of defendants to settle with their creditors. Of 358 executions ordered against Bath debtors between 12 February

---

[17] Sheffield City Archives, Arundel Castle MSS, S 571, Sheffield Court Baron Entry Book, plaints for 5 and 12 December 1808. The Sheffield court functioned both as a court baron and as a court of requests, and was referred to by both names by contemporaries.

[18] Lincolnshire Archives, Stubbs 128/2, Brigg Court of Requests Minute Book, 1808–12, suits for 16 March–8 June 1810.

From courts of conscience to county courts 243

1830 and 12 February 1831, 87 (24%) resulted in payment of the debt in full and 130 (36%) in a compromise between creditor and debtor rather than in the imprisonment of the latter.[19] But execution against the impoverished debtors' goods possessed obvious tactical limitations as an instrument of economic coercion. When the Bristol court levied an execution in 1816 upon the goods of debtor Sperring, who owed his creditor a sum of ten pounds, the sale of Sperring's goods produced only the derisory sum of twelve shillings and sixpence. Of 182 executions against goods levied by the Bristol court in 1817 for which outcomes were recorded, just over three-quarters resulted in payment of the debt; the remaining cases were entered in the court books with the laconic notation 'No goods'.[20] The paucity of debtors' material possessions, the dangers of seizing them and the difficulty of disposing of these goods profitably repeatedly encouraged court personnel to turn to the debtor's body as a means of enforcing payment. Commissioners at the Brigg court of requests ordered immediate executions against the bodies of a quarter of all debtors who came before them from 16 March to 8 June 1810, either because the defendant had failed to appear in court or because the creditor specifically requested this remedy. The widow Hannah Rhodes sued George Moore for a debt of five shillings on 16 March, and the commissioners, 'Upon hearing the Complainant (the Defendant not appearing after having been duly summoned)', ordered an execution against Moore's body at his creditor's request.[21] In London, George Watson of Shoreditch, already threatened with an execution by his landlord, was imprisoned in 1813 at the instance of his baker, who had initially obtained an execution against Watson's goods. As Watson explained in a begging letter to the overseers of his parish of settlement, when the bailiff 'Came into my Place and saw me Ill and my Chilldren [*sic*] almost Naked Looking Round at [my] . . . Things says he Those things are not worth my Taking I must Gett and [*sic*] Execution and Take you and it appears to me you will be as Comfortable in Jail as in your present Situation'.[22]

As Table 6.1 demonstrates, wide variations marked the use of execution orders by the commissioners of different courts of requests. Although commissioners in Newcastle and Stockport were more likely to attempt to elicit payment of debts by executions against debtors' goods than by ordering the

---

[19] *Second Part of the Appendix to the Fourth Report of the Commissioners Appointed to Inquire into the Practices and Proceedings of the Superior Courts of Common Law*, Parliamentary Papers, XXV, part 2 (1831–32), 534–5.

[20] Bristol RO, 09308/1, Bristol Court of Requests Execution Book, 1816–32, entry for *Ashley* v. *Sperring*, 31 October 1816, and suits for January–December 1817. Of 182 suits, 131 (72%) were paid in full, 11 (6%) paid in part and 40 (22%) unpaid owing to the lack of goods upon which to execute.

[21] Lincolnshire Archives, Stubbs 128/2, Brigg Court of Requests Minute Book, 1808–12, suits for 16 March–8 June 1810.

[22] Thomas Sokoll, ed., *Essex Pauper Letters 1731–1837* (Oxford, 2001), 293.

244 Petty debts and the modernisation of English law

Table 6.1. *Courts of requests judgments, 12 February 1830–12 February 1831*

Court	Suits initiated	Executions against goods	Executions against body
Bath	3,711	130	358
Birmingham	7,926	178	1,241
Derby	1,793	66	343
Halifax	22,864	962	2,410
Newcastle	3,921	1,052	282
Norwich	3,938	566	588
Sheffield	11,518	37	3,860
Stockport	1,885	271	203

Source: Second Part of the Appendix to the Fourth Report of the Commissioners Appointed to Inquire into the Practices and Proceedings of the Superior Courts of Common Law, Parliamentary Papers, XXV, part 2 (1831–32).

imprisonment of their bodies, many court officials were clearly impressed by the disciplinary potential of confinement in gaol. Halifax's commissioners – notorious for the severity of their regime in the 1770s – were two-and-a-half times more likely and Birmingham's commissioners nearly seven times more likely to order an execution against the body than against the goods. A defendant who appeared in the Sheffield court was over a hundred times more likely to receive an order of imprisonment than to face the seizure and sale of his possessions. Execution against the body was an unexceptional verdict in the courts of requests. In the jurisdictions listed in Table 6.1, executions issued against the body ranged from a low of 7.2 per cent of all suits (in Newcastle) to a peak of 33 per cent of all debts (in Sheffield).

The increase of many courts' jurisdictions from the original limit of forty shillings to encompass debts of several pounds exerted a decisive impact upon imprisonment for debt. Since the reforms of the 1780s, commissioners had been limited to sentencing debtors to maximum terms of forty days per debt, but their new authority to hear claims for larger sums was accompanied by powers to commit debtors for up to 100 days (for courts with jurisdictions up to five pounds) or 200 days (for courts that adjudicated debts of up to ten pounds). In Bath, where the commissioners were empowered to imprison debtors for up to 200 days per debt, of the 358 debtors who received executions against their bodies, 61 (or 17 per cent) received this maximum sentence.[23] The commitment book for the Spilsby gaol in Lincolnshire suggests the onerous sway that such powers of imprisonment could exert on the lives of small-claims debtors, removing them from work and home for months at a time. From 1827 to 1844, local courts of requests committed 466 petty debtors to the Spilsby gaol,

[23] *Second Part of the Appendix*, 534–5.

From courts of conscience to county courts

of whom 365 (78.3 per cent) served their imprisonment in full. John Frankist, labourer, entered the gaol on 30 March 1828 and was released a hundred days later on 7 July; Ruth Stephenson, labourer, was committed for a hundred days on 22 December 1834 and recommitted for an additional twenty days for a second debt upon the expiration of this term, gaining her release from prison only on 20 April 1835.[24]

Statistical samples cannot convey the trauma that imprisonments such as these inflicted upon court of requests debtors and their families, but the desperate appeals written to local Poor Law authorities for parish relief to help stave off arrest or to piece together the fragments of family life after release from gaol speak eloquently to their plight. Margaret Howell of Ely appealed in desperation to her husband's parish of settlement in Colchester in 1832, undertaking the arduous process of letter-writing to beg assistance for the family during his incarceration. 'I rite to inform You of the trubel i ham now Left in my husband is taken away from me and put in prison for a dad of two pounds seven shillin wich we run for bread for the Children in the Cholery sickners [cholera sickness]', she explained to the overseers. 'It is not in my power to maintain all my Children myself.'[25] As Howell's letter suggests, rather than transforming pauper families into exponents of sturdy independence and individual autonomy, imprisonment for debt by courts of requests underscored the vital importance of cultivating servile relations of obligation. The correspondence of David Rivenhall, imprisoned in the Clerkenwell house of correction in 1824 for a debt of two pounds and committed to Coldbath Fields prison for another petty debt in 1827, is larded with the conventional rhetoric of gift-giving and mutual obligation rather than couched in the language of liberal individualism. 'I am truly sensible of the great obligation which I am under and shall ever feel most grateful for the same...if, Sir, you will under my distressed situation, be pleased in some measure to alleviate the demand against me', Rivenhall wrote to the overseers in Chelmsford in 1824. Rivenhall, who drew attention to his inability to pursue gainful employment while imprisoned for his debts, clearly inhabited a mixed economy in which charitable obligations, market endeavour, luck, misfortune, debt and credit were inextricably intertwined, rather than a world in which individual effort, free contracts and the cash nexus reigned supreme. 'It is with the most profound Sentiments of respect and gratitude that I take the liberty of addressing you Humbly Imploring your Charitable aid for myself and helpless distressed family at this unfortunate period when I am deprived of my liberty or the mains [sic] of doing anything for them', Rivenhall wrote in 1827. Rivenhall's begging letter recalls the sorry tales of personal misfortune

[24] PRO, PCOM2/400, Spilsby Gaol Discharge Register, 1826–48, commitments for 22 January 1829–27 July 1844.
[25] Sokoll, ed., *Essex Pauper Letters*, 497–8.

246   Petty debts and the modernisation of English law

recounted on the doorstep by itinerant traders and recorded in the diaries and memoirs of the consumers who purchased their goods. Before his arrest, he had hoped to 'provide for my poor family by selling oysters in which I have been always Tolerably Lucky but just as the season began I was taken and put into prison for a small sum of twelve shillings and six pence which I have no mains [*sic*] on earth of paying', Rivenhall concluded, situating his willingness to assume personal responsibility for his dependents against a background in which economic misfortune generated by the vicissitudes of the market and the enforced idleness imposed by the debtors' prison had rendered him wholly incapable of so doing.[26]

Withdrawing thousands of able-bodied heads of households from their families and the workforce for months at a time, the expanding small-claims courts propelled new waves of debtor inmates into gaols now increasingly conceptualised – however unrealistically – as sites of rational discipline and punishment. Like insolvents imprisoned by the superior courts, the debtors committed to gaols and houses of correction by courts of requests constituted a fundamental category mistake when viewed from the perspective of contemporary penal ideology and liberal economics. For creditors too, the impact of imprisonment for debt was far from straightforward. Removed from the labour market and exempt from punitive employments in the prison, small-claims debtors were at once powerfully impressed by the sanctity of contracts and liberated from full contractual liability by the terms of their imprisonment. Compelling thousands of debtors to honour their obligations by paying their debts in full, execution orders also convinced many creditors to accept partial compositions in lieu of the full sums for which their debtors were legally liable. The very powers of imprisonment exercised by court commissioners were instrumental in compelling creditors to moderate their contractual claims by accepting partial payment, for the statutory regulation of the courts enacted in the aftermath of the Halifax scandal ensured that plaintiffs who failed to reach an accommodation with defendants saw their debtors liberated from all liability to pay the litigated sum upon their release from gaol.

Politics in the courts of requests

Litigants and contemporary observers were painfully alive to the inherent contradictions of debt recovery in the nineteenth-century courts of requests, but attitudes toward the courts – and efforts to reform or abolish them – were also powerfully shaped by the broader tenor of popular and parliamentary politics. Both support for and hostility toward the eighteenth-century courts of conscience had focused on the twin topics of legal process and economic growth.

---

[26] Ibid., 253. For pedlars' doorstep narratives of misfortune, see above, 93–4.

From courts of conscience to county courts 247

Whereas proponents had urged that the summary courts would promote useful credit among the lesser sort by ridding small-claims litigation of the procedural excrescences, excessive costs and long delays of suits at common law, detractors had attacked courts of conscience as tribunals geared to protect the interests of a range of vested interests by depriving freeborn Englishmen of their right to trial by jury. Although these lines of argument continued to inform nineteenth-century debates over small debt litigation, they were overshadowed in the early decades of the century by arguments that centred more narrowly on the abuse of political power. As radical and liberal critiques of unreformed political institutions gained intensity, the courts of requests (despite their modern provenance and commercial origins) became entangled in heated debates over the persistence of Old Corruption – the nexus of political, legal and economic interests that sustained aristocratic rule within the state.[27]

In jurisdictions where established aristocratic leaders had assumed a degree of oversight over the local courts of requests that operated within their spheres of political influence, the links between the new small-claims tribunals and traditional forms of political authority were immediately obvious to observers. Functioning both as a court of requests and as a manorial court, Sheffield's small-claims tribunal was controlled by the Duke of Norfolk, as lord of the manor of Sheffield, and Earl Fitzwilliam, as lord of the manor of Ecclesall. Norfolk and Fitzwilliam, in addition to enjoying an automatic right to serve as commissioners in the court, held the nomination of all the court's officers in their gift.[28] As political tensions escalated in the era of democratic reform, such control of small-claims courts offered aristocratic politicians a means with which to resist parliamentary encroachments upon their local bases of power. Lord Bathurst, who was lord paramount of the seven hundreds of Cirencester, interfered repeatedly in the affairs of the Cirencester court of requests, resisting local efforts to extend the court's business to include the burgeoning town of Stroud, which lay less securely within his influence. When the Whigs, at Lord Brougham's behest, embraced reform of local courts as a political cause, Bathurst entered the fray against them by attempting to enlarge the powers of the Cirencester court, a ploy that observers interpreted as a nakedly partisan effort to prevent both the creation of 'independent local Courts' and the incorporation of the borough.[29]

In cities, the entrenched interests of urban elites likewise served to associate courts of requests with the evils of unrepresentative oligarchic government. In

---

[27] For the broader context of campaigns against Old Corruption, see Philip Harling, *The Waning of "Old Corruption": The Politics of Economical Reform in Britain, 1779–1846* (Oxford, 1996).

[28] Norfolk's steward, Michael Ellison, oversaw the day-to-day administration of the court and its patronage. See esp. Sheffield City Archives, Arundel Castle MSS, S 478, parts 8–14.

[29] UCL Archives, Henry Brougham Collection, 47,065, John G. Ball to Lord Brougham, 3 April 1834.

248   Petty debts and the modernisation of English law

the City of London, where the court of conscience had been a byword for venality since the eighteenth century, the aldermanic elite's continued refusal to take action against corrupt officers made the authoritarian character of their rule powerfully manifest. Despite the commissioners' frantic appeals to the City's aldermen for redress, Sir Watkin Lewes, high bailiff of Southwark, persisted in outrageous interference in the proceedings of the Southwark court of requests. Channelling fees and debts collected from litigants into his own and his officers' pockets and refusing to discipline officials who failed to levy executions ordered by the court, Lewes also forced repeated adjournments by appearing in the court to denounce the commissioners' conduct.[30] In the provinces too courts of requests were plagued by accusations that vested interests and party politics had supplanted the principles of equity that petitioners and parliamentary sponsors had originally advanced to justify their foundation. In Bristol, where the original seventeenth-century court of conscience was augmented in 1816 by the creation of a parallel court of requests empowered to hear debts of up to fifteen pounds, control of the small-claims courts remained firmly in the grip of the Tory corporation throughout the 1820s and 1830s. Claims that the court's procedures were 'intolerable and illegal', complaints that the commissioners openly trafficked in justice while treating '*misfortune* as if it were a *crime*' and accusations that the court habitually provided the corrupt creditor with 'a license to extract from the pocket of the Defendant such a sum as he may have screwed up his conscience to swear to' punctuated lively public commentary in newspapers and pamphlets, predictably supported by references to Blackstone's strictures against courts of conscience in the *Commentaries*.[31] Party politics guided appointments to the court's roster of paid officials, and protected corrupt officers from discipline. When John Wilcox, the bedridden registrar of the Bristol court of conscience, at long last expired in 1837, £1,800 collected from debtors remained in his possession and could not be recovered from his estate.[32]

Birmingham's court, so lauded by William Hutton in the 1780s, was an object of reform-minded odium by the 1820s and remained a focus of criticism until its abolition in 1846. A campaign waged in pamphlets and local newspapers blended critiques of the commissioners' abdication of their equitable mission with accusations, crafted to complement contemporary political agitation, that their malfeasance could be linked directly to their undemocratic constitution. Richard Jenkinson, a schoolmaster who had been sued by his plumber

---

[30] CLRO, Misc. MSS. 258.4, Minutes of Evidence and Papers re. The Conduct of Sir Watkin Lewes, High Bailiff of Southwark, and his officers, 1815

[31] Charles Houlden Walker, *Letters on the Practice of the Bristol Court of Requests; on Judicial Sinecures in Bristol, and Other Important Subjects* (London, 1820), vi, 2–3, 7. See also, for example, *The Bristolian*, 29 August 1829, 6 January 1830.

[32] Graham Bush, *Bristol and Its Municipal Government 1820–1851* (Gateshead, 1976), 136, 160.

From courts of conscience to county courts 249

and gaoled for four days in 'the *prison-hole* of this *Equity Court*' until his friends remitted his debt and costs, denounced the court passionately in 1827. 'I shall endeavour to describe the hurly-burly in this Court during the short time I was present; and this being the general state of the Court during hours of business, a pretty fair criterion may be drawn of the *justice and equity* likely to proceed from it', Jenkinson expostulated in a pamphlet deriding the court's gross departure from the niceties of common-law procedure.[33] Joseph Parkes, who championed radical reform of the court in *Aris's Birmingham Gazette*, was similarly strident. 'The present inefficient and corrupt state of the Court of Requests has become proverbial', he commented, observing that in such a tribunal, monopolised by a small oligarchy of officers, 'Justice... must be deaf as well as blind.' For Parkes, the commissioners constituted a baneful local manifestation of the political corruption rendered endemic throughout the state by the unreformed House of Commons. '*Capacity* and *integrity* for the duties of this important office are not required in this notable jurisdiction, provided the *self elected* body elect an individual with a certain *purse*', he commented caustically. 'Nor can I omit the reflection... that these facts shew the importance to the town of Birmingham of a PARLIAMENTARY REPRESENTATION; and that if it had possessed that invaluable privilege, the evils now exposed would not so long have been permitted to exist.'[34]

Although the passage of the 1832 Reform Act and the 1835 Municipal Corporations Act failed to liberate small-claims courts from the grip of entrenched urban elites, the partial democratisation of politics in the 1830s did encourage critics of the courts to redirect the focus of their opposition. Antagonists of the new metropolitan tribunals mooted in the later seventeenth and early eighteenth centuries had predicted that the creation of summary small-claims courts administered by local lay commissioners would subject petty debtors to a bastard form of law at the hands of petty shopkeepers, and the political enfranchisement of precisely this class by the First Reform Act served to reinvigorate these concerns.[35] J.E. Collins of Trowbridge, who wrote to apprise Lord Brougham of the evils of 'shopocracy' in the Wiltshire courts of requests in 1839, emphasised not merely the arbitrary authority wielded by tradesmen who conducted the court's business 'in a most slovenly & disgraceful manner', but also the ways in which shopkeepers' social and economic connection with their customers through the credit relation invariably led to collusive relations between the

---

[33] Richard Jenkinson, *Justice in Equity Exemplified: Being the Full Particulars and True Account of the Proceedings in the Court of Requests, Birmingham...* (Birmingham, [1827]), 11, 13, 21.

[34] Joseph Parkes, *The State of the Court of Requests and the Public Office of Birmingham* (Birmingham, 1828), 1, 6, 3, 16. The tract originally appeared as a series of letters in *Aris's Birmingham Gazette*.

[35] For the seventeenth-century predictions, see above, 201. For shopkeepers' influence in politics after the 1832 act, see T.J. Nossiter, *Influence, Opinion and Political Idioms in Reformed England: Case Studies from the North-East 1832–1874* (Brighton, 1975).

250   Petty debts and the modernisation of English law

commissioners and litigants. Although 'persons of property, influence... [and] Education' were appointed as commissioners, the men who chose to serve most actively in the Trowbridge court were a grocer, a baker, a publican and a shoemaker, tradesmen 'intimately connected with many of the suitors, participating in their prejudices & often united by the tie of shopkeeper & customer'. Litigants in the court (both debtors and creditors), Collins claimed, routinely appealed to a commissioner with whom they traded 'to get him to attend at the hearing'. If the tradesman refused, he lost 'the Custom of that Individual & from this practice a very great perversion of Justice results'. Like justice, credit was debased by the operation and coercive powers of the court, which promoted a dangerous form of obligation predicated on the commissioners' powers of execution rather than upon debtors' ability to pay their bills. The court, Collins concluded, 'instead of protecting useful Credit... has, like most Courts of Requests, created a very pernicious Credit affecting both Debtor and Creditor'.[36]

Collins's claim that courts of requests promoted pernicious credit among the lower orders signalled a line of critique that grew increasingly significant from the 1830s. As Old Corruption gradually receded from the forefront of political consciousness, concerns about the tendency of small-claims courts to stoke unnatural consumer desires by promoting false credit became more conspicuous in public discussions of the courts of requests. Considerations of gender figured centrally in these debates, in which credit relations acquired a sexual charge already familiar from the fraught personal debts that animated relations between male and female characters in English fiction. In 1836, attacks upon the '*private interest*' that swayed commissioners' decisions in the Sheffield court were thus accompanied by denunciations of the itinerant pedlars who resorted to the court to enforce their contracts, having entangled innocent defendants in the snares of debt by 'acting the part of the Old Serpent, and fascinating the wives of the working classes' with their cheap finery and alluring luxury goods.[37] In London, court of conscience commissioners not only shared but acted upon this antagonism. J.R. McCulloch, denouncing the false credit promoted by drapers who relied upon the courts to enforce contracts for goods purchased by plebeian wives as their husbands' agents, observed in 1844 that metropolitan commissioners discouraged this system by invoking their equitable discretion and 'ordering claims of *this* kind to be paid by *extremely small* installments, and these at *very distant* intervals'.[38]

---

[36] UCL Archives, Henry Brougham Collection, 3,656, J.E. Collins to Lord Brougham, 20 March 1839.

[37] *Sheffield Iris*, 9 February 1836.

[38] J.R. McCulloch, *A Dictionary, Practical, Theoretical, and Historical, of Commerce and Commercial Navigation* (London, 1844), 1206. Mayhew also noted this antagonism to credit drapers in metropolitan courts of requests. See Henry Mayhew, *London Labour and the London Poor*, 4 vols. (London, 1861–62), I:381.

From courts of conscience to county courts

In Birmingham, the interval between the passage of the county-court act in 1846 and the inauguration of the new courts in 1847 saw local reformers develop this line of attack further at a series of public meetings on the 'glaring abuses' of local debt litigation. Joseph Corbett's claim that the commissioners of the Birmingham court of requests were complicit with the unscrupulous business tactics by which a host of local tradesmen entrapped unwary credit consumers drew loud cheers from the crowd. In Corbett's interpretation, the court fostered a false credit that imposed artificial needs and inflicted unnecessary goods upon plebeian consumers by enforcing debts in defiance of equitable notions of contractual justice. Denying that he sought to 'induce the working people to abstain from the payment of their just debts', Corbett highlighted:

the temptations that beset the needy working people. The 'packman' or Scotch hawker with his temptations; the agents for the sale of articles of every kind of comfort often thrusting them upon their customers ... Weekly payments spring up to the packman, the coal-man, the beer-man, and the huckster, and swarms of them; and they expect to be paid punctually for their high-priced goods, and if not so paid, – then to complete the ruin of an unhappy and falling family, – some vile legal blood-hound is let loose upon them ...

Offering a sharp contrast to the false credit created by the commercial machinations of these tradesmen and their legal harpies was the useful credit that the courts of requests had been established to promote. For like the petitioners who had successfully urged Parliament to create the eighteenth-century courts of conscience, Corbett recognised and accepted credit as an essential pillar of the modern market economy, an instrument necessitated by the market's inevitable 'fluctuations of trade' and competitive profit margins. 'It has been sneeringly observed that the poor ought not to get into debt', Corbett commented. 'How are they to keep clear of it, with earnings when times are good but just sufficient with every economy to make both ends meet?'[39]

Corbett's distinction between the useful credit required to maintain labour markets (by sustaining and reproducing working-class families) and the false credit that often animated the consumer market (by preying upon the acquisitive desires of male labourers' dependants) prefigured key arguments that were to dominate Victorian and Edwardian county-court practice. Hailed by Lord Brougham and his acolytes as modern tribunals of commerce that would break decisively from the corrupt practices of the courts of requests, the county courts were instead to build substantially upon existing practices and to draw significantly from systems of thought inherited from eighteenth- and early nineteenth-century small-claims tribunals. To be sure, the appointment of judges and the

---

[39] *Birmingham Advertiser*, 11 June 1846, 6 August 1846. For the background to this public campaign, see Joseph Allday, *Injustice, Oppression, and Cruelty: Local Courts for the Recovery of Small Debts, and Extortionate and Ruinous 'Costs'* [Birmingham, 1846].

252   Petty debts and the modernisation of English law

right of all defendants and plaintiffs to representation by a solicitor or a barrister added new layers of legalism to county-court practice. But the law itself was as much transformed by its encounter with the small-claims courts as it was effective in ridding petty debt disputes of their equitable dimensions.

County-court practice

Possessing sixty judicial districts sub-divided into a total of 491 local courts, the new tribunals that began to operate in 1847 established a dense reticulation of small-claims courts throughout England and Wales. Judges drawn from the ranks of experienced members of the Bar (later assisted by legally qualified registrars) presided within each of the districts, travelling to every outlying court at least once in the course of the month and holding more frequent sittings in court towns located in major urban centres. Their presence, reformers optimistically predicted, would ensure that small-claims litigation would henceforth be conducted with gravitas and guided by formal legal learning. Now directed by statute to adjudicate disputes in strict accordance with the decisions rendered by superior-court judges, legal historians have argued, the county courts were decisively distanced from the principles of equity and good conscience that had inspired the eighteenth-century courts of conscience. With the passage of the County Courts Act of 1846, H.W. Arthurs asserts, 'the vast armada of local and special courts that largely comprised the English legal system in 1830 was replaced by a new national fleet of county courts...and was securely anchored within the safe harbour of the common law'.[40]

From the outset, partisans of the new jurisdictions laboured assiduously to promote precisely this interpretation of the county-court system. 'I feel that we are entering upon a new era in the history of the law, and I firmly believe that the renovation of County Courts will be regarded by posterity as one of the great improvements of the nineteenth century', the judge of the Warrington court announced to his first suitors in 1847, intent to distinguish his own jurisdiction from 'the exploded Courts of Requests' it had supplanted.[41] The *County Courts Chronicle*, established in 1847 to champion the new tribunals, was especially conscious of the imperative to maintain this essential distinction. 'Courts of Requests were bear-gardens in noise and confusion, and their character was at the lowest ebb', the *Chronicle* proclaimed condescendingly in 1847. Emphasising the pressing need for judges to preserve 'with more than common strictness the dignity and decorum of their courts as regards alike to order and the manner of proceeding' and urging them to assimilate the new tribunals 'to the *tone* of the Superior Courts', the paper warned the newly appointed judges of the 'tendency in all Inferior Courts to depart from the formal regularity that is a distinguishing

[40] Arthurs, *'Without the Law'*, 45, 15.   [41] *CCC*, 1 September 1847, 80.

feature of the higher Law Courts in England, and which is so much an object of admiration with foreigners'.[42] Decades later, Thomas Falconer, county-court judge and avowed disciple of both Bentham and Brougham, continued to reiterate this refrain. Celebrating 'the excellence and economy' of the county-court system, Falconer asserted – quite erroneously – that instalment payments were an innovation of the county courts unknown in the courts of requests, and emphasised 'how enormous was the change effected in 1846 in the abolition of [these] petty and oppressive Courts of Law'.[43]

As the frequency and intensity with which proponents of the county courts reiterated these claims suggest, the divergence between the old and new court systems was not entirely self-evident to contemporaries. Even advocates of the new county courts, indeed, were often wont to describe them in terms that recalled the now defunct courts of requests. A London tradesman who commended the county courts in 1861 as 'One of the greatest improvements of the present time' acknowledged that their judges' 'general tone and bearing is not such as to impress the parties themselves with the serious nature of their statements' and admitted that in consequence 'some have been described as perfect bear-gardens'.[44] In a number of jurisdictions, continuity in personnel helped to ensure that litigation in the county courts continued to display characteristics associated with the disorderly courts of requests. Bath, Brighton, Bristol, Liverpool and Manchester were among the county courts in which the presiding judge had previously been active in the business of the local court of requests.[45] Arthur Palmer, appointed assessor of the Bristol court of requests through Tory patronage in 1839, became the first judge of the Bristol county court and swiftly brought the new tribunal into disrepute. Complaints by lawyers that Palmer permitted agents who lacked formal legal qualifications to represent litigants in his court surfaced in the first months of his tenure in 1847; two years later, the Home Office was compelled to interrogate the judge when Bristol tradesmen petitioned 'complaining of the dilatory and irregular manner in which the business of your court has been conducted'.[46] Elsewhere, the legacy of the old courts persisted into the 1880s. Richard Wildman, who

[42] Ibid., 1 July 1847, 34.
[43] Thomas Falconer, *On County Courts, Local Courts of Record, and on the Changes Proposed To Be Made in Such Courts in the Second Report of the Judicature Commissioners* (London, 1873), 40.
[44] Anon., *Business Life: The Experiences of a London Tradesman with Practical Advice and Directions for Avoiding Many of the Evils Connected with Our Present Commercial System and State of Society* (London, 1861), 155–6.
[45] For this overlap in judicial personnel, see esp. *CCC*, 2 August 1847, 60; John Frederick Archbold, *The Practice of the New County Courts*, 3rd edn (London, 1848), 7–8; Sir Thomas Snagge, *The Evolution of the County Court* (London, 1904), 12.
[46] For Palmer's appointment, see Bush, *Bristol and Its Municipal Government*, 150. His peccadilloes as a county-court judge are noted in *CCC*, 2 August 1847, 54, and PRO, HO 86/2, 19–20, H. Waddington to Arthur Palmer, 22 September 1849.

254   Petty debts and the modernisation of English law

retired from the judgeship of Nottingham county court in 1881, had been active in the Derbyshire court of requests in the 1830s and 1840s; Thomas William Rodgers, clerk of the Sheffield county court from 1847 until his death in 1881, had earlier served as deputy steward of that city's court of requests.[47]

Charges that county-court judges were corrupt or politically partisan were less frequent and more muted than the accusations of venality habitually lodged against the court of requests' commissioners,[48] but denunciations of county-court judges' arbitrary rulings in defiance of the common law were, if anything, even more current than those levelled against their predecessors. At the most prosaic level, age and disability demonstrably detracted from the performance of many judges. H.T. Atkinson of Leeds was, at the age of seventy-three, an active and compassionate county-court judge, but deafness hindered his execution of court business, conspiring with his own persistent financial worries to render Atkinson 'anxious and depressed' in 1878.[49] Government parsimony actively discouraged the retirement of disabled judges from the county-court bench. The Lord Chancellor granted pensions at his discretion rather than by right, a policy which, the *County Courts Chronicle* charged in 1885, ensured that numerous judges appointed in 'prehistoric times' remained in place despite physical or mental incapacity.[50] Freedom from disability, however, failed to guarantee the appropriate conduct of the younger members of the county-court bench. Arbitrary rulings, perfunctory attention to the conduct of court business and refusal to abide by established legal principles featured prominently in the barrage of accusations levelled against the county-court judiciary. The growth of the newspaper press brought these charges to a new and burgeoning audience, lending debate on the Victorian county courts national scope and significance unknown to attacks lodged against the courts of requests.[51]

Although disability, senility and incompetence all fostered arbitrary decision-making in the county courts, the fundamental cause of disparities in judicial behaviour was the broad scope of the equitable and discretionary powers that judges enjoyed by statutory right. Equity featured in county-court practice at two levels. Formally, the county courts were courts of equity by the statutory provisions that gave them jurisdiction over causes normally heard in equity

[47] *CCC*, 1 October 1881, 197–8; *Solicitors' Journal*, 25 (9 July 1881), 682.

[48] Appointment of county-court judges was in the gift of the Lord Chancellor, and the dominance of Liberal ministries lent the Victorian county-court bench a Liberal cast that attracted some accusations of partisan political behaviour. See, for example, *CCC*, 1 March 1886, 353, and 1 December 1886, 594.

[49] Bodleian, MS Eng.misc.e.940, Diary of H.T. Atkinson, 428 (4 November 1878). See similarly *CCC*, 1 June 1881, 117. Atkinson retired in 1880: *CCC*, 1 November 1880, 436–7.

[50] *CCC*, 2 November 1885, 258.

[51] Patrick Polden, 'Judicial selkirks: the county court judges and the press, 1847–80', in Christopher W. Brooks and Michael Lobban, eds., *Communities and Courts in Britain 1150–1900* (London, 1997), 245–62, esp. 248.

courts such as Chancery: the 1865 County Courts (Equitable Jurisdiction) Act, 28 & 29 Vict. c. 99, which conferred an equity jurisdiction over estates valued at up to £500, was the most substantial of these provisions in the pre-war era. Contemporary proponents of the county courts celebrated this formal equitable jurisdiction as a fundamental revolution in legal principles – 'They have solved the problem of the fusion of law and equity long before Chief Justices and Lords Justices had detected the secret', the *County Courts Chronicle* exalted – but this development had little quantitative impact upon county-court practice. While hundreds of thousands of petty debts (valued at or below forty shillings) were pursued in the county courts each year, fewer than a thousand equity cases were entered in the courts per annum.[52] County courts, however, also enjoyed a second, informal equity jurisdiction, familiar from the elastic principles of 'equity and good conscience' that had shaped dispute resolution in the courts of requests. For in addition to endowing judges with authority to exclude (or accept) the appearance of a range of agents – wives, children, servants, employees, debt-collectors and the like – in lieu of plaintiffs and defendants, the County Courts Act of 1846 instructed judges to inquire into the contractual and social circumstances surrounding the defendant's unpaid debt and granted judges considerable latitude in ordering payment and committal to gaol. In wielding their considerable discretion to adjudicate the vexed issues of agency and imprisonment, county-court judges were to build upon equitable principles earlier exercised by commissioners in the courts of requests, rather than to reject these precedents entirely.

Issues of legal agency troubled county-court litigation from the outset. Citing section 91 of the County Courts Act, judge William Walker of the Sheffield, Rotherham and Barnsley courts announced to his first suitors that he would accept arguments made on behalf of plaintiffs by barristers and attorneys but not by debt-collectors, a rule that initially lends substance to the claim that lawyers and legal formalism came to dominate county-court practice. But in addition to these 'regular professional men', Walker accepted the appearance of agents such as 'attorneys' clerks, wives, children, or shopmen', a practice that diminished the tyranny of the law in his courtroom.[53] Nor was Walker unusual in this regard. In his treatise on county-court practice, John Cowburn, an attorney who served as the assistant clerk of the Settle and Kirkby Lonsdale court, highlighted the willingness of judges to entertain suits and testimony from plaintiffs and defendants who lacked full legal agency. Minors, Cowburn noted, could sue to recover unpaid wages in the new courts as if they were

---

[52] *CCC*, 1 October 1885, 235. See Polden, *History of the County Court*, 59–61, for the equitable jurisdiction conferred in 1865. A more limited equity jurisdiction had derived from section 22 of 9 & 10 Vict. c. 95.

[53] *Sheffield and Rotherham Independent*, 17 April 1847, 8. For local debt-collectors' outraged response to their exclusion from his court, see ibid., 24 April 1847, 5, and 1 May 1847, 5.

256 Petty debts and the modernisation of English law

Table 6.2. *Litigants' representatives, Boston County Court, January–June 1848*

Litigant	Litigant's representative in court				
	Barrister	Attorney	Paid agent	Wife	Total
Plaintiff creditor	12 (13%)	49 (55%)	13 (15%)	15 (17%)	89 (100%)
Defendant debtor	6 (5%)	40 (32%)	4 (3%)	74 (60%)	124 (100%)

Source: Lincolnshire Archives, AK 16/2, Boston County Court Minute Book, 1847–48.

adults, and the judges possessed 'full power' to examine interested parties such as the litigants themselves, 'their wives, and agents, as well as all other persons, on oath'. Far from seeking to distance the county courts from their disreputable predecessors, Cowburn specifically invoked the principles of the defunct courts of conscience, arguing that county-court judges would render their judgments 'according to equity and good conscience'.[54]

Debtors and creditors eagerly exploited the opportunities provided by county-court procedure for representation by family members and paid agents who lacked formal legal qualifications. Creditors, although more likely than debtors to hire a barrister or attorney to represent them in the county court, continued to avail themselves of representation by extra-legal agents. In the 399 suits heard in the Boston county court from January to June 1848, 89 creditors (22%) chose to be represented in court by a representative – whether a barrister, an attorney, a paid agent, or their own wife. As Table 6.2 indicates, representation of creditors by individuals with formal legal qualifications predominated in this sample: 68% of plaintiffs who chose to be represented in court were represented by a barrister or solicitor; wives (17%) and paid agents (15%) appeared for the remaining third of represented plaintiffs. Debtors – 124 (31%) of whom chose to be represented in court – were, in contrast, significantly more likely to turn to extra-legal agents to defend their unpaid debts. Nearly two-thirds of debtors who dispatched a representative to the court relied upon the skills of a wife or a paid agent, and just over a third appealed to a member of the legal profession. The minute book in which these suits are recorded makes nonsense of the claim that the county courts were effectively colonised by lawyers. Wives and paid agents who lacked professional qualifications were both frequent and effective litigants in the Boston county court from its first years of operation. William Kates's wife successfully argued her husband's claim against the attorney hired

---

[54] John Cowburn, *The Suitor's Guide to the New County Courts; Being a Plain and Familiar Exposition of the Act and Rules of Practice, Designed to Assist Those Who Desire to Avail Themselves of the Facilities Given for the Recovery of Small Debts, without the Aid of a Professional Advisor* (London, 1847), 1, 11.

From courts of conscience to county courts

by debtor Edward Newton, who was ordered to pay Kates his debt 'forthwith'; John Doughley's wife gained a judgment for her spouse against the claim for unpaid rent lodged by creditor Mary Barwick's agent.[55]

Resort to extra-legal agents persisted – indeed, it appears to have increased – in the Boston county court over time, rather than fading as the legal profession gained its supposed stranglehold upon small-claims litigation. In 1900, 171 plaintiffs in four sampled months sent a representative to the court rather than appearing in person. Only 41 (24%) of these creditors were represented by an attorney; 15 (9%) of these suits were litigated by plaintiffs' wives and 115 (67%) by paid agents. Like creditors, debtors who relied upon a representative in Boston were largely content to leave the defence of their suits to family members and extra-legal representatives. Of the 55 debtors who dispatched a representative to the court in the sampled months, only 14 (25%) employed an attorney. Paid agents accounted for 16 (29%), and wives for 25 (46%), of defendants' representatives. Labourers, who constituted the largest single group of defendants in the 690 sampled suits (191 defendants, or 27.7%), were disproportionately likely to be represented in court by their wives. More than three-quarters of the debtors represented by wives were labourers.[56]

The Boston county court was unexceptional in this respect. The district served by the Shoreditch and Bow county court, home to a working population in which labourers, porters, carpenters and stevedores were prominent, likewise encouraged female participation at all levels of debt transaction and recovery. From the outset, wives appeared as agents for their husbands in a significant number of suits in the Bow court. Of twenty-seven suits heard at Bow in January 1850 in which a defendant sent a representative to court, four attorneys, six agents and seventeen wives appeared on behalf of debtors.[57] Married women continued to play a vital role in the proceedings of the Bow court throughout the century, and appear to have been instrumental in increasing the likelihood that claims against their husbands would be reduced. In 674 cases heard in Bow in April 1892, 203 (30%) were defended by debtors' wives. Cases in which a wife represented a husband were disproportionately likely to result in a reduction of the debt claimed. In 44 of the 106 suits in the sample in which the debt was reduced (or 42%), a wife had appeared on behalf of her husband.[58] In

---

[55] Lincolnshire Archives, AK 16/2, Boston County Court Minute Book, 1847–48, case numbers 161 and 374.

[56] Lincolnshire Archives, AK 16/12, Boston County Court Minute Book, 1899–1900. The sample consists of all suits for the months of January, April, July and October. Of twenty-two defendants represented by a wife for whom a trade was recorded, seventeen (77 per cent) were labourers.

[57] LMA, CCT/AK/15/4, Bow County Court Plaint and Minute Book, 1849–51, January 1850. In this sample, plaintiffs sent a total of thirty representatives to court: three wives, five attorneys and twenty-two agents. For the vital economic role played by wives in Shoreditch and Bow Victorian working-class households, see Ellen Ross, *Love and Toil: Motherhood in Outcast London 1870–1918* (Oxford, 1993), esp. 41, 45, 47, 72, 82, 85.

[58] LMA, CCT/AK/15/8, Bow County Court Plaint and Minute Book, 1892, April 1892.

258   Petty debts and the modernisation of English law

his memoir, Edward Abbott Parry, judge of the late-Victorian and Edwardian Manchester county court, repeatedly underscored the role played by the wives who acted as agents for their debtor husbands in his circuit. 'The wife is the solicitor and advocate of the working-class household, and very cleverly she does her work as a rule', Parry opined. 'The women are the best advocates.'[59]

If wives' appearance as representatives of their husbands was made possible by county-court judges' discretionary interpretations of legal procedure, equitable reasoning was also conspicuous in judges' adjudication of consumer debts that violated their notions of the moral economy. As in superior courts of equity, the enforcement of contracts in county courts was subject to mitigation by the social and moral contexts that surrounded the disputed debts, and many county-court judges used their discretionary powers to signal their hostility to creditors who sought to exploit their contractual rights without reference to their corresponding obligation to act equitably toward their debtors. Judge Crompton Hutton of the Bacup county court, for example, invoked equitable lines of argument in allocating legal costs in a suit brought by a music-seller to enforce payment for a piano, which the creditor had sold to his debtor on the hire-purchase system. 'If [the] defendant would pay the balance due on the piano . . . he . . . should make no order as to the costs to which [the] plaintiff would have been entitled had the sale been a proper one', Hutton remonstrated in delivering his judgment. 'The hire system was one by which people would get a pianoforte, or anything else on enormous credit, extending over a very long time, which was a mischievous system, and open to every kind of abuse.'[60] Money-lenders and itinerant pedlars of drapery goods – the so-called Scotch drapers or tally tradesmen attacked in the 1830s and 1840s for resorting to courts of requests to collect debts owed by husbands for goods thrust upon innocent plebeian wives – were objects of particular judicial censure. A Yorkshire judge who in 1886 counselled a debtor in his court to act the part of 'an honest man' by paying each of his creditors his due 'except the "moneylender and Scotchman"' reflected (and further legitimated) this pervasive antagonism.[61]

Outright refusals by county-court judges to enforce credit drapery debts contracted under dubious circumstances by working-class wives on their husbands' credit punctuate reports of county-court proceedings. In London, judge Ryland

---

[59] Edward Abbott Parry, *Judgments in Vacation* (London, 1911), 56, 61. Significantly, Parry specifically described wives who appeared in his court as 'the Defendants' (56) rather than (as was technically the case at law) as the defendants' agents.

[60] *CCC*, 1 December 1879, 237.

[61] *CDG*, 1 July 1886, 178. For antagonism to these creditors, see Margot Finn, 'Scotch drapers and the politics of modernity: gender, class, and nationality in the Victorian tally trade', in Martin Daunton and Matthew Hilton, eds., *The Politics of Consumption: Material Culture and Citizenship in Europe and America* (Oxford, 2001), 89–107, and G.R. Rubin, 'The county courts and the tally trade, 1846–1914', in G.R. Rubin and David Sugarman, eds., *Law, Economy and Society, 1750–1914: Essays in the History of English Law* (Abingdon, 1984), 241–99.

routinely nonsuited plaintiffs such as the tallyman M'Calla, who in 1850 attempted to recover a debt of eight shillings and sixpence contracted by the defendant's wife. Although M'Calla's agent proved delivery of the goods, the debtor's wife insisted that she had been induced to purchase them against her will. 'The Learned Judge said it was a very wicked mode of carrying on business, and every endeavour ought to be made to suppress such a mischievous system', the *County Courts Chronicle* reported. 'He considered that in such cases tallymen were not entitled to recover.'[62] Antagonising tradesmen and law-makers alike, these equitable tactics persisted for decades. Questioned by a sceptical parliamentary select committee member in 1893 as to the legality of the expedients he used to discourage tallymen and money-lenders from using his county court to collect their debts, judge Edge of Devonshire was adamant 'that I have the power as a judge; because I sit not only as a judge of law, but as a judge of equity; and the Courts of Equity have for years refused as we all know, to enforce these inequitable demands'.[63]

Edge's equitable interpretations of county-court practice were widely current among Victorian and Edwardian judges, but they were hardly universal, for a vocal cohort of judges adhered instead to classical liberal conceptions of economic exchange and personal autonomy. Celebrating free markets and free contracts in their judicial decisions and in a lively pamphlet literature, these judges insisted upon the free will exercised by working-class consumers in their day-to-day purchasing activities. To these men, the unpaid debts litigated in their courts represented fundamental lapses of personal autonomy and character on the part of labourers. Thomas Falconer ridiculed the pervasive charge that credit drapers seduced working-class wives with their cheap finery and thereby ensnared innocent male labourers in debts contracted without their knowledge or volition. 'The man said, "the woman who thou gavest to be with me SHE gave me of the tree and I did eat"', Falconer fumed in 1873. 'So says the cowardly man of to-day: "My wife got the clothes wherewith she clothes herself and even has provided for me, and which covers the nakedness of my children and I could not see what she did nor know of it: she took all even if I have partaken of it".'[64] As a failure of manly self-control and patriarchal household management, personal debt figured in this critique of working-class culture as the polar opposite of personal credit, rather than its complement, and imprisonment for debt provided an essential mechanism with which to impress workmen with this fundamental distinction. 'Men of bad

---

[62] *CCC*, September 1850, 233. See similarly, for example, *The Warehousemen and Drapers' Trade Journal*, 19 October 1872, 345.

[63] *Report of the Select Committee of the House of Lords on the Debtors Act; Together with Proceedings of the Committee, Minutes of the Evidence, and Appendix*, Parliamentary Papers, IX (1893–94) (HL 156), 87.

[64] Falconer, *On County Courts*, 107.

260   Petty debts and the modernisation of English law

principle and drunkenness cannot obtain credit at present', judge Johnes of the Montgomeryshire circuit argued in extolling the salutary effect of county-court imprisonment. 'The trader requires the double security of good character and legal redress in case his confidence should be broken.'[65] Attributing 'the great majority of County Court cases' to 'the results of drunkenness', Johnes argued that while men of character could maintain their credit through labour, sobriety and thrift, 'reckless or unprincipled men' required the harsh discipline of the prison to recognise and fulfill their contractual obligations.[66]

For judges such as these, prison reformers' efforts to render imprisonment for debt fully punitive complemented their own attempts to discipline and punish working-class debtors who had failed either to develop the habits of personal industry or to internalise the conceptions of individual autonomy required by the modern market. Unlike imprisonment by the courts of requests, which had allowed defendants to expunge their debts by serving their sentence in full, completion of a term of county-court imprisonment failed to liquidate the debt, and recalcitrant offenders were consequently liable for repeated periods of increasingly punitive incarceration if they defaulted on their payments. Judge Amos of the Marylebone court made his commitment to the new discipline of rigourous confinement emphatically clear in 1847. 'On the Judge taking his seat he begged of all present to take notice that in every case where default was made in obeying the orders of the Court, he should ... send the parties so disobeying to the House of Correction, where they would have only the gaol allowance, and be compelled to wear prison dress', the *County Courts Chronicle* reported. 'There they would be treated, not as debtors, but as criminals.' Promptly acting upon his threat, Amos sentenced a debtor who had defaulted on a monthly instalment payment to two weeks' imprisonment in the local house of correction and reiterated that 'he would be treated as a criminal' in this prison. When the debtor offered to sell his work-horse 'and pay the money immediately', Amos – determined to enforce the discipline of the market through the prison – adamantly 'refused to allow him' to do so.[67]

In contrast, judges who subscribed to equitable interpretations of county-court practice questioned both the utility and the justice of imprisonment for petty debts. When moralistic speeches from the bench failed to discourage determined creditors from seeking to enforce their contracts through the courts, these judges turned to their arsenal of discretionary powers. Instalment orders set at low levels or at long intervals, repeated adjournments of hearings and suspended sentences all functioned to mitigate the strict enforcement of

---

[65] Arthur James Johnes, *Is Credit an Evil? In a Letter to C.M. Norwood, Esq. M.P.* (London, 1869), 4.
[66] Idem, *Should the Law of Imprisonment for Debt in the Superior Courts Be Abolished or Amended? In a Letter to the Rt. Hon. Lord Brougham and Vaux* (London, [1868]), 4, 5.
[67] *CCC*, 1 October 1847, 85.

contractual relations in these courts. 'Default cases are put at the end of the list and all kind of contrivances are brought in to help in discouraging this class of business', the *County Courts Chronicle* observed with disapproval in 1881. 'The love of exercising judicial power is shown even in hearing cases that are wholly undefended, and also in making orders to pay the debt by absurdly small instalments.'[68] If Andrew Amos was determined to use the Marylebone court to discipline a population of feckless and dissolute debtors, his brother judges in the metropolitan county courts were often inspired by less draconian visions of contractual justice. In 1849 the judge at Westminster county court, citing his discretionary powers under section 99 of the act and an outbreak of cholera at the local gaol, repeatedly refused to comply with creditors' requests that their debtors be imprisoned for failure to make ordered instalment payments.[69]

Regarding debt and credit as two sides of the same coin of payment rather than as antithetical market strategies, these critics of contractual freedom – like generations of novelists, diarists and autobiographers before them – treated personal debt as a species of misfortune rather than as a necessary token of failed character. In this interpretation, the effect of county-court imprisonment for debt was to substitute the false credit of luxurious consumption for the useful credit that preserved working-class domestic life. 'The chief evil of the present system of imprisonment for debt is the undesirable class of trade and traders that it encourages', judge Parry of Manchester concluded in 1911, condemning 'the money-lenders, the credit-drapers, the "Scotchmen," the travelling jewellers, the furniture-hirers, and all those firms who tout their goods round the streets for sale by small weekly instalments relying on imprisonment for debt to enable them to plant their goods out on the weaklings'. Troped as an innocent victim, Parry's debtor required not imprisonment but rather 'the interest of the State' to preserve his domestic life and 'deliver him from temptation'. Resonating with the traditional interpretation of the Lord's Prayer, in which debt (like sin) was an inevitable misfortune of fallen man, this analysis placed the burden of immoral contractual behaviours firmly on the shoulders of tradesmen and drew particular attention to the deleterious social consequences of their false assessments of character. Urging that shopkeepers should deal with labourers in full employment on a strictly cash basis and offer unemployed workers credit only 'if they know the character of the man', Parry charged creditors – not consumer debtors – with trading 'recklessly and equally to those in work and out of work, for necessities, luxuries, and inutilities'.[70] A contributor to

---

[68] Ibid., 1 February 1881, 33.   [69] Ibid., 1 September 1849, 237.

[70] Parry, *Judgments in Vacation*, 107, 113, 224. See similarly the analysis offered by the registrar of Shipton-on-Stour county court, Theophilus Lot, *A Plea for Poor Labouring Men: Shewing that by the County Court Practice They Are Led into Debt, and Compelled to Pay Debts by a Process of Extortion and Oppression Most Prolonged and Harmful, and Also Unjust Because Such Process Is Used against Poor Men Only* (Birmingham, [1888]).

262   Petty debts and the modernisation of English law

Palgrave's *Dictionary of Political Economy* likewise identified shopkeepers and tradesmen as the instigators of false credit relations. 'If a man has neither property nor character it is better that he should not be able to obtain credit by what is practically a mortgage of his body', this writer wrote disparagingly of county-court imprisonment for debt.[71]

The diary kept in 1878 by H.T. Atkinson of the Leeds county court forcefully conveys the moral dilemmas that troubled county-court practice and the antagonism that plaintiffs could encounter when they sought to collect their debts through county-court imprisonment. Atkinson's diary was written against a backdrop of persistent parliamentary concern that creditors as a class – and credit drapers in particular – were prone to abuse the county-court system.[72] References to editorials and press reports dealing with small-claims procedures recur throughout his diary, situating Atkinson's private reflections upon his own legal practices within the wider contexts of parliamentary politics and law reform. On 15 February, Atkinson's registrar drew the judge's attention to the large number – '60 cases!' – of debtors committed to York Castle by the Leeds court since the New Year, and suggested that Atkinson might work to reduce this figure by requiring 'more stringent proof . . . of ability to pay' before acceding to creditors' demands that their debtors be imprisoned. Assenting to this proposal, Atkinson found himself torn between the contractual rights of his plaintiffs and the economic exigencies of his defendants. On 16 February, inaugurating the new policy of 'stringent proof' of ability to pay, Atkinson observed that 'The great difficulty is to distinguish between a truthful and an untruthful statement as to the means of the debtor.' The absence of the male debtor himself from the courtroom typically complicated this determination, for 'The husband generally sends the wife who tells a piteous tale of destitution in the home.' Equitable considerations led Atkinson both to question and to reject the efficacy of county-court imprisonment, not least because the pernicious combination of easy access to consumer credit and strict enforcement of credit contracts threatened to degrade the character of the English workman:

Imprisonment at all for debt seems to me the last lingering relic of a barbarous age and ought no longer to exist. Its abolition would introduce a system of healthier dealing between the shopkeeper & the operative. It would, no doubt, lessen credit being given, but what was given would be founded on the character of the . . . dealings between the parties and would be founded on the confidence which arises from the character of the debtor for probity and the performance of his promises.[73]

---

[71] R.H. Inglis Palgrave, ed., *Dictionary of Political Economy*, 3 vols. (London, 1891–94), I: 505.

[72] See Finn, 'Scotch drapers and the politics of modernity', and Rubin, 'The county courts and the tally trade', for the political dimensions of this antagonism.

[73] Bodleian, MS Eng.misc.e.940, Diary of H.T. Atkinson, 164 (15 February 1878), 165 (16 February 1878).

Where Georgian legislators had grappled with the need to provide legal mechanisms that would promote 'useful credit' among the plebeian population, Victorian county-court judges now struggled to adjudicate the indiscriminate credit dealings that were a significant legacy of the creation of summary small-claims courts throughout England and Wales in the eighteenth century.

Hobbled by Parliament's persistent refusal to abolish imprisonment for debt, Atkinson sought to circumvent its operation in his court by deploying his wide discretionary powers. On 4 May, beset by large numbers of 'judgment summons' debtors who – having neglected or refused to comply with the judgments rendered against them by the court – were due to be imprisoned, Atkinson chose to adjourn their hearings to a later date, 'In consequence of the prevailing distress in all cases where the debtor was unemployed'. Atkinson was no naïve idealist: his strategies for mitigating debtors' contractual obligations were predicated on compassionate and equitable principles, but not upon a facile conception of working-class moral virtue. August 1878 saw Atkinson struggle on yet another of his 'dismal days', with a few hundred wives anxious to negotiate with him to prevent their husbands' incarceration. Acknowledging that such problems were 'In many cases caused by drink and its inevitable companion idleness', the judge noted his continued use of strategic adjournments to avoid imprisoning judgment debtors. October saw no diminution of his adherence to equitable judicial lenience. 'Poverty', Atkinson confided in his diary, 'wants nothing added to its burden and hardness and where there is suffering amounts to cruelty.' In this ethical context, making orders for minimal instalment payments provided Atkinson with another 'means of escape' for his debtor defendants. His judgments of threepence a week or a shilling a month were designed to infuse common-law conceptions of contract with more equitable understandings of status, misfortune and obligation.[74]

Atkinson's dilemmas in the Leeds county court and his equitable responses to them reflect the wider tensions that troubled the enforcement of working-class contracts in Victorian and Edwardian county courts. While providing rapid and relatively inexpensive resolution of most creditors' suits – either by prompting an agreement between plaintiff and defendant or by precipitating a court order through the trial process – the county courts also created a public forum in which judges themselves repeatedly questioned the moral legitimacy of contractual relations.[75] Newspaper press coverage, a vibrant pamphlet literature on legal reform and successive parliamentary investigations of the courts and their

---

[74] Ibid., 244 (4 May 1878); 342 (10 August 1878); 348 (5 October 1878); 409 (16 October 1878).
[75] For the rapidity with which uncontested suits (which formed the great proportion of all plaints) were determined, see Paul Johnson, 'Small debts and economic distress in England and Wales, 1857–1913', *EcoHR*, 46 (1993), 70. Public debates of wives' county-court activities are discussed in greater detail in my 'Working-class women and the contest for consumer control in Victorian county courts', *P&P*, 161 (November 1998), 116–54.

264   Petty debts and the modernisation of English law

proceedings kept these contentious issues in constant public view. Distinctions of class and gender proved especially significant in this context, offering those county-court judges who were inclined to emphasise the equitable aspects of their legal duties a cadre of social rationales for tempering their administration of the common law. Wives' continued presence in the courts as extra-legal representatives of their husbands – like their active role as agents for their menfolk in the consumer market – created repeated opportunities for equitable negotiation of working-class credit contracts even as it underscored the problematic character of individual autonomy and free will in day-to-day retail exchange. In the later nineteenth century, the disciplinary reform of imprisonment for debt, the passage of legal reforms that gave upper- and middle-class debtors access to the less draconian procedures of bankruptcy and wide variations in different county-court judges' use of imprisonment lent the legal anomalies entailed by credit relations contracted by working-class wives particular salience.[76] As reformers' efforts to render imprisonment for debt fully punitive escalated, the disjunction between the legally liable contractual individuals who suffered incarceration – predominantly adult male labourers – and the family members who routinely made purchases with these debtors' credit – particularly their wives – loomed ever larger in the public imagination. Embedded in dense networks of domestic obligation, labouring men's contractual autonomy was constantly undercut by their status as heads of households, for under the law of necessaries their credit in consumer markets was shared by their dependent family members. Cast in liberal theory as autonomous individuals, these debtors often appeared instead before the law courts as social individuals whose economic choices were made at second hand, by members of their family circle. As autonomous individuals, their liability for consumer debts was often clear-cut, but as social individuals it was frequently opaque, a circumstance that county-court judges' equitable lines of reasoning insistently brought to the attention of the legal community, Parliament and the wider public.

Case law, statutory reform and married women in the county courts

Although most county-court suits – and the vast bulk of county-court imprisonments – involved debts contracted by working-class consumers, reportage of small-claims litigation in legal periodicals and the popular press also attracted

---

[76] As in the courts of requests, county-court statistics of incarceration varied significantly by court. As late as 1927, over a quarter of all imprisoned debtors were committed by the five judges of Leeds, Hull, Pontefract, Grimsby and Doncaster. PRO, LCO 2/1145, Alexander Maxwell to Sir Claud Schuster, 18 December 1928. Variation in county-court activity also fluctuated with local and national employment conditions, as amply documented in Johnson, 'Small debts and economic distress', 65–87.

From courts of conscience to county courts 265

public scrutiny to a second category of troubling consumer contracts, the debts of middle- and upper-class wives. Just as reform of the debt law and debtors' prisons brought the tensions associated with male labourers' dual identities as both autonomous and social individuals into new prominence, so too legislative reform of marital relations created new dilemmas for county-court judges who sought to arbitrate the debts of married women at all levels of society. Changes in case law further complicated litigation of these debts. New precedents set in the superior courts sought to reduce husbands' liability for their wives' debts, but county-court judges often proved unwilling to administer justice in their own tribunals according to these novel principles. Equity and law, autonomy and social relations, co-existed uneasily in county-court disputes over both middle- and working-class household debts in Victorian and Edwardian England.

From 1857 to 1902, successive statutory reforms of marital law altered key aspects of economic relations between English husbands and their wives. The Divorce Act of 1857 removed separation and divorce from the dual custody of the ecclesiastical courts and Parliament, establishing instead a civil Divorce Court, located in London. Due to the high cost of its proceedings, the Divorce Court was primarily invoked by middle- and upper-class husbands and wives, but subsequent legislation of 1878, 1886, 1895 and 1902 brought marital separation within the reach of the poor by empowering local magistrates to award non-cohabitation, maintenance and custody orders to wives who had suffered physical abuse at the hands of their husbands.[77] Statutory reforms of property law – most significantly the Married Women's Property Acts of 1870, 1882 and 1893 – further disrupted established legal relations between English husbands and wives. Propertied families had, for centuries, secured their daughters' economic status upon marriage through the creation of equitable trusts, exploiting a legal remedy available under equity – but not at common law – that offered affluent wives a degree of financial security without allowing them to exert active control over the funds set aside as their own separate property.[78] The later Victorian period saw statutory revisions of the common law that extended equitable property rights to progressively wider circles of married women. By the Married Women's Property Act of 1870, wives gained partial powers to control (as their own separate property) earnings and inherited wealth notwithstanding their coverture. In return for these limited rights, wives who possessed separate property were rendered personally liable for debts contracted before – but

---

[77] For the class dimensions of the Divorce Act, see Gail L. Savage, ' "Intended only for the husband": gender, class and the provision for divorce in England, 1858–1918', in Kristine Ottesen Garrigan, ed., *Victorian Scandals: Representations of Gender and Class* (Athens, OH, 1992), 11–42. George Behlmer details the evolution of working-class separations in 'Summary justice and working-class marriage in England, 1870–1940', *Law & History Review*, 12, 2 (Fall 1994), 229–75.

[78] See esp. Susan Staves, *Married Women's Separate Property in England, 1660–1833* (Cambridge, MA, 1990).

266   Petty debts and the modernisation of English law

not after – their marriage. Anathematised by lawyers, legislators and feminist agitators alike for its often incoherent and contradictory provisions, the 1870 act was comprehensively revised by the Married Women's Property Act of 1882. Endowing all married women, regardless of whether their families had settled property upon them through an equitable trust, with the ability to hold and dispose of property in their own right, this act empowered wives to enter into contracts in their own names to the extent of their separate property. Now liable, to the extent of their separate property, for debts contracted after marriage, wives could also sue or be sued in their own name. The Married Women's Property Act of 1893 further provided that, except when explicitly acting as her husband's agent, a wife automatically bound her separate property – both existing and prospective – as security for payment of her debts. Significantly, however, wives' liability attached not to their persons but to their separate property: from 1893, married women sued under the Debtors Act of 1869 could suffer execution against goods included in their separate property, but they could not themselves be imprisoned for their debts.[79]

Occurring in parallel to these statutory reforms were developments in case law that sought to diminish husbands' liability for their wives' debts by revising the provisions of the law of necessaries. *Jolly* v. *Rees*, heard in the Court of Common Pleas in 1864, clarified and substantially enhanced a husband's ability to deny liability for his wife's 'necessary' debts by arguing that he had specifically forbidden her to purchase goods on his credit. Previous precedents had required that a husband make a public disavowal of his wife's agency to the specific tradesman in question to secure freedom from liability for her necessary debts, but *Jolly* v. *Rees* cast the presumption of married women's right to pledge their husbands' credit for necessary goods into substantial doubt. Much to the frustration of tradesmen – who routinely relied upon wives' implied agency to secure credit contracts for an array of groceries, textiles, drapery and household goods – *Debenham* v. *Mellon*, heard and appealed in a succession of courts in 1880, upheld *Jolly* v. *Rees*. Narrowing the provisions of the law of necessaries, this decision confirmed the right of husbands to free themselves from liability for even 'necessary' debts by claiming in court to have privately forbidden their wives to enter into credit contracts as their agents.[80]

---

[79] Lee Holcombe, *Wives and Property: Reform of the Married Women's Property Law in Nineteenth-Century England* (Toronto, 1983), 179–83, 201–5, 223–4.

[80] For legal practice on this issue before 1864, see for example J.J.S. Wharton, *An Exposition of the Laws Relating to the Women of England; Showing Their Rights, Remedies, and Responsibilities, in Every Position of Life* (London, 1853), 368–9. Erika Rappaport expertly details changes in the case law in ' "A husband and his wife's dresses": consumer credit and the debtor family in England, 1864–1914', in Victoria de Grazia, ed., *The Sex of Things: Gender and Consumption in Historical Perspective* (Berkeley, 1996), esp. 169–73, and idem, *Shopping for Pleasure: Women in the Making of London's West End* (Princeton, 2000), 55–65. Customarily cited at the time as *Debenham* v. *Mellon*, the 1880 suit was technically *Debenham and Freebody* v. *Mellon*.

If leading cases had exercised the hegemony in legal practice that they enjoy in legal theory, *Jolly* v. *Rees*, *Debenham* v. *Mellon* and the successive Married Women's Property Acts would mark a fundamental watershed in consumer debt and credit relations in England. But here as in so many aspects of legal culture, judicial interpretations of the law were multiple and discordant rather than uniform and univalent.[81] County-court judges, many of whom had prided themselves on their ability to fuse equity and law long before the statutory reforms of the 1870s and 1880s, played a key part in interpreting these new developments in property relations in the context of litigation. Their reactions to new departures in case law and statutory regulation diverged in two primary directions. On one side stood judges who adhered to the new letter of the law and accepted husbands' diminished liability for their wives' debts; on the other were judges who abided by traditional interpretations of a wife's ability to pledge her husband's credit for necessary goods.[82] Cross-cutting these distinctions were county-court judges' conflicted efforts to distinguish between those contexts in which male and female debtors should be treated as autonomous individuals – as men or women who exercised free will in the market – and those situations in which they must instead be understood to function as social individuals – as men or women who gained rights (or responsibilities) by virtue of their status and connections rather than by virtue of their autonomous identity alone.

Jolly v. *Rees*, *Debenham* v. *Mellon* and the Married Women's Property Acts of 1870–93 provided ample substance for reflection on the county-court bench, but even those judges who consistently sought to shape their rulings to reflect these revisions of the law found that social circumstances constantly intruded upon their determinations of the individual's contractual identity, agency and liability. Judge Crompton Hutton enraged the tradesmen of Oldham, Bolton, Rochdale and Bury in 1874 when he cited *Jolly* v. *Rees* in ruling against shopkeepers and grocers who resorted to his court to recover debts contracted by wives acting as their husbands' agents. Reiterating 'that a trader could not recover a debt if it had been contracted by a woman without her husband's consent', Hutton sought to privilege the autonomous over the social individual. The local tradesmen who convened an angry public meeting in Manchester to protest over his conduct resoundingly rejected this interpretation, emerging as vocal partisans of the social individual. Championing husband and wife as a composite legal entity in which separate wills, acts and responsibilities were necessarily (if not always seamlessly) united, they emphasised the economic losses that awaited tradesmen who failed to acknowledge that credit transactions were embedded

---

[81] For the perils of mistaking case law for a history of legal practice, see A.W. Brian Simpson, *Leading Cases in the Common Law* (Oxford, 1995), esp. 1–12.

[82] Superior-court judges also offered contradictory interpretations of these new rules, albeit their variations appear to have been less common than those in the county courts. See for example the discussion of superior-court cases in Rappaport, *Shopping for Pleasure*, 65–73.

268   Petty debts and the modernisation of English law

in social relations and animated by social distinctions. William Kershaw of Rochdale argued to a cheering audience 'that if tradesmen were compelled to ask ladies who wanted credit whether they had got their husbands' authority for incurring debts, they would insult many of their best customers'.[83] An editorial in the following week's *Warehousemen and Drapers' Trade Journal* elaborated further upon the social life of contractual relations in its critique of Hutton's rulings. Arguing that credit contracts negotiated by wives constituted a natural and normative component of familial relations, it held that tradesmen were 'fully entitled, from a common sense view of the subject, from the practical guarantees afforded by the habits of our social life, to suppose that husband and wife are acting in concert, and the liability incurred by one is accepted by the other'.[84]

Although judge Hutton adduced *Jolly* v. *Rees* to advance the claims of husbands as autonomous individuals, other county-court judges were conspicuous among the exponents of the social individual. Ironically, while equitable reasoning discouraged some judges from committing male labourers to prison for debts contracted with tradesmen of dubious propriety by their wives, equity was also invoked from the bench to sustain wives' right to act as their husbands' agents in the very credit transactions that rendered these men vulnerable to imprisonment. Expatiating upon the significance of *Debenham* v. *Mellon* in 1880, the *Solicitors' Journal* had observed that because a married woman's agency now derived not from her mere status as a wife but from her husband's willingness to endow her with his credit, 'it is impossible to say that an authority derived from the will of the husband can exist contrary to his will, unless the husband has so conducted himself as to make it inequitable for him to deny . . . her authority'.[85] Precisely this equitable caveat offered county-court judges repeated opportunities to deploy their discretionary powers against the grain of contractual individualism.

The rulings made in the Bradford county court by judge Daniel illustrate the instability of the legal framework established by the evolution of case law on married women and debt. In 1880, Daniel heralded *Debenham* v. *Mellon* as a new dawn in household credit relations. He warned his tradesman plaintiffs that whereas 'Hitherto it had been assumed that the wife, in her character of wife, would be entitled by law to pledge the credit of her husband for necessaries – food and clothing – for herself and children', thanks to Mellon's legal success in the appeal courts, 'It was now settled law . . . that a wife, in her character as a wife, had no authority whatever to pledge her husband's credit, even for necessaries.'[86] Three years later, however, the established verities of 'settled

---

[83] *The Warehousemen and Drapers' Trade Journal*, 14 March 1874, 124; 21 March 1874, 136–7.
[84] Ibid., 21 March 1874, 127.   [85] *Solicitors' Journal*, 4 December 1880, 89.
[86] Ibid., 1 January 1881, 172.

law' were less apparent to Daniel, when he attempted to resolve a suit for grocery and drapery goods purchased by a wife on her husband's credit. 'In cases in which a shopkeeper has sold goods to the wife, for which he seeks to make the husband responsible, the onus lies on him to establish the fact of agency', Daniel began his ruling confidently. But having rehearsed the central principle of *Debenham* v. *Mellon*, he promptly subjected this precedent to equitable analysis, and found it wanting. 'It would not be reasonable that a husband should be entitled by law to deprive his wife of her right to pledge his credit for necessaries suitable to her condition by attempting to force her acceptance of an insufficient allowance', he explained, before proceeding to order the debtor defendant in this suit to pay for the 'necessary' portions of the debt contracted on his behalf (but without his knowledge) by his wife.[87]

Daniel was only one among many county-court judges who recognised the continued salience of wives' characters as agents of their husbands even in the legal aftermath of *Jolly* v. *Rees*. In *Hamley* v. *Chetwynd*, heard in the Chester county court as *Debenham* v. *Mellon* wended its way through the appeal system, judge Horatio Lloyd grappled with the issues of agency raised by separation and divorce, newly salient features of county-court debt negotiations thanks to the Divorce Act of 1857 and the Matrimonial Causes Act of 1878. The plaintiff was one of many frustrated local tradesmen who had allowed Mrs William Chetwynd to purchase an expensive hat on her husband's credit. Judge Lloyd, justifying his ruling that William Chetwynd – described as 'an independent gentleman' – must pay his wife's 'necessary' debts, admitted that 'the law may be said to some extent to be in a doubtful state' but experienced 'very little difficulty or doubt' in ruling for the creditor plaintiff. Noting that the Chetwynds lived separately and that this separation had been precipitated by William Chetwynd's marital misconduct, Lloyd assured the court that the defendant's wife 'had committed no fault which disentitles her to share her husband's home, her natural and proper place, and it is by his act that she does not occupy that position, and through no fault of hers'. Because Mrs Chetwynd was 'an innocent person deprived of the advantages of home by the act of her husband', judge Lloyd reasoned, the law had never 'suggested a doubt as to the authority...of the wife to pledge her husband's credit for necessaries'. He admitted that 'At first sight it staggers me to see ladies giving three guineas for hats and getting a great number of them, but I suppose in the times in which we live this is often done, and therefore... I treat them as necessaries.' To be sure, Mrs Chetwynd's purchase of ten costly hats in nine months might seem excessive, but 'I cannot say, on looking over these bills, that there is anything in them which is not necessary to the person occupying the position of Mr Chetwynd's wife.'[88] Mrs Chetwynd's identity as a social individual – her inhabitation of 'the position of Mr Chetwynd's

---

[87] *CCC*, 1 November 1883, 199–200.   [88] Ibid., 2 August 1880, 586–7.

270   Petty debts and the modernisation of English law

wife' – conferred rights and agency upon her, despite her separation from him and notwithstanding his status as 'an independent gentleman'. Lacking the rights of an autonomous individual, she was, none the less, an effective and knowing consumer, acquiring ten hats in nine months (for which her husband was held liable) by virtue of her social status.

Much to the frustration of legislators and superior-court judges, the Married Women's Property Acts of 1882 and 1893 failed to convince many county-court judges to substitute autonomous individuals for the social individuals who appeared before them in the courtroom. When the government, preparing to introduce the Married Women's Property Bill of 1893, sounded judicial opinion on the local administration of debt disputes that involved questions of wives' agency, superior-court judges recited a litany of legal lapses and erroneous judgments by county-court officials, but also dissented from each other's interpretations of the letter of the law. 'I cannot help thinking that the law of necessaries has been misunderstood', judge Heywood opined, lamenting the prevalence of decisions in which 'the distinction has not been well borne in mind between the "necessaries" which may be supplied under the *prima facie* agency of the wife, and those which may be supplied under the true legal agency of the wife, viz., when he has turned her out of doors without provision, and causes of a like kind'. Husbands, in Heywood's interpretation, were autonomous individuals until and unless they failed to provide their families 'with the common necessaries of life', for '*then only*, a presumption of law arises in favour of the agency of the wife, but merely to supply herself and family with such food and clothing as are *absolutely* necessary for them'.[89] Judge Richard Harrington, commenting on Heywood's opinions, agreed that much 'confusion has arisen from the loose and inaccurate use of the word "necessaries"', but proceeded to urge the continued imperative even at common law to account for social distinctions in determining the extent of wives' agency. Noting that the superior-court judgments that served as precedents had 'in every case without exception...been concerned with persons either in a superior grade in society, or at least above that class which lives from hand to mouth', Harrington cautioned against 'laying down a fixed rule of presumption which is to bind equally in the case of a beggar or a millionaire'. The relative norms of social life – what he termed 'the ordinary usage of society' – rather than the absolute rights of the autonomous individual, guided Harrington's understanding of necessary purchases. 'Extravagance in amount, or unsuitability of the articles purchased rebuts the presumption of authority – so I think should the nature and length of credit obtained where it is inconsistent with one's common knowledge of the habits of the thrifty and well conducted of the class to which the defendant

[89] Judge Heywood, *The Law of Husband and Wife* [1892], in PRO, LCO 2/57, Married Women's Bill, Comments on (1892–93).

belongs', he concluded.[90] The practice of everyday life – common sense, common reason and common knowledge, but not invariably strict common law – persistently shaped legal interpretations of the contractual person in the long nineteenth century.

Even the passage of the Married Women's Property Act of 1893 failed to disrupt the hegemony of quotidian considerations in county-court practice. Adjudicating *Fletcher* v. *Williams* in the Marylebone county court in 1899, judge Stonor considered the precedents set by *Jolly* v. *Rees* and *Debenham* v. *Mellon* as well as the legal significance of the separate income enjoyed by the defendant's wife under the Married Women's Property Acts. 'After much consideration and...some doubt', he determined that the husband remained liable for over thirty-eight pounds owed for 'necessary' apparel purchased on credit by his wife. Although it emerged that 'there was an "understanding" between them, and a constant practice, that the wife should pay her own bills out of a small separate income', the judge declined to rule that the wife's separate property should be held liable for her debts. 'In conclusion, to take a common-sense view of this case, the defendant has clearly consented to his wife purchasing goods far beyond the means she possesses, with the understanding that he would... supply the deficiency...and it is surely only common justice that he should be held liable to the tradesman who has provided her with suitable necessaries, with his consent and on his credit', Stonor reasoned.[91] As tradesmen learned to their cost, the liability for debts secured in theory by wives' separate property often proved of little practical value when debt disputes entered the courts. W.H. Whitelock, registrar of the Birmingham county court, reiterated this complaint in 1914. Creditors who failed to establish the liability of husbands for their wives' debts, he concluded wearily, 'could, of course, sue the wife, but, inasmuch as by a ridicuous legal fiction any contract made by her is not personal, but on behalf of some non-existent entity known as her separate estate, he cannot utilise the Debtors Act to enforce his judgment'.[92]

Court records confirm these public protestations. From January 1893 to May 1896, officers of the Thame county court in Oxfordshire sought to levy executions upon the goods of 265 recalcitrant debtors. The eighty-one suits for which the clerk recorded that no goods could be recovered illustrate the ways in which wives' complex identities as social individuals exacerbated the already difficult task of attempting to enforce contracts by seizing debtors' goods. The suits of Joseph Stretton – 'No goods – On the Parish' – and George Jackman – 'no goods...a Pauper' – recall the impoverished conditions of plebeian households

---

[90] PRO, LCO 2/57, Richard Harrington to Mackenzie, 30 November 1892.

[91] *CCC*, 1 February 1899, 33–4.

[92] W.H. Whitelock, 'The industrial credit system and imprisonment for debt', *Economic Journal*, 24 (March 1914), 36.

272   Petty debts and the modernisation of English law

that had encouraged court of requests personnel to execute against debtors' bodies rather than their chattels. But the Thame execution book also illuminates the dilemmas created for county-court officials by the evolution of novel forms of credit and new conceptions of individual ownership. The case of Edwards Hade – 'No Goods whereon to levy – Everything on hire-purchase' – suggests the impediments posed to debt recovery by a new mechanism for credit purchasing already viewed with distaste by members of the county-court bench. The revision of married women's property rights only added further to the complexities of debt recovery. 'No Goods – Everything claimed by Wife', read the entry on Henry Gibson; 'No goods. Things belong to Wife' was the annotation on Thomas Blood's court record.[93]

The new anomalies introduced into county-court practice by later Victorian and Edwardian legal reforms derived from and helped to perpetuate the antinomies that marked the dominant legal fiction of the age, the autonomous individual. In political life, the demise of Old Corruption and the rise of democratic culture drew much of their ideological force from new formulations of manly character, from modern constructions of masculinity that claimed to privilege personal independence over social connections and class distinctions. The central contradiction of the manly individual's independence – his authority over and liability for dependent family members within the household – was habitually repressed in popular political discourse and parliamentary debate.[94] Petty debt litigation, however, ensured that this essential tension rose to the forefront of English legal culture. Legislators and superior-court judges laboured to liberate the autonomous individual from the trammels of social obligation, but the economic and cultural practices of daily life posed formidable obstacles to this emancipatory project. As keepers of the family purse, working-class wives served as natural agents of their labouring husbands in debt transactions and debt disputes, but as social individuals at once protected and disabled by coverture they rendered the notion of free contract intensely problematic. Even as reform-minded officials adduced the newly disciplinary practice of imprisonment for debt as an effective means of enforcing the male worker's contractual obligations, judicial practice constantly exposed the logical fallacies of this individualising mechanism by highlighting the independent labourer's necessary dependence upon his wife's agency in the market and the court. At the upper levels of society, where the insolvency legislation of 1861 and 1869 had now rendered imprisonment for debt a rare occurrence, the 'necessary' credit purchases made by married women charged with maintaining their families'

---

[93] Oxfordshire RO, CCT/3/A06/1, Thame County Court Execution and Commitment Book, 1892–1908, 19, 30, 1, 32, 38.

[94] See esp. Anna Clark, 'Gender, class and the nation: franchise reform in England, 1832–1928', in James Vernon, ed., *Re-Reading the Constitution: New Narratives in the Political History of England's Long Nineteenth Century* (Cambridge, 1996), 230–53.

From courts of conscience to county courts 273

class status also served to thwart the expression of autonomous individualism. William Chetwynd's liability, as an 'independent gentleman' for the purchase of ten essential hats by his fashionable wife signals the free contract's persistent immersion in the mutual obligations that sustained both the credit nexus and the social individual in English consumer markets.

Conclusion

Wives and workmen were not the only consumers whose disputed debts brought the contentious issues of personal liability home to county-court judges. As the consumer market expanded, children and adolescents were increasingly drawn into exchange relations.[95] Among the propertied classes, the proverbial youthful excesses of aristocratic culture were increasingly emulated – albeit within more modest limits – by the feckless sons of professionals and independent gentlemen. Although scholars of English consumer culture have long ignored the nineteenth-century male retail market, Christopher Breward has now recuperated these 'hidden consumers' for historical analysis. Focusing on 'the day-to-day activities' of consumers, Breward rejects 'The Great Masculine Renunciation' thesis posited by previous scholars – the argument that the nineteenth century saw a progressive shift away from fashion-conscious masculine consumer behaviour – and documents a rich range 'of subjective consumer positions that belies any single reading of Victorian and Edwardian masculinities as univalent or static in their visual or sartorial manifestations'.[96] County-court litigation provides additional evidence of this vibrant male consumer culture. For like wives under coverture, male youths of the upper classes who had not yet reached the age of twenty-one were 'infants' in the eyes of the law and avidly exploited their identity as social individuals to gain access to goods and credit in consumer markets.

As university education became more common among the propertied classes, college debts served to induct successive cohorts of genteel youths into consumer credit relations – and thereby ensnared them in consumer contract litigation. The correspondence of John Matthews, an Oxford solicitor, testifies to retailers' willingness to deploy credit to encourage young men at university to develop their consumer sensibilities to the full. In 1836, the executors of Loder & Gunner, an Oxford emporium popular with students, employed the solicitor to collect the shop's myriad outstanding accounts. Now dispersed widely throughout England and Wales, the shop's customers had retained scores of debts

[95] For the inclusion of children into consumer culture in the consumer revolution, see Neil McKendrick, John Brewer and J.H. Plumb, *The Birth of a Consumer Society: The Commercialization of Eighteenth-Century England* (London, 1982), 286–315.

[96] Christopher Breward, *The Hidden Consumer: Masculinities, Fashion and City Life 1860–1914* (Manchester, 1999), 10, 25, 27.

274   Petty debts and the modernisation of English law

from their undergraduate days. From 29 October 1829 to May 1831, Loder & Gunner customer and Oxford undergraduate Lord Glandine had amassed debts to the shop that took over six folio pages to record in the solicitor's books. Still unpaid in 1836, the debts provide a window onto elite male purchasing: they were contracted for 'Perfumery & brushes, China, Glass, and earthen ware, plated and cabinet goods ... Loder and Gunner being dealers in almost all sorts of small articles for men at College'. Aristocrats were hardly alone in considering such goods essential items of masculine consumption. When Matthews wrote to Thomas Clive, Esq., to solicit payment for debts contracted at Oxford by Clive's son, he described Loder & Gunner as 'hairdressers, & perfumers, stationer &c, ... [who] sold such articles as Gent[leme]n of the University cant well do with[ou]t, as you will I think be convinced if you sh[oul]d think proper to enquire; when perhaps you will feel more disposed than at present to discharge the acco[un]t'.[97]

The solicitor's letter to the elder Clive draws attention to a central point of conflict in undergraduate credit contracts, the liability of fathers for their minor sons' debts under the law of necessaries. Entering university before attaining his legal majority, an undergraduate student was entitled to purchase goods 'suitable and agreeable' to his father's 'station and condition in life' on his father's credit.[98] Defined in this elastic manner, necessary items of male expenditure stretched to encompass an extraordinary range of goods and services. In a much-cited eighteenth-century precedent, Lord Kenyon had ruled that livery purchased on credit for the servant of an infant army captain was 'equally necessary for the honour and credit of his station', but that cockades purchased on credit for his soldiers were, unlike the liveried servant, 'not absolutely necessary for his existence'.[99] The law of necessaries placed Oxbridge tradesmen on the horns of a dilemma. Prohibited from insisting on cash sales both by the extended credit cycles demanded by elite consumers and by their desire to entrammel students in debt relations that would continue into adulthood, retailers were forced at once by custom and calculation to contract with social persons who lacked legal autonomy as individuals.

Negotiation and compromise on both sides prevented many of these consumer debts from entering the legal system, but suits that reached the county courts provided judges with yet another platform from which to explore the limits of contractual obligation. In a case heard in the Cambridge county court in 1883, the judge expatiated at great length upon the difficulty of distinguishing necessary from luxurious college expenditure. The defendant's 'infant' son,

---

[97] Bodleian, Eng.MS.lett. c.13, Letterbook of John Matthews, Oxford solicitor, Matthews to agents, 24 June 1836, fol. 380; Matthews to Thomas Clive, Esq., 27 June 1836, fol. 382. The evils of the undergraduate credit nexus are detailed in Anon. [An Oxford B.A.], *Tradesmen and Undergraduates: Or, the Present System of Debt and Credit at Oxford Unveiled* (London, 1844).

[98] Peake, *Compendium of the Law of Evidence*, 278.   [99] Ibid.

From courts of conscience to county courts 275

aptly named Young, had contracted a debt of two pounds seven shillings for sherry, brandy and maraschino consumed at a wine party in his rooms. The judge 'was decidedly of opinion...that the maraschino and brandy were not necessary', but he 'had more hestitation as to the wine, as the quantity was moderate'. Only after inquiring into the student's family circumstances, and learning that he was the eldest of the ten children of a clergyman who claimed (for reasons of economy) to abstain from beer, wine and spirits at his own table, did the judge rule the sherry a 'luxury' for which the plaintiff could not enforce a contract made by a minor on his father's presumed credit.[100]

Conscious of the fine distinctions that worked to maintain status differentials in Victorian society and recognising conspicuous consumption as a perquisite of masculine self-fashioning, judges and juries struggled to assign appropriate levels of expenditure to men whose station in life was determined not by their identities as individuals but by their dependent social status within the family unit. The protracted case of *Ryder* v. *Wombell*, initially heard in a county court in 1864 and subsequently appealed through successive higher courts, demonstrates the wide scope for 'necessary' purchases created by contemporary understandings of class and rank. The younger son of the deceased Sir George Wombell, the debtor defendant of this suit 'moved in the highest society' as an intimate of the Marquis of Hastings and the racing set. Wombell – who lacked a legal guardian – enjoyed an annual income of £500, but was due to inherit a sum of £200,000 upon coming of age. With these substantial resources in expectation, Wombell enjoyed easy access to consumer credit. In 1864, at the age of nineteen, he obtained a pair of crystal, ruby and diamond sleeve-links, a silver gilt antique chased goblet, a bottle of smelling-salts, a pair of coral earrings and gold studs on credit from the Bond Street jeweller Ryder. Declining to pay his bill when it was presented, Wombell was taken to court by his creditor and found liable for his debts, upon which he invoked his infancy, claiming that as the bulk of his purchases were for luxury items, he could not as a legal minor be held liable for payment.[101]

The arguments adduced by the lawyers and judges who grappled with the extended series of suits that ensued from this decision illustrate the often contradictory ways in which age, class and gender expectations shaped Victorian understandings of contractual obligation. Instructed by the judge that they must take the defendant's position in life into account in determining his liability, an initial jury concluded that Wombell's purchases – with the exception of the smelling-bottle and the coral earrings, which were items of feminine consumption – did indeed constitute necessary purchases for a young man of his rank,

---

[100] *CCC*, 1 March 1883, 53.
[101] All material on this suit is taken from Anon., *Reports of County Court Cases and Appeals Decided by All the Superior Courts...* (London, 1868–69), 82–6, 277–8, 311–16.

for which as an infant who lacked a guardian he should be held personally liable. Wombell's barrister refused to accept this logic, arguing that goods such as 'racehorses and diamond shirtbuttons' were inherently luxurious objects of expenditure regardless of the consumer's social status. The suit continued, on appeal, to wend its way through the court system. New evidence on Wombell's social identity further complicated the determination of his ability to enter into consumer credit contracts, when it emerged that he had, at the age of twenty, taken a wife and fathered a son. A series of interchanges between the presiding Chief Justice, Cockburn, and Wombell's QC, Hawkins, drew repeated attention to the instability of contemporary understandings of the autonomous individual. Wombell's marriage and fatherhood – clear indications that he had assumed the social status of mature manhood – potentially weakened his claims to be treated as an infant incapable of entering into a binding credit contract for luxuries. '"You do not think a wife a necessary?"', the Chief Justice queried Wombell's counsel incredulously, raising the prospect that Wombell should be held liable for his purchases of necessary feminine goods, such as a bottle of smelling-salts (presumably obtained on behalf of his wife). Hawkins swiftly rebutted that a wife '"was not [necessary], for a youth of twenty, and that if she were, a baby was not"'. The Chief Justice, not yet fully satisfied, elaborated further upon the troubling status of the coral earrings, which hung suspended in his legal reasoning between the Scylla of luxurious consumption and the Charybdis of necessary expenditure. The earrings, he reasoned, might be construed as luxuries if Wombell had purchased them for another woman during his engagement to his wife, but should be ruled necessaries if purchased for his prospective spouse. Having considered and discarded these complex permutations of Wombell's personal identity, Cockburn concluded by instructing the jury to find on behalf of the debtor defendant, which – no doubt with evident relief – they promptly did.

Theorists of contractual exchange habitually conceptualise modern commodities as inanimate goods that circulate in the market in response to the volition and desires of autonomous individuals,[102] but consideration of the petty debts disputed in English small-claims courts suggests that the commodities that circulated in historical markets obeyed a different logic. Putatively independent and dependent purchasers alike entered credit relations not as autonomous individuals who exercised free choice by entering into free contracts but rather as social individuals who negotiated among their shifting consumer identities to obtain both necessary and luxury goods. Nor did the commodities whose purchase provoked these disputes figure in the courtroom merely as inert material objects. Rather, like the gifts exchanged in pre-modern cultures, like the

---

[102] See the perceptive discussion (and critique) of this model in Arjun Appadurai, 'Introduction: commodities and the politics of value', in idem, ed., *The Social Life of Things: Commodities in Cultural Perspective* (Cambridge, 1986), esp. 4.

problematic presents that animated relations between characters in English novels and like the perpetual traffic in foodstuffs detailed in Georgian diaries and memoirs, these commodities participated in the unstable meanings, strategies, structures and practices of social life. The hats, the wine, the textiles, the earrings and even the quotidian grocery goods purchased by social individuals on credit refused to inhabit fixed and stable positions in the market and the courts. Under the law of necessaries, their identities fluctuated no less than those of the economic agents who sought to acquire them – for themselves or for other selves – through the credit nexus. Necessaries in one context and luxuries in the next, these goods assumed social meanings that reflected the station in life of their purchasers rather than their use value or their exchange value alone. Their history lies not in the triumphal narrative of the rise of the possessive individual but rather in the persistently social life of modern English contract.

7   Market moralities: tradesmen, credit and the courts in Victorian and Edwardian England

For tradesmen who served the burgeoning consumer population, the establishment of a national reticulation of county courts in 1847 had promised a new era of commercial prosperity. Presided over by qualified barristers and governed by national statutes, the new small-claims tribunals had appeared admirably suited not only to easing the recovery of consumer debts but also to effecting a broader transition in social and economic relations from status to contract. The timing of the new courts' foundation was moreover – if only in retrospect – propitious. In real terms, average per capita income in Britain rose only modestly in the first half of the nineteenth century, but the decades from 1851 to 1901 were to see average personal income increase by 75 per cent.[1] Plebeian and propertied purchasers had engaged in vigorous market activity since at least the early modern period, but the Victorian era saw increased standards of living combine with a new and dazzling range of goods, sales mechanisms and retail venues to extend the horizons of consumption – and of consumer debt – in novel directions.

So striking was this perceived development of consumer activity that both contemporary observers and subsequent historians hailed the later nineteenth century as an era of retail revolution. In this interpretation, the 1850s marked a decisive turning point in English consumer culture, effecting a sharp break with established conventions and inaugurating a period of dramatic modernisation in English markets. The appearance of new retail institutions – most notably, co-operatives, multiples and the department store – provided an institutional foundation for this line of argument, suggesting that the personal relations fostered by traditional shops and family firms fell into desuetude from mid-century as large-scale enterprises wedded to high-volume turnover, fixed prices, spectacular displays and aggressive advertising campaigns were in the ascendant.[2]

---

[1] John Benson, *The Rise of Consumer Society in Britain, 1880–1980* (London, 1994), 12–13.

[2] Key examples of this approach include Rachel Bowlby, *Just Looking: Consumer Culture in Dreiser, Gissing and Zola* (London, 1985); William Hamish Fraser, *The Coming of the Mass Market, 1850–1914* (London, 1981); James B. Jefferys, *Retail Trading in Britain: 1850–1950* (Cambridge, 1954); Bill Lancaster, *The Department Store: A Social History* (Leicester, 1995); Lori Anne Loeb, *Consuming Angels: Advertising and Victorian Women* (New York, 1994); Erika Diane Rappaport, *Shopping for Pleasure: Women in the Making of London's West End* (Princeton, 2000).

278

Market moralities 279

Cash sales figure centrally in this model of consumer modernisation. As Erika Rappaport asserts, department stores 'institutionalized cash transactions, introducing a new relationship between buyer and seller, to extricate themselves from older trading practices'.[3] Thus transformed by new retail outlets and novel commercial practices, consumer relations were primed for the advent of the mass market, in which differentials of status were to dissolve in the face of anonymous mechanisms of exchange.

Recent research on early modern consumer markets has cast many of the material bases of this revolutionary model into doubt. Fixed prices, branded products, ready-made garments, seductive window displays and cash sales had all entered the consumer market by the eighteenth century, where they existed alongside (and often complemented) more conventional retail practices.[4] The perception of sweeping change wrought by innovative retail institutions and novel sales strategies now appears to reflect shifts in representational regimes more accurately than it signals a fundamental change in material practice. 'The existence of these innovations should not be confused with their rate of diffusion or overall significance', Michael Winstanley wisely cautions.[5] Geoffrey Crossick and Serge Jaumain distinguish carefully between representations of the department store as an icon of consumer modernity, on the one hand, and the persistence of traditional retail practices in the market, on the other.[6] Trade statistics overwhelmingly bear out this distinction between retail iconography and quotidian experience. In 1915, independent shops were the site of 82 per cent of all retail trade transacted from a fixed address. Co-operatives and chain stores each accounted for a further 8 per cent of fixed-shop retail purchasing, while department store sales represented a mere 2 per cent of such trade.[7]

These revisions to our understanding of retail practice provide an institutional matrix within which the evolving history of personal debt and credit relations

---

[3] Rappaport, *Shopping for Pleasure*, 49–50. See, similarly, Lancaster, *Department Store*, 9.
[4] See esp. Nancy Cox, *The Complete Tradesman: A Study of Retailing, 1550–1820* (Aldershot, 2000); Christina Fowler, 'Changes in provincial retailing practice during the eighteenth century, with particular reference to central-southern England', *Business History*, 40, 4 (October 1998), 37–54; Beverly Lemire, *Dress, Culture and Commerce: The English Clothing Trade before the Factory, 1660–1800* (Basingstoke, 1997); Miles Ogborn, *Spaces of Modernity: London's Geographies 1680–1780* (New York, 1998), esp. chap. 4; John Styles, 'Product innovation in early modern London', *P&P*, 168 (August 2000), 124–69; Claire Walsh, 'The newness of the department store: a view from the eighteenth century', in Geoffrey Crossick and Serge Jaumain, eds., *Cathedrals of Consumption: The European Department Store 1850–1939* (Aldershot, 1999), 46–71; Claire Walsh, 'Shopping in early modern London *c*. 1660–1800' (Ph.D. thesis, European University Institute, 2001). For a broader perspective on these developments, see Margot Finn, 'Sex and the city: metropolitan modernities in English history', *VS*, 44, 1 (Autumn 2001), 25–32.
[5] Michael J. Winstanley, *The Shopkeeper's World, 1830–1914* (Manchester, 1983), 217.
[6] Geoffrey Crossick and Serge Jaumain, 'The world of the department store: distribution, culture and social change', in Crossick and Jaumain, eds., *Cathedrals of Consumption*, 29.
[7] Benson, *Rise of Consumer Society*, 62.

280   Petty debts and the modernisation of English law

must be situated. Conceptions of modernity and active efforts to modernise exchange were vital to contemporary experiences and interpretations of consumption in the long nineteenth century. But the seductive narratives of retail revolution spun by advertising agents, department store magnates and the new trade publications that proliferated in the later nineteenth century must be treated with substantial caution. Obscuring the long genealogy of consumer modernisation, these highly partisan accounts also ignore the extent to which modernity, in its Victorian and Edwardian inflections, was self-consciously assimilated with tradition. As Bernhard Rieger and Martin Daunton have argued, 'Since most current theoretical models emphasize that experiences of discontinuity defined the "modern", a central aspect of contemporary British concepts of modernity has escaped historians' attention: that on many occasions, Britons understood modernity in terms of continuity and *not* exclusively in terms of fundamental rupture.'[8] Credit relations between consumers and retailers (and between retail traders and their wholesalers) confirm that contemporaries' encounters with modernity were partial and highly selective. In flocking to the new county courts to enforce their debtors' contracts, joining trade protection societies that offered to provide systematic credit evaluations of their customers and loudly proclaiming their allegiance to the cash nexus, Victorian and Edwardian tradesmen remained hostages to traditions of consumer activity rooted in credit, character and connection. Their relations with consumers, although powerfully shaped by modern conceptions of contract, continued to be dominated by considerations of status and governed, through personal credit obligations, by social and cultural forms of capital.

Conceptions of credit

Although neither classical nor Marxian economic theory provides a satisfying theoretical framework for historical understanding of the consumer market, contemporary commentary by retailers themselves offers a rich fund of material for the analysis of debt relations. Published in 1819, *The London Tradesman: A Familiar Treatise on the Rationale of Trade and Commerce* is characteristic of one strand of this literature, dismissing as 'jejune' abstract conceptualisations of trade that neglected to account for credit. 'Adam Smith should be read coolly, and with large allowances for his want of *practical* knowledge', the 'Several Tradesmen' who authored this treatise urged. Attributing the success of the *Wealth of Nations* to the mere 'rhetorical merits' of the text and insisting that its audience lay with 'a few fine gentlemen' rather than 'Traders' themselves, they

---

[8] Bernhard Rieger and Martin Daunton, 'Introduction', in Martin Daunton and Bernhard Rieger, eds., *Meanings of Modernity: Britain from the Late Victorian Era to World War II* (Oxford, 2001), 12.

Market moralities 281

expressed 'considerable disgust at the ineptitude of some of his elucidations' and heaped particular scorn on Smith's neglect of retail credit. If the reader asked '"what Adam Smith says upon the subject?"' of credit, the authors cautioned, 'we can give him the usual answer, "nothing at all to the purpose".' 'He does not mention the *word*' credit, they expostulated, neither '*credit*, whereby goods may be obtained, nor *connection*, whereby goods are disposed of again, and profits are made, are reckoned by him in any way whatever'.[9]

Later nineteenth-century commentators echoed and amplified the arguments of the *London Tradesman*, embedding analyses of credit within broader debates on the nature and extent of modernity in English markets. In this school of interpretation, credit, connection and character featured as a trinity of values and practices that lent structure and meaning to modern commodity exchange. 'We may ... say that as soon as we pass from the simplest stage of society in which the individual provides for his own wants ... credit comes to the front', Palgrave's *Dictionary of Political Economy* (1891–94) explained, for 'credit is evidently essential to the full development of competition, and the growth of credit is historically one of the most marked characteristics of the progress of society from status to contract'. Economic resources could account for only a portion of the purchasing activities analysed in the *Dictionary*, because credit dealings ensured that retail exchange was also shaped fundamentally by perceptions of social worth. 'All sound credit should rest on one of two bases, namely property or character', the *Dictionary* pronounced, eschewing purely economic determinations of purchasing power.[10] Many trade publications rehearsed these arguments. In an article advising neophyte retailers on 'Going into Business' in 1908, *The Draper* discounted the significance of purely economic calculations of profit and loss and emphasised the persistence of character and connection in credit relations. 'It is a mistake ... to open trade in a country town where one is quite unknown', the newspaper warned. 'While values count, personalities count much more. Those keen qualities of mind which ... can instantly weigh up values, and take advantage of every turn of the market, are not of such importance in the country as a knowledge of customers, their idiosyncrasies, wants, opinions on politics, and church matters.'[11] Underscoring the disparities

---

[9] Anon., *The London Tradesman: A Familiar Treatise on the Rationale of Trade and Commerce, As Carried On in the Metropolis of the British Empire* (London, 1819), 27, 364–7. For historians' tendency to over-rate the contemporary salience of Smith's theories, see Julian Hoppit, 'Attitudes to credit in Britain, 1680–1790', *HJ*, 33, 2 (June 1990), 305–6. For the efforts of evangelical religious thinkers and businessmen to address the spiritual (as opposed to pragmatic) inadequacies of classical economic theory, see E.J. Garnett, 'Aspects of the relationship between Protestant ethics and economic activity in mid-Victorian England' (D.Phil. thesis, University of Oxford, 1987).

[10] R.H. Inglis Palgrave, ed., *Dictionary of Political Economy*, 3 vols. (London, 1891–94), I: 452, 505.

[11] *The Draper*, 8 August 1908, 764.

282   Petty debts and the modernisation of English law

between the anonymous cash sales posited by economic theorists and the highly personal interactions occasioned by the ubiquitous credit transactions of actual consumer markets, this analysis privileged the role played in exchange by the accumulation and expenditure of social and cultural capital.

A second school of contemporary commentary, however, disputed the necessary linkage between credit and commercial progress. Like many subsequent historians, exponents of this analysis sought to portray credit as an atavistic economic mechanism, arguing that the advent of the co-op, multiple and department store had inaugurated a new, thoroughly modern era of cash sales in retail markets. In 1886, the weekly *Grocer* proclaimed ' "the cash grocer" ... the grocer of the future' and announced triumphantly that 'The long credit system has had its day.' In this view, extended trade credit had been well suited to 'the old times', but had become 'an anachronism' by the later nineteenth century. 'The cash grocer, assuredly, is quite a modern product', the newspaper concluded.[12] Lady Jeune, probing 'The ethics of shopping' in the *Fortnightly Review* a decade later, likewise celebrated the passing of customary retail credit and the advent of the modern cash economy. A quarter-century before, she claimed, 'We bought our goods at ... various shops, and dutifully followed in the steps of our forefathers, paying for the things we had at the end of the year, for no well-thought of firm ever demanded or expected more than a yearly payment of their debts.' The development of modern retail practices, Jeune insisted, had put paid to these conventions: department 'Stores, with their improved facilities for purchasing and concentration of goods, have made credit impossible', she asserted decisively.[13]

Attention to trade records helps to put these competing world views into perspective. For if credit was 'impossible' in prescriptive representations of the modern retail market, it was remarkably prevalent in English consumer transactions at all social levels throughout the long nineteenth century. In contrast to much hortatory literature, descriptive data of economic transactions are – like contemporary novels, diaries and memoirs – replete with references to credit and saturated with considerations of character and connection. Later Victorian retail co-ops provide a case in point. For G.J. Holyoake, pioneer and apologist of the co-operative movement, credit sales appeared to pose an obstacle to the evolution of individual autonomy, and the co-ops' commitment to cash transactions thus represented an essential component of economic modernity. Co-operative principles, Holyoake told the nineteenth annual Co-operative Congress in 1887, formed the basis of a forward-looking cash 'economy which has given our working-class members a new sense of independence – not yet possessed by the middle and upper classes – the independence which pays its

---

[12] *The Grocer*, 20 November 1886, 818.
[13] Lady Jeune, 'The ethics of shopping', *Fortnightly Review*, 307, n.s. (1 January 1895), 123, 126.

Market moralities 283

own way; for he who is in debt is owned by others'.[14] Trade statistics generated by co-operative societies themselves, however, demonstrate the practical limits they confronted in attempting to generate autonomous economic relations through cash sales. For despite their much-vaunted insistence that all transactions occur on a ready-money basis, retail co-ops were routinely forced to extend credit to remain competitive in working-class consumer markets. A report in 1886 revealed that over half of all English co-operatives extended credit to their customers. Although most societies suffered losses from these credit dealings, their representatives argued that market forces precluded strict adherence to cash principles. The receipt of fortnightly or monthly wage payments, members' sickness or temporary unemployment and the circumstance that credit was customary (and thus mandatory) in their locality were prominent among their justifications for this departure from the co-ops' first principles. Pressures such as these, indeed, promoted an expansion of co-operative credit over time. By 1901, almost three-quarters of all co-operative retailers reported granting credit to their members.[15]

Positioned at the other extreme on the moral spectrum of plebeian consumer purchasing was the credit drapery system. Itinerant pedlars who sold textile goods on credit had become an established feature of English consumer culture by the later seventeenth century. Providing the poor with a wide variety of cloth and haberdashery goods, the packmen, hawkers and pedlars who brought the early modern market to the consumer's doorstep had early acquired an unsavoury reputation. A tract published in 1708 epitomised the dominant stereotypes of the trade, associating these tallymen or 'Scotch' drapers with pawnbrokers, pimps and prostitutes and drawing attention to itinerant credit drapers' unseemly willingness to enforce their extortionate contracts with plebeian consumers through the mechanisms of imprisonment for debt.[16] Despite the increasing salience of fixed shops in the retail sector over time, the modern period saw a significant expansion of peddling in general (and credit drapery in particular). Between 1831 and 1911, the number of itinerant traders reported in the Census rose from 9,459 to 69,347, figures that represented an increase in the ratio of pedlars to population from 1:1,470 to 1:520. Troped as foreign

[14] George Jacob Holyoake, *Inaugural Address Delivered at the Nineteenth Annual Co-operative Congress Held at Carlisle* (Manchester, [1887]), 7.

[15] J.C. Gray, *The System of Credit as Practiced by Co-operative Societies* (Manchester, n.d.), 5, 12, 20–1, 25; Martin Purvis, 'Co-operative retailing in Britain', in John Benson and Gareth Shaw, eds., *The Evolution of Retail Systems, c. 1800–1914* (Leicester, 1992), 125.

[16] Anon., *The Misery of Iniquity Luckily Discover'd. Or, a Horrible Plot and Wicked Contrivance against Poor Honest People of This Nation. In a Comical Dialogue between a Pawnbroker, a Tallyman, a Bum-Bailiff, a Town-Miss, a Keeping-Fool, a Vintner's Drawer, and a Sham-Devil . . .* (London, 1708), esp. 7–8. Margaret Spufford details the early modern development of credit drapery in *The Great Reclothing of Rural England: Petty Chapmen and Their Wares in the Seventeenth Century* (London, 1984).

interlopers whose seductive wiles ensnared the wives of honest English labourers with debts for unnecessary items of cheap finery, Victorian and Edwardian credit drapers traded with hundreds of thousands of working-class consumers on a weekly or monthly basis.[17] Whereas proponents of co-operative retailing lauded the modernity of cash dealings, Scotch drapers were vociferous exponents – and active practitioners – of credit as a vital instrument of modern consumer culture.[18] In their public pronouncements, credit drapers touted their trade as a democratising influence on market relations: a Lancaster tallyman speaking to the Northern Central Credit Drapers Association in 1894 compared his trade's extension of credit facilities to the working-class consumer with John Bright's successful campaign to expand the parliamentary franchise from men of property to working men.[19]

Market competition also ensured that middle- and upper-class consumers enjoyed continued access to retail credit in the later Victorian and Edwardian years, notwithstanding the increasingly shrill tone of prescriptive attacks upon the 'traditional' credit system. Where Lady Jeune saw cash supplanting credit in the modern drapery establishments of the 1890s, Fred Burgess's five-volume compendium, *The Practical Retail Draper*, instead discerned the development of multifarious hybrid forms of transaction, as tradesmen adapted both cash and credit terms to meet the new demands of the consumer public. Acknowledging that 'it is very much easier to formulate plans of trading on either one or other of the two well-defined lines – cash and credit', Burgess concluded that 'the experience of most retail shopkeepers, and certainly of drapers, is that this is not possible'. Rather than demolishing credit, the advent of ready-money drapery shops had prompted traditional retailers to offer a range of cash and credit transactions to their customers. 'Thus it was that the dual trading was brought into existence and has to a large extent been retained as a matter of convenience in many shops', Burgess explained. 'The difference between cash and credit trading . . . is of such variable quality and so differently conducted that it is hard to understand the standard principles and their application as exemplified in any one group of shops.'[20] Viewed from this vantage point, credit and cash featured not as polar opposites, one mired in the mutualistic conventions of the past and the other emblematic of the individualistic future, but rather as unstable positions on the kaleidoscopic spectrum of exchange mechanisms available to the modern English consumer.

---

[17] Margot Finn, 'Scotch drapers and the politics of modernity: gender, class and national identity in the Victorian tally trade', in Martin Daunton and Matthew Hilton, eds., *The Politics of Consumption: Material Culture and Citizenship in Europe and America* (Oxford, 2001), 90, 92–3.

[18] See esp. G.R. Rubin, 'From packmen, tallymen and "Perambulating Scotchmen" to Credit Drapers Associations, c. 1840–1914', *Business History*, 28, 2 (April 1986), 206–25.

[19] *CDG*, 21 April 1894, 117.

[20] Frederick W. Burgess, *The Practical Retail Draper: A Complete Guide for the Drapery and Allied Trades*, 5 vols. (London, n.d.), I: 201–2.

Market moralities 285

Trade bills and billheads that document middle- and upper-class purchases offer further evidence of the persistent slippage that obtained between cash and credit sales in this period. At one level, printed trade materials exhibit substantial change over time. Trade-cards, bills and advertisements that proclaim retailers' allegiance to 'ready money', 'cash only' and 'strictly for cash' conditions of sale are infrequent early in the nineteenth century, but become commonplace in the Victorian and Edwardian years. Accepted at face value, this shift from credit to ready money confirms the association between cash and consumer modernity upheld by contemporary proponents of the department store – and by subsequent historians.[21] But a closer examination of trade records reveals the inadequacies of this interpretation. Comparison between the conditions of sale printed at the top of the billheads and the handwritten accounts and correspondence entered by tradesmen beneath these prescriptive formulae brings the dual character of cash and credit transactions into sharp relief. At mid-century Rodgers & Co., retail shirt-makers, announced sternly that 'CASH PAYMENTS ARE STRICTLY ADHERED TO', but a bill for purchases made by H.F. Yeatman, Esquire in 1849 and 1850 is dated 1852. Nor did I.H. Gosling, a drapery establishment in Richmond, require Benjamin Haydon's former patron, the Dowager Duchess of Sutherland, to pay cash for goods, despite its claim to be a 'Ready Money' shop. Purchasing dresses, ribbons and trimmings to a value of nearly fifty pounds in July, August and September 1857, the dowager duchess paid for the goods only in October. Alfred Webb Miles, a tailor at Hanover Square, claimed to sell 'ENTIRELY FOR CASH', but a bill sent to Lady Lambert, dated 24 December 1870, was paid only in July 1871, after a conventional credit interval of six months had elapsed. Like retail co-ops that served the working-class consumer, the new department stores vaunted ready-money principles but rapidly succumbed to credit trading. Mrs Buller's bill for goods purchased in April 1879 from Swan & Edgar's department store – 'Terms, Cash on or before delivery' – was marked paid three months later in July.[22]

So entrenched was the credit system among middle- and upper-class consumers that tradesmen were compelled to offer their customers 'cash' discounts for bills paid with any degree of promptitude after receipt of the goods. In the 1880s Castell & Son, Oxford clerical outfitters, offered discounts of 10% on accounts paid within a week of purchase, 5% for bills paid within four months

---

[21] Fowler, 'Changes in provincial retailing practice', 48, argues that the advent of such assertions on billheads reflects a shift from credit to cash sales precipitated by the reintroduction of smaller coinage in the 1790s, but the evidence below suggests that this transition was largely semantic.

[22] Bodleian, John Johnson Collection, Bill Headings 28 (116); Women's Clothes and Millinery 1; Bill Headings 28 (108); Bill Headings 8 (82). For an excellent introduction to this rich collection of sources, see [Julie Anne Lambert], *A Nation of Shopkeepers: Trade Ephemera from 1654 to the 1860s in the John Johnson Collection* (Banbury, 2001). Rappaport, *Shopping for Pleasure*, 70, notes that Whitely's department store also extended credit to some customers.

286   Petty debts and the modernisation of English law

and 2½% cash discount for payments rendered within six months. Interest-free credit of six to twelve months' duration was the norm for affluent consumers, and longer credit cycles were hardly exceptional. A bill sent in 1837 to the Reverend Mr Jeffrey by Creeke & Ratlett, Cambridge tailors, noted that the shop charged interest only on accounts that remained unpaid fifteen or more months after the date of purchase.[23] Like diaries kept by consumers, the letterbooks of tradesmen and their lawyers testify to the capacious credit enjoyed by middle- and upper-class customers who traded 'on account' – paying a portion of their bill at intervals, but always leaving a balance unpaid as a token of their intention to continue to patronise the shop. When the solicitor John Matthews attempted to collect unpaid debts for Loder & Gunner – hairdressers, perfumers and china dealers to Oxford's undergraduate population – in 1836, many proved, as did the unpaid account of the Reverend Penfold, to extend back more than a decade.[24]

Debt relations such as these were clearly calculated to encourage young men at university to enter the world of masculine consumption through credit mechanisms that would continue to link them to Oxbridge tradesmen across decades – and indeed generations. In her memoir of late Victorian metropolitan culture, Molly Hughes described her lawyer husband's mode of replenishing his stock of apparel as 'simplicity itself'. 'Ever since his Cambridge days Mr Neal of Trumpington Street, had supplied him with clothes', Hughes recalled. Her husband typically paid his old Cambridge tailor five pounds per annum on account, leaving a balance of twenty pounds or so remaining. When Molly Hughes, who confessed to having 'a horror of the smallest debt', suggested that he liquidate this obligation by paying the balance of the account, her husband was appalled. ' "What a blow that would be to Neal! He would think that I was dissatisfied and finished with him" ', Arthur Hughes chastised his wife. 'So I hoped it would never be paid, for apparently nothing but the death of a customer would excuse such an act of discourtesy . . . and now his sons clothe my son Arthur in the same delightful way.'[25] The American journalist R.D. Blumfeld so disconcerted his London tailor in 1900 by telephoning to request a bill for the goods he had purchased on credit over the preceding year that the unhappy tradesman 'came down to Fleet Street . . . and begged me to tell him what was wrong, and . . . hoped I was not leaving him'. 'I could not satisfy him that all I wanted was my bill', a bemused Blumfeld recorded in his diary. 'He went away quite unhappy with my idiosyncrasy.'[26]

---

[23] Bodleian, John Johnson Collection, Oxford Trades 7, and Bill Headings 28 (110).

[24] Bodleian, Eng. MS.lett.c.13, Letterbook of John Matthews, 1835–36, fol. 390, Matthews to Rev. Penfold, 13 July 1836. See, similarly, the account book of Charles Noel, Viscount Campeau, who paid two bills for goods obtained in 1857 in January 1859 and in January 1860 settled one bill dating from 1856 and another from 1857. Bodleian, Eng.misc.f.865, Account Book of Charles Noel, 1858–60, 5 January 1859; 10 and 24 January 1860.

[25] Molly Hughes, *A London Family, 1870–1900* (Oxford, 1991), 541–2.

[26] Ralph David Blumfeld, *R.D.B.'s Diary: 1887–1914* (London, 1930), 85.

Market moralities 287

The language employed by tradesmen in correspondence with their customers indicates the degree to which the operation of this extended credit economy undercut strictly contractual conceptions of exchange. Letters requesting payment of unpaid bills were typically apologetic and truckling in tone. Larded with elaborate justifications of tradesmen's requests for payment, they touched only sparingly and warily upon retailers' contractual right to receive cash for goods sold to consumers. The tone of a bill sent by the 'Cash' tailors H.J. & D. Nichol to the Marquis of Bute in August 1846 for a range of goods purchased since 1844 is characteristic, 'respectfully requesting' payment, 'which they presume must have escaped his Lordship's memory'.[27] The correspondence of Lord Brougham, the chief parliamentary champion of legal reforms designed to ease and speed the recovery of trade debts, is especially (and ironically) illuminating in this regard. In May 1837, Samuel Drummer attributed his request for payment of a bill delivered in December to 'the depressed state of business' rather than to Brougham's legal liability for the account. 'Indeed I most earnestly intreat [sic] this favo[u]r in making the above solicitation [and] trust your Lordship will not consider me too urgent in my application', Drummer concluded worriedly. John Beaumont, writing to Brougham at the end of August 1832, had likewise been loath to press his claims.

I beg your Lordship will excuse my writing to your Lordship in the Country but your Lordship has been so much engaged all the year that I have never been able to see your Lordship, & as the Hire of her Ladyships [sic] Landau was due on the 11th Jan[uar]y last, perhaps your Lordship would be so good as to meet us – the amount, [is] Eighty five Guineas, & I beg to observe, we only had Eighty Five Pounds, last year & my agreement was for Eighty five Guineas & as . . . it is as good a Carriage as we ever built I hope your Lordship will be so kind as to remit us that sum.[28]

Couched in the language of mutual obligation, Brougham's correspondence with his tradesmen speaks forcefully to the halting and fractured triumph of commodity relations in modern England.

Although peers could expect to receive especially favourable credit terms from tradesmen eager to associate their shops with an aristocratic clientele, less exalted middle-class customers were also treated with surprising delicacy by all but the most importunate retail creditors. Notwithstanding his notorious insolvency, Benjamin Haydon was dunned with much hesitation by Andrew Henderson, who had supplied the Haydon family with greengrocery items such as mushrooms, spinach and lettuce to a value of over forty-six pounds between June 1825 and March 1826. In July 1826, Henderson wrote apologetically to request payment:

[27] Bodleian, John Johnson Collection, Bill Headings 28 (110). The bill was eventually paid in 1847.
[28] UCL Archives, Henry Brougham Collection, 9,569, Samuel Drummer to Brougham, 6 May 1837, and 42,692, John Beaumont to Brougham, 31 August 1832.

288   Petty debts and the modernisation of English law

I beg to inform you I have taken the liberty to send your account which I trust you will find correct and which, should it be convenient I shall be truly obliged to you to settle ... [a] severe loss I have lately sustained from the hailstorm obliges me to make this earnest request, the great expense I am at to repair, the damages having had all my glass broken, makes me at present greatly distressed for money and will make me doubly thankful could you discharge the account.[29]

The text of an Edwardian manual for grocers suggests that this reluctance to express legal claims for payment in contractual terms endured into the twentieth century. Sample letters for collecting overdue accounts printed in this text rehearse the hesitant pleas of Victorian tradesmen. 'You will see that it is very much overdue and necessitates our keeping our books open for a period when everything should have been settled and closed, moreover our low prices do not admit of long credit', one letter ventured in justifying its demands. Only in the last instance, the author suggested, should the language of contract be invoked: 'If possible, we wish to avoid the unpleasant publicity of the County Court, at the same time we cannot forego our rights', the fifth and most stringent sample letter finally asserted.[30]

Bound to extended credit cycles by both custom and competition, tradesmen who served much of the consumer market remained wedded to personalised, highly dependent interactions with their customers throughout the nineteenth century. Lacking formal mechanisms for assessing purchasers' capital resources, they continued to rely upon evaluations of personal character as a proxy measure of consumer risk. As urbanisation, contractual labour relations and consumer purchasing grew apace from the later eighteenth century, however, these qualitative determinations of character were increasingly complicated by individuals' social and spatial mobility and their new opportunities for manipulating personal appearance and connection to obtain credit in the consumer market. Encouraging traders to elaborate more systematic mechanisms for assessing risk, these developments failed to displace character from the heart of evaluations of creditworthiness. Just as the advent of 'ready-money' shops had prompted the evolution of hybrid transactional forms rather than a simple transition from credit to cash sales, so too the attempt to formalise credit ratings witnessed an accommodation between traditional determinations of character and a range of novel contractual strategies.[31] A new constellation of

---

[29] City of Westminster Archives, Benjamin Haydon Correspondence, M612/2, bill and letter of Andrew Henderson, 20 July 1826. For the reluctance of small-scale traders and craftsmen to dun their debtors, see David Kent, 'Small businessmen and their credit transactions in early nineteenth-century Britain', *Business History*, 36, 2 (April 1994), esp. 55, 58.

[30] Theo E. Stephens, ed., *Twelve Months Advertising for a Grocer* (London, 1910), 70, 72.

[31] Similarly, the evolution of life insurance in England combined economic calculation with cultural forms of moral calculus. See esp. Geoffrey Clark, *Betting on Lives: The Culture of Life Insurance in England, 1685–1775* (Manchester, 1999), and Robin Pearson, 'Moral hazard and the assessment of insurance risk in eighteenth- and early nineteenth-century Britain', *Business History Review*, 76 (Spring 2002), 1–35.

Market moralities 289

trade protection associations organised by retailers provided an essential institutional base for this process of accommodation, serving both to mediate credit relations in the market and to inform judicial efforts to re-moralise consumer contracts.

Guardian societies and the credit consumer

The development of trade protection societies marked a significant development in retailers' efforts to reduce their exposure to risk without abandoning the conventional credit relations that served to tie consumers to their shops over time and space. The first such society was the Guardians, or the Society for the Protection of Trade against Swindlers and Sharpers, founded in London in 1776. Upon paying an annual subscription of one guinea, members of the London Guardians gained access 'to the support, advice, and assistance of the Society ... without further expense', an entitlement that included access to the Guardians' extensive records and circulars concerning fraudulent consumers as well as legal assistance in prosecuting fraudulent debtors in the courts. A list of members for 1799 demonstrates the broad appeal of these services. Over eighty different trades were represented in the membership, which included such leading lights of the consumer revolution as Josiah Spode.[32]

Remaining unique until 1823, when Liverpool tradesmen formed the first provincial guardian society, the London Guardians laid the foundations of an associational movement which was to extend its myriad tentacles across England, throughout the Celtic fringe and into the wider empire. By mid-century, retailers had formed trade protection associations upon the London model in, for example, Manchester (1826), Hull (1827), Beverley (1834), Birmingham (1845), the West Riding (1848) and Leicester (1849).[33] The membership rolls of the Hull society mirrored the early London Guardians' subscription list in attracting a wide spectrum of artisans, shopkeepers and professionals who accorded credit to their customers. In 1828, the society's 180 members represented 60 different trades, of which drapery, grocery, tailoring and ironmongery together

---

[32] Anon., *Rules and Orders [of] The Guardians: Or Society for the Protection of Trade against Swindlers and Sharpers. Established March 25, 1776* (London, 1816); Anon., *A List of the Members of the Guardians; or Society for the Protection of Trade, against Swindlers and Sharpers, Established March 25th, 1776* [London, 1799]. In form and intent, the guardian society movement shares features with the criminal prosecution societies that proliferated in the latter half of the eighteenth century, as described, for example, by Peter King, *Crime, Justice and Discretion in England, 1740–1820* (Oxford, 2000), 53–7.

[33] There is no comprehensive history of the provincial societies, but essential background information can be gleaned from Anon., *Rules of the Beverley Guardian Society, for the Protection of Trade. Established November 19th, 1834* (Beverley, [1834]); Anon., *The Birmingham Guardian Society for the Protection of Trade: First Report* (Birmingham, 1845); and the centenary history of *The Manchester Guardian Society for the Protection of Trade, 1826–1926* ([Manchester], 1926).

290   Petty debts and the modernisation of English law

accounted for nearly a third of the membership.[34] As more and more local-ities formed guardian societies, concerted action among associations became increasingly appealing to their members. The *Trade Protection Record*, pub-lished by the London Trade Protection Society, observed in 1849 that only a national reticulation of guardian societies would ensure that 'the swindler of to-day in Manchester, could not be the swindler of to-morrow in London or in Glasgow'.[35] Animated by such aspirations, the secretaries of various local soci-eties began to meet annually to exchange information and co-ordinate their lob-bying activities in 1850; a National Association of Trade Protection Societies emerged in 1866, and boasted 76 member organisations with an estimated 40,000 individual members by 1898.[36]

A central aspect of early guardian society activity was the dissemination of information on swindlers who had sought to obtain (or succeeded in obtaining) goods by manipulating the capacious consumer credit system. Local societies compiled and disseminated weekly, fortnightly or monthly circulars describing swindlers active in their area. Although these reports were restricted to sub-scribers, co-ordination among societies worked to broadcast warnings widely among the associated membership. Soon after the development of the provincial trade protection movement, guardian societies began to share information by extending honorary membership to the secretaries of other associations, thereby giving these representatives (and members of their societies) access to their own confidential printed reports on swindlers. The Hull Guardians granted hon-orary membership to the secretaries of trade protection associations of Lincoln, Manchester and Liverpool in 1827. Sheffield, Glasgow, Birmingham, Dublin, Lambeth and south London, Shrewsbury and Wiltshire, Somerset and Bristol trade protection associations were then linked to the Hull Guardians through honorary memberships for their secretaries between 1831 and 1850.[37] The second half of the century saw the density of such information networks in-crease substantially, as local societies in major urban areas appointed hundreds of agents in lesser towns, from whom they derived information on fraudu-lent credit dealings. Already in 1854, the Leicester Trade Protection Society

[34] East Riding of Yorkshire Archives, DDX 424/1, Hull Guardian Society for the Protection of Trade, Minute Book, 1827–44.
[35] *Trade Protection Record*, 7 April 1849.
[36] Leicestershire RO, DE 3512/28, National Association of Trade Protection Societies, Minutes, 1898–1902, 10, printed notice of 'Jubilee Banquet'. The guardian societies' efforts to organise credit trade on a national and international level paralleled the co-operative movement's attempt to nationalise and internationalise the benefits of cash dealing. For the latter development, see Peter Gurney, *Co-operative Culture and the Politics of Consumption in England, 1870–1930* (Manchester, 1996), esp. chap. 4.
[37] East Riding of Yorkshire Archives, DDX 424/1, Hull Guardian Society, Minute Book, 1824–July 1844, 26 July 1827 and 21 April 1831; DDX 424/2, Hull Guardian Society, Minute Book, August 1844–1862, 29 September 1846; 17 January 1848; 2 May 1850; 1 August 1850; 5 December 1850.

Market moralities

boasted connections, through affiliates and agents, with 469 towns, stretching its web of information within England from Amersham, Ashford and Banbury to Yarmouth, Yeovil and York. Imperial towns and cities were also drawn into the Leicester society's orbit: agents in Inverness, Malta, Melbourne and Sligo all numbered among its informants.[38]

The circulars disseminated by guardian societies inadvertently provide a wealth of information on the personal qualities and the strategic practices deployed by consumers to establish a creditworthy status, and demonstrate the wide latitude for fraudulent transactions created by the customary norms of the credit system. Unable to gain access to information on consumers' income, investments and existing liabilities, guardian societies relied instead upon an array of personal characteristics written on or mediated by the consumer's body. Dress and personal appearance surfaced repeatedly as registers of creditworthy status. In 1835, the London Guardians' circular warned members against 'a female of fashionable exterior', whose success in obtaining goods on credit under false pretences was assisted by her 'genteel appearance'.[39] Adrian Beaumont, alias Barlowe, was likewise adept at fashioning a creditworthy character from his personal appearance, genteel accomplishments and family connections. In 1848 the *City of London Trade Protection Circular* reported that Beaumont was 'of gentlemanly deportment, highly accomplished in painting, music, and most of the fine arts, and ... accompanied by his wife, sister, and a little boy of ... rather delicate appearance'. Already successful in duping tradesmen in Cowes, Gosport, Southampton, Chichester, Littlehampton, Bristol and Reading, the Beaumonts were now, worryingly, believed to be active in London. 'The man ... constantly gives out that he is in expectation of a large accession of fortune in right of his wife, whom he represents to be nobly connected', the *Circular* reported. 'The family bear every appearance of gentility, and it is believed that the female portion have a small income, upon the strength of which, credit is obtained for twenty times the amount; when at a convenient opportunity they abscond, considerably in debt to their tradespeople.'[40] Social and economic credit were linked inextricably in the consumer market, where family and status – however fictive – formed the foundation upon which retailers constructed evaluations of profitability and risk.

The Beaumonts' reliance upon association with the aristocracy was indicative of a far wider manipulation of affiliation in English consumer markets, for personal connection formed an essential component of the repertoire of

---

[38] Leicestershire RO, DE 3848/4, Minute Book of the Leicestershire Trade Protection Society, 1854–66, 3; *Fourth Annual Report of the Leicestershire Trade Protection Society* (1854), 16–18.

[39] PRO, C 114/34, Chancery Masters' Exhibitions: Material Relating to the Society for the Protection of Trade against Swindlers, 5th notice for 1835. Many thanks to John Styles for drawing my attention to this source.

[40] *City of London Trade Protection Circular*, 20 May 1848, 3–4.

292   Petty debts and the modernisation of English law

consumer credit strategies deployed by servants, labourers, the middling sort and the upper classes to obtain goods on credit. When Benjamin Haydon was released from debtors' prison for the fourth time in 1836, his patroness, the Dowager Duchess of Sutherland, naturally offered assistance by extending him credit through her connection. 'During the winter and spring she occasionally sent her carriage...to wait at our door, as if she was in the house', Haydon's son later recalled. 'It was all she could afford to do, and she thought it would at least give Haydon credit with his tradesmen.'[41] Again and again trade protection circulars recorded the combined use of credit, connection and character as the levers by which goods could be obtained fraudulently by consumers entirely unknown to unwary tradesmen. The fragmented character of agency in consumer markets clearly exacerbated this problem: the credit purchases routinely transacted by servants, children and wives multiplied the potential for fraudulent credit dealings. In 1798, the London Guardians cautioned their subscribers to guard against 'a Young Woman...having the Appearance of a Lady's Maid' who had 'lately obtained Goods from Two Members, by representing herself as coming from Two Ladies of distinction, to whom she was, in consequence, supposed to be a Servant; but on Enquiry of these Ladies the Transactions turn out to be Impositions'.[42] False claims of personal connection worked to secure swindlers a seemingly endless stream of goods throughout the nineteenth century. A circular from the Liverpool Guardian Society warned against 'A Person calling himself *Hare* and representing [himself] as a Farmer', who had exploited the customary norms of the credit system to obtain shirtmaking materials for his daughters, 'stating that it was not so much for the emolument as to keep them domesticated'. Having returned an initial allotment of shirts, Hare secured a second consignment of goods on credit by assuring the tradesman that he could 'soon have his character as his neighbour (pointing to a House opposite) knew him very well'. Neglecting to make any further inquiry, the tradesman became suspicious only when Hare failed to return with the finished goods, at which time inquiries into his references proved that Hare had concocted both his character and his connections.[43]

Ascriptions of residence and profession further enlarged the scope for consumer credit (and hence for consumer fraud), either by supplementing connection with the superior sort or by providing an alternative basis for determining character when such affiliations were lacking. Countless swindlers gave

---

[41] Benjamin Robert Haydon, *Correspondence and Table Talk: With a Memoir by His Son, Frederick Wordsworth Haydon*, 2 vols. (London, 1876), I: 196–7. For the Dowager Duchess of Sutherland's credit dealings, see above, 285.

[42] Anon. *A List of the Members*, 29. For a splendid case study of swindling and high finance, see Donna T. Andrew and Randall McGowan, *The Perreaus and Mrs Rudd: Forgery and Betrayal in Eighteenth-Century London* (Berkeley, 2001).

[43] East Riding of Yorkshire Archives, DDX 424/12, Hull Guardian Society, Information Book, 1828–46, 7 February 1835.

Market moralities

293

tradesmen false addresses in fashionable districts in an effort to establish their personal credit through the location of their homes.[44] Like location, association with a respectable profession assisted in the creation of a creditworthy status. Priests and ministers – or those posing as such – enjoyed an obvious advantage in retailers' evaluations of risk. Education, verbal facility, genteel manners and the odour of sanctity all combined to lend men of the cloth the character of credit, as many an unwary tradesman found to his financial cost. In April 1848, the *City of London Trade Protection Circular* solicited information on the Reverend T.B. Dymoke, who had left the Southampton area 'in debt to many tradesmen' and also warned its members against 'A Person calling himself the Hon. Rev. B.C.D.F. Fairfax [who] undertook clerical duty at Rawmarsh, near Sheffield, during [a] temporary absence of the incumbent'. Active in soliciting funds for the Society for the Propagation of the Gospel in Foreign Parts, Fairfax had received 'extensive credit' from local tradesmen by talking 'largely of his property and connexions, and made himself highly popular by great activity and appearance of benevolence'. Only when he left the region 'with a great quantity of luggage' without paying any of his bills was Fairfax's true character as a swindler revealed. Where charitable largess had earlier suggested his creditworthy status, Fairfax's false economic identity was now signalled by rumours of domestic sexual impropriety. The *Circular*, belatedly, reported that 'One of his household was suspected to be a female in disguise.'[45]

As the records and circulars of guardian societies attest, retailers were often remarkably generous in awarding credit to persons of whom they knew little or nothing of substance. Writers of didactic literature constantly urged the wisdom of cash dealings, but tradesmen eager to secure custom in competitive markets all too often threw caution to the winds and turned from the supposed verities of cash to the comfortingly familiar vagaries of credit. John Fitzwilliam Thistlewaite, who featured repeatedly in the circulars issued by the London Guardians in 1825, could hardly be accused of misleading tradesmen who were finely attuned to the character of credit: he had, the Society reported, 'for some time past been a Prisoner for Debt in the County Gaol of Warwick, from whence he sends his orders for Goods to various parts of the kingdom'.[46] Appearance, association and address could all be employed to assess risk in consumer relations, but these attributes were also deployed by consumers themselves to obtain goods on fraudulent credit. Tradesmen testifying before a select committee in 1823 repeatedly echoed the claim made by the hatter Francis Carter that false credit was readily obtained by 'people that pass for gentlemen, who in fact are not so, but they meet with gentlemen at different

---

[44] For example, W.F. Fish, *The Autobiography of a Counter-Jumper: In Two Parts: England and South Africa* (London, n.d.), 101–2.
[45] *City of London Trade Protection Circular*, 29 April 1848, 6.
[46] PRO, C 114/34, 9th and 10th correspondences for 1825.

294 Petty debts and the modernisation of English law

places... and make use of gentlemen's names behind their backs'. In his testimony, Robert Taylor ruefully acknowledged that 'where we are deceived most is where gentlemen give us references for other gentlemen' and concluded that it was 'impossible for a tradesman to ascertain the character of those who order goods of him'.[47] Competition for customers of the right class thus ensured that fraudulent activities continued to flourish despite the guardian societies' efforts. As a London tradesman who published a handbook on *Business Life* in 1861 sagely concluded, not even membership in a trade protection association could protect retailers from the fundamental law that '*losses must and will occur in the course of business*'. If debt relations were fraught with risk, he observed, they were also essential sources of profit. 'Many persons can only do a trade by giving credit, and others only by a large, and to a great extent uncertain, credit', he concluded.[48]

Guardian societies and the modernisation of credit

Confronted by both the persistence and the wayward tendencies of customary ascriptions of credit, Victorian and Edwardian traders turned increasingly to collective action. Although late nineteenth- and early twentieth-century shopkeepers are notorious in the secondary literature for their reactionary opposition to modern retail institutions such as co-ops and department stores,[49] their attitude toward market modernity is considerably more complex than this stance alone suggests. Dominated by retailers,[50] trade protection societies stood at the forefront of modernising efforts to reduce commercial risk by strengthening and formalising debt collection strategies, spearheading campaigns on multiple fronts to hold customers fully responsible for their contractual obligations. By establishing debt collection departments to wrest payments from credit consumers, creating credit enquiry offices to improve the quality of credit evaluations and providing legal services to speed their members' debt disputes through the county-court system, local guardian societies and the National Association of Trade Protection Societies sought to mobilise the shared resources of the trading community against the serried ranks of recalcitrant consumer and retail debtors. These efforts added new elements to the complex processes by

---

[47] *Report of the Select Committee on the Recovery of Small Debts in England and Wales*, Parliamentary Papers, IV (1823) (386), 216, 201.

[48] Anon., *Business Life: The Experiences of a London Tradesman with Practical Advice and Directions for Avoiding Many of the Evils Connected with Our Present Commercial System and State of Society* (London, 1861), 123.

[49] See, for example, Crossick and Jaumain, 'World of the department store', 7–8.

[50] As the secretary of the National Association of Trade Protection Societies observed, whereas Chambers of Commerce were dominated by wholesalers, the trade protection movement was more 'intimately connected with retail traders'. Leicestershire RO, DE 3512/25, National Association of Trade Protection Societies, Minutes, 1865–89, circular on Imprisonment for Debt, 8 March 1873.

Market moralities

which personal debts were negotiated in England, but like the guardian societies' earlier attempts to establish the characters of their customers, they failed to dislodge the traditional expectations and practices that had shaped the credit economy since the early modern period.

The growth of specialised trade protection societies and trade publications dedicated to the interests of specific sectors of the consumer market provided an essential vehicle for Victorian retailers' escalating efforts to enforce debtors' contractual obligations. Scotch drapers, who began to organise their own separate trade protection societies in the 1830s and waged increasingly militant campaigns against defaulting plebeian purchasers from the 1870s, established the *Credit Drapers' Gazette and Trade Informant* in 1882; metropolitan tradesmen associated with the London Bakers' Trade Association for Debt Recovery and Trade Protection launched the *Bakers' Monthly Gazette* in 1889. Trade papers such as these routinely solicited information for their 'Lost Customers' and 'Removed Debtors' columns, which broadcast descriptions of consumers who had absconded without paying their bills.[51] In the six months from January to June 1883, the *Credit Drapers' Gazette* advertised for information on the location of 114 defaulting debtors – miners, colliers, carpenters, fitters, furnace labourers, masons, puddlers, railway guards, shoemakers and tinners.[52] Like other trade protection associations, these specialised societies were forced to rely upon physical traits, occupation, family connection and confessional affiliation to identify delinquent debtors in the absence of more formal mechanisms for tracing their evasive movements. Edward Roe, once a lamp-cleaner, was a 'stiff, bowlegged man' and 'used to do a bit of tinkering when near Sheffield five years ago'; Henry Vernon, a miner somewhere in the Leeds region, was married to a woman whose maiden name was Anson and had formerly been in the service of a Mr Farish; Robert Alcock had suffered the loss of a son in the Renisham Park explosion of 1870 and was himself a farm labourer, 'supposed to be...near Burnley'.[53]

More systematic than such efforts to locate debtors who had already absconded was the mounting effort made by trade protection societies to create comprehensive debt collecting networks that would reduce consumers' ability to evade their financial obligations. Local guardian societies began to organise formal debt-collecting departments at mid-century, offering subscribers a range of new facilities for enforcing their contracts without the necessity of entering into protracted, face-to-face negotiations with their delinquent customers. The Manchester Guardian Society and the Leicestershire Trade Protection Society

---

[51] See, for example, *Bakers' Monthly Gazette*, April 1889, 2–3, 13.

[52] *CDG*, January–June 1883. Of the 114 debtors whose trades were indicated, 22 (19 per cent) were miners or colliers. The sample excludes second and subsequent advertisements for a given individual.

[53] *CDG*, 15 August 1884, 37.

296   Petty debts and the modernisation of English law

were pioneers of this development: both established debt-collecting departments in 1850. Leicester's society, with 102 members in 1850 and 1,300 subscribers in 1873, saw its debt-collecting business expand dramatically in the later Victorian period. Members sent in debts totalling £2,769 in 1850, of which the society's collectors successfully recovered £600 (22%). Four decades later, the sums collected were far more substantial. In 1890, subscribers sent in a total of 15,360 debts for collection, and the Leicester society's agents succeeded in recovering debts valued at £58,434 owed to members.[54] Admittedly, the sums recovered for subscribers inevitably failed to match the value of debts sent in for collection: monthly returns for 1854, for example, ranged from a low of 27 per cent to a peak of 76 per cent but averaged only 45 per cent of the submitted claims. As the society's annual report was at pains to emphasise, however, the moral benefits exerted by the debt-collecting department far outweighed its purely economic effect. The debts recovered, the report reminded members, 'are not ordinary accounts, but consist chiefly of claims against the most unprincipled characters, who will not pay by any ordinary means; so that the annexed [statistics] shew a very large proportion recovered by the moral influence of the society'.[55]

Members of other local associations clearly found this line of argument convincing. The Hull Guardian Society appointed Edward Hannah as their first debt-collector in 1854. Two decades later, their collection department was pursuing hundreds of delinquent debtors each year. In 1870, the society accepted 758 accounts for collection and recovered £1,600 in bad debts; in 1880, claimants sent in 1,711 accounts for collection and the society recovered over £4,900 for its members.[56] Larger societies claimed results that far outstripped these achievements. At the annual dinner of the Liverpool Guardian Society in 1908, the president announced that the previous year had seen members apply for the recovery of 15,000 debts, valued at £95,000. Despite the desperate character of the accounts sent in for collection, he observed with satisfaction, debtors contacted by the society had responded by sending over £30,000 to the collection office and had rendered an additional £30,000 directly to their creditors.[57]

---

[54] For Manchester, see *Manchester Guardian Society*, 14. Statistics for the Leicestershire Society are drawn from Leicestershire RO, DE 3848/4, Minute Book of the Leicestershire Trade Protection Society, 1854–66, 3; DE 3848/5, Minute Book of the Leicestershire Trade Protection Society, 1866–80, 22 January 1874; and 7D70/4, Leicestershire Trade Protection Society, Monthly Circulars and Annual Reports, 41st Annual Report (February 1891).

[55] Leicestershire RO, DE 3848/4, Minute Book of the Leicestershire Trade Protection Society, 1854–66, 3.

[56] East Riding of Yorkshire Archives, DDX 424/2, Hull Guardian Society, Minute Book, August 1844–62, 3 February 1853 and 2 February 1854; DDX 424/3, Hull Guardian Society, Minute Book, 1862–76: 3 January 1872; DDX 424/4, Hull Guradian Society, Minute Book, 1876–84, 54th Annual Report.

[57] *The Draper*, 4 July 1908, 669.

Like guardian societies that served a broad spectrum of retailers, the specialised trade protection associations that proliferated from mid-century turned to debt-collection activities in an effort to reduce the cost, difficulty and time required to secure payment from reluctant – and elusive – consumer debtors. Credit drapers' trade protection societies entered into debt collection with particular alacrity. Dealing with a predominantly working-class clientele whose members displayed an alarming willingness to shift their residence to evade their debts, tally tradesmen constituted a natural constituency for the campaign to formalise consumer debt collection. By charging members a modest fee for each bad debt recovered and by accepting commissions from members of other credit drapery associations whose customers had absconded beyond their reach, the salaried agents and solicitors employed by these societies sought to enforce their subscribers' contracts while reducing the level of personal interaction between consumers and creditors entailed by debt collection.[58] Newcastle's Travelling Drapers' Association, which charged a commission of 10 per cent on each debt it succeeded in recovering, had fifty members in 1864 and recovered debts valued at £560. Two decades later, with seventy members, the society was on average collecting £1,288 each year for its subscribers.[59] Statistics from the Manchester Credit Drapers' Association, which appointed its first salaried debt-collector in 1885, mark a similar trajectory. The society accepted 746 accounts valued at £1,355-17-8 for collection in its first year of operation, collecting a modest £68-4-0 from its home members and £19-10-8 for 'foreign' societies. A decade later, the value of the society's debt-collecting activities had risen significantly. At its annual meeting in 1894, the debt department reported paying out a total of £869-9-2 recovered from delinquent debtors to its subscribers and their allies.[60]

The establishment of formal debt-collecting departments with salaried secretaries and agents promoted a parallel development by trade protection associations, the creation of credit enquiry departments (Illustration 9). By combining their own private records of recalcitrant debtors with published press reports of local bankruptcies, insolvencies and county-court litigation, guardian societies amassed a wealth of information on the commercial characters of consumers and tradesmen in their localities. The Hull Guardian Society received 1,865 credit enquiries in 1865, but recorded 4,383 enquiries in 1875 and 7,275 in 1913.[61] The Leicestershire Trade Protection Society witnessed a comparable rise in requests for status reports on local credit buyers. Tradesmen purchased 6,015 credit reports from the society in 1872, 13,619 reports in 1876

---

[58] See Finn, 'Scotch drapers and the politics of modernity', esp. 105.
[59] *CDG*, 15 January 1885, 24.   [60] Ibid., 15 February 1886, 49; 27 January 1894, 27.
[61] East Riding of Yorkshire Archives, DDX 424/3, Hull Guardian Society Minute Book, 1862–76, 3 January 1866; DDX 424/4, Hull Guardian Society Minute Book, 1876–84, 49th Annual Report (February 1876); DDX 424/7, Hull Guardian Society Minute Book, 1906–26, 140.

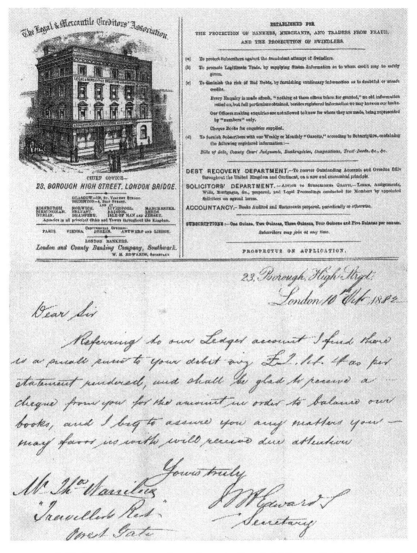

9 Notice and correspondence from the Legal & Mercantile Creditors' Association of London, 1882. By the later Victorian period, debt collection facilities were a standard feature of the guardian societies that sought to protect tradesmen from their wily credit customers. (Reproduced by permission of the Bodleian Library.)

Market moralities 299

and 17,856 in 1890. By 1890, twelve free credit inquiries were included (with the confidential monthly circular) in the Leicestershire society's annual subscription of one guinea; additional reports were available for the modest charge of threepence for the first twenty, sixpence for the next eighty and a shilling for each additional report above that number.[62]

The foundation of the National Associations of Trade Protection Societies in 1865 significantly assisted the wide circulation of credit information collected in this manner. Rule twelve of the new association's constitution specified 'That every Society on admission becomes bound to reciprocate with all and each of the other Societies, in procuring and giving information in answer to enquiries, without undue delay, and to exchange with each other circulars published by them'. A year after the association began to conduct business, it reported receiving 75,000 credit enquiries and returning a sum of over £200,000 from the 80,000 applications for debt collection processed by its agents. Celebrating these statistics, the annual report underlined the association's role in promoting commercial character, concluding that 'These figures represent a vast machinery tending to give confidence to the manufacturer and merchant in the extension of sound, legitimate trading – to furnish additional facilities for credit to the industrious, honest, and frugal, even though it may be small, capitalist – and to prevent losses by bad debts through the reckless, insolvent, or dishonest.'[63] In this emphasis, the association's rhetoric nicely conveyed the extent to which the language of modern contractual relations continued to draw upon the moral tropes of customary market relations.

By 1868, the National Association's 'vast machinery' had extended its reach further into the trading community. The annual report now claimed that the confederation of societies formed 'a network over the greater part of Great Britain, having solicitors, agents, or correspondents in 2,500 towns and places'. Reiterating the association's tendency 'to promote commercial morality', the report underlined the ways in which the modernisation of trade, far from promoting anonymous market mechanisms, tended to reinscribe the conventional economic verities of personal character:

The attentive observer cannot have failed to perceive that the tendency of modern trading has been to outgrow ancient restrictions, and local boundaries; while at the same time the tendency of modern legislation has been to relax the laws relating to trade, and to make it more difficult to recover debts... Hence it follows that character is now much more regarded by prudent traders than legal facilities for the recovery of debts, or outward appearances, as presented to the casual observer; and it is this very requirement of modern trade that has made Trade Protection Societies a necessity.[64]

[62] Leicestershire RO, DE 3848/5, Minute Book of the Leicestershire Trade Protection Society, 1866–80, 22 January 1874; 27th Annual Report (1877); 7D70/4, Leicestershire Trade Protection Society, Monthly Circulars and Annual Reports, 41st Annual Report (1891).

[63] Leicestershire RO, DE 3512/25, National Association of Trade Protection Societies, Minutes, 1865–1880, 12, 17, 38.

[64] Ibid., 60–1.

300   Petty debts and the modernisation of English law

The minutes of the National Association of Trade Protection Societies repeatedly testified to the antinomies of market evolution. Despite its self-conscious emphasis on commercial modernity, the trade protection movement demonstrated the extent to which advances in rationality and systematic routine often worked to reinforce traditional systems of thought, rather than to render them anachronistic.

The incorporation of new technologies by the trade protection movement further illustrates this point. As more and more organisations joined the National Association of Trade Protection Societies, telegraphic communication came to play an increasingly significant part in the guardian societies' endeavours. Allowing the association's secretary to co-ordinate member societies' substantial lobbying activities and to respond swiftly to legislative measures that impinged upon the trading community, the telegraph also afforded a new and fully modern mechanism for the rapid transfer of information garnered by the associations' disparate credit enquiry offices. Like the selective adoption of this technology by the railways, the guardian societies' exploitation of telegraphy 'underlines the cultural and technical contingencies involved in finding a market for the new invention', belying the easy triumph of new business strategies for conducting business.[65] By 1885, the National Association boasted forty-seven affiliated societies, and the secretary devised a 'Telegraphic Code' to encourage the rapid and systematic exchange of information on credit risk throughout this expanding commercial network. The proposed code divided potential debtors into distinct categories of creditworthiness, and assigned each of these divisions a keyword or phrase which, when sent telegraphically from one trade protection society to another, would provide appropriate data for routine, uniform evaluations of trade risk. Economic capitalisation figured importantly in this proposed scheme, but it was constantly modified by considerations of personal character. Respectability was the key organising category of the 'Telegraphic Code', as the first four of the eleven suggested keywords made emphatically clear:

1. 'Safe' means – respectable.
2. 'Good' means – highly respectable and well to do.
3. 'With care' means – respectable, trustworthy and industrious, but with little capital; we think, however, he would not incur any liability he was not able to discharge.
4. 'Moderate' means – respectable, but with little capital; less than the amount named considered advisable.[66]

---

[65] The railway companies' selective adoption of the telegraph is detailed by Iwan Rhys Morus, 'The electrical Ariel: telegraphy and commercial culture in early Victorian England', *VS*, 39, 3 (Spring 1996), 339–78, citation from 341. In the nineteenth-century United States, the development of modern banking similarly relied upon 'traditional' ties of connection. See Naomi R. Lamoreaux, *Insider Lending: Banks, Personal Connections, and Economic Development in Industrial New York* (Cambridge, 1996).

[66] Leicestershire RO, DE 3512/26, National Association of Trade Protection Societies, Minutes, 1879–1891, Report of the 37th Annual Meeting (1885), and printed circular of 21 October 1885.

Market moralities 301

In this manner, by actively promoting new technologies for circulating status reports which themselves incorporated received cultural calculations of economic risk, the National Association of Trade Protection Societies reaffirmed the symbiotic relationship that obtained between character and credit, and between social and economic capital, in English commerce.

The exceptionally rich archival records of the successful London wholesale grocer James Budgett & Son illustrate the operation of this process of accommodation at the level of individual tradesmen, providing detailed information on the credit strategies used by a large, well-capitalised business to attract and maintain trade from retailers. Established in 1857, the firm conducted an extensive cash and credit business with retail traders scattered across the metropolis and throughout the provinces.[67] Their credit ledgers, carefully updated by successive warehousemen into the twentieth century, are replete with estimations of customers' moral and economic worth. Culled from the hearsay evidence of neighbours, commercial travellers and other businesses as well as the more formal reports provided (for a fee) by trade publications, guardian societies and nascent credit agencies, these ledgers demonstrate that even the credit strategies of enterprises that were insulated from the genteel expectations of the upper-class retail market were shaped as fundamentally by evaluations of character as they were by accumulations of strictly economic capital.

Like the retailers whom they supplied, Budgett & Son's employees responded to the increasingly competitive market conditions of the Victorian and Edwardian grocery trade by maintaining a precarious, constantly shifting balance between cash and credit sales.[68] Fully alive to the losses that could accrue from an unwise extension of credit, they were also acutely aware of the profits that would be foregone by an undue or an untimely insistence on cash payment. In 1876, a commercial traveller tendered a negative evaluation of the shop maintained by Sidney Hart of Chatham, denigrating Hart's efforts to stimulate grocery sales by offering customers gifts of chinaware with their purchases. 'We declined to give him credit and he never forgave us', an entry in the ledgers recorded.[69] Frederick Hughes, a Peckham confectioner, was also permanently alienated by Budgett's refusal to grant him a credit account. 'He bullied Williams like a pick-pocket on his calling, says we refused him an account 9 Mo[nth]s or so ago & if we come near the place he is going to put

---

[67] See Chris Hosgood, 'The "language of business": shopkeepers and the business community in Victorian England', *Victorian Review*, 17, 1 (Summer 1991), 35–50, esp. 37–43 and idem, 'The "knights of the road": commercial travellers and the culture of the commercial room in late-Victorian and Edwardian England', *VS*, 37 (Summer 1994), 519–47.

[68] For the atmosphere of anxiety created by fierce retail competition in this period, see Geoffrey Crossick, 'The petite bourgeoisie in nineteenth-century Britain: the urban and liberal case', in Geoffrey Crossick and Heinz-Gerhard Haupt, eds., *Shopkeepers and Master Artisans in Nineteenth-Century Europe* (London, 1984), 62–94, and Winstanley, *Shopkeeper's World*, esp. chaps. 7–8.

[69] Guildhall, MS 20,366/1, James Budgett & Son, Country Customers, 7.

302   Petty debts and the modernisation of English law

us out', the clerk noted in the books.[70] Just as a refusal to grant credit could rankle for years, so too an injudicious decision to dun for payment could bring a longstanding relation with a retail customer to a premature close. When a fire at the premises of Edward Wood on Kentish Town Road prevented his prompt settlement of a small bill, the firm requested payment of the sum before any new orders were executed. Wood's sensibilities were evidently roused by this punctilious adherence to the terms of his contract, and his response rehearsed the indignant reactions of elite consumers of the eighteenth century when presented with an unexpected bill. 'He sends the amount & writes he is surprised at our declining to execute his order, [and] now wishes it cancelled & will not trouble us again', a ledger entry dated June 1896 recorded.[71]

As a large and successful business located in the City and trading throughout the United Kingdom, Budgett & Son had frequent recourse to the new credit mechanisms available to the modernising tradesman. References to and cuttings from the *Grocer* newspaper, established in 1862, suggest the extent to which the later nineteenth-century rise of specialised trade publications assisted in the formalisation of credit evaluations by dispersing information on bankruptcies, assignments and debt litigation throughout the business community.[72] But if formal records of court activity helped to mediate Budgett's credit relations, they acted only as a supplement to more conventional character evaluations made by the firm's many informants. To be sure, when information on economic capitalisation was forthcoming, the company's warehousemen seized upon it eagerly and entered the details into the firm's voluminous credit ledgers.[73] But even when these indicators were available, they failed to provide a sufficient measure of customers' credit status. As the informant who dismissed Stephen Hudger of Greenwich as 'a low common chap' in 1906 commented, 'he has money but his character is not tip top'.[74]

Lacking reliable economic data – or wishing to bolster knowledge of economic resources with evaluations of social and cultural capital – informants turned naturally to affiliation. Just as references to genteel associates and aristocratic patrons consolidated consumers' access to credit, a spectrum of social connections worked to secure retailers' credit accounts. Confessional identity figured conspicuously in these calculations. Themselves Wesleyan Methodists, the Budgetts made frequent gifts to Nonconformist congregations throughout

---

[70] Guildhall, MS 20,367/1, James Budgett & Son, Town References, 40. '10 Bag man but a pig' was the laconic annotation to this report.
[71] Ibid., 51. Hosgood, 'The "language of business" ', offers a nuanced assessment of the extent to which retailers enjoyed (and made use of) freedom from domination by wholesalers who supplied them on credit. For eighteenth-century credit consumer sensibilities, see above, 96.
[72] See, for example, Guildhall, MS 20,364, James Budgett & Son, Records of References, 139–40; Guildhall, MS 20, 365, James Budgett & Son, Account Books, 37, 41.
[73] See, for example, Guildhall, MS 20, 364, James Budgett & Son, Records of References, 62.
[74] Ibid., 10.

England. Chapels in Worcester, Gravenhurst, Leamington, Yeovil, Finsbury, Tottenham and Finchley all benefited from their donations – as, interestingly, did the Hammersmith Jews' Society.[75] Read alongside Budgett's credit ledgers, these gifts hint at the ways in which religious piety might work to promote commercial profit. Budgett's trade informants made frequent – but highly selective – reference to customers' religious affiliations, information that the firm's charitable giving may have helped to elicit (together with credit assessments of these traders) from local religious leaders. Certainly association with confessions known to monitor and police their congregants' economic activities featured prominently in the complex calculus used by the firm to determine consumers' credit profiles.[76] Methodists, Baptists, Quakers and – despite the incidence of anti-Semitic asides in the ledgers – Jews all boasted creditworthy characteristics by virtue of their confessional identities, while Anglican allegiance, significantly, merited no mention. In 1861, E.C. Wright of Sudbury was 'a Quakeress & one of the nicest little customers in our Books [she] can pay cash for everything'; Walker Catt of Chelmsford was considered trustworthy in part because 'Quakers have always stuck to the shop'; and J. Ledbetter & Sons of Dewsbury were, as 'a very old & respectable quaker family', highly regarded in 1895.[77] Joseph Sarjeant of Huntingdonshire combined his business interests with service as a local Wesleyan preacher and was 'always satisfactory', 'a most respectable man in appearance'. For W. Jeremy of Marlborough, Nonconformist affiliations similarly appeared to promise reliable profit margins. Both he and his wife were possessed of 'a little money' but also boasted religious connections that convinced Budgett's informant that they would prosper at Marlborough, 'where there is a good opening especially [as there is] no dissenter grocer – the d[issenters] have promised to rally around'.[78]

Together capital, connection and confession erected a flexible framework upon which Budgett's agents constructed and reconstructed the credit profiles of their customers. Work habits, leisure activities and patterns of expenditure all surfaced as supplementary means for assessing credit as Budgett's employees attempted to process and to reconcile the conflicting mass of information gleaned from disparate trade informants. T.J. Gibson's account was, a traveller reported, 'much overdue' in 1900, but 'at the same time I do not think there is any cause for anxiety as the wife, daughter & 2 sons all work hard in the

---

[75] Guildhall, MS 20,255, James Budgett & Son, General Ledger (1857–71), 116–25.

[76] The role played by religious networks in promoting and policing large-scale enterprises is better understood than the impact of confession upon retail credit. See, for example, Garnett, 'Aspects of the relationship', chap. 2, and Maurice Kirby, 'Quakerism, entrepreneurship and the family firm in north-east England', in Jonathan Brown and Mary B. Rose, eds., *Entrepreneurship, Networks and Modern Business* (Manchester, 1993), 105–26.

[77] Guildhall, MS 20,364, James Budgett & Son, Records of References, 528; ibid., 80; Guildhall, MS 20,365, Account Books, 129.

[78] Guildhall, MS 20,364, James Budgett & Son, Records of References, 431, 207.

304   Petty debts and the modernisation of English law

business & it is not usual for this class of people to come to grief'.[79] The contrast provided by William Burton, who employed twenty men at his substantial provisions establishment, was sharp. After building a large private house for his family – 'it is thought generally that he has spent too much on bricks and mortar' – Burton lost interest in his business, kept his office 'always in a fearful muddle' and (having purchased a yacht) went off 'days at a stretch leaving his store to the tender mercies of his men'. Budgett's informant accordingly suggested that forty pounds was 'plenty to credit him'.[80] Ideally, abstinence, personal oversight of one's business and economic probity – or the absence of these attributes – were mutually reinforcing constituents of character in the ledgers. If such moral reasoning had correlated with economic outcomes more consistently, the project of formalising credit relations would have proven much simpler – and much swifter – than was historically the case. But commercial experience often failed to confirm the expectations raised by received moral stereotypes. Retailer George Reynolds was, an informant observed, 'going on [in] the Buckingham style [with] drink, billiards & gambling, but at present I admit [he is] a good payer'.[81]

As Reynolds's case suggests, self-discipline, habits of industry and the avoidance of excessive expenditure all served as emblems of commercial virtue, but respectability and credit functioned in Budgett's ledgers as fluid, multivalent registers of worth rather than as stable systems of economic valuation. At one level, this instability simply reflected the wide disparities of opinion that could emerge from credit reports that were culled from a far-flung and variegated constellation of informants, but customers' frustrating tendency to display a range of divergent characters over time also fundamentally compromised ascriptions of respectability. When Albert Bootes of Hitchen began to trade with Budgett's in 1871, his credit references variously described him as 'slow' to pay his bills, as 'quite safe' and as 'a worthy little fellow honest as daylight (a Wesleyan) but wants more capital and takes liberties . . . [he] has however promised to mend his ways'. A notation pencilled on the ledger's margin several months later noted that Bootes had 'gone abroad as a missionary without paying his creditors'.[82]

More fundamental was the inherently fluid character of middle-class conceptions of individual character in the context of commercial respectability. Recent scholarship has done much to unpack the complex roles and meanings of respectability in Victorian culture, replacing 'the previous simple portmanteau sense of the term' with a more dynamic understanding of respectability as a cluster of shifting roles in which 'the coexistence of seemingly contradictory modes of behaviour within a single life-style was not an aberration'. Focusing on the instrumental deployment of respectability by plebeian men in

---

[79] Ibid., 43.   [80] Ibid., 24.
[81] Guildhall, MS 20,365, James Budgett & Son, Account Books, 246.
[82] Guildhall, MS 20,364, James Budgett & Son, Records of References, 34.

Market moralities   305

their inter-class relationships with the social groups above them, Peter Bailey has underlined the inability of middle-class observers to recognise the polyvalent character of respectability in working-class culture.[83] But Budgett's credit ledgers suggest that bourgeois businessmen – however oblivious they may have been to the intricacies of working-class negotiations of status – were of necessity well attuned to the internal contradictions that marked conceptions of respectable character within their own ranks. Most telling in this context was the common understanding that a tradesman's previous bankruptcy neither invariably indicated failure to adhere to codes of respectable behaviour nor precluded a rapid return to creditworthy status. The ledgers repeatedly testify to the porous borders that demarcated respectability in commercial relations. The business owned by A. Quilter of Maldon had previously failed, but an informant noted that 'he pays well & they consider him respectable'; A. & J. Dunn, Londonderry confectioners, had been bankrupted in 1895 and paid a dividend of only ten shillings in the pound, yet, already in 1896, a reference from Leicester described the firm as 'thoroughly respectable'.[84] Instability, not stasis, was the hallmark of respectability in Budgett's ledgers as in the wider business world, for commercial characters constructed on the shifting sands of credit existed, at best, in a state of dynamic equilibrium.

As Christopher Hosgood has noted, Budgett & Son became increasingly reliant upon qualitative evaluations of their customers in the later nineteenth century, placing new emphasis on reports rendered by commercial travellers who – in contrast to clerks or warehousemen – boasted personal knowledge gleaned from 'intimate contact with the private lives of their customers'.[85] Particularly from the 1890s, reports compiled by independent credit agencies and by the newly created debt departments of local guardian societies did provide an additional, and ostensibly less subjective, source of data for determining risk. But here as in the wider literature of the National Association of Trade Protection Societies, it is the perpetuation of conventional norms of assessing risk rather than the triumph of a modern language of credit based on purely economic forms of capital that is conspicuous. A report compiled by the credit agency Perry's in 1890 thus described G.W. Grantham of Camden Town in precisely the personal terms habitually employed by commercial travellers. Judged 'an average trade risk', safe to credit of two hundred pounds, Grantham appeared, in the credit agency's estimation, 'to have worked up a fair connection,

---

[83] Peter Bailey, *Popular Culture and Performance in the Victorian City* (Cambridge, 1998), 30, 36, 44.

[84] Guildhall, MS 20,364, James Budgett & Son, Records of References, 381; Guildhall, MS 20,366, Country Customers, 11. V.S. Pritchett's memoir documents his father's repeated bankruptcies, but notes that he succeeded in obtaining goods on credit for successive new enterprises by 'having good connections in his trade'. V.S. Pritchett, *A Cab at the Door: An Autobiography: Early Years* (London, 1968), 87.

[85] Hosgood, 'The "knights of the road" ', esp. 524–7, citation from 525.

306   Petty debts and the modernisation of English law

[and] bears a respectable character'.[86] A report compiled in 1911 by a trade protection association to which Budgett subscribed similarly observed of the confectioner Maynard that 'The people connected are respectable . . . and [their] means are considered adequate for requirements.' A printed statement at the bottom of this typed credit reference form underlined the imperative for traders to seek evidence to supplement the quantitative 'Registered information' – records of bankruptcies, debt litigation, assignments and compositions – upon which their own analyses were based. 'The dispensing of credit with safety being a matter of the utmost discretion, the Subscriber undertakes to obtain information from other available sources, and not to give credit in sole reliance upon any information furnished by the Agency', it cautioned.[87]

A sophisticated City business, Budgett & Son placed continued (and indeed increasing) reliance on the amorphous, unstable and unreliable concepts of respectability, connection and character over time. The persistence of these traditional indicators of credit reflected the demands of the market itself. In an economic environment in which failure was a commonplace occurrence, the language of commercial character offered traders a flexible discursive means for accommodating risk even as they sought to guard against the deceptive credit strategies exploited by swindlers. But the obvious inadequacies of the available alternative mechanisms for determining credit status also encouraged continued recourse to customary and qualitative evaluations of credit. As was the case in the consumer market, the security of profits promised by reliance on cash and capital often proved illusory. Co-ops prided themselves on securing low prices for their members by paying cash to the wholesalers who supplied them, but the entry in Budgett's books for the Burnley Equitable Co-operative Store – specifically cautioning its travellers to 'get the cash before sending any goods' – suggests that such assertions were not to be accepted at face value.[88] In theory, allegiance to modernising market practices simplified tradesmen's calculations of risk, but the hybrid nature of nineteenth-century cash and credit dealings ensured that such claims were, in practice, enmeshed with conventional markers of personal character such as confessional identity, connection and respectability.

Trade protection societies and the county courts

As the National Association's annual report had clearly indicated in 1868, the inadequacies of the legal system loomed large in the collective conscience of

---

[86] Guildhall, MS 20,367/1, Town References, 51. Perry's Original Bankrupt and Insolvent Registry Office for Protection against Fraud, Swindlers &c was established in London in 1810 and published *Perry's Bankrupt and Insolvent Weekly Gazette* from at least 1828.

[87] Guildhall, MS 20,365, James Budgett & Son, Records of References, 15–16.

[88] Guildhall, MS 20,364, James Budgett & Son, Records of References, 102.

Market moralities 307

the mercantile community, and efforts to turn the operation of the courts to the advantage of creditors formed a key part of the guardian societies' programme of commercial modernisation. From the outset, trade protection societies sought to enhance the operation of the debt laws by providing funds and legal advice to creditors who wished to oppose the release of their debtors from custody. In 1834 the Beverley Guardian Society required its governing committee to retain a solicitor to attend meetings and advise its members; subscribers who could demonstrate the justice of their opposition were also entitled to receive 'such legal and reasonable charges as may be incurred in opposing the discharge of such Insolvent Debtors' from the prison.[89] To assist in 'the exposure and punishment of fraudulent practices', the Birmingham Guardian Society similarly granted traders and shopkeepers up to five pounds per case to defray the expenses of opposing a debtor's discharge from prison, and offered its members funds to pay for advice on the labyrinthine complexities of insolvency law.[90] The minutes of various local societies demonstrate that these provisions were actively used by subscribers.[91]

Together, the creation of the county-court system and the escalation of trade protection activity from mid-century encouraged guardian societies to shift the burden of their modernising efforts from the final to the initial phases of debt litigation. Whereas the early guardian societies had provided their subscribers with funds to oppose the discharge of debtors from prison after litigation had run its full course, later Victorian trade protection associations instead employed agents to initiate and expedite their members' suits in the small-claims courts. By offering members the services of clerks and solicitors who were retained to enter plaints in the local county court in bulk and – when the service of a summons failed to elicit payment – would proceed to act as creditors' representatives in the litigation that ensued, the trade protection societies attempted to routinise the legal regulation of contractual relations. Like the societies' debt collection departments, this service was designed to anonymise contractual disputes, obviating the need for the creditor to appear in person in the courtroom. In some localities, this mechanism for depersonalising small-claims litigation met with considerable success, leading guardian societies to play a prominent role in enforcing debts through county-court litigation. The secretary of Hull's Guardian Society obtained county-court summonses for 568 debts (valued at £2,947-10-6) owed to its subscribers in 1878, and succeeded in recovering £1,250-2-4 of that sum (42 per cent). Of the total monies obtained as a result of county-court litigation in Hull in that year, the secretary claimed proudly,

---

[89] Anon., *Rules of the Beverley Guardian Society*, 6.
[90] Anon., *Birmingham Guardian Society*, 4, 15.
[91] See, for example, East Riding of Yorkshire Archives, DDX 424/1, Hull Guardian Society, Minute Book, 1827–July 1844, 1 June 1837; DDX 424/2, Hull Guardian Society, Minute Book, August 1844–62, 1 June 1849.

308   Petty debts and the modernisation of English law

roughly a quarter was obtained through the guardian society's endeavours on behalf of its 717 members.[92]

For creditors, these debt-collecting facilities could offer substantial economies of time and effort, and also eliminate the possibility that their debtors would, by initiating personal negotiations with them (or with a sympathetic judge) in the courtroom, succeed in delaying or reducing their payments. The Ashby de la Zouch branch of the Leicestershire Trade Protection Society, with a membership of 120, entered 600 or so suits on behalf of their subscribers in the local county court in 1867 and was gratified to find that the judge required the plaintiff to appear and testify in person in only forty-seven cases.[93] The activities of the Leicestershire Trade Protection Society itself produced the same happy outcome of reducing county-court debtors' scope for histrionic courtroom pleas. In the twelve months from December 1889 to November 1890, the society's manager lodged a total of 4,484 county-court plaints on behalf of subscribers. In only 101 cases (2.2 per cent) were members themselves compelled to appear in the court to justify their claims.[94]

Leicestershire's society was not exceptional in establishing productive working relations with local county-court judges. The Hull Guardian society was especially assiduous in cultivating its county-court judge, F.A. Bedwell, who responded by treating their interests with much solicitude. In August 1876, the society's quarterly meeting passed a resolution praising Bedwell's 'judicious and energetic exercise' of his powers against debtors; the judge promptly wrote to thank them for their support of the 'debt collection plan' he had instituted in the court.[95] Debtor defendants were fully alive to the potential for such privileged relationships to tip the balance of law in favour of creditors, as the correspondence files of the Lord Chancellor's office reveal. Tom Race of Leeds, repeatedly summonsed to the county court for debts with a tallyman contracted by his wife, wrote obsessively to protest against the decisions rendered by judge Greenhow in the 1890s. Race was convinced the judge's ties to the local guardian society were those of family and 'connection' and was outraged by Greenhow's willingness to provide 'facilities for packmen who are the curse of this West Riding District'. The judge's practice of allowing accountants hired by the guardian society – 'some of them the meanest and most debased persons' – to defend creditors' claims without the personal appearance

---

[92] East Riding of Yorkshire Archives, DDX 424/4, Hull Guardian Society Minute Book, 1876–84, 52nd Annual Report.

[93] Leicestershire RO, DE 3848/5, Leicestershire Trade Protection Society, Minutes, 1866–80, 16 April 1868.

[94] Leicestershire RO, 7D70/4, Leicestershire Trade Protection Society, Monthly Circulars and Annual Reports, tabulation from *Monthly Circulars*, January–December 1890.

[95] East Riding of Yorkshire Archives, DDX 424/4, Hull Guardian Society, Minute Book, 1876–84, 2 August 1876, 6 September 1876. See also 31 May 1877, 14 June 1877, 10 October 1878, 5 and 16 December 1878.

Market moralities 309

of the plaintiffs themselves earned particular odium in Race's denunciations of judgments which he believed to be 'completely at variance with equity'.[96]

Although the Hull Guardians evidently enjoyed close – if not collusive – relations with their local court personnel, trade protection societies throughout England perceived the evolving conventions of county-court practice as major obstacles to their modernising activities. Allegations by traders that county-court judges were dilatory, incompetent or partisan gathered strength as trade protection associations expanded their campaign to enforce debts through the courts, exacerbated by the wide latitude enjoyed by county-court judges and the very limited government oversight to which they were subjected. As Patrick Polden has observed, 'Short of flagrant misconduct the county court judges were more or less free to do as they chose.'[97] Trade protection societies became increasingly sensitive to the foibles of individual judges and to the broader limitations of the court system as their own debt-collecting activities became interlocked with those of other associations. The annual report of the Nottingham and Midland Merchants' and Traders' Association struck a common chord in noting that 'the difficulty of recovering money by County Court process is very great, and [payments are] obtainable generally only by small instalments'.[98]

If some county-court judges provoked guardian societies' hostility through sheer indifference to court business, others elicited this antagonism by responding to trade protection associations' new debt-collecting campaigns with overt counter-measures of their own. Just as guardian societies were intent to stress the strictly contractual nature of their subscribers' relations with their debtors, so too many county-court judges and registrars were determined to preserve the personal character of consumer exchange against these encroachments on their judicial discretion. Refusing to accept abstract conceptualisations of the autonomous individual, they qualified defendants' contractual liability by insisting upon the legitimate role played in economic transactions by social relations. Rather than promoting a uniform transition from status to contract, these judges responded to the challenge of the guardian society movement by urging the continued need to moderate legal obligations by equitable considerations, most notably those of gender and class.

---

[96] PRO, LCO 3/66, Tom Race to the Lord Chancellor, 20 February 1893, and Race to Greenhow, n.d. Greenhow, testifying to a Lords select committee on imprisonment for debt in 1893–94, denied this charge, allying himself with the antagonists of the tally trade and claiming that his 'system has had an extraordinary influence upon subduing credit' and that 'The Scotch draper who travelled round the district does not like my system at all.' *Report of the Select Committee of the House of Lords on the Debtors Act*, Parliamentary Papers, IX (1893–94) (HL 156), 66.

[97] Patrick Polden, *A History of the County Court, 1846–1971* (Cambridge, 1999), 50. See also his 'Judicial selkirks: the county court judges and the press, 1847–80', in Christopher W. Brooks and Michael Lobban, eds., *Communities and Courts in Britain 1150–1900* (London, 1997), 245–62.

[98] Leicestershire RO, DE 3848/4, Leicestershire Trade Protection Society, Minute Book, 1854–66, *31st Annual Report*, 12. See similarly *CCC*, 1 June 1899, 135–6.

310   Petty debts and the modernisation of English law

The actions of the judge and registrar of the Shoreditch and Bow county court illustrate the tensions between tradesman plaintiffs and court officials that were precipitated by the guardian societies' intervention in the ongoing debate over the nature and responsibilities of the legal person. The predominantly working-class area served by the Bow court was prime territory for itinerant traders of cheap drapery goods, who flocked to the court to press their legal claims when debtors defaulted on their instalment payments. In 1884, however, the newly appointed judge, Samuel Prentice, and his registrar instituted procedures designed to wean local tally tradesmen from reliance upon the court's coercive powers. The retail practices to which these officials drew particular attention were precisely those modernising strategies championed by trade protection societies to reduce the level of interpersonal contact between debtors and creditors when disputes arose over payment. By midsummer, Bow's registrar had begun to insist that credit draper plaintiffs meet personally with male debtors whom they had served with court summonses – often for debts contracted by the defendant's wife – to discuss their claims, and dismissed cases in which such negotiations had not transpired. Neither Prentice nor his registrar, moreover, abided by the legal definition of a wife under coverture as merely an extension of her husband's legal personality. Despite clear precedents to the contrary, both officials instructed the court's bailiff to consider a summons served on a wife in lieu of her husband as 'doubtful', thereby preventing the plaintiff from pressing for an immediate judgment.[99]

Conflicts over debts for textile items purchased by wives on their husbands' credit caused particular acrimony as retail tradesmen joined their trade protection societies' campaigns to link the county courts closely with their own debt-collecting agencies. At Bow, Samuel Prentice compounded the frustration caused by his refusal to accept service of summonses on wives by declining to enforce tally tradesmen's debts when they had been contracted without the husband's explicit consent.[100] Prompting an array of local tradesmen – bakers, coal merchants and drapers – who had hitherto resisted joining the ranks of local guardian societies to establish the East London Traders' Protection Association, Prentice's rulings were especially obnoxious to members of the well-organised Scotch drapery trade.[101] Outraged by Prentice's conduct of court business, the London Credit Drapers' Association committed its resources to contesting his paternalistic interpretation of contract law and hired a solicitor to monitor credit drapery suits in the Bow court. In July 1884, the association resolved to appeal a test-case, *Walker* v. *Aldridge*, to the High Court in an attempt to force Prentice to change his mode of operation. The plaintiff, G.W. Walker, had previously come into conflict with the court's registrar for failing to negotiate personally

---

[99] *CDG*, 1 August 1884, 27.   [100] See, for example, *CDG*, 1 November 1884, 101–2.
[101] *East London Press*, 2 and 9 August 1884.

Market moralities 311

with his debtors before meeting them in court and for neglecting to ensure that the husbands whom he sued were fully cognisant of the debts contracted by their wives. Appealing these decisions to Prentice, Walker had succeeded in obtaining judgments for the bulk of his debts, but in one suit, involving a pair of blankets purchased by a wife on her husband's credit, the judge reduced the amount of the claim by five shillings, from twenty-two shillings and sixpence to seventeen shillings and sixpence. Popham, the solicitor retained by the London Credit Drapers' Association, promptly objected to this decision, noting that the debtor husband had not only declined to mount a defence but failed to appear in court at all. 'After a little demur', Prentice agreed to allow the case to be heard by a superior court. The London Credit Drapers' Association called a meeting of its members to support the appeal, which its treasurer estimated would cost subscribers a sum of £150 to prosecute.[102]

Submitted to the Divisional Court of the High Court of Justice, the appeal was heard several months later by Sir Henry Hawkins and Sir Archibald Smith. Here it emerged that the defendant, Jesse Aldridge, was a labourer in receipt of wages of twenty-five shillings a week and was (or claimed to be) entirely ignorant of his wife's dealings with the local tallyman. Walker made no effort to demonstrate that he had negotiated with anyone other than Aldridge's spouse for the blankets, priced at twenty-two shillings and sixpence. The wife had undertaken to furnish this sum in weekly instalments of a shilling, but had ceased to make any payments – while retaining possession of the blankets – after the first month. Upon learning that the plaintiff offered his customers blankets that ranged in price from sixteen shillings and sixpence to thirty-five shillings a pair, judge Prentice – on no evidence beyond his own notions of the proper norms of working-class domestic provisioning – had ruled 'that the wife had an implied power and authority to purchase on her husband's credit blankets to the value and price of 17s.6. but not blankets of greater value or price, as such last mentioned blankets were not suitable and necessary for a person of the defendant's means and condition of life'. The appeal judges not only upheld Prentice's judgment but suggested that, in light of the absence of any evidence that Aldridge had given his wife implied or express authority to pledge his credit, Prentice could (following the precedent of *Debenham* v. *Mellon*) legitimately have refused to enforce the contract at all. Adding insult to this injury, Mr Justice Hawkins concluded his summary of the case by delivering a swingeing rebuke to the tally trade and its campaign to enlist the resources of the court system to collect its debts. Regretting 'that there is leave to appeal given in matters of this sort', Hawkins counselled Prentice to refuse to enforce claims in which a creditor had failed to negotiate directly with the hapless

---

[102] *CDG*, 1 August 1884, 29–30. See also Finn, 'Working-class women and the contest for consumer control', 146–8.

312   Petty debts and the modernisation of English law

husband who was ultimately liable for the payment. 'These men call at the houses of these poor people when their husbands are absent, see the wives and offer them expensive articles without making any inquiry at all into the matter', he asserted indignantly. 'I think it would be a very useful thing if the learned County Court Judge would take the matter in hand and adopt such a course.'[103]

Although court records for Prentice's jurisdiction in the immediate aftermath of this decision do not survive, the plaint and minute books for 1892 demonstrate that Prentice and his registrar continued to render judgments that signalled their unwillingness to accept tradesmen's campaign to absorb the county courts fully into their debt collection networks. Court personnel determined 674 causes in April 1892, and reduced the amount of the claim in 106 cases (15.7 per cent). Significantly, as in 1884, a number of these reductions were made by the court officer despite the defendant's failure either to defend his suit in person or to dispatch his wife to appear on his behalf. On 29 April, for example, M. Abbott & Company, coal merchants, had their suit against the absent Mr Wilson reduced from thirteen shillings and sixpence to eleven shillings and sixpence, to be paid in instalments of two shillings a month; their claim against Thomas Hickey, who also failed to attend the court, was reduced from nine shillings and threepence to eight shillings and threepence; and Richard Brown saw his debt of seven shillings to the coal merchant reduced to only five shillings – or would have done so, had he been in attendance at court.[104]

Credit drapers remained prominent among the court's plaintiffs in the 1890s, but appear to have restricted their use of the court in response to Prentice's strictures.[105] As Table 7.1 indicates, drapers were far less frequent plaintiffs than either coal merchants or the Midland Boot Company – whose paid agents were ubiquitous in the Bow court records. Both the Midland Boot Company and M. Abbott & Company were such frequent litigants that the clerk, to avoid writing the firms' names repeatedly in the 'Plaintiff' column in the minute book, procured rubber-stamps to use in registering their plaints. The relatively high rate – even when compared to the notorious credit drapers – at which these companies suffered the indignity of seeing their claims reduced suggests that Prentice's court remained both hostile to indiscriminate resort to the debt law and committed to deploying officials' discretionary powers to subvert retailers' anonymous, systematic use of the courts to enforce plebeian consumer contracts.

If Samuel Prentice was an especially well-documented practitioner of county-court equitable discretion, his activities clearly formed only a small part of a

---

[103] *CDG*, 15 January 1885, 20–1.

[104] LMA, CCT/AK/15/8, Bow County Court Plaint and Minute Book, 1892, 29 April 1892, plaint numbers 2457, 2461, 2465.

[105] And possibly in response to credit drapers' wider campaign to rehabilitate their reputation, for which see esp. Rubin, 'From packmen, tallymen and "Perambulating Scotchmen"'.

Market moralities   313

Table 7.1. *Debts reduced, Shoreditch and Bow County Court, April 1892*

Company trade	Causes heard	Debts reduced	% debts reduced
Midland Boot	135	16	12
coal merchants	123	26	21
drapers & tailors	44	3	7

Source: London Metropolitan Archives, CCT/AK/15/8, Bow County Court Plaint and Minute Book, 1892.

much broader pattern of judicial practice. Newspaper reports, trade circulars, the legal press and parliamentary inquiries all made the willingness of many county-court judges to limit retailers' rights conspicuously manifest to contemporary observers. When the House of Lords convened a select committee on imprisonment for debt in 1893, many judges were vociferous in defending this right to moderate creditors' legal claims, adducing lines of argument that ran directly counter to the testimony of trade protection society witnesses. Judge Chalmers, who presided in Birmingham over the nation's busiest small-claims tribunal, was unapologetic in declaring that every county-court 'judge works the Act on a different system; it is a purely discretionary system'. Sir Richard Harrington also openly acknowledged that he applied different sentencing principles in the different localities within his circuit, normally imprisoning defendants only for short periods but imposing the full forty-day sentence at Stourbridge, 'Because I think there are a larger proportion of rogues there.' William Renwick, agent of the Bristol, West of England and South Wales Credit Drapers' Association, indignantly denounced the Swindon county-court judge, who exhibited 'a strong aversion to committing to prison at all'. Like judge Atkinson at Leeds, the Swindon judge used strategic adjournments to discourage retailers' undue reliance upon legal coercion. 'He will make a committal order for 3 or 5 days, and suspend it for 150 days', Renwick complained; 'his committals are, if I may say so, ridiculous.'[106]

These judicial appeals to equity, discretion and moral distinctions testify to the persistence in the Victorian county courts of ideals that had inspired courts of conscience since their inception. Notions of 'equity and good conscience' served to link county-court officials to a venerable paternalist conception of just contracts while working to associate the inferior county-court system with the equitable provisions of superior-court practice preserved by the Judicature Acts of the 1870s. Cloaked in these traditions, county-court judges sought to combat the increasingly strident campaigns mounted against their exercise of

---

[106] *Report of the Select Committee* (1893–94), 31, 44, 134.

314   Petty debts and the modernisation of English law

discretionary justice by tradesmen's associations. In doing so, they ensured that a system of dispute resolution intended by its parliamentary proponents to modernise and regularise contractual relations often served – both discursively and in the practice of everyday life – to reinforce notions of mutual obligation between debtors and their creditors that dated from earlier centuries.

Conclusion

Political lobbying developed as a logical corollary of the guardian societies' campaigns in the county courts, and the retention of imprisonment for small debts occupied pride of place in this portion of their expanding list of activities. The minutes of the Hull Guardians document a sustained effort – stretching from the era of the courts of requests to that of the county courts – to convince Parliament that arrest and imprisonment remained vital mechanisms for securing the credit contracts that underpinned modern commerce. From the 1820s, petition after petition issued from the society, urging Parliament to enhance tradesmen's powers to enforce credit contracts, advocating an increase in the Hull court of requests' jurisdiction to twenty pounds and endorsing government efforts to reform the debt law at a national level.[107] Significantly, when Parliament undertook reform of insolvency law in the 1860s, the Hull Guardians accepted the dominant argument that debtors who owed sums of twenty pounds or more should be liberated from the gaol by gaining new access to bankruptcy procedures. But they remained bitterly – and vocally – opposed to proposals to abolish imprisonment for debt for lesser sums.[108]

Local MPs, conscious of tradesmen's electoral significance, entered actively into the guardian societies' political endeavours, working actively to ensure that their complaints were taken seriously in the corridors of power at Westminster.[109] The formation of the National Association of Trade Protection Societies in 1865 added substantially to the volume, stridence and efficacy of the guardian societies' political campaigns. From the outset, the National Association enjoyed ready access to government ministers, contact secured in part through the strategic device of appointing sympathetic MPs as honorary members of their organisation. Already in 1866, delegates of the National Association, accompanied by a supportive cadre of MPs, had waited upon the Attorney-General at the House of Lords to air their views and grievances on

---

[107] See, for example, East Riding of Yorkshire Archives, DDX 424/1, Hull Guardian Society, Minute Book, 1827–July 1844, 21 June 1827; 5 March 1829; 11 June 1829; 18 November 1830; 24 March 1835; 25 May 1843.

[108] East Riding of Yorkshire Archives, DDX 424/3, Hull Guardian Society, Minute Book, 1862–76, 27 March 1865; 7 April 1869; 5 May 1869; 4 August 1869.

[109] See, for example, East Riding of Yorkshire Archives, DDX 424/1, Hull Guardian Society, Minute Book, 1827–July 1844, 6 June 1839; DDX 424/2, Hull Guardian Society, Minute Book, August 1844–62, 2 September 1847.

Market moralities 315

bankruptcy and insolvency reform; as the pace of legal innovation quickened in the following year, the Lord Chancellor's secretary was careful to keep the Association's leadership apprised of developments, and the Lord Chancellor met with a deputation to discuss their concerns.[110] Convinced in 1869 that it was 'of the utmost importance that the power for Imprisonment in County Courts should be retained as at present',[111] the National Association unleashed battery upon battery of circulars, petitions and telegrams when politicians hostile to county-court committals sought to disrupt the status quo. When the Liberal MP Michael Thomas Bass, an active parliamentary advocate of the abolition of imprisonment for debt, secured the appointment of a select committee to review this procedure in 1873, the National Association mobilised its political resources to ensure that the committee – initially packed with Bass's supporters – included a significant contingent of MPs favourable to the trade protection movement.[112] Like the advocates of the courts of conscience who had defended imprisonment for petty debts as a vital aspect of useful credit a century before in 1780, the National Association linked the maintenance of execution against the body firmly to the preservation of plebeian character and morals. Urging in 1874 that 'a limited amount of credit is absolutely indispensable to the vast majority of persons in all classes of society', a petition circulated by the society in opposition to a proposed bill to limit county-court imprisonment underlined the impossibility of executing against the goods of the poor and concluded that there were moreover 'many wives and families to whom an execution [against the goods] is a greater hardship than the temporary imprisonment of the debtor, as the debtors who actually go to jail are almost invariably of a very low class'.[113]

Thwarted in their ambition to modernise contractual obligations in the courtroom itself, the trade protection societies emerged from their legal and economic campaigns as passionate advocates of the retention of county-court imprisonment. Judge Atkinson in 1878 dismissed the county courts' reformulation of this medieval mechanism as the 'last lingering relic of a barbarous age',[114] but tradesmen active in national politics repeatedly – and successfully – countered that imprisonment for debt was an essential tool for effecting the transition from status to contract among working-class consumers. The inaccessibility of customers' banking records – or, for many working-class consumers, the absence of any savings whatsoever – and the legal obstacles that prevented debt

---

[110] Leicestershire RO, DE 3512/25, National Association of Trade Protection Societies, Minutes, 1865–90, 13, 26, 28.

[111] Ibid., 74.

[112] Ibid., printed circulars of 19 February and 1 March 1873 (not paginated). For Bass's campaign, see Finn, 'Scotch drapers and the politics of modernity', 97–100.

[113] Leicestershire RO, DE 3512/25, National Association of Trade Protection Societies, Minutes, 1865–80, 'Imprisonment for debt. To the Honourable the Commons . . .' [1874].

[114] Above, 262.

recovery from wives, servants and children who engaged in daily household purchasing ensured that social and cultural capital continued to play an essential role in retailers' efforts to evaluate the worth and credibility of their clientele. Just as the consumer's person – as manifest in dress, accent, demeanour and style – offered access to the world of goods through the mechanism of credit, so too, for the most lowly of purchasers, the body itself necessarily served as the ultimate guarantee of payment in the modern period.

Conclusion

Preserved within the correspondence of the eighteenth-century philanthropist John Howard is an anonymous didactic tale designed to expose the horrors of the unreformed debtors' prison. 'The Story of Honestus and Constantia' deploys the received conventions of fiction to advance explicitly political ends. The debtor protagonists, like countless characters in English novels, figure as quintessential victims of misfortune, their idyllic marriage shattered because the virtuous Constantia's 'external Charms captivated the rich Corruptus'. Playing upon the conflation between female sexuality and insolvency that had structured literary representation since the financial revolution, Corruptus connives 'to gratify his . . . hellish lust' by extending credit to Honestus. When her husband proves 'unfortunate' in his commercial dealings and is imprisoned for debt by the implacable Corruptus, Constantia is left cold, ill and unprotected. Subjected to the unwanted attentions of her husband's creditor when Corruptus – 'Rank with desire' – enters her home with false offers of charity, Constantia – like Richardson's Pamela when attacked by Mr B – falls into a faint. Death mercifully releases Constantia from further persecution, but Honestus, driven insane by her demise, is liberated from the debtors' prison only to be incarcerated in a madhouse. In a final, gothic twist of fate, his two daughters are adopted by Corruptus, who seduces the girls, and abandons them to a life of prostitution. Such, the author concludes 'was the fate of a worthy virtuous family, all for no crime, who, had they not been Britons, might probably have lived to have been an ornament to their species'.[1]

'The Story of Honestus and Constantia' captures the pervasive intertextuality of the narratives of debt and credit that moulded and made sense of day-to-day exchange relations in English society and culture. The histrionic tones and lurid events that animate this sad saga derive at once from the literary devices and the historical tropes that informed the character of credit; they speak to the overlapping terrain shared by the imaginative expression and the social experience of personal debts in the English past. Rehearsing the dominant plot lines, symbolic

---

[1] Bodleian, MS Eng.misc.c.332, Letters of John Howard, fols. 55–6. Undated, but later eighteenth century.

linkages and sexual preoccupations of fiction, the tale resonates with primary documents that stretch across a spectrum of genres and range over an extended sweep of historical time. As court records, diaries, novels, memoirs, advertisements, personal correspondence, pamphlets and government papers alike attest, the unequal power relations that attached to personal debts and credits were woven into the fabric of contemporary consciousness and permeated the texture of material life. (Illustration 10.) Gender and sexuality recur again and again as the focal points around which these tensions – simultaneously economic, social and political in their content and meaning – were constructed. Constantia's fictional fate runs parallel to the narratives revealed by other archival records: in Randolph Trumbach's sample of fourteen rape prosecutions initiated by married women in eighteenth-century London, for example, five victims identified their attackers as creditors to whom their husbands stood indebted. Betteridge May, assaulted by her husband's employer in 1734, testified in court that she had hesitated to inform her spouse of the rape because her attacker had threatened that if she did so, he would dismiss May from work and imprison him for debt.[2] Later in the century, entangled skeins of economic obligation, sexual strife and legal coercion likewise figured conspicuously in the letters of Samuel Wesley – nephew of the founder of the Methodist movement and a successful musician until debilitating depression and crippling personal debts forced him into premature and impoverished retirement. Defending his future wife, Charlotte Martin, from his family's censure as a youth in 1792, Wesley emphatically denied that she was 'a fickle & unsteady Character' and protested indignantly that 'From me she never received or would accept aught but mere Trifles, although amongst the other diabolical Slanders it was affirmed . . . that I had engaged to liquidate her Debts & administer to her Luxuries'. Finding upon their marriage, however, that Charlotte was 'a determined Spendthrift', Wesley abandoned his wife and children to establish a second household with his adolescent maidservant. Unpaid obligations now preyed on his conscience with new force, destabilising Wesley's already precarious mental balance. In 1817, convinced that he was pursued by creditors set upon him by his estranged wife, Wesley flung himself from a window, falling twenty-five feet to the stones below. Confined to an asylum, he was released in 1818, his financial prospects blighted. 'All is up or down in this whirligig World', Wesley wrote to a friend in 1825, when his earlier delusions of pursuit by Charlotte's creditors proved prescient. 'My loving Wife has caused me to be arrested, & to-morrow . . . I am going to Prison.'[3]

[2] Randolph Trumbach, *Sex and the Gender Revolution, vol. I: Heterosexuality and the Third Gender in Enlightenment London* (Chicago, 1999), 303–5.

[3] Phillip Olleson, ed., *The Letters of Samuel Wesley: Professional and Social Correspondence, 1792–1837* (Oxford, 2001), xxxii, xliii, 366. He was imprisoned in the Cursitor Street spunging-house to which Thackeray later consigned Becky Sharpe's hapless spouse for her debts in *Vanity Fair*.

Conclusion 319

10 Advertisement for a Mortlake tea dealer and cheesemonger, depicting Samuel Johnson paying Oliver Goldsmith's debts to his landlady, to preserve the novelist from the debtors' prison. Narratives of debt and credit drawn from the world of fiction were integral to the daily practices of material life. (Reproduced by permission of the Bodleian Library.)

320   The Character of Credit

In the Victorian era, more stolid observers of social and economic life continued to write the history of personal debt and credit relations as a narrative of sexual transgression and marital infidelity. In a pamphlet advocating reform of imprisonment for debt published in 1858, George Montagu Hicks – the governor charged with introducing a disciplinary regime at London's Whitecross Street prison – recapitulated a familiar and long-lived line of argument when he insisted that 'a stringent line should be drawn between criminality and misfortune'. To illustrate the moral dilemmas that ensued from the innocent debtor's liability to the vagaries of credit, Hicks retailed the story of a wire-worker imprisoned in the gaol by a builder for his unpaid rent. Here as in 'The Story of Honestus and Constantia' and in the life of Samuel Wesley, a husband's path to the prison was speeded by sexual misconduct that disrupted the sanctity of the domestic hearth. The builder, having seduced the debtor's wife, insisted that the wire-worker accept her back into his home, and summarily imprisoned him at Whitecross Street when he refused to accede to this demand.[4] Fiction and melodrama, Hicks's polemical tract suggested, were the very stuff of debt and credit obligations in England, rather than simply literary means by which social and economic experience was represented in signs, symbols and texts.[5]

Character figured centrally and recurrently in English debt relations, both as a metonym for personal credit in moral discourse and as a pragmatic mechanism for obtaining goods and services through the credit nexus. Georgian, Victorian and Edwardian men and women deployed characters – their own and those of the burgeoning fictional canon – along a kaleidoscopic array of radial axes. In prescriptive literature, character acquired static connotations associated with the self-control of autonomous individuals: in Stefan Collini's description, Victorian conceptions of character were marked 'by the assumption that the possession of settled dispositions indicated a certain habit of restraining one's impulses'.[6] But in the market, character constantly displayed a dynamic form, forced by the demands of praxis to flow along fluid lines dictated by desire, strategy and necessity rather than remaining securely within the channels fixed by prescriptive political economy. The identities assembled and reassembled on a daily basis by English consumers at all social levels in a wide array of exchange transactions cast these men and women as irrepressible characters in the market. Unstable constructs contingent upon dress, manner, verbal facility and connection, their characters drew upon the perceived verities of social capital rather than upon the monetary values of the cash nexus alone. The swindlers

---

[4] [George Montagu Hicks], *The Double Doom of the Poor Debtor: To Those Who Owe Money; and Those To Whom It Is Due* (London, 1858), 11.

[5] See similarly the argument that autobiographical writing 'was not just an inscription but a medium of gender relations', in Trev Lynn Broughton, *Men of Letters, Writing Lives: Masculinity and Literary Auto/Biography in the Late Victorian Period* (London, 1999), 78.

[6] Stefan Collini, *Public Moralists: Political Thought and Intellectual Life in Britain 1850–1930* (Oxford, 1991), 97.

Conclusion

who – much to the discomfiture of tradesmen and guardian societies – forged concocted connections to obtain goods on false pretences were clothed in the character of credit, but so too were the multitude of respectable men and women who enjoyed cycles of retail credit that extended for weeks, months and even years at a time by virtue of their status as social individuals.

In the idealised moral cosmologies crafted by hortatory authors such as Samuel Smiles, lapses in personal character led ineluctably to the autonomous individual's loss of personal credit.[7] By contrast, the characters chronicled in novels, diaries, memoirs, prison records and legal documents repeatedly succeeded in sustaining their credit relations despite their economic deficiencies and moral failings. George Gitton of Bridgnorth, a bankrupt printer with a decided weakness for drink, epitomised the inherently conflicted character of credit in the practices of everyday life. The recipient in 1866 of a stream of gifts from friends, patrons and creditors – four cigars presented by his grocer at the New Year, half a sovereign from a kind-hearted justice of the peace, a pork pie gifted by a shopkeeper with whom Gitton traded on account, a 'fine bottle' of old port donated by a local MP and 'a pair of button boots good as new' from Thomas Branson, Esq. – Gitton eked out an existence through a panoply of expedient makeshifts. Cash cadged from all and sundry bolstered the trade credit perpetually extended, redeemed in part and then renewed by the nearby shopkeepers from whom Gitton made his necessary purchases of milk, butter, eggs, meat and porter. Part-time employment reporting county-court suits for the *Bridgnorth Journal* and the *Shrewsbury Chronicle* brought Gitton muchneeded cash income, but court reporting was not his only connection with the legal realm of contract. Sued by his coal-dealer and his ale-merchant, Gitton appeared repeatedly as a defendant in the court whose proceedings he routinely chronicled for the Shropshire press.[8]

The sheer volume of credit relations revealed by the myriad personal, institutional and imaginative sources that document English exchange relations is striking. Comprehensive data on retail debt before the First World War are lacking, but the cumulative evidence from small-claims litigation attests to the centrality of credit-dealing over the course of the very long nineteenth century. As Craig Muldrew has conclusively demonstrated, 'credit was ... extended as a normative part of the tens of thousands of daily market sales and services' already in the sixteenth century: in the early modern period, 'it was credit, above all, which dominated the way in which the market was structured and interpreted'.[9]

---

[7] See, for example, Samuel Smiles, *Thrift* (1875; London 1997), chaps. 12–13, and above, 20–1.

[8] M.D.G. Wanklyn, ed., *The Diary of George Gitton of Bridgnorth for 1866*, Shropshire Record Series, vol. 2 (1998). For his gifts, see 1 (2 January 1866); 10 (26 and 27 January 1866); 31 (31 March 1866); 119 (31 December 1866). For his county-court activities, see, for example, 3 (6 January 1866); 41 (30 April 1866); 49 (24 March 1866); 51–2 (4 June 1866).

[9] Craig Muldrew, *The Economy of Obligation: The Culture of Credit and Social Relations in Early Modern England* (Basingstoke, 1998), 95.

322   The Character of Credit

The borough courts in which the bulk of disputed petty debts had hitherto been tried suffered significant declines in litigation by the early eighteenth century, but the erection – in the face of powerful opposition from exponents of the common-law tradition – of local courts of conscience throughout England and Wales in the century from 1740 to 1840 testified to contemporaries' persistent recognition of the essential role of 'useful credit' in economic life. Notoriously chaotic and often staggeringly corrupt, these equitable small-claims courts laid the foundations of the modern county-court system that came to dominate civil litigation in Victorian and Edwardian England. Although county-court statistics capture only those (relatively few) debt disputes that consumers were unable to resolve through interpersonal negotiation or the offices of debt-collecting societies, they are suggestive indices of the pervasive extent of credit trading in this period. Rising from 396,793 plaints in 1850 to 878,493 plaints in 1875, county-court litigation brought 1,146,418 debtors within the grip of the civil law in 1900.[10] Credit drapers alone boasted tens of thousands of accounts with working-class families. When tally traders active in the northern counties mobilised against a parliamentary proposal to abolish county-court imprisonment in 1873, they conducted a partial census of provincial trade in which 665 credit drapers reported 960,548 heads of household – or several million customers – on their books.[11] Writing in 1914, W.H. Whitelock, registrar of the Birmingham county court, ventured hesitantly that credit dealing was on the decline in urban centres, but none the less had 'little doubt that 70 per cent. to 80 per cent. of the working-class families still supply their requirements on credit'.[12] Middle- and upper-class consumers were no less entangled in the credit nexus than were the lesser sort. As Erika Rappaport has cautioned in analysing purchasing by the propertied classes, 'Informal store credit was so prevalent and so irregular that studies of income levels alone tell us little about the nature of the growth of consumer society.'[13]

A recognition that the English economy was fundamentally structured by credit relations is essential to our understanding of the ways in which the market functioned as a site of praxis. In classical and Marxian economic theory, credit features as an inert composite of cash, time and interest, but in English markets credit acted as a dynamic force, effecting qualitative change in the substance of

[10] Patrick Polden, *A History of the County Court, 1846–1971* (Cambridge, 1999), Appendix 3, Table 1.

[11] Anon., *Abstract Report of a Conference of Delegates Representing the Northern Central Credit-Drapery Association*... (Manchester, [1873]), 8–17.

[12] W.H. Whitelock, 'The industrial credit system and imprisonment for debt', *Economic Journal*, 24 (March 1914), 33. Muldrew, *Economy of Obligation*, 100, estimates that about 90 per cent of trade in early modern England was conducted on a credit rather than a cash basis.

[13] Erika Rappaport, *Shopping for Pleasure: Women and the Making of London's West End* (Princeton, 2000), 54. A logical corollary of this conclusion is that the function of domestic credit significantly problematises historiographical debates over the standard of living.

Conclusion 323

consumer relations. Beyond contributing to the quantitative growth of consumer activity, credit channelled consumption in new directions by empowering economic agents – most notably married women – who were otherwise excluded from circuits of exchange governed by the laws of contract. Under the law of necessaries, wives and infant children obtained a cornucopia of 'necessary' goods through the credit of husbands and fathers, binding these 'independent' individuals through liens of debt to contractual obligations not of their own making. Where autonomous individuals, free contracts and cash exchange dominated economists' conceptions of the market, social individuals, contractual coercion and the credit nexus were familiar – and essential – accompaniments of daily purchasing practices in the historical market. If economic theorists were loath to acknowledge the salience and significance of personal credit, writers of imaginative and autobiographical literature were palpably alive to its implications. In novels, diaries and memoirs, the traffic of goods – gifted, begged, borrowed and cadged, as well as bought for money – was described in loving detail as writers (themselves immersed in the quotidian stratagems and prone to the daily indignities of debt and credit obligations) rehearsed the narrative lines that describe the social life of contract.

The history of social individuals and their credit contracts complicates and challenges models of contractual freedom that attend too insistently to the genealogy of personal autonomy. Sir Henry Maine's classic formulation of the triumphal progress from status to contract wrought by modernisation, Albert Venn Dicey's less sanguine reflections on the rise and fall of freedom of contract in nineteenth-century England and the more recent reinscriptions of these influential paradigms offer essential insights into the changing trajectory of legal regulation over time.[14] But by focusing on the possessive individual to the detriment of dependent social persons, these approaches to the history of contract also distort our understanding of material culture in the past. In labour markets, as Robert Steinfeld has forcefully demonstrated, 'free' contracts between employers and their workers repeatedly 'yielded "unfree" labor' in Georgian and Victorian England.[15] Until 1872, employers could compel wage workers to fulfil their labour contracts by appealing to local justices of the peace, who were empowered by Master and Servant legislation to imprison offenders at hard labour in houses of correction. In consumer markets, the evolution of free contracts

[14] For Maine, see above, 15–16. Dicey's *Lectures on the Relation between Law and Public Opinion in England during the Nineteenth Century* (London, 1905) is situated within the intellectual and political (as opposed to the social and cultural) context of contractual evolution in P.S. Atiyah, *The Rise and Fall of Freedom of Contract* (Oxford, 1979), 231–7.

[15] Robert J. Steinfeld, *Coercion, Contract and Free Labor in the Nineteenth Century* (Cambridge, 2001), 39. See also John V. Orth, *Combination and Conspiracy: A Legal History of Trade Unionism, 1721–1906* (Oxford, 1991), and Douglas Hay, 'Patronage, paternalism and welfare: masters, workers, and magistrates in eighteenth-century England', *International Labor and Working-Class History*, 53 (Spring 1998), 27–48.

324   The Character of Credit

was likewise riddled with contradictions. The decades that saw Parliament enact successive statutes to punish breaches of labour agreements also witnessed the creation of courts of conscience and courts of requests empowered to confine petty debtors to prisons and bridewells for failure to meet their credit obligations in the consumer market. This effort to render the autonomous individual fully liable for his (and eventually her) personal contracts was repeatedly confounded by the dense networks of social relations in which personal identities and contractual persons were enmeshed. In the market, freedom of contract for husbands and fathers was constantly threatened by the freedom from contractual liabilities enjoyed by their dependent wives and children.

Like the history of male workers and consumers in the market, the history of women's contractual identities is habitually told in terms of the rise of the autonomous individual. In standard accounts of the protracted struggle for the reform of married women's property, feminist politics powered by liberal conceptions of individual rights lie at the heart of legal change. Democratic impulses and feminist agendas enjoy pride of place in this narrative of contractual evolution, which identifies the petitioning campaign initiated by Bessie Leigh Smith and her female associates on the Married Women's Property Committee of 1854–56 as the point of origin for the eventual passage of the Married Women's Property Acts of 1870–93. 'The feminists' concerns for the freedom and equality of women placed them in the mainstream of nineteenth-century liberalism', Lee Holcombe has written of these developments; the attempted reform of married women's property legislation in 1854–56, Mary Lyndon Shanley similarly argues, derived from Leigh Smith's passionate belief in 'each individual's claim to equality before the law'. In this description, wives' ability to pledge their husbands' credit for necessary goods constituted only a marginal incentive to reform of marital propertied rights. 'Perhaps as an afterthought calculated to appeal to their parliamentary allies, they added that husbands too suffered under the law, being held responsible for their wives' debts', Shanley observes of the Married Women's Property Committee's petition to Parliament in 1856.[16]

Consideration of the social history of contract, however, suggests the need to augment this liberal narrative of autonomous rights with the competing stories told by social individuals and their market transactions. For the feminist activists of the 1850s had been preceded in 1849 by members of the City of London Trade Protection Society, who had promoted legislation to render married women who were separated from their husbands personally liable for their own debts. February 1849 saw the society print a proposed bill for parliamentary consideration, reciting 'the great impositions and frauds . . . practiced on tradesmen and others, and severe pecuniary losses . . . continually sustained by reason

---

[16] Lee Holcombe, *Wives and Property: Reform of the Married Women's Property Law in Nineteenth-Century England* (Toronto, 1983), 5; Mary Lyndon Shanley, *Feminism, Marriage and the Law in Victorian England, 1850–1895* (Princeton, 1989), 30, 33.

Conclusion 325

of the present state of the law, as regards the defence of coverture to claims and actions founded on contract'.[17] An editorial in the society's weekly circular, supporting this campaign, situated this effort firmly within the modernisation process described by the transition from status to contract. The writer acknowledged that 'in remote times, when the transactions of society were infinitely more simple, and the circumstances of persons well known, and the husband was not only theoretically but practically the possessor of all the property of the wife', coverture 'was not unjust'. But 'modern times' had rendered the law 'wholly unsuited to the present state of society and its relations', subjecting independent male agents to increasingly anachronistic social and economic obligations entailed by the law of necessaries.[18]

Although the City of London Trade Protection Society's short-lived campaign of 1849 proved abortive, guardian societies continued to participate actively in debates on married women's property reform in the following decades. Their interventions were shaped fundamentally by traders' problematic encounters with the myriad married women who acted as social individuals in the market and the county courts. When Parliament debated the Married Women's Property Act of 1893, the National Association of Trade Protection Societies resolved that wives should be held personally liable for all debts which they had contracted. 'The whole of the law with regard to the obligations of married women is in an unsatisfactory state', the association's annual report pronounced gloomily. 'If women are to be allowed the privileges which the Legislature has in recent years given them, then their obligations ought to follow, and be attached to the privileges.'[19] Reflecting tradesmen's mounting frustration with the economic consequences of the halting and piecemeal transition from status to contract in nineteenth-century England, this resolution articulated an alternative model of modernisation. It countered the liberal feminist paradigm, in which the individual's natural rights and freedoms were paramount, with a model of contract more attentive to the pragmatic demands of the credit nexus, in which individual rights were coupled with social obligations, and property ownership figured as a privilege rather than as an essential perquisite of personal identity.

For married women, the acquisition of full contractual rights and responsibilities was to await the interwar years, which saw a concatenation of legal and economic shifts in the formal and informal credit regimes that had dominated market exchange in the Georgian, Victorian and Edwardian periods. Pawnbroking, a staple stratagem in the plebeian wife's economic arsenal, suffered declines during the First World War that were to persist and deepen in the following decades. Hire-purchase agreements, which rose twentyfold between

---

[17] *City of London Trade Protection Circular*, 3 February 1849, 1.
[18] Ibid., 10 February 1849, 1–2.
[19] Leicestershire RO, DE 3512/27, National Association of Trade Protection Societies, Minutes, 1891–98, 45th Annual Report (19 April 1893), 4.

326 The Character of Credit

1918 and 1928, came to account for two-thirds of consumers' larger purchases in this period; instalment plans offered by department stores, clothing clubs, check-traders and mail order firms also brought increasingly routine and formalised credit facilities to an ever-expanding population of purchasers.[20] The resilience exhibited by traditional forms of exchange in the eighteenth and nineteenth centuries – the persistence of gifting behaviours in the era of the consumer revolution, the enduring trope of economic misfortune in contemporary analyses of personal debt and the salience of equitable principles in judicial interpretations of credit obligations – cautions against the assumption that these developments wrought a rapid and wholesale transformation of the social life of contract. But a range of legal evidence none the less points to the interwar years as a period of fundamental change in debt and credit relations. The Married Women and Tortfeasors Act of 1935 (25 & 26 Geo. V c. 30) effectively dismantled the remaining disabilities – and the remaining protections – of coverture, rendering wives personally responsible for their contracts and liable to suffer imprisonment for their unpaid debts.[21] As a device of last resort for enforcing consumer debts, however, imprisonment became an increasingly marginal practice in the interwar years. County-court imprisonment peaked at 11,986 committals in 1906, stood at 5,711 in 1913, dropped to a mere 293 persons in 1918 and rose again to an interwar height of only 4,041 in 1932.[22] Perhaps more significant than these decreasing committal rates were the parallel increases in resort to imprisonment for debt by justices of the peace for defendants' failure to pay maintenance orders, bastardy orders and local rates. When J.D. Unwin, head of the Cambridge University settlement in south London, denounced *The Scandal of Imprisonment for Debt* in 1935, his target was not county-court imprisonment for consumer debts but rather the dramatic interwar rise in the proportion of debt committals ordered by summary police courts.[23] If civil debts contracted with tradesmen on the vicarious credit of male householders by dependent wives and children had been central to contemporaries' understanding of imprisonment for debt in the nineteenth century, committals to prison for failure to pay necessary debts owed to dependent family members and the state emerged as the contentious credit issues of interwar legal processes.

In historical interpretations of English culture and society, the eighteenth century marks a pivotal moment in the modernisation of traditional beliefs and practices, a decisive turning point that saw revolutionary changes in production and consumption, a transformation of notions of time and space and

[20] Melanie Tebbutt, *Making Ends Meet: Pawnbroking and Working-Class Credit* (Leicester, 1983), chap. 6, esp. 179, 186–9, 193, 199.
[21] Holcombe, *Wives and Property*, 224.
[22] Polden, *History of the County Court*, Appendix 3, Table 5.
[23] J.D. Unwin, *The Scandal of Imprisonment for Debt* (London, 1935), 1–4. Imprisonments for failure to pay wife maintenance, bastardy orders and rates roughly doubled in the interwar period.

Conclusion 327

the emergence of newly insistent conceptualisations of the individualist self. Changes in credit relations form an integral component of models of historical change that posit the eighteenth century as a moment of modernisation.[24] The establishment of the Bank of England, joint-stock companies and insurance offices, Craig Muldrew for example argues, worked to shift contractual relations in England away from an economy of mutual obligation in which 'There was not as yet an important social distinction between the utilitarian world of economics and the more "subjective" social world of feelings and events', to a universe in which credit principally depended 'on...rationally determined future profitability and...accumulated physical and monetary capital'.[25] This book in contrast emphasises the protracted nature and partial effects of the eighteenth-century's modernising impulses. The slow pace, unstable trajectories and unintended consequences of cultural, social and economic change are defining features of the character of credit in England from 1740 to 1914. Where Sir Henry Maine saw a modern transition from status to contract, the history of personal debts and credits reveals instead an ongoing dialogue and accommodation between contractual behaviours and the enduring status differentials of gender and of class.

---

[24] See especially the perceptive surveys of eighteenth-century moments of modernity in Miles Ogborn, *Spaces of Modernity: London's Geographies 1680–1780* (London, 1998), esp. chap. 1, and Kathleen Wilson, 'Citizenship, empire and modernity in the English provinces, *c.* 1720–90', in Catherine Hall, ed., *Cultures of Empire: A Reader* (Manchester, 2000), 157–86.

[25] Muldrew, *Economy of Obligation*, 65, 329.

Bibliography

ARCHIVAL DOCUMENTS

Bath City Record Office, Bath
Court of Requests Minute Books, 1829–41

Bedfordshire Record Office, Bedford
QGR/1/15, Reports and Papers, Bedford County Gaol, 1846, 1850
QGR/1/33, Reports and Papers, Bedford County Gaol, 1853

Birmingham Central Reference Library, Birmingham
William Hutton MS
Winson Green Prison Newscuttings, Local Studies, L.43.93

Bodleian Library, Oxford
Eng.misc.c.332, Letters of John Howard
Eng.misc.f.865, Account book of Charles Noel, 1858–60
Eng. MS.lett.c.13, Letterbook of John Matthews, Oxford solicitor, 1835–36
John Johnson Collection of Ephemera

Bristol Record Office, Bristol
09303/1, Court of Requests Proceedings, 1816
09308/1–2, Court of Requests Execution Books, 1816–32

British Library, London
India Office records, Home Misc. series, H/420, 'First Section of the Statistical Report',
  Fort William, Calcutta, 26 October 1798

British Library of Political and Economic Science, London
Sir Joshua Jebb Papers

Cambridge University Library, Cambridge
Add. 9358/7/4, Court of Requests Minute Book, Chatteris, 1785–92

Centre for Buckinghamshire Studies, Aylesbury
Q/DA/95, Pocket Book of G. Stratford

328

Bibliography

City of Westminster Archives, London
M612/2, Benjamin Haydon Correspondence

Corporation of London Record Office
Borough Compter Journal, 1817–23
Composite Printed Minutes of the Court of Aldermen, 1853–70
Gaol Committee Minute Books
Gaol Committee Officers' Reports
Gaol Committee Papers
Letterbook of John Law, Keeper of Southwark Compter, 1819
London Court of Requests Register Book (1786)
Minute Book of the Committee to Enquire into the Practice & Fees of the Court of Requests, 1774–88
Misc. MSS. 258.4, Minutes of Evidence and Papers re. The Conduct of Sir Watkin Lewes, 1815.
Misc. MSS. 342.3, Proceedings before Sir George Carroll and Alderman Cubitt, 12 May 1857
Repertories of the Court of Aldermen: Rep. 162, 179, 182, 222, 227, 250
SC 2/6, Southwark Compter Register, 1809–18

East Riding of Yorkshire Archives, Beverley
DDX 424/1–7, Hull Guardian Society for the Protection of Trade, Minute Books, 1827–1926
DDX 424/12, Hull Guardian Society, Information Book

Gloucestershire Record Office, Gloucester
Q/Gc/18/1–3, Prison Charity Committee Proceedings, 1792–1845

Guildhall Library, London
MS 659, King's Bench Miscellaneous Papers
MS 10,781, Allhallows Lombard Street, Receipts for Prisoners' Relief, Ralph Carter's Charity, 1824–66
MS 13,668/1–2, Christ's Hospital: Dame Mary Ramsey's Gift: Account of Payments, 1824–41
MS 17,009, Ironmongers' Company Charities: Volume of Signed Receipts for Beneficiaries Confined for Debt, 1718–70
MS 17,027, Prison Charities: Thatched House
MS 20,364–67, Papers of James Budgett & Son, Ltd., Grocers
Pam 5339, Rules for the Court Erected by Some of the Prisoners in the King's Bench, Prison (abolished 21 June 1779)

Lancaster Reference Library, Lancaster
D 6351, no. 24, Lancaster Castle Returns and Correspondence
Higgin Family Biography File
Lancaster Castle Census, 1851
MS 133, Special Commission to Inquire into the State, Conduct and Management of Lancaster Castle, 1812–15

330   Bibliography

MS 2311, Account Book of the Rigby Charity, 1783–1800
MS 3218, Punishment Book, Lancaster Castle, 1785–89
MS 6615, Book of Laws to Be Observed by the Court of Lancaster Castle, 17 June 1772
MS 7321, Account of the Prison as Related by Mr. Higgin, Keeper

Lancashire Record Office, Preston
QAL/1, Lancaster Castle Committee Proceedings, 1783–1848

Leicestershire Record Office, Wigston Magna
DE 3512/25–28, National Association of Trade Protection Societies, Minutes, 1865–1902
DE 3848/4–5, Minute Books of the Leicester Trade Protection Society, 1854–80
7D70/4, Leicester Trade Protection Society, Monthly Circulars and Annual Reports

Lincolnshire Archives, Lincoln
AK 16/2, Boston County Court Minute Book, 1847–48
AK 16/12, Boston County Court Minute Book, 1899–1900
CoC 2/1, Minutes of the Grand Jury, 1741–1891
CoC 2/6, Lincolnshire Gaol Sessions, 1858–70
CoC 5/1/1–5, Lincoln Castle Keeper's Journals, 1824–60
R Box L.365.9 HAR, 93/26, Michael Hardy, 'Lincoln County Gaol in 1851' (typescript)
Stubbs 128/2, Brigg Court of Requests Minute Book, 1808–12

London Metropolitan Archives
CCT/AK/15/4, Bow County Court Plaint and Minute Book, 1849–51
CCT/AK/15/8, Bow County Court Plaint and Minute Book, 1892

Oxfordshire Record Office, Oxford
CCT/3/A06/1, Thame County Court Execution and Commitment Book, 1892–1908

Public Record Office, London
C 114/34, Chancery Masters' Exhibitions: Material Relating to the Society for the Protection of Trade against Swindlers
HO 20, Prisons Correspondence and Papers, 1820–43
HO 45, Registered Papers, 1839–1979
HO 49/9, Correspondence to the Law Officers, 1843–55
HO 86/1–3, County Courts Entry Books, 1845–69
HO 119/8, Miscellaneous Reports (Civil), 1827–33
HO 130/3, Prison Statistics and Regulations, 1824–26
LCO 2/57, Married Women's Bill, Comments on, 1892–93
LCO 2/1145, Imprisonment for Debt: Statistics and Costs, 1928–35
LCO 3/66, Imprisonment for Debt, Suggestions on, 1893
PALA 8/70, Palace Court Rule Book, 1801–02
PALA 9/1/25–27, Palace Court Judges' Notebooks, 1843–45
PALA 9/3, Appointments of Officers of the Palace Court
PALA 9/8, Palace Court and Marshalsea Miscellaneous Books and Papers
PCOM 2/293–94, Bedford Prison Governor's Journal, 1852–67

Bibliography 331

PCOM 2/396, Shrewsbury Debtors Register, 1855–61
PCOM 2/400, Spilsby Gaol Discharge Register, 1826–48
PCOM 2/442–4, Lancaster Castle Governor's Journals, 1816–48
PCOM 7/491, Employment and Payment of Debtors, 1899–1900
PCOM 9/61, Memorandum on the Law of Civil Coercion, 1929
PCOM 9/1321, Treatment of Debtor Prisoners, 1945–47
PRIS 9, Queen's Prison: Miscellaneous Books, 1842–62
PRIS 10, Queen's Bench, Fleet, Marshalsea and Queen's Prisons: Miscellanea, 1697–
1862
T 90/66, Prisons: King's Bench and Fleet, 1830–33

Sheffield City Archives, Sheffield
Arundel Castle MSS, Sheffield Court of Requests Materials

Somerset Record Office, Taunton
Q/Agi/7/1, Ilchester Gaol Occurrence Book, 1816–21
Q/Agi/7/3, Ilchester Gaol, Magistrates' Book, 1821–44
Q/Agi/17/1–3, Ilchester Gaol Debtors' Registers, 1808–44
Q/Ags/17/1, Shepton Mallet Gaol, Register of Debtors, 1842–78
Q/Agz/18/1–3, Small Debtors Society Records, 1809–1932

University College London Archives
Henry Brougham Collection

West Yorkshire Archives Service, Wakefield
C118/101, Wakefield House of Correction Debtors' Receiving Book, 1847–49
CC1/2/1, Keighley Court of Requests Judgment Book, 1840–42

York Castle Museum Archive, York
Diary of William Pashley, 1837–48
Printed notice of furniture rentals, York Castle, 1 January 1869
'Rules of the Clifford Club: To Be Observed in Clifford's Buildings by All Debtors',
no date.
York Castle Gaoler's Journal, transcript, 1824–47

DIARIES AND AUTOBIOGRAPHIES

MANUSCRIPT

Atkinson, H.T. Diary of H.T. Atkinson, Serjeant at Law, 1878. Bodleian, MS
Eng.misc.e.940.
Daubney, Miss Dorothy H. Diary of Miss Dorothy H. Daubney, 1900, 1907. Glouces-
tershire RO, D 5130/9/2, D 5130/9/7.
Flinders, Matthew. MS Diary of Matthew Flinders, surgeon, 1775–1802. Lincolnshire
Archives, Flinders 1–2.
Harvey, Edward. Diary of Edward Harvey, Letter-Carrier, 1859–61. Modern Records
Centre, University of Warwick, MS 219.

332   Bibliography

Newton, James. Diary of the Rev. James Newton of Nuneham Courtney, Oxon., 1761–62. Bodleian, MS Eng.misc.e.251.

Shaen, Rebecca. Commonplace Book and Journal, 1800–55. Bodleian, MS Johnson e.7.

Swift, W.E. Diary of W.E. Swift, Schoolmaster of Churchdown, 1897–98. Gloucestershire RO, D 3981/24.

Upcott, William. Diary of William Upcott, Bookseller of London. British Library, Add. MS 32,558.

Waugh, Edwin. Diary of Edwin Waugh, 21 July 1847–10 February 1851. Manchester Central Reference Library, microfilm.

Whitmore, Charles Shapland. Diaries of Charles Shapland Whitmore, County-Court Judge, 1855–83. Gloucestershire RO, D45 F48/1–6.

PRINTED

Anon. *Reminiscences of an Old Draper*. London, 1876.

Ashford, Mary Ann. *Life of a Licensed Victualler's Daughter: Written by Herself*. London, 1844.

Ayres, Jack, ed. *Paupers and Pig Killers: The Diary of William Holland. A Somerset Parson, 1799–1818*. Stroud, 1984.

Bell, Alan, ed. *Sir Leslie Stephen's Mausoleum Book*. Oxford, 1977.

Beresford, John, ed. *Woodforde: Passages from the Five Volumes of the Diary of a Country Parson 1758–1802: The Reverend James Woodforde*. Oxford, 1935.

Blumfeld, Ralph David. *R.D.B.'s Diary: 1887–1914*. London, 1930.

Brierley, Ben. *Home Memories, and Recollections of a Life*. Manchester, [1887].

Broadhurst, Henry. *Henry Broadhurst, M.P.: The Story of His Life from a Stonemason's Bench to the Treasury Bench. Told by Himself*. London, 1901.

Brown, A.F.J., ed. *Essex People 1750–1900: From Their Diaries, Memoirs and Letters*. Chelmsford, 1972.

Bryant, G.E. and G.P. Baker, eds. *A Quaker Journal: Being the Diary and Reminiscences of William Lucas of Hitchin (1804–1861) a Member of the Society of Friends*. 2 vols. London, 1934.

Bullen, Frank T. *Confessions of a Tradesman*. London, 1908.

Burnett, John, ed. *Useful Toil: Autobiographies of Working People from the 1820s to the 1920s*. London, 1994.

Cameron, Clare [pseud. Winifred Burke]. *Rustle of Spring: Simple Annals of a London Girl*. London, 1927.

Charke, Charlotte. *A Narrative of the Life of Mrs. Charlotte Charke (Youngest Daughter of Colley Cibber, Esq.): Written by Herself*. Intro. Leonard R.N. Ashley. 2nd edn. 1755; Gainesville, 1969.

Clive, Mary, ed. *Caroline Clive: From the Diary and Family Papers of Mrs Archer Clive (1801–1873)*. London, 1949.

Cobbett, William. *The Autobiography of William Cobbett: The Progress of a Plough-boy to a Seat in Parliament*. Ed. William Reitzel. London, 1947.

Coltham, Paul, ed. *The Diary of a Prison Governor: James William Newham 1825–1890*. Gloucester, 1984.

Crosby, Alan G., ed. *The Family Records of Benjamin Shaw, Mechanic of Dent, Dolphinholme and Preston, 1772–1841*. Transactions of the Record Society of Lancashire and Cheshire, vol. 130. Stroud, 1991.

Bibliography   333

Crowther, Janice E. and Peter A. Crowther, eds. *The Diary of Robert Sharp of South Cave: Life in a Yorkshire Village 1812–1837*. Oxford, 1997.

Coustillas, Pierre, ed. *London and the Life of Literature in Late Victorian England: The Diary of George Gissing, Novelist*. Hassocks, Sussex, 1978.

Cozens-Hardy, Basil, ed. *The Diary of Sylas Neville 1767–1788*. London, 1950.

Crawford, J.D. *Reflections and Recollections*. London, 1936.

Crick, Throne [pseud.]. *Sketches from the Diary of a Commercial Traveller*. London, 1848.

Davies, Margaret Llewelyan, ed. *Life As We Have Known It: By Cooperative Working Women*. Intro. Virginia Woolf. London, 1930.

Davies, William Henry. *The Autobiography of a Super-Tramp*. London, 1908.

Fendall, C.P. and E.A. Crutchley, eds. *The Diary of Benjamin Newton, Rector of Wrath 1816–1818*. Cambridge, 1933.

Fish, W.F. *The Autobiography of a Counter-Jumper: In Two Parts: England and South Africa*. London, n.d.

Gatliff, H.E., ed. *Stations, Gentlemen! Memoirs of James Gatliff*. London, 1938.

Gray, Mrs Edwin, ed. *Papers and Diaries of a York Family 1764–1839*. London, 1927.

Grylls, Richard G., ed. *A Cornish Shopkeeper's Diary 1843: The Diary of Henry Grylls Thomas, Draper and Grocer of St Just-in-Penwith, Cornwall, and Thirteen Letters Written to His Wife between 1846 and 1854*. Mount Hawke, Cornwall, 1977.

Harris, George. *The Autobiography of George Harris, LL.D., F.S.A., of the Middle Temple, Barrister-at-Law*. London, 1888.

Heath, John, ed. *Diaries of Henry Hill of Slackfields Farm 1872–1896*. Nottingham, 1982.

Hewitt, Martin and Robert Poole, eds. *The Diaries of Samuel Bamford*. Stroud, 2000.

Holder, Marjorie and Christina Gee, eds. *The Diary of a London Schoolboy 1826–1830: John Thomas Pocock*. Plymouth, 1980.

Hughes, Molly. *A London Family, 1870–1900*. 1934–37; reprinted Oxford, 1991.

Hutton, William. *The Life of William Hutton, Stationer, of Birmingham; and the History of His Family*. 1816; reprinted London, 1841.

Jobson, Allan. *The Creeping Hours of Time*. London, 1977.

Jowitt, Jane. *Memoirs of Jane Jowitt, the Poor Poetess, Aged 74 Years, Written by Herself*. Sheffield, 1844.

Kussmaul, Ann, ed. *The Autobiography of Joseph Mayett of Quainton (1783–1839)*. Buckinghamshire Record Society, no. 23. Cambridge, 1986.

Lackington, James. *Memoirs of the First Forty-Five Years of the Life of James Lackington*. 2nd edn. London, 1792.

Lewis, June, ed. *The Secret Diary of Sarah Thomas 1860–1865*. Moreton-in-Marsh, Gloucestershire, 1994.

Liddell, A.G.C. *Notes from the Life of an Ordinary Mortal: Being a Record of Things Done, Seen and Heard at School, College, and in the World during the Latter Half of the 19th Century*. London, 1911.

Liddie, John A., ed. *The Diary of George Bird: Victorian Wheelwright*. [Nottingham, 1982].

Linder, Leslie, ed. *The Journal of Beatrix Potter from 1887 to 1897*. London, 1966.

Mayo, Isabella Fyvie. *Recollections of What I Saw, What I Lived through, and What I Learned, during More Than Fifty Years of Social and Literary Experience*. London, 1910.

334   Bibliography

Morgan, Richard, ed. *The Diary of a Bedfordshire Squire (John Thomas Brooks of Flitwick 1794–1858)*. Bedfordshire Historical Society, 66 (1987).

O'Mara, Pat. *The Autobiography of an Irish Slummy*. New York, 1933.

Owen, Robert. *The Life of Robert Owen: Written by Himself*. Intro. John Butt. 1857; London, 1971.

Parry, Edward. *Judgments in Vacation*. London, 1911.

Penn, Margaret. *Manchester Fourteen Miles*. Intro. John Burnett. 1947; Firle, Sussex, 1979.

Philpot, Terry, ed. *That's the Way It Was: A Working Class Autobiography 1890–1950*. Oxted, Surrey, 1982.

Pope, Willard, ed. *The Diary of Benjamin Robert Haydon*. 5 vols. Cambridge, MA, 1960–63.

Pritchett, V.S. *A Cab at the Door: An Autobiography: Early Years*. London, 1968.

Roberts, Robert. *The Classic Slum: Salford Life in the First Quarter of the Century*. London, 1971.

A Ragged Schooling: Growing Up in the Classic Slum. Manchester, 1976.

[Saxby, Mary]. *Memoirs of a Female Vagrant: Written by Herself*. London, 1806.

Scott, Clement and Cecil Howard, eds. *The Life and Reminiscences of E.L. Blanchard: With Notes from the Diary of Wm. Blanchard*. 2 vols. London, 1891.

Spevack, Marvin, ed. *A Victorian Chronicle: The Diary of Henrietta Halliwell-Phillipps*. Hildesheim, 1999.

Stanley, Liz, ed. *The Diaries of Hannah Cullwick, Victorian Maidservant*. New Brunswick, 1984.

Steel, Frank. *Ditcher's Row: A Tale of the Older Charity*. London, 1939.

Surtees, Virginia, ed. *The Diary of Ford Madox Brown*. New Haven, 1981.

Taylor, Tom, ed. *Life of Benjamin Robert Haydon, Historical Painter, from His Autobiography and Journals*. 3 vols. London, 1853.

Thompson, Flora. *Lark Rise to Candleford*. 1939; London, 1945.

Thrale, Mary, ed. *The Autobiography of Francis Place*. Cambridge, 1972.

Turner, Thomas. *The Diary of Thomas Turner 1754–1765*. Ed. David Vaisey. Oxford, 1984.

Wale, Henry John, ed. *My Grandfather's Pocket-Book: From A.D. 1701 to 1796*. London, 1883.

Wanklyn, M.D.G., ed. *The Diary of George Gitton of Bridgnorth for 1866*. Shropshire Record Series, vol. 2. Keele, 1998.

Wells, H.G. *Experiment in Autobiography: Discoveries and Conclusions of a Very Ordinary Brain (since 1866)*. New York, 1934.

Whitbread, Helena, ed. *I Know My Own Heart: The Diaries of Anne Lister (1791–1840)*. London, 1988.

Wise, Dorothy, ed. *Diary of William Tayler, Footman*. London, 1962.

Woodforde, Dorothy Heighes, ed. *Woodforde Papers and Diaries*, 35–88. London, 1932.

Woof, Pamela, ed. *The Grasmere Journals*. Oxford, 1991.

NEWSPAPERS

Bakers' Monthly Gazette
Bath Guardian
Birmingham Advertiser

Bibliography 335

Bristolian
City of London Trade Protection Circular
County Courts Chronicle
Credit Drapers Gazette
Daily News
Draper
East London Press
Grocer
Monthly Review
New Statesman
Sheffield and Rotherham Independent
Sheffield Iris
Solicitors' Journal
Trade Protection Record
Traders' Herald
Warehousemen and Drapers' Trade Journal

GOVERNMENT REPORTS AND PARLIAMENTARY PAPERS

Hansard's Parliamentary Debates
Journals of the House of Commons
Ninth Report of the Inspectors Appointed under the Provisions of 5 & 6 Will. 4 c. 88 to Visit the Different Prisons of Great Britain. Parliamentary Papers, XXXIV (1844)
Report from Commissioners: Inspectors of Prisons – Great Britain, 2nd Report. Parliamentary Papers, XII (1837).
Report from the Committee Appointed to Enquire into the State of the Gaols of the Kingdom: Relating to the Fleet Prison. London, 1729.
Report from the [House of Commons] Committee Appointed to Enquire into the Practice and Effects of Imprisonment for Debt. London, 1792.
Report of the Select Committee of the House of Lords on the Debtors Act; Together with Proceedings of the Committee, Minutes of the Evidence, and Appendix, Parliamentary Papers, IX (1893–94) (HL 156).
Report of the Select Committee on the Recovery of Small Debts in England and Wales, Parliamentary Papers, IV (1823) (386).
Second Part of the Appendix to the Fourth Report of the Commissioners Appointed to Inquire into the Practice and Proceedings of the Superior Courts of Common Law, Parliamentary Papers, XXV, part 2 (1831–32)

NOVELS

Anon. *The Adventures of a Watch*. London, 1788.
Austen, Jane. *Pride and Prejudice*. 1813. Ed. James Kinsley. Oxford, 1990.
    Sense and Sensibility. 1811. London, 1969.
Burney, Frances. *The Wanderer; Or, Female Difficulties*. 1814. Ed. Margaret Anne Doody, Robert L. Mack and Peter Sabor. Oxford, 1991.
Dickens, Charles. *Bleak House*. 1853. Ed. Nichola Bradbury. London, 1996.
    David Copperfield. 1850; New York, 1981.

336   Bibliography

Little Dorrit. 1857. Ed. Harvey Peter Sucksmith. Oxford, 1982.

The Pickwick Papers. 1837.

Edgeworth, Maria. *Belinda*. 1801. Ed. Kathryn J. Kirkpatrick. Oxford, 1994.

Fielding, Henry. *Amelia*. 1751. Ed. David Blewett. London, 1987.

Joseph Andrews. 1742. Ed. R.F. Brissenden. London, 1977.

Galsworthy, John. *In Chancery*. 1920. Ware, Hertfordshire, 1994.

Gaskell, Elizabeth. *Ruth*. 1853. Ed. Angus Easson. London, 1997.

Gissing, George. *Eve's Ransom*. London, 1895.

Goldsmith, Oliver. *The Vicar of Wakefield*. Ed. Stephen Coote. London, 1982.

Haywood, Eliza. *The History of Miss Betsy Thoughtless*. 1751. Ed. Christine Blouch. Peterborough, Ontario, 1998.

Smollett, Tobias. *The Adventures of Ferdinand Count Fathom*. 1753. London, 1990.

Thackeray, William Makepeace. *The History of Pendennis*. 1850. London, 1972.

Vanity Fair: A Novel without a Hero. 1848. Ed. Geoffrey Tillotson and Katherine Tillotson. London, 1963.

Trollope, Anthony. *Framley Parsonage*. 1861. London, 1984.

Orley Farm. 1862. Ed. David Skilton. Oxford, 1985.

Phineas Finn. 1869. Ed. John Sutherland. London, 1972.

The Struggles of Brown, Jones, and Robinson: By One of the Firm. 1862. Oxford, 1992.

The Three Clerks. 1858. London, 1993.

The Way We Live Now. 1872. Oxford, 1982.

Wells, H.G. *Tono Bungay*. 1909. Ed. John Hammond. London, 1994.

Wilde, Oscar. *The Picture of Dorian Gray*. 1890. New York, 1998.

PRIMARY TRACTS AND TREATISES

Allday, Joseph. *Injustice, Oppression, and Cruelty: Local Courts for the Recovery of Small Debts, and Extortionate and Ruinous 'Costs'*. [Birmingham, 1846].

Anon. *Abstract Report of a Conference of Delegates Representing the Northern Central Credit-Drapery Association, Held at the Clarence Hotel, Spring Gardens, Manchester, April 17th and 18th, 1873*. Manchester, [1873].

An Authoritative Account of the Riots at Birmingham, on the 14th, 15th, 16th, and 17th Days of July, 1791 . . . London, [1791].

The Birmingham Guardian Society for the Protection of Trade: First Report. Birmingham, 1845.

Business Life: The Experiences of a London Tradesman with Practical Advice and Directions for Avoiding Many of the Evils Connected with Our Present Commercial System and State of Society. London, 1861.

A Description of the King's Bench Prison: Being a Brief Review of Its Constitution . . . London, [1827].

An Exhortation to the Debtor Released by the Society for the Discharge and Relief of Persons Imprisoned for Small Debts. London, [1780].

The Gaol of the City of Bristol Compared with What a Gaol Ought to Be: Intended to Diffuse a More General Knowledge of the Requisites of a Good Prison . . . Bristol, 1815.

General Regulations for Inspection and Controul of All Prisons . . . 2nd edn. Gloucester, [1790].

Bibliography 337

[A Hanoverian]. *John Bull Starving to Pay Debts of the Royal Prodigal: A Letter to the House of Peers*. London, [1795].

The Junior's Precedence: Illustrated in a New Impression of Two Acts of Parliament Made in Ireland, for the Recovery of Small Debts... Shewing the Necessity of Courts of Conscience... London, 1750.

The Lady Russel's and All Lords of Mannors, Case and Reasons against the Bill for Erecting a Court of Conscience. [London, 1707]. British Library press mark 1891.d.1 (39).

A List of the Members of the Guardians; Or Society for the Protection of Trade, Against Swindlers and Sharpers, Established March 25th, 1776. [London, 1799].

The London Tradesman; A Familiar Treatise on the Rationale of Trade and Commerce, As Carried on in the Metropolis of the British Empire. London, 1819.

Manchester Guardian Society for the Protection of Trade, 1826–1926. [Manchester], 1926.

The Misery of Iniquity Luckily Discover'd. Or, a Horrible Plot and Wicked Contrivance against Poor Honest People of this Nation. In a Comical Dialogue between a Pawn Broker, a Tallyman, a Bum-bailiff, a Town-miss, a Keeping-fool, a Vintner's Drawer, and a Sham-devil... London, 1708.

A Narrative of the Proceedings of Lord George Gordon, and the Persons Assembled under the Denomination of the Protestant Association. London, 1789.

Observations upon the 'Short State of Facts Respecting the Court of Requests at Halifax, &c. &c. &c.. n.p., [1780].

Reasons against the Bill for Erecting Courts of Conscience. n.p., [1675]. British Library press mark 816.m.15 (2).

The Relative Duties of Debtors and Creditors Considered: Shewing the Indispensable Obligation Debtors Are under to Make the Utmost Restitution to Their Creditors; and Proposing Some Arguments and Reasons for the Gentleness and Compassion of Creditors towards Insolvent Debtors. London, 1743.

Reports of County Court Cases and Appeals Decided by All the Superior Courts... London, 1868–69.

Rules and Orders [of] The Guardians: Or Society for the Protection of Trade against Swindlers and Sharpers. Established March 25, 1776. London, 1816.

Rules of the Beverley Guardian Society, for the Protection of Trade. Established November 19th, 1834. Beverley, [1834].

[A Female Debtor]. *A Summer Holiday in Holloway Gaol*. [London, 1909].

[An Oxford B.A.] *Tradesmen and Undergraduates; Or, the Present System of Debt and Credit at Oxford Unveiled*. London, 1844.

Whitecross and the Bench: A Reminiscence of the Past: By the Author of Five Years' Penal Servitude. London, 1879.

Archbold, John Frederick. *The Practice of the New County Courts*. 3rd edn. London, 1848.

Belae, Catherine Hutton, ed. *Reminiscences of a Gentlewoman of the Last Century: Letters of Catherine Hutton*. Birmingham, 1891.

Blackstone, William. *Commentaries on the Laws of England*. 4 vols. 1765–69; Chicago, 1979.

Burgess, Frederick W. *The Practical Retail Draper: A Complete Guide for the Drapery and Allied Trades*. 5 vols. London, n.d.

338   Bibliography

Buxton, Thomas Fowell. *Appendix to the First Edition of an Inquiry, Whether Crime and Misery are Produced or Prevented, by Our Present System of Prison Discipline...* London, 1818.

  An Inquiry Whether Crime and Misery Are Produced or Prevented by Our Present System of Prison Discipline. London, 1818.

[Caldwell, James]. A Manufacturer. *A Letter to the Manufacturers and Inhabitants of the Parishes of Stoke, Burslem, and Wolstanton, in the County of Stafford, on Courts of Request...* n.p., [1794].

Chesterton, George Laval. *Revelations of Prison Life; with an Enquiry into Prison Discipline and Secondary Punishments.* 2 vols. 2nd edn. London, 1856.

Cowburn, John. *The Suitor's Guide to the New County Courts; Being a Plain and Familiar Exposition of the Act and Rules of Practice, Designed to Assist Those Who Desire to Avail Themselves of the Facilities Given for the Recovery of Small Debts, without the Aid of a Professional Advisor.* London, 1847.

Cresswell, Robert Nathaniel. *Reports of Cases Heard and Decided in the Court for the Relief of Insolvent Debtors...* London, 1830.

Defoe, Daniel. *The Complete English Tradesman.* 1726; Gloucester, 1987.

Dicey, Albert Venn. *Lectures on the Relation between Law and Public Opinion in England during the Nineteenth Century.* London, 1905.

Dixon, Wiliam Hepworth. *The London Prisons: With an Account of the More Distinguished Persons Who Have Been Confined in Them.* London, 1850.

Dornford, Josiah. *Nine Letters to the Right Honourable the Lord Mayor and Aldermen of the City of London, on the State of the City Prisons...* London, [1786].

  Seven Letters to the Lords and Commons of Great Britain, upon the Present Mode of Arresting and Imprisoning the Bodies of Debtors. London, [1786].

Elliott, J.H. *Credit the Life of Commerce: Being a Defence of the British Merchant against the Unjust and Demoralizing Tendency of the Recent Alterations in the Laws of Debtor and Creditor.* London, 1845.

Falconer, Thomas. *On County Courts, Local Courts of Record, and On the Changes Proposed to Be Made in Such Courts in the Second Report of the Judicature Commissioners.* London, 1873.

Francklin, Thomas. *A Sermon Preached at the Chapel in Great Queen-Street, Lincoln's Inn-Fields, on Sunday, March 20, 1774, for the Benefit of Unfortunate Persons Confined for Small Debts.* London, [1774].

Grant, A. *The Public Monitor; Or, a Plan for the More Speedy Recovery of Small Debts; Wherein the Expediency of Erecting County Courts and of Enlarging the Powers of the Court of Request, Is Pointed Out.* London, 1789.

Gray, J.C. *The System of Credit as Practiced by Co-operative Societies.* Manchester, n.d.

Hall, J. *Lancaster Castle: Its History and Associations.* Lancaster, 1843.

Hallifax, James. *A Sermon Preached at the Parish Church of St. Paul, Covent-Garden, on Thursday, May 18, 1775, for the Benefit of Unfortunate Persons Confined for Small Debts.* London, 1775.

Haydon, Benjamin Robert. *Correspondence and Table-Talk: With a Memoir by His Son, Frederick Wordsworth Haydon.* 2 vols. London, 1876.

[Hicks, George Montagu]. *The Double Doom of the Poor Debtor: To Those Who Owe Money, and to Those to Whom It Is Due.* London, 1858.

Bibliography

Higgin, Edward. 'Memoranda relating to Lancaster Castle'. *Transactions of the Historic Society of Lancashire and Cheshire*, 1 (1848–49): 95–102.

Holyoake, George Jacob. *Inaugural Address Delivered at the Nineteenth Annual Cooperative Congress Held at Carlisle*. Manchester, [1887].

Howard, John. *The State of the Prisons of England and Wales, with Preliminary Observations, and an Account of Some Foreign Prisons and Hospitals*. 4th edn. London, 1792.

Hutton, Catherine. *A Narrative of the Riots in Birmingham, July 1791*. Birmingham, [1875].

Hutton, William. *Courts of Requests: Their Nature, Utility, and Powers Described, with a Variety of Cases, Determined in That of Birmingham*. Birmingham, 1787.

  A Dissertation on Juries; With a Description of the Hundred Court: As an Appendix to the Court of Requests. Birmingham, 1789.

Jenkinson, Richard. *Justice in Equity Exemplified: Being the Full Particulars and True Account of the Proceedings in the Court of Requests, Birmingham*... Birmingham, [1827].

Jeune, Lady. 'The ethics of shopping'. *Fortnightly Review*, 338, n.s. (1 January 1895): 123–32.

Johnes, Arthur Johnes. *Is Credit an Evil? In a Letter to C.M. Norwood, Esq., M.P.* London, 1869.

  Should the Law of Imprisonment for Debt in the Superior Courts Be Abolished or Amended? In a Letter to the Rt. Hon. Lord Brougham and Vaux. London, [1868].

Johnson, Marmaduke. *Ludgate, What It Is; Not What It Was*. London, 1659. In *A Survey of the Cities of London and Westminster and the Borough of Southwark*, II: 694–702. Ed. John Stow. 2 vols. 6th edn. London, 1755.

Keane, David Deady. *Courts of Requests, Their Jurisdiction and Powers, under the 'Act to Amend the Law of Insolvency, Bankruptcy and Execution,' (7 & 8 Vict. c. 96) and the 'Act for the Better Securing the Payment of Small Debts,' (8 & 9 Vict. c. 127)*. 3rd edn. London, 1845.

Lot, Theophilus. *A Plea for the Poor Labouring Men: Shewing That by the County Court Practice They Are Led into Debt, and Compelled to Pay Debts by a Process of Extortion and Oppression Most Prolonged and Harmful, and Also Unjust Because Such Process Is Used against Poor Men Only*. Birmingham, [1888].

McCulloch, J.R. *A Dictionary, Practical, Theoretical, and Historical, of Commerce and Commercial Navigation*. London, 1844.

Maine, Henry Sumner. *Ancient Law: Its Connection with the Early History of Society, and Its Relation to Modern Ideas*. London, 1861.

Mallory, John. *Objections Humbly Offer'd against Passing the Bill, Intitled, a Bill for the More Easy and Speedy Recovery of Small Debts, into a Law*. London, 1730.

Mayhew, Henry. *London Labour and the London Poor*. 4 vols. London, 1861–62.

Neild, James. *An Account of the Rise, Progress, and Present State of the Society for the Discharge and Relief of Persons Imprisoned for Small Debts throughout England and Wales*. 3rd edn. London, 1808.

Olleson, Philip, ed. *The Letters of Samuel Wesley: Professional and Social Correspondence, 1792–1837*. Oxford, 2001.

340   Bibliography

Palgrave, R.H. Inglis, ed. *Dictionary of Political Economy*. 3 vols. London, 1891–94.

Parkes, Joseph. *The State of the Court of Requests and the Public Office of Birmingham*. Birmingham, 1828.

Paul, Sir G.O. *Considerations on the Defects of Prisons, and Their Present System of Regulation...* London, 1784.

Peake, Thomas. *A Compendium of the Law of Evidence*. 5th edn. London, 1822.

Pearce, James. *A Treatise on the Abuses of the Laws, Particularly in Actions by Arrest*. London, 1814.

Phillips, Sir Richard. *A Letter to the Livery of London, Relative to the Views of the Writer in Executing the Office of Sheriff*. 2nd edn. London, 1808.

Pollock, Sir Frederick, and Frederic William Maitland. *The History of English Law before the Time of Edward I*. 2 vols. Cambridge, 1895.

Pratt, John Tidd. *An Abstract of All the Printed Acts of Parliament for the Establishment of Courts of Requests in England and Wales, with Cases Decided Thereon*. London, 1824.

Smiles, Samuel. *Character*. 1871; London, 1997.

   Thrift. 1875; London, 1997.

Smith, Isaac. *A Warder's Experience of Lancaster Castle*. Blackburn, n.d.

Smith, William. *Mild Punishments Sound Policy: Or Observations on the Laws Relative to Debtors and Felons...* London, 1778.

   State of the Gaols in London, Westminster, and Borough of Southwark. London, 1776.

Snagge, Thomas. *The Evolution of the County Court*. London, 1904.

Sokoll, Thomas, ed. *Essex Pauper Letters 1731–1837*. Oxford, 2001.

Stephen, James. *Considerations on Imprisonment for Debt, Fully Proving That the Confining of the Bodies of Debtors Is Contrary to Common Law, Magna Carta, Statute Law, Justice, Humanity, and Policy*. London, 1770.

Stephens, Theo E. *Twelve Months Advertising for a Grocer*. London, 1910.

[Stockdale, James]. 'An Old Lancaster Castle surgeon's journal'. *Cross Fleury's Journal*, nos. 109 (September 1905) and 111 (November 1905).

Trusler, Reverend [John]. *The London Advisor and Guide: Containing Every Instruction and Information Useful and Necessary to Persons Living in London, and Coming to Reside There*. London, 1786.

Vincent, William. *A Plain and Succinct Narrative of the Late Riots and Disturbances in the Cities of London and Westminster, and Borough of Southwark*. 2nd edn. London, 1780.

Walker, Charles Houlden. *Letters on the Practice of the Bristol Court of Requests; on Judicial Sinecures in Bristol, and Other Important Subjects*. London, 1820.

Warwick, Sir Philip. *A Discourse of Government, as Examined by Reason, Scripture, and Law of the Land. Or True Weights and Measures between Sovereignty and Liberty*. London, 1694.

   Memoires of the Reign of King Charles I. With a Continuation to the Happy Restoration of King Charles II. London, 1701.

Weston, H.W. *Protection against Imprisonment for All Embarrassed Debtors. Why Not?* London, 1858.

Wharton, J.J.S. *An Exposition of the Laws Relating to the Women of England; Showing Their Rights, Remedies, and Responsibilities, in Every Position of Life*. London, 1853.

Bibliography 341

Whitelock, W.H. 'The industrial credit system and imprisonment for debt'. *Economic Journal*, 24 (March 1914): 33–40.

Woolley, Reverend W. *The Benefit of Starving: Or, the Advantages of Hunger, Cold, and Nakedness; Intended as a Cordial for the Poor, and an Apology for the Rich.* London, 1792.

SECONDARY SOURCES

Alborn, Timothy L. *Conceiving Companies: Joint-Stock Politics in Victorian England.* London, 1998.

Alexander, David. *Retailing in England during the Industrial Revolution.* London, 1970.

Allen, Christopher. *The Law of Evidence in Victorian England.* Cambridge, 1997.

Anderson, B.L. 'Money and the structure of credit in the eighteenth century'. *Business History*, 12, 2 (July 1970): 85–101.

Andrew, Donna T. and Randall McGowen. *The Perreaus and Mrs. Rudd: Forgery and Betrayal in Eighteenth-Century London.* Berkeley, 2001.

Appadurai, Arjun. 'Introduction: commodities and the politics of value'. In *The Social Life of Things: Commodities in Cultural Perspective*, 3–63. Ed. Arjun Appadurai. Cambridge, 1986.

Appleby, Joyce. 'Consumption in early modern economic thought'. In *Consumption and the World of Goods*, 162–73. Edited by John Brewer and Roy Porter. London, 1993.

Armstrong, Nancy Fix. *Desire and Domestic Fiction: A Political History of the Novel.* Oxford, 1987.

Arthurs, H.W. *'Without the Law': Administrative Justice and Legal Pluralism in Nineteenth-Century England.* Toronto, 1985.

Atiyah, P.S. *The Rise and Fall of Freedom of Contract.* Oxford, 1979.

Auerbach, Nina. *Romantic Imprisonment: Women and Other Glorified Outcasts.* New York, 1985.

Bailey, Peter. *Popular Culture and Performance in the Victorian City.* Cambridge, 1998.

Baker, J.H. *The Law's Two Bodies: Some Evidential Problems in English Legal History.* Oxford, 2001.

Barty-King, Hugh. *The Worst Poverty: A History of Debt and Debtors.* Stroud, 1991.

Battestin, Martin C. and Ruthe R. Battestin. *Henry Fielding: A Life.* London, 1989.

Beattie, J.M. *Crime and the Courts in England 1660–1800.* Princeton, 1986.

Behlmer, George. 'Summary justice and working-class marriage in England, 1870–1940'. *Law & History Review*, 12, 2 (Fall 1994): 229–75.

Bellamy, Liz. *Commerce, Morality and the Eighteenth-Century Novel.* Cambridge, 1998.

Ben-Amos, Ilana. 'Gifts and favors: informal support in early modern England'. *JMH*, 72, 2 (June 2000): 295–338.

Bender, John. *Imagining the Penitentiary: Fiction and the Architecture of Mind in Eighteenth-Century England.* Chicago, 1987.

'Prison reform and the sentence of narration in *The Vicar of Wakefield*'. In *The New Eighteenth Century: Theory, Politics, Literature*, 168–88. Ed. Felicity Nussbaum and Laura Brown. London, 1987.

342   Bibliography

Benson, John. *The Rise of Consumer Society in Britain 1880–1980*. Harlow, Essex, 1994.

Berg, Maxine. 'Women's consumption and the industrial classes of eighteenth-century England'. *Journal of Social History*, 30, 2 (Winter 1996): 415–34.

Berg, Maxine and Helen Clifford, eds. *Consumers and Luxury: Consumer Culture in Europe 1650–1850*. Manchester, 1999.

Berry, Christopher. *The Idea of Luxury: A Conceptual and Historical Investigation*. Cambridge, 1994.

Bestor, Jane Fair. 'Marriage transactions in Renaissance Italy and Mauss's *Essay on the Gift*'. *P&P*, 164 (August 1999): 6–46.

Bourdieu, Pierre. 'The economy of symbolic goods'. In his *Practical Reason: On the Theory of Action*, 92–123. Stanford, 1998.

Outline of a Theory of Practice. Trans. Richard Nice. Cambridge, 1977.

Bowlby, Rachel. *Carried Away: The Invention of Modern Shopping*. London, 2000.

Just Looking: Consumer Culture in Dreiser, Gissing and Zola. London, 1985.

Brantlinger, Patrick. *Fictions of State: Culture and Credit in Britain, 1694–1994*. Ithaca, NY, 1996.

Breward, Christopher. *The Hidden Consumer: Masculinities, Fashion and City Life 1860–1914*. Manchester, 1999.

Brewer, John. *The Sinews of Power: War, Money and the English State, 1688–1785*. New York, 1989.

Britnell, R.H. *The Commercialisation of English Society, 1000–1500*. Cambridge, 1993.

Brooks, Christopher W. *Lawyers, Litigation and English Society since 1450*. London, 1998.

Brooks, Christopher W. and Michael Lobban, eds. *Communities and Courts in Britain 1150–1900*. London, 1997.

Broughton, Trev Lynn. *Men of Letters, Writing Lives: Masculinity and Literary Auto/Biography in the Late Victorian Period*. London, 1999.

Brown, David Blayney, Robert Woof and Stephen Hebron, eds. *Benjamin Robert Haydon 1786–1846: Painter and Writer, Friend of Wordsworth and Keats*. Kendal, 1996.

Buck, Anne. 'Buying clothes in Bedfordshire: customers and tradesmen, 1700–1800'. *Textile History*, 22, 2 (Autumn 1991): 211–37.

Burgess, Miranda. 'Courting ruin: the economic romances of Fanny Burney'. *Novel*, 28, 2 (Winter 1995): 131–53.

Bush, Graham. *Bristol and Its Municipal Government 1820–1851*. Gateshead, 1976.

Campbell, Colin. *The Romantic Ethic and the Spirit of Modern Consumerism*. Oxford, 1987.

Cannadine, David. *Aspects of Aristocracy: Grandeur and Decline in Modern Britain*. New Haven, 1994.

Carrier, James G. *Gifts and Commodities: Exchange and Western Capitalism*. London, 1995.

Carruthers, Bruce G. *City of Capital: Politics and Markets in the English Financial Revolution*. Princeton, 1996.

Champion, W.A. 'Litigation in the boroughs: the Shrewsbury *Curia Parva* 1480–1730'. *Journal of Legal History*, 15, 3 (December 1994): 201–22.

'Recourse to the law and the meaning of the great litigation decline, 1650–1750: some clues from the Shrewsbury local courts'. In *Communities and Courts in Britain*

1150–1900, 179–98. Ed. Christopher W. Brooks and Michael Lobban. London, 1997.

Church, Roy. 'New perspectives on the history of products, firms, marketing, and consumers in Britain and the United States since the mid-nineteenth century'. *EcoHR*, 52, 3 (August 1999): 405–35.

Clark, Anna. 'Gender, class and the nation: franchise reform in England, 1832–1928'. In *Re-Reading the Constitution: New Narratives in the Political History of England's Long Nineteenth Century*, 230–53. Ed. James Vernon. Cambridge, 1996.

Clark, Peter. *The English Alehouse: A Social History 1200–1830*. London, 1983.

Clunas, Craig. 'Modernity global and local: consumption and the rise of the West'. *American Historical Review*, 104, 5 (December 1999): 117–44.

Cohen, Jay. 'The history of imprisonment for debt and its relation to the discharge in bankruptcy'. *Journal of Legal History*, 3, 2 (September 1982): 153–71.

Coleman, P.J. *Debtors and Creditors in America: Insolvency, Imprisonment for Debt and Bankruptcy, 1607–1900*. Madison, 1974.

Collini, Stefan. *Public Moralists: Political Thought and Intellectual Life in Britain 1850–1930*. Oxford, 1991.

Copeland, Edward. *Women Writing about Money: Women's Fiction in England, 1790–1820*. Cambridge, 1995.

Corbett, Mary Jean. *Representing Femininity: Middle-Class Subjectivity in Victorian and Edwardian Women's Autobiographies*. New York, 1992.

Cornish, W.R. and G. de N. Clark. *Law and Society in England 1750–1950*. London, 1989.

Cox, Nancy. *The Complete Tradesman: A Study of Retailing, 1550–1820*. Aldershot, 2000.

Craig, Randall. *Promising Language: Betrothal in Victorian Law and Fiction*. Albany, NY, 2000.

Cromartie, Alan. *Sir Matthew Hale 1609–1675: Law, Religion and Natural Philosophy*. Cambridge, 1995.

Cross, Nigel. *The Common Writer: Life in Nineteenth-Century Grub Street*. Cambridge, 1985.

Crossick, Geoffrey. 'The petite bourgeoisie in nineteenth-century Britain: the urban and liberal case'. In *Shopkeepers and Master Artisans in Nineteenth-Century Europe*, 62–94. Ed. Geoffrey Crossick and Heinz-Gerhard Haupt. London, 1984.

Crossick, Geoffrey and Serge Jaumain. 'The world of the department store: distribution, culture and social change'. In *Cathedrals of Consumption: The European Department Store 1850–1939*, 1–45. Ed. Geoffrey Crossick and Serge Jaumain. Aldershot, 1999.

Cunningham, Valentine. 'Unto him (or her) that hath: how Victorian writers made ends meet'. *Times Literary Supplement* (11 September 1998): 12–13.

Daunton, Martin. *Progress and Poverty: An Economic and Social History of Britain, 1700–1850*. Oxford, 1995.

Daunton, Martin and Bernhard Rieger, eds. *Meanings of Modernity: Britain from the Late Victorian Era to World War II*. Oxford, 2001.

Davidoff, Leonore and Catherine Hall. *Family Fortunes: Men and Women of the English Middle Class, 1780–1850*. Chicago, 1987.

Davis, Natalie Zemon. *The Gift in Sixteenth-Century France*. Oxford, 2000.

344   Bibliography

De Bolla, Peter. *The Discourse of the Sublime: Readings in History, Aesthetics and the Subject*. Oxford, 1989.

De Certeau, Michel. *The Practice of Everyday Life*. Trans. Steven Rendall. Berkeley, 1984.

De Marchi, Neil. 'Adam Smith's accommodation of "altogether endless" desires'. In *Consumers and Luxury*, 18–36. Ed. Maxine Berg and Helen Clifford. Manchester, 1999.

De Vries, Jan. 'Between purchasing power and the world of goods: understanding the household economy in early modern Europe'. In *Consumption and the World of Goods*, 85–132. Ed. John Brewer and Roy Porter. London, 1993.

   'The industrial revolution and the industrious revolution'. *Journal of Economic History*, 54, 2 (June 1994): 249–70.

DeLacy, Margaret. *Prison Reform in Lancashire, 1700–1850: A Study in Local Administration*. Manchester, 1986.

DeMaria, Robert. *The Life of Samuel Johnson: A Critical Biography*. Oxford, 1993.

Diamond, Alan. 'Fictions, equity and legislation: Maine's three agencies of legal change'. In *The Victorian Achievement of Sir Henry Maine: A Centennial Reappraisal*, 242–55. Ed. Alan Diamond. Cambridge, 1991.

Dickson, P.G.M. *The Financial Revolution in England: A Study in the Development of Public Credit 1688–1756*. London, 1967.

Dillon, Steven. 'George Eliot and the feminine gift'. *Studies in English Literature*, 32, 4 (Autumn 1992): 707–21.

Dixon, Peter. *Oliver Goldsmith Revisited*. Boston, 1991.

Dolin, Kieran. *Fiction and the Law: Legal Discourse in Victorian and Modernist Literature*. Cambridge, 1999.

Douglas, Mary and Baron Isherwood. *The World of Goods: Towards an Anthropology of Consumption*. 2nd edn. London, 1996.

Duffy, Ian P.H. *Bankruptcy and Insolvency in London during the Industrial Revolution*. New York, 1985.

Duncan, Martha Grace. *Romantic Outlaws, Beloved Prisons: The Unconscious Meanings of Crime and Punishment*. New York, 1996.

Dunlop, C.R.B. 'Debtors and creditors in Dickens' fiction'. *Dickens Studies Annual*, 19 (1990): 25–47.

Easson, Angus. 'Imprisonment for debt in *Pickwick Papers*'. *The Dickensian*, 64, 355 (May 1968): 105–12.

Eastwood, David. *Governing Rural England: Tradition and Transformation in Local Government 1780–1840*. Oxford, 1994.

Elam, Diane. ' "Another day done and I'm deeper in debt": *Little Dorrit* and the debt of the everyday'. In *Dickens Refigured: Bodies, Desires and Other Histories*, 157–77. Ed. John Schad. Manchester, 1996.

Ellis, Markham. *The Politics of Sensibility: Race, Gender and Commerce in the Sentimental Novel*. Cambridge, 1996.

Epstein, William H. *John Cleland: Images of a Life*. New York, 1974.

Erickson, Amy Louise. *Women and Property in Early Modern England*. London, 1993.

Evans, Robin. *The Fabrication of Virtue: English Prison Architecture, 1750–1840*. Cambridge, 1982.

Feather, John. 'From rights in copies to copyright: the recognition of authors' rights in English law and practice in the sixteenth and seventeenth centuries'. In *The*

Bibliography

Construction of Authorship: Textual Appropriation in Law and Literature, 191–209. Ed. Martha Woodmanse and Peter Jaszi. Durham, NC, 1994.

Fine, Ben and Ellen Leopold. 'Consumerism and the industrial revolution'. *Social History*, 15, 2 (May 1990): 151–79.

Finn, Margot C. 'Being in debt in Dickens' London: fact, fictional representation and the nineteenth-century prison'. *Journal of Victorian Culture*, 1, 2 (Autumn 1996): 203–26.

'Debt and credit in Bath's court of requests, 1829–39'. *Urban History*, 21, 2 (October 1994): 211–36.

'Henry Hunt's *Peep into a Prison*: the radical discontinuities of imprisonment for debt'. Forthcoming in *English Radicalism, 1550–1850*. Ed. Glenn Burgess and Matthew Festenstein. Cambridge, 2004.

'Law, debt, and empire in Calcutta'. *Papers of the Faculty Seminar in British Studies*. Austin, 2000: 1–25.

'Men's things: masculine possession in the consumer revolution'. *Social History*, 25, 2 (May 2000): 133–55.

'Scotch drapers and the politics of modernity: gender, class and national identity in the Victorian tally trade'. In *The Politics of Consumption: Material Culture and Citizenship in Europe and America*, 89–107. Ed. Martin Daunton and Matthew Hilton. Oxford, 2001.

'Sex and the city: metropolitan modernities in English history'. *VS*, 44, 1 (Autumn 2001): 25–32.

'Victorian law, literature and history: three ships passing in the night'. *Journal of Victorian Culture*, 7, 1 (Spring 2002): 134–46.

'Women, consumption and coverture in England, *c*. 1760–1860'. *HJ*, 39, 3 (September 1996): 703–22.

'Working-class women and the contest for consumer control in Victorian county courts'. *P&P*, 161 (November 1998): 116–54.

Fletcher, Lorraine. *Charlotte Smith: A Critical Biography*. London, 1998.

Flint, Christopher. *Family Fictions: Narrative and Domestic Relations in Britain, 1688–1798*. Stanford, 1998.

'Speaking objects: the circulation of stories in eighteenth-century prose fiction'. *PMLA*, 113, 2 (March 1998): 212–26.

Fontaine, Laurence. *History of Pedlars in Europe*. Trans. Vicki Whittaker. Durham, NC, 1996.

Foucault, Michel. *Discipline and Punish: The Birth of the Prison*. Trans. Alan Sheridan. New York, 1977.

Fowler, Christine. 'Changes in provincial retailing practice during the eighteenth century, with particular reference to central-southern England'. *Business History*, 40, 4 (October 1998): 37–54.

Francis, Clinton W. 'Practice, strategy and institution: debt collection in the English common-law courts, 1740–1840'. *Northwestern Law Review*, 80, 4 (Winter 1986): 807–955.

Fraser, William Hamish. *The Coming of the Mass Market, 1850–1914*. London, 1981.

Freedgood, Elaine. *Victorian Writing about Risk: Imagining a Safe England in a Dangerous World*. Cambridge, 2000.

Frost, Ginger. *Promises Broken: Courtship, Class, and Gender in Victorian England*. Charlottesville, 1995.

346 Bibliography

Gagnier, Regenia. *The Insatiablity of Human Wants: Economics and Aesthetics in Market Society*. Chicago, 2000.

Subjectivities: A History of Self-Representation in Britain, 1832–1920. Oxford, 1991.

Gallagher, Catherine. *Nobody's Story: The Vanishing Acts of Women Writers in the Marketplace 1670–1820*. Oxford, 1994.

Garnett, E.J. 'Aspects of the relationship between Protestant ethics and economic activity in mid-Victorian England'. D.Phil. thesis, Oxford University, 1987.

Gash, Norman. *Pillars of Government: And Other Essays on State and Society c. 1770–c. 1880*. London, 1986.

Gatrell, V.A.C. *The Hanging Tree: Execution and the English People 1770–1868*. Oxford, 1994.

Gewirtz, Paul. 'Narrative and rhetoric in the law'. In *Law's Stories: Narrative and Rhetoric in the Law*, 2–13. Ed. Peter Brooks and Paul Gewirtz. New Haven, 1996.

Godelier, Maurice. *The Enigma of the Gift*. Trans. Nora Scott. Chicago, 1999.

Goodland, Lauren M.E. ' "Making the working man like me": charity, partnership, and middle-class identity in nineteenth-century Britain: Thomas Chalmers and Dr. James Phillips Kay'. *VS*, 43, 1 (Summer 2001): 591–617.

Gregory, C.A. *Gifts and Commodities*. London, 1982.

Greig, J.Y.T. *Thackeray: A Reconsideration*. Oxford, 1950.

Green, D.R. 'Street trading in London: a case study of casual labour, 1830–60'. In *The Retailing Industry*, II: 115–31. Ed. John Benson and Gareth Shaw. 3 vols. London, 1999.

Green, Thomas Andrew. *Verdict According to Conscience: Perspectives on the English Criminal Trial Jury, 1200–1800*. Chicago, 1985.

Greenberg, Kenneth S. *Honor and Slavery: Lies, Duels, Noses, Masks, Dressing as a Woman, Gifts, Strangers, Humanitarianism, Death, Slave Rebellions, the Proslavery Argument, Baseball, Hunting, and Gambling in the Old South*. Princeton, 1996.

Guest, Harriet. *Small Change: Women, Learning, Patriotism, 1750–1810*. Chicago, 2000.

Gurney, Peter. *Co-operative Culture and the Politics of Consumption in England, 1870–1930*. Manchester, 1996.

Guth, Delloyd J. 'The age of debt: the Reformation and English law'. In *Tudor Rule and Revolution: Essays for G.R. Elton from His American Friends*, 69–86. Ed. Delloyd Guth and John W. McKenna. Cambridge, 1982.

Haagen, Paul Hess. 'Eighteenth-century English society and the debt law'. In *Social Control and the State: Historical and Comparative Essays*, 222–47. Ed. Stanley Cohen and Andrew Scull. Oxford, 1983.

'Imprisonment for debt in England and Wales'. Ph.D. dissertation, Princeton University, 1986.

Habakkuk, John. *Marriage, Debt and the Estates System: English Landownership 1650–1950*. Oxford, 1994.

Hammerton, A. James. *Cruelty and Companionship: Conflict in Nineteenth-Century Married Life*. London, 1992.

Hancock, David. *Citizens of the World: London Merchants and the Integration of the British Atlantic Community, 1735–1785*. Cambridge, 1995.

Hannay, David. *Life of Tobias George Smollett*. London, 1887.

Bibliography

Harling, Philip. *The Waning of "Old Corruption": The Politics of Economical Reform in Britain, 1779–1846*. Oxford, 1996.

Hay, Douglas. 'Patronage, paternalism and welfare: masters, workers and magistrates in eighteenth-century England'. *International Labor and Working-Class History*, 53 (Spring 1998): 27–48.

'Property, authority and the criminal law'. In *Albion's Fatal Tree: Crime and Society in Eighteenth-Century England*, 17–63. Ed. Douglas Hay, Peter Linebaugh, John Rule, E.P. Thompson and Cal Winslow. New York, 1975.

'The state and the market in 1800: Lord Kenyon and Mr Waddington'. *P&P*, 162 (February 1999): 101–62.

Heal, Felicity. 'Reciprocity and exchange in the late medieval household'. In *Bodies and Disciplines: Intersections of Literature and History in Fifteenth-Century England*, 179–98. Ed. Barbara A. Hanawalt and David Wallace. Minneapolis, 1996.

Henning, Basil Duke, ed. *The History of Parliament: The House of Commons 1660–1690*. 3 vols. London, 1983.

Henriques, U.R.Q. 'The rise and decline of the separate system of prison discipline'. *P&P*, 54 (February 1972): 61–93.

Hilton, Boyd. *The Age of Atonement: The Influence of Evangelicalism on Social and Economic Thought 1785–1865*. Oxford, 1988.

Hirsch, Adam J. *The Rise of the Penitentiary: Prisons and Punishment in Early America*. New Haven, 1992.

Hitchcock, Tim, Peter King and Pamela Sharpe. *Chronicling Poverty: The Voices and Strategies of the English Poor, 1640–1840*. Basingstoke, 1997.

Hoffman, Philip T., Gilles Postel-Vinay and Jean-Laurent Rosenthal. *Priceless Markets: The Political Economy of Credit in Paris, 1660–1870*. Chicago, 2000.

Hoffman, Philip T., Gilles Postel-Vinay and Jean-Laurent Rosenthal, 'Information and economic history: how the credit market in Old Regime Paris forces us to rethink the transition to capitalism'. *American Historical Review*, 104, 1 (February 1999): 69–94.

Holcombe, Lee. *Wives and Property: Reform of the Married Women's Property Law in Nineteenth-Century England*. Toronto, 1983.

Hollingsworth, Keith. *The Newgate Novel 1830–1847: Bulwer, Ainsworth, Dickens and Thackeray*. Detroit, 1963.

Hont, Istvan and Michael Ignatieff, eds. *Wealth and Virtue: The Shaping of Political Economy in the Scottish Enlightenment*. Cambridge, 1983.

Hoppit, Julian. 'Attitudes to credit in Britain, 1680–1790'. *HJ*, 33, 2 (June 1990): 305–22.

'Financial crises in eighteenth-century England'. *EcoHR*, 2nd ser., 39, 1 (February 1986): 39–58.

'Patterns of parliamentary legislation, 1660–1800'. *HJ*, 39, 1 (March 1996): 108–31.

Risk and Failure in English Business 1700–1800. Cambridge, 1987.

'The use and abuse of credit in eighteenth-century England'. In *Business Life and Public Policy: Essays in Honour of D.C. Coleman*, 64–78. Ed. Neil McKendrick and R.B. Outhwaite. Cambridge, 1986.

ed. *Failed Legislation 1660–1800: Extracted from the Commons and Lords Journals*. Intro. Julian Hoppit and Joanna Innes. London, 1997.

Horwitz, Henry and James Oldham. 'John Locke, Lord Mansfield, and arbitration during the eighteenth century'. *HJ*, 36, 1 (1993): 137–59.

348   Bibliography

Hosgood, Christopher P. '"Doing the shops" at Christmas: women, men and the department store in England, *c.* 1880–1914'. In *Cathedrals of Consumption: The European Department Store 1850–1939*, 97–115. Ed. Geoffrey Crossick and Serge Jaumain. Aldershot, 1999.

'The "knights of the road": commercial travellers and the culture of the commercial room in late-Victorian and Edwardian England'. *VS*, 37, 4 (Summer 1994): 519–47.

'The "language of business": shopkeepers and the business community in Victorian England'. *Victorian Review*, 17, 1 (Summer 1991): 35–50.

Hudson, Nicholas. *Samuel Johnson and Eighteenth-Century Thought*. Oxford, 1988.

Hudson, Pat. 'Financing firms'. In *Business Enterprise in Britain: From the Eighteenth to the Twentieth Century*, 88–112. Ed. Maurice W. Kirby and Mary B. Rose. London, 1994.

The Genesis of Industrial Capital: A Study of the West Riding Wool Textile Industry, c. 1750–1850. Cambridge, 1986.

Hunt, Margaret. *The Middling Sort: Commerce, Gender, and the Family in England 1680–1780*. Berkeley, 1996.

Hunter, J. Paul. *Before Novels: The Cultural Contexts of Eighteenth-Century English Fiction*. New York, 1990.

Hyde, Lewis. *The Gift: Imagination and the Erotic Life of Property*. New York, 1979.

Ignatieff, Michael. *A Just Measure of Pain: The Penitentiary in the Industrial Revolution, 1750–1850*. London, 1978.

Ingrassia, Catherine. *Authorship, Commerce, and Gender in Early Eighteenth-Century England: A Culture of Paper Credit*. Cambridge, 1998.

Innes, Joanna. 'The King's Bench Prison in the later eighteenth century: law, authority and order in a London debtors' prison'. In *An Ungovernable People: The English and Their Law in the Seventeenth and Eighteenth Centuries*, 250–98. Edited by John Brewer and John Styles. London, 1980.

'Prisons for the poor: English bridewells, 1555–1800'. In *Labour, Law and Crime: An Historical Perspective*, 42–122. Edited by Francis Snyder and Douglas Hay. London, 1987.

James, Wendy and N.J. Allen, eds. *Marcel Mauss: Centenary Tribute*. New York, 1998.

Jefferys, James B. *Retail Trading in Britain: 1850–1950*. Cambridge, 1954.

Johnson, Paul. 'Class law in Victorian England'. *P&P*, 141 (November 1993): 147–69.

Saving and Spending: The Working-Class Economy in Britain 1870–1939. Oxford, 1985.

'Small debts and economic distress in England and Wales, 1857–1913'. *EcoHR*, 46, 1 (February 1993): 65–87.

Joyce, Patrick. *Democratic Subjects: The Self and the Social in Nineteenth-Century England*. Cambridge, 1994.

Keating, P.J. *The Working Classes in Victorian Fiction*. London, 1971.

Kent, David. 'Small businessmen and their credit transactions in early nineteenth-century Britain'. *Business History*, 36, 2 (April 1994): 47–64.

Kercher, Bruce. 'The transformation of imprisonment for debt in England, 1828 to 1838'. *Australian Journal of Law and Society*, 2, 1 (1984): 60–109.

King, Peter. *Crime, Justice and Discretion in England, 1740–1820*. Oxford, 2000.

Kirby, Maurice. 'Quakerism, entrepreneurship and the family firm in north-east England'. In *Entrepreneurship, Networks and Modern Business*, 105–26. Ed. Jonathan Brown and Mary B. Rose. Manchester, 1993.

Bibliography 349

Kostal, R.W. *Law and English Railway Capitalism 1825–1875*. Oxford, 1994.

Kowaleski-Wallace, Elizabeth. *Consuming Subjects: Women, Shopping, and Business in the Eighteenth Century*. New York, 1997.

Kupinse, William. 'Wasted value: the serial logic of H.G. Wells's *Tono Bungay*'. *Novel*, 33, 1 (Fall 1999): 51–72.

[Lambert, Julie Anne]. *A Nation of Shopkeepers: Trade Ephemera from 1654 to the 1860s in the John Johnson Collection*. Banbury, 2001.

Lamoreaux, Naomi. *Insider Lending: Banks, Personal Connections, and Economic Development in Industrial New England*. Cambridge, 1996.

Lancaster, Bill. *The Department Store: A Social History*. London, 1995.

Landau, Norma. *The Justice of the Peace, 1679–1760*. Berkeley, 1984.

Langford, Paul. *Public Life and the Propertied Englishman 1689–1798*. Oxford, 1991.

Laqueur, Thomas W. 'Bodies, details, and the humanitarian narrative'. In *The New Cultural History*, 176–204. Ed. Lynn Hunt. Berkeley, 1989.

Lees, Lynn Hollen. *The Solidarities of Strangers: The English Poor Laws and the People, 1700–1948*. Cambridge, 1998.

Lemire, Beverly. *Dress, Culture and Commerce: The English Clothing Trade before the Factory, 1660–1800*. Basingstoke, 1997.

'Petty pawns and informal lending: gender and the transformation of small-scale credit in England, *circa* 1600–1800'. In *From Family Firms to Capitalism: Essays in Business and Industrial History in Honour of Peter Mathias*, 112–38. Ed. Kristine Bruland and Patrick O'Brien. Oxford, 1998.

Lesjak, Carolyn. 'Utopia, use, and the everyday: Oscar Wilde and a new economy of pleasure'. *ELH*, 67, 1 (Spring 2000): 179–204.

Lester, Mark. *Victorian Insolvency: Bankruptcy, Imprisonment for Debt, and Company Winding-up in Nineteenth-Century England*. Oxford, 1995.

Lieberman, David. 'Contract before "freedom of contract"'. In *The State and Freedom of Contract*, 89–121. Ed. Harry N. Scheiber. Stanford, 1998.

'The legal needs of a commercial society: the jurisprudence of Lord Kames'. In *Wealth and Virtue: The Shaping of Political Economy in the Scottish Enlightenment*, 203–34. Ed. Istvan Hont and Michael Ignatieff. Cambridge, 1983.

'Property, commerce, and the common law: attitudes to legal change in the eighteenth century'. In *Early Modern Conceptions of Property*, 144–58. Ed. John Brewer and Susan Staves. London, 1996.

The Province of Legislation Determined: Legal Theory in Eighteenth-Century Britain. Cambridge, 1989.

Lineham, Peter J. 'The campaign to abolish imprisonment for debt in England, 1750–1840'. M.A. thesis, University of Canterbury, NZ, 1974.

Lobban, Michael. *The Common Law and English Jurisprudence, 1760–1850*. Oxford, 1991.

'Henry Brougham and law reform'. *English Historical Review*, 115, 464 (November 2000): 1184–215.

Loeb, Lori Anne. *Consuming Angels: Advertising and Victorian Women*. New York, 1994.

Lovejoy, Paul E. and David Richardson. 'Trust, pawnship, and Atlantic history: the institutional foundations of the Old Calabar slave trade'. *American Historical Review*, 104, 2 (April 1999): 333–55.

350   Bibliography

Lynch, Deidre. *The Economy of Character: Novels, Market Culture, and the Business of Inner Meaning*. Chicago, 1998.

'Personal effects and sentimental fictions'. *Eighteenth-Century Fiction*, 12, 2–3 (January–April 2000): 345–68.

McCalman, Iain. *Radical Underworld: Prophets, Revolutionaries and Pornographers in London, 1795–1840*. Cambridge, 1988.

McConville, Séan. *English Local Prisons, 1860–1900: Next Only to Death*. London, 1994.

A History of English Prison Administration, vol. I: *1750–1877*. London, 1981.

McDonagh, Josephine. *De Quincey's Disciplines*. Oxford, 1994.

McIntosh, Marjorie. 'The diversity of social capital in English communities, 1300–1640 (with a glance at modern Nigeria)'. In *Patterns of Social Capital: Stability and Change in Historical Perspective*, 121–52. Ed. Robert I. Rothberg. Cambridge, 2001.

McKendrick, Neil, John Brewer and J.H. Plumb. *The Birth of a Consumer Society: The Commercialization of Eighteenth-Century England*. London, 1982.

McVeagh, John. *Tradeful Merchants: The Portrayal of the Capitalist in Literature*. London, 1981.

Mann, Bruce H. 'Tales from the Crypt: prison, legal authority, and the debtors' Constitution in the early Republic'. *William and Mary Quarterly*, 3rd ser., 51, 2 (April 1994): 183–202.

Mascuch, Michael. *Origins of the Individualist Self: Autobiography and Self-Identity in England, 1591–1791*. Stanford, 1996.

Mathias, Peter, *The Transformation of England: Essays in the Economic and Social History of England in the Eighteenth Century*. London, 1979.

Mauss, Marcel. 'A category of the human mind: the notion of person; the notion of self'. In *The Category of the Person: Anthropology, Philosophy, History*, 1–45. Ed. Michael Carrithers, Steven Collins and Steven Lukes. Cambridge, 1985.

The Gift: The Form and Reason for Exchange in Archaic Societies (1925). Trans. W.D. Halls. Foreword by Mary Douglas. New York, 1990.

Meldrum, Tim. *Domestic Service and Gender 1660–1750: Life and Work in the London Household*. Harlow, Essex, 2000.

Mikhail, E.H., ed. *Goldsmith: Interviews and Recollections*. London, 1993.

Miller, Andrew H. *Novels behind Glass: Commodity Culture and Victorian Narrative*. Cambridge, 1995.

Moretti, Franco. *Signs Taken for Wonders: Essays in the Sociology of Literary Form*. Trans. Susan Fischer, David Forgacs and David Miller. London, 1983.

The Way of the World: The Bildungsroman *in European Culture*. Trans. Albert Sbragia. New edn. London, 2000.

Morgan, Rod. 'Divine philanthropy: John Howard reconsidered'. *History*, 62, 206 (October 1977): 388–410.

Morus, Iwan Rhys. 'The electric Ariel: telegraphy and commercial culture in early Victorian England'. *VS*, 39, 3 (Spring 1996): 339–78.

Muldrew, Craig. *The Economy of Obligation: The Culture of Credit and Social Relations in Early Modern England*. Basingstoke, 1998.

' "Hard food for Midas": cash and its social value in early modern England'. *P&P*, 170 (February 2001): 78–120.

'Interpreting the market: the ethics of credit and community relations in early modern England'. *Social History*, 18, 2 (May 1993): 163–83.

Neeson, J.M. *Commoners: Common Right, Enclosures and Social Change in England, 1700–1800*. Cambridge, 1992.

Nelson, Julie A. 'Abstraction, reality and the gender of "economic man" '. In *Virtualism: A New Political Economy*, 75–94. Ed. James G. Carrier and Daniel Miller. Oxford, 1998.

Nicholson, Colin. *Writing and the Rise of Finance: Capital Satires and the Early Eighteenth Century*. Cambridge, 1994.

Nixon, Nicola. 'The Reading Gaol of Henry James's *In the Cage*'. *ELH*, 66, 1 (Spring 1999): 179–201.

Nossiter, T.J. *Influence, Opinion and Political Idioms in Reformed England: Case Studies from the North-East 1832–1874*. Brighton, 1975.

Nunokawa, Jeff. 'The miser's two bodies: *Silas Marner* and the sexual possibilities of the commodity'. *VS*, 36, 3 (Spring 1993): 273–92.

Offer, Avner. 'Between the gift and the market: the economy of regard'. *EcoHR*, 50, 3 (August 1997): 450–76.

Ogborn, Miles. *Spaces of Modernity: London's Geographies 1680–1780*. New York, 1998.

Orth, John V. *Combination and Conspiracy: A Legal History of Trade Unionism, 1721–1906*. Oxford, 1991.

Parry, Jonathan and Maurice Bloch, eds. *Money and the Morality of Exchange*. Cambridge, 1989.

Pearson, Jacqueline. *Women's Reading in Britain 1750–1835: A Dangerous Recreation*. Cambridge, 1999.

Pearson, Robin. 'Moral hazard and the assessment of insurance risk in eighteenth- and early nineteenth-century Britain'. *Business History Review*, 76, 1 (Spring 2002): 1–35.

Peters, Edward M. 'Prison before the prison: the ancient and medieval worlds'. In *The Oxford History of the Prison: The Practice of Punishment in Western Society*, 3–47. Ed. Norval Morris and David J. Rothman. Oxford, 1995.

Pitofsky, Alex. 'The Warden's court martial: James Oglethorpe and the politics of eighteenth-century prison reform'. *Eighteenth-Century Life*, 24, 1 (Winter 2000): 88–102.

Pocock, J.G.A. *Virtue, Commerce, and History: Essays on Political Thought and History, Chiefly in the Eighteenth Century*. Cambridge, 1985.

Pointon, Marcia. *Strategies for Showing: Women, Possession, and Representation in English Visual Culture 1665–1800*. Oxford, 1997.

' "Surrounded with brilliants": miniature portraits in eighteenth-century England'. *Art Bulletin*, 83, 1 (March 2001): 48–71.

Polden, Patrick. *A History of the County Court, 1846–1971*. Cambridge, 1999.

'Judicial selkirks: the county court judges and the press, 1847–80'. In *Communities and Courts in Britain 1150–1900*, 245–62. Ed. Christopher W. Brooks and Michael Lobban. London, 1997.

Polkey, Pauline. 'Reading history through autobiography: politically active women of late nineteenth-century Britain and their personal narratives'. *Women's History Review*, 9, 3 (2000): 483–500.

352   Bibliography

Polloczek, Dieter Paul. *Literature and Legal Discourse: Equity and Ethics from Sterne to Conrad*. Cambridge, 1999.

Poovey, Mary. *A History of the Modern Fact: Problems of Knowledge in the Science of Wealth and Society*. Chicago, 1998.

Making a Social Body: British Cultural Formation, 1830–1864. Chicago, 1995.

Porter, Roy. 'The gift relation: philanthropy and provincial hospitals in eighteenth-century England'. In *The Hospital in History*, 149–78. Ed. Lindsay Granshaw and Roy Porter. London, 1989.

ed. *Rewriting the Self: Histories from the Renaissance to the Present*. London, 1997.

Posner, Richard A. *Law and Literature*. Revised edn. Cambridge, MA, 1998.

Psomiades, Kathy Alexis. 'Heterosexual exchange and other Victorian fictions: *The Eustace Diamonds* and Victorian anthropology'. *Novel*, 33, 1 (Fall 1999): 93–118.

Pugh, Ralph B. *Imprisonment in Medieval England*. Cambridge, 1979.

Purvis, Martin. 'Co-operative retailing in Britain'. In *The Evolution of Retail Systems, c. 1800–1914*, 107–34. Ed. John Benson and Gareth Shaw. Leicester, 1992.

Radkin, Margaret Jane. *Contested Commodities*. Cambridge, MA, 1996.

Rappaport, Erika Diane. '"A husband and his wife's dresses": consumer credit and the debtor family in England, 1864–1914'. In *The Sex of Things: Gender and Consumption in Historical Perspective*, 163–87. Ed. Victoria de Grazia, with Ellen Furlough. Berkeley, 1996.

Shopping for Pleasure: Women in the Making of London's West End. Princeton, 2000.

Raven, James. *Judging New Wealth: Popular Publishing and Responses to Commerce in England 1750–1800*. Oxford, 1992.

Richards, Thomas. *The Commodity Culture of Victorian England: Advertising and Spectacle, 1851–1914*. London, 1990.

Rose, Jonathan. *The Intellectual History of the British Working Classes*. New Haven, 2001.

Ross, Ellen. *Love and Toil: Motherhood in Outcast London, 1870–1918*. New York, 1993.

Rubin, G.R. 'The county courts and the tally trade, 1846–1914'. In *Law, Economy and Society, 1750–1914: Essays in the History of English Law*, 321–48. Ed. G.R. Rubin and David Sugarman. Abingdon, 1984.

'From packmen, tallymen and "Perambulating Scotchmen" to Credit Drapers' Associations, *c.* 1840–1914'. *Business History*, 28, 2 (April 1986): 206–25.

'Law, poverty and imprisonment for debt, 1869–1914'. In *Law, Economy and Society, 1750–1914: Essays in the History of English Law*, 241–99. Ed. G.R. Rubin and David Sugarman. Abingdon, 1984.

Russell, Norman. *The Novelist and Mammon: Literary Responses to the World of Commerce in the Nineteenth Century*. Oxford, 1986.

Sainsbury, John. 'John Wilkes, debt, and patriotism'. *JBS*, 34, 2 (April 1995): 165–95.

Savage, Gail. '"Intended only for the husband": gender, class, and the provision of divorce in England, 1858–1868'. In *Victorian Scandals: Representations of Class and Gender*, 11–42. Ed. Kristine Garrigan. Athens, OH, 1992.

Schramm, Jan-Melissa. *Testimony and Advocacy in Victorian Law, Literature, and Theology*. Cambridge, 2000.

Schwarz, L.D. *London in the Age of Industrialisation: Entrepreneurs, Labour Force and Living Conditions, 1700–1850*. Cambridge, 1992.

Searle, G.R. *Morality and the Market in Victorian Britain*. Oxford, 1993.

Sekora, John. *Luxury: The Concept in Western Thought, Eden to Smollett*. Baltimore, 1977.

Shammas, Carole. *The Pre-industrial Consumer in England and America*. Oxford, 1990.

Shanley, Mary Lyndon. *Feminism, Marriage, and the Law in Victorian England, 1850–1895*. Princeton, 1989.

Shapley, Peter. 'Urban charity, class relations and social cohesion: charitable responses to the Cotton Famine', *Urban History*, 28, 1 (May 2001): 46–64.

Sheehan, Wayne Joseph. 'The London prison system, 1666–1765'. Ph.D. dissertation, University of Maryland, 1975.

Shepard, Alexandra. 'Manhood, credit and patriarchy in early modern England c. 1580–1640'. *P&P*, 167 (May 2000): 75–106.

Sherman, Sandra. *Finance and Fictionality in the Early Eighteenth Century: Accounting for Defoe*. Cambridge, 1996.

Shoemaker, Robert B. *Prosecution and Punishment: Petty Crime and the Law in London and Rural Middlesex, c. 1660–1725*. Cambridge, 1991.

Simmel, Georg. *The Philosophy of Money*. Ed. David Frisby. Trans. Tom Bottomore and David Frisby. 2nd edn. London, 1990.

Simpson, A.W.B. *Leading Cases in the Common Law*. Oxford, 1995.

Slatter, Michele. 'The Norwich Court of Requests: a tradition continued'. In *Customs, Courts and Counsel: Selected Papers of the 6th British Legal History Conference*, 97–107. Ed. Albert Kiralfy, Michele Slatter and Roger Virgoe. London, 1985.

Smail, John. *The Origins of Middle-Class Culture: Halifax, Yorkshire, 1660–1789*. Ithaca, NY, 1994.

Snell, K.D.M. *Annals of the Labouring Poor: Social Change and Agrarian England 1660–1900*. Cambridge, 1985.

Spierenburg, Pieter. *The Prison Experience: Disciplinary Institutions and Their Inmates in Early Modern Europe*. New Brunswick, 1991.

'The sociogenesis of confinement and its development in early modern Europe'. In *The Emergence of Carceral Institutions: Prisons, Galleys and Lunatic Asylums 1550–1900*, 9–77. Ed. Pieter Spierenburg. Rotterdam, 1984.

Spufford, Margaret. *The Great Reclothing of Rural England: Petty Chapmen and Their Wares in the Seventeenth Century*. London, 1984.

Stallybrass, Peter. 'Marx's coat'. In *Border Fetishism: Material Objects in Unstable Spaces*, 183–207. Ed. Patricia Spyer. London, 1998.

Stanton, Judith Phillips. 'Charlotte Smith's "literary business": income, patronage, and indigence'. In *The Age of Johnson: A Scholarly Annual* 1 (1987), 375–401. Ed. Paul J. Korshin. New York.

Staves, Susan. *Married Women's Separate Property in England, 1660–1833*. Cambridge, 1990.

Stearns, Peter N. 'Stages of consumption: recent work on the issues of periodization'. *JMH*, 69, 1 (March 1997): 102–17.

Stedman Jones, Gareth. *Outcast London: A Study in the Relationship between Classes in Victorian Society*. Oxford, 1971.

Steedman, Carolyn. 'Enforced narratives: stories of another self'. In *Feminism and Autobiography: Texts, Theories, Methods*. Ed. Tess Cosslet, Celia Lury and Penny Summerfield. London, 2000.

Past Tenses: Essays on Writing, Autobiography and History. London, 1992.

354 Bibliography

Steinfeld, Robert J. *Coercion, Contract, and Free Labour in the Nineteenth Century.* Cambridge, 2001.

Stirk, Nigel. 'Fugitive meanings: the literary constructions of a London debtors' sanctuary in the eighteenth century'. *British Journal of Eighteenth-Century Studies*, 24, 2 (Autumn 2001): 75–88.

Stone, Marjorie. 'Dickens, Bentham, and the fictions of law: a Victorian controversy and its consequences'. *VS*, 29, 1 (Autumn 1985): 125–54.

Strathern, Marilyn. *The Gender of the Gift: Problems with Women and Problems with Society in Melanesia.* Berkeley, 1988.

Stretton, Tim. *Women Waging Law in Elizabethan England.* Cambridge, 1998.

Styles, John. ' "Our traitorous money makers": the Yorkshire coiners and the law'. In *An Ungovernable People*, 172–249. Ed. John Brewer and John Styles. London, 1980.

'Product innovation in early modern London'. *P&P*, 168 (August 2000): 124–69.

Sutherland, John. *Victorian Fiction: Writers, Publishers, Readers.* Basingstoke, 1995.

Tadmor, Naomi. *Family and Friends in Eighteenth-Century England: Household, Kinship and Patronage.* Cambridge, 2001.

' "In the even my wife read to me": women, reading and household life in the eighteenth century'. In *The Practice and Representation of Reading in England*, 162–74. Ed. James Raven, Helen Small and Naomi Tadmor. Cambridge, 1996.

Tebbutt, Melanie. *Making Ends Meet: Pawnbroking and Working-Class Credit.* Leicester, 1983.

Terpstra, Nicholas. 'Confraternal prison charity and political consolidation in sixteenth-century Bologna'. *JMH*, 66, 2 (June 1994): 217–48.

Thirsk, Joan. *Economic Policy and Projects: The Development of a Consumer Society in Early Modern England.* Oxford, 1978.

Thomas, Donald. *Henry Fielding.* London, 1990.

Thompson, E.P. *Customs in Common: Studies in Traditional Popular Culture.* New York, 1993.

The Making of the English Working Class. London, 1963.

Thompson, James. *Models of Value: Eighteenth-Century Political Economy and the Novel.* Durham, NC, 1996.

Thompson, Lynda M. *The 'Scandalous Memoirists': Constantia Phillips, Laetitia Pilkington and the Shame of 'Public Fame'.* Manchester, 2000.

Titmuss, Richard. *The Gift Relationship: From Human Blood to Social Policy.* London, 1970.

Tosh, John. *A Man's Place: Masculinity and the Middle-Class Home in Victorian England.* New Haven, 1999.

Trumbach, Randolph. *Sex and the Gender Revolution*, vol. I: *Volume One: Heterosexuality and the Third Gender in Enlightenment London.* Chicago, 1999.

Turner, Cheryl. *Living by the Pen: Women Writers in the Eighteenth Century.* London, 1992.

Unwin, J.D. *The Scandal of Imprisonment for Debt.* London, 1935.

Veall, Donald. *The Popular Movement for Law Reform 1640–1660.* London, 1970.

Vickery, Amanda. *The Gentleman's Daughter: Women's Lives in Georgian England.* New Haven, 1998.

Walkowitz, Judith R. *City of Dreadful Delight: Narratives of Sexual Danger in Late-Victorian London.* Chicago, 1992.

Bibliography

Walsh, Claire. 'The newness of the department store: a view from the eighteenth century'. In *Cathedrals of Consumption: The European Department Store 1850–1939*, 46–71. Ed. Geoffrey Crossick and Serge Jaumain. Aldershot, 1999.

'Shopping in early modern London'. Ph.D. thesis, European University Institute, 2001.

Weatherill, Lorna. *Consumer Behaviour and Material Culture in Britain 1660–1760*. 2nd edn. London, 1996.

Webb, Sidney and Beatrice Webb. *English Prisons under Local Government*. London, 1929.

Weiner, Annette B. *Inalienable Possessions: The Paradox of Keeping-while-Giving*. Berkeley, 1992.

Weiss, Barbara. *The Hell of the English: Bankruptcy and the Victorian Novel*. Lewisburg, PA, 1986.

White, James Boyd. *Heracles' Bow: Essays on the Rhetoric and Practices of the Law*. Madison, 1985.

White, Jonathan. 'Luxury and labour: ideas of labouring-class consumption in eighteenth-century England'. Ph.D. thesis, University of Warwick, 2001.

Wiener, Martin J. *Reconstructing the Criminal: Culture, Law, and Policy in England, 1830–1914*. Cambridge, 1990.

Wilson, Kathleen. 'Citizenship, empire and modernity in the English provinces, c. 1720–90'. In *Cultures of Empire: A Reader*, 157–86. Ed Catherine Hall. Manchester, 2000.

Winder, W.H.D. 'The courts of requests'. *Law Quarterly Review*, 207 (July 1936): 369–94.

Windler, Christian. 'Tributes and presents in Franco-Tunisian diplomacy'. *Journal of Early Modern History* 4, 2 (May 2000): 168–99.

Winstanley, Michael. *The Shopkeeper's World, 1830–1914*. Manchester, 1983.

Wunderli, Richard M. *London Church Courts and Society on the Eve of the Reformation*. Cambridge, MA, 1981.

Wyatt-Brown, Bertram. *Southern Honor: Ethics and Behavior in the Old South*. Oxford, 1982.

Zedner, Lucia. *Women, Crime and Custody in Victorian England*. Oxford, 1991.

Zelizer, Viviana A. *The Social Meaning of Money: Pin Money, Paychecks, Poor Relief, and Other Currencies*. New York, 1994.

Zomchick, John. *Family and the Law in Eighteenth-Century Fiction*. Cambridge, 1993.

Index

Administration of Justice Act (1970), 187
advertising, 278, 280
agents, 238, 255–8
  wives as, 239, 266, 269, 272
Amos, Arthur, county-court judge, 260
aristocracy, patronage by, 42, 49, 71–3
Armstrong, Nancy, 27, 33
Arthurs, H.W., 237, 252
Ashford, Mary Ann, 238–9
Atiyah, P.S., 16
Atkinson, H.T., county-court judge, 65, 101,
  254, 262–3
Atonement, the, 73–4
attorneys, *see* lawyers
Austen, Jane
  Persuasion, 48
  Sense and Sensibility, 52, 60
autobiographies, 65–6
autonomy, personal, 37, 86, 87, 95, 188, 259,
  323; *see also* individualism

Bailey, Peter, 305
Bamford, Samuel, 78, 82, 103
bankruptcy, 90, 110, 114, 128, 174, 186, 315
barter, 6–7, 35, 76, 77–8, 79
Bass, Thomas Michael, 315
beadles, 233–4
Bedford gaol, 132, 149, 161, 180
Bender, John, 56
billing practices, 95–7, 228, 285–8
Bird, George, 88, 94, 97–8, 100
Birmingham gaol, 141, 226
Blackburn, William, 120
Blackstone, Sir William, 15, 128, 205, 219–20,
  226
  Commentaries on the Laws of England, 205,
  219, 235, 248
Blanchard, E.L., 75, 97
Bloch, Maurice, 8
Blumfeld, R.D., 286
Borough Compter, 115, 128, 144, 147, 231,
  232

Bourdieu, Pierre, 9, 30
Bradford gaol, *see* Halifax and Bradford gaol
Brantlinger, Patrick, 25, 63
Breward, Christopher, 273
bridewells, *see* houses of correction
Brierley, Ben, 65
Bristol Newgate, 118, 121, 172
Brooks, Christopher, 16, 197, 201, 202, 236
Brougham, Lord Henry, 15, 251, 287
Brown, Ford Madox, 75, 79, 97
Burgess, Fred, 284
Burke, Winifred, 88
Burney, Frances, 48, 55
  Wanderer, The, 35–8
Buxton, Thomas Fowell, 158

Caldwell, James, 220–2
Cambridge Castle gaol, 135, 160
Carrier, James, 9, 89
cash nexus, 84, 95, 105, 211, 221
  economic theory and, 5–6, 12, 35, 38, 45,
  323
  fictional representations of, 36, 40
  limits of, 75, 76, 88, 93, 320
cash sales, 279, 282–3, 301
  contrasted to credit sales, 284–5
Certeau, Michel de, 66
chaplains, prison, 137–8
character, 18–20, 177, 188, 320–1
  Benjamin Haydon and, 74
  and credit, 47, 102–5, 260, 261–2, 281, 299,
  302, 306
  and imprisonment for debt, 102, 162, 163,
  262
charity, 122, 123, 124–8, 161, 209; *see also*
  Prison Charity Committee; Thatched
  House Society
Charke, Charlotte, 93
Chartism, 148, 181
Chesterton, George Laval, 177
Christmas boxes, 84, 88
Church, Roy, 21

356

Index

civil law, 16, 17, 109, 190
Clark, Peter, 77
class differences, 175–6
Cleland, John, 54
Clerkenwell house of correction, 209, 232, 245
Clunas, Craig, 4
Cobbett, William, 80, 89
Coldbath Fields prison, 177, 245
Collini, Stefan, 320
commodification, 31, 63, 76, 87, 89, 276–7
  fictional representations of, 26, 32
  limits of, 67, 76, 88
commodity fetishism, 45
common law, 150, 197, 199, 220
  antagonism to, 14, 204, 224, 225, 264
  contrasted to equity, 199, 201
  procedures of, 198, 201, 235
common side, of prisons, 57, 120, 129
composition, on debts, 162, 163, 185, 186, 246
confessional identity, 302–3
connection, 68, 89, 164, 177, 281
  and credit, 95, 100, 291–3, 305
consumer credit, *see* credit, retail or trade
consumer revolution, the, 4, 16, 18, 19, 197;
  see also retail revolution
contempt of court, 173, 178, 186
contract, 32, 33, 288
  freedom of, 2, 16, 21, 44, 210, 259, 261, 272–3, 323–4
  strict enforcement of, 29, 39, 60, 163, 165, 190, 210, 246, 309
  transition from status to, 15, 32, 281, 315, 323, 325
convicts, 114; *see also* criminal law
co-operative stores, 92, 278, 279, 282–3, 306
Copeland, Edward, 55
county allowances, 122, 171
county courts, 173, 252, 307–9
  Birmingham, 313
  Boston, 256–7
  Bristol, 253
  lawyers and, 237–8
  Leeds, 262–3
  modernisation and, 237
  Sheffield, 255
  Shoreditch and Bow, 257, 310–12, 313
  Shrewsbury, 184
  statistics, 322
  Thame, 271
  see also equity; imprisonment for debt; judges, county-court
Court for the Relief of Insolvent Debtors, *see* Insolvent Debtors Court
courts of conscience, *see* courts of requests

courts of requests, 15, 32, 111
  Bath, 239–40, 241, 242, 244
  Birmingham, 202, 208, 222, 224–5, 244, 248–9, 251
  Brigg, 243
  Bristol, 202, 205, 208, 241, 243, 248
  Calcutta, 112, 235
  Chatteris, 229–31
  Cirencester, 247
  City of London, 198, 220, 232–4
  commissioners of, 111, 199, 218, 220, 222, 229, 230, 235, 239
  defendants (debtors) in, 206–7, 231–2, 240–1
  execution against goods by, 217, 230, 242, 244
  execution against the body by, 243–4
  Halifax, 211–16, 244
  imprisonment for debt by, 172, 182, 186, 208–11, 216, 218–19, 244–6
  Keighley, 240
  London metropolitan, 231, 250
  Newcastle, 202, 236, 243
  Norwich, 202, 208
  petitions to create, 202, 203–5, 210
  plaintiffs (creditors) in, 229, 231, 232, 238, 240–2, 246
  Sheffield, 202, 239, 241, 247, 250
  Southwark, 115, 202, 208, 248
  Surfleet, 206, 229
  Tower Hamlets, 202, 205, 208, 217, 232
  Wiltshire, 249–50
  see also Hutton, William; summary justice
coverture, 14, 21, 62, 272, 325
  imprisonment for debt and, 54, 132, 326
  legal departures from, 225, 239, 310
  see also Debenham v. *Mellon*; *Jolly* v. *Rees*; law of necessaries; Married Women's Property Acts; wives
Cowburn, John, 255
Craven Street Society, *see* Thatched House Society
Crawford, J.D., county-court judge, 102
Crawford, William, 166, 167, 170, 176
credit, 7–8, 9, 21, 37
  false, 250–1, 261–2
  fictional representations of, 37, 46, 48, 49, 51
  public, 5, 12, 25, 27
  retail or trade, 9, 17, 95–8, 280–6
  useful, concept of, 204, 207, 210, 216
  see also James Budgett & Son; pawning
credit drapers, 258, 261, 262, 283–4, 310–12, 322
  guardian societies and, 295, 297

358   Index

credit inquiry departments, 297; *see also*
    guardian societies; National Association
    of Trade Protection Societies
creditors, *see* plaintiffs
criminal law, 18, 109, 114, 197, 203; *see also*
    penitentiary
Cromartie, Alan, 199
Cross, Nigel, 53
Crossick, Geoffrey, 279
Cullwick, Hannah, 83, 84
Curia Parva (Shrewsbury), 198

Daubney, Dorothy, 99
Daunton, Martin, 280
De Quincey, Thomas, 75
De Vries, Jan, 4, 21
Debenham v. *Mellon*, 266, 268–9, 271, 311;
    see also coverture; law of necessaries;
    wives
debt, personal, 28
    Christian conceptions of, 28, 40, 42, 74,
        103, 124–5
    contrasted with crime, 29, 60
    see also insolvency
debt collection, 99, 295–7, 298, 302; *see also*
    guardian societies; National Association
    of Trade Protection Societies
debt law, 29, 99–102, 186; *see also*
    bankruptcy; imprisonment for debt;
    insolvency
debtors, imprisoned, 114–15, 180
    contrasted with criminals, 110, 120, 125,
        149, 157–9, 171, 180, 184, 189
    fraudulent, 128, 162, 173, 174, 176, 178
    and labour, 157, 161, 171, 187–8, 226
    and opposition to prison reform, 171–2,
        178, 185
    penal, 175, 177, 178, 187, 189
    sympathy for, 179–80
    tobacco and, 169–71, 187
    women as, 180
    see also charity; county courts; courts of
        requests
debtors' prisons, 117–20, 138
    alcohol in, 129, 131–2, 136
    classification schemes in, 176, 178, 179, 185
    codes of conduct within, 139–45
    as havens, 148–50, 186, 189
    penal reform of, 154, 156, 166
    women and, 132–4
    see also houses of correction; imprisonment
        for debt; spunging-houses
Defoe, Daniel, 51
DeLacy, Margaret, 135
department stores, 87, 89, 105, 278, 279, 280,
    282

diaries, 64–5, 70
Dicey, Albert Venn, 323
Dickens, Charles, 55, 65, 133, 185
    Bleak House, 40
    David Copperfield, 52, 58
    Little Dorrit, 52, 55, 59, 64, 190, 191, 192
    Pickwick Papers, The, 52, 55, 65, 191
discretion, judicial, 14, 15, 203, 220
    county courts and, 254, 260, 263, 309, 313
    see also equity
Divorce Act (1857), 265, 269
Dixon, William Hepworth, 126
domestic ideology, 11; *see also*
        separate-spheres ideology
domestic service, *see* servants
Dorchester gaol, 169
Dornford, Josiah, 232, 234
double-entry bookkeeping, 76, 80
drapers, 47; *see also* credit drapery; tailors

Eastwood, David, 153
Edgeworth, Maria, 55
    Belinda, 48
Elliott, J.H., 175
equity, 14, 99, 100, 199, 200, 203, 265
    county courts and, 254–5, 256, 258–9, 263,
        268, 313
    courts of requests and, 199, 205–6, 223–5,
        249
    fictional representations of, 32, 37, 44
Evans, Robin, 118, 137, 159
execution, orders of, 111
    against chattels or goods, 111, 112, 271–2,
        315
    against the body or person, 111, 112, 115

Falconer, Thomas, 253, 259
feminism, 43, 44, 66, 324, 325
Fielding, Henry, 52, 53, 70, 116
    Amelia, 48–9, 53, 57
    Joseph Andrews, 46, 52, 53
final process, 111
financial revolution, 5, 12; *see also* credit,
    public
Fisherton Anger gaol, 160
fixed prices, 90, 97, 105, 278, 279
Fleet prison, 53, 118, 130, 136, 176
    charity in, 149
    codes of conduct within, 140
    disorder in, 129, 139, 147
    fictional representations of, 191
    Rules of, 121
    women and children in, 133
Flinders, Matthew, 228–9
Foucault, Michel, 156, 157
Franklin, Thomas, 125

Index

Gagnier, Regenia, 66
Gallagher, Catherine, 55
Galsworthy, John, 25
  In Chancery, 43
garnish payments, 58, 141, 145
Gaskell, Elizabeth
  Ruth, 39
Gatliff, James, 104
gender, *see* masculinity; sexuality, and debt;
  wives; women
gifting behaviours, 7–8, 81, 321
  Benjamin Haydon and, 68, 73
  fictional representations of, 29–32, 34–45
  modernisation and, 8, 9, 33
  see also charity
Gissing, George, 53, 79
Gitton, George, 321
Gloucester gaol, 172
Goldsmith, Oliver, 54, 319
  Vicar of Wakefield, The, 51, 54, 56, 58,
    65, 70
Gordon Riots, 146, 147–8
Graham, Sir James, 179
Gray, Faith, 83
Gregory, C.A., 8
Grey, Sir George, 148, 179
groats, 122, 124, 149
guardian societies, 289–3, 294–9, 305, 307–9,
    310–11, 314, 325; *see also* National
    Association of Trade Protection Societies
Guest, Harriet, 38

habeas corpus, writ of, 122, 181
Hale Commission (1652), 199
Halifax and Bradford gaol, 213
Hallifax, James, 125
Halliwell-Phillipps, Henrietta, 64
Harris, George, 75
Harvey, Edward, 88
Haydon, Benjamin Robert, 19, 67–76, 287, 292
  Chairing the Member, 71
  see also character; King's Bench prison
Haywood, Eliza
  History of Miss Betsy Thoughtless, The, 47,
    51, 60
Hertford gaol, 171
Hicks, George Montagu, 179, 320
Hill, Henry, 97
Hilton, Boyd, 74
hire-purchase, 258, 272, 325
Holcombe, Lee, 324
Holland, William, 81
Holloway prison, 187, 189, 192
Holyoake, G.J., 282
Home Office, 148, 166, 167, 171, 176
Home Secretary, 171, 174

Hoppit, Julian, 152
Horsemonger Lane prison, 134, 137
Hosgood, Christopher, 305
houses of correction, 113, 175, 209, 323
Howard, John, 118, 124, 209, 226, 317
  prison reform and, 112, 155–7, 211
  State of the Prisons, 156
Hughes, Molly, 78, 92, 94, 286
Hull Guardian Society, 289, 290, 296, 297,
    307, 308, 314
Hutton, William, 102, 222–7

Ignatieff, Michael, 145
Ilchester gaol, 122, 129, 160
imprisonment for debt, 110
  abolition of, 18, 25, 168, 172, 186, 187, 315
  county courts and, 260–2, 315, 326
  custodial character (safe custody), 110, 136,
    150, 160–1, 174, 188
  fictional representations of, 29, 56, 152,
    189–93
  legislative reform of, 173, 175
  see also county courts; courts of requests;
    debtors' prisons; insolvency
individualism, 43, 66, 223
  autonomous, 264, 267, 270, 272, 276, 321
  contractual, 9, 21, 237, 268
  economic, 2, 12, 37, 46, 128
  economic theory and, 63, 320, 323
  fictional representations of, 41, 42
  imprisonment for debt and, 260, 324
  possessive, 26, 27, 28, 32, 277, 323
  women and, 270, 324
  see also autonomy, personal
infants, *see* law of necessaries; minors;
    university debts (undergraduate)
Ingrassia, Catherine, 18, 25
insolvency, 111, 114, 174, 176, 180, 314, 315;
    see also debt law
Insolvent Debtors Court, 180, 186
instalment payments, 326
  ordered by county courts, 260–1, 263
  ordered by courts of requests, 211, 217, 230,
    232, 241, 250, 309

James Budgett & Son, 301–6
Jaumain, Serge, 279
Jenkinson, Richard, 248–9
Jeune, Lady, 282
Johnes, Arthur, county-court judge, 260
Johnson, Samuel, 54
Jolly v. *Rees*, 266, 267, 271
Jowitt, Jane, 93
Joyce, Patrick, 104
judges, county-court, 191, 252–4, 258, 263,
    267–71, 309; *see also* discretion, judicial

360 Index

Judicature Acts (1873–75), 14, 313
juries, *see* trial by jury

keepers, of prisons, 134–7, 180
Kent, David, 180
Kenyon, Lord, 274
King, Peter, 203
King's Bench prison, 129, 133, 147, 148, 176
  Benjamin Haydon and, 19, 68, 70, 72
  charities of, 126
  codes of conduct in, 140, 145
  common side, 121
  debtor population of, 115, 118, 121, 181
  fictional representations of, 58
  master's side, 120, 140
  novelists in, 54
  officers of, 136, 137
  Rules of, 121
  women and children in, 133
  see also Queen's Prison

labour, free, 207, 210, 214
Lackington, James, 104
Lancaster Castle prison, 115, 118, 147, 150
  alcohol in, 131
  charities of, 127
  codes of conduct in, 141, 142, 144
  disorder in, 132, 139, 144
  officers of, 135
  reform of, 158
  statistics of imprisonment in, 182
  women and children in, 132, 141
law of necessaries, 14, 239, 264, 266, 270–1,
    277, 323; *see also* coverture; *Debenham*
    v. *Mellon*; infants; *Jolly* v. *Rees*; Married
    Women's Property Acts; wives
lawyers, 12, 62, 255, 256, 273–4
  fictional representations of, 57
  hostility toward, 199, 205
legal fictions, 13, 62, 272
Leicester Trade Protection Society, 289, 290,
    295, 297, 308
Liddell, A.G.C., 101
Lieberman, David, 219
Lincoln Castle prison, 149, 182, 183
  charities of, 128
  disorder in, 131, 132, 139
Lister, Anne, 85–6, 92
Liverpool Guardian Society, 289, 292, 296
lock-up houses, *see* spunging-houses
Locke, John, 8, 201, 210
London Guardian Society, 289, 291, 292, 293,
    324
Lord's Act, 122
Lord's Prayer, 29, 47, 73, 185
Lucas, William, 75

Ludgate prison, 126, 135, 140, 147
luxuries, 5, 10, 216, 261; *see also* law of
    necessaries
Lynch, Deidre, 19

McCulloch, J.R., 250
Maine, Sir Henry, 13, 15, 323, 327
  Ancient Law, 15
Manchester Guardian Society, 289, 295–7
market culture, 26, 34, 39, 45, 46, 62
  Pamela and, 27, 32
marriage market, 11, 35, 44, 48, 61
married women, *see* wives
Married Women and Tortfeasors Act (1935),
    326
Married Women's Property Acts, 265–6, 270,
    271, 272, 324, 325
Married Women's Property Committee, 324
Marshalsea prison, 55, 59, 137, 147, 149, 176
  charities of, 122, 126
  code of conduct in, 143, 144
  debtor population of, 118
Marx, Karl, 6–7
  Capital, 12, 45
Mascuch, Michael, 104
masculinity, 50, 79, 104, 272, 273–6
Master and Servant legislation, 323
master's side, of prisons, 57, 120, 121, 129,
    143, 176
Mauss, Marcel, 7, 9
  Gift, The, 7, 10
Mayo, Isobel, 91
Meldrum, Tim, 76
memoirs, *see* autobiographies
mesne process, 111, 116, 149, 173
minors, 255, 273, 274–5; *see also* law of
    necessaries; university debts
    (undergraduate)
misfortune, 28, 63, 128, 206, 317, 320
  Christian notions of, 103, 125
  imprisonment for debt and, 60, 152, 162
modernisation, 8, 50, 326
  guardian societies and, 307, 309
  legal change and, 15, 200, 323
  paradigms of, 5, 325
  retail practice and, 89–90, 278, 284,
    299–301, 302, 309, 325
modernity, concept of, 280, 281, 294
money-lending, 142, 228, 258, 261
Moretti, Franco, 62
Muldrew, Craig, 17, 90, 198, 321, 327

National Association of Trade Protection
    Societies, 290, 299, 314–15, 325
National Debt, 153
Neild, James, 120, 162, 165

Index

Neville, Sylas, 1
Newgate prison, 119, 135, 143, 147, 209
  debtor population of, 118
  master's side of, 121
  officers of, 135
Newton, Reverend James, 81, 103
novelists
  and critiques of market culture, 25
  and imprisonment for debt, 52
novels, as commodities, 25, 52

Oglethorpe, James, 155
Old Corruption, 87, 247, 250, 272
Oxford, student debts, 286; *see also* minors;
  university debts (undergraduate)
Owen, Robert, 89

packmen, *see* credit drapers
Palace Court, 112, 149, 190
paper money, 80
Parkes, Joseph, 249
Parry, Edward Abbott, county-court judge,
  102, 258, 261
Parry, Jonathan, 8
particular providences, 73, 74
Paul, Sir George Onesiphorous, 157–8, 163, 166
pawning, 7, 17, 69, 78–80, 325
peddlers, 93–5, 250, 258–9, 283; *see also*
  credit drapers
penal discipline, 157, 159, 160, 177–8
penitentiary, 56, 61, 63, 158, 167
Penn, Margaret, 94
Phillips, Sir Richard, 117
Place, Francis, 116, 134
plaintiffs, small-claims court, 315; *see also*
  courts of requests
Pocock, John Thomas, 133
Polden, Patrick, 236, 309
political economy, 5, 26, 63, 207, 211, 320
  cash and credit in, 12, 26, 35, 38
  see also Smith, Adam
Pollanczek, Dieter, 14
Poor Laws, 122, 153, 165, 175, 206, 210, 217,
  245
Poovey, Mary, 67
Posner, Richard, 32
Potter, Beatrix, 87
Poultry Compter, 118, 135, 147, 232
Prentice, Samuel, county-court judge, 310–13
Prince of Wales (George IV), 71, 153
Prison Charity Committee, Gloucestershire,
  163–5, 166
Prison Commission, 187, 188
Prison Discipline Society, 158
Prison Inspectorate, 166, 167, 168–9, 176
Pugh, Ralph, 110

Queen's Prison, 149, 181, 184, 187
  reform of, 176, 178, 185
  see also King's Bench prison

Radcliffe, Ann, 51
Rappaport, Erika, 279, 322
respectability, 300, 304–5
retail revolution, 278, 280; *see also* consumer
  revolution
Richardson, Samuel, 27
  Clarissa, 64, 65
  Pamela, 26–34
Rieger, Bernhard, 280
risk, 9, 223, 288, 289, 291, 294, 301
Roberts, Robert, 80, 91
Rose, Jonathan, 65
Rules (of debtors' prisons), 19, 121, 176, 181
Russell, Lord John, 167, 170, 176
Russell, Whitworth, 167, 170
Ryder v. *Wombell*, 275

sanctuaries, 116
Saville, Sir George, 213
Saxby, Mary, 93
Scotch drapers, *see* credit drapers
seduction narratives, retail, 38, 47, 70; *see also*
  sexuality, and debt
Select Committee on Imprisonment for Debt
  (1893–94), 309, 313
separate-spheres ideology, 38–9; *see also*
  domestic ideology
separate system, of confinement, 166, 167,
  187
separation, marital, 265, 269
sexuality, and debt, 12, 60, 74, 317, 318–20
  fictional representations of, 28, 29, 31, 35,
  36, 38, 39, 48, 49
  see also seduction narratives, retail
servants, 19, 32
  gifts to, 30, 82–4
  payment of, 76, 238
Shanley, Mary Lyndon, 324
Sharp, Robert, 78, 80, 87, 94, 100, 101
Shaw, Benjamin, 103
Sheffield gaol, 139, 141, 168
Shepton Mallett house of correction, 183, 184
Smiles, Samuel, 20, 321
Smith, Adam, 5, 11, 210, 216, 280–1
  Wealth of Nations, The, 5–6, 12, 280
Smith, Bessie Leigh, 324
Smith, Charlotte, 52, 54
Smith, William, 157, 232
Smollett, Tobias, 54
  Ferdinand Count Fathom, 51, 58
sociability, retail, 90–2, 98
social capital, 20, 282, 301, 302, 316, 320

362   Index

social individual, 67, 264, 267, 268, 276–7, 321, 323
    infant as, 273
    wife as, 269–70, 271, 272–3, 324, 325
Society for the Discharge and Relief of Persons Imprisoned for Small Debts, *see* Thatched House Society
solicitors, *see* lawyers
Solly, Rebecca, 65
Southgate, Walter, 100
specie, shortages of, 76, 77, 212
Spilsby house of correction, 183, 184, 244–5
spunging-houses, 1, 49, 58, 60, 116–17, 134, 147, 318
stages system, 188
Stallybrass, Peter, 6
Steedman, Carolyn, 66
Steel, Frank, 94
Steinfeld, Robert, 323
Stephen, Sir Leslie, 86
summary justice, 18, 113, 198, 203, 220; *see also* trial by jury
surgeons, 137, 242
Surveyor-General of Prisons, 167
Sutherland, Duke and Duchess of, 72, 285, 292
Sutherland, John, 62
Swift, W.E., 97
swindlers, 290–4, 320; *see also* credit, fraudulent

Tadmor, Naomi, 28
tailors, 46, 61, 68, 92, 286; *see also* credit drapers
Tayler, William, 99
Thackeray, William Makepeace, 53, 55
    Pendennis, 48, 52, 53, 55
    Vanity Fair, 49, 52, 58, 116, 318
Thatched House Society, 161–2, 211–17
Thomas, Sarah, 82, 86
Thompson, Flora, 84, 92
Thompson, James, 37
trade protection societies, *see* guardian societies
treadwheel, 159, 161
trial by jury, 10, 18, 190, 201, 220–2; *see also* summary justice
Trollope, Anthony, 42, 53, 56, 115
    Framley Parsonage, 42, 52, 56, 190
    Orley Farm, 191
    Phineas Finn, 56, 190, 191
    Struggles of Brown, Jones and Robinson, The, 50
    Three Clerks, The, 52, 56, 60–2
    Way We Live Now, The, 50
truck system, 77

Trumbach, Randall, 318
Turner, Thomas, 64, 77, 92, 95–6, 99
turnkeys, 138

university debts (undergraduate), 60, 273–5, 286; *see also* infants; law of necessaries; minors
Unwin, J.D., 326
Upcott, William, 84

Vickery, Amanda, 38

wage norms, 76–7, 204, 216
Wakefield house of correction, 183
Wale, Thomas, 81, 85
Walsh, Claire, 90
Warwick gaol, 171
Warwick, Sir Philip, 200
    Discourse of Government, 200
    Memoires, 200
Waugh, Edwin, 104
Webb, Sidney and Beatrice, 155
Weiner, Annette, 8
Wells, H.G., 80
    Tono Bungay, 51
Wesley, Samuel, 318
Whitecross Street prison, 129, 145, 150, 187
    charities, 126
    disorder in, 137, 140, 143
    fictional representation of, 191
    reform of, 175, 185
    social composition, 127, 182
Whitelock, W.H., registrar of Birmingham county court, 271, 322
Whitmore, Charles, county-court judge, 101
Wiener, Martin, 188
Wilde, Oscar, 43
    Picture of Dorian Gray, The, 43
Winstanley, Michael, 279–80
wives, 14, 49, 258–9, 265–73, 310–12
    as agents, 239, 242, 256–8, 262
    see also coverture; law of necessaries; Married Women's Property Acts; women
women, 32, 225, 324; *see also* coverture; law of necessaries; Married Women's Property Acts; wives
Wood Street Compter, 147, 232
Woodforde, Reverend James, 82, 85, 91, 94, 96, 103
Woodforde, Nancy, 85, 91

York Castle prison, 118, 129, 131, 135, 262
    codes of conduct, 141, 144
    reform of, 171